SUNSHINE
AND
SHADOW

SUNSHINE
AND
SHADOW

JAN HOWARD

RICHARDSON & STEIRMAN

NEW YORK

ACKNOWLEDGEMENTS

A special thanks to Stewart Richardson and Hy Steirman for believing in this book and having faith in me and my ability as a writer. And for words of encouragement along the way.

And thanks to Bob Robison for reading a skimpy outline some years ago and recognizing the potential for a book.

*To Corky with much love
and without whose encouragement
and understanding this book
would never have been written.*

BOOK

ONE

I can feel the cold. A shiver runs through my skinny little body as the wind drives the rain under the flaps of the flimsy tent where the graveside services were being held for my baby sister, Peggy Sue, nine months old. Seeing her there in her tiny casket, I wondered why everyone was crying. To me, she looked like she did when she was asleep. Death had no meaning for me at two and a half.

Mom was dressed in a thin cotton house dress and a shabby coat that couldn't hide the fact that she was already big with another child. Sue sat in a rickety chair someone had placed there for her, just rocking back and forth . . . moaning softly. Daddy, his gray work shirt buttoned up to the neck, sitting next to her, just stared straight ahead. His work-worn hands lay folded in his lap.

My grandma tried to shush me when I started to cry. I wasn't crying because Peggy Sue had died . . . I was crying because I was cold . . . and I wanted to go home.

Home, at that time, was a brown, weather-beaten house that had seen better days, on 27th Street in Kansas City, Missouri. Where we all slept, I don't know . . . there were so many of us. Mom, Daddy, Beulah (almost fourteen), Pete (ten), Tiny (eight), Junior (six), and me. And sometimes Mom's mother and step-father, Grandma and Grampa Ward. I asked Mom one time how we all fitted in, and she said she just hung us all up on nails.

It was the mid-thirties and the Depression was supposed to be about over. If it was, the news never reached our house. There was talk of soup lines. Daddy, being a proud man, refused to go. Then I suppose the hungry look on his children's faces made him pick up his bucket, join Mom and the older kids and go stand in line to bring home food we wouldn't have otherwise had.

3

The welfare lady came once a month bringing grapefruit, prunes, flour, rice, oatmeal, cornmeal, and a few canned goods. There must have been a lot of cornmeal because I remember eating mush a lot. Hot, like cereal, in the morning, and fried for supper.

The clothes Mom brought home had to have been donated by someone a little but not much more fortunate than we were. Dresses were all cut from a "one size fits all" pattern and made from the same feed sack material. Shoes were either men's or boy's. No little dainty girls' shoes. Big, high-topped things that your feet swam around in. I was too little to pay attention to shoes, but Tiny would cry as Mom tried desperately to find something she could wear that didn't swallow her.

Daddy was a stone and brick mason by trade, but no one was building anything. If it hadn't been for the WPA (Works Progress Administration, or PWA, Public Works Administration), something Franklin D. Roosevelt started to help destitute men feed their families during the Depression, we'd have probably starved to death. But Daddy wasn't alone. There were men with college degrees working with him.

I can see him now as he was in those days. Sitting, still in his work clothes, in a rocking chair, smoking his pipe. Not saying a word. Just rocking. Sometimes, he'd motion to me and I'd crawl up onto his lap to feel the security of his arms and smell the aroma of his pipe tobacco. My name was Lula Grace but he never called me anything but "Baby Girl."

Some say Daddy looked mean. Well, maybe he did to others. His swarthy complexion, deep-set eyes, and high cheekbones probably added to a "mean" look. He smiled very seldom. Probably because he had very little to smile about. But he had a twinkle in his eyes that extinguished the gruffness in his voice and the frown on his face. But he cussed a lot! To him, saying "son of a bitch" was like saying "good morning." Mom used to say, "Now, Roll (short for Rolla), does that help?", which would bring forth a string a cuss words a lot worse than the first one. But he had a tender side. Especially with me. Like carrying me to the outside toilet in the middle of the night because I was too scared to go by myself and too shy to use the slop jar under the bed. He had a lot of magic cures, too. My earaches, which I had frequently, were cured the instant he blew warm smoke on them.

And dog bites or a scraped knee were sure to get kerosene poured on them. Tobacco juice was the only thing for a cut. It's a good thing there were home cures because there sure wasn't money for a doctor. When someone was sick the county health nurse would come bearing whatever was necessary. She only came as far as the door, though. Grandma, being one quarter Cherokee Indian, usually ignored the nurse and concocted her own remedies. Water kept boiling on the back of the wood stove, fat meat poultices and rags, dipped in some awful-smelling stuff, put on our chests and covers pulled up till only our eyes were visible. It's a wonder we all didn't die of suffocation.

Bill, Mom's son by a former marriage, and the oldest of the kids, had joined the CCC (Civilian Conservation Corps, formed by Roosevelt in 1933 to provide work and training for young men), and Beulah had married. But they had just made space for another child, Dick, born when I was three. When he was two, for some reason known only to them, Mom and Daddy decided to leave Kansas City.

Heaven only knows how they found the places we lived in. Have you seen the movie *Grapes of Wrath*? Well, the Joads were nothing compared to us! It must have been a sight to see our Model T Ford chugging along the road with sticks of furniture piled as high as it would go and kids hanging out of both windows and sitting on top.

Daddy wouldn't drive at night so along about sundown he'd find a campsite and Mom would dig out pots and pans and cook supper over an open fire. Daddy would pull off mattresses, which always lay on the very top, and make makeshift beds. Usually we'd go to sleep counting stars or trying to guess what the hoot owl was saying. Tonight was different, though. As soon as I was down off the truck (it used to be a car but Daddy had cut off the backseat and made it into a pickup), I made a run for the woods to go to the bathroom. As little as I was, six years old, I still didn't want anyone to see me. Hardly out of sight of the camp, I saw a concrete block building in a clearing. With a child's normal curiosity, I decided to take a look inside. What I saw sent me screaming for Daddy. A lot braver with him beside me, I led him back to the building and inside. On each side of the door was a small room, both with bars on the opening cut out of the side.

One big room, empty except for a rope with a noose at the end hanging from a rafter. Under the noose, on the floor, was blood . . . fresh blood. Daddy took a quick look around, grabbed my hand, and headed back to the campsite. He was walking so fast my little legs could hardly keep up. After saying something to Mom, he loaded up the car, piled us all back in, and headed out . . . fast. Dark or not. I kept asking questions but the only answer I got was that we had been somewhere we had no business being. To this day, I don't know what that building was but I have my own ideas.

Birch Tree is a small town in south central Missouri. And when I say small, it should be in capital letters. I think the population *now* is around five hundred. Considerably less in 1937, I'm sure. The town consisted of dirt streets, a drugstore, a grocery store, and a one-pump gas station. And *we* lived in the country! I don't know if that was the planned destination when we left Kansas City or if that was just as far as we got before it was time for Mom to give birth to Bob, my youngest brother. Bobbie Laird . . . that's really his name. I guess Mom didn't know, by spelling it that way, he'd be stuck with a girl's name. She really *did* come up with some names. Besides Bob, there was Richard Eugene (that one's not too bad), Lula Grace (me), Larrance Junior (we skipped the Larrance . . . he was always "Junior"), Minnie Harriet (I don't know how she came to be "Tiny"), Ralph Leon (to us, he was "Pete"), Beulah Louise (she always hated Beulah but that's what we called her), and William Grady (he was named after his father, William Grady Watson). Needless to say, we called him Bill. There were two more. Snooks (I never knew his real name), who died when he was thirteen. And Nadine, who died at the age of two. Both Snooks and Nadine died of infantile paralysis (polio). And within two weeks of each other. I've been told that Mom had to choose between attending Nadine's funeral and taking care of Snooks, whom she'd been told could die at any moment. She chose the living. Besides, Junior and Tiny also had the disease. It's a miracle, with the lack of medical help, that anyone survived.

A lean-to shanty . . . one room with a kitchen built onto the side . . . with dirt for a yard . . . was to be home for about a year. I don't know how we lived. Daddy strictly wasn't a farmer and had no use for "them that was." We did have a few chickens. I remember that well because it was my job to bring in the eggs and one night I forgot and Daddy made me go out, after dark, to the henhouse. Scared to death, I opened the door, felt my way to the nest, stuck my hand in and felt something like a pin stick my finger. I screamed and ran back to the house. Daddy, with a flashlight, came back with me. Shining the light on the nest, we saw the biggest black snake I'd ever seen. It was not only on one nest but stretched all the way across the room. My feet couldn't move fast enough to get me out of there and back to the house. After that, it was only with the threat of a whipping with a "hickory limb" that I collected the eggs.

From somewhere, a baby calf turned up. Every minute I could, I'd feed it and pet it till I almost wore out its coat. Then, one morning, just as I was coming out of the house, I saw Daddy shoot it. I must have been in shock because I stood there and watched as he strung it up by its two hind legs and, with a knife, slit open its belly. I'd heard people talk about butchering but I had no idea what it meant till now. And I never dreamed it would be "my" calf. I know now that we had to have the meat to live but at that time every time Mom would put some of it on the table, I'd start crying and get sick.

We went hunting a lot. Rabbits, squirrels, possums. Even at seven years old, I had learned to shoot a twenty-two rifle and could bring down a squirrel from the highest tree. That came from having older brothers, I guess. Or maybe it was the early sense of survival. Anyway, these wild creatures were the base for the watered-down gravy we ate for breakfast.

We had an old red tick hound that was always having "running fits." But, on his good nights, we'd go possum hunting. One night, he was barking and carrying on so that Daddy thought for sure he had one cornered in a hollow log laying on the ground. Me, being overly brave, said, "I'll get it!" and proceeded to crawl in after it. Suddenly, the awfullest stink I'd ever smelled hit me full in the face. It was a *skunk!* On the way back to the house, no one would walk anywhere near me. And even though it was cold, Mom stripped me bare naked outside and made me get in the rain barrel, where she scrubbed me till my skin was raw. Then she took my clothes and burned them. It still took several days before the smell wore off.

Up the road about half a mile lived a family who was heavy

into praying. Every so often Mom would take some of us kids up there (Daddy wouldn't go because he wasn't into praying too much) and all I remember them doing was praying. We didn't dare not bow our heads when they started but as soon as they did, their son, about my age, and I would watch and snicker till we knew it was about time for them to quit, then we'd bow our heads again and say, "Amen."

School was about two miles down the road and every morning Junior, Tiny, and I had to walk past the "praying" house. I was only in the first grade but I was more afraid of walking past that house than I was of school. I always made Junior and Tiny walk closest to it. Some folks said the woman who lived there had "fits." One morning, just as we got even with the house, we saw the woman out raking the yard (they had *grass!*). Suddenly, the rake went flying through the air and she began dancing around and hollering in a language I'd never heard before. As fast as our legs would carry us, we ran back home. After hearing what we'd seen, Mom said the woman was talking in "tongues." That scared me even more because now I thought she had *two!* A short time later, with a switch Daddy was carrying touching our legs every few steps, we were on our way back to school.

With what she had, Mom did the best she could. But one day, when Bob was a few weeks old, she wasn't able to cope. He was crying and when she picked him up I thought she was going to rock him. For a few minutes she stood there looking at him and listening to him screaming at the top of his lungs. Then *she* screamed and threw him across the room. The rest of us kids ran out of the house to get Daddy. I remember Mom being sick awhile with what they said was a nervous breakdown. Bob survived with no apparent injuries. I guess he also had the survival instinct.

Beulah and her husband, Buster, came for a visit a few months later. I thought they must be rich because their car didn't have the back cut off. It had two full seats! I'd been told to stay away from it but when no one was watching, I couldn't resist. I climbed in and sat down on those big soft seats, pretending to drive. Then, hearing Mom calling my name, I got out but forgot to take my hand off the door before slamming it. It closed and locked on my left thumb. I was screaming so loud everyone came running. Everyone but Buster, who had the keys. Beulah ran to the barn, where he and Daddy were, to get him. Mom was crying almost as loud as I was. I think she expected when the door opened for my hand to be left hanging there. It wasn't, but my thumb was as flat as a flitter, turning black and had all the skin scrapped off. Daddy took me into town to the nearest thing to a doctor's office there was . . . the drugstore, sat me up on the counter, and held me as the druggist twisted my thumb one way and another, then poured iodine all over my hand. They thought I'd been screaming *before!!!*

It wasn't long before we moved into "town." Up on a hill behind the few little stores. The house was better this time. It was white (at one time) and two-storied. Out back there was a barn with a loft which I like to climb up in and hide. Pete was in the CCC's but Tiny and Junior were always teasing me. Besides, if I was out of sight, I didn't have to take care of Dick and Bob.

Daddy got work building a small, one-room jail. I guess they needed it to put the men who drank a little too much "white lightning" on Saturday nights. I loved to take Daddy his lunch, then spend the afternoon watching him carefully "key" around the stones he'd place in the cement. I learned that "keying" was outlining every rock with cement he put on a small round tool. He took as much pride in building that jail as he would have in the finest building. I asked so so many questions and got in his way so much that, when he got the walls up, he'd lock me inside till he got ready to leave. To me, it was like a big playhouse and I was happy to stay in there for hours. With my great imagination, I had plenty of company. I'd play games where, instead of looking like me, dark brown straight hair with bangs that hung down in my eyes (a haircut I got from Mom putting a bowl over my head when she cut it), eyes that were so dark brown they were almost black, set in a little round face, and a skinny little frame that set it all off, I'd look like a little girl I had seen in town. Pretty, blond curly hair, very fair, and always with a freshly ironed dress on. I liked her better than me. She never got in any trouble. I always was.

One day Mom was baking a cake and asked me to go to the henhouse and bring her two eggs. I deliberately brought two the hen was setting on . . . half chickens. After innocently handing them to Mom, I ran to the barn loft. I was halfway there when I heard her scream, "Grace! Come here to me!" I wasn't about to.

As fast as I could, I climbed the ladder to the loft . . . Mom right behind me. I knew she couldn't get through the small hole at the top, though, and once through there, I was safe. She stood at the bottom and said angrily, "Grace, come down here!" I knew I was fixing to get the whipping of my life and decided to take my chances with Daddy. "Not till Daddy comes home!" I hollered back down. I watched through a crack in the wall till I saw her go back into the house. Then I sat there till I saw Daddy walk in the yard. I could see him talking to Mom. After a few minutes, he walked to the barn. I knew I was safe and climbed down. Not so. I still got a whipping but, bad as it was, I knew Mom's would have been worse.

The next day was Sunday, and whenever she could, Mom always sent us to Sunday school. I hated it and was always the last to get dressed. This morning was no exception. Tiny and Junior were ready and Mom was combing my hair. I'd always been tender-headed and was crying. The more I cried, the harder she pulled. Finally, I jerked away and started for my favorite place . . . the barn. I wasn't quick enough. She grabbed me, gave my hair a final jerk, stuck a penny for collection in my hand, and with another whipping on my small butt, sent me tagging after Junior and Tiny. On the way down the hill, they took my penny away from me and threatened to beat me up if I told. I couldn't win for losing. The final straw was the day a neighbor (the mother of the little blond girl) gave me one of her daughter's dresses. Even though it was prettier than any I had, I resented it. Immediately, I climbed up in the mulberry tree and got it thoroughly stained. On purpose. It wasn't long before I had a name tag around my neck and I was on a train by myself headed for Oklahoma City, where Grandma lived. I was seven years old.

Grandma and Grampa Ward had left Kansas City when I was about three and moved back to Oklahoma City, where they had lived once before. Grampa had died shortly after I got there. Now Grandma lived alone in a two-room apartment that was in the middle of others that all looked the same. If I went outside by myself, I had to count apartments from the end to make sure I got home.

Grandma, even though she was Mom's mother, was as different from her as night and day. Where Mom was very fair with light red hair, Grandma was very dark with black hair. Mom took after her father, a redheaded Irishman named James Shirley (a cousin to Belle Shirley, who later married Ben Starr . . . thus . . . Belle Starr). Grandma, although she was only a quarter Indian, looked full blood. And where Mom wouldn't allow liquor or cards in the house, Grandma loved to spend her days in a tavern with her cronies playing "high five," "pitch," drinking beer, and dipping snuff. She'd take me with her and I'd sit for hours watching, fascinated. Especially, the snuff. I thought it must really taste good. One night behind her back, I tried it. Taking a teaspoon, I filled it and stuck it in my mouth. Suddenly, I couldn't spit *or* swallow. My mouth felt like it was swelling up like a balloon and I was getting sick. Grandma turned when she heard me gagging. With one blow, she sent me *and* the snuff in my mouth flying across the room. Most of it came out but some went down my throat. The next few days I spent between the bathroom and the bed.

At Grandma's, I learned to iron. She went to a secondhand clothing store and bought me a pleated skirt. After washing it, she said, "If you wear it . . . you iron it." Fixing a stool for me to stand on, she showed me how to iron the pleats. Up and down . . . down and up. Every time I'd mess it up, she'd wet it and I'd start again. Before I finally got it right, I decided from then on I'd have skirts that were straight . . . no pleats.

When it was time for me to go home, my ticket wasn't for Birch Tree but West Plains, Missouri, a town about fifty miles away where Mom and Daddy had moved.

Compared to Birch Tree, West Plains was a big city. The "Avenue" (that's all it's ever been called) runs all the way from the railroad station at the bottom of the hill (about a half mile) through the "square" and on to the south another mile or so (maybe more now). To the east and west is Broadway. Right in the middle sits a big red courthouse. All up and down the Avenue and around the square, stores (most of which I never saw the inside of) lined the streets. At the bottom of the hill on the Avenue was Richard Brother's store, a combination grocery, feed, and dry goods store, where everyone got credit . . . for a while. On one side of the square was the only department store, Aids, which sold everything from "soup to hay." The population in 1938 was around 6,000 good folks. And a few who weren't so good.

Daddy went back to work for the WPA, working on a new school that was being built. With that income, and money earned doing stonework on houses, we had a decent living for a change. I don't know what his wages came to but, whatever it was, it was more than we'd ever had. We still had the Model A Ford with the truck bed in back so he could haul his tools to work. The first house we lived in was on the Siloam Springs route, west of town a few miles. By local standards, it probably wasn't much but, to us, it was *fine!* After all, it had *two* bedrooms! The bottom half was stone and the top was something that resembled stucco. Maybe just rough cement. Anyway, it had a roof and a yard that had a few sprigs of grass and a couple of trees. I had been born eight years before not far from here.

Not long after we moved to West Plains, Tiny married a man nine years older than she was, Freddie Downen. She was two weeks over fifteen. For a while I had a bed to myself. Then the newlyweds' house burned and they moved back in until Freddie could build another one. I had the choice of a pallet on the floor or sharing a bed with Dick. I chose the pallet because Dick wet his bed a lot.

Friday night was our big bath night. Dragging out the old galvanized washtub, filled with water which had been carried from a spring or pond, whichever was nearest, and heated on the wood cook stove. We each took turns. By the time the last one got in, the water was so dirty you couldn't tell if he (or she) were clean or not. On Saturday mornings, putting on our "town clothes," we'd pile into the car-truck, or whatever, and, whether we had any money or not, head for town. If Daddy had made enough money that week, we kids would get a dime to go to the "show" and a nickel for ice cream. If not, we'd walk up and down the Avenue and around the square all day long. Just looking in windows or wandering through stores. I was fascinated by things I never dreamed of owning.

One Saturday, lying on a table in one of the stores, just waiting for me to come by, was a bright, shiny yellow pencil. I'd never had one with the end not even sharpened. None of the other kids at school had one either. I thought, *This is just what I need.* Looking to see that no one was watching, I slipped it into the pocket of my feed-sack dress and quickly walked out of the store and up the Avenue. The farther I walked, the faster I walked. I knew everyone could see it shining through my dress. Mom always said if you stole anything you got put in jail. I expected any minute for a policeman to grab me and haul me off in handcuffs. I turned and, as fast as I could, made a beeline back to that store, laid my forbidden treasure back where I'd gotten it, and ran for the nearest exit. Years later, I thought about stealing. But not anything as small as a pencil.

Mom and Daddy had friends, Mr. and Mrs. Atkins, who lived on the other side of town. That summer they sent me to stay with them. Their older children were the ages of Pete, Beulah, and Bill but they had one son, Bobby, the age of Junior (four years older than me). I loved Mr. and Mrs. Atkins, they were almost a second set of parents, but Bobby was constantly teasing me, a typical brother. Yet again, it was my job to gather the eggs. Their hens had the habit of laying eggs in the barn loft. One day, with my little bucket hanging over my arm, I climbed the ladder to the loft, gathered the eggs, and, without looking for the ladder, swung down again. But, this time, Bobby had taken it away. I fell to the floor with a crash . . . eggs went everywhere, including on top of my head. My leg was cut from the fall and I was screaming at the top of my lungs. In the meantime, Bobby had put the ladder back up before his mother got to the scene of the crime, and was standing there laughing. I could have killed him! Yet, all in all, it was an interesting summer and one of the most pleasant I remember. Aside from the egg incident, there were other, more amusing, times. Like Mr. Atkins letting me ride on the horse while he plowed. And the time I got the horse close enough to a fence to climb on and rode it through the orchard, every limb hitting me in the face. Then he stopped in the middle of a pond and dumped me off. I remember crying because Mr. Atkins wouldn't take me fox hunting. Not wanting to miss anything, after everyone was asleep, I slipped out of the window, climbed a tree, and sat there till daylight listening to the dogs bark excitedly. Then one time Bobby and I helped a retarded boy named Harold Weeks climb a tree to get peaches we couldn't reach, then ran off and left him there. But, best of all, I remember Mrs. Atkins's homemade cottage cheese, watching her squeeze the whey out of the curdled milk through cheesecloth, then adding the cream and salt and pepper. Then she'd let me have the first bite. I'd sit for hours watching her bake pies. I also turned the handle of the butter churn she'd put on the floor for me. But, all too soon, it was time for me to go home.

Daddy's work had stopped and he, along with a neighbor and every kid who was big enough (including me), went to Arkansas to pick strawberries. The pay was a nickel a box. All day long we'd pick, then collect our meager wages and go back to the place where we, and several other families, had set up camp. There was very little money for food so I was always still hungry after supper. One night, from the direction of another family's camp, I smelled beans cooking. With my empty bowl in hand, I walked over and asked, "Could I please have some beans? I'm hungry." Daddy found me scarfing up their beans and potatoes, thanked the people, and led me back to our campsite. There was such a sad look on his face, I wished I had stayed hungry.

It must have been awfully hard on Mom and Daddy not being able to give their children the things they needed and wanted . . . especially at Christmas. Usually, in our stockings were an apple or orange and some little homemade or secondhand toy. We were glad to get anything but the thing I wanted the most was a doll. I had never had one and, rich or poor, all little girls are the same. They need a doll to love and cuddle. I never dreamed of having one, though. They only came from Santa Claus. And Santa Claus was for rich kids. But, each Christmas, I hoped.

We'd moved again. (Don't ask me why. Maybe the rent was due.) This time we moved to another house on the same road. This one had an upstairs where we all slept. It was Christmas Eve and all the kids had been sent to bed early. Even poor as church mice, we still had Christmas anticipation. I was eight years old and knew this would be the last time I could hope for my doll. I could hear Mom and Daddy talking softly downstairs. Tiptoeing to the top of the stairs, I watched as they carefully put something in each of our stockings. Then I saw it! Laying there on the floor was my beautiful doll! Small but beautiful! I was so happy I almost squealed. Running back to bed, I jumped in and closed my eyes so I'd hurry and go to sleep. I couldn't wait to get my hands on my dream. I was so excited I like to never went to sleep. Yet, I must have because Mom was shaking me gently. She must have been as proud as I was excited. She knew how much I wanted a doll. Daddy was waking the other kids and we all ran downstairs. Now I could squeal out loud! I grabbed my doll and was rocking her back and forth. Dick was jumping up and down saying, "Let me see . . . let me see!" Before I could stop him, he grabbed the doll and, just as quickly, dropped it. As it hit the floor, the head and one arm broke off. The other parts lay in pieces. Of course Dick got a spanking, but it was too late. My doll was gone. Whatever else I got didn't matter. My Christmas was ruined and my eight-year-old heart was broken.

Daddy loved music. He had a French harp which he'd play sometimes. Mostly Red River Valley. And Mom said when she was a girl she had learned to play the piano. I couldn't imagine it. All I could imagine Mom doing was cooking, washing dishes, scrubbing floors, and washing clothes on the scrub board. She was forty-three years old and hard work was taking its toll. Her hair was still a pretty red but there were lines in her face that shouldn't have been there. She had said when she was young she had an eighteen-inch waist. But that, too, was long gone. Probably several kids ago. She had a temper. I saw evidence of that one time when she threw a cup at Daddy. But she was loving and kind, too. Even with her reserved ways of not showing affection, we knew it was there. Daddy was seventeen years older than Mom, but sometimes it seemed the opposite. One day he came home with a battery radio. There was barely money for food but he wanted to listen to the news and, on Saturday nights, the Grand Ole Opry. But only long enough to hear his favorite, Texas Ruby. Her voice was so deep, I thought it was a man with a funny name. Sometimes a neighbor who lived down the road would come to listen. He'd been there so much I thought of him as part of the family and I'd crawl up on his lap. After a while, Daddy told me not to. He said I was too big for that. I could sit on *his* lap but not the neighbor's. I was confused.

At home, I wore mostly overalls like the boys, but to school I wore one of the few dresses I had. All hand-me-downs . . . either too big or too small. And long cotton stockings which Mom insisted upon and which I hated. Grimmet, a one-room school-church house, was about a mile down the road from where we lived. And, once out of sight of the house, I'd stop and roll down my stockings . . . clear to the ankles. After all, I was *almost* nine years old. And I was *almost* in the fourth grade. A few months one way or the other didn't make that much difference. Besides, there was a boy named Robert in the sixth grade that I kinda liked. And from the way he'd been pulling my hair and taking my biscuit and syrup sandwiches away from me, I knew he liked me, too. Junior, who was in the seventh grade, and Dick, just barely old enough to go to school, were always with me. They threatened to tell Mom but they never did. Maybe because I said I'd tell some awful lie and get them a whipping, either at school or at home. So, off we'd go, swinging our lard buckets with our lunch in them.

Coming home one evening, they decided to stop and climb a persimmon tree. But, since I'd already had my bout with falling out and getting the breath knocked out of me, I decided to pass and walked on by myself. Daddy had told me, time and time again, to always stay with Junior and Dick, but, since I didn't always do what I was told, I walked on, Junior hollering after me, "You'll be sorry!" He just knew I'd get another whipping.

Out of sight of them and home, I stopped in my usual place to roll my stockings back up. I felt someone watching me and looked up to see the neighbor who always came to listen to the radio with Daddy. I wasn't afraid . . . especially when he handed me a stick of red peppermint candy. It was natural for him to take my hand and walk along beside me. I noticed he kept looking around, kinda strange-like, but didn't pay much attention. His hand was getting tighter and I tried to pull away. I couldn't. Suddenly, I was afraid and started to cry. A field with stacks of hay ran along side of the road. With a jerk, he pulled me across the ditch and into the field. I was crying hard now. "Please . . . I want to go home!" I looked back to see if Junior and Dick were anywhere in sight. They weren't. The man kept pulling me toward the center of the field, where the biggest haystacks were. After taking another look around, he pulled me behind the biggest one. The same one Junior and I would hide behind when Mom was mad. He was pulling at my clothes and I heard the sound of cloth tearing. In my little girl mind, I knew I'd get a whipping for tearing my dress. He threw me to the ground and fell on top of me. And though I fought tooth and nail, I couldn't scream . . . his hand was over my mouth. My body was violated and my mind was damaged in a way I wasn't to know the full extent of for years to come. Finished with his crime, and after warning me if I told *anyone,* he'd do it again, he left me there . . . crying. Holding my dress together where he'd torn it, I ran across the field and up the hill to the house. When I got in sight of the yard, I saw the man there talking to Daddy . . . just like nothing had happened. He looked at me, smiled, and said, "Hey, how's my girl today?" I turned and ran into the house. Mom, taking one look at my dress, grabbed my arm with one hand and the ever handy switch with the other. "What have I told you about climbing trees!" she said as the switch hit my already bruised body. I clinched my teeth and didn't cry a tear. I knew it was no use telling her what had happened . . . she wouldn't believe me. Later, Daddy tried to get me to tell him what had happened but I ran from what had always been my place of comfort . . . his arms. The next few days, I'd catch him looking at me with a puzzled look on his face. I had changed from the rambunctious little girl to a quiet, scared little rabbit. As the man's visits declined I began to be more normal, but Daddy must have put two and two together. It wasn't long before we moved to Oklahoma City.

The house we moved to was out in the country. All I remember is that it sat up on pilings about three feet high. That was fine with us kids because we could play underneath. The dirt yard was small and surrounded by weeds taller than I was. I heard Daddy talking about animals going mad and remember him tying a little dog we had to one of the iron bedsteads inside and him lying out on top of the car with a shotgun in his hands. The Model T had been replaced with another kind of car. But, as usual, the back had been cut off and replaced with a truck bed. They all looked the same to me.

On the way to school one day (for some reason I was by myself), I saw a big dog coming toward me. I stopped in my tracks. Daddy had told us a mad dog would be foaming at the mouth and weaving because he would be blind. He said they could tell where we were by sound. This dog looked just like the one Daddy had described. The road was dirt and home was as far in back of me as school was in the other direction. About a half a mile. Looking around, I saw my hiding place. A concrete culvert that ran underneath the road. Quickly, I scrambled down the ditch and into the culvert. I sat there barely breathing, afraid he'd hear me. I could hear the dog growling . . . he was right over me.

For what seemed like hours, I sat there. Finally, the growling stopped. After a while, I ventured a peek outside. He was gone. I climbed out and ran. Not to school but back home. I told Daddy what I had seen. He said something about "this son-of-a-bitchin' country," and within a few days we moved again. Back to Kansas City. To another house on 27th Street. I was eleven years old and it was 1941.

The house had two floors. Bedrooms upstairs, and downstairs was some kind of living room and a kitchen. Somewhere, Junior had learned to dance. When Daddy wasn't listening to the news, he'd turn the radio on and dance all over the room. I begged him to teach me. Finally, he did. We had a ball until one day we were practicing the latest jitterbug step. He threw me between his legs and I was supposed to land on my feet. Instead, I landed on my head and was knocked as cold as a Christmas turkey. That ended my dancing for a while.

Junior was my idol. Even with all his teasing, I knew he loved me. And I thought he was the handsomest thing walking. Sandy-colored hair and laughing brown eyes. Not too tall but, after all, he was only fifteen. I ran to him with all my problems. One morning, I woke up and, seeing blood all over the bed, thought I was dying. I ran screaming to Junior. Gently, he sat me down and told me that I was becoming a woman and that it was natural. Then he told me to go to Mom. She seemed embarrassed to talk about it. All she said was that it would happen every month and started tearing up sheets for me to use when it happened. It was up to me to figure what to do with the sheets. She just handed them to me and went on with whatever she was doing. I felt like a leper. Every time it happened I would hide in my room as much as possible till it was over. Daddy listened to the radio more than he usually did. I kept hearing him talk about "war" and "Hitler" but it didn't register. I didn't know what either one was. Pete and Bill, my older two brothers, were in the Army, but I didn't know what that meant, either.

We made another move. This time to a house on Paseo Boulevard. A *big* house which had, at one time, been a fine home. But Mom turned it into another kind of home. A home for old people. In every bedroom was someone who was old and sick. *We* were crammed into what was left. Daddy was working and I couldn't see why Mom had to take care of them. I knew she got paid, either by their pension checks or by their families, but I resented them. She even got a black woman, Sara, in to help. And when I say *black*, I mean black. I'd never been around many black people and she scared me to death. I was so afraid I'd run into her in the dark and not be able to see her. I say "black people" now, but at that time the word I used was "nigger." It's the only one I'd heard to describe them. One day Sara's two young sons came by the house and I called them "chocolate drops." They turned around and called me "white trash." Their mother heard us and told me if I didn't get out of her kitchen she'd "cut your gizzard out." I knew she meant it!

There was one room upstairs (almost in the attic) that Mom said I could have if I wanted to fix it up. Before she could snap her fingers, I was gathering scraps of wallpaper and odds and ends of paint from anywhere I could find it. My sister Beulah came over now and then and offered to help me but, as always, I wanted to do it myself. Mom showed me how to make paste out of flour and water and I'd stand on a chair holding a strip of wallpaper as straight as I could, then slap it to the wall. There was no thought about matching anything, I just wanted it to *stick!* For days I worked up there until I'd be so tired I could fall asleep in the middle of my mess. I wouldn't let anyone see my handiwork. "Wait till I get finished," I said. Finally, after four days, I was ready for the "grand showing." Standing proudly outside the door, I watched Mom, Daddy, Beulah, Junior, and whoever else happened to be there parade into "my" room. Expectantly, I waited for their praise. Instead, all I heard was laughter. I couldn't see what was so funny. Sure the wallpaper was a little crooked, in fact it kinda resembled a fan, but it looked all right to me. If I didn't look at it too long at a time. Anyway, with all the different patterns, it was colorful. And no one would be in it but me. That was the most important thing.

Easter came and my first trip to a "real" farm. We'd lived in the country and Tiny and Freddie lived on a farm but I'd heard so much about Uncle Bert (Daddy's brother) and Aunt Mary's (his sister-in-law) farm I couldn't wait to see it. Daddy never talked much about his family. Maybe because he'd been disowned for selling the horse he was plowing with for fourteen dollars and running away when he was fourteen to join the Merchant Marine. But that was such a long time ago. He was sixty-four now. I'd heard stories of other things he'd done, but they just made him seem more exciting. Things like serving in the Spanish American War under someone else's name. Then keeping that name (Clyde Fisher) after it was over. His real name was Rolla Henry Johnson. Clyde Fisher didn't fit. Mom was his third wife (the first one had borne him a son, Tracy. She *and* his son had died of tuberculosis when the boy was sixteen). He was married again and when he'd tell about it he'd say, "I put her on a train and she went a thousand miles one way and I went a thousand miles the other way." Daddy was a great storyteller. Us kids would sit on the floor and listen for hours as he spun tales we didn't know whether to believe or not. Tales about living in Hong Kong, China, and Yokohama, Japan. About being a faro dealer in a gambling club in San Francisco. Junior said one time that Daddy told him he'd accidentally killed a man caught cheating and, rather than go to prison, took a "four-year camping trip." He'd also worked for the railroad as a brakeman under the name Clyde Fisher for many years. That's when he met and married Mom. Under the name Fisher. That's even the name on Beulah's birth certificate. And I don't ever remember Grandma Ward ever calling him anything except Clyde. Sometimes, Mom would, too. I didn't try to figure it all out. I just hoped that someday I'd get to go to all those places.

I didn't know why after all these years Daddy decided to visit his brother, but when he asked if I wanted to go, I jumped at the chance. He told me to bring some clothes so I threw what little I had in a paper sack and set out on our adventure with excitement.

Brookfield, Missouri (where their farm was), was only about a hundred and fifty miles away. Maybe not that far. But it took us all day. Daddy wouldn't drive over thirty-five miles an hour. I didn't care, though. I'd been back and forth between Kansas City, West Plains, and Oklahoma City so many times I could tell you how many telephone poles there were. But I'd never been to this part of the country. Sometimes Daddy was talkative, sometimes he was silent. This trip, he was silent. I contented myself with staring out the window at all the beautiful farms we passed and wondering if Uncle Bert's was like any of them. Finally, along about sundown, we stopped in front of the biggest white farmhouse I'd ever seen. We'd lived in two-storied houses before but none *this* big! I couldn't imagine only three people (Uncle Bert, Aunt Mary, and their nineteen-year-old son, Willard) living there. Daddy got out of the car as a man who looked a lot like him came around the corner of the house. I couldn't get a good look at him but knew it must be Uncle Bert. Daddy motioned for me to stay in the car. I watched as he walked over and shook hands with the man. From where I was sitting I could see their faces and wondered why neither of them was smiling. They just stood there talking. I turned my attention back to the house. *Gosh, I wonder what's it's like to live here?* I thought. There was a porch that ran the full length but there was no porch swing. A porch swing always makes it seem friendly. The yard was well kept, and out back behind a white fence was a huge red barn. Inside the barnyard I could see some cows and a white horse. I wanted to get out where I could see better but, for once, I did what Daddy told me to do.

A neat but stern-looking woman came out of the house. The way she was dressed made my mouth fall open. Her dress came all the way to the top of her shoes. And over it, she wore an apron just as long. The only thing I'd seen that long was Mom's nightgown. She walked over to the car, took a long look at me, then walked to where Daddy and Uncle Bert were talking. Every now and then, they'd glance back at me. I felt like a monkey in a zoo. They all three came back to the car. Daddy opened his door, got out my sack, and handed it to Uncle Bert. Aunt Mary opened my door and said, "Come, child. You're going to stay with us awhile." I grabbed the car seat, but she took my hand and gently but firmly pulled me from the car. I started to run to Daddy but she held on to my hand. Daddy came back to the car but, instead of coming over to me, he walked to the other side and got in. "Daddy," I said, almost crying, "I want to go home." For the first time, he looked at me. "They need you to help out for a few days. They'll send you home on the bus." He didn't look happy . . . he didn't look sad. As he drove away, tears fell down my face. I kept looking, expecting him to turn around, but he never did. I felt so alone and deserted. I couldn't believe my daddy had left me there. He must have known when he asked me if I wanted to come. But not one word had been said to prepare me. Now I knew. I wasn't here for a visit but to work. I followed these two total strangers into the house I'd been so curious about. Now, I just wanted to run away.

Uncle Bert and Aunt Mary weren't that bad, really. Just hard-working people who never smiled very much. Or any. Almost before the sun was completely down, Aunt Mary said it was time for bed. I wasn't about to disagree with her. With a candle in hand, she led me up a long stairway. I felt like I was walking the last mile. At the top, she opened one of the three doors and led the way into the biggest bedroom I'd ever seen. And the ceilings were so high I thought they surely must touch the sky. Right in the middle of the room sat a huge four-poster bed piled high with a feather mattress. While I was wondering how I was supposed to get in it, Aunt Mary pulled a chair over to the side of the bed. She pointed out the pitcher of water and washbasin on a stand in the corner and the slop jar under the bed, then stood there while I pulled my dress over my head, put on my thin cotton nightgown, and got up on the chair. Standing there, I wondered what she'd do if I jumped in instead of crawling in. I chose to jump! Landing flat in the middle, I sunk to where all I could see was the flicker of the candle on the ceiling. After a minute, I saw the light begin to disappear and then heard the door shut. It was pitch-black. Blacker than Sara who worked for Mom. My heart was pounding so hard I thought someone would surely hear it. I'd always been a little afraid of the dark but afraid didn't describe this feeling. Terrified was more like it! Every ghost and horror story I'd ever heard came back to me. I lay there afraid to move. I must have slept because the next thing I knew, Aunt Mary was shaking me. "Time to get up," she said. *She must be crazy,* I thought. *It's still dark.* But I crawled out of bed and got dressed. When I got to the kitchen, I looked at the clock. It was four-thirty!

First, I was told to set the table. Three places . . . Willard was gone somewhere. Then Aunt Mary told me to go get some pre-serves from the "cellar." I didn't know what the heck she was talking about. Handing me a lantern, she pointed out to the backyard. I'd never even been out there, but I walked where she had pointed. Coming upon a door kinda slanting up out of the ground with some dirt piled high over it, I knew this must be the cellar. Setting the lantern on the gound, I tugged and tugged and finally got the door open. It weighed more than I did. Stepping inside, I turned to reach for the lantern but, before I could reach it, the door slammed down on my head, knocking me backward. I screamed and screamed but my only answer was the echo of my own voice. I crawled back to where I thought the door was, found it, but couldn't get it open. I'd thought I was scared the night before! I imagined snakes and spiders everywhere! About the time I decided I was going to be buried here forever, the door opened and Uncle Bert stood there. "Why'd you leave the lantern outside?" he asked. That was about the dumbest question I'd ever heard!

No sooner was breakfast over and the dishes washed than we started cooking dinner. I'd never seen so much food in my life. Aunt Mary didn't talk much but she *did* explain that they had several hired hands working for them and they all ate dinner there. She told me to set the table for six so I figured there were only two working for them. Wrong! There were four. I found out quick that the men sat down to eat and we waited on them. Uncle Bert, Willard (he'd come back sometime that day: a tall, dark-haired, good-looking man about nineteen, with a weird sense of humor, I was to find out later), and four hired men. Aunt Mary and I ate after they went back to work. All day long we cooked and washed dishes . . . washed dishes and cooked. Now I knew why they went to bed so early. That night I had no trouble falling asleep. A goblin could have carried me away and I wouldn't have cared. I knew, no matter how bad it was at home, my stay here was going to be a short one. I'd made up my mind.

After about a week and when Aunt Mary's back was turned, I sneaked out of the house and decided to explore all the things Uncle Bert had told me to stay away from. First off . . . the barn. He'd said a white bull named Tony was penned up in there. Also, a mean ram. I didn't even know what a ram was. No one was in sight as I climbed over the barnyard fence. Standing there, looking up, the barn looked taller than ever. *I wonder what's in the top,* I thought, and spied a ladder leading to an opening way up there. I climbed up and crawled in. *Heck,* I thought, *it's just another old barn loft!* Then I saw a rope hanging from the ceiling. Walking over to where it was, I couldn't resist pulling it. Suddenly, the floor opened beneath me and I was on my bottom sliding down some kind of chute to a stop in one of the stalls.

Facing me was the biggest white bull I'd ever seen. I don't know which one of us was more surprised, me or the bull. As far away from him as I could get, I scrambled over the stall and ran for the gate at the far end. Just as I got to the top I heard a noise in back of me. Turning around, I saw the ram . . . with horns out to *here!* I heard Uncle Bert holler, "Get off that gate!" but, before I could, the ram hit it full force and sent me flying. Thank God, I landed on the other side. I don't know which would have hurt more, the ram or the way Uncle Bert grabbed my arm. "I told you to stay away from this barn, didn't I!" With that, he shoved me into a room filled with dried ears of corn and some sacks of what I assumed was feed, and locked the door. "You're gonna *stay* here till I finish the chores!" He sounded just like Daddy did when *he* was mad.

Sitting down on one of the sacks, I saw a machine with a handle. "I wonder what that's for," I said to myself, and decided to find out. After experimenting, I learned that it ground up corn. By the time Uncle Bert came back, the whole floor was covered. The minute he opened the door, I knew I was in for it. He was *mad!* Dragging me back to the house, he said, "Damn it, Mary, *I told* you to keep this girl in the house!" He sounded even *more* like Daddy. Considering the alternative, I was glad to go to bed without supper.

Being good a few days at a time was all I could handle. Besides, I hadn't ridden the white horse. Willard had told me its name was Nellie and had promised to let me ride it, but that was the last I'd heard. Watching for my chance, I slipped out of the house and ran to the barnyard. Nellie was standing peacefully right where I wanted her . . . beside the fence. Just as I got ready to jump on her back, I saw Willard come out of the barn carrying a pitchfork. I started back down but he said, "Go ahead. Climb on." He was smiling so I guessed it was all right. Deciding not to jump, I slid very carefully onto her back. She didn't even move. Not, that is, till Willard screamed and jabbed her with the pitchfork! Suddenly she made an awful noise, reared up on her hind legs, and took off, clearing the fence with one jump, and ran at breakneck speed across the field, me hanging on for dear life. My screams didn't help matters. Just as suddenly as she had started, she stopped, and sent me flying past her head. As I scrambled away from her, she just stood there munching grass and looking at me. Halfway back to the house, I met Uncle Bert coming after me. The look on his face told me more than a fortune-teller could have. I was going home . . . quick!

It was no surprise to learn we were moving again—back to Oklahoma City. Us kids just took it for granted that we'd only be in a school a few months or weeks at a time. Never even long enough to learn the other kids' names. But Daddy said he had to go where the work was and work, right now, was in Oklahoma City. Or, at least, that was his excuse. But I knew he just wanted to leave Missouri. He said all the whole state was good for was to "raise a crop of rocks." Mom hated Oklahoma just as much. I guess, where we lived depended on who won the argument.

The house, this time, was on N.W. Tenth Street. It was pretty if you didn't get close enough to see the paint peeling and the cracks in the walls. In a way it reminded me of Uncle Bert and Aunt Mary's house. Big, what once had been white, and two stories. Lots of rooms. I had visions of one for my very own till Mom started filling them up with old people again. Then, as usual, we were crammed into two rooms. And now there were two more added to the family. Pete had married an Oklahoma City girl by the name of Betty and they had a nine-month-old baby, Betty Faye. He was away at camp, so they stayed with us. Beds were everywhere! And when it came time to eat, it was "everybody grab a plate and sit wherever you can find a place."

Eleven years old is a hard time for a girl. Not quite a woman but not a child, either. But then, even though I didn't think of it often, I hadn't been a child for three years. Maturing early didn't help. Ever since my periods had started, my body had blossomed considerably. So much so it embarrassed me. My breasts weren't big but certainly larger than those any eleven-year-old should have. And with "baby fat," I weighed a hundred and twenty pounds. At five feet two inches tall, I was downright chubby. I'd been wearing Tiny's size ten handmedowns for some time.

Pete came home on leave, and knowing how much I liked music, he bought me a Hawaiian steel guitar. Why he chose that instrument, I don't know, but Daddy scraped together enough money so I could take lessons. A dollar a lesson. Once a week. Everything went fine until the teacher found out I was playing by

ear instead of learning to read music. He'd put this music in front
of me, then sit down and play what it was supposed to sound like
after a week of practicing. I'd go home, never look at the music,
and play it the way he did. Of course, the pieces weren't compli-
cated (things like "Mary Had A Little Lamb"), so I didn't put
forth much effort. I wanted to learn songs like "Deep In The
Heart Of Texas" and "Chattanooga Choo Choo," which I had
heard on the radio. Another one of my favorites was "Born To
Lose." It wasn't long until the teacher gave up on me. But I'd sit
around and pick out melodies and try to sing the songs I knew.
Daddy was the only one who listened.

Tiny came for a rare visit. I was so glad to see her. Even
though she was six years older than I was, we seemed almost the
same age. From somewhere I got another kind of guitar. The
kind I'd seen Freddie play sitting out under the walnut tree in
their front yard when he'd had a few beers or some homemade
wine. He'd sit there and pick and·sing old Jimmy Rogers yodeling
songs by the hour. He must have taught Tiny, because she could
play his guitar. We'd gather around and she'd pick and we'd
harmonize on "Born To Lose" and "El Rancho Grande." One day,
we got the idea to audition for WKY, the local radio station. I don't
remember how we got the nerve, but we just *knew* we were going
to be the "stars of tomorrow."

For a week, we worked getting our outfits together. Begging,
borrowing, and sewing, we came up with red skirts, red vests,
and white blouses. The great day finally came. The audition was
set for two in the afternoon. The closer it came, the more nervous
we got. And the more nervous we got, the more we giggled. At
the radio station, a man with an irritated look on his face showed
us into a glass-enclosed room and shut the door. He went into
another room where we could see him but not hear him. He
pointed his finger at us and we knew it was time to sing. I
couldn't say a word. Neither could Tiny. We looked at each other
and it was all over. Both of us got so tickled we couldn't stop. The
man came around, jerked open the door, and said, "Don't ever
come here and waste my time again!" We were quickly ushered
out of the station. All the way home on the streetcar, we laughed
till we were almost sick. Passing a building with a sign out front
that said "The Nut House," we decided that would be just the
right place for us to get a job. All I had to do was lie about my age,

and I was good at that. We rang the bell and got off on the next block. When I told the man inside the building I was sixteen, he didn't bat an eye. Just told us to report for work the next day.

We found out immediately why it was called the Nut House . . . it was filled with nuts . . . on a conveyor belt. Handing us our aprons, the boss told us as the nuts came down the belt to pick out the bad ones. Well, I couldn't pick for eating. By noon, I was sick to my stomach. By quitting time I had stomach cramps something awful and had taken a lot of bathroom breaks. I had eaten enough nuts to stock a grocery store. I think Tiny lasted three days but one was enough for me. There had to be something better. I decided baby-sitting was easier. After all, I'd taken care of Dick and Bob all my life.

The first job was for a Navy commander and his wife. They had four of the most ornery kids I'd ever seen. While I was trying to feed one, two more would be fighting and the fourth would be taking his clothes off in the front yard. That's when the parents came home and decided I wasn't old enough to handle their children. From the way the kids acted, I figured the parents could use some lessons on how to raise kids.

Next was a tiny baby for a preacher's wife. As soon as the preacher would leave, for wherever he was going, his wife would get all dressed up and go out. Shortly before he got home, she'd change back into what she'd had on when he left. One night she got caught. He came home sooner than she expected, and he found me there alone with the baby. He'd figured out I was there to keep her company, or help with the baby. That was the end of that job.

Next, and last, was the four-year-old son of a bank executive and his wife. The man came to pick me up in the fanciest car I'd ever seen. It was black and looked like it was a mile long. We drove to the richest part of town and stopped in front of the prettiest house I'd ever seen. It looked like one of the houses I'd seen in the movies, what few I'd been to. Inside, it was the same. Shining clean and not a magazine out of place. The furniture was soft and velvety. In a way, it was kinda spooky. So big. And so quiet. Before they left, the woman showed me where everything was and said I could eat anything in the refrigerator I wanted and that their son was asleep. She pointed to his room at the top of the open stairway. I waited till I heard the car leave, then headed for the kitchen. Busying myself with making a sandwich, I heard a nosie behind me and turned quicky. There stood a little boy with the weirdest eyes I'd ever seen. They were normal-size and all but the look in them was mean. Real mean. It sent chills down my back. Gathering my wits about me, I said, "Hi. I'm Grace." He didn't answer. Just walked over to the refrigerator and opened the door. "I want some milk," he said.

"Sure. I'll pour it for you." At least we were talking. I reached for a small glass.

"No," he said, "I want a big glass." Okay. So he wanted a big glass. I poured it full. He took it from me, then, looking me right in the eye, poured in on the floor. I grabbed a dish towel and him at the same time.

Now it was *my* time to look mean! "Okay, young man, you clean up every drop of it." It didn't bother him at all. He took the towel, cleaned up the milk, and walked back upstairs. But not into his room. He stood at the top of the stairs looking at me. Any normal four-year-old would have cried, screamed for "Mommy," or something. Not him. I went up, took his hand, and led him into his room. He still didn't say a word as I tucked him into bed and covered him up. Just looked at me with the eyes that were old beyond his years. I shut the door and went back downstairs to retrieve my sandwich and read a book. All the lights were out except a dim one over the stairway and my reading lamp. Engrossed in my book, I suddenly felt a cold chill down my back and got this eerie feeling. I turned just in time to dodge the butcher knife plunged into the sofa where I'd been sitting. The little monster was standing there grinning. As scared as I was, I was also *mad!* Not too gently, I grabbed his arm and practically pulled him back up the stairs and into his room. Throwing him on the bed, I walked out and shut the door. When his parents came home, they found me sitting on the floor right outside their son's room. I wasn't going to turn my back on him again. I told them what had happened and they offered no explanation. I got the feeling that they had run out of baby-sitters and that's why they had resorted to an eleven-year-old. I was really relieved to get back to my crowded room at home.

When it was time for Tiny to go home, I rode with Daddy to the bus station. That's when I got the idea for my next job. A waitress. It was still a few weeks before school would be out, so I bided my time before mentioning it. As little as I was *in* school, I needn't have bothered. Being overly self-conscious about my clothes, I skipped school more than I went. I'd leave home pretending to go off to school, my paper sack filled with a peanut butter sandwich (if I was lucky), and I'd head for the park. Sometimes it would take a week or more before the truant officer would catch me and take me home. Then I'd have to attend school for a while. You could always count on me staying away though when my "woman" days came. I was so afraid some stain would show on the old white skirt I had to wear day after day. The red skirt I'd worn on the audition had vanished. Mom was always giving something away to "someone less fortunate than we were." I knew she had to have looked long and hard to find someone poorer than we were.

While I was waiting for school to be out, I'd watch Betty put on makeup and fix her hair. Then, out of everyone's sight, I'd practice it. At first, I looked like something in a Frankenstein movie. Black eyeliner out to my hairline and bright red lipstick. Then I began to look more normal. Still too weird. But I didn't know the difference. I just knew, from what I saw in the mirror, I looked a lot older. When I was through practicing, I'd wash my face and hide my makeup (stuff I'd taken from Betty's leavings when she wasn't looking). I even practice rolling my shoulder-length brown hair around my fingers into rolls around my face.

I first mentioned my job idea to Daddy. He was always my go-between with Mom. At first he refused. But, with a little time and me saying *"Please,* Daddy," he finally gave in. He knew how much I wanted decent clothes. And he knew why I skipped school so often. But there would be no extra money if I didn't work. I guess even he knew, I wasn't a little girl anymore.

The manager didn't question me when I said I was sixteen and asked for a job. He told me to come to work at eleven that night. "Eleven? At night?" I asked. I'd never thought of working at night. But I said I'd be there. I'd handle Daddy and Mom when I got home. It wasn't as easy as I'd thought it would be. Daddy threw a fit. And Mom cried. But, with the understanding that Daddy would put me on the streetcar and meet me when I got off, they finally agreed. I was so eager to learn, it took me about an hour that first night before I was hollering, "BLT and hold the mayo!" with the best of them. As the nights wore on, though, I

was so tired I had trouble staying awake. There was so much
noise at home, I couldn't sleep and I'd go to work nearly as tired
as I was when I got off work. Every morning when I climbed on
the streetcar, I'd see the look of pity on the conductor's face. I'd
fall asleep immediately and he'd let me sleep to the end of the
line, then wake me at my stop on the way back. I must have
looked pitiful. The eyeliner and lipstick I'd carefully applied the
night before by then was smeared all over my face. Girls not
much older than I was and who looked a lot like I did the
morning after I'd worked all night, came in the bus station
sometimes. I guess he thought I was one of them. I had no idea
then what kind of work they did.

My job came to an abrupt end one night when Daddy came in
unexpectedly. He sat at the end of the counter watching me. I'd
never seen Daddy drunk, but I knew he'd had a few beers. His
face was sullen and angry. Maybe upset at himself for letting me
work there. There was a naval base not far from Oklahoma City
and the counter was filled with sailors. Usually I'd joke with
them like the other waitresses, but not tonight. Suddenly, one of
them grabbed my arm and said, "Hey, baby, how about going out
with me?" That did it! Daddy had grabbed that sailor by the collar
before he knew what was happening. "Get your hands off my
eleven-year-old daughter, you son of a bitch!" You could have
heard a pin drop. I took off my apron, took Daddy's hand, and
walked out of the bus station. A couple of weeks later we moved
back to Kansas City. Back to 27th Street again.

I entered the sixth grade at Askew School. It was strange. I
felt so old. Not like the girls in my class. All they talked about was
boys. They seemed so childish. But then, they *were* children. But
I wasn't. As I settled in to the routine, I began to be more like
them. At least, I tried to be. I even had a crush on a boy. But he
had a crush on someone else. And I hated her. One evening
walking home from school, I could hear them laughing as they
walked behind me. "Grace is ugly," they'd say. Or, "Grace wears
ugly clothes."

I stood it as long as I could, then stopped and waited for them
to catch up. When they did, I grabbed the girl by her hair and
threw her to the ground. Sitting on top of her, I pounded all my
hate and embarrassment into her face. The boy was long gone.
Then I heard the words she was screaming. "You only hate me

because my mother's crippled!" I'd never even *seen* her mother! I stopped pounding and started laughing. When I let her up, she ran down the street yelling "I hate you! I hate you!" I didn't really care one way or another.

One night Daddy was listening to the radio and us kids were making so much noise he couldn't hear. Suddenly, a different voice came on the air. It even got *our* attention. Franklin D. Roosevelt was saying something about Pearl Harbor being bombed. War. Mom started crying and Daddy looked awfully serious. Within two weeks Junior, with Daddy signing the papers, enlisted in the Army and was gone. We had a small flag with three stars on it in our window. Not long afterward, two more were added—Freddie, Tiny's husband, and Buster, Beulah's husband. Soon, all of them were overseas. Junior, Bill, Freddie, and Buster were in Europe and Pete was in the South Pacific. Mom waited and watched each day for letters that came so seldom. That summer I was sent to stay with Tiny in West Plains. With Freddie gone, I would be company for her, they said.

It wasn't like going visiting. Their farm was like a second home to me. Nothing had changed. Except now, there was just me and Tiny to do the work. Since the house consisted of one room and a lean-to kitchen, housework didn't take much of our time. But feeding the cows and chickens, and working in the garden, did. I never learned the art of milking a cow so that job fell to Tiny. But when it came to washing clothes, I did my part. With Freddie gone, there weren't too many clothes to wash. Tiny and I combined had very few dresses. Since we both wore the same size, we traded off. That way we had twice as many dresses.

They had about six cows, a couple of plow horses, and a few chickens. The ones that didn't produce eggs ended up in the pot. One time I told Tiny that I'd love to have fried chicken for supper. She said, "Well, go kill one." I'd watched her do it so figured it was easy. After choosing the one I was condemning to death, I ran it down. For something so little, they sure could run fast. Grabbing its neck, I swung it round and round like I'd seen Tiny do. The only difference was, when she did it the head came off. With me doing it, the neck just got longer. The poor thing was squawking and carrying on something terrible. I was crying and kept wringing. Finally I threw it to the ground and ran into the house. "Tiny!" I cried. "You've got to do it! It's flopping around out there half killed!" Calmly, she went out, got the ax, caught the chicken, laid it across a log, and chopped its head off. There was still a good six inches of neck left.

Without Freddie there, it seemed strange and lonely. He had always seemed like a second father to me. He was a good-looking man, blond, with wavy hair and blue eyes. Not too tall, probably five eight or nine, thin and wiry. But he laughed a lot. And could *he* square dance! People who lived out in the country would often clear all the furniture out of their houses and hold a square dance. Word would get around and folks from miles around would come bearing fiddles, guitars, and banjos. And lots of food. Not everyone was welcome, though. No "town" people or strangers. One time two soldiers from Ft. Leonard Wood (about seventy miles away) came and made the mistake of asking some local girls to dance. They ended up with their heads busted in. Not dead . . . but hurt bad enough so they'd never come back. But now, it's all different. The only music in the house is when Tiny and I try clumsily try to pick out the three chords we know (C, G and F) on the guitar Freddie left behind.

We were eight miles from town with no car. All week we'd stay on the farm by ourselves. Then, on Saturday, we'd hitch a ride to town with a neighbor who was good enough to stop by. Each Saturday we'd switch dresses. That way we always had something different to wear.

Water we used to drink and cook with was hauled in big barrels on the back of someone's truck from a farm up the road. They were lucky enough to have a cistern, or well. Any other water was way up a hill in a spring down past the barn, about a quarter of a mile away. We carried water two buckets at a time.

Wash day was *really* interesting! Carrying a basket of clothes between us, we'd walk down to the spring, where Tiny would build a fire under the washtub there. Carrying the water, we'd fill the tub and put the clothes in to boil. After making sure the fire was burning good, we'd go back to the house or pick blackberries nearby. I was *always* ready for a blackberry pie. When it was time, we'd head back to the spring, carrying a washboard and lye soap. Scrubbing until our hands were raw, each taking turns till the laundry was done. Then the water had to be emptied and refilled to rinse. When you knew your back would break and there was nothing but bones left on your hands, it was time to carry the wet clothes back to the house and hang them on the line. After a few wash days you learned to wear your clothes as long as possible.

I'd completely forgotten about school but Tiny hadn't. I was twelve years old and should be in the sixth grade. I say *should,* because I'd been in school so seldom and because we'd moved so much. Each new school would just put me in whatever grade my age called for. This one was no different.

The school was about two miles away, across a field and through some woods. Each day I dreaded that walk. There were cows and a bull in that field and I didn't want to get acquainted with any of them. But, as luck would have it, the time came sooner than I thought it would. Climbing over the fence to the field, I saw them . . . right where I had to cross. As I skirted around them, the cows didn't pay much attention. But the bull was a different story. He looked at me and started pawing the ground. I knew that meant trouble! My legs wouldn't move as fast as I wanted them to as I ran for the fence on the other side of the field. The bull was right behind me! Finally, out of breath, I reached it. As I scooted under, the bull stopped, as if to say, "Ha! Scared you, didn't I!" There must be a better way to get to school.

Recess was my favorite subject. The teacher was only five years older than I was. I doubted if she had *any* kind of certificate. She was a dumb-dumb. If the answer to a question wasn't in a book, she didn't know it. Therefore she didn't hold my attention a lot.

All the schools out in the country were one room and did double duty. School on weekdays, and church on Sunday. Our student body consisted of twelve kids but that was enough for a softball game. Everybody was drafted. It didn't matter if you were six or sixteen. Catcher was my position. That is, till a bat, with a boy attached to the other end, connected with my head. I came to lying across one of the seats inside the school and swearing to kill the boy who had hit me. He just happened to be Freddie's nephew. For two weeks, his mother walked him to school and came after him. Maybe she was afraid that I'd carry out my threat.

One thing that made the short time I stayed in that school memorable was the fact that one of the little bastards transferred his head lice to me! Tiny noticed me scratching my head, held me down, and searched my head for those crawling monsters. When she found what she was looking for, she said, "Don't touch my comb!" The next trip to town, she bought a fine-toothed comb. Then, after scrubbing my head raw with lye soap and kerosene, she sat me down, made me lean my head over a newspaper, and ran that comb through my hair, time after time. As I watched, I could see tiny little black specks hit the paper and start crawling. When my head was raw, she poured more kerosene on. It hurt so bad I was beginning to wish she'd just light a match and get it over with. No wonder my hair is thin!

I never returned to Kansas City. A letter came, saying it was time for me to come home. It was from Oklahoma City. Inside the envelope was ten dollars for my bus ticket.

That winter was better than many others before. For one thing, the house wasn't filled with old people. I think Daddy had put his foot down. Instead, Mom worked in a private home taking care of the elderly mother of a woman by the name of Nicholson. Their home was neat and pretty and I'd stay there as much as they'd let me. Especially since they had a son, Jack, who was six feet five inches tall and played basketball (what else?). Sometimes, at his mother's urging, he'd take me roller-skating. We must have looked like the "odd couple." I was all of five feet four inches.

Daddy came home one night in a rare mood. He was mad as hell! For days he'd been building a huge brick chimney on the outside of a woman's house. I'd gone with him a couple of times and seen how high it was. All the way from the ground to way past the top of the house. When he finished, he asked her to come out and inspect it before paying him. This was his policy. Another policy was that he wanted to be paid cash. She came out, looked his work over critically, then pointed to a place clear at the top. "That brick's out of place," she said. From the way he told it, Daddy said, "I'll fix it," went back to his truck, got a sledgehammer, and tore the whole thing down. Then he got in his truck and came home. All that work wasted, but he got his satisfaction. I think it's called "Cutting off your nose to spite your face."

I'd heard Mom and Daddy have heated disagreements before, but in the spring of 1943 they had one *hell* of a fight! It ended with Mom taking me, Bob, and a lot of cardboard boxes tied with string and rope, and going, on a bus, to West Plains.

Dick was old enough now to be of some help to Daddy. He stayed with him. I was thirteen years old and had lived in more than twice that many houses.

Tiny, on her one visit to see Freddie before he went overseas, got pregnant and was staying with her in-laws. So, as soon as we got off the bus, Mom looked in the paper (*The Daily Quill*) and found a house to rent. I don't know how she did it. We had no money. Maybe it was a promise of "a check in the mail." Anyway, with our pitiful belongings, we moved in. There was no trouble finding a place to put things because there was no furniture except a couple of beds and a few odds and ends. Usually, the houses we rented came "partly furnished." That meant beds, a few chairs, and a dresser or two. And a table to eat off. Not this time. The floor would have to do for the eating place. That is, if we'd had any food.

Mom sat on the side of one of the beds and counted out the small amount of money she had. Not even enough to buy groceries. I saw tears come into her eyes.

I vaguely remembered that there was a café on the square. The next day I walked in and asked the owner for a job. Without looking up from wiping the counter, he said, "Don't need no help." Refusing to take no for an answer, I leaned down to where my eyes were level with his. "I'll do anything," I said. "Even wash dishes." He never stopped wiping the counter.

"Don't need a dishwasher."

"Look, mister," I pleaded, "I'm hungry. My mom and my brother are hungry." My voice got louder. "*I need a job!*" For the first time, he looked at me and must have seen the desperate look on my face.

"Well, I can't pay you, but I can give you food to take home."

"I'll take it!" I said, almost before he got the sentence out of his mouth. Before he could change his mind, I was behind the counter.

The place wasn't very big, just a few booths along one wall, some tables in the middle of the floor, and the counter with about six stools. But it was enough to keep me hopping.

All day long, I tried to prove how much he needed me. When I wasn't waiting on customers, I was cleaning or scrubbing. I did everything but cook and handle the money. Since he knew I was hungry, he didn't trust me with either. At the end of the day, he filled a medium-sized bucket with vegetable soup left over from lunch, gave me a bottle of milk and some bread, and told me to be back the next morning.

After a few days, Mom got a job cleaning house and I knew it was time to negotiate my pay. I held out for ten dollars a week, and got it.

Things went along pretty nicely. Furniture even started appearing at the house. I never asked where it came from, just assumed Mom had begged, borrowed, or bartered it.

All summer, I worked at the café. I even began to like it. And even though I didn't have much to say to them, the customers were nice. I just did my job and collected my pay.

Daddy came back for a visit and brought Dick so he could start school. But he didn't stay long. There was just no work for him in West Plains. He went back to his beloved Oklahoma City. Each time he came and left, I wondered if I'd ever see him again. Mom was adamant in her refusal to go back with him. But that's not saying she stayed put in West Plains. I came home one night to find some men I'd never seen before loading our stuff on a truck. I thought we'd been evicted! But Mom said she'd found a better house closer to the square. By better, she meant bigger. I knew what she had in mind. Sure enough, room by room, our new house began to fill up with old people.

The house itself wasn't bad. Really, kinda pretty. Or it had been. It was a block from the square, a half a block from the Davis theater (the only one in town), near the funeral home, and a block from the high school. It had several rooms, both upstairs and down, but only two were reserved for us. All along one side there was a porch. I liked it. And the yard was decent. Yet, even when we'd lived there several months—outside of friends or relatives of the old people or Tiny—we never had any company. Speaking of Tiny, she was at the house one night when I was singing "Mairzy Doats and Dozey Doats and Little Lambzy Divey" at the top of my lungs. She got irritated and said, "Shut up! Who do you think you are . . . Kitty Wells?" Hell, I doubt if Kitty Wells ever heard that song!

One night, I had my ears glued to the radio and almost didn't hear the knock at the door. I knew it was a stranger because no one came to the *front* door. The living room had been turned into a bedroom. The only access was at a side door. I walked outside and around the porch to see a man standing there. From the way he was dressed, in a suit, he was either a bill collector, or lost.

"Is there a Mrs. Johnson living here?" he asked.

"Yes," I replied, "that's my mom. I'll get her." I knew it! A bill collector! I wished now I had said she wasn't home. He followed me back around the porch.

"Mom!" I hollered, "there's someone here to see you!" I left the man standing there, and went back to my radio.

Mom came out of the kitchen wiping her hands on her apron. I ignored them till I heard "Do you have a thirteen-year-old daughter by the name of Grace?" This got my attention! Straining my ears, I listened as he told Mom that it was the law that I had to be in school until I was sixteen. Oh, no! Not again! I thought I was through with all that. I'd already decided to quit. After all, I didn't need a high-school diploma to work as a waitress. Besides, I'd only attended the total of one school year the past two! He said that I would be given a test the next day to determine what grade I should be in, told her when school started, then looked at me, and said, "Be there!"

The next morning, promptly at nine, I was in a room at the high school taking a test I just knew I would fail. Afterward, I sat there waiting for the teacher to grade my paper. When she looked up and smiled, I thought, "Oh God, I've passed! Now, I'll have to go to school!"

School or no school, I still had to work, and since I couldn't work at the café any longer, I got a job, after school and on Saturdays, cleaning and doing odd jobs around the house for a Mrs. Dorothy Robertson, the owner of the funeral home. One of these jobs was washing out lingerie. I'd never seen such pretty underwear. It was a shame it had to be worn under her clothes. She showed me how to soak them in cold water, then gently squeeze the water through the fabric. Somehow, though, I couldn't imagine Mrs. Robertson (very dignified and always dressed in a suit) wearing those things. Then I found out they belonged to her daughter Jo, who had been married but was living at home and was very sick. I saw her now and then. She was totally beautiful! She would fit the underclothes.

Even though I liked my job, I was uneasy being upstairs where all those dead people were. I jumped at every sound. One day, I was emptying milk from the five-gallon can a man brought from their dairy farm once a week. The radio was on and I was singing, "I Want To Be A Cowboy's Sweetheart" right along with it. A door slammed behind me and the can went crashing to the floor . . . milk everywhere. I turned to see Mrs. Robertson standing there . . . calmly watching the milk slide all over her spotless floor, under cabinets . . . everywhere. Grabbing the mop, I tried desperately to clean it up. Not the least bit flustered, she smiled and said, "Grace, why don't I talk to Mr. Green at the drugstore about a job for you. I think you'd do better there."

Working in the Model Drug was fun. Sometimes I'd get to wait on customers in other parts of the store, but mostly I was behind the soda fountain, where I ate all the ice cream I could hold. Before I'd gotten my fill, I'd balooned up to a hundred and twenty-five pounds. That was fat. Or at least I thought so. I suddenly became very conscious of how quickly a person can gain weight, when my sister-in-law, Ronnie (Veronica), whom Junior had married in England, came to live with us. When she arrived she weighed a hundred and eighteen pounds. Within six weeks, after eating three ice-cream sundaes at a time, whole stalks of bananas, and five pounds of chocolates at a sitting, she went up to a hundred and sixty-three pounds. A blimp! She explained it away by saying she was starved for sweets.

I'd been in school for quite a while, but it was at the drugstore that I began to make a few friends. One was a girl named Lila Lee King. Petite, blonde, and pretty. To me, that described everything I wasn't. My lack of self-esteem reached from my toes to the top of my head. Sometimes I'd look into the mirror and say to the reflection looking back at me, "Okay, what can you do to improve yourself?" The hair was all right, I decided, brown with red highlights showing through. For makeup I used only lipstick, and I still hadn't gotten *that* right. I knew the shade was too red but then every shade I'd tried was too something. I decided to go *au naturel*. But then when samples came in at the store, I'd bring some home and start over.

Even though some of the kids asked me, I still wouldn't go out with them—for two reasons. One, I didn't have nice clothes like they did, and, two, Mom had started going to a church that didn't believe in anything. No movies, dancing, or roller-skating.

Nothing! One girl I went to school with attended the church, and after sneaking out to go to a movie, the congregation found out about it and convinced her that she was surely going to hell. Now, everywhere she goes she carries a Bible with her. I just used the excuse that Mom wouldn't let me, and let it go at that. I'd never even asked her.

One night I decided to take a chance. Mom had gone somewhere and Lila Lee came over and asked me to go to a movie. *Jane Eyre* was playing. My sister Beulah had come from Kansas City for a visit. She could stay with the old people. I told her where I was going. She said I couldn't go. In anger, I turned and said, "You're not my mother and you can't tell me what to do!" I slammed out the door. I knew I'd have hell to pay later, but I decided to enjoy the movie. We got more than our money's worth. Our seats were right on the aisle, and right in the middle of the movie, I saw a big fat woman walking up the aisle. Just as she got even with us, she stopped. I looked at her just in time to see her bloomers fall to the floor. She stepped out of them and, without once looking back, walked on up the aisle. I looked at Lila, she looked at me, and we both went into hysterics. The woman never did come back. I guess someone told the usher because, before long, he came up the aisle, and like he was picking up a copperhead snake, picked up the bloomers and carried them out.

When I got home, I ignored Beulah and Mom's tirades, went to bed, stuffed cotton in my ears, and went to sleep.

Among the kids who used to come in the drugstore was a boy named Mearle Wood. I'd seen him at school and knew he was on the football team, but he was a senior. Since I was a freshman, we only exchanged "Hello's." His best friend was Lila's "steady" boyfriend, Bob Claxton, captain of the team.

Mearle seemed nice enough and I was flattered that he even noticed me. I'd definitely noticed him. Lila described him as one of the "best-looking" boys in school. I could see why. He was tall, about five eleven, dark curly hair and a ready smile. The thing I noticed most, though, was that he took longer to drink a Coke than anyone I'd ever seen.

Little by little Mr. Green let me work more in other sections of the store. One thing he was finicky about was letting him ring up the sales. It was as though he didn't trust me with the cash

register. This was odd because it was only the register on the far
side of the store that he was worried about.

One day, as he was leaving to go next door to the bank, he
said, "If anyone comes in, just tell them I'll be right back." The
door had barely closed behind him when a man came in and
headed right for the back register. Feeling full of unauthorized
authority, I walked up and said, "May I help you, sir?" He was
looking toward the back of the store. I knew he was looking for
Mr. Green.

"Where's Mr. Green?" he asked.

"Oh, he's gone to the bank, but I can help you," I said
confidently.

Looking slightly uneasy and fidgeting from one foot to the
other, he said, "Well, under the cash register in a drawer, there's
some little boxes . . . gimme one."

"What's the name on the box?"

"Never mind the name. Just gimme one," he said impatiently.

Opening the drawer, I saw several small square boxes. Taking
one out, I read the label. "Pro . . . fa . . . lac . . . tics. What's that?"

Not even answering me, he grabbed the box, threw a dollar on
the counter, and rushed out the door, almost bumping into Mr.
Green as he was coming in.

"What the hell did *he* want?" he asked.

"Oh, just something called pro . . . fa . . . lac . . . tics. He told
me where to find them, and there's a dollar on the counter." I was
quite proud of myself.

Turning beet-red, Mr. Green said, "If you go near that drawer
again, you're fired!"

I couldn't see what the big deal was about, but after that I
contented myself with making the best ice-cream sundaes in
town.

On weekdays, my hours at the store were from four to six. By
the time I got home, Mom had the supper trays prepared to serve
to the old people . . . That was *my* job. As much as I hated it, I
knew I was a lot more able to climb stairs and carry trays than
Mom was. And, even though I was embarrassed by the way we
lived, I still felt compassion for those old people whose families
had left them to the mercy of strangers. Some of them had no
visitors for months at a time. One lady hadn't seen her daughter
in twenty years. I couldn't imagine it.

I always left a woman at the end of the hall till last. She was weird! Stockily built with coarse gray hair sticking up like horns all over her head, she'd pace back and forth in her room, which she always kept dark. If you raised the blinds, she started screaming. It was easier to leave them down.

Balancing the tray with one hand, I carefully opened the door. Not being able to see too well, I stood there and tried to locate the table. Every night she moved to a different place in the room. Suddenly I heard this piercing scream and saw this creature coming at me from across the room! The tray crashed to the floor and I started to run. I wasn't quick enough. Grabbing my arm, she spun me around and with one blow knocked me across the room. Scrambling up, I gathered all the strength of my Indian and Irish ancestry, doubled up my fist, and let her have it! Right on her warty and hairy chin.

Leaving her standing there, astonishment and anger written all over her face, I went back downstairs and said, "I don't care if I starve to death and sleep in the streets, I'll *never* serve another tray!" And I didn't.

With Lila Lee's help and influence, I was asked to be on the "Pep Squad." There was only one drawback . . . I had to have a red skirt, white blouse, and a red and white sweater with the word ZIZZORS (the name of the team) across the front. So, every week, I hoarded my meager pay ($8.00) until finally I had enough. The very next game, I was in the stands yelling my head off. Every game thereafter, I was the first one there . . . not because I loved sports, but because it was the only occasion I could wear my outfit.

Mearle started hanging around a lot. Knowing just how to get around Mom's objections to me going anywhere, he started coming over to the house pretending he just came to talk to her. I could see him winning her over. Besides, she knew his mother, who worked at Eads clothing store. And with his uncle owning a car dealership, she thought I was making a real good catch. Knowing how Mom felt about a girl getting married as soon as possible so she didn't "get into trouble," this worried me some but I figured I'd handle that when the time came. Right now, all I was interested in was being part of "the gang" and having fun. I'd already decided I was going to be a nurse.

The rest of the school year was filled with football and basketball games, working at the drugstore, and a few parties. Mom still hadn't given in much to that, but as long as I was with Mearle, she let me go. She would have had a fit if she'd known what went on at those "parties." Most of them ended up with the kids pairing in twos and disappearing into the dark. All except Mearle and me. I'd have no part of the necking scene. The other kids made fun of me, and Mearle got mad a lot, but I didn't care. Something far back in my mind made me cringe at more than a casual kiss.

Mearle's graduation was coming up and all the girls talked about was what they were going to wear. Being a dreamer, I asked Mom if I could buy the powder blue suit and coat I'd seen in a store window on the square. It was thirty dollars.

When she said she didn't have it, my hopes were dashed. Then I thought of Daddy. Without telling Mom, I wrote to him. Starting the letter off with "Daddy, do you love your baby girl?" I thought I might have a chance. Always before, when I'd asked that, he'd said, "What do you want?" . . . I'd see if it would work this time. I went on to explain my dire situation, mailed the letter, and hoped. A week later his answer came . . . a thirty-dollar money order. Mom threw a fit! But, with money in hand, I purchased the only real nice thing I'd ever had. They even threw in a hat to match!

Along with Mearle's diploma came his draft notice. The air was filled with excitement and going-away parties. Secretly, though, I was sort of glad he was leaving. I liked Mearle but had grown awfully tired of Mom talking about us getting married. Maybe, with him away, she'd forget about it. Besides, there was another boy at school I was hoping would ask me for a date.

One day, about two weeks after Mearle left, this boy came into the drugstore. The first thing he said was, "Why didn't you tell anyone?"

"What are you talking about?" I asked.

"I ran into your mom and she said you and Mearle got married before he left."

"*What!*" I almost dropped the sundae he'd ordered! "That's not true!" From the smirk on his face, I knew he didn't believe me.

As soon as I got home, I faced Mom with what he'd said. "What do you mean telling people that Mearle and I are married!"

"Well . . . you have been talking about it."

"No . . . *you're* the one that's been talking about it! Not *me!*" I slammed out of the house and went to find Lila Lee. She'd heard the same thing. No matter how much I denied it, the seed was planted. I just hoped it would die of starvation.

My freedom had come to an abrupt halt. Once more, the only freedom I was permitted was school and work. And I hated school! When the teacher wouldn't let me join the Glee Club because I couldn't read music and wasn't good enough, I deliberately tried to get expelled. I was selected to be the sophomore representative to the Junior Chamber of Commerce, but couldn't do it because I flunked Citizenship. The Home Ec teacher refused to help me hem an ugly skirt I had to make, so I cut it in half. One day, in cooking class, she made me eat a shrimp cocktail (to me they looked like grub worms) and I got sick. To get back at her, I dumped a whole can of red pepper in the vegetable soup she was making for the other teacher's lunch. I waited outside the door until I heard them holler. In study hall one day, I was eating those little Boston Baked Beans (candies) when the sack burst and they rolled all over the floor. The teacher made me get down on my hands and knees and pick up every one of them. When her back was turned, I crawled out the window, down the fire escape, and went home. One thing led to another. I would do anything to get kicked out. Then I could go and live with Daddy, who was still in Oklahoma City. But I failed. I got suspended a few days at a time and a passing grade of I −. Daddy showed up in West Plains just in time to help Mom move to a run-down house on Missouri Avenue.

This house was much worse than the last one. Smaller. Every inch of space was crammed with old people. My little corner was literally that. Part of what was once the dining room, with sheets hung around it for privacy.

Having turned into a real rebel, I sneaked out every chance I got to go to the Echo Club and George's Round Up, strictly teenage hangouts. On any night, if you were within a block of it, you could hear The Andrews Sisters singing "Rum and Coca-Cola" or Tommy Dorsey's "Boogie Woogie" blaring from the jukebox . . . And I loved to dance!

One night, in the middle of a hot jitterbug, Mom walked in. The music never stopped, but it might as well have. Everything else did. Some of the kids snickered and backed off to a corner, leaving me standing in the middle of the room by myself. Even my partner had disappeared. Grabbing me by the arm, and loud enough for everyone to hear, Mom said, "What's a married women like you doing in a place like this!"

"*Mom!* You know I'm not married!" I screamed.

"Well, you might as well be. Now get on home!"

"I'm not going!" I saw it coming but didn't dodge quick enough. Her hand connected with my face and it sounded like a bomb going off! I was so embarrassed I wished the floor would open and swallow me.

Trying to keep back tears, I followed Mom out the door.

All the way home, I could hear her mumbling something about sending me to a convent, or a girls' home. I didn't answer but thought to myself, *The sooner the better!*

Daddy's dream was to own a brand-new car before he died. The closest he came was a 1940 Hudson Teraplane. He still has his Model A makeshift truck for work, but the Hudson was his pride and joy. No one dared touch it.

One day, he couldn't get the Model A started and decided to give me my first driving lesson. With my brother Bob, then eight, and my nephew Sonny (Beulah's nine-year-old son, who was staying with us) in the truck bed, Daddy sat me under the wheel. One by one, he showed me everything he thought I needed to know . . . how to guide it . . . how to shift gears . . . very little else. "Now when I push it and you feel it start, just pull over to the side of the road and stop," he said. Daddy got in the Hudson. Very carefully he eased forward until the bumpers connected . . . I started to move . . . slowly at first . . . then faster and faster. The oncoming cars gave me plenty of room. From the way I was weaving, they knew there was a novice at the wheel. Suddenly the car jerked and I took off like greased lightning! Bob and Sonny were screaming at the top of their lungs! Daddy had shoved the gas lever, which was connected to the wheel, all the way to the top . . . he didn't say anything about bringing it down when the car started. The car was going at breakneck speed down Missouri Avenue and I was holding on to the steering wheel with all my might! I knew there was a sharp curve coming up right ahead of me. Daddy pulled around to where he was about even with me and was making all kinds of motions with his arms. He kept pointing to the steering wheel. The curve was getting closer and I could see the gas station which was located there. Just before I got to it, I realized what Daddy was saying, pull the gas lever down! I did but, not knowing anything about the brakes, it slowed me down very little. There was just one thing to do . . . and I did it! Aimed the car right for the empty lot in back of the gas station. As the car jumped a ditch, Bob and Sonny almost left the truck bed . . . not of their own free will. Finally, thank God, we rolled to a stop a few feet in front of a concrete wall. Daddy pulled to a stop behind us, cussing a blue streak! Jumping out of the truck, the kids ran to him screaming, "We don't have to ride back with her, do we?" I just sat there, shaking all over. Daddy walked over to where I was glued to my seat and at first started to chew me out, then he started laughing. "Well," he said, "I guess you just learned to drive." The ride back home was a lot smoother. I drove the truck and Daddy, with Bob and Sonny in the car, following me.

Soon after, he had to return to Oklahoma City and since he needed the truck to work with, left the Hudson parked in the driveway. Making sure all the doors were locked, he stuck the keys in his pocket and gave one last warning: *"Don't touch my car!"*

He was barely out of sight before I was trying to figure out how to get the doors open and the car to running. A bright idea came to mind. Freddie's nephew was a mechanic. I'd heard some boys talk about "hot wiring" a car. With Tiny's help, we got him over and watched as he removed the radio from the dash, stored it up behind the seat (it only had one), and put two wires together. Lo and behold, sparks flew! He got it started. "Okay, girls," he said, "it's all yours. Just don't ever tell your dad I did this."

For one solid month (over Mom's many objections) I had a ball! Suddenly, I was the most popular girl in town. Since gas rationing was on, all the kids chipped in with all the coupons they could scrounge. Up and down the Avenue we'd cruise. Around the square, to George's Round Up and up the hill to the Echo Club. Anywhere we could think of, just so we were on the move. Mom finally gave up telling me I couldn't go. She just said, "You'll have your daddy to answer to." Shoot, I knew he wouldn't be back for a month and that was a long time.

A small airport had been built a few miles out of town . . . just big enough for crop duster planes. Sometimes, I'd go out just to watch them take off and land. It looked so exciting! One day, one of the pilots walked over to where I was hanging over the fence watching. "Wanta go for a ride?" he asked. I looked from him to the plane, which looked a lot like the one the Wright brothers had used when they made their first flight. "Sure," I said, a lot braver than I felt.

If you exaggerated a little, you could say the thing had two seats. The back one was barely big enough for me to fit into. The pilot strapped me in, and crawled into his seat. About the time he got the engine started, I decided to back out. "Wait!" I yelled, "I've changed my mind!"

"Too late," he yelled back at me, laughing. We began to roll down the dirt runway. Faster and faster, then we were airborne. As scared as I was, it was the most exciting feeling I'd ever had! My hair was flying in the wind: I held on for dear life! Then it started. The plane dipped . . . rolled . . . turned upside down . . . did everything but stay straight and level. I began to feel sick. We finally landed and I couldn't get out fast enough. I vomited all over his precious plane. It served him right! Then and there, I decided it would be train, bus, or walking from now on.

On the way home, it began to rain. The clay dirt road was slick as glass. Suddenly, the car headed for a ditch and I couldn't stop it. The ditch was like a triangle cut out of the ground. The car ended up with the right side leaning up against red clay on the other side. Forcing open my door, I climbed out and looked at the damage. Lord, Daddy's gonna kill me, I thought when I saw the fender dented and red clay over the rest of the car. I must have looked pitiful standing there in the rain looking at the damaged car. A tractor I had passed a ways back came to a stop beside me. "Need some help?" the man asked as he climbed down from his seat. Answering his own question, he got out some kind of hook, attached it to the front bumper, and pulled me out. "This your car?" he asked.

"My dad's," I replied. Climbing back on his tractor, he said, "Good luck," and drove off. He knew I was going to need it.

Since the Avenue was a steep hill and it was pouring by now, I drove there, parked slantwise, got a rag up from behind the seat, and started trying to get the clay off. It was the only car wash in town! There was nothing I could do about the dent.

On the way home, I smelled something burning. Mearle's father, Tabor, worked in a gas station. I made it to there. Smoke was pouring out from under the hood. He took one look and said, "When was the last time you put oil in?"

"Oil?" I said. I'd never thought about that.

"Too late anyway," he said, "the engine's burnt up." Oh, God! I got back in and, after several tries, the motor started. If I can just get it home, I thought. I almost made it. About two blocks from home, I saw the one person I certainly didn't want to see, Daddy, who was coming to meet me. He was furious! I knew I'd had it!

"Get the hell out of my car!" he hollered. I'd already done that. As he walked round and round the car, he looked like he might start crying at any moment.

He got in and chugged off down the street. Leaving me standing there feeling like the lowest thing on earth. A worm would have looked down on me. I loved my dad and by my selfishness had hurt him terribly. I deserved whatever punishment I got. But the only thing he said was, "Don't ask me for anything, or to do anything, for a month." He made me feel worse.

From the radio news, we knew the war was almost over. Germany had surrendered, but Japan was hanging on. My two brothers-in-law, Freddie and Buster, and Junior were already home but Pete was still in the South Pacific. And now, Mearle's mother called to say he would be home in two weeks. I didn't know how I felt. I was glad he hadn't been wounded but that was true for anybody I knew who was in service. Mearle's mother said she wanted me to go with the family to meet the train. I tried to come up with an excuse but they all seemed too feeble.

The train was due in at two in the afternoon. Mearle's folks said they would pick me up. "After all," they said, "you'll soon be part of the family." I was tired of arguing about it. In a way, though, I was looking forward to seeing him. My life hadn't exactly been a bed of roses since he'd been gone.

The small railroad station platform was crowded with all of Mearle's family . . . his mother, Verna, his father, Tabor, his brother, Bill Jay (Bob was in the Army); aunts, uncles, and cousins. And lots of friends. Everybody was laughing and joking and suddenly I was caught up in welcoming back a hometown boy who had been fighting for his country. That's how everybody referred to everyone coming home these days. It didn't matter what they had been before the war or what they might be afterward. They were hometown heroes.

Seeing Mearle swing down from the train, I was suddenly overcome with shyness and hung to the back of the crowd. All the time he was hugging his mother, shaking hands with his father and little brother, I could see his eyes searching the crowd. Spying me, he ran over, picked me up, swung me around, and kissed me! Right there in front of God and everybody!

Later that evening, after all the family get-togethers were over, standing in our front yard, I said, "I really *am* glad you're home." I knew he wasn't too sure from the way I'd withdrawn my hand each time he'd tried to hold it. Reaching in his pocket, he brought out a tiny box . . . opened it and took out a small diamond ring. Dumbfounded, I just stood there. He reached for my hand.

"Well, since everybody thinks we're married already, don't you think we oughta do it?" Was this a proposal? I'd always thought "I love you" went along with it. We'd each signed our letters "with love," but I did that with my brothers! Suddenly it took on a different meaning. Love between a man and a woman. But I wasn't a woman. I was fifteen. He slipped the ring on my finger. It *was* pretty . . . and I'd never *had* a ring before. I decided to keep it . . . just for a week or so. And I could just see the other girls' faces blush with envy when they saw it. Even though I knew there wasn't going to be a ceremony, we were talking about two weeks from Sunday for the wedding.

Mom was thrilled! It was exactly what she had been waiting for. Now I'd be safe. For the next ten days it was as if Mearle had never been away. Lots of parties and running around with "the gang." Time drew closer, though, and I knew I had to give back the ring. I liked Mearle but I didn't love him. I didn't know what love was!

As I knew he would, Mearle got mad when I told him. I figured he'd get over it. And if he didn't, it didn't really matter. But I wasn't prepared for Mom's anger. Noticing the vacant spot on my finger, she asked, "Where's your ring?"

"I gave it back."

"What do you *mean* you gave it back!"

"Mom, I can't marry someone I don't love!" She walked over, stood where her face wasn't a foot from mine, and said, "Love's got nothing to do with it! Besides, after what's been going on, you *need* to marry him!" I knew what she meant. But she was wrong. I *hadn't* been to bed with him. I never *wanted* to go to bed with him. He'd tried many times but, so far, what little honor I had left was safe. But I was hurt by her words . . . and angry. Maybe the reason she wanted me to marry him was so I'd have a better life . . . I didn't know. I didn't know what to do. Mearle called . . . his mother called . . . Mom kept at me. Everybody but Daddy. From the first, he'd never liked Mearle. And now, even less. It never dawned on me to just refuse and let it go at that. I called Mearle and said I'd marry him on Sunday. Mom signed the papers for the marriage license. Only one signature was needed.

The wedding was set for noon in the Church of Christ where Mom attended. I dressed in the only good dress I owned, a pale blue cotton. It should have been green to match my complexion. I felt like I was dressing for a funeral. And in a way, I was. The funeral of my girlhood.

Mearle came to pick me up. As we walked out of the house, I saw Daddy sitting in the yard, his back to the house. He'd refused to go to the wedding. He'd wanted great things for me and this was breaking his heart. I couldn't go without asking him one more time.

Walking over to where he was sitting, I put my hands on his shoulders. He looked up, and I saw tears in his eyes. I'd never seen my daddy cry before.

"Don't do it," he said, "don't marry him."

"I have to, Daddy. It's too late to back out now."

"It's never too late. I'll send you to nursing school. You'd like that, wouldn't you?" He was almost begging me. I looked back to where Mearle and Mom were waiting for me. It *was* too late. I just patted him and walked away.

As the car pulled out of the driveway, I looked back. He hadn't moved, but his head was buried in his hands.

The ride to the church was one I had taken a few but not many times before. At Mom's insistence, I'd attended with her a few times. And one day, just because it seemed the thing to do, I'd been baptized. It had no meaning for me, though. All I thought was that the preacher was trying to drown me. I'd never liked water over my head. Not since I'd almost drowned in a river when I was thirteen.

Mearle's family was all there. The only members of mine were

Tiny, Freddie, and Mom. Several friends . . . all with that know-ing smile on their faces. The closer I got to the altar the more nervous I became. And the more nervous I got, the more I started to giggle. When the preacher asked me to repeat after him, I turned and looked at Tiny. That was the wrong thing to do. I started laughing. You should have seen the shocked looks! Not only from the preacher but from everybody. All except Tiny, who was laughing, too. Freddie nudged her and she quit, but I couldn't. I wonder if anyone's ever done that before? When it came time to say "I do," I wanted to say "I won't" but didn't. It was over. I was Mrs. Mearle Wood. July 22, 1945.

Someone had done the dirty work of tying tin cans and old shoes onto the car Mearle had borrowed from his uncle. There was a threat of a "chivaree" (a down-home party which ends up with someone "kidnapping" the groom), but Mearle managed to outmaneuver them and headed straight for the only hotel in West Plains . . . a big white-frame building about a half a block from the square.

The only thing Mom had told me about what I was in for was that there were "wifely" duties which I would have to put up with. I wasn't stupid. I knew what she meant. But I didn't know the extent of the terror which grabbed me the instant Mearle touched me. Suddenly, I was eight years old and fighting for my life. There was no tenderness or understanding on Mearle's part—just anger. I hated him! Afterward I felt dirty and used. As he dressed to go out somewhere, he looked back to where I lay crying on the bed and said, "Do you want to come along?" I just shook my head. I was so ashamed I could die. There was no way I could face anyone. I wished he would go away and never come back. As the door shut behind him, I pulled the covers up over me, trying to hide from myself.

The next morning, while he was still asleep, I dressed quietly, took my little dimestore suitcase, and slipped out the door. Mom and Daddy's house was at least a mile from the hotel but I walked. Daddy wasn't home but Mom was in the kitchen. When I walked in, her eyebrows raising asked the question. "Mom," I said, "I can't live with him. I want to come home." I stood there waiting for her answer. Drying her hands on a dish towel, she said, without even turning around . . . almost as if *she* was ashamed to face me, "There's just some things that you have to put up with. You'll get used to it. Now, you'd better get on back."

Walking back to the hotel, I'd never felt so alone in my life. Alone and resigned.

Three days later and for the rest of Mearle's leave, we stayed with his folks in their small four-room house on Cass Avenue. There were only two bedrooms. Mearle's mother, father, and brother (Bill Jay) slept in the back one off of the kitchen. And to get from the kitchen and bathroom to the living room, you had to walk through our room. Some mornings, Mearle would be up before everyone left for work. But whether he was up or not, until everyone was gone I'd lay with my face to the window. Would this feeling never end? I knew I had to accept my life. I was married and that was that.

Mearle had been assigned to Fort Leonard Wood, Missouri. Two weeks after he left, he called saying he had a place for us to stay and for me to catch the next bus.

The heat that stultified the air in Waynesville, Missouri, hit me full in the face as I stepped off the bus. There was no sidewalk and the dirt, where the driver sat my suitcase down, was as hard and dry as cement. I stood there and looked around. Very few trees. In fact, very few buildings. A few sleazy bars, a small grocery store where those who were stupid enough to shop there got charged twice as much if they happened to be military, a couple of gas stations, and last but not least, some thrown-together cabins they had nerve enough to call motels. Since the base was just a few miles away, this was the "halfway house" for personnel waiting for on-base housing. As I was to find out, the local people took every advantage of it.

Mearle was nowhere to be seen, but since it was the middle of the day, I hadn't really expected him. Dragging my suitcase, I walked to where a beat-up cab was sitting. The driver barely looked up from the book he was reading as he asked, "Where to?" I guess he got all the business he wanted and didn't care that my suitcase weighed as much as I did. He sure didn't offer to help. As I was getting me and it settled in the back seat, I said, "Can you take me to the Temple Tourist Court?" This was the first time he looked at me. "You goin' there?" He sounded surprised.

"That's where my husband told me to go if he didn't meet me."

The cab started off with a jerk as he turned around and

headed back in the direction from which I'd come. I couldn't
believe my eyes when he stopped in front of a place I'd seen from
the bus. As we'd passed, I'd thought, *Gosh, I'd hate to live there!*
No wonder I hadn't seen the sign. It was a lot smaller than the
one that read "Vacancy . . . by hour or day." Inside, the cabin was
just as bad as I'd thought it would be. The man in the office had
barely looked up when I'd told him my name and said we were
supposed to have a room there. I don't imagine he had many
permanent tenants. In a monotone voice, he said, "Number
seven," and slid the key across the desk. I hadn't expected a
marching band to welcome me but this was almost more than I
could handle. I took the key, went out, and started searching for
the room that matched the number. Finally, way in the back, I
found something that resembled an outside toilet. And the key
fit!

The bed was old, iron, had seen better days and a lot of use.
The floor was covered with faded linoleum. Against one wall was
a beat-up chest of drawers and in the corner sat a straight-backed
chair. There was one small window, up high over the chest of
drawers. Climbing up on the chair, I found there was no way it
could be opened. The bath consisted of the essentials and a metal
shower covered with a plastic shower curtain that had what
looked like slime all over it. Sitting on the side of the bed and
looking around, I knew that as bad as I'd wanted to get away from
home, this was *not* what I had in mind.

Mearle came in a while later and found me still sitting there.
When he told me that we might have to be there awhile, I got up
and started doing what I had done in a lot of places I'd lived . . .
making it livable.

Within a couple of weeks, our name came up for on-base
housing. I couldn't have been happier. With nothing to do but
read and walk around this crummy little town, I was looking
forward to getting some kind of job on the base. But the rule was,
to work on the base, you had to live there.

Since Mearle was at work, I took the base bus to 107 Magnolia
Court . . . an address I had envisioned as a cute little cottage.
But, when the bus stopped, I saw what resembled a row of
cardboard boxes. On the right, in front of me, was the number

107. *Well,* I thought. *This must be home.* At least it was one hundred percent better than the Temple Tourist Court.

The door was halfway open. A woman was standing in the kitchen. Thinking I must be in the wrong house, I said, "Oh, I'm sorry," and started to leave. Before I could, she came over and said, "You must be Grace. I'm Billie. I've been expecting you." Seeing the question in my eyes, she went on to explain that there was such a shortage of housing that two couples had to share one house. She and her husband had been there a couple of weeks. Picking up my suitcase, she led the way to the bedroom that was to be ours. I'd never shared a house with a total stranger before but she seemed nice. And it *would* be nice to have company.

The next day, Billie and I both went to the base employment office, both hoping to get on at the PX . . . a sort of everything store for military personnel. Whatever you could get in town, you got here a lot cheaper. The clerk told Billie to report to the PX first thing the next morning. Then she turned to me. I was to report to the *laundry!* I had never seen the inside of one, let alone worked there.

My first assignment was to sort dirty laundry. Believe me, you haven't lived until you've handled dirty shorts and socks all day long. After a few days, though, I was promoted to a six by six cubicle where the cleaned and ironed clothes were to be wrapped, tied in bundles, and given to the "will call" counter.

The laundry was not only a place of employment for a lot of soldiers' wives but a work detail for German prisoners of war. And I was scared to death of them! Only twenty feet away, I'd watch them folding sheets in a precise way they had, looking at me and laughing among themselves. I figured it was best I didn't know what they were saying. Coming back one day, I walked around my little cubicle and came face to face with one of them. His arm was raised high and in his hand was a hammer! I just knew I was fixing to be brained! I went running to my supervisor! With a disgusted look on her face, she explained that he was only fixing the shelf on my table. I felt like an idiot. But I was still a little nervous, especially when I heard that thirteen of them came down with venereal disease. Since they were under guard all the time, no one could figure out how (and where) they got it. I guess where there's a will there's always a way.

For a few weeks, things went along fairly smoothly. I had even gotten used to Billie and Fred (her husband) being around. And Mearle was on his best behavior. I'd never seen him so conscious of his manners and dress when Billie was around. I just hoped it lasted. It did. Until I came home very early one day and found the two of them wrapped in a tight clinch on the sofa. I stomped into the bedroom, threw my clothes in the suitcase, and walked right past them. Damned if I didn't notice that Mearle was smiling! I didn't even feel the weight of the suitcase. Hell, I'd have carried solid cement to get away from the house. Even though I waited several hours in Waynesville for a bus to West Plains, Mearle never came looking for me. All the way home, I was between tears and anger, and yet glad to be going home.

No one was really surprised to see me. After telling Mom what had happened, she said, "Well, that's just part of being a man, and a wife has to accept it." I flipped my lid!

"To hell with that! If I'm going to live up to *my* part of this so-called marriage, he damned sure is going to live up to *his*. Or there'll be no marriage."

The next few weeks I stayed home. Sometimes going out to Tiny and Freddie's, where Daddy was helping them with some construction work. I was there when VJ Day came. All day long Daddy and Freddie sat under the walnut tree drinking home-made wine. It was the only time I'd seen either one of them drunk.

Mearle had been transferred to Little Rock, Arkansas. Knowing I couldn't continue staying at home, I boarded the bus. *Maybe everything will be better,* I tried to convince myself.

Staying in a motel each day while Mearle was at camp, I'd scan the papers for apartments. The ones we could afford were all terrible. I was about to give up when I saw an ad I couldn't resist checking out. "For rent. Guest cottage on grounds of retired Army officer. Military personnel only." Afraid it would be gone by the time Mearle got home, I took a bus to North Little Rock.

Standing there looking at this huge white mansion with a tall white fence around it, I knew I must have the wrong address. But the number on the mailbox and in the paper were the same.

Very carefully, I opened the gate and almost tiptoed up the flagstone walk to the door. All the time gaping at the well-kept grounds . . . beautiful trees and flowers everywhere. And right in the middle of it all stood a flagpole with a flag waving softly. I almost felt I should stop and salute.

I'd forgotten I'd rung the doorbell and was startled when a soft voice said, "Yes?" through an opening in the door.

"I . . . I've come about the apartment," I said. It was too good to be true. I just knew she'd reject us. The lady who opened the door matched her voice. Tall, dignified, with soft gray hair waved gently around one of the kindest faces I'd ever seen. I knew she was looking me over and wasn't sure whether she liked what she saw or not.

"The colonel is out but come with me. I'll show you the apartment." I breathed a sigh of relief.

The minute I stepped inside, I fell in love. It was so pretty! Twin beds (which suited me fine) with matching bedspreads and a soft rug between; some tables covered with crocheted doilies; a bathroom that was so clean it didn't look like it had ever been used. There was no kitchen but, in one corner, with a beautiful Oriental screen around it, was a small table, two chairs, and a small refrigerator. It was perfect! I couldn't wait to tell Mearle! That evening, with me hurrying him every step of the way, we moved into our fairyland cottage.

The next day, I got a job in a restaurant just down the street . . . ten to one and five to ten. Midday, when I came home, there were always fresh flowers and a pitcher of ice water or lemonade waiting for me. I wanted to stay forever!

I began to be tired all the time. And sick. For one who had always bounded out of bed, now it was a real effort. And taking one look at food would set my stomach to rolling. By the time I got off at one, it was all I could do to make it home and in the bed. And, more and more, I'd sleep until I began to be late for the evening shift. Mrs. Parker (the colonel's wife) worried about me and insisted I see her doctor.

"Pregnant? I just can't be!"

Looking at me over his horn-rimmed glasses, he said, "Are you sure you're married?"

"Of course, I'm married but . . . I just *can't* be pregnant!" My tears were beginning to show, and they weren't tears of joy. Mearle had been staying at the base a lot lately and when we were together it wasn't too pleasant.

His reaction at the news was just what I'd expected. And not the kind you see in a Doris Day movie. "We don't *need* a damned baby!" he exploded. Giving me a condemning look, he slammed back out the door he'd just come through. I stood there for a minute, then went to the main house and asked to use the phone. Finding out there was a bus leaving for West Plains in two hours, I told Mrs. Parker what had happened and went back to pack. As pretty as this place was, happiness had never been there. Just as I was finished there was a soft knock on the door. Mrs. Parker had come to take me to the bus station.

The apartment I rented was only two drafty rooms on the third floor of an old house on Broadway, but it was all *mine!* Mom and Daddy and Mearle's folks tried to get me to live with one of them but, knowing I'd just hear more of "it'll all work out," I refused. Several times, though, I thought about reconsidering. Missouri is cold and wet in the winter, and with only a small electric heater that warmed about three feet of space, many nights I'd lie in bed covered with whatever was handy and still be cold.

I'd been having cramps all day. With my completely illogical reasoning, I thought, *Maybe I'm not pregnant after all. Maybe I'm fixing to start my period.* Feeling feverish, I crawled into bed wishing Mom or somebody would come over. Feeling the urge to use the bathroom, which was out the door and down the hall, I tried to get up but couldn't. I was so terribly weak.

From what seemed a long ways off, I heard Daddy's voice. Suddenly, with a crash, he burst open the door. "Please, help me to the bathroom," I said weakly. Gently, he helped me out of bed. All the time, under his breath, he was saying, "That son of a bitch!" The pain in my stomach and back was so bad I couldn't stand up straight. Closing the door, I made it to the stool. It felt like my insides were falling out. When I stood up, I knew why. The stool was filled with blood. I screamed, "Daddy!"

Bundling me up in a quilt, he carried me downstairs to the car and to the hospital. Vaguely, I heard the doctor say that I was three months pregnant and was having a miscarriage. Then something about not being able to pass the fetus and having to perform a legal abortion.

Two weeks is a long time to lie and think, but that's what I did. I knew my marriage was on the downhill grade, but I didn't know what to do about it.

Before I was out of the hospital, Mearle arrived on leave before being transferred to Fort Carson, Colorado. Over and over he apologized. But I didn't believe a word he said. I hoped he was telling the truth, but I didn't believe him.

One day, about a week after I was installed in the bedroom at the Woods', I got up to eat breakfast. As I was getting back into bed, my heart felt like wings of a bird fluttering in my chest. It was beating so fast I couldn't get my breath. I felt myself falling. Mearle came running in, put me in the car, and drove to the hospital. By the time we got there, my heart was beating fast but normal. The doctor said it was just nerves and because I'd lost a lot of blood and sent me back home. Mearle was irritated that I'd made a "fuss over nothing."

Looking into the mirror one day, I was shocked at what I saw. My God! I was so thin. And the look in my eyes was old. My hair, which I'd always tried to keep curled, now hung in limp strands around my face. I didn't want to see myself anymore. Six weeks later I was on my way to Colorado Springs.

The ride across Kansas was never-ending. But I'd heard that Colorado was beautiful and was looking forward to it. Mearle had even promised that once we were away from both our families things would be better. I really hoped so.

As the mountains began to come into sight, I got excited. I'd never seen anything so beautiful. Maybe this was a good sign.

When the bus pulled to a stop, I looked out the window and saw Mearle waving. Maybe he *was* glad to see me, after all. I waved back and thought, *He is very good-looking in his uniform.* I'd always heard "a uniform makes a man." Maybe it would be true in Mearle's case.

From the letters he'd written, I'd assumed we'd move right into the apartment on the base. Not so! Our first stop was the "guest house." Actually it was just barracks converted into temporary one-room apartments, filled with couples just like us— waiting for housing. We'd live there until our name came up.

The first night, after getting settled in, we walked around town and Mearle showed me some of the sights. After eating dinner, we headed back for the barracks. As we got closer, I said, "What are all those people standing around for?" Looking up, I (and everyone else) saw a couple, stark naked, making love! The shades were all the way to the top and the lights were on! I wished desperately that the ground would open and swallow me.

Running to the top of the stairs and down the hall to our room, I ran into the room and pulled the shades down as far as they would go, sat down on the bed and cried. Then I realized I could hear someone talking and laughing . . . plainly. I could hear every word they said! The walls had to be like tissue paper!

"I'm not staying here!" I said hysterically, as Mearle came in the door.

Laughing, he said, "It's the only place there is." And he started undressing.

"But if we can hear them, they can hear us!"

"You'll get used to it," he said as he crawled into bed.

Taking a long time in the bathroom, I hoped he'd be asleep when I came out. He wasn't. My feeling about sex hadn't changed. It was something I had to put up with.

After a couple of weeks, the great news came. Our apartment was ready. I couldn't wait. When Mearle came home that evening, I was already packed. Of course, it didn't take much doing since all we owned was what I'd brought from home in two suitcases.

I had been to the base . . . the PX and other buildings. But I never knew that a barracks, like the one we were staying in, was where our apartment would be. The only difference was that, instead of individual rooms, it was cut up into two- and three-room apartments. Two if you had no children, three if you had a child (no more than one was allowed). The walls were paper-thin. You could stand in one apartment and, straining a little, carry on a conversation with someone next door.

The rooms were furnished in Government Issue. Two hard cots, a plain chest of drawers, a small square table and two chairs, one skinny floor lamp, and a plastic sofa. The bare essentials. There was no kitchen and cooking was not permitted. This was supposed to be done in the mess hall about a building's length away.

You've never cooked until you've cooked on one of those huge stoves where meals for hundreds had been prepared. The refrigerators lined the walls and each family was allowed one or two shelves. At night, it was a big family reunion. Everybody cooking at the same time and eating at those long tables designed for about twenty-five people. It was sort of fun, though, and provided a place to get acquainted.

The mornings were the funniest. About six o'clock, you'd see people traipsing back and forth in their robes and pajamas. In the winter it was really funny! Petty soon, we got wise and, rules or no rules, started carrying things for breakfast back with us after supper.

At first Mearle and I got along pretty well but after the newness wore off we were back where we started.

By this time, he was a sergeant, and started hanging out at the Noncommissioned Officers' club a lot. "It's just a bunch of guys drinking beer. Nothing you'd like," he'd say. Anyway, I was never invited.

Bob, Mearle's brother, just eighteen months younger, and also in the Army, got transferred to Fort Carson. I was never so glad to see anyone! He and Mearle were complete opposites. Mearle had dark brown curly hair, Bob was a blond. While Mearle was sullen most of the time and quick of temper, Bob was always laughing and making jokes. He was fun to be around. Sometimes he'd drop by and, finding me alone, would stay and play five hundred rummy with me till Mearle came home.

One night, Bob dropped in and, seeing I was alone again, asked, "Where's Mearle?"

"You can probably find him at the NCO club," I said.

"Why didn't you go?" he asked.

"He said it was just for guys," I said, surprised that he didn't know.

"Like hell it is! Hasn't he ever taken you?"

"No."

He looked around. "Where's your coat? We're going to the NCO club!"

I said, "I don't think Mearle's gonna like this." But I pulled on my coat anyway.

"To hell with him," Bob said. "Come on."

Walking into the club, I stopped . . . trying to get my eyes adjusted to the darkness. Suddenly, Bob said, "Maybe this wasn't such a good idea. Come on, I'll take you back home."

"No." The band was playing loud and the place was packed . . . Guys *and* girls! Hearing a familiar laugh, I turned to where it was coming from. There was Mearle sitting at a corner table with

a woman I had never seen before. Before Bob could stop me, I
walked over to where they were sitting. As he looked up, I saw
Mearle's face darken with anger. "What the hell are you doing
here?" My Irish and Indian temper surfaced.

"More like what are *you* doing here!" I said. Not even thinking, I picked up the beer sitting on the table in front of him and
threw it in his face. The bastard! It was less than he deserved!
Bob grabbed my arm and hurried me out of there.

On the way home, he said, "I shouldn't have taken you there."

"No, Bob, you're wrong. You should have taken me a long
time before now."

Sometime later, I heard Mearle come in. From the way he was
stumbling around, I knew he was drunk. I was already in bed and
turned my face to the wall pretending to be asleep.

The next morning, hearing the alarm go off, I didn't budge.

Mearle asked, "Aren't you going to get up and fix breakfast?"

"Get your own damned breakfast," I said and turned back to
the wall. As he left, he slammed the door hard. I thought, *Now
the whole world knows we've had a fight*. I didn't even care.

Of all the women in the building, one I had gotten to be good
friends with was Molly Cash, who lived next door with her
husband Jim (a Tech sergeant) and eighteen-month-old baby.
She'd told me that they had three other children back home with
her folks in Minnesota, staying there until their larger quarters
were ready. Older than I was (by eleven years), she was still so
much fun I loved to be around her. One day she'd said, "The
same doctor delivered all my babies. The last time when he said
he had to put stitches in, I said, 'Hell, Doc, just put a zipper in
that thing!'"

Before marrying Jim, Molly had been an entertainer going by
the name Molly O'Day. Her forte was Irish songs, of which she
knew what seemed like a thousand. All day long you could hear
her singing at the top of her lungs. She sang everything—from
ballads to more raunchy songs. Some people complained but I
loved it!

This particular morning, as was her custom, she knocked on
the door. Not waiting for an answer, she bounced into the room.

"Hi, honey. I heard the commotion. You two have a little
fight?"

I couldn't help it. Bursting into tears, I told her what had happened.

"Well now," she said. "What you need is to come shopping with me. I've got to buy a baby bed. So you get dressed and I'll be right back." Not waiting for an answer, she went out the door.

I thought, *Well, why not!*

Before shopping, Molly suggested lunch at a place she said served "the best drinks in town." I presumed they also served food.

The waiter (I'd never seen a man waiting tables before) said, "Cocktails, ladies?"

Before I could answer, Molly said, "Sure. Bring me a martini and she'll have a Singapore Sling."

The waiter, not even looking at me, turned to go fill the order.

"Molly!" I said, "I've never even tasted alcohol. Besides, I'm only sixteen!"

Smiling, she said, "Just keep your mouth shut, honey, and he'll never know."

Looking over the menu, I didn't recognize half of it. Molly, seeing my confusion, said, "I'll order for you, okay? How about fried oysters?"

Not wanting to show my ignorance, I nodded my head. I'd never seen an oyster!

The drinks came and mine tasted like lemonade. Being thirsty, I drank it right down and ordered another one.

By the time lunch came, I could hardly see the plate, let alone the oysters. Holding on to my plate with one hand, I'd wait until one stopped spinning around and stab it with my fork. Everything got funny. I couldn't eat for laughing. But every so often, Molly would stick an oyster in my mouth. Lord, help! The room was spinning around something awful! But I was still laughing!

Parking in front of the furniture store, Molly insisted I stay in the car. I guess she was afraid my wobbly legs would betray me. Leaning back in the seat, I wished the world would stop spinning. It was worse with my eyes closed, and I opened them just in time to see Mearle and his lieutenant pass in front of the car.

Opening the door, I almost fell as I got out. "Hi!" I said in a more than slightly slurred speech. "Molly and I just had lunch!"

Not bothering to introduce me, Mearle looked as if he could kill me.

"You're drunk!" he said, unbelievingly.

"Well . . . maybe just a little."

Shoving me back inside, he said, "I'll see you when I get home!"

As they walked away, I thought, Hell, what's he so mad about. He does it all the time!

By suppertime, my head was clear but throbbing slightly. Mearle didn't show up and I knew he was at the NCO club. He spent more time there than he did at home. Just as I started to get ready for bed, he walked in drunk. Very drunk! Grabbing me by the arm, he swung me around and slapped me full across the face, knocking me to the floor. "What the hell do you mean embarrassing me in front of my lieutenant!" He hit me again, this time with his fist! Just as his arm raised for another blow, the door burst open and Bob lunged across the room at Mearle. Slamming him against the wall, Bob drew back his fist. "No, Bob!" I screamed. I'd never seen them fight, and knowing I was the cause, didn't want to now. "It's all right! It's my fault! Let him go!" Bob dropped his arm and Mearle went out the door, slamming it after him.

Walking into the other room, I looked into the small mirror over the chest of drawers. Before, I'd complained because I couldn't focus on it . . . now I could see only too well. My mouth was bleeding, inside and out, and one eye was beginning to swell. I looked awful! Bob came in and said, "There's no reason good enough for him to knock you around."

"It's all right, Bob. He won't do it again."

After he left, I sat on the bed and counted what money I had. Not much but enough for a train ticket to Kansas City. I'd had enough!

As I'd thought, Mearle didn't come home all night and the next day, at two in the afternoon, I boarded the train.

I'd already called Beulah collect. When she met the train, I could see she was concerned . . . especially when she saw my face, which by now was black and blue.

"That son of a bitch! What did he do to you!"

Not bothering to go into details, I just said I was leaving and asked if I could stay with her for a while. I knew she had a small house and two children, but I figured if I paid half the rent and groceries, I'd be paying my way. Besides, I didn't know where else to go. She agreed on both counts.

Knowing I had to have a job, I lied about my age, saying I was eighteen (I was sixteen), and got one at the telephone company where Beulah worked.

About a month later, just when I was getting used to the routine, I began to be sick a lot. Finally, at Beulah's insistence, I saw the company doctor. I was totally shocked at his diagnosis. I was two months pregnant. I knew I'd missed a period but that was nothing unusual. I was totally terrified! Somewhere, in the back of my mind, I just knew I'd die if I had a baby. Maybe the experience with the miscarriage had something to do with it, I don't know. Pregnant or not, I was not going back to Mearle!

Each day became more difficult. More and more, I took days off. Even when I was at work, I had to take a lot of sick breaks. Even Beulah was getting tired of hearing me throw up every morning.

Mom wrote often but after a while I dreaded opening her letters. Filled with the "Wages of Sin," and "You should go back to Mearle," Mom was convinced I was out every night at some honky-tonk.

Three months had gone by and I was five months pregnant. One night, sitting alone pondering my situation and wondering what the hell I was going to do, the phone rang. Absentmindedly, I picked it up.

"Hello."

"Grace?" It was Mearle!

"Yes. What do you want?"

"I hear you're pregnant."

"How did you find out?"

"Never mind how I know. What I want to know is, who does it belong to?" I couldn't believe my ears!

"You insensitive bastard! What do you mean!"

"Well, you sure didn't look pregnant when you left here."

"Are you ignorant enough to believe you swell up like a balloon immediately?"

He laughed.

"I'll bet that's what you look like." Holding the phone out, I looked at it as if I was holding a snake in my hand. I couldn't believe I was carrying on this stupid conversation! Slamming the receiver back on the hook, I thought, *I hope it bursts your eardrums, you son of a bitch!*

By the time I was six months along, I realized my working days were coming to an end. I was gaining so much weight and having real problems with my kidneys, the doctors suggested bed rest. It was impossible.

Tiny had written and suggested I come stay with them. Deciding it was the only solution, I boarded the bus for West Plains.

Welcome or not, it sure was crowded. Their house had burned and Daddy had helped Freddie build a garage (big enough for one car), which they were living in until the the new house was finished.

Talk about wall-to-wall people! Tiny, Freddie, Mickey (four years old) and me. All in a six-by-nine-foot room. Besides the beds, there was a wood cook stove, a small table, and a couple of chairs. Clothes were hung from nails driven into the wall. Big as a barn and getting bigger every day, I took up most of the room.

They always had a vegetable garden so our days were filled with picking and canning vegetables to be stored for winter. Not being able to do much of the picking, my contribution was stringing and breaking green beans.

July had always been hot and this day was no exception! My chair and tub of green beans were placed out under the walnut tree so I could get as much breeze as possible. Sitting there breaking and stringing away, I didn't pay much attention to the cars going by. Not until one pulled around the corner and stopped. It was Mearle. I was too big to run so I sat there and waited for him to walk over to me.

Looking me over from head to toe, he said, "Gained a little weight, haven't you?" I was suddenly conscious of the way I must have looked. The last time he'd seen me, I weighed a hundred and twenty pounds. Now, at a hundred and fifty-three, I must have resembled a blimp. And not only was my body swollen, but because of the kidney disorder, my face was swollen and blotched all over.

"What are you doing here?" I asked.

"I thought we should talk."

"I can't think of a thing we've got to talk about." I went back to breaking beans.

"What are you gonna do when the baby's born?" I looked at him, hoping he could see the hate in my eyes.

"Since you don't think it's yours, what do you care?"

Seeing Tiny come out of the house, he turned to go. "Well, if you change your mind, I'm at home." Home being his folks' house. I'd heard he'd been discharged and was staying there but I could have cared less.

To his back, I said, "I won't."

Mearle's folks weren't all that bad. In fact, they'd always been nice to me. His mother, Verna, was a tall, dark-haired, dignified lady who always had a quick smile for everybody. Often, I'd wondered why, because her life certainly wasn't that easy. Her husband, Tabor, was, to put it bluntly, the town drunk. I couldn't stand him. Whenever he was around, if at all possible, I made it a point to be somewhere else.

Bill Jay, Mearle's youngest brother (ten years old), extremely jealous of my intrusion on his close relationship with Mearle, did everything he could think of to make my existence as miserable as possible. I had absolutely no intention of going back to that little house on Cass Avenue.

Waking up one morning when I was eight months along, I felt lousy and could hardly get out of bed. My feet were so swollen I could hardly get my shoes on. And my hands looked as if you could stick a pin in them and they'd deflate like a balloon. I knew I had to see a doctor.

Since there was no electricity, ironing wasn't the easiest job. Hot or not, a fire had to be built in the wood stove, then the irons (heavy cast iron) placed on the stove until they became hot enough to sizzle if you touched them with a finger dipped in water or spit. Not room enough for an ironing board, we used the table with an old cloth of some kind spread on top. We'd iron with one until it became cool, then switch to the other. Back and forth.

Finally, getting dressed in one of the only two maternity dresses I had, we left for town.

After examining me, Dr. Thompson, white-haired and the picture of a country doctor, asked, "How far do you live out of town?"

"About eight miles," I answered. He thought for a minute.

"Is there any way you could stay in town till this baby's born?"

I could see he was concerned. "How about staying with Mearle's family?"

"I can't do that, Dr. Thompson. Mearle and I are separated."

"Well, I'm going to give you some medicine and if you have any trouble at all, get in touch with me immediately." He started writing on a prescription pad.

The next few days were miserable. Staying in bed and doing without salt didn't seem to help. I began to worry about my baby.

Late one afternoon, I heard a car stop. Looking out the window, I saw Mearle and his mother coming toward the house. *Oh, no,* I thought. *I'm not up to this.*

Verna came in first. Walking over to the bed, she sat down. "Grace." Her voice was gentle. "We've come to take you home with us."

"Verna, I can't go back to Mearle. He doesn't even think the baby's his."

"He knows the baby's his. But that's beside the point. You're sick and you've got to be in town till this is over."

Mearle walked in from where he'd been talking to Tiny outside. Sitting down on the bed beside his mother, he said, "Come home with us. Just till the baby's born. I promise you, it'll be all right. After that, we'll see. All right?" Strange. He actually seemed concerned.

Tiny, who had followed Mearle inside, said, "You know you can stay here but I really think you should think about the baby. You can always come back." All of them were waiting for my answer. There was really no choice. I had to go.

Once more, we were given the front bedroom. Actually, it was just me. Mearle slept on the sofa. And never tried to touch me in any way. I'm sure he knew that would be the wrong thing to do. He was more considerate than I'd ever known him to be. *Maybe the baby would make a difference,* I thought. I just didn't know.

The doctor had said the baby could be born anytime during the last two weeks in August. By the middle of the month, I was getting anxious—and afraid. A lot of polio was going around, and the radio was full of news of where to go and not to go, mentioning all the symptoms and warnings for pregnant women.

Tiny, who visited often, suggested we hurry this child along with a little castor oil and quinine. I was game for anything.

Watching her mix this concoction, I gagged just thinking about drinking it. But, determined as I was, I downed every drop . . . then ran for the bathroom. God, it was awful!

As I walked back and forth (she said that was the thing to do) I thought, *Surely this, combined with that shit I drank, will do the trick.* I walked . . . and walked . . . and walked. Mostly back and forth to the bathroom, since I now had diarrhea. Finally, when I felt I had completed a marathon, I went to bed. The next morning . . . I was still pregnant.

The next night was hot but, tired of staying home, I insisted on going with everyone else to the softball game. Mearle was on the team and wouldn't miss a game for anything.

Taking all kinds of pillows and blankets to sit on, I lumbered into the car. My back had been hurting all day but I knew if I complained I'd have to stay home.

We'd no more than gotten settled down to watch the game when I began to have stomach cramps. Slight at first, then harder. *My God!* I thought, *I must be in labor!* I remembered what the doctor had said about timing the pains. When they became fairly frequent, I turned to Verna and said, "I think you're going to be a grandmother before morning."

Quickly, she gathered up our things and drove me to the hospital. Since I'd been told this could be a long process, I told her Mearle could come when the game was over.

All night long the pains kept getting harder and closer together. If I'd known it would be this bad, I might have put it off awhile. Suddenly, though, I wasn't afraid. I just wanted my baby to be healthy.

Finally, I was promoted to the delivery room. Lying on that cold table, with my legs strapped in a very uncomfortable position, I heard the nurse say, "Think of something else, dear." Was she crazy? How was I supposed to think of something else when I felt like I was being torn apart.

Hearing Dr. Thompson say, "All right . . . we're ready for the ether," I started telling them how to make baking powder biscuits.

At six-thirty A.M., my first born son was laid in my arms. Seven pounds, twenty-one inches of screaming humanity! He was named James (for Mom's father) and Van (for Mearle's uncle). James Van Wood . . . Born August 27, 1947.

The first day at home, after two weeks in the hospital, was scary. This precious little bundle was mine and I didn't have the faintest idea how to take care of him. I just knew he'd break, strangle, or something. A "new mother" instruction book was handy at all times. No matter how long or loud he cried, if it said feed him every three hours, he didn't get fed one minute sooner. And if his diaper was slightly damp, he got changed. He was bathed at eight o'clock every morning and again at two in the afternoon. Still he cried.

On his first checkup, the doctor asked, "Are you still breast-feeding him?"

"Yes," I said proudly, "I've got lots of milk."

"We'll see," he said, and took a sample of my milk.

Minutes later, he was back. "Hell! No wonder this baby is screaming. Your milk is like water!" He wrote out a formula which was to be started immediately.

Jimmy was one month old when Mearle announced he had decided to go to college in Pittsburgh, Kansas. An Army buddy of his lived there and said it was a great teacher's college. And since Mearle had decided he wanted to be a high school coach, it was the place to go. He went on ahead and said he'd call when he found an apartment.

Mearle had been so considerate since Jimmy had been born. And really seemed to love the baby (especially after he'd seen there was no way he could disclaim him). Neither of us had mentioned separating again.

The apartment Mearle had rented was two rooms in the basement of a private home. Dark and damp. Being November, it was also cold. The rooms were not adjoining. To go from one to the other, we had to first go through part of the basement.

The furniture consisted of one hard sofa that made into a bed, a lamp and chair, and the baby bed we'd bought on time payments. The kitchen had a gas stove, a metal cabinet which held enough dishes for two people (if you didn't have more than a one-course meal), and a table and two chairs. The floor was concrete covered with linoleum about half the size of it. There was no need for an ice box. It was so cold, milk would keep for a couple of days. And we didn't have that much food on hand, anyway.

Christmas came and, unexpectedly, so did Mom, Daddy, Tiny,

Freddie, and Mickey. I was embarrassed. Not because of our living conditions . . . but because I only had money enough to buy one skinny chicken for Christmas dinner. And the Christmas tree was a scrawny branch they'd given me at the grocery store and I'd stuck it in a pot. Pitiful. Jimmy was too little to notice, though, and Mearle and I didn't matter. The money we'd scraped together for presents went for a teddy bear for Jimmy.

The minute she walked in the door, Tiny saw the bare cupboard, and went out and bought groceries! Santa Claus comes in many forms.

Jimmy was constantly sick. Croup; three-day measles; colds; everything. I knew we had to get out of that apartment. Once a week, I'd get a paper, take Jimmy, and walk to nearby apartments. By this time, we'd also bought a stroller on credit. Then a high chair.

One day, I found it. Three bright cheery rooms up over a grocery store. Besides our apartment, there were two other apartments in the building. All leading off from an open space in the middle. It was perfect! So clean. And, for once, the furniture was nice. The rent was only slightly more than where we were living now. We moved immediately.

A young couple with a small baby lived across the hall. We never became friends and hardly ever met but it was nice knowing someone else was around.

One day, not dreaming anyone could hear me, I was bathing Jimmy and singing a soft lullaby. There was a knock at the door. Opening it, I saw my neighbor from across the hall.

"Was that you singing?" she asked.

"Oh, I'm sorry," I said, "I didn't mean to disturb you. I won't do it again."

"Oh, no. Please do. Have you ever thought of singing on the radio?"

Embarrassed, I replied, "No. I'm afraid lullabies are as far as my singing will ever go."

Turning to go, she said, "I hope not."

Price Minor, a friend of Mearle's from school, was at the apartment a lot. He kept talking about a college in Greeley, Colorado. "If you want to be a teacher," he'd say, "that's the place to be." I didn't pay too much attention to him.

One afternoon, as I stood looking down at Jimmy's face, smiling in his sleep the way babies do, I thought, *Things are too good to last*. Mearle had even gotten a night job as a cook in a restaurant and at least we were making ends meet—though barely. Then I heard Mearle and Price's voices outside the door. They were supposed to be in class. Their faces told me something was up.

"Guess what?" Mearle said. "I've decided we're moving to Colorado. Price is going with us." My feeling had been right.

"And have you also decided where the money is coming from to make this move?" I asked sarcastically.

"No problem," he said. "I've already called Mom and she'll loan us the money." That was always Mearle's answer—call Mom.

"When do we have to leave?" I asked.

"Well, school starts in two weeks . . . guess you'd better start packing."

Verna sent a hundred dollars. With Price promising to pay half the expenses, we headed west for Greeley. The '41 Buick we'd bought on the "dollar down and dollar when you catch us" plan was packed to the hilt with everything we owned. From pots and pans to baby furniture.

Except for "tourist" stops near Canyon City, Colorado, where we walked across the swinging bridge over the Royal Gorge and another when we drove to the top of Pikes Peak, it was constant driving. The car ran pretty good except for a couple of steep roads up those mountains when I thought it had huffed its last puff.

The third day, Greeley came into sight. Just fifty miles north of Denver, I expected it to be like Colorado Springs. I was disappointed . . . there was not a mountain in sight. The nearest one was twenty miles to the west, near Loveland. Greeley looked like Kansas, flat and uninteresting.

The college housing which Mearle had promised was unavailable. The nearest thing to it was a twenty-seven-foot house trailer. But even it looked good after being packed like sardines in the car for several days.

After helping unload the car, Price went to find himself a room. Thank God! For a while I thought he expected to stay with us. He was nice but a little too attentive to suit me. Mearle said it was my imagination. I didn't think so. Even so, there was noplace to put him. With a double bed at the back, a small stove and table in the middle, and Jimmy's bed in the front, there wasn't an inch to spare. The high chair sat half in the middle of the room and everything else had to be stored in an outside shed.

Figuring out our financial situation, we knew we couldn't begin to make it unless I got a job. Mearle said he had too big at load at school to work, so with the baby-sitting offered from the woman in the next trailer and thanks to my previous experience, I got a job at the local telephone company. Split shift. Ten to one and five to ten.

One day ran into another. Up at six, breakfast for Mearle, then get Jimmy and his things ready for the baby-sitter. Work at ten; home at one; wash baby clothes; hang them on the line (there was no such thing as a dryer); clean the trailer, and back to work. Sometimes Mearle would take care of Jimmy at night . . . sometimes not. When he didn't, it was after eleven before I got him home and in his own bed. Poor little thing, the minute I'd lay him down, he'd breathe a big sigh and fall asleep.

Two months after we'd arrived in Greeley, when Jimmy was fourteen months old, I discovered I was pregnant again. Great timing! The only good thing I could think of was that now they'd *have* to give us campus housing.

Envisioning campus housing as a row of gingerbread houses, I was disappointed to find the familiar converted barracks. But compared with the trailer, it was fantastic! A living room, two bedrooms, a bath, and kitchen. And with the furniture we requisitioned from the college and a little paint and powder, it wasn't too bad. Especially if you didn't look real close. Then you would see the cracks in the walls where we had to tack up cardboard to keep the freezing wind from coming leaking in during the winter. Winters were something else! Sometimes the wind-chill factor was fifty below zero. Many times diapers would freeze before I could get them on the line. Sometimes the wind would blow them dry; if not, I'd take them in and lay them across the gas heater in the living room. Jimmy was notorious for his scorched diapers.

The pregnancy hadn't been an easy one. At five months, I just couldn't handle working and taking care of the house and Jimmy, too. Mearle finally got a job as cook in a drive-in, working from five until ten in the evening. But, though he was off work at ten, sometimes it was midnight before he came home. If I questioned him, the answer was always the same. "I played a few hands of poker with the guys."

Sometimes scraping together rent money wasn't easy but I insisted upon paying it on time. When the stranger standing at the door said he'd come to collect two months' back rent, my heart fell to my feet. "You must be mistaken," I said. "It's always paid on the first."

"Do you have your receipts?" he asked.

"No, but I'm sure my husband does." I desperately *hoped* he did!

"Well," he said, "all I can say is, if you don't pay the back rent or come up with the receipts in ten days, you'll have to move out."

"Yes, sir. But I *know* I'll find the receipts." I hoped he believed me . . . I didn't.

Closing the door, I thought, *Surely he paid the rent*. But my intuition told me he hadn't. And I knew where the money had gone.

Usually I was in bed when Mearle came home but not this night. Sleep was the last thing on my mind.

Sitting at the kitchen table drinking a cup of coffee (I drank at least three pots a day), I heard Mearle's key in the lock. Surprised to see me there, he said, "What are you doing up?"

"Waiting for you. Tell me, where have you been?"

"I've told you before . . . playing poker. Why?"

"Poker?" I asked calmly.

Looking a little more than uncomfortable, he replied, "Sure," and headed for the bedroom.

"Did you lose?" I asked, following him.

"Not much," he said. Avoiding my eyes, he began to undress. The anger that had been boiling inside me exploded.

"How much!" I yelled . . . not caring if I woke Jimmy or not. "About two months' rent?"

"I lost a little but I'll win it back."

"And in the meantime, how do we pay the back rent?"

"Don't worry about it. I said I'll get it, and I'll get it." He went into the bathroom and shut the door.

Once more, I knew where the money would come from. His mother. God, I hated to ask her. Although she never seemed to mind, I knew it was two weeks' hard-earned wages for her. And, damn it all, she shouldn't have to send it to us.

School was out in June and Mearle thought it would be a good idea to go home for the summer. For once, I agreed with him. The government check of $135.00 would stop during the summer and at least in West Plains, I wouldn't have to worry about groceries. Besides, the baby was due sometime in July and I needed help with Jimmy.

The college had a warehouse for people who left in the summer. We put everything in there, except the bassinet and our clothes, and started the long, uncomfortable, hot trip to West Plains.

Even though it was more crowded than ever at Mearle's house, it was good to be there. I'd missed seeing Tiny and Freddie. And Bill Jay, who had once been so obnoxious, now couldn't do enough for me. He loved Jimmy, and when I needed help, he was the first one there. Verna was the typical, proud grandmother. Even Tabor was tolerable.

The old saying about craving is true. Or at least, it was with me. With Jimmy, it was watermelon. Now, it was canned tomatoes. And the closer it got to my time, the more I ate. At least two big cans a day. There was one difference, though. Instead of gaining thirty-three pounds, I only gained twenty. In my ninth month, I weighed one hundred and forty pounds.

Everything was ready. The bassinet, which had been Mickey's (Tiny's son) first bed, and Jimmy's, was now freshly painted white and trimmed in blue ribbon. All it needed was a baby.

The pain that woke me was familiar. Slow, steady back cramps. And, now and then, a painful knotting in my lower abdomen. The baby was one hard knot. I knew I was in labor.

By the time Mearle stopped in front of the hospital (the same one where Jimmy had been born) the pains had slacked off. Dr. Bailey, a kind and gentle man, said it might be false labor. At this news, Mearle was slightly irritated that I'd gotten him out at two o'clock in the morning for nothing. But I was insistent. "This baby will be born tonight." I just knew it! "You can go back home if you want to but I'm staying here!"

Sure enough, about an hour later, the labor began again. This time, there was no letting up. Dr. Bailey was a firm believer that you didn't take to the bed any sooner than necessary. Therefore, until almost delivery, I walked the floor.

Once more, in the delivery room. When the pains got so bad I was screaming with every one, the familiar ether mask was laid over my face. I felt my baby being born. And, somewhere in the distance, I heard Dr. Bailey say, "It's a boy." . . . Six twenty-five. July 20, 1949.

Just after I woke up, the nurse carried this precious little bundle . . . all five pounds, five ounces, in her hand. Looking down on his face, she said, "Now, isn't this a corker." And laid him in my arms. He was indeed! Later that day, with everyone's help, he was named Carter (for Tabor's father) and Alexander (for Verna's father). Carter Alexander Wood.

When she first saw him, Tiny said, "Poor little thing. You'll never grow with a name like that."

All summer long, Mearle had promised to get a temporary job so we'd have money for the trip back, but for one reason or another, he never did. He was content to let his folks support us. He spent the summer playing baseball and running around with his buddies. Except for being reminded when he saw us that he was a father, I think he thought he was back in high school. Therefore, when Corky (the name had stuck with him) was a month old, we had to borrow more money. I use the word "borrow" loosely because whoever loaned us money knew it would probably never be paid back.

Things hadn't changed in Greeley. The same dismal barracks, surrounded by rocks, dirt, and a few sprigs of grass for a yard. And along one side was an irrigation ditch. I'd always had the fear that Jimmy would wander out of my sight and fall in. Hopefully, by the time Corky was old enough to be outside we could move.

Mearle started back to school and worked at the drive-in. One day ran into another. Winter was coming on and I dreaded the thought of the long days of being cooped up in the dismal apartment. But, worse than that, since Jimmy wan't yet toilet-trained, there were twice as many diapers to be washed and no way and no room to dry them. It was a constant battle between me and the weather.

When Corky was seven months old, there was no getting out of it, I had to go back to work. There just wasn't enough money to survive. Mearle was up to his old tricks of bringing home half his pay, the rest spent on God knows what. For a while, we had credit at a nearby grocery but, when a couple of months went by without the bills being paid, it was cut off. With a new baby, I thought surely he would settle down and show more responsibility, but that word wasn't in his vocabulary.

Spring came. And on my days off, I'd take the boys to a nearby park every chance I got. I pushed Corky in the stroller and Jimmy ran along beside us. One day, as luck would have it, a wheel broke. There was nothing to do but take a cab home. The driver was black. Ordinarily, there is nothing unusual about that, except that Jimmy and Corky had never seen a black person. In West Plains, what few black people there were lived in another part of town. Come to think of it, I'd wondered myself where they got groceries and things . . . I never saw them in any of the stores.

Jimmy couldn't take his eyes off the driver. Suddenly, at the top of his lungs, he yelled, "Mama! Look at that black face!" Whirling around in his seat, the driver gave me a look that made me even whiter than I was. Because my hand was over his mouth, Jimmy kept squirming. But, every time I'd start to remove it, he'd start with, "Mama, look at . . ." My hand would cut off the rest. Finally, in front of the apartment, I was trying to hold Corky, the stroller, and Jimmy, and pay the driver. Suddenly, Jimmy bolted and ran, yelling as loud as he could, "Guess what! I just saw a black man!" to anyone within hearing distance.

I started feeling sick again. This time, worse than ever. Having no money for a doctor, I put off going as long as possible. I'd missed a couple of periods and just prayed I wasn't pregnant. I just couldn't be! Lord! Corky was just a little over a year old! How in the world would we live?

After the examination, the doctor walked in with this big smile on his face. I knew what he was going to say and I didn't want to hear it. I couldn't help it, I started to cry.

"Now, now, Mrs. Wood," the doctor said. "You're going to have a healthy baby." He didn't know I couldn't pay for this visit, let alone another baby. I went home with my spirit in the bottom of my shoes.

Mearle, who'd been watching Jimmy and Corky, said, "What's the matter with you?" Looking at him, hate must have shown in my eyes. It was obviously in my heart.

"Shit!" he said. "You're not pregnant *again!*"

My voice deadly quiet, I said, "Yes, you bastard, I'm pregnant again." As many times as I had begged him, he'd refused to use any kind of prevention and now he was surprised I was pregnant! I knew that all he was worried about was that I wouldn't be able to work.

Sick or not, there were still things that had to be done. Every day, while the boys were taking their naps, I'd drag out the washboard and wash their things in the sink, I'd clean the house as best I could. Then I would try to rest until they woke up. Once a week, with some quarters for the machines in my pocket, I'd pile the rest of the clothes (tied in a sheet) and Corky on the stroller and Jimmy tagging behind and walk a block to the laundromat. It was okay walking down but coming back it was all uphill. One day, my back started hurting real bad. It was all I could do to get home. I knew something was bad wrong! The lady next door, seeing me struggle up the steps, came out and said, "Where's that son of a bitch you're married to! Why doesn't he help you with this?" Helping me into the house, she insisted I see the doctor.

From the way the doctor was looking at me, I must have looked pitiful. Picturing myself through his eyes, I saw a girl, just barely out of her teens, who looked a lot older; and even though she was pregnant, she was skinny. A hundred and fifteen pounds. The only thing big about me was my waist. Just big enough so I was back into the same old skirt and maternity top I'd worn through two other pregnancies. Pride took over. Straightening my back, I looked him square in the eyes. I didn't want pity from anyone.

"Mrs. Wood," he said. "You're going to have to have almost complete bed rest or you're going to lose this baby."

"But, Doctor, I have two other babies."

"Isn't there anyone who can help you?" My answer was the blank look in my eyes.

All the way home, I thought, *Who can I call? Who can I call?* That evening, I called Mom. With Grandma living with them now, I knew she couldn't come but I asked for brother Bob, who was fifteen. A few days later, he arrived, prepared to stay.

With my supervising, Bob took over the care of Jimmy and Corky and, with a little help from me, even did the cooking. I literally couldn't lift a broom. Twice, when I tried, I ended up in the hospital with labor pains. The doctor said it would be a miracle if I carried the baby to term. Having gained so little weight, he said, every day would help. I barely weighed a hundred and twenty pounds.

Easter came and we got the boys one of those little ducks I saw in the stores at that time. They were fascinated! Bob built a small pen right outside the front door where it could be in the daytime. At night, with chairs and newspaper, we'd improvise an indoor pen. I had no idea what we'd do when it got bigger but, right now, the boys loved just watching it. Corky, especially.

One day, they were outside (Corky, Jimmy, and the duck) and I was sitting at the kitchen table peeling potatoes. Every now and then, I'd look out to see if they were all still in sight. Corky had a habit of taking off all his clothes and wandering off . . . only to be brought back by a neighbor. Glancing up, I saw Jimmy playing with a neighbor boy but no Corky . . . and no duck. As I opened the door, I saw them. Corky had crawled into the pen and was holding the duck's lifeless body by its neck. Looking up at me, puzzled, he said, "Gucky don't peep no mo, Mommy." No wonder. Its neck was broken. Gently, I took it from him, walked around to the back of the house, and gave it the only burial I could. I threw it in the irrigation ditch. So much for pets in the housing project.

Mailtime was the highlight of my day. Usually it was mostly bills but, every now and then, there was a letter from home from Tiny, Mom, or Verna. This time, it was Tiny. Anxiously, I tore open the letter. Expecting the usual, "We're fine . . . hope you're the same," I was surprised when it started, "Hope you received the money all right." What money? I wondered. Reading on, I learned that, some time ago, Mearle had written saying I was sick, we had run out of credit, and couldn't feed the babies. They had mortgaged their farm and sent five hundred dollars. Five hundred dollars! My mind was whirling. From what she said, they had also sent a promissory note, which he had promised would be signed by both of us, and they had received it back . . . with my signature on it. Mearle had told them that his aunt and uncle were going to co-sign with us but when Tiny had called them, they knew nothing about it. I was dumbfounded! If he had received the money . . . where *was* it? What had he done with it?

When Mearle came home that night, I was waiting for him. "Mearle . . . where's the money Tiny and Freddie sent?"

"What money?" he asked. It had never ceased to amaze me the way he could lie and look you right in the eye.

"There's no use to lying," I said. "I got a letter from Tiny today." He just shrugged his shoulders.

"So?" I couldn't believe it. He was actually daring me to question him! Telling him the details of the letter, I demanded an explanation.

"I don't have to tell you what I do with my money!" That did it!

"*Your* money! *Your* money! This time it isn't *your* money. It's money borrowed from my sister!" I knew I was screaming. "Tell me what you did with it!"

Ignoring me, he turned to leave the room and ran into the gas heater. I knew he'd been drinking. Furious because he'd burned himself, he whirled around and drew back his fist. I just stood there, hating him intensely.

"Go ahead, you bastard," I said, quietly. "That's about the only thing you're man enough to do. Hit a pregnant woman." Bob walked in rubbing the sleep out of his eyes. Mearle dropped his fist and, without saying another word, slammed out the door. I hoped to hell he never came back!

Walking in to where Jimmy and Corky lay sleeping, I looked down at their innocent faces and wondered what was going to become of us.

Usually the sun woke me up. This morning it was pain. Down low in my back. But since it wasn't in my stomach, I wasn't too concerned. Getting up, I went in to start the coffee and then in to change Corky's diaper. He was twenty-three months old and I had never been able to potty train him. He was doing pretty good, though, usually going into the bathroom with Jimmy to see how it was done till, one day, I heard him screaming. Running in, I found him holding his little penis, kicking the stool and screaming, "The wid fell on my talywacker!" After that, it was like pulling eye teeth to get him into the bathroom.

Lifting him out of bed, I felt a stabbing pain in my stomach. I couldn't ignore it any longer. I must have screamed because Bob came stumbling off the couch which was his bed. "What's the matter?"

"I've got to get to the hospital."

"Where's Mearle?" he asked.

"I don't know. Go get the lady next door." The pain was getting worse. There was hardly any time from one pain to another . . . and it was way too soon for that.

The neighbor came over and said she had already called a cab. "Now, don't worry about the boys. I'll take care of them." Having a couple of her own, I knew she would. I kissed Jimmy and Corky . . . With Bob carrying my suitcase, we left for the hospital.

Walking to the desk, I asked what floor the maternity ward was on. Her concentration on the gum she was chewing, the receptionist said, "Visiting hours aren't till two this afternoon." She went right on chewing.

Another pain hit! Loudly I said, "I'm not visiting! I'm having a *baby* and *now!*"

After a quick examination by the nurse, they rushed me right into delivery. The doctor said the heartbeat was so faint they wouldn't be able to give me anything for pain. The pains all ran together. Then I heard the doctor say, "Okay . . . now one more big push." I felt my body give up the baby I had been carrying. Being wide awake, I listened for the cry. Nothing. Turning my head, I saw the doctor holding the baby and rubbing its stomach. He turned to me. "You have a beautiful baby boy." He held him out to where I could see. Even with all that goop on him, he *was* beautiful. He hadn't cried but his eyes were wide open. Almost as if to say, "Here I am, world . . . I made it!" June 2, 1951. This time I chose the name myself . . . David Bryan. Not after anybody. Because the county hospital didn't believe in keeping you any longer than necessary, three days later I was home.

The day after David was born was the first time Mearle had seen him. It was old hat by now and he just didn't seem to give a damn, especially when I told him David hadn't cried.

For the next few days I watched David constantly. And when I wasn't, Jimmy, Corky, or Bob was. When he wasn't sleeping, he just lay there. I was so afraid he'd choke and I wouldn't know it. The doctor hadn't seemed too concerned but I was just sure he was mute.

One day, fixing formulas, I thought I heard something. My heart pounding, I stood there to see if it came again . . . Yes! A baby's crying! Dropping the bottle, I ran into the bedroom. Jimmy and Corky were standing there wide-eyed! "We didn't do anything, Mommy," they said. I didn't know who to hug first! David kept on screaming . . . and I let him. Just stood there loving the most beautiful sound in the world. A few nights later, that sound probably saved our lives.

It was rare that Mearle ever came home before midnight or after. And since I went to bed right after I got the boys down for the night, I was usually sound asleep. But not that sound asleep. I couldn't wake up. I could hear David crying but I couldn't open my eyes. Something was choking me! Almost against my will, I struggled out of bed. My God! The room was filled with smoke! Thank God, I always pulled a light blanket over David's bassinet. Grabbing him, I ran into the other room. Shaking Jimmy and Corky, I kept crying, "Wake up . . . please wake up!" Bob came into the room, coughing and stumbling. I could hear sirens! Me carrying Corky and David . . . and Bob carrying Jimmy, we ran from the house. The kitchen was in flames!

Suddenly the yard was filled with neighbors. Someone took David and Corky from me and began to walk me around the yard. Gradually, I came to myself. "Where's my babies!" I screamed. Then I saw Jimmy and Corky huddled around the woman next door, who was holding David. Together, we stood there while the firemen ran in and out of the house. Finally the fire was out. But everything in the kitchen was destroyed.

As we were standing there, Mearle drove up. He walked to the door, looked around, and turned back to me. He didn't say a word. Just stood there condemning me. The next few nights, the kids and I stayed with one neighbor, Mearle and Bob with another. I was still very weak. David was not two weeks old and now I had to try to make a burned-out house livable. Actually, the only thing that burned up was the refrigerator and stuff in the kitchen. But everything else was black with smoke. I didn't know if I could face it. Somehow, though, strength came from somewhere.

Thank God for that neighbor! Without her to take care of the
boys, I don't know what I'd have done.

About the second day into the cleaning, she hollered in
through the screen, "Grace, you have a long-distance phone
call!"

Running next door and past where the kids were playing on
the floor, I grabbed the phone. Out of breath, I said, "Hello?"

"Grace?" It was Mom. "Junior and Ronnie had a bad car
wreck. She's hurt real bad and they don't expect him to live." I
almost fainted! She was crying but went on to tell me they had
been driving from Fort Bragg, North Carolina (where he was
stationed with the Air Force), were fourteen miles from her
house, and had a head-on collision. Ronnie (my sister-in-law)
had been thrown through the windshield . . . her face all cut up.
And Junior had almost every bone in his body broken. Patty, their
fifteen-month-old daughter, was in the backseat and had only
suffered a broken leg.

Mom begged me to come home. Since David was just ten
days old, I didn't know how I could. But knew I had to.

When Mearle came home, I told him what had happened and
asked him to get an advance on his pay for gas money. He said he
couldn't. He already owed more than he had coming. Desperate,
I went to my neighbor and asked to borrow seventy-five dollars.
She went into the kitchen and came back holding out sixty
dollars. "This is all I have but if it'll help, it's yours." Gratefully, I
took the money, hugged her, and ran back home.

Mearle said he would stay in Greeley, work, and keep the
apartment. That evening, with the old Buick, which had somehow held together, loaded with what was absolutely necessary,
me, Bob, Jimmy, Corky, and with David in his bassinet in the seat
beside me, started the long drive to Humansville, Missouri.

Driving straight through, it was still almost eighteen hours.
Sometimes, when I was totally exhausted, I'd let Bob drive. But I
was so nervous, it wasn't for long at a time. Arriving, I left the
kids with Mom and went directly to the hospital. God, I hardly
recognized either one of them! Ronnie's face was horribly dis-
figured and Junior's head was so swollen, I thought the nurse
had given me the wrong room. The priest had already given him
the last rites.

For days, we took turns living in the hospital corridor. Then, a miracle happened . . . they both took a turn for the better. The doctor said it would be a long haul but they would get well. Thank God!

After about two weeks, I took the boys and drove to West Plains. Mearle's folks and Tiny and Freddie had never seen David. And they were all eager to see Jimmy and Corky.

We had just gotten settled in when Mearle called and said he was coming home. "But what about your job?" I was afraid to ask.

"I quit. I can always get another one." I tried another approach. "What about the apartment . . . and our things?" He dodged the issue.

"They'll be all right till we get back. Gotta go. I'll be in sometime tomorrow." I knew there was more to be said but he'd already hung up. Sleep didn't come easy. Somehow, I knew that whatever we'd left in Greeley would stay there forever.

Mearle avoided the subject as long as he could. Finally, at my insistence, he told me, "I'm not going back to school."

"What do you mean, you're not going back?" Surely I hadn't heard right. After all we'd gone through so he could get a teaching certificate! "What about our things?"

"Hell, there wasn't much worth bringing."

"Maybe not, but it's all we've got." I was almost in tears. Except for a few I brought with me, he'd even left the boys' pictures.

When David was three months old, Mearle broke the news that he'd gotten a job teaching in a one-room school in Dora, Missouri. Dora! That was forty miles from here! And in the middle of nowhere! He'd already rented a house and was to start teaching in a week. No wonder he'd gotten the job. Down there, all a teacher needed was a high school diploma and to be able to read and write.

The house looked as if it had been deserted for some time. It was out in the country. The nearest neighbor was a quarter of a mile away. As I stood there looking at what was to be our home, what spirit I had sank. Waist-high weeds surrounded the house in what was supposed to be the yard. And around the whole thing, a rusted barbed-wire fence. We couldn't stay here! Yet, we had no place else to go. We had to stay.

The house consisted of three rooms and a kitchen and bath.

Furniture was the barest of necessities. Old iron bedsteads that had seen better days and a mattress that looked like someone with serious kidney problems had slept there; a dresser with three legs (the fourth was propped up with a block of wood); a couch that you could only sit on two sides of (springs were sticking out in the middle); and a chair in the same condition. The floor was covered with linoleum that was so faded you couldn't tell if there had ever been a pattern. In the kitchen, there was a three-burner oil cook stove and that was it! No table or chairs! Not even a high chair. That, along with the baby bed, had been left in Greeley. Heat came from a wood stove in the middle of the "living" room. That is, when there was wood. And if I could get the fire started. Sometimes, after burning all the paper I could find . . . pouring kerosene on it . . . blowing till I was blue in the face . . . it still wouldn't burn. I'd sit on the floor and cry. Then I would start all over again.

First thing on my list of "things to do" was borrow a sickle from the neighbor down the road and try to clear the weeds from around the house and the path to the toilet. The only blessing cold weather brought was the fact that they wouldn't grow back until spring. God willing, I wouldn't be here then.

The days were endless. Never seeing a soul, I thought I'd die of loneliness. Once in a great while, the neighbor down the road would stop by but not often. Folks down there have a way of keeping to themselves. I was always afraid something would happen and I wouldn't be able to get help. Mearle took the car to school and, when he was gone, there was no escape. I was terrified of snakes and wouldn't let Jimmy and Corky outside. All day long, except when they were asleep, I'd think up little games to play with them. It kept them occupied.

Outside the kitchen door, I kept a can of kerosene for the cook stove and to start fires with. Over and over, I'd cautioned the kids to stay away from it. But, one day while I was changing David, Jimmy came running into the bedroom. "Mama, Corky's drinking out of that can!"

"What can?"

"That one you told him not to." My God, it was the kerosene! Practically throwing David on the bed, I ran out expecting to find Corky choking to death or dead. But he was just standing there making a face. Grabbing him up, I ran down the road to the neighbor's. She had lots of kids . . . she'd know what to do.

Between breaths, I told her what had happened. Taking him
from me, she smelled his breath (the odor was strong) and made
a face. "Whew!" she said. Then, after looking him over, "Well, he
seems all right. Just don't light a match around him." I guess
she'd been through a lot of emergencies such as this, but I didn't
know how many more *I* could stand.

Mearle wasn't supposed to get paid for another week. And
though I'd tried to make them stretch, the groceries had run out.
We had no food . . . not even milk. The man who ran the small
country store had refused to give us credit. There was only one
place to go. Putting my pride in my pocket, I walked to the
neighbor's house. Before I got more than a few words out of my
mouth, she began putting bologna, bread, and potatoes in a sack.
And milk in a bucket. She even put in some hard Christmas
candy for the boys.

After supper, I gave Jimmy and Corky each a piece of the
candy and sat them down to play. Mearle was gone somewhere
and we were there by ourselves. Corky came running into the
kitchen, where I was washing dishes. "Jimmy . . . Jimmy," he
said and pointed to the living room. Dropping the dish I had in
my hand, I ran in to find him lying on the floor, his face a bluish
color . . . he wasn't breathing! Panic-stricken, I grabbed him up
and hit hard on his back. Nothing! His body was completely
limp! Turning him upside down, I shook him as hard as I could.
Still nothing! I knew he'd die if I didn't do something quick.
Instinctively, I ran my fingers down his throat as far as I could
and felt the candy. Suddenly, he started gagging and, after a few
times, threw up the candy and a lot of blood. But, thank God, he
was breathing! My legs wouldn't hold me. I sank to the floor, held
him, and rocked back and forth. Oh, dear God, next time we
might not be so lucky.

Long after the boys were asleep, I waited for Mearle to come
home. Finally, I heard the car. I met him at the door. The minute
he walked in, I smelled the beer. The son of a bitch! No money
for food but he'd found the money for beer! I could have killed
him. I didn't bother to question him about the beer, though.
There was something more important.

"Mearle, we've got to move closer to town. Jimmy almost
choked to death tonight." The bastard didn't even answer me.
"Did you hear what I said?"

"Yeah . . . I've already decided that. I'm too damned good to teach in a one-room school." His answer didn't surprise me. But I was so glad to hear it, I didn't question his motives. The only thing was, we had to wait till after Christmas for them to get another teacher. And that was two weeks away.

David was a good baby but for the past few days he'd been crying constantly. I knew he had a cold and was running a slight fever but I was doing all I knew to do. Kept water boiling on the stove for steam; Vicks on his chest; and broke aspirin in tiny pieces, mashing it in water and giving it to him every few hours. Still he didn't get better. With him sick, I insisted Mearle ride to school with a neighbor so I could have the car at home.

The fire had gone out in the wood stove. For a while, I'd left the kerosene stove going but the fumes got so strong I had to turn it off. The house was so cold, I'd bundled Jimmy and Corky up in coats and sweaters till they could hardly move. And David was wrapped in so many blankets, all you could see was the top of his head. His little face was hotter than ever. I knew I had to get him to a doctor. That meant the forty-mile drive to West Plains. I didn't know if there was enough gas to make it. But with Jimmy and Corky in the backseat and David on the seat beside me, I started out.

The roads weren't the best in the world, to say the least. Dirt, one-lane roads with ruts almost as deep as the ditches that ran alongside. About fifteen miles from town there was a steep hill that ran down to a bridge that crossed the river. I'd always been afraid of that hill. And now, even more so. There had been rain mixed with snow and the only part of the road that wasn't dirt . . . was ice. As I topped the hill, I stepped on the brakes . . . my foot went all the way to the floor! I had no brakes! I threw the car into low gear. But even that didn't help much. The car was gaining speed and it was all I could do to guide it around the sharp curves. Suddenly, the roaring waters of the river came into sight and I could see the curve at the bottom that was almost impossible to make if you were standing still. I knew I couldn't make it! Just before the curve was a house on the right and a barn on the left. There was only one thing to do . . . head for the barnyard! I must have been praying because I heard myself saying over and over, "Oh, God . . . oh, God." As we crashed through the fence I heard Jimmy and Corky scream and my head hit the steering wheel.

A man was shaking me and saying, "Are you all right?"

"Where's my babies!" Then I saw David, still wrapped in his blankets, on the floor beside me. Turning around, I saw Jimmy and Corky crawling up from the floor in the back where they'd been thrown. Both with bloody noses. But they weren't crying. I guess they were too surprised.

When I explained to the man why I was going into town, he said he'd take me. At least David had stopped crying.

At the doctor's office, the nurse asked, "May I help you?"

"Yes. My baby's sick. But he's asleep now. And has been for quite a while." In fact, I thought, since the accident. She took him from me, looked at his face, and disappeared through a door. It seemed like forever before she came back and motioned to me.

"Mrs. Wood," the doctor said gravely, "your baby has pneumonia. Also, he wasn't asleep, he was unconscious." Oh God! I told him about the accident. Evidently he had hit his head when he fell from the seat. The doctor told me to take him to the hospital immediately.

For the next ten days, with Mearle's folks taking care of Jimmy and Corky, I spent every minute at the hospital. I told his mother that I would never go back to that house and sent word for Mearle to bring our things into town.

David recovered quickly, much quicker than I did. Sometimes, I'd listen to a train whistle and think, I'd like to be on that train and gone. But, right now, the only part of me that was going anywhere was my mind—a little at a time.

The only place we could find that was cheap enough for us to rent was a small house about two miles out of town. On the same road Tiny lived on. It was run-down but at least someone passed by now and then. Tiny and I nailed together orange crates to make up for furniture that wasn't there. Everything from dressers to a table and chairs.

For some time now, I hadn't been able to handle the slightest crisis. I was scared all the time. Any time I was alone with the babies, I knew something terrible would happen. All I did was cry—whether anything was wrong or not. There were times my heart would pound so hard I thought it would pop out of my chest.

Tiny came by one day, found me sitting on the floor rocking David back and forth and crying. When she asked where Jimmy and Corky were, I just kept rocking and crying. Loading us all into the car, she took me to Dr. Rollin Smith, the same doctor who had taken care of David. He said I was having a nervous breakdown and prescribed phenobarbital four times a day. Also, he said, it wouldn't be safe to leave me out there alone with the boys. I had to be where someone else was around.

After a couple of weeks of us staying with his folks, we found a basement apartment on Grace Avenue. And Mearle got a job at the Model Drug—the same place I had worked when I was in school.

The apartment wasn't fancy but a whole lot nicer than anything we'd had in a long time. Furnished fairly nicely and with a real rug on the floor. Thanks to the medicine and moving into town, I wasn't scared anymore. But I still cried a lot.

It was springtime and I'd fixed a pallet in the yard for the kids to play on. Cautioning Jimmy and Corky to watch David, I went back inside to fix supper. Hearing Tabor (Mearle's father) talking to the kids, I thought, *I hope he isn't drunk.* When he walked down the steps, I could see he was. I busied myself frying potatoes. I could barely stand him when he was sober, let alone drunk! Coming into the kitchen, he was right behind me every move I made. Suddenly, quick as lightning, he grabbed me and pushed me up against the cabinet. "You bastard!" I screamed. "Get your hands off of me!" Pushing against him with one hand, the other was reaching for the iron skillet in back of me. When he saw the skillet about to connect with his head, he dodged, lost his balance, and fell. Before he could recover, I ran to the phone and called the police. Then ran outside and took the boys to the other side of the house. It didn't matter about Tabor but I didn't want the boys to see the police take their grandfather away in handcuffs. Looking around the corner, I saw them taking him out. He looked so pitiful, I almost felt sorry for him. But not quite. As he got in the car, he called out, "Call Vern! Call Vern!" He knew I could hear him. I thought, *You're damned right I'll call Vern, you creep. And I'll tell her what you did.*

After I calmed down, I tried to think what I was going to tell Mrs. Wood. Sometimes I'd call her Verna but most of the time it was Mrs. Wood. I liked her. She'd always been good to me and now I'd had her husband thrown in jail. Before I could get my thoughts together, she walked down the steps.

Seeing me struggle with my words, she helped me by saying, "It's all right. It'll do him good to spend thirty days in jail." She sounded relieved. Then she said something I didn't expect to hear. "Grace, if you ever decide to leave Mearle, I'll help you all I can." Before, I'd just liked her. Now, I began to love her.

"I've thought about it many times but I've got three babies. Where would I go?"

"I don't know," she said, "but I don't want you to live your life like I have lived mine. Mearle's just like Tabor. No good."

After she left, I thought a long time about what she had said. I didn't know when or how but she was right. One day I would leave him.

The boys were asleep and I was still thinking about what she'd said. The door burst open and Mearle came directly across the room to where I was sitting listening to the radio. For I often wished for a television for the boys, but I was content to close my eyes and lose myself in music. Right now, Johnny Ray was singing "Cry." And I was softly singing along with him. But not for long. With one blow Mearle knocked me from the sofa to the floor. I screamed and he came toward me again. "You bitch!" he said. "I'll teach you to have my father thrown in jail!" His fist hit the side of my head! I could taste blood! I could hear the boys crying but I couldn't get up. At that moment, when I knew Mearle was going to kill me, Tiny walked in. Mearle, seeing her, walked past and out the door. She ran into the bathroom, got a wet cloth, came back, and started bathing my face. Taking the cloth from her, I said, "Please, see about the boys."

For a long time we talked. "One of these days," she said, "he's going to kill you." I didn't know what to say. I knew she was probably right. Yet, I didn't know what to do. I knew he'd calm down and apologize. I also knew it would happen again. The reason Tiny came by was to show me the pictures she had taken a week or so before. As I looked at the one of me and the three boys sitting out in the yard, I thought, *Lord, I'm twenty years old and I look forty.*

A lot of people in West Plains were moving to Cairo, Illinois, to work in canning factories. Mearle joined them. Two weeks later (as was always the case) he called and said he'd rented an apartment and for me to bring the kids on the bus. Like an old woman, I began to pack.

The minute I saw the "apartment," I knew I wasn't going to

stay there. Cairo itself was a hellhole, but the place he'd brought
us to live in was worse. The only way it differed from the Temple
Tourist Court in Waynesville, Missouri, was that the room was
slightly larger, yet just as dirty. There was no way my little boys
were going to live in this dump. Since there was no bus out that
night, we had to stay there. But after the light was out, I could
hear the relatives of the bugs I'd killed making plans of attack.
The next day, we went back to West Plains. Mearle followed a
week later.

Within a week, he came in and said, "How would you like to
live in Kansas?"

"I wouldn't."

"Well, you're going to. I've got a job there starting next week."

"What kind of job?" I asked. For the first time in a long time,
he smiled.

"A coaching job in a high school."

Sunflower, Kansas, was not all its name implied. At least, where
we lived: a row of gray, one-story prefab houses that looked a lot
like a newer concentration camp. There were two apartments to a
building—one at each end. The furniture was much like what
we'd had at Fort Carson. Except for another baby bed and high
chair we'd bought on time. But furniture was furniture. And I
was glad to have any at all.

For the first time in a very long time, Mearle seemed reason-
ably happy. And it made for a lot better atmosphere at home. He
seemed to like his job although he never talked much about it. I
was glad for whatever had brought about this change. Maybe,
just maybe, this would be the turning point.

Christmas was coming, and I decided to get a part-time job.
Our "Santa Claus" day had always been so sparse, I wanted it to
be different this year.

In a place like this, there was always someone available to
baby-sit. The only reason I was working was to make extra
money. I didn't have to look far. The woman next door had three
children and said she wouldn't even notice three more.

Since Sunflower had no stores to speak of, I headed for the
nearest town . . . Lawrence.

J.C. Penney was my first stop. Lucky for me, they had an
opening. In men's clothing, not children's, which I asked for. Not

wanting to lose this opportunity, I said I had all kind of experience. They must have been very short of help because the
manager didn't even question my long list of references, which
were all lies.

I did fine for a few days—after all, how many kinds of clothing
do men *wear*? And, unlike women, they weren't too picky. That is
until a man who weighed at least four hundred pounds asked for
some long-handled underwear. I searched . . . and searched . . .
and searched. Up on ladders, down on my knees, I found there
was nothing in his size. Finally, giving up, I said, "Sir, have you
ever thought of having them specially made?" The look he shot at
me would have cut an elephant down to size. But, hell, he was
probably Scrooge on Christmas, too! No Christmas spirit at all.

Since part of my pay was a discount of anything I bought, I
went through the store like a dose of Epsom salts. Spending
every dime I made on toys, clothes for the kids, decorations . . .
anything that had to do with Christmas. I wanted this to be the
best ever.

Christmas Eve, we put together the children's toys and placed
them under the tree. Then fixed their stockings, which Mom had
made and embroidered the names on each one, and carefully
placed them so they'd be the first thing they saw when they woke
up. Later, sitting at the table having a cup of coffee together,
Mearle and I decided we would both try harder to make something of our marriage. We both knew it was falling apart, but he
swore this was a new beginning. Things were going to be different from now on. I was willing to try anything.

The next morning, seeing the boys run from one toy to another and gobbling up the goodies Santa had left them, I even
began to like Sunflower, Kansas.

Winters in Kansas were a lot like those in Colorado—cold as
all get out and snow knee high to a giraffe. The wind would
darned near knock you off your feet. But, cold or not, it was still a
battle to keep Corky from taking off all his clothes. Always, just
before I went to bed, I'd sneak in to take one final peek to make
sure they were covered up. Tiptoeing in to where Jimmy and
Corky slept (David slept in our room), I could hear Corky talking
softly to himself. He hadn't seen me yet and I stood in the
doorway loving the scene in front of me. Except for one thing—
he had all his clothes off! Laying there, naked as a jaybird and

with his bare butt shining, playing with his blanket. Then I caught what he was saying. "Look at the horsies."

Walking over to the bed, I said, "What horsies?" and reached to retrieve the pajamas from the floor.

"On the ceiling, Mommy. See the horsies." I touched him and gasped! My, God, he was burning up! He'd been okay when I'd put him to bed, Now he was burning up with fever. As quickly as I could, I dressed him and told Mearle to stay with Jimmy and David. I would take Corky to the hospital.

In the emergency room, I watched anxiously as they took his temperature. It was 106! For no reason! Except for the fever, they couldn't find a thing wrong with him. Quickly, the nurse got out a small bathtub, filled it with water and ice cubes, and slowly put Corky in it. It broke my heart to watch his little body shivering and hear him cry, "*Mommy*, I'm cold." All night long, between the nurses and me, we bathed him in ice water. Every hour they'd take his temperature. Finally, it came down to 104. After examining him again, the doctor still couldn't find any reason for the fever but suggested Corky remain in the hospital for observation. After two days, it left as quickly as it had come. There was never any explanation for it.

I knew things were going too good to last. Mearle began to get edgy. Nothing satisfied him. He was constantly yelling at the boys over trifles. And when he did speak to me, it was always about something I had done wrong. I figured it was some problems at school. Not wanting to upset the applecart, I tried to ignore his bad moods.

Hearing the door slam, I came out of the bedroom where I'd just put the boys down for their naps. It was Mearle. "What are you doing home so early?" I asked.

Not bothering to answer, he walked over to the ice box, where he kept the ever-present supply of beer. Following him, I asked, "Is school out early?" I was afraid of the answer.

Taking a swallow of beer, he sat down at the kitchen table. "I got fired," he said matter-of-factly. It was like a bomb going off in my head!

"Why?" I asked. Then the look I knew so well came into his eyes. The look that said, "I don't want to talk about it." Picking up his beer, he walked out the door and slammed it after him.

I walked in, looked down at my sleeping babies, went back to the living room, and cried. It really was over. I knew I might as well start packing.

Dark came and still Mearle hadn't come back. The boys were playing on the floor and I was busying myself with fixing supper. I heard a knock at the door. Opening it, I saw my next-door neighbor. I guess something in my face betrayed the false cheerfulness in my voice when I said, "Hi."

"Are you all right?" she asked.

"Of course I'm all right. Why?" It wasn't the first time I'd kept my feelings to myself.

"I heard Mearle got fired," she said.

"How'd you know?"

"Honey, *everybody* knows," she said. Then went on to tell me the sordid details.

Since it was a small community, a lot of the teachers lived in the project but I'd never met any of them. Each time there was some function going on, Mearle had always found some excuse to exclude me. But, not wanting to rock the boat, I didn't push it. The culmination of what my neighbor told me was that Mearle had been having an affair with the female physical education teacher, and they got caught. Evidently it had been going on almost from practically the first day we arrived. And everyone knew. Everyone but me.

For the next three days, I didn't know, and didn't care, where Mearle was. Groceries and money were running low and I was too ashamed to stick my head out the door. In between fits of crying, I packed. I didn't know where we'd end up but I knew we'd be leaving Sunflower. The eviction notice had come the day before.

Mearle came home looking, for all the world, like he'd been on a three-day drunk. A three-day growth of beard on his face, hair that hadn't seen a comb, and clothes that definitely had been slept in. Standing there looking at him, I thought, *He looks just like Tabor*.

Not even bothering to apologize or offer an explanation, he said he'd talked to a friend of his from the Army who lived in Verdonia, Kansas—not far from Pittsburgh—and he'd gotten a job there repairing railroad tracks. I thought, What a waste for a man with three years of college. But at least it was a job.

Verdonia itself wasn't much more than a ghost town. In fact, it wasn't even on the map. A few basic stores scattered along one main street. The only word to describe it was "dirty." The houses had old tin roofs and outer walls that had never been painted. The color came with age. I felt as if I had lived in the town since the Civil War. And I was twenty years old.

First things first, the minute we pulled into town we had to find a place to live. And since there weren't many calls for apartments in Verdonia, we rented the only place available. Upstairs over the grocery store. The only entrance and exit was down rickety stairs in the back. God forbid there should be a fire! But, when I opened the door, I realized that a fire was probably the best thing that could have happened to that place. The former occupants were still there—cockroaches. The biggest cockroaches I had ever seen. Mearle just unloaded our few belongings and left for his friend's house. Standing there looking around, I saw no hope of making this place livable. And I darned near didn't have the heart to try. There was one large room furnished in "early empty." A couple of iron bedsteads, a beat-up old sofa, a rickety table and chairs, and an oil cook stove. The kind where you pour kerosene into a tank at the side and hear (and watch) it bubble as the oil is used up. Since it was used for both cooking and heating, it went empty quickly. The louder the bubbling, the more frightened I became. There was no money to buy more. There was no ice box but it didn't matter. There was never money enough to buy more then food for one meal at a time, anyway.

We'd lived there about a month and I never left the apartment except to go downstairs to the grocery store. Mearle would be gone for two or three days at a time. Every day I'd count the few dollars I had left and prayed it lasted until payday. David had long since been weaned from baby food . . . he was now expensive to feed. The only food I bought, outside of milk and bread, was canned soup. And once in a while, hamburger meat or wieners.

It was not unusual for Mearle to be gone a few days, but when it turned into a week, I began to get scared. The money was gone and the only food we had left was a half quart of milk and one can of vegetable soup.

There was about a quarter tank of gas in the car so Mearle had ridden to work with his friend. All day, I anxiously watched out the window for the sight of his truck. As I watched, I saw the landlord coming around the side of the building . . . straight for the stairs. Since there was no way of avoiding him, I opened the door at his knock. He'd always looked unfriendly but today his face was lined with frown wrinkles. He had to of been a hundred and ten if he was a day.

"Where's your husband?" he asked angrily.

Nervously, I answered, "He's at work."

"I've come for the rent." He sure didn't mince words.

Trying to bide for time, I said, "I'm sure he'll be home tonight. We'll have it for you then." I didn't know whether we would or not.

"I don't want it then . . . I want it now!" The bastard! He could have cared less that there were three babies playing on the floor and I had no food and no money. "I'll give you just twenty-four hours to come up with the rent or you have to get out!" On that note of good cheer, he walked back down the stairs.

That evening, I opened the last can of soup and put the boys to bed. I'd never been much for praying but I prayed that night. There was nothing to eat for breakfast.

The next morning, thank God, the kids slept later than usual. Dreading for them to wake with the usual "We're hungry, Mommy." Then I spied a ray of hope—the kids' piggy bank, where I'd stashed a few pennies now and then. Eagerly, I broke it open. Thank you, Lord, there was enough for a quart of milk and some cereal.

All day I waited. Still no Mearle. That evening, with not a dime in my pocket, I loaded the car, and telling the boys that we were going to a drive-in movie, headed out for God knows where. There wasn't a thought in my head. Thank God, Mearle hadn't taken the car. And thank God, the people we owed for it couldn't find us to repossess it. Or maybe it was so old they didn't want it back.

The kids were all excited. What do you tell three little boys? We don't have any food? We don't have a place to sleep tonight? I'm going to run this car off a cliff with you and myself in it? In an irrational moment, I might have except that there wasn't a hill high enough in this damned country.

Coming to the outskirts of a small town called Frontenac, I drove up and down streets looking for a house that seemed friendly. One with a porch light on. That, to me, always meant "welcome." As I searched, I thought, *I wonder if all these people know how lucky they are.* I doubted it.

The boys, never mentioning the drive-in, had long since fallen asleep. I was thankful because I couldn't bear to hear them say they were hungry. Knowing what I had to do, I searched for just the right house. Up and down streets. I had to make a decision soon as the gas tank was registering empty. I saw it. Pulling into the graveled driveway of a neat, white-frame house, I stopped, put my pride in my pocket, and walked to the front door. All the time expecting a dog to come bounding around the corner and take my leg off.

I knocked on the door . . . afraid no one would answer . . . then afraid someone would. I didn't know what I'd do if we were turned away. Just as I was about to give up, the door opened and a lady who looked like she might be someone's grandmother stood there. I sure hoped she was! Smiling, she said, "Yes?"

Before I could swallow them back down, the words came tumbling out of my mouth. "I'm sorry to bother you but I have three little boys asleep in the car . . . no money and no place to sleep. Can you help me?" Not knowing what to expect, I stood there praying silently.

Pushing open the screen door, she glanced toward the car, turned around, and said, "Henry, come out here and help this lady bring these children into the house." I could have kissed her!

Me carrying David, the man carrying Corky, and with Jimmy still half asleep stumbling along beside us, they led us to a small but comfortable room off the screened-in back porch. "We fixed this up for our grandchildren," they said. I knew I had been guided to that house.

After helping me get the boys into the bed, the woman said, "You get some rest. We'll talk tomorrow." Her husband didn't say much but his eyes said all I needed to know—they said "welcome." Softly, they closed the door behind them. Suddenly, I realized I didn't even know their names. And they hadn't asked mine.

David's crying woke me. Poor little thing, his diaper was soaked and he hadn't had a bottle since last night. Jimmy and Corky jumped up from the floor where they'd been playing their silent games. "Mommy, we smell breakfast. Can we have some?" Pulling them to me on the bed, I tried to explain how and why we came to be there and asked them to promise to be as good as possible and not to bother the people any more than they had to. With eyes very solemn and much older than their years, they said, "We promise."

A soft tap came at the door and a woman's voice said, "Breakfast's ready." Carrying David, and with Jimmy and Corky standing patiently beside me, I knocked at the kitchen door. Quickly it opened and the woman's cheerful smile greeted us. "Bring those babies in here," she said, and took David's empty bottle from me. Suddenly very shy, we just stood there. Giving the boys a gentle push, she said, "Go on." Then the wonderful aroma of biscuits, gravy, and eggs took over. Seeing the boys eat like they were starved was more than I could take. Tears rolled down my face. The woman came around the table, patted me, and said, "I'll feed the baby. You eat."

While we were eating, she told us their names—Henry and Sarah Norton—and said they had lived there ever since they were married, fifty years before. I tried to tell her how much I appreciated everything and she said, "Shush now. It'll be good to have children around the house for a while."

As the days went by, I began to feel as if we belonged there. But, knowing we didn't, I wrote to Mom and Daddy asking for money to come home. Waiting for an answer, I tried to do everything I could to help out without getting in the way.

The house was small but extra neat. And in the back was a workshop where Mr. Norton spent most of the time working at his hobby of refinishing furniture. Something he'd started when he'd retired several years ago. "It keeps me out of trouble," he'd say, laughing. I'd bet you a million dollars that man had never been in trouble a minute of his life.

In the front was a porch that ran all the way across with a porch swing on it. From there you walked into the living room, which was furnished with old but comfortable furniture. Most of it they'd probably had for many years but, from the way it looked, I could tell it had been lovingly cared for. On the backs of the sofa and chairs and on the small tables scattered around were lace doilies which Mrs. Norton had made. A big wood stove stood on one side of the room and in one corner was an organ. Their bed was covered with a patchwork quilt which she had also made. The floors, except for the parts covered with braided rugs, were all shiny wood. There was a dining room but no one ever ate there. "Except when we have company," she said. Next came the kitchen, where the hub of activities took place. A big wood cook stove on which something always seemed to be cooking, a round table with four round-backed chairs, and lots of cabinets which I was told Mr. Norton had built. Then there was the screened-in back porch off of which was the bedroom where we slept. I could tell there was, and had been, a lot of love in that house.

It sounds as if we were there a year and I wish we could have been, but after two weeks the mailman delivered the "moving on" money. Early the next morning, after tearful good-byes, we headed for Springfield, Missouri.

Crowded or not, it was good to be home. Playing cards with Grandma (who was living with Mom and Daddy now), hearing Daddy tell stories to the boys and talking to Mom, who, through the years, had changed her mind about Mearle. I didn't even mind serving trays to the few old people she boarded.

Within a few days, I had a job in a dress shop on the square making twenty-seven dollars a week. With Mom's help, I went to the Goodwill and bought a few secondhand clothes to work in. They weren't the best, but a lot better than I had. I don't know what the shop owner saw in me but she did something I'd never heard of before and haven't since. Each day she'd put together an outfit for me out of stock and let me wear it until closing time. She called it "modeling" but I knew it was charity. But I didn't care. I loved my job and the pretty clothes. Little by little I began to learn about materials, what colors to put together and what looked good and what didn't. The owner also told me it was better to have one good outfit than a dozen odds and ends but, since I knew it would be a long time before I'd have to concern myself with either one, I didn't worry too much about that.

It had been a month since I'd seen or heard from Mearle and I began to breathe easier. Maybe he was gone for good. Once in a while the boys would ask, "Where's Daddy?" but not often. I started thinking about getting our own apartment. Before I could, though, all three of the boys came down with the German measles. For three weeks, Mom and I kept the halls hot going from one bed to another. David on a cot in the hall, Jimmy in Grandma's room, and Corky, since he seemed to have the worst case, in a room by himself. Since the doctor said not to let the light hit their eyes, we kept the shades pulled night and day. But still, if I even opened his door a little bit, Corky screamed, "My eyes! My eyes!" Slowly, and with a lot of help from chicken soup, they began to get better. The day they were able to be outside was a great day, celebrated with a big Dairy Queen ice-cream cone. I didn't even care if it dripped all over their clothes.

The apartment I found was close enough so I could drop the kids off at Mom's on my way to work. It probably wasn't much, by most folks' standards, but, compared to what we had lived in, it was a mansion. Three rooms (living room, bedroom, kitchen, and bath) in a private home. And, most important, a yard for the boys. The furniture was old but in good shape. And the floors were covered with linoleum, which I kept shining. I loved it! My favorite times were at night. After bathing the boys, we'd all pile up in my bed and tell stories to each other. I say to "each other" because they always had to relate the latest "Grandma and Grandad" stories and tell me what had happened in their day. When they got sleepy, we'd all say "Now I lay me down to sleep" together. Afterward, I'd say my own prayer of thanks.

By way of Tiny, I learned that Mearle was back in West Plains. I knew it was only a matter of time before he showed up and I dreaded it with a passion. Sure enough, when I came home from work one day, he was there on the porch waiting for me. Just as if he'd come from work and not been gone for weeks. The kids jumped up and down saying, "Daddy's home! Daddy's home!" Kneeling down, he gathered them all in his arms and gave me a look which said, *"See, what are you going to do about it?"* He was right. All the things Mom had told me about what a wife had to put up with came back in full force. I felt beaten . . . right down to my toes.

After the kids were in bed, he told me this farfetched story which I didn't believe a word of. Something about coming home, finding us gone, and going on a three-week drunk which ended in West Plains. There, he had gone to see Tiny, who had told him where we were. I guess, since he was my husband, she didn't know what else to do. He said he had waited this long to come back to give me time to get over my "mad spell." "Besides," he said, "I've got a job teaching school here and, I swear, this time it'll be different." How many times I'd heard those words.

The joy had gone out of me and my job. Every day was the same. Get up, take the kids to Mom's, go to work, come home, fix supper, and go to bed. Even my boss noticed the difference and asked what was wrong but I couldn't talk to a stranger about my personal life. Before, I'd looked forward to every customer; now I dreaded putting on my false smile. Tension was my constant companion. Even though Mearle was teaching, he found fault with everything and everyone. His job, the other teachers, but, most of all, me and the boys. Before, they had been happy and laughing all the time. Now all they did was cry and fight with each other. And Jimmy, who was five, had started wetting his bed.

Struggling in the door with a sack of groceries in one arm and David in the other, I heard the phone ringing. Quickly, setting both of my loads down on the floor, I ran to answer it. It was Mom just wanting to know if I got home all right. Hearing the boys laughing, I turned just in time to see David break the last of the dozen eggs into the carton. "Mom, I've got to go. David's just broken a whole dozen eggs." Before I hung up, I heard her say, "Well, boys will be boys." Grabbing David up, I spanked his bottom and put him on the bed. Jimmy and Corky, still laughing, climbed up on the sofa to watch me clean up the mess. "This is *not* funny," I said, "groceries cost money!" I didn't know why I was hollering at them . . . they were too young to understand. But, I was tired . . . so damned tired.

At that moment Mearle walked in. Seeing the groceries still sitting on the floor and me down on my knees cleaning up an obvious mess, he yelled, "What the hell's goin' on! Can't you do *anything* right? I suppose you expect me to buy some more. Well, to hell with it!" I knew I was in for one more hell of a fight. And I just didn't have the strength for it. Looking him straight in the eye, I said, "Mearle, I don't expect or want you to do anything except stay out of my sight." Then it dawned on me. It was too early for him to be home. "What are you doing home, anyway?"

"I quit my job," he said. I wasn't even surprised.

"What was it this time?"

"I'm not taking orders from some dumb ass who knows less than I do," he said. That was Mearle all right. All that mattered

was his false pride. It didn't matter that we had less than ten
dollars between us, and the rent was due. David had started to
cry and Jimmy and Corky were listening to every word that was
said. Their eyes were big as saucers. I had visions of him dragging us off to some other godforsaken place while he went off
chasing some rainbow that was never there.

"Not this time," I said, my voice deadly quiet.

Whirling around, he said sarcastically, "What do you mean
. . . not this time. You'll go wherever I damned well tell you to
go," and turned to go into the kitchen. I started for the bedroom
to quiet David. Before I had taken two steps, Jimmy screamed,
"Mommy!" Not even bothering to look where I knew Mearle was
standing, I went back and kneeled in front of Jimmy and Corky.
They were scared to death and I couldn't stand it. But they
weren't looking at me . . . they were looking behind me. Not
turning around, I said, "I've had it, Mearle. I can't take any more
of this. I'm leaving. If I have to support children, I'll support three
instead of four."

Grabbing me from behind, he pulled me to my feet with one
hand . . . a butcher knife was in the other. Holding the knife
against my throat, he said, "I'll see you dead before I let you
leave." I could hear the boys screaming and felt the sharpness of
the blade. He was just crazy enough to do it. I'd always heard that
a trapped animal fights. But I didn't. I knew I was dead but
somehow didn't think he'd harm the boys. "Go ahead," I said, "I'd
rather be dead than live with you." I think I really meant it. My
back was to him but I felt his hold tighten. At that moment, there
was a knock at the door. The saying "God protects fools and
children" came to my mind.

Startled, Mearle dropped the knife and I ran to the boys. "It's
all right," I said, trying to calm them, "Daddy didn't mean it."

Mearle went to the door and said, "What do you want?" A
voice I didn't recognize answered.

"We're supposed to meet that guy. Did you forget?"

Turning to me, Mearle said, "I'll be back in an hour. I'll talk to
you then."

As he closed the door, I said, "You wanta bet?" Running to the
phone, I called my folks. Daddy answered. "Daddy, I'm taking a
cab to your house. Will you pay for it?" The panic was plain in my
voice.

"I'll meet you out front," he said. Daddy hated Mearle from the day I married him and had never changed.

Realizing what had almost happened, my heart was beating so fast I could hardly breathe. Stationing Jimmy at the door to tell me when the cab came, I started throwing things in the two cardboard suitcases we had.

Hearing the blessed sound of a car horn, I grabbed suitcases, kids, and what ever else I could carry and ran out the door . . . never looking back. Halfway there, I realized I'd left the most precious things . . . the only decent pictures I had of the kids. But I was afraid to go back.

Until midnight, Mom and Daddy kept us hidden. Then, with as much money as they could spare, we boarded a Greyhound bus for Oklahoma City, where my brother Pete and his family lived.

Within a few days, I had a job as a waitress in a café close to their house. Not much money but enough to help with the groceries. The kids seemed to take everything in stride. They were so used to being dragged from one place to another, they just adapted to wherever they were.

Knowing Mearle would eventually find us, I'd jump every time the phone rang. One night, I heard Pete say, "No. You can't talk to her! Haven't you done enough?" I knew we had to leave. I never wanted to see Mearle again.

My brother, Junior, had not only recovered from the car wreck but had rejoined the Air Force. Ronnie (his wife) had also recovered but their marriage had fallen apart. Now, he was remarried and stationed at Lockbourne Air Base near Columbus, Ohio. When I called him, he said, "Sure, come on out. We'll find room."

Junior and Ida (his present wife) had only been married a short time and I felt so bad about having to move in with them. Especially since they already had two boys (hers by a former marriage) and were having a rough time getting by on his Air Force pay. So we made a deal. Ida would stay home, take care of the kids, and I'd work and buy the groceries. They'd pay the rent.

The only job I could find was clear across town. Being chief cook and bottle washer (literally) in a small, one-man-operation restaurant; the entire place consisted of three tables in the middle of the room and six stools at the counter.

Since I had to open up at six, my day started at four A.M., when I'd get up, tiptoe around so as not to wake anyone, put myself together, and walk two blocks in the dark (most of the time) to the nearest bus stop. Half the time I dozed off during my thirty-minute ride. It always amazed me how many people were up at that time of day. Some of them, I think, just wanted to see the world before it had time to get dusty.

First thing, I'd start a pot of coffee and clean the grill. In case an early customer wandered in. The only early customers were people who worked nearby. Since we weren't in a busy business area, I never had anything that resembled a rush hour. And unless their taste was for hamburgers, cheeseburgers, french fries, or bacon and eggs (the only things I figured I couldn't mess up too bad), they were out of luck anyway. Many times, hours would go by with maybe one customer wanting a cup of coffee and directions to a "good" restaurant.

My only company was a jukebox filled with country music. Since I hadn't listened to the Grand Ole Opry in years, most of the songs were unfamiliar to me. The only ones I recognized were "Jambalaya" and "Your Cheatin' Heart" by Hank Williams . . . and only because they were popular everywhere. I was more into "Wheel of Fortune" by Kay Starr. But the more I played "A Fool Such As I" by Hank Snow, "Just Out Of Reach" by Faron Young, and "I Forgot More Than You'll Ever Know" by the Davis Sisters, the more I liked them. Once I discovered how to "trip" the jukebox, it played constantly.

There was no such thing as having to worry about carrying the money to the bank. There was never enough to bother with. I'd just take what few dollars I earned home with me and have it to open up with the next morning. Many weeks I'd barely take in enough to pay my fifty-dollar salary, which, except for bus fare, went to Ida.

Junior didn't have a car to go to and from the base, so he'd bum rides with different people. Most of the evenings, it would be his Tech. Sergeant, whom Junior called Smitty, who brought him home.

There was no way any red-blooded American girl would not notice T/Sgt. Lowell Alexander Smith (Smitty). Including me. By far, he was the best-looking man I had ever seen. He wasn't really tall (about five nine or ten) but had an almost perfect physique—

wide shoulders, narrow waist, and muscles. Blond, wavy hair, perfectly trimmed mustache, and brilliant blue eyes. And seeing him step out of his red and white Lincoln Continental in his perfectly pressed and tailored uniform started my heart beating double-time. I'd never known this feeling before and didn't know what to do with it. Especially since Junior had told me he was already married. Separated yes, but still married.

More and more, about the time for me to close the restaurant, Smitty would show up to drive me home. It got so I'd look for him and be disappointed if he didn't show up. *This is crazy,* I thought, *I'm married, too.* Oh, well, it was nice to have a friend anyway. Especially a friend who looked at me the way he did—like an attractive woman. He made me *feel* attractive. I began to take more notice of the way I looked. Where before, I'd just run a brush through my hair, wash my face, and let it go at that . . . now, I'd painfully sleep all night in those horrible pin curls so my straight hair would have some curl to it. I'd apply a little mascara and lipstick—as much as I knew about makeup. Usually the lipstick would be too dark, though, and when he'd mention it, I'd wipe most of it off. Since I had no money to waste on clothes, I made do with what I had—a few simple blouses and skirts. But I took a lot more pains when I ironed them.

Smitty began hanging around at night, playing cards or taking me and the kids to a drive-in movie or out for ice cream. Those were special times. The boys loved his car—so did I. We'd never even seen one like it, let alone ridden in one. It seemed a mile long. And since it was Smitty's pride and joy, I was always a little nervous when the boys ate ice cream in the car. He'd never been around little kids, but from past experience, I knew that accidents were bound to happen. But Smitty really seemed to like the boys and was never anything but good with them. It wasn't long before they, too, began to look forward to seeing him.

As much as I was beginning to like Smitty, I still had to work and keep up my end of the bargain with Junior and Ida.

One day, at the restaurant, thinking the man who walked in the door was a much-needed customer, I walked over, smiled, and said, "What'll you have?"

"The keys," he said.

Thinking I'd misunderstood, I said, "I beg your pardon?"

"The keys," he repeated. "I'm closing you down."

"What for!"

"Because the man that owns this joint ain't paid a bill in months," he said. He held out his hand.

I knew there was nothing else to do. "Is it all right if I keep what money there is for my pay?" I asked hopefully.

"Hell, no! What's in the till stays in the till!"

"All right," I said. "I'll leave soon as closing time comes."

"Sister, you'll leave now! And I'll lock up after you." Collecting my empty purse, I walked out the door.

Trying to figure out how I was going to tell Ida that I had no money for groceries, I was absentmindedly looking out the bus window. The bus stopped at a busy intersection. Suddenly, right in front of me was my answer, a sign that said "White Castle" . . . and, better yet, another sign that said "Help Wanted." The bus started to move. Quickly, I ran to the front. "Please. I have to get off!" Totally ignoring me, he kept right on going. Two blocks later, I got off the bus and walked back.

I needed the job and couldn't turn down the only hours that were available . . . eleven at night until seven in the morning. But I figured it would still work out. Better, probably. Except for sleeping a few hours in the mornings, I could be with the boys all day, have supper with them, and be there to put them to bed. If I could only hold up.

I knew it would be hard but not nearly as hard as it was. Unlike the place where I'd been working, this place was constantly busy. When I wasn't waiting on customers, I was cleaning something . . . pie cases, grills . . . anything to keep from standing around, which the management didn't allow. There was one thirty-minute break for "lunch" and whatever else you had to do. At three in the morning, when I was trying desperately to stay awake, they found the perfect solution. Lift all the heavy wooden slats that covered the floor behind the counter and in the kitchen and mop. By seven in the morning, with every muscle in my body aching, it was all I could do to drag myself home and into bed.

Always, when I got home—no matter how tired I was—I'd have breakfast with the boys, and talk to Ida awhile. This morning, I knew there was something on her mind. Figuring the boys had done something wrong, I said, "Okay, Ida . . . spit it out. What's wrong?" She hesitated. Teasing a little, I said, "Come on . . . it can't be that bad."

"Well . . ." she started. Ida talked so soft, half the time I had to strain to hear her.

"Well, what?" I coaxed.

Not looking at me, she said, "I'm pregnant."

"That's wonderful!" I said.

"But I can't take care of the boys anymore." That wasn't wonderful!

"The doctor says with Gary and Billy [her two boys] it would be too much for me." All thoughts of sleep left my mind. It was too cluttered with "What am I gonna do now."

"Don't worry about it, Ida. We'll find someone." I couldn't keep the depression out of my voice. I remembered what a rough time I'd had carrying David. I was sympathetic, really. But a baby-sitter was crucial.

I read newspaper ads, I made several phone calls, then rode the bus to check out the only two who sounded decent whom I could afford. It wasn't much, two rooms upstairs in a private home, but when the woman said she could take care of the boys while I was at work, I signed her up. Besides the outside entrance, there were stairs that led down to the living room. That way, Jimmy and Corky could sleep upstairs, and she could keep David down there with her. That evening, I called Smitty and asked if he'd move us.

After making several trips up and down the stairs getting our "junk" in, I noticed the boys were extra quiet. Then Jimmy started to cry.

"Why do we always have to move, Mommy?" God, it broke my heart. Kneeling down to where they sat on the floor, I gathered them all in my arms and cried with them.

When Smitty had the last box in, he said he had to leave and asked me to walk to the car with him. Leaning against the car door, he gently drew me to him and put his arms around me, tilting my face up to his.

"Grace, you know I love you," he said. He'd said it before but always in a joking manner. This time he was serious.

"Yes, I know."

"Do you love me?" I searched my heart. Was love this closeness I felt . . . this terrible needing feeling? If it was, then I did.

"Yes . . . I do. Will you marry me."

As much as I wanted to shout, "I *will*," I laughed instead.

"Seems to me, we both have divorces to work out first." This brought a smile to his face.

"Yes, I know. I'm working on mine. Will you do the same?"

"As soon as I can. I promise." This kiss was different from any of the others we'd shared. Bonding. Walking back upstairs, even as tired as I was and facing a night at work with no sleep, my heart was lighter than I could ever remember it being.

One morning, two weeks later, I came home to find all three of the boys huddled together in the bed upstairs. The woman was nowhere in sight. David and Jimmy were crying. Corky was just laying there wide-eyed.

Rushing over to them, I said, "What's the matter?"

"We're hungry," Jimmy said.

"Haven't you had breakfast?"

"No," Jimmy said, "and we don't get to eat when you're not here."

"What do you mean . . . you don't get to eat?" They had never lied to me. I knew they weren't lying now.

"They eat the good stuff and we get soup. Mommy, we're hungry." That did it!

Furious, I dragged them with me downstairs to the kitchen. By damn, I'd paid for these groceries and we were going to eat. In the middle of fixing bacon, eggs, and pancakes, the woman walked in and demanded to know what I was doing.

"I'm fixing my children something to eat, *that's what*," I said, my anger clearly showing.

"They get food," she said.

"What, cereal and soup? Jimmy said you save all but that for yourself!"

"Well, grown-ups need more food. Kids don't need anything more than soup!" I could have slapped her ugly face!

"Don't worry, lady. We'll be gone shortly. But, first, we're going to eat!" I went right on fixing breakfast. Afterward, taking everything we could carry, I took the bus back to Junior's and did something I'd never done before—called Smitty at work.

He came on the line. "Sergeant Smith here."

"Smitty?" I couldn't keep the tears out of my voice.

"Grace, what's the matter?"

"Will you loan me the money to go back to Springfield?"

"To get the divorce?" he asked.

"Yes." I went on to tell him what had happened.

"I'll bring it over tonight." Before hanging up, he said, "Grace . . . I love you." That's all it took to bring on serious crying.

Back in Springfield, we stayed with Mom and Daddy. They were so glad to see the boys. Even Grandma, who was never overly fond of children, especially boys, was happy to see them. I remembered when Jimmy was born and I asked her, "What do you think of him, Grandma?" She looked at this little red, wrinkled person I was holding and said, "If it was mine, I'd drown it." I was never sure whether she was joking or not. Looking a lot more than the quarter Indian she was, sometimes I'd thought she'd be happiest with a tomahawk and a teepee.

Wanting to get divorce over with as soon as possible, I went to the Legal Aid Society. I had no idea where Mearle was. They said the procedure was to run an ad in the legal section of the newspaper and wait thirty days. If there was no answer, then a court date could be set. Each day, starting with July 1, I marked an X on the calendar.

The boys were down for their naps and Daddy came out to join me on the porch where I was reading a letter I'd just received from Smitty. Good news. He had gone to Litchfield, Kentucky (his hometown), and gotten his divorce. He said his wife had never shown up. Wanting to share my happiness, I told Daddy what the letter said. His face was serious. "It's about time you were happy, baby girl," he said. I got up and hugged his neck. Of all the people in the world, after my children, I knew my Dad loved me best.

Looking up, I saw Mearle walking toward the house. "Oh, God. It's Mearle," I said, and started shaking all over. Daddy walked into the house. I couldn't move.

As Mearle walked up the steps, Daddy came back out carrying his double-barreled shotgun.

"Daddy. *No!*" I screamed.

Leveling the gun right at Mearle's head, he said, "Get off my porch, you son of a bitch! Or I'll blow your brains out!"

"Don't, Daddy!" I cried. "He's not worth it!"

Never budging an inch or lowering the gun, Daddy said, "I'm gonna die anyway . . . I might as well die doing the world a good deed."

Mearle got the message. When he turned to go, he said, "Get

the damned divorce if you want to but I'll see those kids starve to death before I give you a dime!"

Finding my legs, I grabbed the gun from Daddy. As Mearle disappeared around the corner, I was still trying to figure out how to fire the damned thing.

Court day was August 15. As much as I wanted the divorce, I dreaded seeing Mearle again. He never appeared. After declaring forty dollars a month child support, the judge said: "Divorce granted to Mrs. Wood." Walking out of the courtroom, I vowed, if it took the rest of my life, I'd make Mearle pay for what he'd said.

A week later, Smitty came to take the boys and me back to Columbus. Seeing how happy I was, Mom and Daddy took to Smitty immediately. "This time," they said, as we were leaving, "you'll be in good hands."

Smitty and I were married on September 2, 1953. Jimmy had turned six on August 27, Corky was four on July 20, and David was two on June 2. And I was twenty-three years old. Smitty was thirty-one.

Houses near the base were hard to find. The one we moved into was fairly nice but it had a dirt yard. Since boys will be boys, after a short time outside, they were filthy. Knowing how Smitty cared about cleanliness, I'd have them, me, and the house shining when he got home. Much as I loved him, he was strictly military and inspected his home as though it were a barracks. He just didn't tolerate dirt. I'd never seen this side of him, nor his temper. The evidence of that came one evening while I was fixing supper. Smitty was sitting in a chair holding David on his lap, and Jimmy and Corky were sitting on the floor nearby. I had just thought, "I wish I had a camera," when suddenly Smitty said, "Son of a bitch!", jumped up, pulled David's pants down, and slapped his bottom so hard it sounded like a gunshot. At the same time David screamed, so did I. "Smitty!" Jimmy and Corky ran for the bedroom.

Running over, I grabbed David and tried to quiet his screams. Turning to Smitty, I said, "Damn you! Don't *ever* do that again!"

"The little brat pissed on me!" he said.

"Don't you call my son a brat! He's not a brat, he's just a two-year-old baby!" Smitty had never seen my temper before, either. I walked into the bedroom with David . . . finally his sobs stopped.

Smitty stood in the doorway. I knew he was sorry but it didn't help. Walking over, he took David from me, held him, and rocked him back and forth saying, "Daddy's sorry. Daddy loves you." Later that night, we had come to a firm understanding. Spankings were one thing, but whippings were out! The end of the conversation came when I said, "Smitty, as much as I love you, if you ever hurt one of my children, I'll kill you." He knew I meant it.

One thing I didn't understand was why my allotment hadn't started. Junior said when there was a divorce involved it took longer. It had for him. I had to accept it. But, accept it or not, we couldn't manage on Smitty's take-home pay. They were still taking out money for his former wife's allotment. I didn't understand any of it. But I knew I had to get a job.

I got a job in the tea room at the Morehouse Fashion Department Store from ten in the morning until two in the afternoon. Perfect! But the tips were bad. Since most of my customers were little old ladies, and employees, the most they ever left me was a quarter. And those were *big* tippers! Yet, if I made enough to buy groceries, I was satisfied. My salary (twenty dollars a week) went to the baby-sitter. Smitty's pay went for the rent and the payments on his Lincoln. It had come as a surprise to me, after we were married, when he told me it wasn't paid for.

After that one explosion of temper, Smitty couldn't have been more loving to me and the boys. And when I began to feel sick a lot, he was really concerned. Since I hadn't missed a period, I knew I couldn't be pregnant. But, still, every morning I'd barely make it to the bathroom before losing everything. I started losing weight. Before, I'd worried about my size eight clothes getting a little tight . . . now, they hung on me. I was tired all the time. Smitty would usually come home, fix supper for himself and the boys, and put them to bed. Soon, he insisted I see the base doctor.

"Pregnant?" I asked. "How can I be?" He smiled indulgently. Embarrassed, I said, "No . . . I've never missed a period."

"Well, that's unusual but not unheard of." I remember Mom telling me this had happened when she was pregnant with some of us.

"Are you sure?"

Nodding his head, he said, "Yes. Mrs. Smith, I'm sure. But you've got to take care of yourself. It will probably not be an easy pregnancy."

All the way home, I kept saying to myself, "Three months pregnant . . . three months pregnant. What am I going to tell Smitty?"

Waiting till after supper, I went over, removed David from his lap, and sat down. Wondering if my words would erase the smile from his face, I said, "How would you like to be a 'real' father?" It took a minute to register. Then, almost dumping me on the floor, he sat up straight, turned me so I was directly facing him, and said, "Do you mean it? Are you really pregnant?" I was so glad he was smiling. "So that's why you've been sick?" I nodded my head. He broke out laughing. "Hey, boys! We're gonna have a baby!" Suddenly, it was a happy madhouse. The boys started chanting, "We're gonna have a baby sister . . . we're gonna have a baby sister." A brother was never mentioned.

The allotment money still hadn't started and I was worried about giving up my job but Smitty said not to worry, it would be straightened out immediately. In the meantime, he'd borrow enough money for us to get by on.

Christmas was an effort but it was a happy time. How unlike so many Christmases past. We put up and trimmed the tree together and placed the carefully chosen presents around it. Smitty was like a little kid himself. He was impatient for Christmas Eve so he could play Santa Claus. I loved watching from the sidelines. Christmas morning, after the kids had opened their presents and were playing with their new treasures, Smitty went into the bedroom and brought out a tiny, wrapped present and placed it in my hand. Feeling guilty because all I'd been able to get him was a cheap billfold, I opened it. There, against the black velvet, was the smallest . . . most beautiful diamond ring I'd ever seen. Placing it on my finger next to my plain gold wedding band, he said, "If you're a good girl, I'll get you a larger one for our twenty-fifth anniversary." Nothing could stop my happy tears.

The first of January, my allotment money started; so did premature labor pains. After spending overnight in the hospital, the doctor said, "If you're going to carry this baby, you're going to have to have complete bed rest." The only thing to do was to call Mom.

She'd planned to stay only a few days but after seeing how sick I was, she stayed with us for two weeks. A couple of days before it was time for her to leave, she sat down beside me on the bed. "I have an idea," she said.

"What's that."

"Well, Smitty and I have been talking it over and I'd like to take the boys home with me for a while." I sat bolt upright.

"No!"

"Now, be reasonable," she said, "it'll only be for a little while . . . till you get better. And Daddy and I will take good care of them." I knew they would but, after all we'd been through together, it just wasn't fair for us to be separated now. But I knew she was right . . . I couldn't take care of them. Jimmy was in the first grade and school clothes had to be washed and ironed . . . besides all their other things. Meals had to be fixed and a jillion other things to be organized. I was too sick to think about them. It was the best solution. But, oh God, how it hurt.

Smitty wouldn't hear of all of them taking the bus. Getting the woman next door to stay with me, he drove them to Springfield, turned around, and came right back. All the first night, I cried. I'd never been lonelier in my life. Except for the tears, every other part of me was dead.

Mom wrote often, thank God. She wrote me everything she could think of that the boys had done. Everything from Corky being Grandad's helper to David hiding doughnuts in his bed and saying they were "pleepin'" and Jimmy spilling soup on his sweater just before the school pictures were made. That story made me cry even more. I'd take out the little dime store picture I had of the three of them together and spill tears all over it. Religiously, once a month, I'd call just to hear them say, "I love you, Muvver." And sometimes, in between, Mom would let them call me. I missed them so very much.

Smitty tried, every way he knew how, to make up for the boys' absence. Since I wasn't allowed to do housework, he'd come home at night, fix supper, clean house, take care of everything that had to be done. Once a week he'd take the laundry to the base. In the mornings before he left, he'd make sure all the numbers where he could be reached were left next to my bed. After my check-up, the doctor said I could now be up and dressed but I still should not do any housework. The nausea was gone and I began to feel almost as good as new. Every now and then, slight cramps would start and I'd panic. It turned out that they were nothing more than that.

One night, Smitty and I had talked so much about what we

were going to do when the baby was born and when the boys came home, neither of us could sleep. About midnight, I turned to him and said, "I sure would like to have a steak and a hot fudge sundae."

"Are you serious?" Smitty asked, laughing.

"I'm serious!" He got up and started pulling on his pants.

"Why are you laying there? Get up and get dressed. We're going out for a steak and hot fudge sundae."

"Really?" This was above and beyond being a considerate husband!

"Really!"

By the time we got to the only place we knew to be open, it was two in the morning but it didn't matter. We ate and laughed like teenagers. It had been so long since I had laughed that way.

Smitty always went to sleep immediately, while I lay wide awake. Either the steak or hot fudge wasn't laying lightly on my stomach. Then, down low in my back, I felt the cramps start. Slow at first, then they began to move around to my stomach. Thinking I had overdone too much, I was certain they'd go away if I stayed still.

Oh, Lord, I have to go to the bathroom again, I thought, and started to crawl out of bed. The minute I moved, a strange sensation like a balloon deflating began in my stomach. But, if it *was* a balloon, it was filled with water which I felt escaping from my body. Smitty woke and said, "What's the matter?"

"I don't know," I said and made it to the bathroom. The liquid was still coming. Turning on the light, I saw the blood. "Smitty!" I screamed. He came running in. "Oh, God, we've got to get you to the hospital!"

There was no stopping the pains. They came often and hard. "Oh, please God, not now . . . not now!" I prayed. Arriving at the hospital, Smitty jumped out and ran for a wheelchair. He came back with the wheelchair. A nurse and doctor were with him.

Suddenly, I was in a room with brilliant lights shining in my eyes. Nurses were undressing me! Doctors pulling on gloves and barking orders! There was no stopping my baby from being born. "Mrs. Smith," the doctor said, "we're having difficulty hearing a heartbeat. We can't give you anything for pain. Just hold on." Dear God, I didn't want anything for pain . . . I just wanted my baby to be alive.

Within a few minutes, it was over. Miracles of miracles, I heard a faint cry and heard the doctor say, "It's a beautiful baby girl." *Thank you, God!* Giving me only a glimpse of her, they rushed her into an incubator. I heard someone say . . . "Two pounds, ten and a half ounces."

When I awoke, Smitty was holding my hand and his eyes looked like he had been crying. "Is the baby dead?" My heart stood still.

"No, but it will be forty-eight hours before they'll know if she'll make it."

"Can we see her?"

"They said we should wait," he said.

I started to cry hysterically. I screamed, "I don't *want* to wait! I want to see her now!" Smitty called for a nurse.

Every time I'd open my eyes, I'd start crying and someone would stick a needle in my arm. I stopped asking.

Hearing someone open the door, I kept my face to the wall. "Mrs. Smith," a soft voice said, "are you awake?" Expecting another needle, I turned over. But she was smiling. "How would you like to see a beautiful baby girl?" Life flowed back into my voice.

"Do you mean it? Can I see my baby?" I was already half out of bed.

"Here, let me help you," the nurse said. *Hurry, hurry,* my heart said.

As we walked out the door, Smitty came running down the hall. There was a smile as big as Texas on his face! Grabbing my hand and propelling me as fast as we could walk, we hurried to the nursery. On the way, the nurse explained that a pediatrician had been flown in from Philadelphia especially for our baby. He was on call twenty-four hours a day. Also, that Janet Louise (a name we'd chosen when I became pregnant) was holding her own.

We stood there, arms around each other, looking down at our miracle baby. She was tiny. I'd always heard that six-month babies had no hair or fingernails but it wasn't the case. Her fingernails were clearly visible and she had a shock of black hair. So much so that the nurse said they were going to give her a "Toni" before she went home. And she was *strong!* Even as tiny as she was, the nurse said, she would scoot till her head touched the top of the incubator crib, and they had to keep moving her down. She was naked because even an ounce of cloth would drain her strength. As soon as she weighed three pounds, she would wear a diaper. *More like a tiny handkerchief,* I thought. As we were standing there, the doctor came by and told us that, if all went well, we could plan on taking her home in about a month. With another lingering look, we went back to my room.

Smitty had already called my folks and the boys but I couldn't wait to talk to them myself.

The phone had just started to ring when Mom answered. "Hello?"

"Mom . . . she's gonna make it."

"Thank God!" I could hear the boys in the background in unison: "We wanta talk . . . we wanta talk." "All right. Here's your mama."

One at a time, I told each of them that as soon as we brought their baby sister home, we'd come and get them. They weren't concerned with that—only with "baby sister." Smitty was smiling indulgently as I ran up the phone bill. Hanging up, I stood there looking at the phone, then turned to Smitty—big, strong, military Smitty—and saw tears in his eyes.

My stay in the hospital was longer than usual . . . two weeks. And every minute they'd let me, I was down at the nursery staring through the window at my baby. Each day, the nurses had something new to tell me. She'd lost her birth weight . . . she was gaining so many ounces . . . how much she ate (they must have fed her with an eye dropper). One night, as Smitty and I walked up to the window, a sight greeted us that set us both to laughing. She had on a diaper! Of course, it was folded in fourths and then in a triangle . . . but she *did* have clothes on! And in her hair was the tiniest pink ribbon. Something else we noticed that we hadn't before were two things that clearly said she was Smitty's child. A tiny dimple in her chin and at the tip of her nose, exactly like his.

Since the baby was progressing so well, they let me go home. I hated to leave, but knowing Janet Louise was in good hands helped me to take that one last look before leaving the hospital.

April 15, 1954. It had been exactly a month since Janet Louise was born. Every night since I'd been home, Smitty and I had gone to see Janet Louise at the hospital. And the previous night we'd received the greatest news—we could bring her home in a week. I was so happy I couldn't bear it. Another bit of good news. A few days earlier, Smitty had told me we were being transferred to Sedalia Air Force Base near Warrensburg, Missouri, only fifty miles from Kansas City. The timing was perfect. Usually, after Smitty left at six-thirty, I went back to bed, but not this morning. I was so excited I couldn't think of sleep! The bed was made, the dishes washed, the furniture polished . . . I was looking around for something else to do to use up time until I could go see the baby. Ever since Janet Louise had been born, Smitty had ridden to work with someone, leaving the car for me. He was always sure it had gas. He left the keys on the bedside table.

Nervous now, I switched on the radio to a country station . . . the only one we listened to now. Red Foley was singing "Steal Away." A song about a little Negro baby's funeral. I thought, *That's the saddest song I've ever heard.* The phone rang. Thinking it was Smitty, I ran to answer it.

"Hello?"

"Mrs. Smith?" It was the doctor.

"Yes?" My heart was beating in my throat.

"Your baby's had a cerebral hemorrhage. If you want to see her alive, come to the hospital immediately." The phone went dead in my hand.

I screamed into the emptiness. For a second, I stood there not believing what I'd heard. It was a nightmare. Then, I grabbed the keys and ran out the door.

As I screeched to a stop at the emergency-room entrance, a military car pulled up beside me. Smitty jumped out and grabbed my hand, and we ran down the corridor to the nursery.

Holding each other for strength and support, we stood there. For nine solid hours we watched the nurses and a doctor gathered at the tiny incubator. They injected needles into her tiny arms, moved them up and down, turned her over. Each time she drew a labored breath, I didn't breathe again until she did. Suddenly, I realized everyone was looking at me! I looked at the baby. Why wasn't she breathing? Why weren't they working on her? Smitty's hold on my arm tightened. They were closing the top of the incubator. The realization hit me. My baby was dead. The nurses were crying—the doctor was walking toward me.

Screams filled my ears. They were *mine!* "No! Let me touch her! Please . . . let me hold her!" Smitty and the doctor were leading me down the hall. A priest came toward me. Over my screams, he said, "God took this little angel home to save her from any hurt in this cruel world." Someone stuck a needle in my arm and as it took effect I heard the doctor telling Smitty, "She might have been retarded—she might have been—she might have . . ."

Why they permitted it, I don't know. It's against the law. But somehow, the people at the funeral home agreed to let us take the baby back to Springfield to bury her. With the transfer, I couldn't bear to leave her in Columbus.

The next morning, with the baby in a tiny casket in the backseat, we left for Springfield. If we had to stop for anything, one of us stayed in the car. The one thing that kept me sane was the thought of seeing my boys again.

Mom and Daddy lived in Collins, about thirteen miles from Springfield, and ran a small grocery store–filling station. There wasn't much room for living quarters, just a couple of bedrooms and a kitchen, but in a front room was a portion closed off with a drape where Mom kept a lot of plants and flowers. This was where we put the tiny casket and opened the lid. My tears had all been used up and as I stood there looking down at her, I thought, *She seems asleep, just like she did in the hospital.* The boys stood silently looking at her. How could I explain death to them when I didn't understand it myself?

The next day, with Tiny, Freddie and Mickey, and my brother Pete and his family in attendance, Janet Louise was buried next to Grandma, who had died just a few months earlier.

Two days later, after a tearful good-bye to the boys and a promise to come for them in two weeks, we headed back to Columbus. I never wanted to see that damned town again but we had to pack for the move to Warrensburg.

Thick fog enveloped the car. Smitty crept along slowly. Suddenly red lights were flashing in front of us. Smitty braked to a stop . . . just in time. A man came running up to the car and said, "There's been a terrible accident. Can you help?"

"Stay in the car," Smitty said to me and ran up to what I could see was a tractor trailer truck with a car halfway underneath . . .

the whole front and top crushed. After a quick look, he ran back. "Do we have a blanket or anything?" I reached in the back and gave him the handmade quilt Mom had given to me just before we left.

Watching from the car, I saw Smitty lift a small form out of the car, wrap it in the quilt, and lay it gently on the ground. Then, putting all his weight against the seat, he broke the frame and lifted a woman's body out of the car. I could hear a man screaming.

About this point, an ambulance arrived. After talking with the attendants a minute, Smitty walked back to the car and got in. He saw the questions in my eyes. He said a four-year-old boy and his mother were dead. The husband, who was pinned beneath the steering wheel, had both legs broken. I cried uncontrollably, "Please, don't drive." All I could see was one of my sons in the form of that small body Smitty had laid on the ground.

Very slowly, he drove to the nearest motel. As he walked in the light of the door, I saw for the first time the blood that covered his clothes.

Warrensburg, Missouri, was a nice little town, not far from the Air Base. The three-bedroom house we rented was old but nice. It was just a few blocks from a school where Jimmy was in the first grade. It was great to have the boys home, and for a while we indulged their every whim. Then, things got back to normal, spankings included. Nearby was a small delicatessen, where they served sandwiches and drinks to students from the college. After asking Smitty several times, he finally agreed to let me work there. We could use the extra money and I needed something to keep my mind busy. The job didn't last long. I'd only been there a couple of weeks when I came down with a bad cold. *Well, I'll take care of this quick*, I thought, and went to the doctor for a penicillin shot. Leaving the doctor's office, I walked to work. By the time I got there, my feet didn't feel like they were touching the pavement. I began to tingle all over. My boss took one look at me. "My God, girl . . . you're white as a sheet!", and sent me home.

Jimmy was at school and Corky and David were with the baby-sitter, who lived next door. By the time I walked into the house, my legs felt like sticks . . . no feeling. Walking to the phone, I tried to dial Smitty's number at work. I couldn't make my legs function. Making it to the bed, I lay down and felt the numbness take over the rest of my body . . . all except my face. By the time Smitty came home, I didn't know I had a body.

Scared to death, he called an ambulance and I was rushed to the base hospital. The diagnosis was an "allergic reaction to penicillin."

After two days, feeling started coming back—first my feet— then my hands—then all over. As I was leaving the hospital, the doctor said, "*What*ever you do, don't *ever* let anyone give you penicillin! Next time, it may kill you. By all rights, it should have this time."

Next came the mumps. Jimmy first . . . ten days later, Corky . . . then, ten days later, David. For thirty days we had mumps in every room.

Corky had always been a loner. A lot of times, Jimmy and David would be playing together and Corky would be off to himself playing with a little stick or a toy car in the dirt. Lately, I'd noticed he wasn't even doing that. Just sitting on the porch watching the other kids play. Seeing him sitting there, his chin in his hands, I walked out and said, "What's the matter. Don't you want to play?"

"I'm tired," he said. "I wanta take a nap." This just wasn't like Corky. Usually, I had to force him to take a nap.

I took him into the house and almost before I got his clothes off, he was asleep. Reaching down to push back the curls that lay on his forehead, I touched him. His face was warm . . . too warm. "Tomorrow, young man," I said to myself, "you're going to the doctor."

After listening for what seemed like a long time with a stethoscope, the doctor said, "Has he ever had rheumatic fever?"

"No."

"Has he ever had an extremely high fever for no reason?" Then I remembered Sunflower, Kansas, and told the doctor.

"Well, he has an extra sound in his heart that usually comes from rheumatic fever but I can't be sure. We need to watch him closely for the next few months to see if there's any change." Then, seeing Corky looking at him intently, the doctor smiled and touched Corky's face. "Tell me, where did you get those freckles?"

Never taking his eyes off the doctor's face, Corky said solemnly, "A suntan through a screen." Heaven only knows where that came from. I was glad that was all that came from his innocent mouth—because the doctor was black. I knew that was why Corky couldn't take his eyes off of him.

After cautioning me to watch for signs, such as his fingernails turning blue, I was told to bring him back in two weeks.

For the next six months, every two weeks, we were in the doctor's office. At first, when the doctor would joke with him, Corky would respond. Now, he just sat listlessly. At home, I was constantly checking his fingernails, which always had a tinge of blue in them. He didn't play at all. He just watched television or slept.

One day the doctor called and asked if I could take him to Kansas City. "Of course," I replied.

"There's a specialist there I'd like to take a look at Corky. I've made a tentative appointment for next Monday. Can you make it?"

"Yes."

He said, "I think it's best."

Since Daddy's surgery, a few weeks before, he and Mom had moved to Kansas City and were living with my brother Junior and his family (Junior had gotten his Army discharge shortly after Smitty and I left Columbus).

Dropping Jimmy and David off there, I drove Corky to the Children's Hospital. After a lengthy examination, the doctor said, "Mrs. Smith, I want you to be prepared. There's every possibility your son may have to have heart surgery." Seeing the fear in my eyes, he went on. "Now, it's not a certainty. But if he doesn't show considerable improvement in the next few weeks . . . possibly we'll have to bring him in for an operation."

"Are you going to keep him?" I asked fearfully.

"No, but I want to see him in two weeks."

Another six months went by punctuated with trips every two weeks to Kansas City. Each time, the doctor had good news. Corky was improving. He had no explanation either for what was wrong or for Corky's improvement. I just thanked God.

Finally, I heard what I'd been waiting to hear. "Well, young man," the doctor said to Corky. "It looks like you and I won't be seeing each other for a while."

"Does this mean what I think it does?" I asked.

"It sure does. Bring him back in six months."

That evening, driving back to Warrensburg, I actually had to threaten Jimmy and Corky with a spanking for wrestling in the backseat. But I didn't shout loud enough for them to hear me.

With all the trips back and forth to Kansas City and all the times I hadn't been home when he got there, Smitty never said one cross word. That's why his outburst took me by surprise. I was just hanging up the phone after talking to his lieutenant, who had called to inform him of an alert on the base. Each practice was carried out as though it was real, and every man was called in. Smitty walked in the door.

"Who were you talking to?" he asked angrily.

"Your lieutenant. He called to tell you of an alert." I couldn't understand his anger.

"Why the hell did you talk to him so long?"

"I didn't. Just long enough to take a message."

"Well, if he calls again, just tell him I'm not home and hang up!" I looked at him in astonishment. He must be worried about something at the base. He never discussed problems with me but he'd never acted this way before, either.

All evening, he sulked. But by the time the boys were in bed he had cooled off. Putting his arms around me, he said, "You're beautiful. You know that?" A shyness I hadn't felt in a long time came over me.

"Sure. And you're crazy. Did you know that?" Gently, he ran his fingers over my face.

Later, after everyone was asleep, I went into the bathroom and looked into the mirror. Beautiful? Me? My hair was the same brown it had always been, except that now it was a little messed up. My eyes were the same small brown eyes I'd always had, though they were a little brighter now. My cheeks and lips had a natural glow to them. Looking at my body, I was pleased with what I saw. What little weight I'd gained when I was pregnant was gone and I was back to a size eight. *Funny*, I thought. *Before I met Smitty, I don't ever remember really looking at my body. I was always a little ashamed of it.* Now, secure in Smitty's love, all that was gone. Maybe I was beautiful. I certainly *felt* beautiful. And if he thought I was . . . then I was. Happy, I went back to bed.

A new housing development, to be rented to military personnel only, had been built near the base. Every Sunday, we'd drive out, just looking. I fell in love with a frame house with yellow shutters, an attached garage and a concrete driveway, with a fantastic yard with the back part fenced in. I'd ask Smitty to stop in front and I'd sit there looking at it longingly. It was perfect! But I didn't say a word. I didn't have to.

Smitty broke the silence. "There's just no way."

"No way for what," I asked innocently. I knew he wanted the house as much as I did.

"No way we can afford the rent." An idea struck me!

"What if I get a job?"

"Where?" he asked.

"At the Skyview Restaurant near the airport. They've been advertising for a dinner waitress," I said hopefully. I'd seen the ad several times and hoped it was still available.

"Well . . ." I could "hear" him thinking. "See what you can find out about it."

Leaping across the seat, I hugged him and mentally started arranging furniture we didn't have.

Housework was labor of love. Each day, I lovingly dusted the furniture we'd bought on credit. Bunk beds for the boys' room, a bedroom suite for us, a sofa, a chair, and a television set for the living room, and a shiny chrome dinette set for the kitchen. The stove and refrigerator came with the place. The floors were covered with new carpet and linoleum. I'd never lived in a new house before. And with our new furniture, I felt like a princess in a castle. Smitty had been reluctant to go into debt but I promised him I'd work until every stick of furniture was paid for.

Mom had visited us a few times but Daddy had never seen the house. One day he called and said, "You gonna be home for a few days?"

"Sure, Daddy. Why?"

"Well, I thought I'd come over for a few days if it's all right?" There was a question in his voice.

"What do you mean, if it's all right? Of course it is." Daddy and Smitty liked each other and we'd tried, several times, to get him to come for a visit. Each time he'd say, "Some other time."

"Well, can you come and get me?"

"As soon as Smitty gets home, we'll be on our way." I was thrilled!

Ever since the operation, Daddy had seemed to go downhill. He went back to work for a while, but finally had to give it up. Besides, the only food he was allowed to eat were raw eggs, milk, Jell-O and pudding—anything soft and easily digestible. It seemed to take the life out of him. He said he was hungry all the time. At mealtime, he'd always sit in another room where he couldn't see the food. It hurt me, to see him that way.

For the two weeks he was with us, he was almost like his old self. He laughed and played with the kids and had long talks with Smitty. He even cussed a lot—happily. It was great watching him holding David on his lap and, with Jimmy and Corky sitting on the floor in front of him, listening to his tall tales about his past, or mine. They were fascinated! Every few minutes, I'd hear one of them say, "Really, Grampa, did you do that?" Or "Did Mommy do that?"

He told them about the time, when I was eleven, he'd made me take a swallow of beer to see if I would turn out to be a drinker. And when I'd spit it out, he had said, "Okay, that's enough." He told a true story about the time I'd shot his shotgun and it had knocked me six feet backward off the stump I was standing on; about the time he'd pulled me out of a pen where an old sow and her new litter of pigs were, just as I was about to get my head chomped off; and about the time I ate a lot of green apples out of the tree after he told me not to—even though I was the one who got sick, I lied, saying Junior and Tiny had done it. The stories he told about me were true but I wasn't so sure about the stories he told about himself. Such as the time he was dancing with a one-eyed Mexican woman and her glass eye fell out and rolled around the floor. Even Smitty laughed at that one.

Daddy wasn't known for patience. One morning David got a sample of that. My hands were full fixing breakfast and getting Jimmy ready for school, so I asked Daddy to feed David, who was in the "Terrible Twos" and pounding on his high chair. I had fixed oatmeal, which wasn't his favorite, and every bite Daddy would put in David's mouth he'd spit out. For a while Daddy tried coaxing him: "Come on, open up—that's a good boy." Out it would come. At the end of his short patience, Daddy turned the bowl full of oatmeal over David's head. "Okay, son," Daddy said. "If you want oatmeal all over you, that's what you've got." He got up and walked out of the room. David looked at me in surprise. Jimmy and Corky were rolling on the floor laughing. I couldn't help it, laughing, too.

One of Daddy's favorite pastimes was sitting quietly and listening to music. Especially Tex Ritter's "High Noon" and "Green Grow the Lilacs." And, on Saturday night, everything came to a halt while he listened to the Grand Ole Opry.

Then, he decided it was time for him to go back to Kansas City.

"What for, Daddy?" I asked.

"Your mama might need me," he said. All these years, I'd wondered if they really loved each other. Now, I knew they did.

Mom worked at a nursing home and, with Junior and Ida both working, he was alone a lot. And, as often as possible, I'd make the fifty-five-mile trip from Warrensburg just to spend a few hours with him. I loved him and knew our time together was going to be short.

Just before Christmas, I was visiting him and asked what he'd like for lunch.

Expecting the usual answer of Jell-O or pudding, I was surprised to hear him say: "Pumpkin pie."

"Daddy, you know you can't have pumpkin pie."

"Damn it! I want pumpkin pie!" Then his voice changed . . . almost begging me. "Please. I've been hungry too long. I'd like to die with a full stomach." I couldn't bear to see my dad begging like a little child. Without another thought, I was out the door and on my way to the restaurant down the street. Quickly, I glanced at the pie case. They had pumpkin pie. "Give me the whole pie," I said. Carrying it carefully, I went to the house. As I walked in the door, I had to stop and laugh. Daddy was already at the table . . . his plate and fork at the ready.

Christmas in our new house was the best ever. Having already decided that the house was our present to each other, Smitty and I concentrated on the kids. Not a lot of presents but just enough for "Santa Claus." The great thing was that we were all together, we were all well, and Daddy was getting better. After the pumpkin pie episode, I'd expected him immediately to get worse. But it had been just the opposite.

A couple of weeks later, I was getting ready for work when the phone rang. It was my sister, Beulah. "Grace, Daddy's in the hospital. He's real bad." Somehow, lately, I'd put the thought that Daddy might die out of my mind. She went on to tell me that the Red Cross was trying to get Bob home from Korea and Bill home from Germany. Pete and Dick were already in Kansas City. And Tiny was on her way from West Plains. Mom, who had had a gall bladder attack a few days before, was in the hospital, on a floor above Daddy's room.

General Hospital was a big, imposing red brick building that looked like a prison. The first time I walked into Daddy's room— gray and smelling of antiseptic—I wanted to turn and run.

The only furniture was a straight-backed chair and the bed Daddy was lying on. His arms were stretched back over his head and tied to the bed. There were needles in both his arms and a tube in his nose. His eyes were staring blankly at the ceiling. *Oh, God, I mustn't cry.* But I can't stand to see him like this!

Hearing him moan, I walked over to the bed, leaned down, and kissed his forehead. Looking right at me, he said, "Please untie my hands." My heart cried out.

"I can't, Daddy. They said you keep pulling the needles out."

"If Grace was here, she'd untie my hands," he said.

"This is Grace, Daddy." He looked at me again.

"No, you're not. But if you are and you don't untie my hands, you're not worth a shit!" Now, that was like Daddy. I smiled. After a few moments, he said, "Come to think of it, you never were worth a shit!" With that, he turned his face to the wall.

For over a week, we took turns sitting by his bed. And, when they'd let her, we'd bring Mom down. She'd just sit by his bed, hold his hand, and cry.

Even though Mom was Protestant, Daddy had been raised Catholic. But something happened—he never said what—when he was sixteen and he had never gone to church since. He could quote the Bible but he said, "I don't need no preacher telling me what's right and what's wrong." Someone asked if he'd like to see a priest. Shaking his head, he said, "No. It's too late."

The doctor said Daddy could linger on for weeks so I decided to go home and check on the boys. Smitty had assured me they were all right but I wanted to see for myself.

The next morning Beulah called. "Grace, I wish you could have been here last night. Daddy was his old self. When we took Mom down, he said, 'Linnie, you're as pretty as ever.' The doctor now thinks he might pull through." With all my heart, I wanted to believe her but I was afraid to. That night, trying to look at the positive side, I told Smitty I was going to wait a few days before going back.

The next morning, the minute the phone rang, *I knew.* It was Beulah. Daddy had died at seven that morning. He was alone. Like me, everybody had gone home to get some rest.

At the funeral, hearing a preacher—who had never laid eyes on Daddy—say inane things that meant nothing to anyone there was more than I could bear. He simply repeated what he had read in the obituary, leaving out any mention of Bill—my half brother— as one of the survivors. I tried not to listen.

Realizing the preacher had finished talking and everyone was getting up, I followed them like a robot to the casket. Leaning over, I kissed Daddy on his forehead and said, "Oh, Daddy, I'm so sorry I can't take you back to Oklahoma. I'm sorry they've put a damned necktie on you. I love you. Please, forgive me." Then I walked away.

On the way to the cemetery, I thought of all the times he'd said, "Don't bury me in the damned state of Missouri. Hell, you can't dig a hole six feet deep in rock!"

When we got there, I saw a priest standing by the graveside and refused to get out of the car.

The following Memorial Day, I asked Beulah to drive me out there. The minute we entered the gate, I knew it was a mistake. I couldn't breathe. Quickly laying a rose on Daddy's grave, I whispered, "Forgive me, Daddy, but, I'll never come back. You are not here."

I soon began to have all the symptoms of pregnancy. Not sick, as I'd always been, but just the usual morning sickness. Smitty and I had often talked about having another baby but, after the trouble I'd had carrying David and Janet Louise, I was more than a little scared. Besides, because we still owed for a lot of the new furniture, I needed to work. I kept my secret until the doctor definitely confirmed it. "Mrs. Smith, you're two months pregnant."

Later, after the kids were in bed, I sat down on the sofa next to Smitty, who was watching a great show on television.

"Smitty," I said hesitantly.

"Shhhh," he said. I'd picked the wrong time. As I started to get up, he grabbed my arm.

"Wait a minute. Come back here. What is it?" I sat down. He looked at me and switched the television off. "Now. What is it?" he said gently. I gathered my courage.

"Remember when you said you wanted to be a 'for real' father?"

"Yes." He began to smile.

"Does that still stand?" The smile spread clear across his face.

"It sure does, baby. It sure does." He reached for me. I jumped up.

"No, you silly!" I laughed. "I'm trying to tell you I'm pregnant!"

"Well, why didn't you *say* so!" He wanted to tell the boys immediately but I asked him to wait. He knew what I meant.

For the first time, I was healthy as a horse. Nothing seemed to bother me. At the restaurant, they said I could work as long as I felt like it. And I felt like it!

When I was six months along, Smitty brought home the news that he was being transferred to the Panama Canal Zone. I'd known when we were married that we would be moving a lot but this time it was bad timing!

I cried and cried. But the more Smitty told me about the nice house we'd have there and household help for almost nothing (Imagine *me* with a maid!), I began to get adjusted to the idea. Still, it tore my heart out to sell our furniture for half of what it was worth. We had no choice. The furniture company refused to take it back and, after inquiring, we found we couldn't take it out of the country until it was paid for. The only thing we held on to was the blond console television, which the kids loved and which we planned to leave with Tiny and Freddie.

Carefully, I packed everything I could do without and shipped it to Smitty's overseas address. That way, he could already have it there when we went to join him. He promised it would be soon.

Until we got to Panama, we would be staying with his brother and sister-in-law, Pete and Gladys Smith, in Louisville, Kentucky.

It was hot! So hot I could see the steam rising from the pavement on the driveway! Having accepted the fact that we were leaving the only real home they'd ever had, the kids just stood and watched as first one man and then another carried out pieces of our furniture. Then, they turned and started playing on the floor of the garage with some precious marbles they'd stashed in their pockets. I think they were afraid the movers would take them, too.

Smitty and the boys were in the car waiting impatiently while I took one last look around. I knew it was hot but I just had to have this final moment. Walking from room to room, I recalled every happy hour shared here. I didn't want to leave but, hearing the car horn, knew it was time. Lord. I dreaded the drive to West Plains!

For a while, everyone was silent—just watching the scenery go by. Then, seeing some cows in a field, Corky said, "Look at the cowboys!" He broke the ice! Suddenly, everyone began talking at once.

This time at the farm seemed a lot different from the many times I'd been there before. This was a visit . . . not a case of necessity. For a few days, we put the imminent separation out of our minds—or tried to. The kids loved to go to the barn with Smitty and Freddie when it was time to milk the cows. All the way to the house, I could hear them squealing. I knew they were getting squirted with milk. One evening, though, Smitty was sitting in the yard with me when Corky ran to him screaming. "Daddy! Daddy! That cow barked at me!" They were definitely not farm boys.

Time was getting short. In a few days Smitty would leave and, wanting to get me settled at Pete and Gladys's, we left for Louisville. During the drive, we made plans. Plans for the baby. Plans for the future—just plans. We'd never been separated except for a few days at a time. Now it could be weeks, or months, before we saw each other again. He was going to try to come home when the baby was born but wouldn't be sure until the time came.

Pete and Gladys were sitting on the porch of their big white house. Their children—a boy and girl about Jimmy and Corky's age—were playing in the yard. After being cooped up in the car, it felt good to get out and stretch our legs. Within a few minutes, the kids were all playing like they'd been together all their lives. It would be lonesome without Smitty but I knew the decision to stay here was the right one. It was close to a military hospital and the house was big, so we'd have two rooms to ourselves. They had even gone to the trouble of buying new curtains and bedspreads.

Smitty was dressed and ready to leave. As he held each of the boys on his lap and asked them to promise to be good and take care of Mommy, he didn't seem to notice that his uniform was getting wrinkled. As I had done so many times before, I wondered how I could have been so lucky to have him fall in love with me. As he held me to him and promised to write every day, my heart was so full of love it was beating very fast.

Having already made arrangements to have the car shipped, he started to back out of the driveway. "Smitty! Wait!" I cried, and ran to the car. Seeing the tears rolling down his face was all it took for me to fall completely apart. Pete arrived and gently pulled me away so he could leave. Standing there, I watched until the last sign of the red and white Lincoln faded from sight. Both the sun and my tears were blinding me.

Each day, I'd sit on the porch waiting for the mailman. Two weeks went by without a letter. It got so the mailman would say, "I'm sorry, Mrs. Smith, nothing for you." I was puzzled. He'd promised to write. He'd *promised!* Something must be wrong with the mail. Perhaps tomorrow . . . Aside from a letter about my support check, nothing. *I should have my check by now.* Right after the last check, I'd sent in the change of address. I wasn't really worried but I was now low on money.

The mailman, instead of stopping at the mailbox, was walking toward me. My heart in my throat, I ran to meet him. Thinking the letter was from Smitty, I grabbed it from his outstretched hand. Not even looking at the return address, I tore it open. "Dear Mrs. Smith," it started. Damn! It was some kind of form letter! Without continuing, I looked at the envelope again. The return address was The United States Government. I went back to reading the letter. As I read, I stumbled to the porch swing to keep from falling. Most of the legal words I couldn't understand, but what it amounted to was that Smitty's ex-wife had gone back to court in Litchfield, Kentucky. She said she was a Catholic and didn't believe in divorce and Smitty was the father of her year-old son. The judge, eighty years old, had set aside their divorce. Therefore, my marriage to Smitty was null and void. All checks, from now on, would go to her, and whatever amounts I had received after the judgment would have to be repaid.

Gladys came out of the house all smiles. "Well, I see you got your letter," she said. I couldn't even speak. I just handed her the letter. As she read, the smile disappeared from her face. *"Oh, my God!"* I was crying so hard, I couldn't talk. She led me to the bedroom.

When Pete came home, he read the letter and immediately tried to reach Smitty in Panama, but no one seemed to know of his whereabouts. He left messages everywhere. "Tell him to call home immediately. It is an emergency!" After three agonizing days, there was still no word. Pete and Gladys were still nice but didn't know what to say. I guess they felt helpless, as I did. The boys, sensing something was wrong, stayed close to me. Most of the time, they were in my room with the door closed.

The house was empty. Pete was at work and Gladys had taken her children shopping. Picking up the newspaper, I scanned the "Apartments for Rent" ads. After making several calls and circling the ones that were "By Week or Month," I called a cab. I couldn't afford it but there was no way I could carry our suitcases on the bus. The carefully worded thank-you note left propped up on the kitchen table was the only evidence that we'd ever been there.

Watching the meter click off precious dollars, I knew I'd have to make a decision soon. The next house looked like orange crates stacked on top of each other and was not in the best of neighborhoods. I told the cab to stop. The woman who answered the door wasn't too thrilled about renting to a very pregnant woman and three kids but after I told her we'd only stay a very short while, she agreed.

The stairs that led to the apartment were outside of the house. And, as I climbed them, I wondered if I'd live to come back down. I felt that bad. The two small rooms were hot and stifling even with the windows open. When the boys were asleep, I lay there trying to muffle my sobs in a musty-smelling pillow.

Nausea woke me and I barely made it to the bathroom. My stomach felt like a rock. The baby, evidently feeling my tension, was in a tight, hard ball. I walked back to the bed and sat down. The night before, I hadn't bothered to look around. Now I did, and realized what we had come to. What was advertised as two rooms was actually one room, with a makeshift kitchen at the end of it. The furniture consisted of the beds we had slept in; an old sofa and a stand-up lamp; a rickety card table and two metal chairs; a metal cabinet containing a few plastic dishes and some pots and pans; and a two-burner gas stove with the oven to one side. It was a long descent from the little white house in Warrensburg. How long ago had we left there? A hundred years.

Taking the boys with me and cautioning them to be careful, I walked down the stairs. Just as we got to the bottom, the landlady—I use the word loosely—came out and said, "I want you to know your kids have got to be quiet! My husband works at night and needs his sleep!" I knew our stay there would not be pleasant. "Also," she added," they can play in the yard only if you're with them!" I looked around at the dirt with a few sprigs of grass here and there and thought, *What yard?* But, not being wealthy, I couldn't afford to make waves by telling her my thoughts. The rent was only ten dollars a week.

The boys, who were usually so good, suddenly began fighting and crying constantly. Coming back from the store where I'd bought just enough food to survive, I was putting it away when Jimmy and Corky ran out the door and down the steps. David, who had started wetting his pants again, was crying to be changed. As I reached for him, I heard Jimmy scream! Halfway down the steps, I saw Jimmy coming around the corner . . . blood streaming from a cut on his head. Corky was right behind him, carrying a brick in his hand. Looking up at me, he said, "I didn't mean to, Mommy." I took them both back upstairs and bathed the blood away. It was just a small cut but I put both of them to bed anyway. Jimmy was still crying. Corky kept patting him and saying, "I'm sorry. I'm sorry."

That night, after the boys were asleep, I sat down and wrote Tiny asking for train fare to West Plains. There was no way I could explain why in a letter. So I ended it, "Please hurry." Then, I wrote Smitty the longest letter I'd written in my life. I wrote of everything we'd been through together: Good and Bad, Happy and Sad. I told him of the love we'd promised forever, of the baby we'd lost, and the one that would be born in two months. "Oh, God, Smitty, if you're alive, please write me at Tiny's." Running out of words and tears, I sealed both envelopes and walked to the corner mailbox and dropped them in the slot.

It was a fifteen-hour ride (with a transfer) from Louisville to West Plains. Leaving at midnight, we were scheduled to arrive at two the next afternoon. I'd packed a few sandwiches but since the boys were too excited to sleep, they ate them immediately. About daylight, we chugged to a stop in the station where we were supposed to change trains. The kids awoke crying. Having already counted my money, I kept them quiet with promises of pancakes and milk. Inside the diner, I thought *The hell with it* and ordered bacon and eggs. But, instead of the potatoes, they brought grits, which the kids had never seen before and refused to eat. Knowing it would make me vomit, I didn't waste money on food for me.

As the train pulled into West Plains, I saw Tiny and Freddie standing on the platform with very worried looks on their faces. They didn't ask any questions. I waited until the kids were out of hearing range, then told them the entire story. Tiny's face turned white.

"I can't believe it! He was so good to you. He loved you so much!" Freddie sat quietly. His face was a dark cloud.

Day after day, I waited for the mailman. Night after night, I cried myself to sleep. "Oh, God, Smitty, where are you? How could you do this to me?"

Tiny worked at the shoe factory, and since Freddie was in the fields all day and they didn't have a phone, she'd drop us off at her sister-in-law Vera's house—about two miles from town. I'd recently been having some pain and she was afraid to leave me alone. Since I was emotionally dead, I didn't care where I was.

For days now, I had not felt the baby move. It had never been too active so I wasn't really worried. But, as I sat in a chair watching the boys play, I felt the nagging pain start in my back. Thinking it would go away, I tried to ignore it. Then, it reached my stomach. From past experience, I asked Vera to call Tiny. By the time she got there, I was doubled over in pain. With her help,

I walked up the steps of the same hospital where Jimmy and Corky had been born.

After examining me, the doctor said, "I hear a faint heartbeat. We're going to give you a shot and try to stop the labor." The needle pierced my arm. After awhile, the pains eased and stopped. The baby still wasn't moving but the doctor told Tiny she could take me home.

Four days later, the pains started again and I was rushed back to the hospital. This time, even with the shots, there was no stopping them. Vaguely, out of the fog that was engulfing me, I heard the doctor say, "I can't give you anything for pain." Then: "Damn! It's a breech birth!" I couldn't open my eyes but I could feel Tiny's hand and hear her saying, "Hold on to me. Just hold on." It sounded like she was crying. After an eternity, the doctor said, "It's a girl." Then, "The baby is dead." I felt her weight as they laid her across my stomach. Over and over, I heard myself screaming, *"Smitty! Smitty!"* Then, thank God, I lost consciousness.

Tiny told me that the baby had looked just like Jimmy. Without ever having a name and without me ever seeing her, Tiny and her son Mickey stood with me, and a local minister I had chosen, as she was buried in a cemetery near the hospital.

I knew I was always welcome at Tiny and Freddie's. But I also knew we couldn't stay too long. I needed to work and the only work there was at the shoe factory or at a few cafés where no one ever heard of tipping. Being a waitress was what I did best. The nearest restaurant was in Springfield. Never having heard a single word from Smitty, I vowed, even though my heart still hurt for him, my mouth would never again speak his name.

Accepting what little money Tiny and Freddie could spare, three weeks after the baby had been born, we left for Springfield. It was just after Jimmy's birthday on August 27, 1955. I was twenty-five years old. I felt a hundred and twenty-five.

Immediately after getting off the bus, I bought a newspaper and started calling about apartments. My basic questions were "Is it clean?" and "Is it cheap?" With two suitcases, three little boys, and my back hurting like crazy, a bus was out of the question. Narrowing the list down to two, we walked over to a cab parked at the curb.

The apartment I decided on consisted of one room upstairs in a private home. Unlike the one in Louisville, it was comfortable and clean and the landlady was available for baby-sitting. That evening I circled every "Waitress Wanted" ad, and bright and early the next morning I went off with my best "What'll you have?" smile. The first place I applied to, hired me. I would be a car hop. The hours were perfect—eleven A.M. to seven P.M. *(Daytime, for a change)*. By the end of the first week at work, I knew the only thing I'd get plenty of were insults and sexual propositions from customers who were too cheap to leave a tip. My weekly pay was thirty dollars a week.

Jimmy was seven and in the second grade but Corky was fixing to spend his first day in kindergarten. The school was two blocks away and while I walked with them in the morning, I worried about them walking home by themselves in the afternoon. Over and over, I drilled instructions into their heads. "Don't talk to strangers! Wait for the school patrol to tell you when to cross the street! Wait for the green light!" Corky finally got tired of listening, put his fingers in his ears, and made noises like a race car.

The first day, Jimmy dressed himself, but trying to dress Corky was like catching a bouncing balloon. He was all over the place. It amounted to a wrestling match. Finally getting every button buttoned and his boots on the right feet, I declared myself the winner. I explained that there would be black children in school and they were not to treat them any differently from the way they treated anyone else. I needn't have worried. Since they were asleep when I got home, I had to wait until the next morning to ask about school the day before. As I was again trying to corner Corky, I said, "Well, how was school yesterday?"

Jimmy said, "Fine," and went on dressing.

Corky said, "You know those black kids?"

"Yes?"

"Well, they had on boots and jeans just like I did!" That's all there was to it.

The alarm clock was set for six but I didn't need it to wake up. The chills, fever, and coughing had done that all night long. Trying to get out of bed, the room turned upside down and, weakly, I lay back dov 1 pulling the blanket up to my chin. *God, I can't be sick! I have to work!* The boys were still alseep and I dozed off again. The alarm was ringing but it just droned on and on and finally quit. Trying to wake up, I never quite made it and drifted in and out of sleep.

The sound of dishes clanking together made me open my eyes. For once I was glad we were in one room because, from where I lay, I could see Corky and David playing quietly on the floor. Turning my head toward the small alcove kitchen, I saw Jimmy, with one of my aprons tied around him, standing on a chair washing dishes. Seeing I was awake, he climbed down, came over to the bed, and, patting me gently, said, "Don't worry, Muvver, I'll take care of you." Suddenly, the flood of tears that I'd kept dammed up inside me for the last few weeks poured down my face. Corky and David crawled up beside me and tried to console me. I cried until I couldn't cry anymore. Then and there, I made up my mind that as soon as I was well enough, we would leave this place forever.

A few days later, I placed a collect call to Mom, who was living with my brother Pete in Gardena, California, thirty miles from L.A. I asked for the bus fare to make a new start in Los Angeles.

When the money arrived, there was barely enough for the ticket. I forgot meals for the three-day trip. There was only one thing to do.

Leaving the boys with the landlady, I walked to the corner phone booth and looked up "Pawn Brokers" and discovered there was one three blocks away.

The shop was filled with everything imaginable. A young man, about my age but looking a lot younger, was handing over his watch to the man behind the counter. I stood there and waited until he left; then, trying to act like I'd done this a dozen times before, I walked over and said, "Do you give money for rings?"

The man looked me over, smiled, and said, "Well now, little girl, that depends on what kind of ring you've got." I held out my hand with the tiny ring Smitty had given me on it.

"Would you slip it off for me?" he asked. Taking it off, I laid it in his outstretched hand. He reached for some kind of glass and looked at it through it. Then he said, "You'd better keep it. It's not exactly the Hope diamond." He handed the ring out to me.

"Please," I said, "whatever you can give me is all right." I could see him thinking.

"Well," he said, running his hand through his shock of gray hair, "the most I can give you is twenty-five dollars."

"I'll take it," I said before he could change his mind.

He laid the money in my hand and started writing out a ticket.

"I won't need that," I said, and turned to walk away. Then, taking off my plain gold wedding band, I walked back and said, "How much for this?"

Again, he looked at the ring, then at me. "How old are you?" he asked.

"Old," I said. "And I need money."

"You know, you can buy these anywhere for ten dollars," he said, and started to hand it back. Then, he said, "Would five help?"

I nodded.

As I walked back to the apartment, feeling the empty place on my finger, I tried not to remember how happy I'd been when Smitty had placed the rings there. But that was over now. The only thing that mattered was survival.

I'd thought the trips to and from Greeley were long but, compared to this one, they were a ride in the country. Texas alone took forever to cross. The bus was packed . . . every seat full. We were jammed into two seats, Jimmy and Corky in one and me, holding David on my lap, in the other. Two sailors sitting in back of us were smoking, and the smoke swirled around us like a fog. Corky, who hated smoke, coughed, choked, and held his breath until I thought he was going to turn blue. Suddenly, before I could stop him, he stood up in the seat, turned to the sailors, and said, "Would you please put out those cigarettes, they're choking me to death!" I was so embarrassed I could die! Jerking him down, I was scolding him when one of the sailors leaned over the seat and said to Corky, "Hey, buddy, we'll make a deal. We won't smoke if you'll come back and sit with us." He looked at me as if to ask my approval. I nodded my head. Corky was already halfway over the seat. For the rest of the trip, he was their constant companion.

With Mom plus the four children, Pete and Betty's two-bedroom apartment was already overcrowded. With us there, it was like fifty sardines in a ten-sardine box. In one bedroom alone there were three sets of bunkbeds where Mom and five kids slept. Two more little ones plus Pete and Betty in their room, and me on the couch. Talk about tight quarters! Mealtime was stand up, stand in line, Army style. "Keep moving, don't hold up the line!"

With several big poker clubs, Gardena was known as Poker City. My first job application was to the biggest and nicest one—the Rainbow Club. Figuring "chip girls," who carried big trays of chips and money strapped around their necks to the tables, made a lot more tips, I tried for that first. When they put one around my neck and I sank to my knees, I inquired about a job as a cashier in the restaurant. When the manager said, "We'll call you if there's an opening," I went to the next club. Each time I heard the same story. After several failures, my spirits began to sag, and my feet were sore. Stopping at a family-style restaurant, I was sitting at the counter scanning the want ads, when the waitress said, "What'll you have, honey?"

"A glass of iced tea and a job." I was only half joking.

"Are you serious?" she asked.

"About the iced tea?"

"No. The job!"

"Sure, I'm serious!"

"Well, hold on," she said, "Let me get the man with the money!"

Before I left there I had a job, beginning in the morning.

Mom took care of the boys and for the next three weeks, except for some money to Pete and Betty for groceries, I hoarded every cent I made. Each night, I counted the quarters and dimes I'd made in tips. When there was enough, I'd roll them in papers I got from the bank and stash them away. I was determined to have an apartment of our own.

My fourth week on the job, I was patiently standing in the line of the bank waiting to cash my check. Handing it to the teller, I expected her to hand back cash. Instead, she handed back the check. It was marked "Insufficient funds."

Hurrying back to the restaurant, the manager gave me some feeble excuse and said, "Hold it until tomorrow. I'll make it good then." Being a trusting soul, I stuck it back in my purse. The next morning, prompt little waitress that I was, I arrived at work thirty minutes early. The door was padlocked. And, on it, a sign read: "Closed by Order of the Sheriff."

I must have had thirty jobs in the next thirty days. For one reason or another each one turned sour. The first was a job in a hot pastrami sandwich stand. But, after burning my hands several times trying to get the pastrami out of the steamer, I decided to move on. My next job was in a Mexican restaurant where, after I spilled a plate of hot enchiladas on a customer, the manager said "Buenos noches." In the next place they demanded I give them four dollars for a name tag.

"What for?" I asked.

"So the customer will know your name," he said.

"I don't *have* four dollars," I said. "I promise that if a customer wants to know my name, I'll tell him."

"No good," he said. "No four dollars, no job. That's the rules."

My rule was "Never hit a manager in the face no matter how much you want to."

Home was a four-room apartment, just like Pete and Betty's, which I'd rented the week before, for two weeks at a time. The address was 15713 Brighton Ave., Apartment 13. The stove and refrigerator were provided but the rest—some beds; a table and chairs, a well worn sofa, and a small television set—were compliments of the Salvation Army. Mom moved in with us and when I either worked or looked for work, she watched the boys. A small park was about half a block away and every afternoon either Mom or I would take the boys there to play. David headed for the swings or the sandbox and Jimmy and Corky for the ball field. So long as anyone was playing, they were content to watch.

There was a gas stove in the apartment, and since the pilot light was always going out, I was scared to death of it. Each time I'd light the oven, I'd hold my breath until the flame caught. David had a fascination for matches and several times I caught him. Once he set fire to the boys' clothes in the closet. I spanked him and put him to bed. Always threatening to do something more drastic the next time. Leaving what it was to his imagination.

One day, catching him watching me when I lit the oven, I cautioned him never to go *near* the stove.

While making up the beds, I heard the explosion that rocked the house! Running into the kitchen, I saw the oven door blown off and David picking himself up off the ground outside. His hair was singed and black stuff covered his face and clothes. Grabbing him up, I gave him the spanking of his life, put him to bed, and banned television.

Sometimes, since the park was so close, I'd let the kids go to the park with the neighbors' kids or their own cousins. Each time, making them promise never to talk to strangers!

One day, Jimmy and Corky came home alone. "Where's David?" I asked.

"We don't know," Jimmy said. "He wasn't in the sandbox."

I ran back to the park and searched everywhere . . . he was nowhere to be found. Having heard stories about children being kidnapped in parks, my imagination went wild. Back at the house, I called the police, then ran back to the park, Jimmy and Corky with me. We searched for five hours. Finally, at eight o'clock that night and five blocks away from home, we found him . . . playing in a sandbox with another little boy. Seeing me run toward him, he got up and said, "It's all right, Mommy, I'm tired anyway." Seeing him standing there, one boot missing and knowing he was headed for the bed, I didn't have the heart to do anything but hug him.

Nothing else seemed to be working out, so I decided to try the Rainbow Club again. As I walked in, the manager looked up and, recognizing me, said, "Hey . . . I tried to call you." I'd given them Pete's phone number, but they'd moved to another part of town.

"You mean there's an opening?"

"Well, I'll have one in a week. The gal that's here now is pregnant and says she can't hack it."

"Well, I can!" I said.

"Okay. Be here at nine sharp Monday." I was out the door before he could change his mind!

All the way home, I was walking on air. Fifty dollars a week! Gosh. Two hundred dollars a month! I could pay the rent, buy groceries, and have some money left over! I couldn't wait to tell Mom and the boys.

To anyone else, the Rainbow Club might have been a cheap poker club but I was fascinated! From where I sat in my cashier's cage, I could watch everything that went on. One man, especially, captured my attention. He was there every morning when I went to work and still there when I got off at six. The thing that really got me was that he never went to the bathroom. I couldn't understand it. He was big and fat, so I figured most of it was bladder! Finally, my curiosity got the best of me and I asked one of the chip girls.

"Oh, you mean Nick?"

"Is that his name?" I asked.

"Yeah. Nick the Greek they call him. He's been a millionaire and a pauper more times than anyone can count." The name didn't mean a thing. What I wanted to know is . . .

"How come he never goes to the bathroom?"

Laughing so hard I thought she was going to drop her tray, she said, "Honey, let me tell you a fact of life. Do you know what a catheter is?" Hell, yes, I knew! When one of the babies was born they had catheterized me and it hurt like crazy. Nodding my head, I thought, *What's that got to do with it?*

"Well, he has one and the tube goes down to a bag strapped to his leg."

Thinking about it for a minute, I said, "Gosh, that must hurt a lot. I hope he wins." She walked away laughing and shaking her head.

After that, I couldn't take my eyes off him. The chip girls would bring his food but he never took his eyes off his cards— he'd drop a chip on their tray and go on playing. He went on for four days, after which I never saw him again.

I learned an important thing while working there. Gambling Fever . . . It was a real sickness. Day after day, I'd see the same people come in. Many of them housewives who I knew were gambling with grocery money.

Another good thing about working in the restaurant was that I could eat all my meals there and save on groceries at home. Still weighing a hundred and twenty-nine pounds, I put myself on a strict diet. Green vegetables, lean broiled meat or fish, salads with just vinegar, and potatoes with just salt and pepper. And no sweets. It really wasn't hard to do and in six weeks I was down to a hundred and eight pounds . . . more than I'd intended to lose. Not all of it was the diet. The other reason was sleepless nights.

Even though things were going fairly well, I still missed Smitty. And I still loved him. If only I could hear from him. I had not tried to contact him since Louisville. I started making excuses. He might not know where we were. I faced everything except the truth. I couldn't bear the truth.

The mailman never brought anything but bills so I wasn't happy when he'd drop something in our box. The furniture company in Warrensburg had found me and dunned me regularly. I tore the notices up. Surely, they wouldn't put the mother of three little boys in jail . . . would they? The other reason I hated to see the bills was the fact if they could find me, so could Smitty.

Seeing the return address on the envelope—T/Sgt. Lowell A. Smith—my heart almost jumped out of my chest! Tearing it open, I began to read.

" 'My darling, I've written a thousand letters and torn up each one. What can I say?' "

I read hungrily. But, as I comprehended what I was reading, the happiness began to fade and tears dimmed my vision. There must be some mistake! I read it again. He was telling me that Joan (his wife) had joined him in Panama and he was trying desperately to get her to agree to another divorce. *How are you going to accomplish that, you bastard,* I thought, *while you're in bed together?* Bitterness and hatred were filling my heart. I read on. " 'Since I know you need transportation to work, I've traded the Lincoln for a yellow and black Mercury and am having it shipped to you'." *Well, wasn't that generous of the son of a bitch! Of course I had to make the payments! Well, let him send it! I'll keep the bastard until they repossess it!* Ironically, the last line was, "Please wait for me. All my love, always . . . Smitty." Bullshit! I was crying so hard I couldn't see, and screaming a stream of cuss words that would have made a sailor blush, I tore the letter into shreds, lit a match to it, and stood away from the sink where I'd thrown it so my tears wouldn't put out the fire as I watched it burn. My heart was in as many pieces as the letter.

I'd been at the club about seven months when the boss came to me and said: "Grace, I'm gonna have to let you go."

"Why? What have I done?"

"Nothing. But you remember that girl whose place you took?"

"Yes."

"Well, she's had her baby and I told her when she left that if she wanted to come back, she could."

"Well, you didn't tell *me!*" I was trying not to cry.

"Hey, I didn't think she would! But now she does and I feel obligated to keep my word."

"Can I stay two weeks?" I asked, figuring that would give me time to find another job and another paycheck. "Sure. Two weeks." That was that. Back on the streets.

I'd always heard cocktail waitress made a lot of tips. So, even though I didn't know one drink from another, I decided to try it. With time and someone else's patience, I figured I could learn anything.

The sign out front said "Rusty's Bar." *Maybe it'll look better in the dark,* I thought. *Right now, it looks like a deserted shack.* Lacking the courage to approach a really nice place, I ventured in. Once inside, I had to stop and get my eyes adjusted to the dark. When I did, I didn't like what I saw. The place was filthy! And sitting at the tables were some men who looked like they hadn't been home since the night before. I knew it was my imagination but I felt their eyes were undressing me as I walked to the bar and asked to see the manager. The bartender, looking me over, said, "I'm the manager. What can I do for you?"

"Well I . . . uh . . . do you need a waitress?" He laughed.

"Do you wait tables as slow as you talk?"

"No, sir."

"Can you start today?" he asked.

"Yes, sir."

"Okay," pointing to a room in the back, "you'll find some uniforms in there. One of them should fit."

A couple of girls were changing clothes. Seeing what they were wearing, or rather, what they weren't, I said, "Am I supposed to wear that?" They didn't answer . . . just pointing to a rack filled with skimpy costumes like the ones they were wearing. But it was a job! The white top didn't look like it would fit a two-year-old but I squeezed my thirty-four D's into it thinking, *If I take a deep breath, every button will pop.* The skirt wasn't much better . . . black, flimsy, and just barely covering my bottom. Taking my waitress shoes out of the paper sack and putting them on, I turned to the mirror on the back of the door. *Gosh,* I thought, *I can't go out there like this!* But thinking of the great tips I was gonna make made me change my mind. *I'd better make great tips.* The pay was only eighty-five cents an hour!

The bartender and I had a system and, as the evening wore on, I began to get used to it. As he sat my orders on my tray and if

I could remember who had ordered what, I was okay. I hated the job but knew I had to stay until I could find something else.

My hours were five in the afternoon till one A.M. Every day, the same obnoxious man was there. He looked (and smelled) like he hadn't had a bath in a week, and I avoided waiting on him.

My fourth day, every time I'd walk past, he'd reach out and pat my bottom. "Don't do that, sir," I'd say firmly. It didn't faze him. In fact, each time he'd laugh louder. The other customers got a big kick out of it. And he sat right where I had to turn in my orders at the bar.

His back was to me, and he was talking to some man who had joined him at his table. Now was my chance. Now I could slip by without his knowledge. Just as I got past his table, he reached out, grabbed me and, losing my balance, I landed on his lap! With him holding on, it took several tries before I made it back up. "Sir! Do you see this tray?" I was angry!

"Yeah . . . what about it?"

"Well, the next time you touch me . . . whatever is on it goes on your head!" Turning to anyone that might be listening, he said, "Hear that! The little lady is gonna dump something on my head!" He roared with laughter.

Sure enough, he was daring me. My tray was loaded. Deliberately, I walked right past his table. As he reached out (as I knew he would) I dumped the whole six drinks on his head. "Sir," I said calmly. "Maybe you'll find one of these to your liking." Within a few minutes, I was changed and out the door. There had to be something better. I'd also been fired.

There were lots of waitress jobs but most were either too far away or the hours were impossible or the place was too fancy or a dump. Huff's Coffee Shop was on my rounds and, during the day, I'd stop there for a glass of tea, usually around noon. One day, looking around, I thought, *This place is really busy.* Then, it dawned on me. Why not try for a job here? I asked to see the manager.

"Could you use another waitress?" I asked. I'd seen him every time I'd been in there so it wasn't like asking a total stranger.

"As it happens, I might. What's your experience?"

Making up a fast lie, I told him I'd been a banquet waitress in a hotel in Springfield and had just moved here. I knew he wouldn't check.

When I left there, I had a job starting the next day, eight A.M. till four P.M. Glory be! Perfect! I could get the boys up, dressed, have breakfast with them, and I could also be home in the evenings. It would leave Mom free to do baby-sitting where she would be paid.

Every now and then, I'd get a letter from Smitty but I never answered them. What was the use? Each one vowed his undying love for me and begged me to wait for him. But his wife was still with him in Panama and of course he was still married. I'd read the parts I liked over and over. Then I would tear the letter up and burn it. I never even wrote him when the car arrived. It was almost laughable. Here I was with an almost new Mercury and I didn't have enough money to buy gas for it. Junior (my brother, and Smitty's best friend) lived about forty miles from me and occasionally came to see me on Smitty's behalf. When I said I was never going back to him he got mad and left.

Huff's was a busy place and darned hard work but the other waitresses were nice and the boss was tolerable. Pretty soon I got to know a lot of the regulars. It made me feel good when they'd stand in line and wait at my station. The only drawback at Huff's was that if you turned in an order, you'd better make sure it was correct. Otherwise, you paid for it. Literally.

Some of the regulars were ambulance drivers. Nice guys but always teasing me. Sometimes, I'd get their orders mixed up but they took pity on me and ate whatever I brought them. All except one of them.

"What'll you have?" I asked.

"A chocolate shake," he said.

"Coming up," I said, and turned to the fountain. The minute I put the malt in, I realized my mistake. *But, what the hell,* I thought. *He won't know the difference.* Pouring it into a glass, I turned, smiling, and set it in front of him. "Here you are, sir."

Tasting it, he said, frowning, "This is not a shake . . . it's a malt!" And pushed it back . . . almost off the counter.

Catching it just in time, I said, "You know, a lot of people say our shakes taste like malts. It must be the ice cream. Here, try it again." I set it back in front of him.

Taking a sip, he said, "Damn it, lady, this is a *malt!*" and started to hand it back to me. From the cash register where he stood, the boss was watching.

"Sir, you're right. It is a malt. I made a mistake and we have to pay for any mistakes and I just can't afford it. Please, won't you drink it?" I must have sounded awfully pitiful because he tipped the glass up and, like it was medicine, drank every last drop, threw a quarter on the counter, got up, and walked out, never to be seen again. Or at least, not at my station.

Several times, it was sheer luck that I wasn't fired. A certain couple came in every Friday night. He was handsome and slim and she was pretty and fat. One of my favorite pastimes was to mentally match people together. But no way could I imagine how she'd gotten or kept him. Each night, their order was the same. Steak, french fries and a salad. Then, to top it off, he'd have sherbet and she'd have a hot fudge sundae loaded with whipped cream, exactly the opposite of what they should have had.

One night, when she ordered the sundae, before I could stop myself, I said, "Ma'am, you really don't need a hot fudge sundae. How about sherbet?" The look she gave me indicated I'd made a terrible mistake!

"Miss," she hissed. "I'll have whatever I damned well please!"

"Yes, ma'am." I went to get the sundae. As I sat their orders down in front on them, I caught the husband smiling. She never looked at me. But, after they left and I went to clean off the table, there was a dollar under his plate, and she hadn't touched the sundae. Never expecting to see them again, I was surprised, the next Friday, to see them back, waiting for my station. I sent another waitress over but they sent her back and motioned to me.

"Yes, folks, what'll you have?" I asked nervously. He spoke up with the usual order. I turned to her.

"Let me see," she said. "I'll have a steak, medium. Cottage cheese and a salad with lemon juice." I almost dropped my order pad.

"Yes, ma'am!" I couldn't wait for the end of the meal.

"The usual?" I asked.

"No," she said, smiling. "He'll have the hot fudge sundae and I'll have sherbet." After that, there was always a dollar tip and, as the weeks went by, I began to see the results.

Right after the boys were asleep, I'd hit the hay. I was usually so darned tired I'd fall immediately to sleep. This day had been one of the hardest. A nagging pain in my back had made every tray

I'd carried seem like it weighed a ton. Asking Mom to please take care of the kids, I fell into bed, only to be awakened in the middle of the night with the worst pain I'd ever felt—on the right side of my back.

Driving myself to the emergency room at Harbour General (a county hospital), I learned I had a kidney stone. As they gave me a pain shot, I thought, *Oh, God, how am I going to pay the rent!*

After ten days in the hospital, I was drained. Mentally, physically, emotionally, and financially. Even if my job was still there, the doctor had said I couldn't return to work for ten days. Except for what Mom made baby-sitting, we had no money and the rent was due. Every day, we'd figure exactly what we had to eat to survive and carefully ration that. My brother Dick had moved in with us but hadn't gotten a job yet. But he did help with the boys, and that meant a lot.

I couldn't sleep. Each night, I'd wonder if the next day we'd get our eviction notice.

All the years, even when things seemed hopeless, I'd avoided welfare. Oh, I knew about it but couldn't bring myself to ask for help. Today, pride had to take a backseat. I left the car at home . . . for two reasons. One was that I doubted if they'd think I needed help very badly if I could drive a car like that. Also, I didn't want to use up gas.

I took the bus to downtown Los Angeles to The Children's Aid Society. The first thing they asked was, "Do you receive child support?" After hearing my story of the divorce and what Mearle had said, she said, "Well, we'll see about that!" Explaining that there were laws against fathers abandoning their children, no matter what the circumstances, she got out her pad and pencil, wrote down the family names I gave her, and said she'd get to work on it immediately. In the meantime, I was given emergency grocery and rent money and was told that I would receive twenty-seven dollars every two weeks.

Before the first two weeks were up, I was back at work. Thank God, my job still existed.

One day, the boss walked up and said, "Grace, how would you like the hostess job?" That was only four hours during dinner! And they didn't make any tips! I panicked!

"You mean give up the day shift?"

"No. I mean in addition to that. Do you think you could handle it?"

Without even hesitating, I said, "You bet I could!" The extra four hours meant an extra four dollars!

The weeks dragged on. Soon it was months. I'd been there over a year . . . most of the time working twelve hours a day. Eight until four and six until ten. I'd have breakfast with the kids . . . go to work . . . back for supper and get them ready for bed . . . then back to work. Jimmy and David seemed to accept my absence but not Corky. He fought me all the way. Every night it was a battle, and it tore my heart out to see him crying. One night, he flat refused to lay down in bed so I could cover him up. I'd lay him down and he'd bounce right back up. "I'm *not* going to sleep!" he cried.

"What are you gonna do?"

"I'm gonna sit right here till you come home!"

"It'll be hard to sleep sitting up." I couldn't keep from laughing. It made Corky even angrier.

"You'll see! I'll be sitting right here when you get home!" I wondered if there'd ever be a time when I wouldn't have to leave them.

When I got home, I tiptoed in to kiss each one and cover them up. Corky was lying across his pillow, tears dried on his little checks. I leaned down to kiss him and, as I touched him, he sat straight up in bed. "See? I told you I'd be sittin' right here!"

"That's right, darlin'," I said as I laid him back down. "Mama's home now. You can go to sleep." I cried the rest of the night.

I only had two days off a week, one devoted to cleaning house, and catching up on washing and ironing; the other doing whatever was inexpensive with the boys. My days did not vary much.

I'd finished my eight hours and came home to change into my "hostess" clothes. Usually the boys were outside to meet me but not today. I wondered if Mom or Dick had taken them somewhere. I walked into the house, expecting it to be empty, and stopped cold in my tracks! Smitty was sitting at the kitchen table holding David on his lap, and Jimmy and Corky were hanging onto every word of what he was saying. My heart felt like a jackhammer in my chest. One part of me wanted to run to him and the other part of me wanted to run as fast as I could away from him. Paralyzed, I couldn't move in either direction.

Putting David down, he walked toward me. "Aren't you glad to see me?" he asked, holding out his arms. I started toward the bedroom.

Following me, he grabbed me and kissed me. For just a moment, I gave in to the feeling I'd wanted for so long—his arms around me. Then, suddenly, all the hurt, anger, grief, and disappointment of the last year and a half came out. Jerking out of his arms, I started pounding on his chest screaming, "Damn you. Damn you." I'd lost all control. Turning to the dresser where for some strange reason his picture still sat, I grabbed it, took it out of the frame, tore it into shreds, and threw it at him! "That was all that was left of you. Now it's gone," I screamed. "Now, get the hell out of my house!"

I didn't even see it coming. With the full force of his hand, he slapped me clear across the room! My head hit the baseboard and I lay there dazed. He started toward me. There was a look I'd never seen on his face before. Total, insane, anger!

"Who were you going out with?" he demanded.

"No one. I was going back to work!" This couldn't be Smitty? This man was a stranger!

"Like hell you were! You were going out with some man!" With one hand, he jerked me off the floor. I could hear the boys screaming! God, where was Mom? Where was Dick? I felt his hands go around my throat and I knew he was going to kill me. And there was nothing I could do about it.

I came to lying across the bed. My head hurt . . . my throat hurt . . . but I was alive. As strong as Smitty was, I didn't know what had kept him from finishing the job, unless he thought he had.

Calm now, I walked to the edge of the kitchen. His back to me, Smitty was kneeling in front of the kids, trying to quiet them. "Daddy will take care of you," he said.

"No, Daddy won't take care of you. Mommy will," I said. His back stiffened.

The kids said, "Mommy!" And they ran to me. Slowly, Smitty got up and turned around.

"Smitty," I said, "I waited all these months. Sometimes loving you . . . sometimes hating you—but—I waited—Now I just hate you. I want you out of my life and out of my house. Don't ever come back." I walked over and opened the door.

As he walked past me, he stopped. "Grace, I'm sorry. Please forgive me." I turned and walked into the other room. Hearing the door shut, I went back, looked out the window, and watched until he was out of sight. He was gone.

The next few weeks, I was like a robot at work. With Smitty gone, something else was gone, too. All emotion. I couldn't feel a thing. All the customers were the same. They accepted my blank look along with their check. All except one. Don Britton.

From the few words we'd exchanged, I'd learned he was a salesman for the Brother International Sewing Machine Company. His daily challenge was to try to make me smile. He teased all the girls but he seemed to delight in picking on me. I wasn't in the mood for it and, sometimes, I was downright rude. It didn't seem to faze him.

Seeing him come in the door, I turned to another waitress and said, "Hey, I can't take this guy today. How about you waiting on him."

"Sure, honey," she said. She turned to Don, who had seated himself at the counter. "Hi, Don. How's it going?" He didn't even answer her.

I had gone to the end of the counter. He came and sat down on the stool right in front of me. "What's the matter?" he said, smiling. "Don't you need my quarter tip today?"

I started to walk away. He reached across the counter and touched my arm. "I'm only teasing."

"I know. I'm just not up to it today. What'll you have?"

All through lunch, he kept watching me. It was obvious there was something on his mind.

As I gave him his check, he got up, laid a quarter on the counter, and started to walk away. After a few steps, he came back, laid another quarter on the counter, smiled, and walked out.

The next day, after almost the same routine, he said, "How would you like to quit this job and be a secretary?" Mission accomplished. I started laughing.

"Fine! There's only one drawback. I can't type or take shorthand."

"Not even a little bit?"

"Not even a little bit!" *Me? A secretary? It was a laugh!*

"Well," he said, "give me your number anyway. I'll have my boss call you."

I'd heard a lot of lines but this was a new one. Somehow, though, he wasn't the type. In all the times he'd been in here, he'd never made a pass or said anything out of the way. Just for the heck of it, I gave him my number.

Much to my surprise, a few days later, a man by the name of Dave Boder called and asked me to come in for an interview. "You mean he was on the level?" I asked. Then went on to explain that I couldn't type or take shorthand and it would be a waste of his time and mine. He insisted. This was ridiculous! I'd tried many times to *get* a job but never to get *out* of one! "Mr. Boder," I said, "I've told you I have no qualifications for a secretarial job. Why do you want to see me?"

He laughed. "Don Britton has never recommended anyone before. I just want to see what it is you've got!" At least he was honest. We set an appointment for the next day.

Sitting in the outer office, I began to get nervous. *What am I doing here?* I thought. *This man is only going to laugh at me.* Too late. A man was walking toward me. Holding out his hand, he said, "Mrs. Smith? I'm Dave Boder." He looked just like his voice . . . friendly.

All the time he was asking me questions, I kept telling myself to relax. After all, he wasn't going to bite me! He didn't seem the type. Not exactly fat, he was what you'd call "chubby." Well dressed (gray tailored suit, white shirt, and shiny black shoes) and, except for a rim of graying hair around his head, bald. The thing I noticed the most was his beautiful, kind smile and twinkling blue eyes. I liked this man.

For thirty minutes, I told him all the reasons he shouldn't hire me. Ignoring me, he kept writing on a pad. Handing it to me, I read, "Can you report for work Monday morning?" I couldn't believe it! That meant I was hired! I was going to be a secretary! Explaining my duties, he said I would mostly handle the salesmen's contracts, complaints from customers, bank deposits, make "leads" for the salesmen . . . just, in general, be his Girl Friday. And, since I'd told him of my previous experience as a telephone operator, once in a while I would relieve the switchboard operator. My pay would be sixty-five dollars for five and a half days . . . nine to five Monday through Friday and nine to twelve Saturday mornings. No more working nights! I could be home to get the kids off to school in the mornings and be home with them at night.

The car, which I'd managed to keep by making one payment out of every four, was parked across the street in the parking lot. As I got in and drove home, I felt like I was floating on air. Even though it was pouring down rain, for the first time in a long time,

I felt the sun was beginning to shine. I could have kissed Don Britton.

My brother Dick, who was still living with us, was dating a beautiful, auburned-haired girl by the name of Dee Hood. Her skin was like porcelain, and she had the tiniest waist I'd ever seen. They were primarily friends. Sometimes she'd come over when Dick wasn't even home, and we'd just talk. It was good to have someone to talk to . . . someone my own age. As we got to know each other, I asked her questions about makeup, hair, and woman stuff. She always looked so neat and pretty. I needed all the help I could get. It had been so long since I'd even cared but now, with this new job, I had to try to look nice. For hours at a time, she'd work with me . . . showing me how to do my eyebrows, use a lighter color lipstick and rouge in the right places. And coats and coats of mascara to enlarge my small, dark brown eyes.

Many times, being in a hurry in the morning, I'd get it on wrong and Mr. Boder would suggest (with a smile) that I go wash my face. I gave up and went back to *au naturel*.

Now and then Dee would mention that she, her mother, and her sister, Barbara, would go to a place called Cowtown on Sunday afternoons to listen to Wade Ray. The name meant nothing to me. Several times she asked me to go with them but I wanted no part of it for two reasons. One, I didn't think it was right to go in a place like that without a man. Two, I didn't care that much for country music anymore . . . not since Smitty. I didn't want to be reminded of him.

It was Saturday morning. Dee called and asked me to go with them to another club called The Shedd to hear Wynn Stewart and his band.

"Who's he?" I asked.

"He's really good. You'll like him," she said. "Besides, I'm dating him and I want to see what you think."

"Well, I don't know."

Mom, hearing part of the conversation, said, "Go on and go. It'll do you good." That surprised the heck out of me, because she didn't approve of any place that sold liquor.

After more coaxing from Dee and Mom, I said, "Okay . . . why not! It might be fun." Except for work and taking the kids somewhere, I hadn't been out of the house in eighteen months.

As we pulled into the crowded parking lot, I could hear the loud music coming from inside. I almost backed out. "Dee," I said, "we can't go in there."

"Sure we can. Come on." She was already out of the car.

I followed her, still resisting. "I really don't think we should." They didn't pay me any attention—just kept on walking. Not wanting to wait alone in the parking lot, I followed.

The place was dark and smoky and filled to the rafters. On the bandstand was a five-piece band and, in front, the lead singer was singing "Love Me Tender," an Elvis Presley song. As we walked past, the whole band smiled and waved, and I knew that I was in the company of regular customers. Seated in a booth at the edge of the bandstand and almost inside a speaker, I knew I'd go deaf if we stayed more than ten minutes.

Everyone but me ordered Vodka Sevens. I stuck with plain Seven-up. Men started coming up and asking me to dance. Embarrassed, I'd shake my head no, point to one of the others, and scoot a little farther to the back of the booth. Finally, they quit asking. As I watched, though, I envied the ones out there on the dance floor. They seemed to be having so much fun. I'd forgotten how to have fun. But I did enjoy the music. It wasn't bad. In fact, it was pretty darned good.

At intermission, the whole band came over and, one by one, I was introduced to Ralph Mooney (the steel player); Pete Ash (the piano player); Tony somebody or other (the drummer); and Wynn Stewart. After saying a brief hello, everybody left except Wynn, who sat down next to Dee. And from the bits and pieces of conversation I heard, I knew they were more than casual friends.

By the end of the evening, I was actually enjoying myself! I even danced once. The band was on a break and the jukebox was playing Elvis Presley's "Hound Dog" when a big fat guy came over, and before I knew what was happening, he'd grabbed my hand and pulled me out on the dance floor. At first, I was awkward, but he was such a good dancer he just guided me around the floor. Before long, I was beginning to think he was a fat Fred Astaire and I was Ginger Rogers!

When I walked into the house, guilt took over. I hadn't been home to put the boys to bed.

The next night, to make up for it, I took them to a Mexican restaurant—a rare treat. Before I could stop Corky, he'd reached into a bowl of hot peppers, stuck one in his mouth, and bit down on it. "Corky! No!" I said, and tried to get him to spit it out. He just shook his head and, with tears rolling down his face, went right on chewing.

I liked my job. Dave Boder was a jewel and the salesmen (all thirteen of them) sort of adopted me. They knew I had three children to support and wasn't interested in anything except making a living. Their "passes" consisted of laughing, joking, and teasing me. I think they would have seriously hurt anyone who carried it further. And they brought me so many "goodies" from home, I saved money on lunches. In fact, I very seldom took a lunch break.

The showroom, right outside my office, was filled with display models of sewing machines. And every day, when Mr. Boder was at lunch, the same woman came in, wandered around, and asked me questions about them. I kept telling her that she'd have to talk with Mr. Boder but she'd always disappear before he came back. *Oh, well,* I thought, *she's not the type to sew anyway.* Her long, manicured fingernails didn't fit the image. She interested me, though. I'd never seen anyone like her. Very well dressed, every hair in place, and makeup you could tell she spent hours on. What the heck did she want with a sewing machine? I told Mr. Boder about her but he'd just smile and change the subject.

Well, here she comes again, I thought as I heard the door chimes. But, before I could get up, Mr. Boder walked in the door and went over to her. He seemed angry, which wasn't like him. She glanced at me and he pointed to the door. Well, that's the last of her!

The next day, before noon, the phone rang. In my best secretarial voice, I said, "Brother International."

"Grace? This is Phyllis." Phyllis? Oh, yes. The woman from the showroom.

"Yes. What can I do for you?"

"I'd like to take you to lunch. There's something I'd like to talk to you about."

"What's that?" I couldn't imagine what someone like her would have to talk to *me* about.

"Well . . . I don't think we should talk over the phone but it's about a job."

"But I already have a job."

"I know. But the job I'm talking about can make you a lot more money." Money! The magic word.

When Mr. Boder came back, I told him I was going to lunch with Phyllis. "Who?" he asked.

"You know . . . the woman from the showroom. She wants to talk to me about something."

His face was livid. "That bitch!" He came around the desk, put his hands on my shoulders, and leaned down real close to my face. "You're not going to lunch with her . . . not now or any other time!"

Timidly, I asked, "Why not?"

He seemed exasperated! "Grace, do you know what a prostitute is?"

"No, sir."

"Well, it's someone that sells sex for money. That's what she is, and I don't ever want you talking to her again." He didn't have to say any more. I was naive, not stupid! Knowing that's the job she was talking about, I was also embarrassed.

Since the night at The Shedd, I'd gone out with Dee several times. She was still dating Wynn and said she hated to go alone. So, when neither her mother nor her sister could go, she'd call me. I loved the music and it had gotten so I never wanted for dance partners. And it didn't cost a cent. They never charged us to get in and she bought my single Seven-up.

This Saturday night, the place was more crowded than usual. Bodies were packed together on the dance floor like sardines. During intermission, Wynn came over and, with him, this tall, undernourished-looking guy . . . who was more than a little drunk. As the stranger stood there, weaving and grinning stupidly, Wynn said, "Grace, I'd like for you to meet my best friend, Harlan Howard." I couldn't believe he'd brought this creep over to introduce him to me.

"Hello," I said, not really looking at him. I'd seen all I wanted to.

"Would you like to dance?" he asked, in a voice so slurred I could barely understand him.

Wynn was standing there, grinning, waiting for me to dance with his friend. Slowly, I got up. I wasn't looking forward to it.

From the first step, I knew that dancing was not Harlan's thing. He walked around the floor, mostly on my feet. After he stumbled a few times, I was afraid he would fall down and take me with him. I walked off the floor and back to the booth. Harlan just turned and weaved toward the exit.

Wynn apologized. "I'm sorry, Grace. I didn't know he was that drunk or I wouldn't have brought him over. He is really a nice guy when he's sober."

I had no intention of finding out.

Three weeks went by and I had forgotten Harlan Howard. The phone rang. "Grace . . . this is Harlan." Harlan? The voice sounded familiar.

"Yes. The drunk dancer. I called to apologize. Wynn told me what I did, but I don't really remember."

"That's not surprising. Did you make it home all right?"

"Hell, no! I slept in Wynn's car! He found me in the backseat when he got off work." I could just imagine this tall, gangly guy trying to curl up in the seat of Wynn's little Ford. "Would you like to go to a movie?" he asked.

I thought, *Well, now that's he's sober, he sounds kinda nice.* "Sure," I said. "I think I'd like that." I hadn't been to a movie in a long time.

"If you promise not to eat anything at the movie that costs more than a corter (the way he pronounced quarter), I'll pick you up in an hour." I could see right now that this was going to be an interesting evening!

As he pulled into the drive-in theater, he gave me one more instruction. "You sit on your side of the car and I'll sit on mine," he said, smiling. What a character! He didn't know he was perfectly safe with me.

Afterward, we went back to the house and talked over coffee. I learned that he worked at Pacific Press, Inc., a place where magazines such as *Time, Life,* etc, were printed. From the things he said and the way he said them, I gathered he hated his job. "Somehow, someway," he said, "I'm going to be a songwriter." He'd wanted to write songs since he was seventeen.

Harlan had been born in Detroit, Michigan, but he was named after Harlan County, Kentucky, where some of his folks had lived. A few years before, living in Tucson with his wife and daughter, Jennifer (about David's age), he had come down with polio. Eventually, they had divorced and his wife and daughter had moved to L.A. From the expression on his face when he talked about them, I had an idea that they had lot to do with him moving to Los Angeles. I certainly understood him because, even after all that had happened, I still hadn't forgotten Smitty. But some loves die of starvation. Others because you kill it.

Harlan wasn't handsome, he wasn't even good looking. But there was something about him—like a puppy that had been kicked once too often. He was about six feet three and downright skinny with a shock of thick, dark brown hair which he wore in a crewcut. You could always tell when he needed a haircut when sprigs of hair started popping out all over his head away from the gel he used to keep the sides down and the top standing straight up. But he was good-natured, with laughing eyes and . . . was also kind.

After the movie date, he was at the house constantly, and the boys seemed to take to him more and more. Sometimes, we'd play cards with Dick and Dee (they were just friends now) and, sometimes, he'd bring over his guitar and play, as long as the songs didn't require more than three chords, which was all he knew. He would sing his latest music, which he called his babies—his "brainchildren."

He was happiest when he was around music. We often went out to see some of his friends—Buck Owens, Bobby Bare, Wynn Stewart, and a lot of others wherever they happened to be playing. They were all struggling, too, just trying to get a break. Most of them were recording but had never had anything really big. Except the gang at *Town Hall Party*, a three-hour weekly stage and television show. The first time he took me there, backstage, no less, I thought, *This guy knows everybody!* On stage stood people I had seen in movies, on television, and heard on record, but never ever thought I'd meet. Tex Ritter (Daddy's favorite), Johnny Bond, Skeets McDonald, The Collins Kids, Jimmy Wakely, Joe and Rose Lee Maphis, Freddie Hart, and a pretty sixteen-year-old blonde who had a voice as a big as all get out by the name of Jeanie Sterling. I couldn't believe I was there!

Harlan and I had been dating exactly thirty days and, to celebrate our "anniversary," we went to The Shedd. Dee was there and we all sat together in a booth. During intermissions, Wynn came over and joined us. Harlan and Wynn were drinking beer and, in honor of the occasion, I joined Dee in a vodka seven. One lasted all evening.

Harlan was always joking. It was one thing I liked about him. He made me laugh. When he said, "Why don't we get married," I thought it was another joke.

"You're crazy!" I said. "We've only known each other thirty days!"

"I know it," he said, "but I think we'd get along." Wynn and Dee agreed.

"Sure! We could drive to Vegas and be married in the morning!"

Looking from one to the other (they were all waiting for my answer), I thought, *Hell! . . . why not!*

Eight o'clock in the morning isn't the ideal time to see Las Vegas. Well, I guess it depends on whether you've had a good night's sleep or are looking at Vegas through bleary eyes, red from lack of sleep—like ours were. Tired and hungry, we went to one of the casinos for breakfast. It was cheap. Since the owners want you to spend money gambling, they charge very little for food. My stomach was in knots. As hungry as I was, I ate almost nothing. I wanted to back out but didn't know how. Harlan looked like he was having second thoughts, too, but neither of us made the move. Leaving the coffee shop, I dropped a nickel in a slot machine and lost. *This is not a good sign,* I thought.

The courthouse opened at nine, and it took about ten minutes to get a marriage license. Then, driving up and down the street, we chose one of the many small white buildings that had a sign "Wedding Chapel" out front. As we pulled to a stop, we saw someone bringing flowers out of a back door and taking them in the front. That way, everyone was supposed to think the flowers were especially for their ceremony . . . not used over and over again. The whole performance was phony. If there was a laugh in me, it should have come out then.

We must have been a pitiful sight, standing there in the wrinkled clothes we'd driven all night in. In front of a so-called minister who had probably been educated in a correspondence course. Wynn was still in his stage clothes, and Dee stood up with us and on May 11, 1957, Harlan Perry Howard and Lula Grace Smith were pronounced man and wife. The words "I love you" had never been uttered by either one of us.

On the way out, a woman, holding a plastic disk toward us, said, "Don't you want to buy a recording of your ceremony?" She put it on a machine and played it for us. You could barely hear Harlan say "I do" and couldn't hear me at all. I wasn't sure I had. We didn't buy the recording. Besides, it cost ten dollars and we'd blown most of what we had on the license, the minister, and breakfast. Wynn had just enough for gas back to L.A.

Driving to Vegas, everyone had been laughing and joking. Now, there was only silence. I kept thinking, *God! What have I done?* I knew Harlan was thinking the same thing. Sitting as far on opposite sides of the seat as we could get, we kept our heads turned from each other. Finally, to keep the tears that I felt welling up in my eyes from rolling down my cheeks, I leaned back and closed my eyes. I woke up when Wynn stopped the car, turned around, and said, "Okay . . . which way do I go?" I didn't say a word. Harlan said, "Just drop me off at my place." He lived in a rooming house in Huntington Park.

As he got out of the car I thought for a minute he was going to walk away without a word . . . and he started to. But then, he turned around and said, "We both know we've made a mistake. But I'll call you." I nodded my head.

Three weeks went by. I was beginning to hope that this could be resolved without us ever having to see each other again. Then he called.

"Grace? This is Harlan."

"I know."

"How are you?" We were like two strangers.

"I'm fine. And you?"

"Well . . . I think we need to talk. After all, we are married." *Lord, don't remind me!,* I thought.

Later that evening, he came over and we had the most serious talk we'd ever had. We both knew we weren't in love. Yet, like me, he was lonesome and needed somebody. I hadn't really forgotten Smitty, I never would, but that part of my life was over. And the kids needed a father. Weighing all the pros and cons, we decided to try to make a go of it. When we broke the news to Mom and the boys, they were thrilled. That is, everyone but Harlan and me.

Walking out to his old, black '49 Ford with him, he put his arm around me and said, "L.G."—the nickname he had given me and the closest thing to an endearment—"I'm really gonna try."

"I will, too," I promised.

Talk about crowded! Our small two-bedroom apartment was crammed with wall-to-wall people. Mom and the boys in one bedroom, Harlan and I in the other, and Dick on the sofa. After a while, Dick moved out but he still came around a lot.

Little by little, we began to adjust to each other. Every now and then, I'd see one of the boys crawl up on Harlan's lap, and it wasn't long before they started calling him "Dad." Funny, give a child a little bit of love and he'll turn to you every time. I guess the same went for me. But it didn't go for Harlan's daughter, Jenny. We'd driven over one day to take her for ice cream and to give us a chance to get acquainted. But everytime she'd look at me, she'd say, "I hate you!" I didn't have a chance. She'd been well coached by her mother, I presumed.

One night in the middle of dinner the phone rang. "Hello," I said. No answer. Starting to hang it back up, I heard, "Grace?" It was Smitty. Just hearing his voice started my heart pounding. Harlan looked up.

"Who is it?" he asked.

"Smitty," I answered. Harlan went back to eating.

"Grace, are you there?" I could tell it was a long-distance call.

"Yes, I'm here." I couldn't bring myself to hang up.

"I'm calling from Cheyenne, Wyoming. I'm stationed here." I didn't answer. "I know, after what I did, you probably hate me, but the divorce is worked out and I want you and the boys to come to Cheyenne. Please say you still love me." My hand was shaking so I could hardly hold the phone. "Oh, God, Smitty," I said. "Why did you wait so long?" I looked at Harlan, who was watching me but he hadn't said a word. I had to say it. I had to force the words out of my mouth.

"It's too late, Smitty. I got married a month ago."

"No!" he cried. Gently, I laid the phone back in the cradle and stood there looking at it. It was finally over. I walked into the bathroom.

Drying my face, I put on a smile that never reached my eyes, and walked back to the kitchen. "Was that Daddy?" the boys asked.

"No. That was Smitty." I touched Harlan's hand. "This is Daddy."

When Harlan and I married, the Children's Aid money stopped. But with his pay—fifty-five dollars a week—and mine, we managed. We budgeted so much for rent, so much for groceries, and so much for emergencies. If we were careful with money, we even managed to take trips to Marineland, Disneyland, and Knotts Berry Farm. And there was always the beach. Harlan was wonderful to the boys, I couldn't help but love him. Maybe I'd never have that terrible, passionate love for him that I'd had for Smitty but our marriage had only gotten me hurt.

Tiny wrote me that Mearle's mother Verna had divorced Tabor and was living in Bell, only a few miles from us. Even though I hated Mearle, Verna had always been good to me. I decided to take the boys to see her.

After the hugs and kisses were over, we began to talk of the past.

"Have you ever heard from Mearle?" she asked

"No. And I don't want to except by way of child support."

"Well," she said, hesitating, "if you should want to contact him, he's living in San Jose. He married a girl named Peggy who was stationed with him at Fort Carson." I remembered the girl in the NCO club that night. Mearle's brother Bob told me her name was Peggy.

"What's he doing now?" I asked. She knew I was pumping her but went right on.

"He's a sergeant in the Marine Corps." Before I left, I had got his address.

The next day, I called the base commander. "My name is Lula Grace Howard. I'd like to speak to you about Sergeant Mearle M. Wood."

"Concerning what?" he asked brusquely.

"Concerning four years' back child support," I said.

"What!"

I told him the whole story.

"Send me the children's birth certificates, your marriage certificate, and your divorce decree, and I'll look into it," he said. After giving him my address and phone number, I hung up. I was already planning how I was going to use the over five thousand dollars Mearle owed me.

Three days later, he called me back. "Mrs. Howard, you'll be glad to know that Sergeant Wood had been dishonorably discharged from the Marines and he's already off the base." Damn!

That wasn't what I wanted! I'd thought sure they'd make him pay the child support . . . not kick him out! He went on to tell me that Mearle had joined the Marines with a fraudulent discharge from the Army saying he'd never been married and had no minor children. Also, that he was presently married and his wife was expecting a child. I could have cared less.

A few days later, Mearle called from his mother's house. "I guess you're happy," he said. "You got me kicked out of the Marines."

"No, I'm not happy. I thought they'd make you pay us the money you owe us," I said bitterly. "You know, you can go to jail!"

The tone of his voice changed. "Yes, I know, but if you'll give me a few days, I'll come up with the money." This surprised the hell out of me!

"You've lied too many times, Mearle."

"This time, I mean it. Give me four days."

"All right. Four days. No more." Was I being a fool again?

"I'll call you," he said, and hung up.

At the end of the four days with no call, I called his mother. "Didn't he call you?" She sounded surprised.

"No, he didn't."

"Well, he's gone back to Montoursville, Pennsylvania, where his wife's folks live." I knew it! To Mearle, lying came as easy as breathing.Before hanging up, she gave me his phone number.

Dialing the number, and listening to it ring, I stood there tapping the edge of the table, all the hate and anger waiting to explode when someone answered.

"Hello?" a woman's voice said.

"I'd like to speak to Mearle Wood, please." I didn't want her to hang up before I got him on the line.

"Who's calling?" Good. He was there!

"The ex-Mrs. Wood!" I heard her screaming, "Mearle! Your ex-wife's on the phone!"

"Hello?" He was calm as a cucumber!

"You dirty, rotten bastard!" I said. "You wanted four days to have time to get out of town, didn't you?"

"You guessed it."

"I'll make you pay, you lying son of a bitch! Just wait and see!"

"You can't talk to me like that! My wife's just had a baby!" What a stupid damned thing to say!

"Who cares! Let her and the brat starve the way we did. Besides, idiot, all you've got to do is have the guts to hang up!" Before he could, I slammed down the phone . . . hoping it burst his damned eardrums!

The next morning, I was at the district attorney's office. After hearing my story, he said, "That young man's got a shock in store for him. The law's been changed and a man can no longer get out of child support just by skipping the state."

"You mean, even with him living in Pennsylvania, he can still be made to pay?"

"Yes, ma'am. I'll be in touch with the district attorney in Montoursville immediately, and you'll hear from me within two weeks."

"Good!"

Coming home from work, I had changed clothes and started supper. Jimmy and Corky had gone to the park. But since we sometimes called David "lightning"—because one minute he's there and the next minute he's gone—I'd kept him at home.

Glancing out the window, I saw him playing with the little girl next door. The radio was on, I was singing along with Elvis, *Just wanta be . . . your teddy bear . . .* and went on peeling potatoes. Thinking I heard someone at the door, I stopped and listened. Nothing. I went back to singing and peeling. I heard it again. As I opened the door, David fell at my feet. My God, his face was blue! Grabbing him up, I threw him in the car and drove like mad to the nearest emergency room, about two blocks away. When I ran in, David in my arms, a nurse took him and disappeared through a door.

It seemed like hours before the same door opened and a doctor, blood all over his white coat, came toward me.

"Mrs. Howard?"

"Yes," I said anxiously.

"Your son is going to be all right." Not knowing what had happened, I looked at him blankly. He said, "He had a piece of hard candy lodged in his throat and we had to do a tracheotomy."

"A what?"

"A cut in his windpipe so he could breathe. The only problem is that the candy was in pieces and I'm not sure we got it all."

"What does that mean?"

"It means that he could develop pneumonia. As a precaution,

we've put him in an oxygen tent. We should know within forty-eight hours."

Walking into the room, I saw the plastic tent that covered the bed and David lying inside, asleep. A bandage around his throat. Pulling up a chair, I sat down and didn't take my eyes off him. I remembered vividly when Jimmy had nearly choked to death. After a while, David began to move and started to cry. I leaned over and said, "It's all right, darlin'. Mommy's here. Don't talk." He dozed back off.

Sometime during the night, I heard him again. He was trying to talk. He was very frightened. "David, don't try to talk," I said. He was still trying. I leaned closer. "Mommy," he said, "I never want any more hard candy."

"Don't worry. There'll never be another piece in the house."

Thank God he didn't get pneumonia. After three days, he was home. But I wondered what was going to happen next!

Lately, I hadn't been feeling well. I was so weak! My menstrual cycles were so messed up . . . one period ran into another. There were days when I just couldn't make it to work. Dave Boder, bless his heart, just said, "Don't worry about things here. Just get well."

I hated to waste money on seeing a doctor but, when the bleeding got so terribly bad, I had to. I hadn't seen a doctor since we'd been in California. I chose the nearest one, an osteopath down the street. It took him all of ten minutes to tell me that I was having a miscarriage and needed surgery immediately. I was hemorrhaging. Not having sense enough to get a second opinion, and after calling Mom to tell her I was going, I went straight to the hospital.

I felt myself gagging, and someone pushed a basin toward my face. It was Harlan. Jimmy was standing on a stool, holding my hand, and leaned down to kiss me. He was too young to be there but Harlan had sneaked him in. The smell of ether was so strong! Suddenly, Jimmy turned green and started to sink from sight . . . his arm clearing everything from the bedside table as he went down. Water pitcher . . . flowers . . . everything.

The nurse ran in yelling, "Get that kid out of here!" Harlan had already picked him up and was on the way out the door.

A week after surgery, I was still in nearly as bad a shape as I was when I got to the hospital. The doctor said more surgery had to be done. I was too weak and scared to object. Ten days after I was released, I was still bleeding and went back to the doctor. "You're anemic," he said, and pushed a prescription across his desk. *Hell, no wonder,* I thought, *if I don't get better soon, I'll die and won't have to worry about it.*

I'd been off work so long and, even though I'd talked to Mr. Boder several times and he'd assured me my job was intact, I felt guilty about not being at work. I called him. "Mr. Boder? I don't know when I'll be able to return to work. I think I'm just going to have to quit."

"Can't you get it through your head I don't *want* another girl in this office!"

"But . . ."

"No buts! I'll get another girl to fill in for you." His voice changed from hollering to gentle. "In the meantime, I want you to go to the best gynecologist in this city. My wife has checked it out and says to see a Dr. Earl Hyman at U.C.L.A. Medical Center. Don't worry about your pay check . . . it'll be there every week till you come back. I don't care how long it is." I started to cry. No one had ever been this good to me. "What are you waiting for," he said, back to his blustery self. "Get on the phone! It's dull around here without you."

During the examination, Dr. Hyman said, "My God! What butcher has gotten hold of you!" Afterward, he told me that when the damage from the stillborn baby was combined with the botched operation, if I didn't have cancer now, I would have in six months. He then told me to get two more opinions. Which I did.

Later that week, I called and said "Okay, when do I go in?"

After the surgery, which required removal of the uterus, I couldn't stop crying. "It's not like you needed more children," he said. "You have three healthy boys. Be thankful." He was right.

Three weeks later I was home and on the mend but I didn't return to work for eight more weeks. I felt old . . . Far beyond my twenty-five years.

Harlan was still hard at work on getting his songs recorded. Having succeeded with a few, he haunted the offices of Cliffie Stone at Central Songs, Ken Nelson at Capitol Records, and Johnny Bond and Tex Ritter, who had their own publishing

companies. Every minute not at work, he was at home, strumming on his guitar, or out "where the action is."

Feeling almost human again, I was restless and switched on
the TV. But all the news was bad. Vice President Nixon was in
South America having all sorts of trouble. There was something
about Fidel Castro starting a war in Cuba, and about somebody
named Khrushchev. I switched it off, went into the kitchen, and
started washing dishes. Harlan had left to go over to Wynn
Stewart's. Soapsuds up to my elbows, I was singing away. I heard
the door slam. Thinking it was one of the kids, I ignored it and
went on singing. Turning around, I was startled to see Harlan
standing in the doorway. "I didn't know you could sing," he said.

"Well, if you call it singing," I said, a little embarrassed.

"Come on, let's see if you can sing with a guitar!!" Practically
dragging me into the living room, he handed me the words to a
song called "Daddy For A Day." I looked at him questioning. "Just
change the word from *Daddy* to *Mommy* and sing," and he began
to strum and sing the melody. After a couple of times through, I
joined in.

"Hey, that sounds pretty good!" he said. "Let's see how it
sounds on tape." He started his small Wollensack tape recorder.
Suddenly, I couldn't open my mouth! With a little coaxing, a little
bitty voice came out. It didn't sound a bit like me. "Wait a
minute!" he said, "let's see how it sounds in the bathroom. The
echo's better in there."

Feeling more than ridiculous, I stood in the shower and, with
Harlan standing, one foot on the stool, playing the guitar, we
taped "Mommy For A Day." Listening to it back, I thought it was
about the worst-sounding thing I'd ever heard! Tossing the words
"I've got work to do" back over my shoulder, I went back to
something more useful . . . washing dishes. But, within a few
days, Harlan had set up a demo session—a rough recording of
the song to be presented to an artist to show the melody and
lyrics—at a small studio in Whittier (another suburb of L.A.).
With the help of Wynn Stewart's band and words of encouragement from everyone, I sang the song. Listening to it back, even
though I didn't let on, I thought it was the greatest thing since
buttermilk! It was actually *me* singing! Later that night, I took it
over for my friend Dee to hear. Listening politely for a while, she
then stopped the tape and said, "Do you want my honest opinion?"

"Yes!" I said, expecting her to praise my singing ability.

"It's the worst I've ever heard!" My ego was totally deflated. Putting the tape away, I refused to listen to it again. She was right. It was bad.

Harlan watched for the mail every day. As bad as it was, I couldn't believe he had sent it to a publisher in Nashville. But he had. It was no surprise to me when they didn't reply, but he was so dejected, I kinda wished they had.

One day, it came, with the news that Kitty Wells was going to record his and Buck's song. Gosh!

After that, every spare minute and dime was spent at the studio in Whittier. And every song that could possibly be sung by a female was given to me to demo. Harlan told me that he played them for Tex Ritter and Johnny Bond and they had asked who was singing. When he told them it was me, they said, "It's pretty good but she's too old to start singing. We're looking for eighteen-year-olds." I was twenty-six. Just for kicks, though, they had a couple of songs written by Ned—the writer of "From A Jack To A King"—and Sue Miller, and asked if I would demo them at a session they had set up in Bakersfield (about ninety miles north of L.A.).

Usually, at the sessions, there was only the band and us. I was expecting this one—except for Tex and Johnny and Louis Tally, the owner—to be the same. But when I walked in the studio and saw the whole staff from Town Hall Party plus Ricky Nelson there, I damned near fainted! To them, it was just another demo session but, to me, a little girl from West Plains who had never sung in front of anyone until recently, it was like being in front of a bunch of critics! And they would all know I was lousy. God, get me out of here!

After several tries, with me messing up the lyrics each time, Tex came out of the control room and over to me. Seeing I was about to burst out crying, he said, patting me on the shoulder, "Now, now, little girl. Forget about all those people. Just pretend they're not here, and sing the song to me. Okay?"

Looking into his kind, gentle eyes, I knew that's what I'd do— sing the song for him. And sing, I did.

Harlan wrote another song called "Pick Me Up On Your Way Down" and fired it off to the same publisher, Pamper Music, in Nashville. Not long afterward, we received word that Charlie

Walker was going to record it. He was on a roll! The demo sessions got more frequent and it seemed when I wasn't in the office, I was in the studio. He even got a bug about me recording. Going in with Wynn's band and with the drummer playing on a cardboard box, we recorded two songs, "Pick Me Up On Your Way Down" and "I Wish I Could Fall In Love Again." Pressing up ten records, we took them around to our friends at local radio stations. One of them, Charlie Williams at KFOX in Long Beach, actually played it—once.

Mr. Boder knew Harlan was writing songs because I was always talking about it. "What are you messing around with this hillbilly stuff for?" he'd ask. Being a real highbrow, he hated it. But, still, each time I'd ask for time off to do something, he'd say, "Take off!" I hoped he wouldn't, but expected any time, for him to fire me.

One time, I thought for sure it was all over. On Saturdays, when I worked a half a day, the only people in the office were me—and sometimes one of the kids I'd brought with me—Mr. Boder, and the salesmen. We'd just clear up Friday's contracts, check out the leads for that day, and leave.

Bernard Etzin, a young man in his late twenties who looked a lot like a young Cornell Wilde and who also owned the whole shootin' match, was hardly ever there on weekdays, let alone Saturdays, but he was that day.

Ever since I'd been there, which had been about a year and a half, my main strategy was to stay out of his way. If I saw him coming anywhere near my desk, I'd busy myself with anything within reach to try and look as indispensable as possible. I don't think he even knew my name.

Just as I was doing the last contract, he walked into the office and over to my desk. Mr. Boder, whose desk faced mine, glanced up and said, "Hi, Bernie." Mr. Etzin acknowledged with a short nod, then turned to me.

"I'd like for you to take a letter to Japan," he said. Mr. Boder almost choked!

Very slowly, I looked up and said, "By slow boat or plane?" I waited for my answer to sink in.

"What do you mean?" he asked.

"Mr. Etzin," I said. "I can't take shorthand." Mr. Boder unsuccessfully tried to hide the grin that was peeking through.

"Oh," Mr. Etzin said. "Well, I'll talk slow and you can type it."

At this, Mr. Boder got up and walked to a part of the room where Mr. Etzin couldn't see him laughing.

"Mr. Etzin, sir," I said, sounding slightly pitiful, "I can't type."

"You can't?" he asked. I shook my head. He turned and walked out of the office.

Mr. Boder, leaning over a desk, was laughing so hard he couldn't talk. I began to clear out my desk. *Well, Grace,* I thought. *You've messed up again, it's back to the streets.*

Mr. Etzin walked back in and this time, he was laughing as hard as Dave Boder.

"Dave," he asked. "How long has this girl been here?"

"About a year and a half," Mr. Boder answered.

"How much is she making?"

"Sixty-five a week."

Mr. Etzin turned and looked at me, smiling. "Well," he said, "raise her to eighty-five. Anyone who can be here a year and a half and not know typing or take shorthand must have something on the ball." He winked at me and walked out of the office. My sigh of relief must have sounded like a wind tunnel! Thank God!

Wynn and I demo'd a song of Harlan's called "Yankee Go Home." Harlan had taken the song to Joe Johnson of Challenge records, which Wynn recorded for, and said he could have the song if he took me with it. Knowing he could always replace my voice, Joe agreed.

The session was set for one o'clock. All morning at work, I couldn't keep my mind on what I was doing. Wanting my throat to be in really good shape, I tried not to smoke. The less I smoked, the more nervous I became. By session time, I was a wreck and said, To hell with it, and started chain-smoking.

The same musicians were there except for Gordon Terry, a new fiddle player they had added. The only person who made me nervous was Joe Johnson. But after a while, his friendly smile made me begin to relax. I even enjoyed it. When we finished and were listening to the playbacks, Joe said. "You know, we might just have something here." Nevertheless, I was tired and wanted to go home. It had been a hectic and exciting day but I still had to go to work early the next morning.

Going to clubs got to be a regular thing. With two songs recorded, Harlan was basking in the recognition he was getting.

And I would have enjoyed it, too, if I hadn't known that sometime during the evening I would be asked to sing. Stage fright, to me, is one of the most horrible feelings in the world. About the time I knew I would be called, I'd get chills, start shaking all over, my mouth would get as dry as cotton and I'd get a sick feeling in the pit of my stomach. Then I would break out in a cold sweat! Lord, it was awful! I'd stand there at the microphone like a knot on a log and my voice, which in the studio was fairly strong, would come out sounding like Minnie Mouse. Wynn, standing behind me, would say, "Sing out, damn it!" But I couldn't. And, if Wynn and I sang together, since he was no taller than I was and had a complex about it, I'd have to take off my shoes. That made it worse. *If they'd just let me sing in the studio and forget this live business,* I thought, *I'd be all right.*

Harlan and I had been married two years and everything was coming up roses. I was still on edge for some reason. Looking around me, I saw nothing but good things. Jimmy and Corky were on ball teams, David was in the Cub Scouts, my health was good for a change, the rent was paid on time, and Harlan was writing like crazy. What in the world could go wrong? But I couldn't get rid of the worry.

Jimmy was always playing sick to get out of going to school so it was nothing unusual for him to complain of not feeling well that morning. Feeling his forehead, I told Mom, "He's a little warm but he'll be all right once it's too late to go to school." Nothing to worry about. Kids were always coming down with something.

As I started to leave for work, I glanced back at Jimmy. He looked a little peaked. Walking back to him, I leaned over and kissed his forehead. It was warm. "I've changed my mind," I told Mom, "I'm not going to work."

"Now, that's silly," she said, "I'll call you if he gets any worse. It's probably just a cold."

"Well . . . you're probably right, but I'll call you in an hour."

All the way downtown I kept thinking I should turn around and go back. As soon as I got in the office, I called. "Mom, how's Jimmy?"

"Well, I don't know. He's complaining of his legs hurting."

Thank God it was Saturday and I'd only have to be a here a half a day. And Harlan was home if Jimmy should have to go to the doctor. But, after thinking about it, I decided to ask Mr. Boder if I could leave early. I had just turned to ask when the phone rang. "Brother International," I answered.

"Grace." It was Mom. "I think you'd better come home. Jimmy is throwing up and his fever is higher. Also, his legs seem to be drawing." It hit me! Dear God . . . Polio!

"I'll call you back, Mom." Hanging up, I called the office of Dr. Nambu, a Japanese pediatrician who had seen the kids a few times. In fact, just recently, he'd given them their polio shots.

"I'm sorry," the nurse said in her best professional manner, "Dr. Nambu is off today."

"But you've got to find him!" I said, and told her the symptoms.

"I'll call you right back," she said, and hung up. I started walking the floor. Maybe it was my imagination. Maybe it wasn't polio. But what if it was! The phone rang.

"Dr. Nambu is on a fishing boat off Long Beach." My heart sank. "But he's having a helicopter pick him up. Bring the child to the emergency room immediately!"

I called Harlan and he said he'd bring Jimmy and meet me there. Not even stopping to explain to Mr. Boder, I ran out of the office and broke every speed limit on the thirty-mile drive to the hospital. The freeway was crowded and I was crying so hard I couldn't see.

As I ran in the door, Harlan grabbed me. "They've taken him in to do a spinal tap." *Oh God! Please, God. Take care of my Jimmy!* I knew He was up there . . . I just hoped He was hearing me.

The doctor came out of the operating room removing his mask. From where his smock stopped, I could see he still had on his fishing clothes. I held my breath. "I'm sorry," he said. "Your son has spinal meningitis. The tap was full of it." My knees almost buckled. The doctor was still talking. "We've got to get him to U.C.L.A. Medical Center immediately . . . I'll arrange for an ambulance."

"Please," I pleaded. "Please let me see him!"

"All right, but you mustn't touch him. It's very contagious."

I rushed past him into the room he had come out of. Seeing

Jimmy lying there, his back bowed like a horseshoe, tears streaming down his face and his eyes filled with fear, no one could have kept me from touching him. Running to him, I took both his hands in mine and kissed them gently. I wanted to cry but knew if I did, it would frighten him more. "I'm scared, Mom," he said.

"I know, baby. But, it'll be all right." It *just had to be all right! Please God!*

The ambulance attendants came in, and when Jimmy saw them, he screamed, "Mom, don't let 'em take me! Don't let 'em take me!" I looked desperately at Harlan. He left the room to return a few minutes later with the doctor.

"We've decided we'll take him in the car with a police escort."

Gently, they laid him, on his side, in the backseat and, with sirens screaming, we drove across town to U.C.L.A. All the way with me leaning over the seat holding his hands.

Doctors and nurses were waiting at the emergency entrance and, before even taking him out of the car, began giving him shots. Suddenly, he was in their hands and God's. I couldn't get near him. As they wheeled him down the corridor, I could hear Jimmy screaming!

We were shown to a waiting room where we sat and paced for what seemed like hours. Finally, a doctor came in and motioned for us to sit down. I braced myself.

"Mr. and Mrs. Howard, I hate to have to tell you this but, at the outside, your son has four hours to live." My mouth choked off a scream! I was numb.

"No! You're wrong! He's not going to die!" The doctor went on to tell us that Jimmy was in isolation and very critical. Spinal meningitis was almost always fatal, but they would do everything possible. He suggested we go home. No way! A team of mules couldn't have dragged me from that hospital. I intended to stay! At almost daybreak, Harlan went home to bring me back some things I would need.

For nine days, I walked the corridor and stood outside the glass enclosure where Jimmy lay. His back was still bowed and his eyes were filled with pain.

In the cubicle next to Jimmy lay a small baby, his stomach terribly swollen. When I asked the nurse what was the matter with him, she said, "Leukemia. He's dying." I felt so selfish. At least Jimmy had a chance of survival . . . this baby had none.

When he wasn't at work, as much as he could be Harlan was with me at the hospital. We'd stand and watch as the doctors and nurses went through their routine before entering Jimmy's room. Going into an anteroom outside the enclosure, they'd don masks, gowns, rubber gloves, and caps. Then before coming out, they'd remove everything and put it into a container which would be taken out and burned.

I knew Jimmy was better because his back had begun to straighten, but the doctors usually had little to say. Tonight was different. The one who saw Jimmy regularly walked over to us and said, "How would you like to go in and talk to your son?" They were the most beautiful words I'd ever heard!

He explained and stressed the fact that we were never to take off the masks, gowns, caps, or gloves while in the room. And under no circumstances were we to touch Jimmy. Then, after cautioning us about leaving the things in the container, he said, "You can stay five minutes."

Even after what the doctor had said, it was all I could do not to hug and kiss Jimmy. But, for now, I was content just to hear him say he didn't hurt too bad. He was so grown up. When he said, "Mom. I think you should go home and get some rest," I knew he was going to get well. *Thank you, God!*

On the way home, Harlan and I talked as though we hadn't seen each other in a year. But then, it seemed like a year. I couldn't wait to see Corky and David. I knew they'd been all right with Harlan and Mom but I wanted to hold them. The doctor had said since the disease was so terribly contagious, it was a miracle the other boys hadn't come down with it, too.

In the midst of our conversation, Harlan had some good news he'd been holding back. First, the song Wynn and I had recorded was getting a lot of play. Second, and most important, he had gotten a royalty check on his songs and suggested we start looking for a larger house. Lord, I had forgotten all about the music business! With the $27.50 a month that the law was forcing Mearle to pay, and with my pay and Harlan's, we were doing all right. But there was no way we could afford to move without Harlan's song royalties. All the hard work was beginning to pay off.

For some time I'd had my eye on a house on Gardena Boulevard. Two bedrooms, living room, dining room, and kitchen; a small front yard (mostly filled with some sort of vines but it had a tree), and a big backyard with a fig tree in it. Along the side was a graveled driveway and a run-down garage. Best of all, it was furnished. Since Mom had gotten her own apartment, it was all the room we needed. By most standards, it was very ordinary but it was heaven to me. The drawback was that the rent was $150.00 a month, twice what we'd been paying. With careful figuring, we decided we could afford it, and went to check it out.

The owner lived in Chula Vista (a hundred and fifty miles away) and a real estate company handled the leasing. On hearing we had three children, he started to withdraw the hand reaching for the deposit. "We'll take real good care of the house," I said.

"All right, then. But if there is any damage, you'll have to pay for it." He took our money.

Four weeks later, Jimmy came home from the hospital to a new home. It was a whole new beginning. We had much to be thankful for.

Things were back to normal, by which I mean working all week, and going to one of the clubs on Saturday night—especially if there was a guest artist. It was usually a recording star from Nashville. It became normal for me to meet people such as Roy Acuff, Marty Robbins, the Glaser Brothers, Wanda Jackson, Jim Reeves, and George Jones. One night, it was Ray Price, part owner of Pamper Music in Nashville and instrumental in getting Charlie Walker to record "Pick Me Up On Your Way Down." By now, he had recorded a song of Harlan's, "Heartaches By The Numbers." After the show, he went home with us and we sat up all night listening to him sing songs like "Let Me Talk To You" and "Many Dreams Ago," a song I had recorded. Then he'd either ask me to sing with him or hand the guitar to Harlan and ask me to sing by myself or Harlan to sing him another "hit." By the time he left, we were both so high on music, it was hard to go to sleep.

There was never a lack of clubs to go to. Los Angeles was filled with them! But a couple of our regular stops were Bonnie Price's Foothill Club and George's *Round Up*, both in Long Beach. Occasionally, we'd go to hear Skeets McDonald or Joe Maphis—Town Hall Party regulars. One night, we were sitting at the bar—the bandstand was *behind* the bar—listening to Joe. His expertise on the guitar amazed me. Sometimes he'd play so fast, his fingers were just a blur. And all the time he was playing, he was grinning a big infectious smile that covered his whole face. Suddenly, right in the middle of a song, he stopped, looked down at me, and said, "Did you know that you're as pretty as a speckled pup?" and went right on playing. Everybody was looking at me and laughing. I was embarrassed. But it pleased me. Not since Smitty's time had anyone told me I was pretty. I sure didn't think of myself that way. Oh, I tried to fix myself up more now but I still didn't know beans about makeup. I'd practice and practice and still end up with my eyebrows way too dark and lipstick too red. Other than that, all I wore was a little powder and rouge—no eye makeup. I'd tried that a few times and ended up resembling a clown. One thing I'd been thinking about, though, was changing the color of my dark brown hair. For two reasons; I'd been told it would add body to my fine hair and I wanted to bring out the red highlights that I inherited from Mom. Soon, I thought.

It became accepted that well-known recording artists would now call Harlan but the praise he valued the most came from other songwriters. One night, we were in bed when the phone rang. Half asleep, Harlan answered, "Hello?" Then, he sat straight up in bed and, holding his hand over the mouthpiece, whispered, "It's Bill Anderson and Roger Miller!" Catching one end of the conversation, I gathered they were on their way to L.A., where Bill was going to be working at a club. Harlan said we'd be there.

Bill's voice was different, to say the least. It was just above a whisper. He talked a lot of his songs. His weak voice was due, he explained, to a terrible sore throat. Being "Miss Fix It," I invited him to come stay at the house, where I'd doctor him with my homemade remedies. After three days and much Vicks salve, honey with lemon juice, and chicken soup, he decided he'd better leave if he were to have any voice left at all.

A frequent and favorite guest was Bobby Bare, who fended for himself. If the couch was occupied, he'd say, "Give me a blanket. I'll sleep in the bathtub." Which he did.

Every three months, another royalty check came in, each one larger than the last. At first two figures . . . then three . . . then four. It was more money than either of us had ever seen before. We were like kids with new toys. Suddenly there was money for new bicycles for the kids—which unfortunately got destroyed

when a fire burned down the garage where they were stored—
new clothes, and more frequent visits to Disneyland. We even
bought a new car. Trading in the Mercury (which I had arranged
to have put in my name) and Harlan's old Ford, we bought a
shiny new, red 1959 Chevrolet Impala. We were uptown! Next
came a vacation! Since Harlan had never met Tiny and Freddie,
nor had I ever met any of his family, we decided to take a
southern route through Arizona, New Mexico, and Oklahoma, to
Missouri. We then planned to drive north to Michigan. For three
weeks we drove a few hours a day, went sightseeing, stopped
whenever we felt like it, and, in general, had a ball.

On the way back, we stopped in Deadwood, South Dakota,
where the kids visited the graves of Wild Bill Hickock (Hiccup, as
Corky called him) and Calamity Jane, and got real cowboy hats.
We went on to Mt. Rushmore, outside Rapid City, South Dakota,
and Las Vegas. This trip we were able to invest slightly more than
a nickel in the slot machines. We were living well.

While the vacation was great, it was good to be home. Suddenly,
Harlan was not only my husband but my agent. Everytime I
turned around, we were going to some club where he'd already
arranged for them to have me sing. And, if I refused, he got
angry. "Damn it!" he'd say. "You've got a talent! How many
people do you think would give their eye teeth to be where you
are!" I knew that and felt bad about it, but I was tired! With
everything I had to do at home, and working at Brother International, I was on a treadmill all the time. But I'd had my fill of
being poor, and if this was what it took to have a decent life and
financial security, I'd certainly do my part.

Visiting *Town Hall Party* one night, though, I nearly changed
my mind. By this time, we were friends of all the cast and were
usually backstage catching up on all the news. The show was in
full swing. Suddenly, I heard my name, not backstage, but
onstage. At first, I didn't think of myself as Jan Howard. (The
record company thought Grace a cold-sounding name and insisted I change it to Jan.) I didn't pay much attention, then I
realized Joe Maphis was introducing me to sing! Hearing it
again, I panicked. The band started "Pick Me Up On Your Way
Down" and someone pushed me onstage. After that, everything
was a total blank. If someone hadn't told me that I sang every

word, not missing a note, I wouldn't have known. I do know one thing, though. If I'd been given a warning, I'd have been long gone!

With the success of the duet Wynn and I had recorded, Joe Johnson decided to invest in a single of my own. Everyone mutually agreed it should be a song called "The One You Slip Around With," written by Harlan and Fuzzy Owens (unrelated to Buck). With that one and one more, we went into the session, which was no different from the others except this time Wynn used half the time and I used the rest.

When Joe asked if I could sing the third-part harmony I said, "I guess so," and stepped up to the microphone. They seemed amazed, but it was just natural for me. I thought everyone did it. It wasn't for a long time that I learned some people just don't hear harmony at all.

A few weeks later, while driving down the freeway, I turned on the radio and heard the results of that session. I darned near wrecked my car. For once, I was proud of what I heard but it was as though I was listening to someone else, not me.

Buck Owens called to say there was going to be a country music show in Bakersfield and would we like to drive up. The kids had become bored with all the music talk and would rather have stayed at home. Since it was important for Harlan to meet the people on the show—Roger Miller, Faron Young, Skeeter Davis, and June Carter—we decided to go. At ten o'clock that Sunday morning, we loaded up the car and began the two-hour trip. The show started at two.

The whole show was great. yet I especially enjoyed Skeeter Davis. June was supposed to be the comedian but I thought Skeeter stole the show. The minute she got onstage, except for a few songs, she never stopped talking. Rattling on about being tired and going to bed and those "mean ole boys just going off and leaving me laying there." The audience roared! Skeeter just looked confused and kept saying, "What are you all laughing at?" I don't think she actually knew!

Talking with June Carter, she said, "You know, if you really want to be a part of country music, you ought to move to Nashville." *A seed was planted.*

Things began to move fast. Ray Price's recording of "Heartaches By The Numbers" reached number one on the country charts of the trade magazines, and Guy Mitchell had just recorded it for the "pop" field. It didn't take long to find out what was going to happen next. We received an invitation from Broadcast Music Incorporated—a licensing company which pays royalties to song-writers—to attend an awards dinner during the National Disk Jockey convention held in Nashville in October. This particular dinner was the most prestigious affair of the convention. We had arrived.

When I asked Mr. Boder for the time off, he said, "When are you going to quit messing with this hillbilly crap and settle down to work?" Nevertheless, he okayed it.

I felt like Cinderella going shopping for the trip. My friend, Molly Cash, at Fort Carson, let me try on one of her long dresses. I'd never owned or even worn a long dress. Now, I was to have one of my very own! Going from one shop to another, I finally settled on a baby blue chiffon, with little cap sleeves. It fit closely to the hips, then flared out into a full, full skirt. To go with it, I bought a white fake fur stole. Another first: I went to a hair-dresser!

First she applied some gooey-looking stuff to my hair, then had me sit for twenty minutes while it did whatever it was supposed to do. I was a nervous wreck. I knew my hair would either turn green, or fall out. But, when it was removed, I was pleasantly surprised to find it was a pretty shade of auburn. Darker than I really wanted it but exciting, nevertheless. Then she whacked off my shoulder-length hair to my neck level and cut little, short bangs. Leaving there, I felt like *somebody*, but . . . didn't know exactly who.

The convention was an amazing experience. With great anticipation, Harlan, Wynn Stewart, and I started for Nashville. Arriving three days later, we checked into the Andrew Jackson Hotel, the hub of the convention activities. I'd never seen anything like it. Fans from every walk of life and stars of every stature were milling around together in the lobby, flashbulbs popping. They didn't know me from Adam, but they took my picture just in case I was someone important. Harlan was the "star" as far as I was concerned, but every few minutes, a disk jockey would stick a microphone in my face and say, "So you're

Jan Howard!" They made it sound like I came from Mars. "Tell us about yourself," they ask, "and how you got into the business." I must have repeated the same story dozens of times. And no one believed me.

All over the hotel, different record companies and recording artists had "hospitality rooms." Whether you were anyone or not, you could just wander in and eat their food and drink their drinks. A town in China could have been fed with the money spent on booze. The greats, near greats, and never were and never-to-be-greats were all there because of their common love of country music.

Every inch of space in the hallways, lobby, and even the elevators was covered with posters put up by record companies, or singers, thanking the disk jockeys for making their record a "hit." Some of the songs and the singers were unknown to me.

The elevators were not supposed to hold more than nine people. They held so many that people missed their floors, because they couldn't get out. The people were so high on life—or something else—they didn't seem to care when the elevators broke down between floors. Having more than a slight case of claustrophobia, I decided one night to walk down eleven flights of stairs. On the way down, I passed a man, carrying a fully set-up steel guitar, walking up the stairs. If you've ever seen a steel guitar, you have to believe that man really wanted to pick.

Everyone who had ever been to Nashville always said, "Whatever you do, don't miss Tootsie's Orchid Lounge." Walking into this hole-in-the-wall bar and hamburger joint right across the alley from the backstage doors of the Grand Ole Opry, I thought, *Is this it?* But, seeing all the pictures of all the famous country recording artists plastered all over the walls, and some of them sitting around at tables having a beer or talking with friends, I decided it was a great place. Many nights you could drop in at almost any hour and listen to a jam session in full swing.

Down a few steps below the room we'd entered from the alley was a larger room with tourists. And a longer bar behind which stood "Tootsie," a short chubby lady with a big smile and a snappy come-back for any wisecrack that came her way. Tootsie stories abounded. She helped many broke musicians or singers with food or money. She never asked to be repaid. Yet she could be tough if necessary! She has been known to physically throw

out obnoxious customers. Judging from the crowd, she'd have
her hands full the next few days.

Tuesday night was the big night—the BMI dinner. I spent all
afternoon getting ready and hoping the dress I'd bought would be
suitable. This was Harlan's big moment, and I sure didn't want
him ashamed of me. Besides, the only "Country Club" I knew
anything about was a bar where they played country music.

Driving up to the door of that big, impressive place, I felt like a
princess going to a ball at the palace. I was all eyes! Every big star
in the world was there! Hanging on to Harlan's arm, I tried to act
as if I belonged there. Once inside, I was never so insecure in my
life.

As the names of the award winners were announced, and
Harlan's name was getting closer, it was all I could do to sit still.
Drawing on all the dignity of panic, I vowed I wouldn't scream or
faint. But as his name was finally announced, and not just for
one award but two, I couldn't help it. I stood up and applauded
until my little "clap clap" was the only one in the room. This was
what life and success were all about. The many nights in smoky
bars, hanging out with other writers and artists, had paid off.
Harlan had made it.

Ray Price was hosting the network radio portion—*The Prince
Albert Show*—of the Grand Ole Opry, and had arranged for me to
be a guest. But, the closer it got to Saturday night, the more
nervous I became. Several times I considered backing out, but I
didn't know how. Did anyone ever give up a chance to be on the
Opry? I don't think so. And knew if I did, I'd probably have to
hitchhike home. Looking out from the side of the stage, I could
see the huge audience and feared that I would surely faint. All
the other artists were milling around, talking to each other and
not paying the least attention to what was happening onstage.
But they were regulars, and I was an amateur at the Opry. I felt
more like a tourist. Then, Ray introduced me and my legs somehow carried me to center stage. As I passed him, he said, "Tear
'em a new one, hon." The only thing I could think of tearing was
my guts!

Via "the grapevine" we heard that Ralph Emery, host of the
all-night radio show on WSM which was heard all over the
country, was playing my record and said good things about it. I
was looking forward to thanking him.

The studio was packed with visiting celebrities and "just folks." For hours we sat there while he visited with everyone but me. I felt like someone who was starving and had been denied a scrap of food. Embarrassed, that little ego I had was deflated like a flat tire.

The next day I met the petite, blond, and very outspoken Jean Shepard. A Capitol recording artist who had had several hits to her credit and had covered (recorded) "The One You Slip Around With," which I had recorded first. My company, Challenge, didn't have super distribution so, while I was getting the glory, Jean Shepard was getting sales. Laughing, she said, "Hey, piss ant, I'll take the money anytime!" I would have gladly traded places with her.

By Sunday, it was all over. After coffee and several "So long till next year"s we loaded the car. The excitement wore off at the city limits of Nashville. We floated back to Los Angeles.

By spring, the seed that June Carter had planted had begun to grow. Not a day went by that we didn't talk about Nashville. But moving there was a "someday" thing. Then Harlan's BMI check came. My God! It was almost twenty thousand dollars! More money than I thought existed in the whole world. Harlan immediately resigned from Pacific Press.

When I told Mr. Boder that we were moving to Nashville, he said, "Nashville? What on earth for!"

"Come with me," I said. With a puzzled look on his face, he followed me to the parking lot. "Okay, which car is yours?"

Pointing to a two-year-old Chevy, he said, "That one."

Walking over to a brand-new white Cadillac, I said, "Well, this one is mine. That's why we're moving to Nashville."

He stared at the Cadillac in disbelief. "Son of a bitch," he said.

We weren't leaving Los Angeles until June so when I got an offer to do a three-day tour with Wynn starting in Lubbock, Texas, for two hundred dollars a day—a little less than I'd made in a month as a secretary—I accepted. Or rather, Harlan accepted for me. They never talked to me.

On the way to Texas, I thought *What in the hell am I doing this for?* Well, I knew: the money. But we didn't need money now. Why put myself through this misery? But Harlan and Wynn were so excited about being on the same show with Archie Campbell and Johnny Horton that I tried to keep up the pretense.

But I was scared. Except for occasional club appearances and one time I had ridden a train for a week to be on Red Foley's "Ozark Jubilee" in Springfield, Missouri, my experience was nil. I demonstrated it in Lubbock!

During rehearsal, I asked the local band we were going to work with if they knew the songs. "Sure," they said. "We don't need to rehearse." I was warned about going onstage unrehearsed, but, being shy, I didn't insist.

Show time came but my courage did not. While I was dressing in the blue skirt with rhinestones around the hem and the white satin blouse that Mom had worked so hard to make, I wanted to run away. Looking at myself in the mirror, I thought I looked exactly like what I was—an amateur. I knew my costume wasn't right, but one I'd paid fifty dollars for at Nudies—a costume designer for *real* stars—had looked like a cheap satin slip. I'd thrown it away.

Backstage, I felt my stomach churning and knew I was going to throw up any minute. Lord, where's the door! Johnny Horton walked over to me. "Jan, do you have a cigarette?"

Startled, I said, "No. I'm sorry. They're down in my dressing room." Someone told me later that he didn't even smoke. Wynn was on stage and I was to be next! Johnny leaned down real close and said, "Jan, do your eyes bother you?" Lord! Now, my eyes are on crooked! That didn't surprise me. I'd never learned to put on mascara.

"No, why?"

"Well, they sure do bother me." I know now, that was an old line and he was just trying to put me at ease. But it didn't help. My name was announced and he pushed me onstage.

From the first note, it was evident the band didn't have the faintest idea how the songs were supposed to go. They hit every wrong chord in the book. Turning around, I said, "You idiots! I thought you said you knew these songs!" That was exactly the wrong thing to do. After that, it was every man for himself. They tried to make me look bad. And I was. I left the stage in tears but had learned a valuable lesson. You get to catch more flies with honey than you do with vinegar.

By the time school was out, we were all packed and ready to leave. Everything we owned, except a few suitcases of clothes, was shipped by truck to Nashville. I hated to leave Mom, I couldn't have made it without her, but my brothers Dick, Bob, and Pete were there so she would never be alone. After promising to write, asking her to come to Nashville as soon as we were settled, I turned to look at the place where we'd been happy and in which so many good things had happened to us. I knew, for the sake of business, the move was necessary. Yet I'd been leery from the beginning. The bubble had burst before.

With Harlan driving the recently purchased blue and white '56 Ford convertible and me the Cadillac, the boys traded from one to the other. The ride across country was fun. Trying to make a mini-vacation out of it, we stopped every day about four o'clock so the boys could swim. Well, Corky and David anyway. Jimmy had never learned how.

Sitting by the edge of the pool, Harlan and I were watching David and Corky playing in the water. Jimmy timidly stood on the side. Suddenly, not being able to stand it any longer, he jumped in . . . right into the nine-foot part! Down he went . . . once . . . twice. I couldn't swim, either, but was going to learn! Harlan grabbed my arm. "What's the matter, son?" he asked calmly as Jimmy came up sputtering and spitting water.

In between breaths, Jimmy said, "I'm drowning, you fool!" and went down again. The next time he came up, it was like someone down under had given him lessons . . . he started swimming for the side.

In Tulsa, we separated. Harlan went on to Nashville to rent a house and get the "feel of things" . . . and the boys and I went to West Plains to spend a few days with Tiny and Freddie on the farm.

We'd already checked out, and Harlan had long since left. Taking the kids for breakfast in the coffee shop, I watched the sky, which was roiling and dark. All the storms I'd been in when I was a kid rushed back vividly to my mind. I remembered in Birch Tree, when I was six, laying behind a woodpile hugging the ground and watching the wind tear trees out of the ground. And when I was twelve, in Kansas City, watching a tornado literally tear a house off its foundation and turn it into matchsticks. It had been a long time since I'd seen a storm like that. I didn't want to see one now.

The kids began to get antsy. "Come on, Mama, let's go!" They were eager to get to the farm. *Well,* I thought, *maybe it'll blow over.* We got into the car.

I had no more than pulled onto the Oklahoma Turnpike than the sky opened up. The rain came down so hard I couldn't see the front of the car, which was being whipped this way and that by the wind. I was paralyzed with fear! David, in front with me, began to whimper. Jimmy said, "Don't cry. Mama's got enough on her hands." He and Corky didn't say another word.

Everything on the turnpike was stopped . . . everything but me. Creeping along at five miles an hour, I glanced out my window and saw it . . . a funnel! Whirling, with all its fury right along side of the turnpike! The wind was so strong I thought the steering wheel would be jerked out of my hands. All the things to do when caught in a car in a tornado left my mind. I couldn't remember anything. I just knew I couldn't stop. If I did, we would die! But I did remember how to pray. And Lord, how I prayed! I never looked out the window again but the rain began to lessen and the wind began to die down. And we were alive. Thank God!

The farm had never looked so good when I pulled into the driveway. For four days, the boys had a great time going to the barn with Freddie, getting reacquainted with the animals, eating homemade ice cream, and doing all the things you just naturally do on a farm. I knew we should leave, but every time I'd think about getting back into that car, I'd start shaking. Tiny kept asking if I was sick. I told her about the experience on the turnpike and I begged her to go to Nashville with me. On the sixth of June, 1960, we pulled into the house Harlan had rented on Grinstead Avenue in Inglewood, a suburb of Nashville.

The house was not a mansion by any means but it was better than most I had lived in, had two bedrooms, a living room, and kitchen. At the side was an attached garage which we planned to turn into Harlan's writing room. In the back was a fenced-in backyard which would be perfect for Annette, the little black poodle we'd bought shortly before leaving Los Angeles. The dog was being flown here. The house was furnished, but until the household goods arrived, it was a paper-plate life. At Sears, Tiny helped me buy essentials to get by with. A couple of days later, saying she had to help Freddie with the work, she left for home.

The heat was sweltering and the humidity was worse. After five years in Los Angeles, I'd forgotten how hot it could be. Four days after we arrived, a severe electrical storm hit. Before it was over, I was on the floor in the bedroom screaming. The kids were comforting *me*. On the news later, we heard that an eleven-year-old boy had been struck by lightning and killed.

A week after the storm, at a house only a block away, a woman opened her mailbox and a bomb literally blew her face off. I couldn't eat. I couldn't sleep. The last time I weighed myself, I was down to ninety-seven pounds.

While I was trying to make the house into a home, Harlan was out making the rounds. Always saying he was "pitching songs." He was not home much. I didn't blame him, though. The house was so damned hot you couldn't breathe.

Many nights, after the kids were in bed, I'd pace the floor. I had horrible fears that something bad was going to happen; it possessed my mind and wouldn't let go. I knew it was ridiculous, but I couldn't shake it. I was afraid of being closed in. I was frightened of open places, of heights, and of the dark. For some time, I'd been having a lot of trouble with my heart getting out of rhythm. I feared I was going to die. Every doctor I'd been to said it was either my imagination or nerves. Hell, I knew my nerves were shot—I didn't have to pay for that information.

The boys were asleep. Harlan was supposed to come home and take us out to eat but, as usual, he neither showed up nor bothered to call. It was nine o'clock. There was always something to keep me busy. Setting up the ironing board in the only cool place in the house, the hallway between the bedrooms, where I'd put a big fan, I decided to iron. The phone rang.

"Hello?" I said, expecting Harlan. Since I didn't know many people here, the calls were usually Harlan or someone wanting to talk to him.

A woman's voice I didn't recognize asked, "Is this sweet little Jan Howard?"

Irritated, I said, "Well, I don't know about the sweet part but this is Jan Howard."

"Well," she said, "I just thought I'd let you know that, if you don't watch out, you'll be singing 'I'd Rather Be the One You Slip Around With' to your husband."

"I don't know what you're talking about." I was angry. "My husband's out with some writer friends of his." Now, I was angry at myself for making excuses to some creep without a name.

"Well, you might think he's pitching songs, honey, but he's pitching woo with Wanda Jackson in the Andrew Jackson Hotel." There was a click and a dial tone. Standing there with the dead phone in my hand, I stared at it stupidly. Then slammed it back on the hook!

Hearing a car door slam and people's voices brought me back to reality. Surely to God, he wasn't bringing someone home without letting me know! Yes, he was. Men and women. Shit. Leaving the ironing board right where it was, I ran into the bedroom, jumped into bed, covered up with a sheet, and pretended to be asleep. Listening closely, I recognized the men's voices—Harlan, Hank Cochran (a songwriter), and Roger Miller —but not the women's.

The bedroom door opened. Keeping my eyes squeezed shut, I heard someone tiptoe over to the bed. "Jan," a voice cooed softly. I opened my eyes. It was Wanda Jackson. "Why don't you get up and make some coffee," she said. Throwing back the sheet, I walked past her into the living room. They were all there. Harlan, sitting on a chair, Roger and Hank on the sofa, and the voice I hadn't recognized, Norma Jean. I'd seen her on television and heard her on records but we'd never met. This was hardly the time. They went right on laughing and talking as though I didn't even exist. I was furious. Turning to Wanda, I said, "You're darned right I'll make coffee. And put arsenic in every cup. Now, all of you, get the hell out of my house!"

Everybody except Harlan took me at my word and split— quickly. He just sat there with a drunk, stupid grin on his face. I reached out and grabbed the first thing in sight . . . a fifty-dollar ashtray I'd bought in Carmel, California. The first symbol of our "new" money. With all my strength, I aimed for Harlan's head and threw it! He ducked, and it hit the wall behind him . . . shattering into a thousand pieces. Walking over to the door, I opened it and said, "You, too, out!"

The car was still out front—they probably guessed Harlan would be joining them—and, as they drove away, I could hear them all laughing. Sitting on the floor, I tried to glue the ashtray back together. But glue doesn't mix well with tears and the pieces wouldn't stick. Finally, I gave up and threw it away. I felt like my marriage was just as fragile. Before leaving California, I had grown to love Harlan—not a fairytale sort of love but a love I'd begun to feel secure in. Now, he had changed. Oh, he was still good to the kids and, most of the time, considerate of me, but it wasn't the same. His mind was somewhere else. But, thinking back over my previous marriages, and realizing I had a lot to be thankful for, I decided I was acting stupid. The more I thought about it and the more I remembered the shocked looks on their faces when I'd made that statement about the arsenic, the funnier it got. I knew an apology was in order.

The next afternoon, Harlan came home. But, instead of acting sorry, he acted as if nothing had happened. Neither of us apologized. We just let it lay.

Harlan said he had made an appointment with a doctor and was taking me there. I knew I had been yelling at the boys and him a lot lately and I knew I was sick but, when I saw this big, red brick building he had pulled up to, I thought, *Not this sick.* It was a private sanitarium! "Harlan, I'm not going in there," I said.

"Now, honey, it's only for two weeks and they can help you."

"No!" I was losing it.

"But it's for your own good," he said. What good! He wouldn't even look at me. A nurse came out, opened my door, and held out her hand to me. Had it come to this? Slowly, I got out of the car. As Harlan drove away, I thought, *How could he do this to me?* I felt I didn't have a friend in the world. Maybe I didn't. Maybe I was crazy. I certainly had been acting like it.

I was led into a room that was bare except for a bed and one chair. The nurse picked up my purse, which I had laid on the bed, opened it, removed one tube of lipstick and a hairbrush, and put everything on the bed. She stuck the purse under her arm and stood there while I changed into the hospital gown laying across the bed. Then, without saying a word, she took the purse, my clothes, and my dignity and left the room. It's funny what taking one's clothes does to a person—it leaves them bare, in more ways than one. Sitting down on the bed, I looked around and saw the thing that really sent me into orbit . . . bars on the windows! Quickly, I jumped up and tried the door. As I suspected, it was locked. My claustrophobia took over and I screamed until someone came and gave me a shot guaranteed to put anyone *close* to six feet under.

Except for a walk in the morning and one at night, both times with a nurse in attendance, I lay in that bed. There was nothing else to do. The meals were served on plastic dishes with spoons but no knives or forks. For some weird reason, they suspected I was going to kill myself. The idiots. Didn't they know I had an unreasonable, terrible fear of dying? I had three little boys at home and had no idea who was taking care of them. I wanted to go home.

The only break in my routine came when a doctor—usually the same one—came in. After looking at me and saying "Hmmm" a lot, he'd leave and that was that for another day.

Lying with my face to the wall, I heard the door open. I didn't turn over. I heard footsteps coming toward the bed. "Mrs. Howard? I'm Dr. Goldner." *A new one,* I thought. I heard a chair screech across the room.

Turning my head slightly, I thought, *He looks like a doctor. I wonder what kind of pills he hands out?* Not saying anything else, he took out a chart and began reading. While he did, I looked him over. Not very tall, red curly hair, nicely dressed . . . and friendly eyes behind his glasses. He was different.

After a minute, he asked, "What brought you here?"

I laughed. "Not what but *whom.*" That brought a smile that matched his eyes. And I sure needed a friend. Slowly, he drew out of me my life history. After examining me, he said, "What you have is Paroxysmal Tachyarrhythmia, and a very run-down condition."

"You mean it has a name? It's not my imagination?"

"No, it's not your imagination. And this can be controlled with medication. But the first thing we've got to do is get you out of here. You definitely don't belong *here.*" As he walked to the door, he said, "I want to see you in my office Monday morning . . . okay?"

"Yes!" I didn't care if he was married and had twelve kids. I loved this man! Especially because he left the door open.

Shortly after Dr. Goldner left, the nurse brought my clothes. The instant she laid them on the bed, I had them on and was on my way out the door. Walking past the desk, I had the tremendous urge to do something obscene like giving them all the finger, but I thought better of it. Instead, very nicely, I asked where I could call a cab.

On the way home, I thought about Harlan's motives in bringing me here. Maybe it was the only way he knew to help me. I didn't know. Anyway, whether that was the case or not, because of my meeting Dr. Goldner, he had. All I wanted was to be home and see the boys. My feelings toward Harlan were next.

Monday morning, bright and early, I was in Dr. Goldner's office waiting for the magic cure. After a long talk, he asked if I would consent to see a psychiatrist. *Well,* I thought. *He does think I'm crazy,* and told him so.

"No, I don't think you're crazy. But you do have every phobia known to man, and he can help you get rid of them. Are you willing to try?"

"Dr. Goldner," I said, "right now, I would go to the moon if you asked me to."

He laughed. "I don't think that will be necessary. Just take this medicine every morning as soon as you wake up. It will help to keep your heart in rhythm."

I left there feeling the whole world was my oyster—filled with pearls.

Even though I wasn't a regular member of the Opry, quite often Mr. Vito Pelliterri, the stage manager, would call and say, "Give me two songs." He looked so formidable and had such a brusque voice, I was scared to death of him. Not physically, but I would never dare question a thing he said. It was like standing before a judge . . . You said, "Yes, sir." Quickly, I'd rattle off whatever came to mind. If it happened to be a song somebody else had recorded, he said, "What the hell are you doing *their* songs for? Do your own!" I'd change my songs.

I'd been told, by a longtime member, that the best way to stay out of trouble at the Opry was to do your spots and leave . . . don't hang around. I couldn't possible understand what trouble I could get into but, taking their advice, that's exactly what I did.

The old Ryman Auditorium wasn't noted for its facilities, air-conditioning, or heating but amenities didn't matter—it was the home of the Grand Ole Opry. The minute you walked in, the charisma of tradition took over. It didn't matter that you had to change clothes in the rest room. People who were lucky enough to play there would have gladly changed clothes outside in the freezing rain just to stand on that stage. And I felt the same way.

Sometimes, if a certain artist was on, Patsy Cline, for instance, I'd stay just long enough to hear them. Tonight, it was Patsy and I wasn't about to leave before hearing her sing. When she walked on stage in her fringed cowgirl outfit and her white cowboy boots and sang "Walking After Midnight," I thought, *Now, that's show biz.* Suddenly, I felt frumpy in my gingham dress. It wasn't what I felt good in, but I'd been told that was what I should wear if I was going to be in country music. I couldn't wait to take it off.

I was right in the middle of changing when the door opened and Patsy stood there, both hands on her hips, looking at me. Having never actually met her, I started to say hello. But, before I could speak, she said, "Well, you're a conceited little son of a bitch!" My words hung in midair. I didn't think I'd heard right.

"What did you say?" I asked

"You heard me. Who do you think you are anyway! You just waltz in here, do your spot, and leave without saying hello, kiss my ass, or anything!" I had heard right!

"Now wait just a damned minute!" I glared right back at her. "Where I come from, it's the people's responsibility who live in a town to welcome a newcomer. And not one person welcomed me here."

Anyone a block away could have heard her laugh! "You're all right, honey. Anyone that'll talk back to the Cline is all right. We're gonna be good friends!" With that, she turned and walked out the door, leaving me speechless! If she only knew how much I needed that. After that first anonymous call, I had received several more. Everything from "Go back where you came from" to "We don't need you here." I figured it must be someone at the Opry but had no idea who. Anyway, I wasn't a threat to anyone.

Harlan was writing like crazy. As soon as he'd get up, he'd head for his room and, within a few minutes, I'd hear the sound of his guitar and the same three chords. He told me if he learned any more, it would ruin his style. Every couple of weeks we'd be in the studio cutting demos. That seemed to spur him on even more. He loved being in the studio. And each time, I listened to see if one was suitable for me. I'd recorded several songs, but none of them made me jump up and down and whistle Dixie. Usually, I never chose them. Harlan did. He and my producer would talk as though I wasn't in the room. Often, I wasn't.

Hank Cochran, another writer for Pamper Music, was at our house a lot. One day he came over with the title "I Fall To Pieces," and he and Harlan retreated to the den. Pretty soon, Harlan called. "L.G., come see what you think of this!" From the first word, I loved it! I knew this one was mine. "Can I have it?" I asked. Harlan and Hank looked at each other.

"Sure," Harlan said, "but, first we'll have to demo it." A session was set up right away. I couldn't wait to play it for my producer, Joe Johnson.

For days after the session, I went around singing, "I fall to pieces . . . each time I see you again . . ." It laid perfectly.

One day, after being downtown all day, Harlan came home and said, "Guess what? Patsy's gonna do 'I Fall To Pieces!'"

"But that's my song."

"It's too pop for you," he said. "Besides, she'll make us a lot of money." In other words, I wouldn't. I didn't care about the money, he'd promised me the song!

"All I'm good for is to make your demos," I said. He didn't bother to answer. After a while the hurt dimmed and I cooled off. After all, he was trying to make a good living. And I wanted to stay home anyway. What did it matter?

From the day we'd moved to Nashville, we'd talked about buying a house if we found just the right one. After buying the new Cadillac, combined with moving expenses, we figured we could put down about three thousand dollars and still have enough money to live on until the next royalty check came.

After weeks of searching, we wanted the very first house we looked at. Ten-seventeen South Graycroft in Madison (about eight miles north of Nashville). It was perfect! Four bedrooms, living room, dining room, a large kitchen with a window that overlooked the backyard, and a daylight basement that was finished as a den. The house was on an acre lot filled with beautiful trees. And, to top it off, the elementary school was within walking distance, and the bus for the high school stopped at the front door. I just knew the house had a lot of love and happiness left in it.

October first was moving day. The excitement of having the first house we owned took the work out of it. The kids would run from one room to another, hollering, "This one's mine . . . This one's mine!" Having always been crammed into one room, they couldn't believe they were each one going to have a room of their own.

We didn't have much furniture—we'd bought just a few pieces. So each day I'd scan the garage and moving sale ads in really good sections of town. Sometimes I found some good buys. But, for things like our bedroom suite and the living-room furniture, we went to a discount furniture warehouse and splurged. Piece by piece the house was furnished in what I called "early comfort." We even bought custom-made drapes. That house was my pride and joy! All the painful years faded into forgotten bad dreams.

Our poodle Annette was so quick she could always evade you in a minute. The first thing we planned was a fence in the backyard for her.

Standing at the sink washing dishes, I was thinking *God's in his heaven and all's right with the world*. Suddenly I heard tires screech and someone scream, "Annette!" Harlan and I ran to the door and saw a car at the side of the street and Corkey kneeling down, with Annette's head in his lap, crying. A man was standing by helplessly. Harlan grabbed Annette and, with me holding her on my lap, we drove to the nearest veterinarian. After examining her, he said it would be merciful to have her put to sleep. Her spine was broken.

All the way home, I cried and wondered how we could break it to the boys. We never had to tell them anything. They were standing out in the yard waiting for us. Seeing us get out of the car without Annette, Corky ran into the house and up to his room. Jimmy and David said nothing.

Corky stayed in his room for four days, not talking to anyone. Harlan thought he was sick because he was running a fever of a hundred and two and suggested I take him to a doctor. But I knew the only cure for heartbreak was time.

The boys had never seen snow and we had lots near Christmas. It was 1960, and folks said it was the worst winter since 1951. But we didn't care. We loved it! The closer it got to Christmas, the more we prayed for snow. It was so great watching the kids build snowmen and have snowball fights, I didn't care if spring never came.

Christmas had always been special to me. Even when we had nothing. I wanted this one to be just right. And I knew that for it to be just right, we should go to church. In California, the kids had attended Sunday school spasmodically. But now, since this was to be our "forever" home, I wanted us to find a "forever" church. And the only one I knew about was the one Mom attended, The Church of Christ. Christmas was on Wednesday, and on the Sunday before, the kids and I (Harlan didn't go), dressed in our Sunday best, walked into church. The service was nice, the singing was beautiful, but I felt something was missing. At the end of the service, I found out what it was. The minister said, "Even though we do not celebrate the Twenty-fifth of December as the birth of Christ, we wish you a happy holiday." The kids looked at each other, then at me. I couldn't believe what I'd heard! Jimmy said, "What does he mean, Mom?"

"I don't know," I said, "but, whatever he means, don't pay any attention to him." We got up and walked out.

Driving home, Jimmy said, "Boy, that's a fine thing. You take your children to church, then tell them not to pay any attention to the preacher."

"Well," I said, "everybody has their own belief and mine happens to believe in celebrating Christmas as the birth of Christ! That's that!"

Harlan and I shopped carefully for everything in the boys' letters to Santa Claus. But one thing that Corky had asked for, they didn't sell—peace and quiet for Mom and Dad.

By Christmas Eve, everything was ready. The tree, which we'd all had such fun decorating—with a beautiful angel on the very top—reached to the ceiling. Presents were everywhere. A fire was roaring in the fireplace and the dinner which I'd spent all afternoon preparing was ready to be served. Snow was falling outside and Christmas carols were playing on the radio. It was like a scene from a Bing Crosby movie. The one thing missing was Harlan. Early that morning, after promising to be back by six, he'd left to make the rounds of office parties. Six came and went. Dinner was getting cold, the candles had burned halfway down and were dripping wax on my new tablecloth, the kids were hungry, and I was angry! At nine, I gave up and said, "Let's eat!" Just then the phone rang.

"L.G.?" It was Harlan, and I didn't need to hear another word to know he was drunk!

"Where are you, Harlan," I asked, but since he wasn't at home, I didn't care.

"I'm at Monument Records . . . come and get me." No excuse, nothing. I was supposed to be his damned chauffeur.

"Harlan, it's snowing like crazy. Where's your car?"

"Hell, I don't know. Just come and get me!" He hung up.

Throwing a coat on, I went down and started the car. The cold didn't bother me. I was hot enough under the collar to ward off a blizzard!

Several times, while inching my way along the snow-covered streets to Hendersonville, where Monument Records was located, I started to turn back. Then I thought, *Oh, well, it's Christmas. He probably got carried away.* I wasn't going to let something like this spoil it.

The parking lot was filled with cars. When I opened the door, my anger came back full blast. The room was crowded with people . . . all drinking and having a merry old time. Maybe it was supposed to be the Christmas spirit but, to me, it looked like just another drunken party.

Searching the room, I saw Harlan leaning up against the wall talking to some girl I'd never seen before. "Hey, Harlan," someone said. "Here's your ride!" Everybody laughed like they were sharing some big joke. No one even spoke to me.

Harlan started toward me, grinning stupidly. That was all it took. Even he thought it was funny! Waiting until he was within hearing distance, I said, "No, Harlan, your ride's not here. Get home the same way you got here." Then I walked out.

By the time someone dropped him off at home, the boys were already in bed asleep. He walked over, ate the cookies and drank the milk the kids had left for Santa Claus, and went to bed. I hoped they made him sick.

But the next day was Christmas. And who can stay mad on Christmas. Before daylight, the kids came bounding down the stairs and into our room yelling for us to get up. As we went into the living room and turned on the tree lights, all thoughts of the night before disappeared. The kids calmed down from seeing what Santa Claus left—they knew he'd been there because he ate the cookies and drank the milk—and Harlan handed out the gifts we'd chosen for each other. Then, when we each had our stack, we took turns opening them. Seeing the happiness on my boys' faces was all the gift I would ever ask for.

As I was fixing everyone's favorite breakfast, pancakes, Harlan and the boys put on their coats and said, "We'll be right back." I couldn't figure out where they could be going on Christmas morning.

When they came back, all smiles, I could see Harlan was hiding something under his coat. That "something" was whimpering. He pulled out a beautiful silver poodle and handed it to me. I started to cry. It was precious, but I'd already decided if we ever had another dog, it would be a *dog* dog . . . one that could be outside. Knowing they had planned this as a wonderful surprise, I didn't tell them how I felt. Maybe I would in a few days. We'd see. For the moment, we had another dog.

Later that day, Harlan and I talked about the night before. He said he was sorry and it would never happen again. I believed him. Then he told me what Fred Foster (owner of Monument Records) had said. "Now, I know where she got the name Jan— from January. The icicles formed on the ceiling the minute she walked in. All she needed was a gun on each hip." He was right about one thing. That *was* where the name Jan came from— short for January.

Having a little fame is a lot like having a swimming pool. Suddenly, you have more friends and relatives than you knew you had. People seemed to think we were rolling in money. I wished we had enough money to support the world, but for a while we tried to. Having been without money for so long, it was hard to turn anyone down. Yet we knew we had to draw the line somewhere. We'd been hearing from people we hardly knew, and for only one reason—money. Having the phone unlisted didn't help. They had ways of finding it.

"Hey, Grace, how're ya doing?" It was an old friend I hadn't heard from in years.

"Fine . . . and you?" I knew what was coming next and waited.

"Oh, pretty good. But I got laid off last week."

"That's too bad," I said, looking at Harlan for help. He shook his head but didn't offer to take the phone. The silence at the other end told me he was waiting for me to offer our help.

When I didn't, he asked, "Do you think you could lend me two hundred and fifty bucks?"

Well, here goes.

"Gosh, I'm sorry, but we just don't have it right now." That ended the pretense of friendship.

"You no good bitch! I hope you fall flat on your face in Nashville! I'll never buy another one of your records you . . ." I hung up. He'd probably never bought one of my records anyway.

It was against his principles to sign with any one company, so Harlan remained a free-lance writer. If one company got him a record, they'd get a few more songs. If not, he'd move on to the next publisher on his list. Since artists knew his reputation as a songwriter, he'd just go to see them or they'd come to our house and he'd either sing the songs himself, or have me sing them, or play one of the many demos we'd made.

As from the time in California, I'd never seen much of Ray Price, but admired his talent tremendously. One night, in a combination of business and pleasure, we'd were invited to his house for dinner.

Driving out to their house in Hendersonville, I was a little nervous. "What's his wife like?" I asked.

"I don't know," Harlan said. "I've never met her."

"It was nice of them to invite us to dinner." Imagining some big ranch, I couldn't wait to see their house. But, when we drove in the driveway, I thought, *The only thing "ranch" about this house is the style.* Once inside, though, with his awards and photographs everywhere, I was very impressed.

Settling down in the den, Harlan got out his guitar and yellow legal pad, which he used to write on, and sang one song after another, each time waiting for Ray's positive comment. After listening awhile, Ray said, "Let Jan sing 'em." Harlan handed me the lyrics.

Linda, Ray's wife at the time, was different from anyone I'd ever met, to say the least. Attractive in a "hard" way, she was petite, very blond, and *very* unfriendly.

After I finished singing, I walked out to the kitchen to see if I could help with dinner. She never acknowledged my presence. "What can I do to help?" I asked. Nothing. "Would you like for me to make the salad?" She turned and gave me the once over. Twice. Then she started taking stuff out of the refrigerator.

"You like my husband a lot, don't you?" she said.

"What?"

She started tearing up lettuce with great gusto. "You're just like all the other 'girl' singers," she said. "All whores."

"Linda, you're wrong! All girl singers are not whores. Besides, I'm married and have three sons." I was careful to stay out of the way of the knife she was chopping up tomatoes with.

"I don't care how many kids you've got," she said. "The first chance you get you'll be in bed with my husband!" This woman had problems.

"Get one thing straight, Linda. As an artist, I admire your husband very much. He has a beautiful voice. Outside of that, I have no interest in him." She totally ignored me. *To hell with it,* I thought, and joined Harlan and Ray on the patio. Within a few minutes, Linda came out and it was my turn to do a double take. She was sugar sweet! All evening, I kept watching for some sign of the Linda I'd seen in the kitchen but it never surfaced.

On the way home, I told Harlan what she'd said. "It's just your imagination," he said. "You're too sensitive. Anyway, Ray's gonna record one of my songs."

The Country Music Association was brand new. And in order to raise money, a big benefit show was being held in Miami. I was asked to go. Everyone else was flying, but, since the psychiatrist hadn't gotten rid of that fear of mine, I had to drive, and wasn't looking forward to it. Then, the perfect solution came up. Ferlin Husky, a top artist whom I had heard many times before moving to Nashville, was on the show and going down on his bus. I could ride with him.

I'd heard of Ferlin's alter ego, Simon Crumm, but had never been in his company. I thought it was strictly an act for stage but . . . not so. To Ferlin, he was a real person . . . in other words . . . two people in one body. I wasn't ready for it.

Shortly after leaving Nashville, I became well acquainted with Simon. He was a hateful, sarcastic bastard! Gentle, nice Ferlin was nowhere to be found. In his place was this character with a baseball cap turned backward on his head, who seemed intent on making me cry. "Just because you got a couple of awards don't make you a singer!" he said. He was right but, being too shy to answer, I just kept looking out the window at row after row of orange trees. The band just ignored him and told me to do the same. But how do you ignore someone who's in your face every minute? Glory be! We were stopping at a truck stop!

I was the first one up front waiting for the door to open so I could get off the bus. Right behind me was Simon. As I jumped down, I heard him say, "Where're you going so fast?" I'd had all I could take. Turning around, I said, "Damn you, get off my back! What have I ever done to you?" Then, I stopped. The baseball cap was gone . . . Ferlin was back. All he'd wanted to do was walk with me. The rest of the trip he was a completely different person. He was Ferlin.

The next day, preparing to leave, I asked someone where Ferlin's bus was. "Oh, he's gone. Didn't you know?"

"Gone!"

"Yes . . . looks like you'll have to fly." I had a feeling this had been cooked up before I ever came down.

Gathering all my courage, I boarded the plane with the other passengers . . . a lot of whom were people who had come down from Nashville for the show. Wesley Rose, co-owner of the Acuff Rose publishing company, was my seat partner. "Do you want the window?" he asked.

"No thanks." I didn't want to witness the crash. My eyes stayed glued to the spot on the wall in front of me.

We began to roll. Oh God, help me! We'll never make it! And, if we crash, it'll be my fault 'cause I'm not supposed to be on this thing! If my heart weren't beating so hard I could hear it in my ears, I'd have sworn it had stopped.

Wesley, seeing I was terrified, began to tell me everything I would feel and hear. Suddenly, the engines weren't as loud, and I had the feeling of stopping in midair. "Wesley! What are we stopping up here for!" I screamed.

"No, Jan," he said calmly. "We've reached altitude and the pilot has throttled the engines back." I wondered if anyone had ever been this scared and lived through it. Leaning back, I closed my eyes so tight I saw stars . . . and it was daylight.

Hearing the stewardess ask if we'd like something to drink, I opened my eyes. Wesley said, "Bring me a martini."

"Bring me the same," I said. I'd never even tasted a martini but the occasion seemed to call for drastic measures.

When she brought the drinks, mine was in my hand and down my throat . . . all in one big gulp. Like one big streak of lightning, it hit my toes and bounced back again. Struggling to get my breath, I thought, *If the plane doesn't kill me, this martini will!*

The pilot announced we were fixing to land in Atlanta, and I was listening to every word Wesley said. Suddenly, getting up the nerve to look out the window, I started screaming. "Wesley! The wings are falling off!" Everyone around me was laughing.

"No, Jan," he said, trying to disengage my clutch on his arm, "he's just lowering the flaps to decrease our speed." God, please! Just get me off this thing. If man were supposed to fly, God would have given him wings! If anyone could have been more glad than I was when that flight was over, it was Wesley.

Jimmy was fourteen, in the eighth grade at Madison High School, and was a natural at making friends. But Corky wasn't quite that open. He never had been. One day, his teacher called and said, "Mrs. Howard, I need to talk to you about Carter."

"What's wrong?" I asked.

"Well, nothing particularly wrong. I just need your help with something." We made an appointment for the next day.

Expecting him to say Corky had done something really bad, I asked, "What's Corky done?"

"Oh, nothing," he was quick to answer, "it's just that he won't talk in class and he'll play with just a few of the children." I promised I'd have a talk with him.

That evening, I said, "Corky, your teacher says you won't talk in class. Why not?"

"I will when I have something worth saying," he said. That made sense to me.

"He also says you won't play with all the children."

"Well, do you like everyone you meet?"

"No."

"Well, I don't, either." I couldn't find anything wrong with either of his answers. The next day I called his teacher and told him so.

David was getting bad grades and had to be put back a year. I couldn't understand it. He studied. But still his grades were failing. And he complained of headaches a lot. Finally, at his teacher's suggestion, I took him to an eye doctor, where I learned he needed glasses. I'd never even thought about it. Later, wearing the glasses, David kept saying, "Boy! Look at that!"

"David, you mean you've never seen that before?"

"No."

"Does this have anything to do with your failing grades?"

"Yeah, I guess so. I never could see the blackboard." Lord. I felt terrible!

"Then, why didn't you say so?" I asked.

"I thought everybody saw it that way." I'd never thought about that.

After that first experience in the Church of Christ, we began to look around for just the right church. One with a good youth program. Each Sunday we'd try a different one. I'd never been to church much but somehow knew it was important for my kids. Once I got them settled into one, I figured I could go when it was convenient. Finally we found it. City Road Methodist. It was not too big and not too small. And the people there were like a family who adopted us immediately. Especially the kids. From then on, they wouldn't dream of missing Sunday school and church— even Sunday nights. It became a way of life.

Washing dishes and watching out the window at the kids playing ball in the backyard, I didn't pay a lot of attention when Harlan walked in and sat down at the kitchen table. "I talked to Hubert Long today about booking some dates for you."

Absentmindedly, I said, "What?"

"I met with Hubert Long about being your booking agent," he repeated.

"What do I need an agent for?"

"Well, if you're gonna be in the business, you have to work the road." This got my full attention.

"Harlan, I don't want to work the road. I want to stay home!"

"Well, you shouldn't have gotten in the damned business then!" He was highly irritated. So was I.

"I didn't get into the damned business. You got me in it." Immediately I was sorry for the remark. I knew he wanted what was best for me. But he didn't understand that I just wanted to be home with my family. "Harlan, we don't need the money." Walking over, I sat down next to him and tried to make a joke out of it. "Why can't I just stay home and bake cookies?" He didn't smile. Just got up and walked out of the kitchen. I had a feeling I was going to learn something about being a "star." Up to now, my experience was occasional appearances on the Opry and demo sessions. And a very few television shows. Watching one of them one day, I thought I resembled a robot. "Just sing, Jan," somebody said. And that's what I did. Just sang. Never moved . . . never took my eyes off the camera . . . just opened my mouth and sang. My hair was still in the little short cut I'd gotten in California. My makeup was all wrong. Everything was wrong, including the dresses. I decided to do something about all of it.

Catalogs were a good reference. I'd pore over them and try to put together outfits that resembled the ones I saw. Then, going to the best shops, I'd get acquainted with the salespeople, and ask their advice. About clothes, accessories, makeup—anything that would make me look better. On television, I'd watch all the "how to" shows and practice what they preached. For hours, I'd walk around with a book on my head and all what I thought was garbage. But, little by little, it began to come together. Nothing pleased me more than when I was dressed to go somewhere and the kids would say, "Hey, Mom, you look pretty sharp." Even Harlan, who was usually in jeans, began to branch out a little by ordering three custom-tailored silk suits from Hong Kong. One black, one blue, and one brown. Yep, we were now ready to take our respective places in the music business society. Everybody called us the perfect couple.

One of the first tours I worked was in Florida . . . ten days. Me, Faron Young, Buck Owens, and George Jones. What a crew! The first date was Miami. For that show June Carter and Skeeter Davis were added. The promoter was Cracker Jim Brooker, whose introductions left a lot to be desired. For June it was "And now, for the comedy portion of our show—*June Carter*." For Skeeter, it was "Here she is!" For me, it was, "And now, *Jan Howard*." For George, it was another "Now, here's George Jones." But the greatest was his introduction of Buck. "Ladies and gentlemen . . . you've all been waiting for Faron Young!" The audience broke into applause. "Well, *Faron's here!*" The applause got louder. "But, first, the man in the watermelon suit . . . *Buck Owens.*"

After the first date, June and Skeeter left the show and I was to ride on Faron's bus with Buck and George the rest of the tour. I'd heard stories about Faron and his filthy mouth but decided if I ignored him, he'd leave me alone.

One day, on the road, Buck, George, and I were sitting halfway back in the bus singing three-part harmony to a song Buck had written. Faron, standing up front, was yelling obscenities at every woman we passed. We went right on singing. Suddenly, Faron turned to me and said, "What would you say if I said that to you?" He seemed amused.

I stopped singing and said, "I wouldn't say anything, I'd knock the hell out of you." Buck joined in.

"Yeah, and if she didn't, I would!" Then George.

"Yeah, and if he didn't I would!"

Faron, ignoring them, looked right at me and said, "You know, I believe you would."

"Never doubt it, my friend," I said, then back to singing.

The last night of the tour was at Vero Beach, Florida. I was glad it was over. Every night, I'd had stage fright to look forward to. It never seemed to get any better. Perhaps not as bad as it used to be, but, still, for the first two or three songs my heart beat louder than the drums.

The motel we pulled into was the Driftwood Inn . . . the spookiest place I'd ever seen. Right on the ocean and made entirely from driftwood. Since I was the only female in the bunch, the desk clerk put me clear on the opposite side of the motel from the men. Walking along the outside hallway to my room, I saw a long, rectangular-looking box set up on pedestals. "What's that?" I asked the bellboy.

"An antique coffin."

"Are you serious?" He nodded his head.

Without hesitating or stopping, I made a U turn back to the desk. "Put me on the other side of the motel," I told the clerk.

"But that's where all the men are."

"That's right. I want to be right in the middle of them."

"Okay." She sounded as though I wouldn't like where she was going to put me—at the end, right on the ocean. Or perhaps I should say right *in* the ocean. At high tide, the balcony was just a few feet from the water. And the door wouldn't close. "Oh, well, nothing like some fresh ocean air."

The room was huge! Rafters about two feet down from the ceiling and all the way across. In the middle was a big four-poster bed with claws for feet and a stool to climb up onto it. It reminded me of the one, years ago, at Uncle Bert and Aunt Mary's farm. As I left for the show, I couldn't get the outside door to close, and had to leave it ajar.

After the show, with my arms full of stage clothes, I backed into the dark room and reached for the light switch beside the door. At the same time the light came on, so did the sound of laughter . . . from above me! Looking up, I saw Darrel McCall and Johnny Seay, two entertainers on the show, sitting on the rafters. They were higher than kites . . . in more ways than one. "Boy, Jan," Darrel said, "you got a great room." Both he and Johnny were rocking back and forth.

"Watch you," I yelled. "You're gonna fall!" They just kept rocking.

"Can we sleep here?" Johnny asked.

"You really like this room, huh?"

"Yeah," they both said.

"Give me a minute. If I can get another one . . . it's yours." I ran down to the desk.

The clerk looked at me like I was crazy. "What's the matter, lady—you got a problem with rooms?" But he assigned me another one. I dashed back. Johnny and Darrel were still rocking.

Gathering up my things, I said, "Okay, fellows, it's all yours." Glancing back, I thought, *I think they mean to roost instead of sleep.*

The room they gave me was between George Jones and Faron Young. Not what I would have chosen but I wasn't about to go back to the clerk. Anyway, the door closed.

I no more than got to sleep when the sound of a door slamming woke me. It was in George's room, and I could hear Faron and him arguing. Oh, shit! Now I'm gonna be awake all night! Even covering my head with pillows didn't keep out the sound of them calling each other every name in the book.

"I'm gonna knock the hell out of you!" That was Faron.

"Go ahead, you bastard!" That was George. Crash! Somebody hit the wall. I assumed it was George.

"Stay down there, you little bastard, or I'll do it again!" That was Faron.

"No, don't hit me again!" George.

"Okay . . . get up." Faron. Then, it started all over again. Then, it stopped. Good. Maybe now, I can get some sleep.

Just dozing back off, I heard a soft tap at my door. "Jan," a meek little voice said. "Are you awake?"

"Who is it?"

"George." Damn!

"What do you want!"

"Have you got a cigarette?" Oh, hell. I crawled out of bed, got a cigarette, opened the door, and burst out laughing. There stood George in somebody's jeans that were a mile too big for him and tied around the waist with some kind of rope. No shirt and no shoes. And with his crew cut and eyes that were enlarged by something besides booze, he looked like a monkey.

Still laughing, I handed him the cigarette. "Now can I get some sleep?" I closed the door.

Just as I was getting back into bed, there was another tap. I jerked open the door and said, "What do you want now?"

He stood there, cigarette hanging from his lips, and said, "You gotta match?"

"Yes. Do you need help smoking it?"

The walls were so thin, I could hear him walk into his room and shut the door. I'd thought Faron had gone to his room, but, when the fighting started again, I changed my mind. Then something hit the wall that jarred my bed. I heard someone moan. Then, it was quiet.

Even after my flight from Miami, I still didn't fly unless I had to. I was going home on the train at ten the next morning. Since George had asked me to wake him before I left, I walked over and knocked on his door. After knocking twice and still no answer, I started to leave. Then, I heard a moan. "George, are you all right?"

"Jan, is that you?" He sounded awful! "Push open the door . . . I need help." The sight that met my eyes was enough to make anyone stare. George was lying on his stomach, covers down to his waist. And the print of the gas heater was burned into his back.

"Lie still," I said. "I'll go to a drugstore and be right back."

As I very carefully rubbed on the salve the druggist had given me and put the bandages on, he said, "Jan, will you take me with you? I can't make it by myself." I helped him on with his shirt. "Can you get your pants on?" He grinned. He wasn't *totally* disabled. "I'll be outside in the cab."

I already had a bedroom booked and got an adjoining one for George. After one try at going to the dining car and him moaning every time the train jerked, we decided the best thing for him to do was to stay in his room and I'd bring his food.

For twenty-four hours, we played cards, talked, read, and slept in our separate rooms. Just before we pulled into Nashville, George said, "Jan, do me a favor?"

"What?"

"Don't tell anybody I spent twenty-four hours on a train with you and never made a pass. It would ruin my reputation."

Looking out the window, I saw Harlan waiting on the platform. As I got off, with George right behind me, he did a double take. He knew George's reputation, also. But, after seeing what shape he was in, he took my suitcase and said, "How ya doin', buddy?" His question didn't require an answer.

For three days, George stayed in Jimmy's room until he was well enough to travel. "Why do they always take *my* room?" Jimmy asked. "Why not Corky's or David's?"

"I don't know. Maybe you should keep a log book. After all, they are kinda famous."

"If they're so famous, why can't they afford a motel?" he asked. I wondered about that myself.

Buck Owens often stayed with us so he and Harlan could write together. At that time, he brought one man with him, Don Rich, a great fiddle player and harmony singer. And Buck, who hung on to the first dollar he ever made, was not one to waste money on foolish things like motel rooms if he didn't have to. Once, since he was only going to be gone a few days, then back again, he asked if he could leave a paper sack with me. "Sure," I said, and stuck it in Jimmy's dresser drawer. When he came back, that's the first place he headed for. Opening it, he poured the contents on the table. It was money. I told him I'd never check luggage again, suitcases or paper sacks!

Another guest was Freddie Hart, one of the artists I'd met in California and who had recorded several of Harlan's songs, "The

Key's in the Mailbox," for one. But Freddie was not only a record-ing artist, he was also a judo and karate expert. In fact, he instructed the Los Angeles police department in the martial arts. Also, he had a school that instructed handicapped children. With this little bit of history, I don't have to tell you the size of Freddie's arms. They were the size of logs! And hard as steel.

Right after Freddie arrived, Harlan went fishing for a week, leaving him here with me and the boys. I didn't mind because I liked Freddie, but all day long he'd walk around with a pad to write song ideas on. And everytime he got what he thought was a genius idea, he'd come to wherever I was, hit me on the arm, and say, "Jan! What do you think of this!" After a week, my arms were black and blue.

One night, he was giving the boys judo lessons in the den. Washing dishes, I wasn't paying a lot of attention. Then, Jimmy came to the kitchen and, holding out his arm, said, "Mom, grab me right here." I did. Before I could blink an eye, I was on my back on the floor. I don't know who was more surprised . . . Jimmy or me.

Limping down to the den, I said, "Freddie, do me a favor . . . no more judo lessons. Okay?"

Mom came from California and was living with us. It was good to have her and she loved doing for the boys. But I knew she got on Harlan's nerves. He didn't complain and was good to her but, more and more, he was spending every possible moment away from home. And when he was home, Mom would retreat to her room. When we tried to get her to join in whatever we were doing, she'd just say, "I'll just be in the way." A lot was her imagination but, either way, I was in the middle. She tried her best to help and did, especially when I was away. Since I hadn't been able to find a housekeeper, I don't know how I'd have managed without her. No one wanted to take on a four-bedroom house, three children, and three adults—and I couldn't say as I blamed them.

I had just returned from a Hap Peebles—a promoter in Kan-sas City—tour in Nebraska, Kansas, Iowa, and points north, east, south, and west. With two and sometimes three shows every day, it was very hard work. The only thing that made it bearable was the other artists on the show and the funny things that happened along the way. Omaha, for instance. I was looking forward to seeing my brother Junior, who lived there. I was hoping he would come to the show. He had not taken it lightly when I'd married Harlan instead of going back to Smitty.

All crummy hotels look the same. This time, it was the Hill. When I opened the door to my room, I saw what looked like a walk-in closet. I went back to the desk and asked for another one. "The only one we have left is the bridal suite," the clerk said.

"I'll take it." It was much larger but it definitely didn't look like a room in which I'd want to spend my wedding night. The carpets were filthy, the bed had lumps in it, and the drapes looked like they'd been up since 1900.

Junior couldn't come to the show but he called to say he'd be over the next morning. He didn't sound happy. Before getting into the shower, I called room service and ordered breakfast. When the knock at the door and a funny-sounding voice saying "Room service!" came, I opened it to find a table being pushed by none other than Ferlin Husky (who was with the show). On the table was a big lump covered with not a tablecloth but a sheet! Jerking the cloth off, Ferlin said, "Surprise!" There lay Little Jimmy Dickins! You remember how I described Fredie Hart? Well, Little Jimmy was the opposite. About four feet eleven but a dynamite entertainer. After they'd had their laugh and left, I returned to get dressed.

As I waited for the elevator, two men walked up. Looking me over, they said, "Did you work here last night?"

"Yes," I said. They looked at each other and grinned.

"Do you work by yourself?"

"No, there's several others with me." I wished the elevator would come.

Finally . . . the elevator. They followed me in.

"You gonna be here again tonight?" they asked.

"No, we have to leave." They were standing too close for my comfort. The doors opened and there stood Junior. The men walked away, grinning. Junior glared!

"What are you so upset about?" I asked.

"Do you know what kind of hotel this is?" he asked.

"No. Except that it's a crummy one."

"Well, it's a cat house." Seeing my stupid look, he said, loudly, "A whorehouse." Damn! No wonder all those questions from those men. And their stupid grins when they saw Junior—they thought he was a customer! Another day another dollar!

My first album session for Challenge was set up a few days after I got home. My throat felt like raw hamburger. Going to a specialist, I expected him to hand me a magic cure. Instead, he suggested I cancel the session.

"You can't!" Harlan said. "Joe's going back to California tomorrow and there's no telling when he'll be back!"

"Harlan, I can barely talk, let alone sing!"

"We'll just get the tracks . . . you can overdub later."

By the time we got to the studio, I was burning up with fever and my throat was like sandpaper. But, with a lot of help from hot coffee and honey, I forced my voice to sing for six hours. My producer Joe Johnson promised if we could get it down, he'd release it as soon as he got back to L.A.

The next morning, I woke gasping for breath and my chest felt like a brick was laying on it. I was having hot and cold chills! I went directly to the doctor.

As soon as I got home, I took two of the pills he'd prescribed and lay down on the sofa. Within minutes, I was tingling all over and seeing the room from a far distance. I could hear someone talking but couldn't answer. All feeling was gone from my arms and legs. Someone was lifting me and I woke up in the hospital with an oxygen tent over me. Asking a nurse what had happened, she said I'd had a bad reaction to the medication and that I had bronchial pneumonia. Good heavens!

Still having a high fever, I slept except when my medicine was brought in. About three in the morning, I woke up just as the nurse pulled back the sheet and jabbed a needle in my hip. Sleepily, I said, "I hope that wasn't penicillin."

"Why?" she asked.

"Because I'm allergic."

"Damn!" she said, and went running out the door. A few seconds later she was back and jabbed another needle in my hip. "There . . . that'll counteract the penicillin." I sat bolt upright in bed.

"You mean, with 'Allergic to Penicillin' in red on the front of my chart, you gave it to me anyway! What the hell's the matter with you!" I got on the phone to my doctor. Since I wasn't going to sleep the rest of the night, he didn't need to, either!

The next morning, with me insisting that Mother Nature was a lot safer than their hospital, I was released.

I tried to find a housekeeper everywhere. I just couldn't keep up the pace of working and trying to do everything at home, too. Two or three had come and lasted a couple of days, then didn't show up again. But they were useless anyway. At the end of my rope, I called a friend. "I've *got* to find someone!"

"Well, my housekeeper has a daughter-in-law that can help out for a while but she won't work full-time."

"What's her name!"

"Solona Dotson. But, I'm telling you, she won't work full-time."

"Just call and ask her to come and see me—I'll take it from there."

The minute Solona, a beautiful brown-black lady with a soft gentle voice, walked in the door, I knew I liked her. And even more when she started opening cabinet doors and said, "Now you just stay still and let me get these boys some supper." All the time she was cooking, she was explaining that she could only stay until I got on my feet. I hoped, by that time, we'd win her over.

Joe Johnson had promised that the album would be released immediately, but each time I talked to him, he made excuses. Finally, he told me that Capitol Records had bought my contract. Harlan knew all about it. The reason he hadn't told me, he said, was, since Harlan had negotiated the whole deal, it was his place to tell me. I agreed with him! It wasn't that I was unhappy. Gosh, anybody would like to be on Capitol, but I thought I should have been consulted. It seemed funny that Ken Nelson, one of the A&R (Artist and Repertoire) men for Capitol, had been to the house many times and had never mentioned anything to me.

When I got the contract, I pored over the fine print. I'll admit I wasn't too knowledgeable, but the part about five thousand dollars being paid to Challenge and coming out of my royalties bothered me. For once, acting on my own, I took it to an attorney, who said the only one coming out well with that contract was Joe Johnson. He suggested I sue.

The court date came and, since I was the only one who showed up, the judge decided in my favor. I'd also found out a few other things. Such as, I was supposed to be paid for doing the sessions and never was. Sure, it was to come out of my royalties, if any, but the fact remained—everybody got paid but me. And I was mad.

I didn't have long to wait for Joe's phone call. To say he was upset is putting it mildly. "But Harlan gave me his word."

"His word about what?" I asked.

"He said if I released you to Capitol, he wouldn't let you sue me."

"Joe," I said, "it's about time someone realized I have a mouth perfectly capable of speaking up, and it's my money, not Harlan's."

That evening, I told Harlan the whole conversation. He picked up the phone and called Joe. I couldn't believe it when I heard him say his word was worth five thousand dollars and he would get me to drop everything. His word, my ass. I wanted my money! But, even though I didn't like it, to keep peace in the family, I agreed to drop it.

My first session for Capitol was a disaster! Ken Nelson, who lived in L.A., didn't come in and assigned another man to produce it. He was drunk and the songs were lousy.

The second one, with a different producer, was the same except for one difference. He was sober and didn't have that excuse.

I called Ken and told him if I was going to record *for* him, I wanted it to be *with* him. He agreed to set up a session in L.A. And "don't worry about songs," he said. "We'll find them when you get here."

Looking down from the plane as we were landing, I thought, "L.A. looks a lot bigger than it did when we left."

Getting into my small rental car, I stopped by a supermarket to get a few essentials for the apartment that had been rented for me. Since I was scheduled for ten days, they thought that would be better—and less expensive—than a motel.

Coming out, my arms full of groceries, I looked to where I thought I'd parked the car. Nothing looked familiar. But then, I couldn't remember what color or kind it was. I'd gotten used to the smaller markets at home and this looked like a used-car lot with all of them the same. Walking up and down row after row, I finally went back in, called the rental company, and waited for them to come and find my car. I started to give it up and call a cab but couldn't since my luggage was in the car.

For days, I went back and forth to Capitol. Ken was nice, introducing me to everybody, but we weren't getting anywhere. The man who handled the foreign product said I was "pop" and shouldn't be recorded country. I didn't understand it. They had bought my contract for what I had done on Challenge—which was strictly country—and now they wanted to change me. It didn't make sense. Another thing I didn't understand was that the only songs Ken played me were from Central Songs. Why not another publisher? Something was definitely wrong! I was so depressed, I passed up a chance to watch Judy Garland record. *Wonder if she started this way,* I thought.

After ten miserable days, we settled on the four "best of the worst." Two standards and two new songs, none of the songs I really wanted to sing. To top it off, Ken hired Hank Levine, an arranger. In Nashville, the musicians did what they called "head arrangements." Everybody gathered around while the demo of the song to be recorded was played. Then, with suggestions from all concerned, they'd come up with what suited the song best. While they were doing this, other voices, if any, would be standing over to one side working out their parts. Here, I was finding out fast, it was very different.

Each evening, I'd call Harlan and tell him what was going on. "Don't worry about it," he'd say. "The people out there know what they're doing." I doubted that.

It was Friday. Ken called and said since the session wasn't scheduled until Monday, I was free for the weekend. Big Deal. The only place I'd been except Capitol was the grocery. I'd just hung up from talking to Ken when June Carter called from Las Vegas, where she was working with Johnny Cash, doing four shows a night at the Mint for two weeks. "Why don't you come over here. John's real hoarse and we don't know if he can do the show tonight. We sure could use your help." It was all I needed. I had to call Harlan, though, and tell him where I'd be. As I was talking to him, there was a knock at the door. "Hold on," I said. "Someone's at the door." There stood Roger Miller. I didn't even know he was in L.A. Inviting him in, I went back to the phone. "Guess who's here?" I said. "Roger." Harlan wanted to speak to him. Handing Roger the phone, I heard him say he was working that night at some club in Pomona, about sixty miles from here. Seeing he was at the end of their conversation, I reached for the phone but Roger was placing it back in the cradle. Harlan had hung up. Evidently he didn't have anything more to say to me.

After an uncomfortable silence, Roger said, "Hey, I've got a great idea! Why don't you come with me to do the show, then we'll both go to Vegas!" I'd told him June had called. Why not!

The club, a big ballroom type of thing, was owned by Willie Nelson and Tommy Alsup. And the headliner was Bob Wills, the king of Western swing. I was looking forward to watching a legend at work.

Roger opened the show. He was a great writer, writing songs like "Half a Mind" for Ernest Tubb, but onstage he did what he thought he did best—goofy songs. Since he'd never had a "hit," the audience was just a little more than polite and it was obvious that Roger just wanted to get it over with.

Afterward, he said, "Come with me while I get paid. Then we'll get the hell out of here."

Backstage, in a dimly lit hallway, we started to follow Tommy and Willie up the stairs to the office. But they turned and said, "Wait here." Thinking they were talking to me, I backed down. But they were talking to Roger, too. As we stood there, I could see Roger was mad and I didn't blame him. I think he had a feeling he wasn't going to get all of his money.

Standing there, looking around, I saw a box that controlled all the lights in the building. Roger walked over, looked at the box, then at me. Great minds work together. After taking a quick glance up the stairs, we started switching tapes. Stage lights were now marquee lights . . . ceiling lights were now outside lights . . . every tape that said what light it was under was switched. Someone said, "Okay, Roger, you can come up now." They didn't include me so I busied myself switching tapes on other boxes. Served them right! Roger came back down, money in hand, and we ran for his car.

For several miles, we laughed about the confusion there would be at the club the next evening, then we settled into a tired silence. It was three o'clock in the morning and we weren't even to Victorville yet. Not even halfway to Vegas! A motel sign appeared ahead. We looked at each other. It was out of the question. Even if our rooms were a mile apart, word would get back to

Nashville that we'd spent the night together. Thank God! A truck stop! After several cups of coffee—which I didn't even like—Roger got up and made a phone call. Coming back, he said, "We're goin' back to L.A. There's a plane at seven o'clock."

Halfway back, we realized that by the time we got back to L.A. we could have been in Vegas. That bit of stupidity kept us going until we were on the plane. Then, as I always did, I leaned back, closed my eyes, and prayed us off the ground. Since Roger's eyes were closed, I assumed he was doing the same thing. Then I heard him say, "Seven minutes. Seven minutes."

"Seven minutes, what?" I asked.

"The first and last seven minutes are the most dangerous." With that bit of encouraging news, he was fast asleep.

At the show, John never showed up. It consisted of June, me—a couple of songs—but, mostly, it was Roger at his best. Afterward, Roger, Luther Perkins, the guitar player, and Margie his wife, and I played blackjack until seven the next morning. No one had had any sleep. Luther and Roger had something to keep them going but I was like a walking zombie. That evening, I flew back to Los Angeles to sleep until Monday morning.

All day Monday, I was a nervous wreck. I wanted the session to go well but every negative feeling in the world assaulted me. Three times I'd left word for Harlan to call me but he never did. *Okay, Jan*—I talked to myself a lot lately—*it's up to you.*

Opening the door to the studio and seeing about fifty musicians, I thought, I must be in the wrong place. Then I saw Hank Levine. What the hell was this? It was supposed to be a country session and there sat ten string musicians (not fiddles) and over in the corner stood nine singers. The Johnny Mann Singers, no less' *Hell's bells, what was I doing here?* Ken came out of the control room and tried to assure me everything was going to be okay, but I couldn't share his enthusiasm. None of the musicians (except Hank) spoke or acknowledged my presence in any way. My confidence was at ebb tide.

During the first song, everyone in the studio acted like wind-up toys . . . just did what was written out. They'd never heard of me. What did they care? That was the impression I had.

The second song came and went with Ken just using the best take. In the middle of the third song, I knew the key was too low. Turning to Hank Levine, I said, "We'll have to raise it a tone."

One of the singers, a blond chick who thought she was Marilyn Monroe, came over and said, "You can't do that! I can't hit my note!" *I'd had it!*

"Well, honey," I got right in her face, "that's your problem. If you can't hit the note, then hit the door!" I turned to face everyone else, as if to say, "Who's next!" No one said a word. I started singing the song again. After a few times, with it not getting any better, I stopped. It was a lousy song. I hated it, and everyone here. Knowing I was going to cry, I ran out of the studio. Ken followed me. "Now, honey," he said. "It's going to be good."

"No, it isn't. And you know it," I cried. Looking back toward the studio, he said, "Well, I'll admit it isn't Nashville."

"No, it isn't." Going back into the studio, I grabbed my things, walked back to where Ken was standing, and said, "And that's where I'm going. Nashville!"

The plane left at one-thirty A.M., and by the time I got to Nashville, I knew why they called the flight the "red eye." We were supposed to land in Dallas, but, due to icy conditions, we couldn't. We flew back to El Paso, where we sat on the ground for four hours. Then, back to Dallas, where we changed planes, and on to Nashville. I arrived at two-thirty in the afternoon. Eleven hours without sleep. To make matters worse, leaving Dallas I had taken my shoes off and couldn't get them back on. I was so darned tired, I just ignored the shocked stares as I got off . . . wearing a fur coat and carrying my shoes.

Harlan was furious and fit to be tied. "What the hell do you *mean* walking out on a session!"

Ignoring him, I walked into the bedroom. I didn't want to argue. I wanted to sleep. "I'm not going back, Harlan," I said calmly.

"The hell you're not! Ken's called twice. The next time he calls, you're gonna speak to him!"

I was taking off my clothes when the phone rang. Harlan answered and handed the phone to me. "Hello, Ken." I was totally detached.

"How do you feel?" he asked. I almost laughed. He thought I was sick. I guess no one had ever walked out before. "Now, don't worry about the session. We'll do the next one in Nashville."

"No, Ken. We won't do it again. Not now. Not ever. I don't

want to record for you anymore. In fact, I don't want to record for anybody." Harlan was listening. His face was dark with anger. "Let's quit while we're still friends."

Ken said he would call again tomorrow, but I knew I wouldn't change my mind. Nothing would change my mind. I was through. Through doing what everybody else wanted me to do. I was going to do what I wanted to do for a change—stay home and be with my boys. It had gotten to where they didn't bother to say good-bye when I left or hello when I came home. And I was tired of getting off airplanes with no one to meet me and going home to a house where no one had missed me.

Harlan thought that time would change my mind, but it didn't. What little confidence I'd had was gone. I wouldn't even work the Opry or sing in front of the kids. A couple of times, I tried to sing at demo sessions. After goofing up and having to stop the tape several times, Harlan said, "Damn! Can't you get anything right?" Later he apologized and said, "You know I didn't mean it. You know you're my right arm." But he was right. I couldn't do anything right. I tried to tell him how I felt but he wouldn't listen. Just said it would pass and that I had an obligation to sing. *An obligation to whom?* I thought.

Little by little, we fixed up the basement into a combination rec room, den, and office. A sofa, chairs, round, braided rug, jukebox, pool table, desk, typewriter, and everything we needed to pre-demo songs.

The mornings were Harlan's writing hours and I loved sitting there listening to his latest creations, sometimes helping out with a melody or a line here and there. Sometimes, I'd jokingly ask, "How about putting my name on this one?" But he'd say, "What's the difference, it all goes into the same pot." I didn't think it was too much to ask. If anyone else contributed anything, their name went on the song. But, he was absolutely right, it all went to the same pot.

After school, the room would be filled with the boys' friends. One thing about it, I never had to wonder where they were. They, and ten or twelve others, would be either playing basketball at the goal we'd put up at the end of the driveway, playing ball in the backyard, playing records or pool. It was great! But sometimes I'd

think, *They're growing so fast . . . they'll be gone before I know it.*
I begrudged every minute I had to be gone.

The afternoons were my time in the den. And that's where my
singing was confined to these days. Sitting alone by myself, I'd
strum the three chords I'd learned from Harlan and sing soft
ballads. On my records, the keys were so high I had to scream
. . . here, I could be myself.

Sometimes, I'd sit and dream about nothing in particular.
Nothing seemed to be my favorite subject lately. Maybe it was my
imagination, but I'd been thinking, it didn't matter to anyone if I
was here or not. Harlan went fishing a lot and the boys had their
friends. I was grateful for that, but I felt left out. I wanted us to be
a family and we seemed to be drifting further and further apart.

Making an attempt to restore the "togetherness" I missed, I
asked Harlan if he would take me fishing with him. He did, but
he wasn't too enthusiastic about it. Since I'd never been, I had to
ask questions about how and what to do. After about an hour, he
headed the boat back to the dock. "If I'm goin' fishing, that's what
I want to do. Not to answer a lot of stupid questions." It's a good
thing I didn't carve my name on the reel.

I remember going to the den one particular afternoon and
nothing after that until eleven that night. I was lying on the sofa
and someone was trying to get me to drink tea. From what I was
told, I pieced together the missing day.

Jimmy had come home from school and found me in the den
strumming the guitar and singing a morbid song about "When
the last breath of life is gone from my body." He'd spoken to me
but I'd gone on singing. He'd led me upstairs to the sofa and tried
to talk to me. When I wouldn't answer, he called Harlan. From
what they said, I had gone through the house, taken every
picture, award, or anything that reminded me of me, packed it
away in a box, and stored it in the farthest corner of the fallout
shelter we'd had built in the basement.

The psychiatrist, whom Harlan insisted I see, said since I felt
no one knew I was there anyway, I'd remove myself every way but
physically. He called it "temporary amnesia" and said it would
probably never happen again.

Laying my feelings on the line, I talked to Harlan. This time,
he listened. "It's not that I'm not grateful," I said. "I am! My gosh,

we've got more than we've ever had in our lives. I'm not slinging hash in some dump and the kids have the first decent home they've ever had!" He didn't say a word . . . just listened as I told him I loved him. And I really did! Maybe not a passionate, wild kind of love but I had grown to love him, deeply. And I knew, in his way, he loved me, too. Enough, I hoped, for him to understand my feelings. As he'd said, we were a team. I went on. "I want a chance to be a mother again. Go to PTA meetings, ball games at school, be a den mother, bake cookies. Just be here when the kids come home from school." I was almost pleading. I stopped waiting for his answer.

"Okay, L.G. If that's what you want, that's the way it will be." His words were like bricks being lifted off my shoulders.

Since the boys had been going by the name of Howard anyway, Harlan suggested we make it legal. But there was only one hitch—Mearle. Even though he hadn't paid child support for years, we still had to have his permission. Our attorney contacted the district attorney in Montoursville, Pennsylvania—where Mearle was still living—who brought him in and gave him an ultimatum. Either he pay up in full or forever relinquish all rights to the boys. He signed the paper. The day we received their new birth certificates was a great day. Now we were a real family forever.

Christmas that year was extra special. We were all together . . . and healthy and had so much to be thankful for. To add the finishing touch, we gave the boys a perfectly marked thoroughbred collie puppy. Unanimously, we named him "Bucko" after Buck Owens.

As big as the house was, it seemed to be overflowing with people. Us, Mom, and now my brother Dick and his three-month baby, Keith. His wife had deserted him when the baby was three weeks old and, not knowing what else to do, he'd come to us. After three months, we could adopt him. I was getting too attached. He agreed and he, Mom, and the baby got a small apartment not far from us. I knew, for Mom's part, she'd be happier there. Nothing I could say changed her mind about "being in the way." And she didn't have a lot of use for people in the music business. To her, they all thought they were better than anyone else and nothing could convince her otherwise. She wouldn't even acknowlege the name "Jan." As far as she was concerned, I was given the name Grace when I was born and that's who I was . . . now and for all time. I never bothered to tell her I'd had it legally changed. The day I had to go to court, the judge asked me if there was a specific reason for this request. I said, "Judge, if your name was LuLa Grace, would you have it changed?"

"Request granted," he said.

After talking to several builders and getting a price we could afford, we decided to build-on a twenty-eight-by-eighteen-foot den and a redwood sundeck over the patio. We'd only paid $19,500 for the house and didn't figure another $10,000 was going overboard.

After three months, it was finished. At one end was a huge fireplace with a raised hearth and bookshelves on both sides. At the other was a large, curved, built-in desk with all the latest recording equipment and shelves above to store our record collection. The wall facing the backyard had a big picture window and the one facing the front had two smaller windows. The red carpet and beige drapes trimmed in red set it off. It was the homiest and prettiest room I'd ever seen. And it was ours.

Just before Easter in 1962, the boys said they wanted to be baptized on Palm Sunday. Nothing could have pleased me more. The next day, the minister called and said he wanted to talk to me. Figuring it was concerning the baptism, I made an appointment for the next afternoon.

"Mrs. Howard," Brother Austin said, "you know your sons are being baptized on Palm Sunday."

"Yes, sir."

"Well, I think it would be a good idea if you were baptized, too." He waited for my answer.

"But, Brother Austin, I've been baptized. And even though it was when I was a child, I figure once you're baptized, you're baptized." What I didn't tell him was that I felt totally unworthy. I worked in clubs where liquor was sold, didn't go to church regularly, and did a lot of things I knew I shouldn't and didn't do many things I knew I should. I felt as if it would be a sin to kneel beside my sons, who didn't have a sin in the world, and take the same vows they did. I knew that God loved me. How else would I have made it this far? But deep down I felt in a lot of ways I'd let Him down.

That Sunday, before baptism, he said, "It's nice to have their mother, Jan Howard, visiting with us." His words accomplished what I felt they were meant to. I felt so ashamed and guilty. But proud of my sons.

There were always a lot of writers and artists at the house. One of the most frequent was Hank Cochran, co-writer of "I Fall To Pieces." Everybody loved Hank. You couldn't help it. He was like a stray puppy. And, since he and his wife Shirley were on the outs a lot, he was homeless. Everytime he got kicked out, he'd call and say, "It's me, Hanktum, can I come home?" Here he'd come carrying his clothes in a "hope it" (hope it doesn't rain) suitcase and take over Jimmy's room. He'd had the same success as Harlan but was still wearing the same double knits he'd worn when I met him.

"Hank, why don't you buy some new clothes? You can afford them," I'd say.

"What for? These are still good." He was amazed I should ask such a silly question.

This time he was sick and, like one of the kids, I took him to the doctor. For three days he lay in bed and waited for someone to bring him food on a tray. I felt part of his "sickness" was wanting to be babied. All it took for him to get well was for me to say, "Don't worry, darlin', Mama will take care of you." Miraculously, he recovered.

The first time he was out of the house, I thought, *Now's my chance*. Calling the Goodwill to come after them, I put all his clothes in a cardboard box and gave it to the man who came to the door. The kids all knew about it and, knowing Hank would scream when he saw his clothes gone, waited until he came home.

Just as we thought, the minute he got upstairs, he yelled, "Jan! Someone stole my clothes!" He ran back down in a panic.

"No, Hank. I gave them to the Goodwill." I thought he was gonna choke!

"You gave my clothes to the Goodwill!"

"Yes. Now you have to get some new ones."

"But they were still good." I thought he was going to cry. Poor Hank.

After recovering, he left, and it wasn't long before he was back, hollering, "Come see my new suit!" from the car to the door. Before he could get in the door, Bucko, who had grown quite a bit by now, jumped up and, from Hank's head to his toes, licked and slobbered all over him. Looking very pitiful, Hank said, "Bucko loves my new suit." We loved Hank—he was one of the family.

There was something different about this demo session. And the difference was a song that Harlan was most excited about and wanted to record himself, and not just on a demo. A song called "She Called Me Baby." Well, why not? His voice was as good as a lot of others, sort of husky and soft. Practically the whole session was spent on that song and with good results. A record company agreed to release it. A few weeks later, we got word that it was a regional hit in Houston. Nowhere else. But in Houston, Harlan was a star. Suddenly, calls started coming in for him to do a show somewhere. "Hell, I'm just a writer, not a singer," he'd say. But from the smile on his face, I knew he was deeply flattered. Always, when they'd ask his price, he'd give some ridiculous figure he thought no one would accept. One day, someone did— for three thousand dollars! Harlan said he'd work only if I were on the show.

It had been so long since I'd even tried to sing, and when I did I sounded like a hoarse frog. And just the thought of going on-stage again made me break out in a cold sweat. I went to see Dr. Goldner. He looked at my throat, hemmed and hawed a bit, ran a few tests, and said my thyroid wasn't working and gave me some pills. I didn't know what my thyroid had to do with my throat but was willing to try anything. I had a feeling he thought it was all in my head and maybe it was but, either way, I couldn't sing.

On the way to Houston, we stopped overnight in Mobile to visit with Anita Carter and Don Davis. Anita was the youngest daughter of Mother Maybelle Carter, whom I'd met when she was in Nashville. Her husband Don was a longtime musician who had played steel guitar with a lot of artists. They now lived in Mobile, his hometown, and did a local television show there.

During an evening listening to him talk, I was impressed with

Don's business sense. *I wish we had someone like that,* I thought. All we knew was write songs, demo them, get records, and spend the money. And lately we'd been doing a lot of the latter.

Arriving in Houston, we were given the "star" treatment. At least Harlan was, and that was fine with me. "She Called Me Baby" was number one on all the radio stations and we made the rounds. As Harlan was being interviewed, I'd sit by silently. Once in a while they'd mention that I was his wife but otherwise I was ignored. That was fine with me. If there was only some graceful way to get out of going onstage—

Back at the hotel, I ran water in the tub until the room was filled with steam and sat in there till my body looked like a prune. Then filling the sink with hot water, I wrapped a towel around my head and almost suffocated trying to get the steam farther down my throat.

That night, as I listened to my introduction, it was like my first show in Lubbock, Texas. Sick at heart, emotionally and physically, with a terrible case of cold feet. I just knew I would flop. I did. I could barely get a sound out. What applause I got was from sympathy. God, it was awful! If I'd thought I wanted to quit before, I was doubly sure now!

For Harlan, though, it was a different story. Even though he wasn't a performer, all he had to do was sing the hits he'd written. At the beginning of each one, the audience would break into applause. And when he closed with "She Called Me Baby" they went wild. I was far more proud of him than I would have been for myself.

On the way home, he said he'd had it. He was going to quit while he was ahead. I think, for the first time, he now understood a little of what I went through each time I went onstage.

Back home, we settled into a routine. Then came income tax time. Ever since we'd been in Nashville, we had used the same accountant. One who was used to working with "nine-to-five" people. Our income totally mystified him. But everyone said he was competent and we just turned everything over to him, never dreaming that he didn't have the faintest idea what he was doing. A rough way to find out was the way we did. A letter came from the Internal Revenue saying we owed twenty thousand dollars in back taxes. Holy cow! Only a short time ago, we'd been worried about paying the rent and now this! Typical "new money" people. Get it and spend it. We had a lot to learn.

Putting our heads together, we came to several conclusions. Like it or not, I had to go back to work. Second, we needed a business manager. Third, we had to borrow twenty thousand dollars. Our finances were down to zilch!

When we were in Mobile, Don Davis mentioned that if a job opportunity came about, he might consider moving back to Nashville. Well, he needed a job and we needed a manager. I suggested Harlan call Don. With an agreement that Don was to receive a certain percentage of Harlan's earnings, it was settled.

I'd resented it when Harlan had decided I needed a booking agent but, since he had, I was sure glad he picked Hubert Long. Not only did Hubert know his business, having learned the ropes from Colonel Tom Parker, Elvis's manager, but he also owned his own talent agency—The Hubert Long Talent Agency—with clients like Bill Anderson, Ferlin Husky, Roy Drusky, Faron Young, and several others in his "Stable of Stars." But, more important, he was the kindest, most caring person I'd ever met. Whether you were a superstar or a beginner, he treated you the same. He was my friend.

After telling Hubert our situation, he started booking dates immediately. I hated to leave the boys again but they understood. "After all," they said, "Solona's here." She'd stayed, thank God. "Besides, Mom, you've been hollering a lot lately." I hadn't noticed. I'd thought I was just a normal mother. I guessed things had upset me more than I'd realized. The boys knew I'd tried the PTA and, after I'd disagreed with a lot of things they said, hadn't been invited back. I'd even tried the den mother bit, but the kids soon dropped out of the Scouts. The only thing I was good at was showing up at Jimmy's ball games, coaxing David in the Children's Theater, which he'd become interested in, and being the brunt of Corky's "scare" tactics when he'd put rubber snakes and tarantulas in my bed. My screams thrilled him no end. But I was a fairly good demo maker! Maybe *I was* supposed to be an entertainer.

The yard was my pride and joy. I'd spend hours planting flowers, seeing that the shrubbery was trimmed, and anything else I could do to make it resemble *House and Garden* magazine.

For some time, I'd been eyeing the big oak tree in the front yard. I knew all it needed was a flower bed all around it and a white picket fence to set it off. Eight hours and eighty dollars later, the ground was dug up and the flowers planted. And just in case the dogs loved it, too, dog repellents were hung all around the picket fence. Exhausted but pleased, I went into the house to wash up for supper.

While we were eating, one of the boys asked, "Mom, when are you going to plant something in that dug-up ground around the tree?" I knew the flowers were small but not that small!

"What do you mean, *when* am I going to plant? Didn't you see the flowers?" It hit me . . . the dogs!

I ran out to what had been my beautiful flower garden. All that was left was stubs! The damned dogs had eaten every one. They'd even eaten the dog repellent! It was the last straw!

That evening, a man came to see the washer and dryer I had advertised for sale. His son, about seven years old, kept playing with the our beagle hounds. I got a brilliant idea! "Do you like dogs?" I asked the man. He nodded his head and looked at the boy. "Would you like to have two beagle hounds?" He nodded his head again. "Tell you what . . . if you'll take the dogs and give them a good home, I'll lower the price ten dollars."

As they drove away, the dogs firmly encircled in the little boy's arms, I felt a little guilty. Maybe, in a week or so, the boys would speak to me again.

It had been almost two years since I'd left Capitol. But since Challenge had released several of the things I'd recorded for the album and with getting another "Most Promising" award, I was still in demand for public appearances.

One of my first shows was in Michigan, where I almost found out what would have happened if I'd taken a "bennie" (Benzedrine).

Standing backstage waiting to go on, I was drinking my ever-present Pepsi. When my name was announced, I put it down on a nearby table. Coming off stage, I went to retrieve it. But just as I was fixing to put it to my lips, something told me to stop. Holding the Pepsi, I looked around at the people standing there. One of them was grinning from ear to ear. Walking to him, I said, "Did you put something in my Pepsi?"

"No! I wouldn't do a thing like that!" I knew he was lying.

"Okay . . . if you say so. But I want to tell you something. If you did and I drink this Pepsi . . . it could kill me." Having no intention of following through, I started to put the drink to my lips.

"Damn, Jan! Give me that!" Grabbing the Pepsi, he said, "What the hell do you mean, it could kill you!"

"I have a rapid heartbeat. And if I should ever, by accident or otherwise, take anything like a bennie, that would be all she wrote." His face turned white. "So I hope you've learned a valuable lesson."

"Oh, yes. God, yes! I promise I'll never do it again." The Pepsi hit the nearest trashcan.

From that day to this, if I have anything to eat or drink in my hand and set it down for any reason, that's where it stays.

One of the next shows was in Florida. The cast (besides me) was six-feet-four-inch Merle Kilgore. Big, handsome crazy Merle Kilgore was in the "spirit world" most of the time and totally eccentric. Except for the time I'd gone over to help out when his wife had the flu, I enjoyed having him around. That particular time, after calling and asking for my help, he just disappeared.

Going into the house, I found his wife upstairs in bed with a high temperature, his kids running wild, and the house in a mess. Digging in, I changed the bed linens, washed clothes, fed the kids, and cleaned house—everything except taking out the garbage. At that moment, Merle walked in. "Hey, Merle," I said, "how about taking out this garbage?"

Looking at me like he thought I'd lost my mind, he said, "Me? Do menial labor with my hands? You're not serious!" He turned and walked into the sparkling clean den.

My first thought was, *Why, you egotistical bastard!* Then I realized that was typical Merle Kilgore.

One thing about it, with Merle riding to Florida with me, it wasn't dull! All the way there and from town to town, he kept me entertained with his stories. But, as the days wore on, I began to be anxious to get home. For some reason, I felt a sense of urgency.

Finally, the last show was over and we started home. But first we had to detour a hundred miles out of our way, to visit the Stephen Foster Museum, where Merle Kilgore spent almost every dime he'd made on the tour buying things like door chimes that played "Way Down Upon The Swanee River."

Driving all night, we arrived in Nashville about eleven A.M. After taking Merle home, I walked into the house dead tired. The boys were at school and the only one home was Solona. "Where's Harlan?" I asked.

Looking a little uncomfortable, she said, "He's not home, Mrs. Howard." Well, that was nothing unusual.

Irritated, I said, "Solona, I *know* he's not home, but did he say where he was going?" She wouldn't look at me. Just started washing dishes.

"Solona! Answer me!"

"I don't know, Mrs. Howard. He wasn't here when I came this morning."

"Did the boys say what time he left?" I asked.

Turning to face me, she said, "They said he wasn't here all night."

"You mean he left them alone all night?" That wasn't like Harlan. Surely, he'd have an explanation. Well, I can't ask him if he isn't here. I started in to go to bed.

As tired as I was, a nagging feeling in the back of my mind wouldn't let me sleep. Giving it up, I got up and washed my hair. The phone rang and I heard Solona say, "Howard residence." Coming into the bathroom, she said, "It's for you, Mrs. Howard. It's Mr. Howard."

"Jan, are you home?" Well, that was a brilliant question!

"What do you mean? Of course I'm home." His voice had sounded odd. "Where are you?" I figured the other questions could wait.

"Joe Allison's in town and I'm down in his room at the Downtowner." Well, that explained it. Joe was an old friend from California and produced a lot of records for different artists. Harlan was pitching songs. "Do you want to come down?" Harlan asked.

"No, I'm tired. We drove all night. Besides, I just washed my hair."

"Okay. I'll be home after a while." Hanging up, I thought *He sounded relieved.* I went back to finish rolling my hair. Slowly at first, then faster. Suddenly, I knew I had to go to the Downtowner.

Ordinarily, I would never have gone out of the house with big plastic rollers in my hair but today, there was something more important than my appearance at stake.

Tying a scarf around my head and dabbing a little makeup on, I dressed and drove downtown.

As I knocked on the door of Joe's room, I could hear the sounds of several people laughing and talking. I knocked again and waited. Suddenly, the door was thrown open and the smile on Joe's face froze. The room fell silent. Walking in, I said, "Where's Harlan?" No one answered, but I didn't need their answer. Walking over to the door of the adjoining room, I opened it. There, in a chair, sat Harlan. In two other chairs were men that had been at the house many times, both writers. And sprawled across both beds were three women I had never seen before. I knew Harlan had spent the night with one of them.

The only acknowledgment Harlan gave me was a nervous laugh. The men looked as though they wished they could disappear. And would have except that I was standing in their way.

"Why, Harlan?" I asked.

Looking like he'd been struck dumb, he didn't answer. I turned to the women, and my eyes went to the ugliest one of the three. Her matted hair looked like it had never seen a hairbrush, and black mascara was smeared around her eyes. Her face had paled considerably. Turning back to Harlan, I said, "If you had to go to bed with one of them, why did it have to be the pig of the bunch?" I looked back at the woman and noticed something else. Shit! No wonder she couldn't look me in the eye . . . both of hers were going in different directions! She was crosseyed. *I've got to get out of here before I throw up,* I thought. Without another word, I walked out the door and drove home.

There was no way I could go back to bed. Instead, I walked out to the pretty white swing we'd installed in the front yard, sat there, and looked over the supposedly serene scene. The house we were so proud of, the flowers I'd planted, the perfectly mowed and trimmed yard . . . everything we'd worked so hard for. How could he do this? Harlan's blue and white Ford convertible turned into the driveway. Walking over, he sat down beside me, and when I didn't say a word, began to talk. Funny, he didn't deny anything. I don't know how I knew to go down there but I knew exactly what had happened even before he told me. The picture was clear in my mind. I even knew the "girls" were from Bowling Green, Kentucky! That surprised him even more.

He told me he had just gotten caught up in drinking and didn't know where the girls came from and more crap like "I didn't make love to her in the normal way," I'd had all I could take. He begged me not to divorce him and destroy our "perfect couple" image.

Looking at him with all the disgust and revulsion I felt inside, I said, "No, Harlan, I'm not going to divorce you, not now, at least. I've got to think. But I'll tell you one thing—don't come near me or try to touch me in any way. I hate your guts!" Walking into the house, I went into the bedroom, slammed the door, and threw myself across the bed. I didn't know what I was going to do or how I could live with this but I knew one thing: I was not going to destroy my sons' lives and give up everything I'd worked my ass off for because of some whore.

The boys knew something was wrong. Where before there'd been laughter and a lot of kidding around, now there was strained silence. Harlan threw himself into writing. The only good thing that came out of the whole mess was a hit song called "Life Turned Her That Way." A few of the lines hit home. "If she seems cold and bitter, I beg of you. Just stop and consider all she's been through. She was crying when I met her, she cries harder today. But, don't blame her . . . life turned her that way." The chorus fit to a T. "She's been walked and stepped on so many times. And I hate to admit it but the last footprint's mine."

Harlan was on the board of directors of the Country Music Association. He asked me to accompany him to a meeting in Chicago. It had been several weeks since the Downtowner incident and nothing had changed between us but, for appearances' sake, I agreed.

Joe Allison, also on the board, was there, but since he'd been a party to what had taken place, I didn't want to talk to him. My God, how many times he'd been at the house, ate at my table, and played with my sons! How could he condone this?

During a break in the meetings, Joe asked me to have lunch

with him. He said he had to talk to me. To give him the benefit of
the doubt, I agreed.

In silence, I picked at my food. "Jan, how long do you think
you can go on like this?" Joe asked.

"I don't know, Joe."

"You know, everyone's entitled to one mistake," he said. I just
looked at him. "Don't throw your life, and what you've built
together, away because of this."

"I don't want to, Joe. But I don't know if I can ever live with
him as man and wife again. The trust is gone."

"Just try. Just say you'll try."

Standing up, leaving my food almost untouched on my plate, I
said, "All right, damn it, I'll try!" and walked out the door.

Even after my talk with Joe and promising I'd try, I still couldn't
forget. Each time Harlan would leave the house, I'd think, *Yeah,
he says he's going to pitch songs, but I wonder where he's really
going?* Harlan, on the other hand, acted as if nothing had happened. And the kids had their own things going. Everything was
back to normal—everything but me.

A ten-room house with one person in it is very lonely. Oh,
there were signs of people living there, but I was in a world of my
own, a world I'd created in my mixed-up mind.

For hours I'd sit in my bedroom trying to figure out why
things had happened and wishing we could be back the way we
were. All the time knowing we could never be. Lately, my mi-
graine headaches had become more frequent, and the one I had
this day was a dilly!

Going to the medicine cabinet, I looked for the red cap of the
Tylenol bottle. Instead, my eyes caught the label on the bottle of
Seconal, sleeping pills that Dr. Goldner had given me more than
a year before. Not one had ever been taken. *That's what I need
. . . sleep,* I thought as I poured one out in my hand. Then, I
poured two more out. Not thinking of anything except my misery
and self-pity, I took the bottle and a glass of water and went back
to my bed. One by one, I swallowed all the pills and began to feel
their effect. Suddenly, my fuzzy mind thought *My God! What
have I done! I don't want to die! I want to see my sons! Jimmy
. . . Corky . . . David! Where are you!*

Hearing someone in the kitchen, I tried to move but nothing

in my body was working except my mind. My screams were silent
. . . except in my head. I was beyond thinking or fighting.
   There were no sirens. *I must be in a car,* I thought. There
were voices but I couldn't distinguish anyone. Cold, wet
towels were put on my head, and a tube ran down my throat. My
guts were being torn out as I gagged . . . and gagged . . . and
gagged. Finally, it stopped. A woman's voice kept saying, "No,
dear, you can't sleep. Talk to me . . . talk to me." She never
stopped. I couldn't hear anyone talking but her. I wanted to talk
but couldn't. Then, she said, "Just imagine a big tree with one
limb hanging down. Reach up, grab it, and hang on." Mentally, I
could see the tree and the limb. With all my mind power, I
reached up, grabbed it, and hung on for dear life!
   Someone came in and said, "Marilyn Monroe has just committed suicide." Someone else said, "Damn it! Get the hell out of
here!" Then, "Your husband's outside. Do you want to see him?"
I shook my head no. I couldn't speak but heard a voice ask, "How
is she?" The nurse said, "Let's just say she's critical. Her blood
pressure is as low as it can go." Then she started pouring water
down my throat . . . replacing every drop I threw up. Finally, I
opened my eyes to see Mother Maybelle Carter sitting by my bed.
She began feeding me fresh peaches she'd brought from home.
Little by little, I felt stronger and knew, thank God, that I was
going to live.
   When I went home, no one mentioned a word as to why I'd
been in the hospital, and I was glad. Sometimes, when I was
alone, I'd walk from room to room saying, "Thank you, Lord."
   The first time I turned to Harlan instead of away from him, he
said I'd never be sorry.
   For quite a while we'd been talking of starting our own publishing company. Even had a name for it—Wilderness Music.
With my working, we'd been able to put all of Harlan's royalties
toward the bank loan. Now, it was finally paid off and the time
was right.
   We found an old house, 913 17th Avenue South (on Music
Row), and figured, with some fixing up, we could have several
offices, some storage rooms, and a demo studio. It would take all
we had plus an advance on royalties, but that would be our
retirement. An agreement was made between Harlan and me. All
of his royalties would go into the business and I would work the
road and support the family. Even the checks I received for doing

the demos would be signed by me and turned back over to the company. That was the only thing that wasn't new. Don Davis handled everything.

The thought *This is for our future* was the only thing that kept me going when I'd come home after cleaning, scrubbing, painting, wallpapering, and anything else that had to be done to get Wilderness into shape, so tired I couldn't carry on a decent conversation. Harlan was strictly into writing and pitching songs. I was into making drapes, buying office furniture (at sales and warehouses), carpet (at discount stores), converting the attic at Wilderness into Harlan's office, and seeing what I could take from our house to that house, to make it more comfortable. The same work went into Don's office downstairs. Mine was the reception room out front.

When I wasn't scrubwoman, I was at Broadcast Music Incorporated learning the ropes of how to run a publishing company. Soon, I was bookkeeper, secretary, demo maker, gopher, chief cook and bottle washer, and *tired!* In my spare time, I was mother, wife, housekeeper, and sometimes "star."

The wife and mother part, I enjoyed. The "star" part was something else again. Oh, I loved doing the Opry, but the road was something I never learned to look forward to.

The Opry was not only a place I loved to perform (even though I was more nervous there than anywhere else), it was a place to see all our friends and watch my favorites. Usually, Harlan would go with me and, in between spots, we'd go over to Tootsie's and sit around and talk. One night, Harlan and I were sitting at a table with Patsy Cline and her husband, Charlie Dick. Faron Young came over, leaned over the table, and said loud enough for everyone in the place to hear, "Harlan, you don't ever have to worry about me going to bed with Jan. It would be like going to bed with my secretary. I'd have to look at her the next morning."

"Faron," I said, "even if there had never been a Harlan Howard, you still wouldn't have to worry about going to bed with me." I knew he just said it to get attention and a rise out of me but it embarrassed the hell out of me anyway. It got so I avoided Tootsie's Orchid Lounge.

I don't know about other "girl singers," but from the stories I'd heard, I was given slightly different treatment. After all, the men

I worked the road with were all Harlan's friends. And mine, too. It occurs to me they just might not have found me that appealing to their manly instincts, but I prefer to believe it was respect that kept anyone from making a pass at me. They were more like bodyguards. One girl, worried about traveling on a bus with nine musicians, asked my advice. "If you act like a lady, you'll be treated as one," I told her. I believe that to this day.

One night, after a show in Chicago, a man from the television station, hearing me say I was starving, offered to take me to eat. One of the musicians heard him, came over, and said, "Where we going?" Taking him aside, I said, "*We're* not going anywhere. *I'm* going to eat."

"Not alone with him, you're not!" he said.

At the restaurant, knowing the television man was going to pay, the musician ordered the biggest steak on the menu. I think my order of a grilled cheese sandwich was probably welcome.

All the motel rooms look the same. Red, orange, or green carpet, drapes that wouldn't close together. I always had to pin them to keep the daylight out. There was the standard, horrible, cheap-looking picture on the wall, a bed, dresser, and chair. And *lonely*.

It got so I could close my eyes and find anything in the room. I'd never learned to pack right (and still haven't) and would end up with my suitcase weighing more than I did. Since it was a "no no" to ask anyone for help, if I couldn't find a bellman, I'd call on God for strength to carry it myself.

Everyone who hasn't worked the road said, "Yeah, but look at all the great places you get to go and all the sight-seeing." Places? Yes. But the only sight-seeing was out the window of someone's bus or car, or the window of an airplane. There was never time for anything else. Sometimes we'd work a show, ride all night to get to the next one just in time to check in, take a bath and do a matinee, then start all over. It went on for days at a time.

The only sleepwear I took on the road was a pair of men's pajamas and an unsexy robe. If I was lucky enough to be on somebody's bus, that was the only sensible thing. Usually, since I was the "outsider," all the bunks would be taken and I'd curl up on a seat and feel like hell the next morning. My teeth itched and the previous night's makeup felt like mud caked on my face. I was not sexy.

I *did* become a fair poker player, though. With nothing else to do after getting tired of counting telephone poles and watching the white line on the highway, it was a way to pass the time. If it got over a quarter limit, though, I dropped out. I'd learned that the hard way by losing fifty dollars in the first hand, playing with Bobby Bare, Cal Smith, and Ernest Tubb.

On a tour of Michigan, George Jones (my all-time favorite singer) was on the show. Having been drinking from day one, he was wild! But, drunk or not, he could outsing anyone I'd ever heard.

Since we had to leave fairly early, I went to bed as soon as possible. But the sound of someone pounding on my door woke me. Sleepily, I said, "Who is it?"

"George! Let me in. I've gotta talk to you." I looked at the clock. It was four A.M.

"Go away! It's four o'clock in the morning!"

"I don't care," he yelled. "If you don't open the door, I'll break it in!" Hell, he was going to wake the whole motel!

Getting out of bed, I threw on a robe and opened the door. "What the hell do you want!"

Not answering me, he walked to the other side of the bed and turned the radio on. I shut the door, walked over, and sat in the middle of the bed, my feet tucked up under me. Twirling the knob of the radio, he ignored me. "Shit," he said. "I can't get no country music!" Suddenly, he threw the radio against the wall!

"Damn you, George, this is *my* room and I'm not going to pay for your damage! You said you wanted to talk. Now talk!"

He leaned back in the chair and looked at me. Without warning, he bounded from the chair to the bed . . . I moved just in time. He went across the bed and onto the floor. Before he could get up, I was across the room and had the door open. "Okay, get out! If you want to talk, go wake Kilgore."

Picking himself up from the floor, he walked past me and out the door. I slammed it after him.

The walls in this motel were so thin you could almost hear the person next door breathing. And the person next door to me was Merle Kilgore, also on the show.

I heard the familiar pounding and Merle's feet as they hit the floor. "God!" he said. "It's the end of the world and I'm not ready." Laughing so hard I was crying, I never went back to sleep. Even putting cotton in my ears and a pillow over my head didn't keep out the sound of their laughing and talking.

Even though I never mentioned the incident to George, for the rest of the tour he avoided me like the plague.

Eight months later he came to Nashville and called Harlan and me to come after him at his manager's house. We were used to that. Particularly if he was drinking. He'd come and hole up in Jimmy's room to recuperate.

George crawled into the backseat. Harlan and I were in front. About halfway home, he started crying and leaned over the front seat trying to put his arms around Harlan. "Harlan . . . you oughta kill me," he said.

"What for, buddy?" Harlan asked.

"I tried to make love to Jan."

I almost went into shock. "George!" Harlan and I just looked at each other. I knew what George was talking about but had never mentioned it to Harlan. There's some things just not worth repeating.

"Well," Harlan said. "You didn't, did you?"

"Hell no! She kicked my ass out!" George said, and started crying again.

The boys had overnight friends, and all the beds except the bunk beds in the basement were full. George found his way to one of them and passed out. Later in the night, I heard what sounded like a fight in my bathroom! Harlan said, "It's just George," and went to see what was going on. I heard them talking and Harlan taking him back downstairs. Coming back, he laughed and said, "George got in a fight with the shower curtain." The next morning, judging from the mess the bathroom was in, I assumed the shower curtain had lost.

Each time he left, after about three weeks he'd call and apologize. "What for?" I'd ask.

"I don't know but there must have been something awful." He never admitted to remembering anything.

One time he was completely sober. It was three o'clock in the afternoon. The boys were due home about four and Solona and I were the only people home. Looking out the kitchen window, I saw a car pull around to the back. George and a girl I had never seen before jumped out and ran into the basement. "Jan, come here quick!" George hollered.

Thinking someone was hurt, I ran down the stairs. The girl stood there looking embarrassed and scared. The only way to describe George's look is panic-stricken! "Her husband's coming after her and he's got a gun!" he said. "You've gotta tell him we're not here!"

"I'm not telling him anything," I said. "I'm calling the police," I ran back upstairs. Within a few minutes another car pulled in the driveway, this time stopping out front. A police car was right behind him. Neighbors on all sides were standing in their yards trying to see what was going on. *Oh, good,* I thought. *Now they'll know for sure all entertainers are crazy.*

The policeman walked to the car, talked to the man, then came to the steps where I was standing. "Mrs. Howard, if George Jones is here, will you tell him I'd like to talk to him?"

George, hearing what the policeman said, hollered, "Hell, no! I'm not coming out! He's got a gun!"

The policeman was getting a kick out of this but I wasn't. My kids were due home any minute. He said, "It's all right, Mr. Jones. I have a gun, too. Now, you just walk with me to the car and we'll settle this peacefully."

He, with George a few steps behind, walked back to the car. I sat down on the steps and hoped the school bus was late. I could hear what was being said.

"I just want my wife," the man said. "Just bring her out and we'll leave. But if I ever catch you messing around with her again, I'll blow your damned brains out!"

George said, "Hell, man, you can have her!" He ran back into the house and practically dragged the poor girl out to the car. "There!" he said, and stood there grinning.

I thought, *Why, you no good bastard!*

The girl got in the car and they left.

The policeman shook hands with George and, smiling, went back to his car. George, not even saying another word to me, said, "Damn! What a day!" But, it wasn't over.

About an hour later, the girl called. "Mrs. Howard," she said. "Do you know where George is?" I couldn't believe her!

"No, I don't. And if I did, I wouldn't tell you."

"Well," she said, "if he calls, will you tell him I'll be at my brother's?" I hung up. The poor, stupid groupie!

The sixties were a great time to be in country music. There was a lot of closeness and friendship among the writers and entertainers. Many times, at our house or someone else's, we'd all get together for "pickin'" parties. A microphone would be set up and, before the night was over, everyone there would have taken the "hot seat." Writers would sing their latest creations and everyone else played what was requested, or what they wanted to. Sometimes strays would hear about the parties and try to crash. One night, at our house, seeing two women I'd never seen before, I asked Harlan, "Who are those women?"

"I don't know," he said. And no one else did either.

Walking over to the women, I asked, "Would you mind telling me who invited you?" I could see they were already sloppy drunk.

"No one!" they said. "We just heard there was a party goin on' and figured we'd get a free beer." I ushered them out the door.

That night was a night to remember. The guests included Hank Cochran (our sometimes live-in), Roger Miller, Joe Allison, Jean Shepard and Hawkshaw Hawkins (man and wife), Patsy Cline (pregnant with her second child) and her husband, Charlie Dick, Roy Clark and his wife Barbara, Vic McAlpine (a writer), Tom Pall and Chuck Glaser (two of the Glaser Brothers trio), Charlie and Ira Louvin, and Justin Tubb. One thing I regret is that a tape recorder wasn't going when Charlie, Ira, Patsy, and I were singing four-part harmony.

Except for a few stragglers, everyone had gone home by three o'clock in the morning. Leaving Harlan talking with them, I went to bed.

Since Jimmy had his driving permit, it was his job to pick up Solona at seven-thirty. If we weren't up, she'd always be real careful to keep everything quiet. Not so this morning. I heard her scream, "Mrs. Howard!" and jumped out of bed. I knew something had happened to one of the boys! She was standing outside the bathroom . . . almost white!

"Solona . . . what's the matter?" I asked.

Pointing to the bathroom, she said, "Lordy, Mrs. Howard, there's a body in the bathtub!"

"What!" Surely not! Slowly, I opened the door. The shower curtain was pushed aside and there lay Justin Tubb . . . asleep. Closing the door, I said, "It's all right, Solona, it's just one of the guests," and went back to bed.

The boys loved to tease Solona, but she never got irritated. Not even when they'd call her salami, bologna . . . everything but

Solona. She'd just smile and go right on ironing and watching her soap operas. Because that's what she was usually doing. And it began to get to me. The kids, saying Solona was wearing out their clothes by washing them so much, would hide their favorite things. And, after she washed a cashmere sweater and pair of pants of mine, shrinking them up to fit a two-year-old, I did, too. To me, it seemed she was letting a lot of other things go just so she could iron and watch her soaps. Every time I'd come home from the road, I had to pitch in and clean house. And I figured that was what I was paying her for. When I asked her about it, she said, "I can't do everything, Mrs. Howard." *Well,* I thought, *she should be able to,* and fired her. *Hell, I've got two weeks off, I'll do it myself.*

After a few days, I found it wasn't that easy ironing twenty to thirty shirts a week and that many pairs of pants, cleaning a ten-room house, grocery shopping, cooking three meals a day, and washing that many dishes, plus everything else that had to be done. I called her house.

Solona and her husband were separated and she lived with her mother-in-law, "Big" Frances, a woman who weighed about four hundred pounds and was head honcho for the black neighborhood where they lived, Big Frances's husband, her two children, and five more who belonged to Solona's sister-in-law who, according to Solona, had never been married.

Big Frances answered the phone. "Hello?"

"Frances, this is Mrs. Howard. Is Solona there?" I asked hopefully.

"Why no, Mrs. Howard. Solona's in Florida."

"How dare she go to Florida when I'm here going crazy! What's she doing there?"

"Well," she said. "These nice folks were going down and asked Solona to go, take care of the children, and sorta have a vacation."

"Well, ask her to call me the minute she gets back, please!" For two weeks I almost went out of my mind! But the kids pitched in, and with them taking care of their own rooms, each taking turns running the vacuum, emptying the garbage, and anything else that had to be done, all that was left for me was cooking, grocery shopping, washing and ironing, and forty thousand other things.

One thing I didn't mind doing was cooking. My collection of cookbooks took up one whole cabinet. Trying to think up interesting things to cook, I'd pore over them as though I were studying for my master's degree.

One of the cookbooks was called *World Cookery*. The ingredients for Tasmanian Rabbit couldn't be bought at Krogers'. But I did find one for Shrimp de Jong that sounded interesting.

I had to go all the way across town to buy the fresh shrimp, fresh scallops, and fresh oysters the recipe called for. But, figuring everyone would be thrilled with this deviation from the same old meat and potatoes, I set about making my masterpiece.

Waiting until everyone was seated at the table, I proudly brought my creation out of the oven. As I set it down, I said, "Okay, dig in," and waited for their praise. Corky bravely took the first helping. After the first bite, he made a face and said, "Ugh! What is this stuff!"

"What do you mean . . . stuff!" I said indignantly. "It's called Shrimp de Jong!"

"Well, it tastes more like Shrimp de Junk!" he said, and pushed his plate back.

One by one, I got the same opinion from everyone. I put a spoonful in my mouth and had to go to the bathroom to get rid of it.

Coming back, I set the bowl in front of Bucko, who was lying on the floor. Taking one sniff, he got up and walked out of the room.

"Okay!" I said. "Everyone for Morrison's Cafeteria, follow me!" So much for exotic food!

Up to my elbows in dishwater, I answered the phone. "Hi . . . how ya doin'?" a very welcome and familiar voice said.

"Solona, when are you coming back to work?" From the tone of my voice, I know she detected the word *please*.

"Your money's my pleasure, Mrs. Howard," she said, then promised she'd be there the next morning. Thank God!

You could count on Solona for several things—among them, not showing up on most Mondays. Either she was sick, her kids were sick, or something. I asked, "Solona, how come this only happens on Mondays?"

"I don't know, Mrs. Howard."

Laughing, I said, "Why don't you just admit you've got a hangover?" Being an avid churchgoer, she'd never admit to such a thing, even if it were true. But, after that last experience, I wasn't about to let a little thing like not coming to work interfere with keeping her.

One Monday, her excuse was different. "I got to go to the doctor," she said.

"What for?" I asked, expecting sickness of some sort.

"I got shot," she said.

"You got what?"

"Shot," she said, matter-of-fact-like. "Last night, I was sittin' in this place down on Jefferson Street talking with this man, and his wife came in waving a gun."

I was glued to the phone . . . it was like one of her soap operas! "What then?"

"Well, she shot at him and missed, but the bullet hit the wall and ricocheted and went through my leg." I couldn't help it; I laughed.

"Solona," I said, "I'm sorry to laugh, but get yourself to the doctor, then to work, okay?" What next!

There was no one like her. My favorite place to pay bills was at the kitchen table so she could tell me all the gossip of her neighborhood and everything that had happened on her soaps. I couldn't have cared less, but I loved her stories.

One Monday, instead of Solona calling with an excuse, someone brought Big Frances to help out. There was no way I could ask that huge lady to go up and down stairs, so I got her a chair and gave a stack of the ever present ironing.

As soon as Jimmy got home, I asked him to please take her home. Harlan had taken the Cadillac and they walked out to the little Ford convertible. Hearing Jimmy laughing, I walked to the door. There they were—Big Frances half in the car and Jimmy pushing, trying to get the other half in. "Hey, Jimmy!" I called. "What are gonna do if you get her in and can't get her out?" He fell on the ground in hysterics! Finally, with both of us pushing, we got her in. I whispered to Jimmy, "If you have trouble getting her out . . . call a wrecker." Afterward, if Solona couldn't come, we did without.

Harlan and I had discussed several times having his daughter, Jenny come for a visit. Things were so much different now and a lot of time had passed, surely we could be friends. With her and David the same age (eleven), I thought they'd have a lot of fun together. Harlan made the call. In fact, several calls, each time talking to his ex-wife a long time, which I didn't think was all that necessary. But, having never asked if any of the old feeling was still there, I didn't now. What good would it do? It was decided Jenny would come the last two weeks in August. The closer it got to the time, the more nervous I became. Harlan, trying to reassure me, said, "She's bound to love you."

"Why," I asked.

"Because I do," he said. That made me feel better.

David moved his things to Corky's room. And in David's I put frilly curtains and a feminine bedspread, flowers on the chest of drawers, and a welcome sign on the door.

The day she was to arrive, we decided Harlan would pick her up and I'd fix a special dinner and see that the boys were "spit and polished." But, from moment one, it was a "no go."

When Harlan was around, she was sweet as sugar, but when he wasn't she was a pint-sized bitch! I tried to ignore things like "I don't know why Daddy married you . . . you're so ugly." It hurt like hell. Maybe it will get better, I hoped.

One thing you can always count on a girl to like is shopping. I knew I could win her over! Going to Chester's—a store in Madison where I bought most of the boys' clothes—we shopped for a complete school wardrobe. It would take a couple of new suitcases to get them all home, but I didn't care. If I had to buy her friendship . . . so be it!

The day before she was to leave, I had some shopping to do in downtown Nashville and took Jenny and David with me. After we three had lunch, I suggested they might like to see a movie while I did what I had to do. "Yeah!" they both said. After finding out what time it was over, I told them to meet me in front of Grace's—an exclusive dress shop—at four o'clock. That way we'd miss the heavy traffic back to Madison.

Four o'clock came and went. So did four-thirty . . . and five. I was frantic! What could have happened! Finally, I saw them sauntering down the street. Meeting them halfway, I said, "Where have you been?"

David, knowing he was in serious trouble, said, "I'm sorry, Mom, we stopped for ice cream." Jennifer was getting a kick out of me being upset and David, getting blamed, was laughing.

When we got home, I said, "Okay . . . out! Both of you, go straight to your rooms and don't come out. No television. No nothing! Your dinner will be brought to you." David, knowing he was getting off easy, escaped my sight as quickly as possible. Jenny said, "When Daddy comes home, tell him I want to see him," and walked slowly to her room. She was enjoying herself.

I told Harlan what had happened and asked him to please stand behind me. To Jennifer's amazement, he did.

The next day, all was forgotten. By everyone except Jenny. When it came time to take her to the plane, she looked at me and said, "Does *she* have to come?"

"She'd like to," Harlan said.

"I don't want her to," she said, "I hate her *guts*." I was stunned.

"It's all right, Harlan," I said. "I won't go." Turning to Jennifer, I said, "Good-bye, Jennifer. I hope you'll come back sometime." With a satisfied smirk on her face, she turned to Harlan and said, "Let's go, Daddy."

With trying to make ends meet and with dates coming in faster than I wanted them to, it seemed I was on the road more than I was at home. When I'd think I was going to have a few days at home, there would be a new booking. It was great to be wanted but it was also demanding. I remember calling Hubert. "You're supposed to be my friend! I thought these days were open."

"Well, they were, but Harlan called telling me to book you. He wants to go fishing."

"Hell, he can go fishing anytime he wants to," I said. "Why do I have to be out of town?" Hubert laughed.

"Maybe he feels safer. If you're out of town, you can't check up on him."

"That's not funny, Hubert. Why would I check up on him?"

"Just kidding," he said. "But he did say he was going fishing." Hell, that's no news flash. Between three or more days at Center Hill Lake, about seventy miles from Nashville, and the office, he was hardly ever at home. Harlan said he needed time to clear his head. If that was the case, it should be nearly empty by now.

The perfect booking came in—four days in Panama City, Florida. Thinking it was a great way to combine business with pleasure, I suggested the whole family go down. We really needed the time together. Besides, the promoter was paying expenses.

Driving down, the tension of Nashville slowly faded and the car was filled with "vacation" atmosphere. It was like old times.

Every day until it was time for me to get ready for the show we'd spend out by the pool or on the beach. Swimming, laying in the sun, building sand castles. Even Harlan began to relax.

The first day there, an event happened that caused some dissension on the show. And, as far as I could see, I was the only one who thought it was funny.

The other entertainers—Porter Wagoner, Archie Campbell, Jim Reeves, Webb Pierce, and myself—had to visit the radio stations to promote the show. It was part of the contract. The stations were selected by the promoter. At the first one, a station that played only "pop" music, the receptionist gave us a blank look and said, "May I help you?"

Since Jim Reeves was the headliner on the show, we had decided he would be the spokesman. Stepping up to the desk, he said, "Yes. I'm Jim Reeves." He expected some sign of recognition. None came. He went on. "This is Porter Wagoner . . . Archie Campbell . . . Webb Pierce . . ." He got no reaction. The girl said, "Did you say Webb Pierce?" She seemed excited now. Jim was completely flustered but started to continue. The girl jumped up from her desk and said, "Excuse me, I'll be right back," leaving Jim with a puzzled look on his face. Webb was smiling.

The girl came back. With her, a man who was searching the room with his eyes. "Which one of you is Webb Pierce?"

Webb stepped forward and they shook hands. For all the attention he paid to the rest of us, we could just as well have stayed on the beach. The reason for all the attention was that Webb's record "I Ain't Never" had crossed over the "country" category, and was being played "pop." None of the rest of us had been that lucky. Jim was so mad he flatly refused to go to the other stations. And that night, instead of Jim closing the show, it was Webb, at the radio station's request.

While we were in Panama City, everything was great, but the closer we got to home, the more edgy Harlan got. He said many times that he shouldn't have been out of town, because he probably missed getting a song recorded. Monday was the day that *Billboard* came out. We had to stop to buy one. I now felt guilty for even suggesting the trip.

We'd been home only a few days when Corky got sick. He'd had tonsillitis several times, but this time, the doctor said they had to come out. Corky almost backed out. But when I talked to him about not having any more sore throats, he agreed to have it done. Then we agreed on something else.

Jimmy and David had been circumcised when they were born but not Corky. And since he'd had some problems, we decided now was the time. Forgetting all about the tonsils, I overheard him questioning David. "What do they do when they circumcise you?"

David very nonchalantly answered, "Nothing to it . . . they just pull it out and cut it off."

Corky yelled, "Mom! I've changed my mind!"

The doctor reassured Corky that both operations were very "every day" and simple and he would be out of the hospital in no time. I watched as they gave him a shot and wheeled him down the corridor. *Nothing to worry about,* I thought. As the doctor says, they do it every day. Nevertheless, I anxiously watched the door to the operating room. After about an hour, the doctor came out.

"Your son is fine. He should be out of recovery in about an hour." He suggested I wait in Corky's room. I started to, then changed my mind and sat back down.

Looking at my watch, I realized it had been almost two hours. That seemed like an awfully long time for him to be in Recovery. The doors opened and the doctor who had operated on Corky came out again . . . this time with blood all over the front of his white coat. He was walking toward me! I jumped up. "What's happened?!"

"It's all right, Mrs. Howard. He's back in recovery."

"What do you mean back in recovery! You said that two hours ago!"

"Well, he hemorrhaged and we had to take him back in. But he's fine now and will be out shortly."

Back in his room, I sat beside Corky's bed and held his hand. He was still out cold, bless his heart. There were tubes and packing everywhere. I was told it was going to be such a routine operation. And now this. Leaning over, I kissed his forehead . . . He moaned. "Don't try to talk, honey. I'll be right here," I said. He was making motions toward the end of the bed. "Are you hurting?" Vigorously he was shaking his head no. Yet I knew he was. What in the world did he want? He was still trying to talk. I leaned over so I could hear. In a hoarse whisper, he asked, "Did they circumcise me?" So that's what he was worried about! I pulled back the covers. "No! They didn't!" He started to cry. "Don't tell them. Please don't tell 'em!" It was all I could do not to laugh. With all the pain I knew he was in, he was more concerned about whether they had "pulled it out and cut it off."

The phone woke me out of a sound sleep. Before picking it up, I glanced at the clock . . . it was 1:00 A.M. "Hello," I said.

"Jan?" It was Hank Cochran. "Are you all right?" I could hear concern in his voice.

"Yes, Hank. What's the matter?"

"Well," he said. "If it's not you, then it's Patsy."

"Hank, what are you talking about?"

"Fred Foster and I are sitting here in his office. You know those shelves in back of his desk?"

"Yes. What about them?"

"Two albums fell out . . . yours and Patsy Cline's. If you're all right, then something's wrong with Patsy." I knew those shelves. They had been made slanting down toward the wall so nothing could fall out. "Stay by the phone," he said, "I'll call you back."

Waiting for his call, I tried reading, gave it up, and turned on the radio.

An all-night disk jockey, Ralph Emory, was saying something about a plane being lost. Then he mentioned the names of the passengers. *Oh, my God.* It was Patsy, Hawkshaw Hawkins, Cowboy Copas, and Randy Hughes. Cowboy Copas's son-in-law, Patsy's manager, was the pilot of the plane. The phone rang again. Before Hank could talk, I said, "I've just heard . . . I'm going over to Jean's." Jean Shepard was married to Hawk and expecting a baby any time.

Driving over, I thought, *God! How could this be happening.* We were playing cards with Jean and Hawk just a few nights ago. That night, Hawk had asked us to go out to the barn with him where he kept his show horses and we watched as he put them all through their paces. One of them, he hadn't worked in eight years. When we asked why he was doing it then, he said, "Just so they won't get rusty."

Harlan was destroyed! He loved Hawk like a brother. The feeling was mutual. When Hawk would call Harlan, anyone listening in might not have gotten that impression. "Let me speak to that ugly son of a bitch you're married to" was Hawk's way of asking to speak to Harlan. Any other way wouldn't have been normal. He was so much a man, with a smile that reached from "here to yonder." It was unbelievable to think that anything could have happened to him.

A few nights before, Patsy had called and asked if I was coming to her recording session. "No, I hadn't planned to," I said.

"Why not?" she asked.

"Well, it might bug you."

"Hell, it won't bug me! Get your ass down there!" Then her voice took on a different tone, one I'd never heard before. "In fact, I'd like to have you there. Will you come?"

"Wild horses couldn't keep me away," I said.

After the session, everybody went to Owen Bradley's office. He was her producer. We listened to the playbacks. She'd recorded several but my favorite was "Faded Love." Lord, what a voice! Patsy was so proud. She'd laugh and say, "Play it *again*."

After listening to them over and over, she went into the adjoining office. Coming back, she held up a record. "Well, here it is, folks! The first and the last!"

"Patsy! Don't say that," I said.

She laughed that big laugh of hers. "Oh, hell, I just meant the first one and the most recent one." Nevertheless, her statement bothered me.

The next day, I saw her at the beauty shop getting her hair done to go to Kansas City to do a benefit. She seemed tired. "As soon as we get back," she said, "Charlie, Randy and Kathy, and I are flying to the Bahamas. I need a vacation."

"Are you going in Randy's plane?" I asked. It was a single-engine plane.

"Sure. What else?"

"I sure wish you wouldn't fly in that little thing," I said. "What if that one engine goes out?"

She laughed. "Well, I guess if the little bug goes down, I'll go down with it."

At six-thirty in the morning, we learned they had crashed near Dyersburg, Tennessee. All on board had been killed. The country music industry was shrouded in grief. For days, it was one funeral after another. Jack Anglin, one half of the Johnny and Jack duo, was killed in a car wreck on the way to Patsy's funeral.

The world had lost some great entertainers, but we had lost some dear friends.

Leaving the boys and Harlan in Solona's care, I rode to Elkins, West Virginia, with George Hamilton IV (another entertainer on the show). After the show, the only place to eat was a small café on the one main street. Starved, I ordered ham and eggs. Charlotte, North Carolina, was the next stop, and we were taking off as soon as we finished eating.

Barely out of town, I started getting sick. I'd remembered that the ham tasted funny but, hungry as I was, I'd eaten it anyway. Every few miles, whoever was driving would stop the car so I could throw up. Up and down the West Virginia mountains and around curves—oh, God, I was sick! All night long, I lay on the backseat with my head in George's lap, crying. "Well, Jan," he'd say, "I wish I could do something to help you."

We finally reached Charlotte about nine in the morning. I called a doctor immediately. The doctor suggested buttermilk and crackers. Ugh! All day long I'd sip awhile and throw up awhile. I called Hubert. "Hubert, I'm terribly sick and I've been throwing up all night. I'm so weak I can't move. How can I ever sing tonight?" I knew he'd understand.

"Sure you can, Redhead [with each successive trip to the hairdresser, my hair became more red than brown]. Just take a hot bath and you'll feel better. See you tonight." He hung up.

As I walked into the auditorium, he said, "See, I told you you could make it!"

"Yeah, Hubert," I said. "But I haven't tried to sing yet."

Onstage, every time I'd reach for a high note, I was positive the audience was going to be splattered with buttermilk and crackers. As I came off stage, Hubert said, "I thought you said you were sick? You never sang better!" He didn't mention the fact that I was green.

I'd planned to sleep in and catch a late flight, but when Hubert suggested going on a seven A.M. flight with him, I agreed. Still being scared to fly, I liked to have someone along for reinforcement. He said he'd pick me up at six.

I was up, dressed, and in the lobby waiting for him. As we got into the cab, he said, "I've got bad news."

"What's that?"

"Faron and Webb are going with us."

"What's bad about that?"

"They're both drunk," he said. "And still in their stage clothes. We have to pick them up at their motel." I didn't know if I was up to that pair this morning.

Pulling up to their motel, we saw them before they saw us. Sure enough, Webb still had on a black tuxedo and Faron was in a blue-sequined Western outfit. What a pair.

Hubert, Webb, and I sat in the backseat facing the driver. Faron, being his true, obnoxious self, was on a jump seat facing us. All the way to the airport, he used the foulest language he knew. "Just ignore him, Jan," Hubert kept saying.

Finally, I'd had all I could take and, ignoring Hubert's advice, said to Faron, "Shut your damned filthy mouth!" That was what he'd been waiting for.

"What's the matter? You too good to hear those words?"

Hubert tried to stop me, but I wouldn't be shushed. "Yes, too damned good!"

Faron turned to Webb—drunk or sober, Webb had always been a gentleman in front of me. "Who in the hell ever told you you could sing!" Faron said. "Where in hell would you have been without my band to back you up last night!"

Webb, not flustered at all, smiled and said, "I'd a just got up there and sang my thirteen number-one hits in a row." At that moment, we pulled in front of the airport.

Almost before we stopped, I jumped out and ran for the ticket counter. Without reservations, the only seats left were in Tourist. But I didn't care if it was on the wing . . . I grabbed my ticket and ran for the gate. Faron was right behind me. "I see you trying to run away from me," he hollered.

The plane was an Electra. First class was in the back and Tourist was in front. Handing the agent my ticket, I ran up the steps to the plane and quickly sat down in the first seat behind the bulkhead. I prayed Faron wouldn't see me when he got on. He just walked on back to First Class. Hubert and Webb came on next. Now that they were past, I turned to see where they were seated. Hubert sat down, but Webb and Faron were still standing there. The stewardess was trying to tell them that Tourist was up front and that's where they'd have to go. Faron threw a fit! "I *never* fly Tourist!" he said. "And I'm not going to now." By now, every passenger was watching. Suddenly, the plane started to move . . . Faron lost his balance, grabbed the stewardess, and they both fell to the floor! I've never seen a woman so mad in my life!

The stewardess ran up the aisle to the cockpit. The plane stopped immediately. In a few minutes, two policemen came aboard, walked to the back, and handcuffed Faron. As they started to do the same to Webb, he said, "I'll leave like a gentleman, thank you," and walked up the aisle toward the door. Faron was headed out, too, but with help of a police escort.

Another stewardess was standing next to my seat. "Do you know those people?" she asked.

"Never saw them before in my life," I said.

Then, just as Faron got even with my seat, he leaned down to me and said, "Jan, I want you to know you're my wife Hilda's favorite singer." The policeman then moved him along toward the exit.

In the back, I heard the stewardess say to Hubert, "You, too! Out!"

"Young lady," I heard him say, "I'll leave if you insist. But if you're asking me to leave because you think I'm drunk, you'd better look for another job." He stayed aboard. As Mom was fond of saying, "Such is life in the Far, Far West." I don't know what that meant but it seemed an apt remark.

The word was that no airline would let Webb and Faron aboard, so they chartered a plane home. It had been an expensive drunk.

As soon as I'd get home from a tour, I'd figure what I had made and begin dividing it up. So much for groceries; so much for house payments; so much for the boys' allowances and school expenses; so much for Solona and household expenses; so much for this and that. If anything was left over, it went to reduce the house mortgage. The only difference between here and California was that here we lived in a bigger house, drove a bigger car, paid bigger bills, and spent a lot of time away from home.

My Opry spots became spasmodic. Once in a while I'd work it, but not often. And I knew why. Not long before, I was asked to meet with a man of some importance in country music. "It's concerning the Opry," he said. I guessed I was going to be asked to become a member.

Sitting in his office, I anticipated the all-important question. "Jan," he said, "would you like to be a member of the Opry?" *Of course I would. Who wouldn't!* I tried to hide my excitement. Calmly, I said, "Yes, sir."

He leaned closer. "Well, you could be if you were a little nicer." It took me a minute to catch on. But when I did, I stood and said indignantly, "Sir, if I'm ever a member of the Opry, it will be on my singing talent—nothing else!" I walked out and drove home knowing I'd never be asked again.

From the day we'd had the basketball hoop installed at the end of the driveway, Jimmy had practiced every spare minute, every minute he wasn't playing golf, that is. His freshman year, he sat on the bench, his sophomore year he played now and then, by his junior year he was on the "A String" of Madison High's basketball team, and now he was a senior and captain of the team. Lord, they were growing up so fast. On the dining-room facing we'd scratched marks showing the boys' growth. And it seemed like lately I was the shortest one in the house (five feet four inches). I wasn't ready for this. Jimmy's goal was to be six feet tall. He now lacked only a couple of inches. Every time I'd have to buy him new clothes because he'd outgrown all the others, I'd wish his goal would wait awhile. To me they were still little boys and yet Jimmy was fixing to graduate.

One day, when I was standing at the sink washing dishes, I found how much Jimmy had grown. He came in, grabbed a wet dish towel, and popped it right on my rear end. Damn! I screamed, grabbed the dish towel away from him, and chased him down the hall, through the living room. Suddenly he stopped . . . and I stopped. Standing there with his hands on his hips, he grinned and said, "Tell me, what are you gonna do if you catch me?"

I stood there looking up at him, six inches taller than I was, and said: "The question never came up before."

"Well, it has now." He grabbed me around the waist and literally tossed me to the ceiling.

"Jimmy, put me down!" When he did, he ran out the door laughing. I stood there watching my tall, lanky son disappear around the corner of the house and thought, *From now on, I'll have to find a better way.*

As deeply as Jimmy was into sports, Corky was into the outdoors. He loved sports and attended every game. Had started to play football, but getting his tailbone fractured in his first game ended that. He still played baseball but his real love was to be out in the woods "listening to nature," as he put it. When he was thirteen—after his uncle Freddie had a heart attack—he spent the whole summer on the farm in West Plains, helping out. He loved it. Riding horses, haying, just being a farm boy.

Corky had a mind of his own, always did. From the time he was little, if his mind was made up nothing could change it. He kept his feelings inside. Many nights at two or three in the morning, I'd make the room rounds to cover them up or take a last minute look to make sure they were all right. Corky would usually be there lying on his back, arms folded beneath his head, staring at the ceiling. "Corky," I'd say. "What are you doing anyway?"

"Just thinking," he'd say.

"About what?"

"Just thinking."

David was a lot like me, easily hurt and overly sensitive. He was also very talented. From the time he was little, he was fascinated with music, art, and drama. Sometimes he'd watch operas or ballet for hours on the educational television channel. He liked classical music. At ten, we bought him a piano and his piano lessons continued until he was thirteen. But, like most kids, he didn't like to practice and quit. The thing that amazed me, though, was that even though he could play things like "Theme from Romeo and Juliet" by reading music, he couldn't play anything by ear. I used to be so puzzled by this. "Why not?" I'd ask.

"I don't know," he'd say, "I just can't." I didn't understand. But why shouldn't I? I couldn't read a note of music.

Because of his love of the "arts," Jimmy and Corky used to tease David a lot. I told them: "You'd better let up on him, one day you may have to borrow money from David."

Things were going so well between Harlan and me, I didn't even mind the guests we always seemed to have at the house. If a new writer whom Harlan was working with came to town, instead of going to a motel (which most of them couldn't afford), Harlan would bring him home. Yet I was as interested as he was in listening to their songs and watching talent begin to surface.

While we were still living in California, we used to go to a club where a young singer named Delane Bramlett worked. He was very good looking and had a fine voice, but he just couldn't seem to get anything going. We'd kept in touch and he showed up in Nashville . . . for two weeks. We thought if he made some demos for Harlan, someone would listen and see the same potential we saw.

Delane's hair was beautiful—brown, naturally wavy—but came down to his shoulders. Figuring that it would go against him, I said, "The hair has to go." He let me take him to a barber shop. Later, I felt bad when I'd catch him looking in the mirror and examining where his hair used to be. He wasn't nearly as thrilled as I was with his new collegiate haircut. "*Anything* for a recording contract," he said. But it didn't happen. After two weeks and polite listening from record company executives, he went back to Los Angeles. I decided next time I'd leave his hair alone.

Harlan was still on the board of directors of the Country Music Association. Their next meeting was in New York and he asked if I would like to go. I'd never been in New York and really looked forward to it. We were to be there only three days, but decided to make the most of it.

Checking into the Americana Hotel, our room was on the twenty-ninth floor. It scared the hell out of me! Since I was so horribly afraid of heights, I'd keep the drapes closed so I wouldn't have to look out the window. Standing by the elevator shaft, the wind sounded like a tornado. I didn't know which was worse, staying in the room or being caught in the elevator going down.

One day, Mrs. Charlie Lamb—her husband was also on the board—and I decided to go shopping at Saks Fifth Avenue. I needed some plain black satin pumps to go with a dress I'd brought with me.

I've always disliked large stores and this experience was no exception. Everything was so darned expensive, and there were floors and floors of it. All I wanted was to buy my shoes and get out.

Seating ourselves in the shoe salon, I looked around at all the nonsmiling faces and thought, *Gosh, did everyone get up on the wrong side of the bed this morning?* The shoe salesman walked over and, as if he was irritated that I was there, asked, "Yes . . . what can I get you?"

"I'd like some plain black satin pumps," I said.

Coming back a few minutes later, his arms were burdened down with boxes. "Are those all plain black satin?" I asked.

"No . . . of course not," he said.

"But that's all I'm interested in."

Taking out a pair that was covered with rhinestones, he started to put one on my foot. "Try this," he said, completely ignoring me. A scowl was on his face.

"Sir," I said, slipping my foot back into my own shoe, "I've figured it out."

"Figured what out?"

"You've never been to smile school."

Staring at me like I'd lost my mind, he said, "What school?"

Leaning over close to his face, I touched the corners of my mouth and lifted them into a smile. "See, that's the way it's done, now you practice and after you've learned, maybe you can teach everyone else in this store. It's really easy and things will look up." I got up and walked away. But, before reaching the door, I turned. I saw the shoe salesman scratching his head and smiling. I guess he'd never met anyone from Tennessee before.

It was 1965. Even without a contract, I was still doing okay. Maybe I wasn't a big star, but with the experience I'd gotten, I was able to hold my own with anyone else on the show. I'd love to have had my own band, but there wouldn't have been much money to bring home if I had. Ego had to take a backseat. Five or six hundred dollars a night (which was a lot of money to me) wouldn't go very far toward paying a band, transportation, and expenses. Marty Robbins told me one time, "Jan, don't ever work without at least one man." I couldn't afford to. I knew when I sang the songs onstage, they didn't sound like the record, but I just hoped the audience would understand. One inspirational song I sang, "Where No One Stands Alone," received encores more times than not. Eventually, it became my closing song. The words told me that God would be there holding my hand, "every day, all the way." It was the one song that my boys asked me to sing for them.

One day, Harlan came home with the news that he had spoken to Owen Bradley and that Owen was interested in signing me. I couldn't believe it. He was one of the greatest producers in the business. But then I thought, *Jan, you're being silly. A man like that doesn't go to artists . . . they go to him.*

Gathering up what demos we thought would be suitable for me, Harlan and I went to Owen's office, where we discussed the songs. I sat there like a bump on a log waiting for their decision. One of the songs chosen was a song called "What Makes a Man Wander," which Harlan had written and arranged and I had made the demo on. Of the four, it was my favorite.

Going into the studio with Owen was a lot different from my last experience. Giving the deceiving appearance of being easygoing, he was all business. And that was important to me.

Owen is a great musician, and once had had his own orchestra. Sitting at the piano, he'd play the song, I'd sing it, and the musicians would get an idea of how it went. Then, when Owen got up to go into the control room, it was time to get down to business.

I was surrounded with some of the top musicians: Grady Martin on guitar, Bobby Moore on bass, Buddy Harmon on drums, Floyd Cramer on piano, Owen's brother Harold Bradley on bass guitar, and Buddy Emmons on steel guitar. The voices were the great Jordinaires. I couldn't have been happier. When it was over, we knew "What Makes a Man Wander" was a hit! Harlan and Owen had been right.

Jimmy graduated in June 1965 and you've never seen a happier, prouder family. Harlan parted with his jeans for the occasion and was dressed in a dark suit. I wore a white linen dress, and Corky and David wore their Sunday best. Sitting there in the auditorium of Madison High School watching Jimmy as he walked down the aisle, tears filled my eyes. *My son,* I thought. *It's been a long, hard row but we made it.*

Afterwards we hurried to get back to the house before Jimmy so we could see his reaction to the baby blue Corvair we'd bought for his graduation present. Waiting on the sun deck, we heard Jimmy hollering before we even saw him. As he jumped out of his friend's car he'd seen the Corvair, which was tied with a big red ribbon! He ran over, sat in it, patted it, and kissed it— everything but put his arms around it—and he tried that. Then he came running up the steps. He threw his arms around Harlan and me and said, "You're the best Mom and Dad in the world!" Harlan handed him the keys and said, "It's all yours, son." Oh, God, I was so happy!

Being on the road so much and with lots to do at home, Harlan and Don suggested we hire a secretary for Wilderness, a girl named Donna Gail who was divorced and had a child to support. She seemed like a good choice to me. But when I saw her, I got a strange feeling. She looked a lot like me! How weird. Of course her hair was a lot darker, but there was something about her. Her eyes, maybe.

After I'd spent a couple of weeks training Gail, Harlan said there was no need for me to come to the office anymore except for demo sessions. I felt as though I'd been dismissed. And I had been.

That summer, it came as a surprise to the kids when I told them that part of growing up was earning their own spending money. Obviously, it had never occurred to them.

Jimmy got a job at a tool and dye company and despised it. The only dirt he cared about was what he picked up when playing football. Factory dirt was different. When he got home, he never even said hello until he'd showered for ten minutes and changed clothes. The vigor with which he threw his clothes in the laundry indicated he was wishing it were an incinerator.

Corky was just the opposite. Lying about his age, he got a job as a laborer on a construction gang. Coming home, he'd have enough cement on him to pave a driveway and stayed that way until a place was refused him at the dinner table until he showered and changed. He could have cared less. And if I washed his jeans, he say, "But they were just getting broke in!" Jimmy called him a slob . . . but Corky also called Jimmy a snob. True brotherly love.

After a few weeks, Corky's boss found out how old he was and had to let him go because he was "child labor." But he called and said, "As soon as he's old enough, I want him back. I've never seen such a good worker." After he lost the job, Corky got out the lawn mower and went to work mowing lawns for anyone who would pay his price.

Being young, David got off easy. But, so he wouldn't feel left out, I'd hire him to do things around the house and yard. Jobs or no jobs, there were still rules to be followed at home. After Solona's two-week "vacation," I'd realized that I couldn't do everything, and assigned specific jobs to everyone.

Each boy was responsible for his own room. If he wanted to live in a "pig pen," it was up to him. Once a week, Solona or I would "rake" it out, but otherwise we didn't enter.

If they had dirty clothes, they put them out in the hall. That way, the clothes that they'd put on but then changed their minds and didn't hang up, didn't get washed. It saved a lot of unnecessary ironing. Since they used the rec room, they cleaned it up.

Each night before Solona left, she'd have dinner ready on the table. Afterward, each of the boys took turns washing dishes.

I took care of our bedroom and mine and Harlan's clothes, did what cooking Solona didn't do, and whatever else was necessary. All in all, it worked out fine. In fact, it was fun having everybody pitching in together.

Sunday was the "day of rest." For a while, I tried to cook a big Sunday dinner, but when I found that I was spending half the day cooking and the other half cleaning up instead of doing things with my family, we decided it was either Morrison's Cafeteria or "everyone for themselves."

One of the entertainers I worked a lot with was Bill Anderson. Ever since he'd stayed at our house in California, we'd been good friends. And now that we were both being booked by Hubert Long, it was natural to put us together.

Sometimes between shows, or if I happened to be riding on his bus, we'd sit around and sing to pass the time. We often sang a song called "I Know You're Married But I Love You Still"— strictly country. The more we sang it, the more we liked it and began talking about the possibility of recording it together. After all, we were both on the same recording label, Decca, and our voices seemed to blend.

After discussing it between ourselves and with Harlan, we decided to approach Owen. Since Bill and I both had had hit singles and it would only double our exposure, he agreed to a trial single.

After listening to tons of songs, we went with "I Know You're Married" and another Harlan wrote called "Time Out." After listening to the words of the latter, "Let's take time out to get acquainted again, we're man and wife, we might as well be friends," I wondered if Harlan had written it for us.

As soon as the record was released, it began to climb the national charts and Hubert was asked, more and more, to put us on shows together. This was great with me. Working with Bill, I didn't have to face the poor local bands which I had ended up with night after night. Even when I was working with a great band, if they didn't know my material, the results weren't good.

Ever since I found that I was able to do it, I loved to sing harmony and did it every chance I got. Even on other people's sessions. Especially, Johnny Cash, whom I'd known since 1957, and who gave me some of my first work on the road—and Porter Wagoner. Porter and I were from the same hometown, and I liked his music. But Owen was not in favor of it: "The uniqueness of your voice is the reason I signed you, not so it could be spread all over other people's records." When I said I'd just blend in and not try to stand out, he agreed. Later, when I told Jimmy Capps, another musician, that, he laughed and said, "Jan, your voice would stand out in the Mormon Tabernacle Choir." Some people had described my voice as strong. Tommy Jackson, a fiddle player, said I must be three fourths lungs. But I couldn't see it. Different maybe, but not strong.

One night, I was scheduled to work a Johnny Cash session and decided to wear my brand new strawberry blond wig. They had just become the "in" thing and mine was real hair and cost four hundred dollars! But, damn, what you had to go through to get it on! First, I had to cut off the top of a stocking, cram all my hair up under it, then put the wig on, and secure it with bobby pins all around. It was so tight, I felt I'd pinned it to my scalp instead of the stocking. I sure didn't want a gust of wind to come along and take it off.

The Cash sessions were supposed to be closed, but there was always a lot of his favorite people hanging around. One of them was Tom Pall Glaser.

As I joined the group around the piano, I heard Anita Carter say, "You'd better not, she'll kill you." I went right on singing my part. Suddenly Tom Pall grabbed the wig and jerked it off! I screamed and grabbed my head . . . not so much from embarrassment, but I thought I'd been scalped! And I was furious! Grabbing the first thing in sight, a beer bottle, I leveled it at Tom and said, "You dirty son of a bitch. I'll *kill* you!"

He was already almost out of the door but I followed him screaming, "And don't ever come near me again!" I ran to the bathroom. Since my hair was such a mess from the stocking, there was nothing else to do but put the damned wig back on.

It was obvious I had been crying. One of the musicians, coming out of his startled silence, said, "The bastard."

A few days later, two dozen long-stemmed red roses, each one with a typewritten "I'm Sorry" in it, were delivered to my house. My head had quit hurting, and I couldn't help it, I laughed. Picking up the phone, I called Tom Pall's house. As he answered and heard my voice, there was silence. Then, hearing me say, "You're forgiven," he said, "Oh, Jan, I'm sorry! It was a sick joke. I thought it would be funny but I had no idea that damned thing was pinned to your head!" He said he had left the studio and it was three days before someone found him drunk in a motel room. We agreed on two things. He would never touch my head again and I would never wear the wig again. I gave it to David to use for a prop in The Children's Theater.

For a couple of years now, we'd belonged to a private club in Madison called Oak Valley. Swimming pool, badminton, roller-skating, Ping-Pong, picnic grounds—everything for family fun. In the summer, when the kids weren't at home, they were there. After a few times, though, Harlan got bored with it and said he preferred fishing. That was all right. Corky and David liked to fish, too and sometimes he'd take them along. But Harlan and Jimmy's "sport" was playing chess. For hours, they'd sit, staring at that board, before either of them would make a move. I tried to learn the game, but after a few times gave it up.

All three of the boys loved to swim. They got their life-saving badges. Good, because I was frightened to death of water after literally almost drowning three times—once in a river when I was thirteen, once when some boys threw me off the high diving board, and once in the ocean off Malibu beach in California when I'd gotten caught in the undertow. If my brother Junior hadn't been watching and called the lifeguards, I'd have been a goner. All I remember about it, besides not being able to breathe, is coming to in one of those little red rescue units with an oxygen mask over my face. Now, except for washing my face and taking a shower, I don't like water over my head

Jimmy had taken a job of lifeguard at Oak Valley. I was all dressed to go onstage at the Opry but had promised one of his friends I'd drop by the pool and bring him a message. It was the last day the pool was open.

Walking around the pool to where Jimmy was, I saw three of his friends coming toward me, smiling. Jimmy came down from his perch and joined them. Without warning, they all grabbed me and, stage clothes, shoes, and all, threw me in the water . . . in the deep end! Each time I came up, I hollered, "I'll brain every one of you!" They stood there laughing and Jimmy said, "Look, Mom! You're swimming!" Then, they jumped in to pull me out.

There was no way I could work. Calling the Opry manager, I said I had a bad cold. He'd never have believed the real story.

September came and Jimmy started college at M.T.S.U. in Murfreesboro, Tennessee, about thirty-five miles from home. For a while, I'd worried that he might want to go off somewhere but he loved his home and church too much for that. We paid for a room in the dorm but it was a waste of money. He came home on Wednesday afternoon and went back Thursday morning. On Friday afternoon he was back till Monday morning, I was actually glad, for a lot of sunshine was missing when he wasn't there.

One day, he and I were standing out on the sun deck watching our dog Bucko stretched out in the sun in the backyard. He had grown so big, he resembled a lion. Weighing a hundred and thirty-nine pounds, the vet said he was the largest thoroughbred collie he'd ever seen. Jimmy said, "You know, Mom, we should have an oil painting done of Bucko. You never know when something might happen to him."

That Christmas, the portrait of Bucko was our special gift to the boys, and it was hung over the fireplace in the den.

Bucko was the gentlest dog ever, but with the rough way my boys and all their friends played with him, he had to be rough to hold his own. His favorite game with Corky was "tug o' war," where Corky would get a stick, Bucko would sink his teeth into it, and drag him all over the yard. If Corky didn't have a stick, Bucko would use his jeans. A lot of time was spent sewing up the legs of jeans.

The boy who delivered the cleaning was scared to death of Bucko and would pick up a stick to ward off any attempt at friendliness. Bucko, seeing the stick, would make right for it. "Honey," I said, "he thinks you want to play. If you won't carry that stick, he won't bother you."

"That's fine if you're right, Mrs. Howard," he said. "But what if you're wrong and I don't have my stick?" I had to admit he had a point.

The only time Bucko ever attempted to harm anyone was when a boy shot him with a BB gun from a bicycle. With one leap, Buck grabbed the boy's jeans in his teeth and dragged him halfway across the yard. When the boy finally got loose, he ran screaming down the street. I knew, shortly, I'd have an angry mother on my hands. Sure enough, within a few minutes, a car screeched to a stop in the driveway. A woman jumped out and, wagging a finger in my face, said, "You've got a vicious dog."

"No, lady. You've got a vicious kid. If you keep him penned up, I'll do the same with our dog."

As she angrily backed out of the driveway, I yelled after her, "Are you sure your son has had his rabies shots?"

For safety's sake and to avoid any further incidents, we had a chain-link fence installed around the backyard. At the cost of six hundred dollars, it was finished and Bucko was in his private "prison." We all stood and watched to see how he would take to it. He'd look at us, walk around the yard a bit from the fence to the middle and back again, then look at us again. About the time we were all feeling a bit guilty, he went back to the middle . . . stood there a minute . . . then in a few well-measured bounds came toward the fence at a dead run and cleared it! When he did, he turned to look at us as if to say, "There."

The next day the fence was torn down and given to Anita and Don Davis.

Don Bowman, one of the writers for Wilderness and a darned good comedian, came to the house a lot. Mostly to try to get Harlan to help him with a song. But Harlan, except for rare occasions, wouldn't co-write with anyone and would hand the song to me, especially if it needed a melody. One night, when Don had written the complete lyrics and I'd put the melody to them, I asked Harlan if I could have my name on it instead of his. "What for?" he said, giving me the same old answer. "It all goes in the same pot. Besides, it'll mess up the bookkeeping."

Don brought Harlan a tape made by a friend of his, Waylon Jennings. Waylon lived in Pheonix, Arizona, but he and Don had known each other since they both lived and worked as disk jockeys in Lubbock, Texas. Harlan, playing the tape for me, asked, "What do you think?"

"I love it," I said. "His voice is different." We both agreed the songs were worth investing the money in for a demo session.

With some positive reaction from the session, Harlan suggested that Waylon come to Nashville, do his own session, and see if they could get some attention for him as an artist.

He stayed at the house for ten days and he and Harlan made the rounds. His hair was long, like Delane Bramlett's.

For some time now, Harlan had been edgy. He didn't have a decent word to say to anyone, especially me. Nothing I did was satisfactory. The way I dressed. The way I wore my hair. Several times, I tried to talk to him but, denying anything was wrong, he refused. "My mind's messed up with songs," he'd say. Or, "I'm having a dry spell." That meant he wasn't writing. "It'll wear off," he'd say. Or, "I need to go fishing." Anything but talk. I suggested my quitting the road. It was the wrong thing to say! "Don't be ridiculous! We need the money!" Hell, we didn't need the money. Practically every song we demo'd got recorded and the publishing company was going great. Money was pouring in. "That money can't be touched," Harlan said. "It belongs to the company." I heard the thousandth time: "It's for our retirement." Hell, if I had to work until I was sixty-five to enjoy some of it, why bother.

A demo session had been set up for six o'clock to do some of Waylon's songs and some of Harlan's. Solona was off, and while I was doing housework and fixing dinner, they were in the den going over songs.

As they were eating, Harlan said to me, "You know, the session's at six."

"I know, Harlan, but I can't do everything. I'll just have to be a little late."

After they left, I changed clothes, put myself together, and drove myself to the studio, arriving about six-thirty. As I walked in, Harlan handed me some lyrics and said, "The band already knows this, see if you can sing it."

I looked at the title and said, "Harlan! I've never even heard this song!" He knew I could learn a song in five minutes, but five minutes hadn't elapsed. I asked the band to run over it with me. After once or twice, I walked to the mike and started singing what I thought was the melody.

Harlan came out of the control room, jerked the lyrics off the music stand, and said, "If you can't sing the damned song, I'll get someone who can!" He handed the lyrics to Anita Carter, who was always there to sing harmony. That did it. Trying not to show how much he'd embarrassed and hurt me, I said, "Okay, Harlan, if that's the way you want it, I'll go home. Furthermore, I'll stay home from here on. You can do the damned demos yourself!" I walked out.

Much later, after I was in bed, he came home. I could tell by the smell and the way he walked that he'd been drinking. I lay there, pretending to be asleep. I felt him turn down his side of the bed and crawl in. Then he reached for me. For weeks he'd acted like I was the most unappealing woman in the world and now he'd decided to make love to me! Getting no response from me, within minutes he was asleep and snoring. I lay there wondering what had happened to the "perfect couple." I knew one thing—I was tired of being used, misused, and mentally abused! Before I drifted off to sleep, I knew that we had to talk, and soon.

Up before he was, I was waiting for Harlan in the den. He came out, coffee in hand, and sat down at his desk.

"Harlan," I said, "we've got to talk." He looked uncomfortable but didn't answer. Trying to make it easier, I walked over and sat down on the desk facing him.

"I'm sorry, L.G.," he said.

"I know you are, Harlan, but you've used the same words so

many times, they've lost their meaning." He started to pick up his guitar, but I stilled it with my hand. "No, Harlan . . . don't pick up the guitar. We've got to talk this out—now."

He still hadn't said a word. I had another idea . . . one I'd been thinking about for quite a while. "Remember that trip to New Orleans we've been talking about? Let's take it—just us." That brought some response.

"Yeah," he said, "that's a good idea. Let's do it." He wasn't jumping up and down but it was a start.

We packed that night and planned to leave bright and early the next morning for the drive down. Before the kids were awake, we went out to put the luggage in the car. There, on one of the suitcases, was a note. *Dear Mom and Dad,* it read. *We want you to have a good time and don't worry about us. Solona's here and we'll be fine. We love you.* Signed, *Your loving sons, Jimmy, Corky, and David.* Bless their hearts. They knew something was wrong and thought this would fix it. I desperately hoped so.

At first, the trip was strained, but the farther we got from Nashville, the better it got. Every few days, Harlan would call Don Davis or the secretary and we'd call the kids and Solona, but other than that no one knew where we were. It was great! Spending the days sight-seeing and the nights having dinner in one of the wonderful New Orleans restaurants and wandering around the French Quarter, we really started to unwind. I think it was the closest we'd ever been. On the drive home, we made a pact. Nothing, or no one, would come between us again.

The kids could tell the difference immediately. They tried so hard to give Harlan the quiet he needed to write so he could be home instead of at the office all the time.

The last couple of sessions I'd recorded hadn't been what we'd wanted. Maybe the songs just weren't good enough. Or, if they were, they didn't fit me. And Owen, since I wasn't Brenda Lee or Loretta Lynn, didn't really know what to do with me. I asked him to just accept me for what I was—Jan. I couldn't be anyone else if I tried. We agreed not to record again until the right song came along. Harlan wrote that song. One called "Evil on Your Mind." The lyrics were sort of tongue in cheek about a man telling his wife she should go and visit her sister "way out West." But she caught on and said the only reason he wanted her to go was that he had "evil on his mind." We laughed about it. Not so long ago that had almost fitted us, but not anymore.

We demo'd seven songs and Owen chose three of those for my next session. Within weeks, "Evil" was number one in the nation. There was a picture of me in the paper which Frances Preston of BMI cut out and mailed to me with this caption: "A cute gal with a great song! Congratulations!"

Now, the dates poured in. If I thought I'd been busy before, it was a vacation compared to now. And every time I'd refuse one, Harlan would call Hubert and tell him to ignore me. "You've got to make it while you can in this business," he'd say. I hated to be away from home so much, but the boys took it in stride. Now and then, when I'd get to a motel, there would be a dozen roses waiting for me—from Jimmy, Corky, and David. I'd get the bill when I got home, but it was the thought that counted.

I was asked to do a tour, along with several other artists, that ended at the Hollywood Bowl, in L.A. The promoter was Jerry Purcell—a slick New York type and not really likable. In Louisiana, Texas, and New Mexico, primarily due to the lack of promotion, the shows were losers. By the time we got to L.A., he was fit to be tied.

Rehearsal for all seventeen acts was set for two-thirty. The night before, I'd stayed with Joe Allison and his wife, Audrey. I called a cab in plenty of time, but I waited and waited. And waited some more . . . No cab. I hate to be late for anything, and knowing how mad Purcell was going to be didn't help. Finally, the cab arrived and when we got to the Hollywood Bowl, I said, "Just let me out here. I'll run the rest of the way!"

Jumping seats and running down aisles, I saw a whole bunch of people onstage. *Good,* I thought, *they're all waiting to rehearse.* Climbing up on the stage, I asked one of the musicians if I was too late and he said, "Hell, no! We've only rehearsed one! There's sixteen to go." I turned and ran smack dab into Jerry Purcell! "Hi, Jerry!" I said, smiling.

He lit into me like a match to a Roman candle! "Where in the hell have you been? Do you know you've cost me two hundred dollars in overtime? I'll see that you never work another show!" and so on. So embarrassed I could die, I turned and ran to the dressing room. When someone came and said it was my turn to rehearse, I went out and was told to do eight minutes. Exactly!

When I finished, Purcell looked at his watch and said, "Be here at six-thirty!" I was so mad I could have killed him.

Later, when I arrived from Joe's house, I walked up to Jerry Purcell and said, "Look at your watch, Mr. Purcell! It's six o'clock and I'm here." Leaving him with a blank look on his face, I turned and went into the dressing room.

Standing, waiting to go on, my anger at Jerry Purcell was the only thing I could think about. It's just as well. If I'd thought about appearing at the Hollywood Bowl, I probably would have succumbed to stage fright.

After my last song, "Evil on Your Mind," the audience broke into applause and my satisfaction was complete. Almost. Jerry walked up to me and said, "Jan, could I talk to you?" His tone was entirely different from that afternoon.

"No, Jerry, you said all I wanted to hear, and more, this afternoon."

"That's what I want to talk to you about. Would you step outside?"

I walked outside the dressing rooms where they sold hot dogs and hot chocolate, got one of each, and sat down on a nearby bench. Jerry sat down next to me.

"Jan," he said, "I want to apologize."

After that tour, I was ready to be home for a while, and get back to normal. An entertainer lives in a "fantasy" world. The real world is with real people. Being treated like a "star" was okay on the road, but at home I was just "Mom" or "L.G." and that's the way I liked it. The kids had even been brought up to know that entertainers were just people who made their livings a different way. No better, no worse than everybody else. Corky brought home one of my albums one day and said, "Coach Anderson wants you to sign this." "Why."

"Let's humor him," I said as I scrawled my name.

David had been in the theater for a couple of years and I never was sure when he was acting. "David," I said. "You've got to learn to come off stage."

"I don't know what you mean," he said.

"Okay, here's a good example. Yesterday, I was in Detroit singing in front of twenty-four thousand people. Today I'm home washing dishes. That's what they call 'coming off stage.'"

I was out in the den plunking away on my three chords when Harlan walked in. "Listen to the song I just wrote!" I said, all excited. Reluctantly, he sat down. Halfway through, I saw that he wasn't paying the least bit of attention. "Won't you please listen and at least give me your opinion?"

When I finished, I said, "Well?"

"Well, it's nothing to write home about," he said, and got out his legal pad to do his own writing.

"Will you help me with it?"

"L.G., why don't you leave the writing to me?"

"But, you help other writers." I was disappointed.

"But you're not a writer! Stick to singing!" End of conversation.

Not being one to give up, a couple of days later I asked if he would play guitar for me to put it down on tape. To humor me, he did. Then I had one more favor to ask. "The next time you play songs for Owen, will you play this for him?" Surprisingly enough, he did. Secretly, I suspected it was to get a turndown so I'd forget it. But it didn't turn out that way. Owen chose it for Kitty Wells's next release. I knew it was no "Stardust" or "Deep Purple" but also knew it was a heck of a lot better than some demos I'd made.

Hubert called and asked if I wanted to go to Charlotte and be a guest on Bill Anderson's TV show. Ever since it began a year before, Jean Shepard had been a regular but now she was going to quit, and several different females were guesting the show. I was beginning to think he'd never ask me.

The show went so well, I jokingly told Bill, "If you ever want another girl singer, let me know."

After the fiasco at the Hollywood Bowl, I never expected to hear from Jerry Purcell again. But I got my list of dates and, low and behold, there was one for him in Islip, Long Island. I called Hubert and said the only way I would do it was for double the money. No one was more surprised than I when he accepted it.

Warner Mack was also on the show. He and I flew up to New York together. The weather was bad and we arrived late. To top it off, the only way we could get out to Islip, Long Island, was to go into New York and transfer to an "Island" cab. But, once there, when the drivers found where we wanted to go, they all shook their heads. "Doesn't anyone here go to Long Island?" I asked.

"Yeah . . . by helicopter," one driver said. This was crazy! Looking across the street, I saw a limousine and ran over to it. "Are you busy?" I asked. He shook his head. I was beginning to wonder if anyone could talk. "Do you wanta be?" He nodded his head. "How much to Islip?" He held up six fingers. "You gotta deal!"

As we entered the racetrack where the show was being held, I saw Jerry Purcell looking out the window of the trailer set up for temporary dressing rooms. Asking Warner for thirty-seven fifty, I counted out my half, gave the driver a fifteen-dollar tip, jumped out, and ran up to Jerry, holding out my arm and pointing to my watch. "See, I'm here and I'm not late!" Nevertheless, it turned out to be the last date I ever worked for him.

Harlan, once again, was on the board of the Country Music Association and was going to their meeting in Los Angeles. This time, I had to ask him if I could go.

Not very long after getting back from New Orleans, the pact we'd made was forgotten, Harlan had slipped right back into his old routine of staying three or four days a week on Center Hill Lake and the rest of the time at the office. Lately, he didn't even bother coming home to change. He kept clothes at the office. Sometimes, the kids wouldn't see him for three weeks at a time. If he were home, he'd be asleep when they left for school and gone when they got home. They often asked about him, but eventually I ran out of excuses. I just said, "I don't know." Not since New Orleans had he attempted to be a husband.

In front of other people, we tried to act like nothing was wrong, but in the privacy of our bedroom it was different. We couldn't talk without arguing. I usually ending up crying. Suddenly, after a phone call from Harlan's manager, Don Davis, he did a complete about-face. I was so happy, I didn't even question it.

Harlan's explanation was, "I've just had so many things on my mind, I guess I took it out on you and the boys. Can you forgive me?" He didn't have to ask twice.

By the time we got home, things were almost like normal. I didn't understand. Did we have to stay out of town to get along?

Usually, if I was working a Johnny Cash session, Harlan would be right in the middle of it, but not tonight. He said he had some work to do and didn't explain further. Pitching songs, I supposed.

Right in the middle of the session, John said, "Jan, do you know the words to that song of Harlan's?" I knew the one he was talking about, the one he'd been holding for seven years.

"No, John, but I can run over to the office and get them. I'll be right back." The office was only five minutes away. Anita Carter went with me.

Opening the door with my key, I turned on the light in the reception room and went to the file cabinet. Then I saw a light coming from under the door to Don Davis's office. *Guess he's working late,* I thought, and began going through the files. Suddenly, I heard a woman laugh. Then, Harlan. Walking back to the closed door, I opened it and saw a sight not meant for my eyes. A woman was sitting on Don's desk with her dress up around her hips and Harlan was standing in front of her with his arms around her. I couldn't have moved if I'd tried.

When Harlan saw me, even in the dark his face turned white. It was like everyone in the room had been turned to stone. Then I found my voice. Surprisingly it was calm.

"Don't you have a home?" I asked. She, too, had found part of her body and was trying to pull her dress down. Harlan hadn't moved. I turned, went back to the files, got the lyrics, and went back to the studio. Neither Anita nor I said a word. I guess she was too embarrassed and I couldn't talk.

Walking into the studio, I handed the lyrics to John and went over to the microphone where the rest of the singers were standing. Anita whispered something in John's ear. At that moment, Harlan walked in the back door. But, before he got across the room, John said to him, "Harlan, I think you'd better leave." There was no way I could finish the session and, after a few minutes, I left and went home.

All night I waited and thought. And thought. I'd seen some signs on his clothes. With so much at stake, I kept hoping I was wrong. Our lives, the boy's lives, our home . . . everything.

The next day, after the boys were gone, he walked up the steps to the sun deck. Trying to keep busy, I was sitting at the kitchen table paying bills. He motioned for me to follow him into the den. Shutting the door, I watched as he laid his head on the desk and began to cry. I couldn't stand it. I was so hurt my insides were bleeding, but I had never seen Harlan cry before. Walking over, I put my arms around him and said, "What's happened to us, Harlan?" He didn't answer. Just held on to me. After he calmed down, he took my hand and led me over to the sofa. "L.G., I don't know what got into me. I swear to you, it's over. I fired the girl. She won't be back in the office." I didn't believe him, but he thought I did. It's hard to let something drown that's trying to survive. That time in Chicago, Joe Allison had said a man deserved a second chance. What about a third, a fourth?

For two weeks, Harlan stuck to the house like glue. He took the boys fishing, all of us out to dinner and to the movies. He couldn't do enough for us. I thought, *He is really trying. Should I dare believe him?* I didn't know.

One day Don called and asked me to meet him and Harlan at the office of Bill Carpenter, our attorney, something about the Internal Revenue, and Wilderness being a holding corporation. I couldn't surmise what had come up now.

When I walked in, I could see all three of them huddled in a deep conversation. Seeing me, they stopped talking and, very businesslike, Harlan offered me a chair.

"Don, what's this all about?" I asked.

"Well, Jan, the Internal Revenue has raised the question, since you and Harlan own equally all the shares to Wilderness, as to whether this makes it a personal holding corporation." I didn't know what the heck he was talking about.

"What's this got to do with me?" I looked questioningly at Harlan, but he was sitting there running his thumb and first finger around each other in a nervous habit he had.

"Well, until we get this straightened out, we need you to sign over your fifty shares." Seeing my look of concern, he quickly added, "It's nothing to worry about. Just the usual formality." He shoved some papers across the desk to me.

"What about Harlan's shares?" I asked.

"Oh, they'll be handled a little differently, but it'll end up the same." Once more, I looked to Harlan for help. But he got up and walked over to the window and stood there with his back to me.

"Harlan, what do you think?" I asked.

Without turning around, Harlan said "Well, L.G., you know Don handles all the business."

"Okay, Don," I said, "I'll take these home, look them over, and bring them to you when I get back in town Monday." I started to put the papers in my purse but Don stopped me.

"Jan, I hate to insist, but we only have until midnight tonight to get these in the mail. It'll be all right, I promise."

I wish I knew more about this stuff, I thought, *but surely Harlan knows what he's doing.* I signed "Lula G. Howard" where the X was. "Are you finished with me?" I asked.

Don was putting the papers I'd just signed in an envelope. "Yeah, Jan. You can go now." He was smiling. For the first time since I'd walked into that office.

All the way home, I thought what a strange meeting that had been. Bill Carpenter and Harlan had neither one said a word. They just let Don do all the talking. But, then, when Don was around that's the way it usually was.

The kids were all gone somewhere, and by the time I was ready to leave for the airport, Harlan still wasn't home. Quickly, I wrote a note. "Dear H.P. I hate to leave before you get home but I have to. Have a good weekend and I'll see you Monday. Love, L.G." Laying it on his pillow, I lugged the suitcases out to the car.

The past two days had seemed like a month. Even Bill had noticed my nervousness. "What's the matter with you?" he asked.

"I don't know," I said, "but something isn't right at home. I just know it." *This is crazy,* I thought. I'd called and talked to David and Solona. Everything was all right except that Harlan hadn't been home. He was probably up on the lake. Somehow, though, I couldn't get that feeling out of my gut.

Bill and the band were going on somewhere else from there, and I took the first flight out.

My car was at the airport and the suitcases, which had weighed a ton when I left, now seemed to weigh nothing as I ran to where it was parked. I had to get home!

Usually, I drove around to the back but today I parked in front. And not even bothering with the luggage, I jumped out and ran in the front door. Bucko was the only one there to greet me. Not even Solona. But this was Monday. Well, everything looked normal. Perhaps it was my imagination after all.

Walking into the bedroom, a note, laying on my pillow, caught my eye. Thinking it was from the kids telling me where they were, I picked it up and began to read. "Dear Jan (not L.G.?): I want to travel. I'm going to Mexico. I prefer to forget you and the boys ever existed. Don't try to find me. Harlan." Quickly, I ran to the den. His guitars were gone. Back to the bedroom. I opened his side of the closet . . . his clothes were gone. I read the note, which was still in my hand, but my brain couldn't comprehend what it was saying! Slowly at first, then like a flood, the tears rolled down my face. "How could you do this, Harlan? How could you do this?"

I was still sitting on the bed, the note in my hand, when Jimmy came in. Seeing the look on my face, he took the note and read it. "That son of a bitch!" he said. Then he sat down, put his arms around me, and let me cry my heart out.

Four days later, I hadn't washed my face, taken a bath, combed my hair, or come out of my room. The only food I ate was what the kids and Solona forced me to eat. It might as well have been cardboard.

The house, which usually was filled with laughter, was filled with whispers from the kids and Solona. It was as though a death had occurred.

The kids would come in, sit on the edge of my bed, and, not saying anything, just pat me or kiss me, or let me cry. I knew I was upsetting them but couldn't help it. The world I'd tried so hard to preserve had crumbled around me and, once more, my sons' lives and mine had been torn apart. Oh, God!

Harlan had bought a boat house on Center Hill Lake. He hadn't told me but, in conversation, someone else had. It was Friday and I knew he'd be there.

On the seventy-mile trip, I tried to rehearse what I was going to say. Surely, by now, he must be having second thoughts. No one could just walk out without a backward glance!

Driving up to the dock, I asked for directions to Harlan's place. The man pointed to something that looked like a Quonset hut sitting in the water at the edge of the lake. My hand was shaking as I knocked on the door.

It opened and Harlan's smile froze. "What the hell are you doing here?" he asked.

"Harlan, we've got to talk," I said, and started to walk past him. But he grabbed my arm.

"You're not welcome here! Didn't you get my note?"

"Hell, yes, I got your note! Why do you think I'm here!" The control I'd sworn to have was slipping from my grasp.

"I want you to get your ass out of here now." I'd never seen ice in his eyes until now. The man who was talking to me was a total stranger. Before I could say another word, he had pushed me out the door and slammed it. I turned and walked back to my car.

As I drove back up the hill, I passed a familiar car. It was his secretary. I should have known. He had only transferred her from the office to his bed.

On the way home, I was crying so hard I came close to missing some of the sharp mountain curves, and didn't know why I tried. Only for my sons.

The kids, knowing where I'd gone, were waiting on the sun deck. But, without a word, I walked past them into the bedroom and shut the door.

For one solid month I never left the house and came out of my room only when no one was at home. For hours, I'd sit on the chaise longue in my bedroom and stare out the window at nothing. If the phone rang when I was alone, I didn't answer it. If it rang and someone else answered, I still wasn't there. I refused to talk to anyone. "Just tell them I'm sick," I said. That would be the truth.

Jimmy walked into the room. Glancing to see who it was, I turned back to the window. Usually, with that silent dismissal, he'd leave the room but not today. Walking over to where I sat, he lifted me up and shook me and my head rattled. "Damn it!" he said. "My mother has more guts than anyone I know of. Now, for God's sake, get up and show some of them!" More gently than he had picked me up, he sat me back down and sat down beside me. I could see tears in his eyes.

For a brief moment, I sat there and looked at him. He was right. I couldn't just stay in my room and mildew. There was life in my body and I had three wonderful sons. Thank God!

Without another word, I got up, went into the bathroom, took a shower, and got dressed. Even put on a little makeup. Then I walked to the kitchen for dinner. The kids saw their mother again.

The next day, I called Hubert and asked if he was free to see my any time that afternoon.

"For you . . . I'll make time," he said.

As the story unfolded from my lips, the smile that had been on Hubert's face was replaced with a look of astonishment. "Why didn't you come to see me before now?" he asked.

"I didn't want anyone to know, Hubert." It was crazy but I felt like a cast off who nobody wanted.

"Whether anyone knows or not isn't important," he said. "What is important is that you see an attorney!"

Remembering my last visit with Bill Carpenter, I said, "I don't have one, Hubert." I could see him thinking.

"What you need is the meanest divorce attorney in this town, Jack Norman, Jr." He picked up the phone and made an appointment for me the next afternoon. "Now, let me ask you this . . . have you checked your bank accounts?"

"No, what for?"

"Just in case," he said, and asked for the account numbers. One by one, he called and got the same answer. Closed! Every dime had been withdrawn. I didn't even have money for groceries. It had been fixed so Don Davis, the son of a bitch, was the only person who could write a check on Wilderness.

As I stood up to leave, Hubert took out his checkbook and wrote me a check for five hundred dollars. "If you need more, call me," he said.

My appointment was for two and all morning I tried to decide on something suitable to wear. *What's the appropriate dress to wear when you have to spill your guts to a stranger?* I thought. Finally, I chose a black silk suit, white blouse, black patent shoes and purse, and white gloves. I was pale as a ghost but that's the way you're supposed to look if you're in mourning, right?

Sitting in his reception room, I was a nervous wreck. I knew Jack Norman, Jr., and Hubert had been friends for years but I'd never met him and had no idea what to expect.

BOOK

TWO

Idly, thumbing through a magazine, I heard Norman's secretary say, "Mrs. Howard, you can go in now."

The office was impressive, to say the least. Oriental rug, two leather chairs, a big desk covered with legal-looking papers, and, behind it, a wall covered with shelves full of law books and mementos. Behind the desk sat a man who fit the office. Distinguished . . . proper and very lawyer-like. Getting up, he came around the desk, held out his hand and said, "Mrs. Howard . . . I'm Jack Norman." His voice was soft, not mean sounding at all. He motioned me to a chair and went back around the desk. Suddenly, his manner did an about-face and he began firing one question after another at me. "Who are you dating? Are you seeing anyone? What was your sex life like?" He went on and on while I sat there with my mouth open staring at him. Then I got mad.

I stood up. "How dare you ask questions like that of me! I'm not some whore who walked in off the streets! And I'm not on the witness stand and don't need a third degree!" I started for the door. But, quickly, he was around the desk and in front of me. He was smiling. "I don't think it's funny!" I said. Unwelcome tears came into my eyes. "I'll go to Vegas and get the damned divorce!" The statement came out of thin air. How in the hell could I go to Vegas when I couldn't even buy groceries!

Taking a handkerchief from the inside of his coat, he handed it to me and led me back to the chair. "I just wanted to see what kind of client I had," he said. "I don't take losers."

Little by little, he drew the story from me, all the time leaning back in his chair with the corner of his horn-rimmed glasses in his mouth. When I got to the part about the bank accounts, he said, "He must be a real bastard!"

After telling him all I could, he said he'd set up a hearing as soon as possible and call me.

273

Friends started dropping by the wayside. People who had been to the house, some of whom I'd thought would be friends for life, suddenly stopped calling. I felt like a leper.

But there were a faithful few. Almost every day Hubert called to say hello and see if there was anything I needed. "Friends," I said. I didn't need one hand to count them on.

Two of the few were Bobby and Jeanie Bare. I'd known both of them since 1957, when Bobby used to sleep in our bathtub and Jeanie was a featured singer on *Town Hall Party* in Los Angeles. A couple of years ago, they had gotten married and moved to Nashville, not far from us. I gave Jeanie her first cookbook, and when she got pregnant with Little Bobby (who was now three months old), I gave her a "baby-get-acquainted-with-Nashville shower." There was no way they could know how much it meant when they came over one day just to see me. Bobby was one of Harlan's best friends, but not once during the visit did he mention him.

About a month after Harlan left, Jeanie called and said the whole inside of their house had burned and asked if they could stay a few days until they found something temporary.

"Temporary, my foot!" I said. "You're gonna stay here until it's ready to move back into!" I needed them as much as they needed a place to stay.

With a precious baby around, there was no way anyone could be down in the dumps. My boys loved Bobby and Jeanie and they argued over who was going to take care of the baby and Keri, Jeanie's four-year-old-daughter by a former marriage.

For three months, no one mentioned Harlan's name. Not me, not Bobby or Jeanie. No one, except the boys. Every now and then, one of them would ask, "Have you heard from Dad?" When I had to say "no," I began to hate Harlan.

Rhinestones were one thing Bobby hated and never wore on-stage. One day, when he was due home from a tour, Jeanie and I planned a special surprise.

Going to the dime store, we bought a bunch of sparkle stuff and sequins. All afternoon we sewed the sequins on Little Bobby's pajama feet. Then, taking the tiny toy guitar we'd bought, we took glue and the sparkly stuff and wrote "Bobby Bare, Jr." on it. We did the same thing to his stroller. Just before we knew it was about time for Bobby to walk in the door, we dressed the baby in his "stage" outfit, and sat him in the stroller right where he'd be the first thing Bobby saw. The look on Bobby's face, and the laughter that filled the room, was worth all the effort. Lord, it was good to laugh again! I hated the thought of them leaving—for more reasons than one. The boys needed a man around the house, at least until they got used to the idea that Harlan wasn't coming back.

Not sleeping much, I got up before daylight and went out to the kitchen. Expecting it to be empty, I was surprised to see Jeanie sitting at the table with her head in her arms, crying.

Walking over, I put my arms around her shoulders and said, "Hey, babe, what's the matter?"

She raised her head. "Oh, Jan, I had the awfullest dream!"

"What about?" I asked. She began serious crying!

"I dreamed I burned your house down!" I started laughing.

"Well, you didn't! So dry up and let's have some tea."

There are so many things a boy needs a father for, one of them, the Father and Son Talk I didn't know if they'd ever had.

I called Dr. Goldner. "Just buy a book called *For Boys Only,*" he said. "That will answer all their questions." I could hear the smile in his voice. *He can smile,* I thought. *He's there to answer questions.* Nevertheless, I bought the book.

That evening, I told the boys what I'd done. "Now, I'm going to read it and when I finish, I want you to read it. Then we'll have a little quiz. Okay?" They just looked at each other, grinning. I could see this was going to be a lot harder on me than it was on them. Lord, they were fourteen, sixteen, and eighteen years old! *Well, better late than never,* I thought.

That night, as I lay in bed reading the book, I thought, *Gosh! I can't ask questions about this!* but went right on reading. There were things I didn't know.

The book was passed from one to the other, and when they'd finished, Jimmy, being spokesman, came and said they were ready for the quiz. *They* might be but I wasn't.

After we were all settled in the living room, I began. "Okay now, why shouldn't you engage in heavy petting sessions?" No answer. Not admitting defeat, I went on. "All right . . . why shouldn't you engage in long kisses?" (dragging out the word "long" out like I was stretching bubble gum).

"Aw, Mom!" Jimmy and Corky said in unison.

"Well?" I said. David was giving the question serious thought. I turned to him.

"David?"

"Well, I guess you couldn't breathe too good," he said. Jimmy and Corky broke out laughing.

"Okay, Mom," Jimmy said. "We've read the book . . . you've done your part. Now, we'll take it from here." He and Corky left the room laughing. I looked at David. After a few seconds, he shrugged his shoulders, got up, and left, too. I said, "Lord . . . I tried."

A session had been set up and I knew I had to start thinking about songs. One I liked very much was the one Waylon had pitched to me when he was at the house.

Since Waylon was one of those who had stopped calling, it took a lot of guts to call him. "Waylon, this is Jan."

"Yeah, how ya doin'?" he asked, not very enthusiastically.

"I'm fine," I lied. "What I called about is . . . remember that song of yours I liked?"

"Yeah."

"Well, I'm fixing to record and I wondered if you could drop off a demo the next time you're out this way?"

"I don't think I'd better do that," he said in his slow Texas drawl.

"What do you mean?"

"Well, since Harlan's not there, somebody might see me and think I was trying to make out with you."

I was stunned. "Are you serious!"

"Yeah."

My Irish and Indian temper came to the surface. "Why, you egotistical bastard! What makes you think you could make out with me? I'm good enough to cook for you, wash your damned clothes, and do demos on your songs, but I'm not good enough to record them, right?" I waited for his answer. When none came, I went on. "One more thing, Waylon. From here on, all I have to say to you is go to hell." I slammed up the receiver. It was going to be a long, rough road.

Jack Norman called and said he had located the money Harlan had withdrawn from the banks. It was in a bank in Franklin—about twenty miles from Nashville—in Harlan's name. The soonest he could set up a hearing was a month from today. What was I going to do until then! Even with putting everything I could on hold, it still took money to run a ten-room house and support three teenage sons. Like it or not, I had to go back to work.

At first, it was mostly Bill's TV show. Thank God for that to help me get my feet wet. When he asked if I'd like to be a regular, it was the answer to my prayers. It would mean a lot of hard work but it was what I needed the most. We even began talking about working all our dates together, but until that could be worked out, we both had contracts that had to be filled separately.

Just before I was to leave to work a week at a hotel in New York City, Joe Allison called and asked me to have lunch. I liked Joe. In spite of everything, I knew he was still my friend.

I guess, from the moment we'd said hello, Joe had noticed the change in me. But, until we'd finished eating and all the small talk we could muster, he never brought up what I knew he wanted to ask.

"Jan, are you all right?"

"Sure, Joe. Why wouldn't I be?" I said, avoiding his eyes.

"You seem so hard. It's not like you."

"You mean not like the 'old' me, don't you?"

"I guess so," he said. "Now, there seems to be a wall about a foot thick around you."

Leaning across the table, I said, "That's right—a glass wall. People can see in but they'll never get close enough to hurt me again."

"Be careful, Jan," he said. "Remember, if you don't leave yourself open to hurt, you also close the door on love."

"No, Joe. I've survived so far. Next time, they could destroy me. I've had it. I guess the only answer is shatterproof glass." My laugh sounded hard even to me.

Since I was going to be in New York a whole week, I hired a guitar player friend, Red Lane, to go with me. Not only did he play fine guitar but he was also a darned good songwriter and singer. With him along, he could show the band how the songs

went and take some of the load off of me. And I'd have someone
to eat with.

The band was fine but, since New York wasn't into country
music, the crowds were only fair. Of course, the fact that I wasn't
exactly a "super star" didn't help.

Each night, I couldn't help but notice the same man was
there. Never applauding, hardly ever smiling, just standing in
the back room watching me. He began to make me nervous. I
asked Lee Arnold, a local disk jockey, about him.

"Oh, you don't have to worry about *him*," he said. "I know
him."

"Who is he? And why is he here every night?"

"Well, you might say he likes your work." I decided to let it go
at that.

The last night, during intermission, the man came over and
introduced himself as Jerry "somebody or other" and asked me to
have dinner with him later.

"Thank you, no," I said. "I'm not hungry. Besides, I don't
know you."

"Just ask Lee Arnold. He'll vouch for me," he said.

"I don't have to ask Lee. I'm not interested." I was close to
being rude.

"Please," he said, "there's some people that want to meet you.
It could mean a great deal to your career." I didn't understand
this at all.

"Excuse me," I said, and walked over to where Lee was
standing. After telling him what "Jerry" had said, he said, "Go.
These people are important and he's right. It would mean a lot to
your career. Believe me, you'll be safe."

Walking back to the man, I said, "Okay, but I can't stay long. I
have an early morning flight."

The cab stopped in front of a club of some sort. The sign out
front said "Jilly's" but that didn't mean a thing to me. The door-
man looked at my companion, gave us a nod, and we walked into
a room so dimly lit, I had trouble adjusting my eyes. But, when I
did, they almost popped out of my head! There, at one of the
tables, sat Judy Garland and Joe E. Lewis! At several of the other
tables, I saw faces that I recognized but couldn't think of the
names. Jerry took my arm and led me over to a table by the bar.

No sooner had we sat down than a big bruiser walked over.
When he leaned down to say something to Jerry, his coat fell

open and there was the biggest handgun I had ever seen nestled against his shirt. *What kind of place am I in?* I thought. At that moment, another man walked up and Jerry jumped up so fast he almost knocked his chair over backward.

The only way this man acknowledged Jerry was to motion for him to sit back down. Then, turning to me, he smiled and said, "Miss Howard, I'm so glad you decided to join us."

"Well," I said, "it was almost like a command performance." I tried to laugh.

At that moment, he turned to the bruiser with the gun. "What have I told you about carrying that. The next time, you'll stay there!" It was almost like a Humphrey Bogart movie! Just as quickly, his tone changed and he was talking to me again.

"Miss Howard, I didn't get to see your performance but Jerry tells me you have a beautiful voice."

"Thank you." What else could I say?

"We're very much interested in country music and I'd like to know more about you. I'd like to invite you to a party tomorrow afternoon on the Island."

"What island?" I asked.

He looked amused. "Long Island."

"Oh, that island," I said. "Well, I'm sorry but I'm going home tomorrow."

"But I insist. You'll meet a lot of interesting people." I'll just bet I would!

"Well, I'll think about it, but now I think I'd better go back to the hotel."

I stood up and the man stood (he looked at least seven feet tall) and held out his hand. "I'll see you tomorrow," he said. It was not a question, but a statement.

On the way back to the hotel, I said to Jerry, "That man at the table . . . he looked awfully familiar." Jerry didn't answer. "And who was 'the man' that I heard several people say would be there any minute?"

"If you hadn't been in such a hurry you'd have met Frank Sinatra." Holy cow!

The cab stopped at the hotel. "Please don't get out," I said. "And thank you for a very interesting evening."

"I'll call you in the morning," he said. "Please plan to go to the party . . . you won't be sorry."

As the cab drove away, I looked after it and thought, *Maybe I should go to the party. No one has ever been this insistent for my company.*

As I opened the door to my room, my foot moved the newspaper lying there. When I did, it flopped open. And there, staring right at me, was the man from the club . . . the man who had invited me to the party. Picking it up, I read something about "indictment" and "godfather." I didn't need to read any further. No wonder his face had been so familiar. It had been before my eyes every time I'd picked up the paper the whole week!

Quickly, I called the airport and booked Red and me on the first flight out. I remembered the last time I'd made friends with the Mafia.

When my record of "Evil on Your Mind" was hot as a firecracker, the Decca promotion man was taking me around to visit the jukebox operators. At one place, he said, "Now, be real nice to this man . . . he can either make or break you in this area."

"What do you mean?"

"Never mind. But he's a big fan of yours and that's a plus."

As we walked into the store, the man coming toward me looked like anybody's grandfather—in face he *was* a grandfather. When we got to talking and I said I had three sons, he brought out his billfold and showed me his family . . . including his grandchildren.

"When are you going to Phoenix?" he asked.

"Before too long, I think. I'm supposed to work a place called Mr. Lucky's."

He wrote something on a piece of paper. "Here's my brother's name and address. Send him a picture and let him know when you'll be appearing there. He'll take good care of you." Absentmindedly, I stuck it in my purse.

Later, in the car, I looked at the paper. Joe English. The name didn't mean a thing to me.

"Just be sure and send that picture," the promo man said.

"Why is it so important?" I asked.

"Jan! That was one of the English brothers you were talking to! They run Chicago!"

"But he was just a nice man," I said.

"Well, just be glad he was smiling."

After mailing the picture, I forgot all about Joe English until Hubert called and said the date at Mr. Lucky's was firm. I would be there four days.

Opening night, at first intermission, Bob Sucorra, the owner, came over and said nervously, "Jan, do you know Joe English?"

"Well, no. But I met his brother in Chicago. Why?"

"He's over there." He motioned to a table across the room. "Go over and talk to him . . . be nice." I wasn't in the habit of being anything else.

Before I got to the table, a nice-looking man in his fifties stood up.

"Mr. English?"

"Miss Howard, I'm so glad to meet you." We shook hands and he introduced me to the lady with him by her first name. I assumed she was his wife.

"How long you gonna be here?" he asked.

"Four days."

"Where you staying?" I told him the Ramada Inn. He handed me a card.

"Call me in the morning when you get up." I figured this was a lunch date which I could pass up, but tucked the card in my cigarette case anyhow.

All through intermission, we talked. The woman never opened her mouth, but Mr. English told me what a fan he was and that he had been following my career.

When it was time for me to go back to work, I stood up, held out my hand, and thanked him for coming. *That's that,* I thought as I walked away. But he stayed the whole four shows.

As I was fixing to leave, Bob Sucorra came over and said, "All this time, he's never been to my club and it took you to bring him here." I got the feeling he wasn't too happy about it.

The next morning, I was still asleep when the phone rang at ten. "Miss Howard, this is Joe English."

"Oh, yes, Mr. English," I said sleepily. "How are you?"

"Fine, thank you. I've made arrangements for you at another hotel. I think you'll be more comfortable there." I came wide awake!

"Oh, no. This is fine. It really is."

"There'll be a car for you in an hour." Before I could answer, he had hung up. Well, he was certainly a man of few words!

In an hour, there was a knock at my door. Opening it, I saw a limousine and a chauffeur!

We pulled up in front of the jazziest motel I'd ever seen. It was like Hawaii! Flowers everywhere! Not even stopping at the desk, the chauffeur took my bags to one of the cabanas by the pool. When he opened the door and stepped aside, I walked into a beautiful suite. On the table was a huge flower arrangement with a card that said "Have a nice stay . . . Joe English." The dream wasn't over. Outside was parked a georgeous red sports car which was mine to use. And, to top it off, a hairdresser was on standby when I needed her. I didn't know what to make of the whole thing. But one thing I did know was that I was definitely going to enjoy the next few days!

Joe English was at the club every night. Sometimes I'd sit with him, sometimes I wouldn't. When I tried to thank him, he dismissed it as though it was nothing.

After leaving Phoenix, I never saw or heard from him again. But, when I told Hubert the story, he said, "Jan, they never give something for nothing." I couldn't figure what in the world they would ever want from me!

On the way home on the plane from New York, I wondered if I should have gone to that party. It might have been interesting.

I'd never heard from Harlan, but word of mouth had it that he was living at the Versailles, a Nashville apartment complex on Hillsboro Road. Like an idiot, I had to try one more time.

I don't know what I expected but certainly not the smile he wore when he opened the door. "Hey. L.G., come on in!" He motioned toward the living room.

Before coming, I had decided to put my hurt and anger on the back burner to see if we could talk like two civilized people. I walked in and sat down in the nearest chair.

"Can I get you something to drink?" Harlan asked as he went to the refrigerator and pulled out a beer.

"No thanks." We were talking like strangers.

He came back, sat in a chair across the room, and said, "Well, how ya doin'?"

"That's a stupid question, Harlan." But not nearly as stupid as I felt for coming here. "I only came to see if we could talk this out."

"There's nothing to talk about. I just want to be free. Obligations are interfering with my writing. It's as simple as that." He leaned back and sucked on his beer.

"To hell with your writing. Are you ready to give up all we've worked for?"

"I'm not giving up anything, Jan." Now he sounded more like Harlan.

"Don't we count at all?" I sounded like I was begging, and I hated myself for it. He got up, walked to the kitchen, and set the beer bottle down.

"Wanta see the apartment?" he called.

"No, Harlan, I don't want to see the apartment."

Walking back in, he leaned up against the door facing. "Gotta king-size bed big enough for two," he said. I got the implication and stood up.

"Yes, Harlan, I'm sure it is." Opening the door, I turned to where he was still standing. "Good-bye, Harlan." It was finally over. The man I had been married to for ten years no longer existed.

September came and the boys started school. Jimmy to M.T.S.U. in Murfreesboro, Corky was a senior in high school and David, who had been put back a year, was a freshman.

The Disk Jockey Convention was the first week in October. Before, I'd always looked forward to the parties and dress-up affairs but not this year. Until now, I'd avoided crowds and the whispers that I knew were going on behind my back. But NARAS (the National Academy of Recording Arts and Sciences) had nominated me for an award for my performance of "Evil on Your Mind," and the song I had written, "It's All Over but the Crying," which Kitty Wells had recorded, was receiving a BMI award for being one of the most frequently played. If nothing else, I had to attend those two events, but I dreaded them. It all seemed ironic. A friend had told me that Harlan said the reason he had left was that he didn't want to be married to a competitor, he wanted someone who was content to stay home and bake cookies. I wondered if he ever remembered the times when I'd begged him to let me do just that. It was too late now.

A couple of days before the BMI dinner, Harlan called and said since we both had to attend this thing, we might as well go together . . . after all, he was the publisher on my song. I wasn't stupid, I knew his reasoning was "the perfect couple" ploy. A lot of people still didn't know what had happened. I decided to go along with his little game.

I immediately set out to buy the most striking dress I could find. I decided on a long, gold-sequined knit trimmed with black mink. Since I still wasn't getting any money, it took five hundred dollars out of what money I had left. But I wanted our last appearance together to be a good one. Besides, I didn't want him to think, just because he'd left me, that I couldn't make it. Pride can be stupid.

Jimmy had come home for the weekend, and all three of the boys looked with approval when I walked out of the bedroom. It was no secret to me that they thought tonight might get Harlan and me back together. Yet I knew their hopes were in vain.

Harlan wouldn't come to the house. I met him at the office at six o'clock. All the way to the Belle Meade Country Club, I'd catch him looking at me. *Wonder what he's thinking?* I thought. *Second thoughts.* I was glad I had splurged on the dress.

When we walked in, the people who knew the situation had a surprised look on their faces—the ones who didn't said, "Hey, it's good to see you two!"

Trying to look normal, I looked around to see who was there. Well, what I was really looking for was a friendly face. What I saw was a *back* that looked familiar. Suddenly, he turned to the girl standing next to him and I saw his face. Damn! It was Delane Bramlett! The young man who had stayed at our house who I had made get his hair cut! What was he doing here? "Delane?" I said. Turning to see who had spoken his name, he saw me.

"Jan!" he said, and came over to hug me.

"Delane . . . what are you doing here?" He laughed and touched his hair, which he wore long.

"Think I need a haircut?" he asked, smiling.

"Delane, will you please tell me what is going on?" The last time I had seen him, he was down and out and headed back to Los Angeles to work in that dive they had the nerve to call a club.

"You really don't know, do you?" His smile covered his whole face.

"No!"

"Well, I think I'll just let you find out for yourself," he said. With that he kissed me on the cheek and went back to join the girl he had been talking to.

Harlan had disappeared into the crowd so I went to the table where we had been assigned to sit. Leaning over to Bobby Goldsboro, who was sitting next to me, I said, "Bobby, see that man over there?" He looked to where I was pointing.

"Yes. Why?"

"What's his name?" I knew . . . but I wanted to see if anyone else did.

"Delaney," he said.

"Delaney who?"

"Just Delaney . . . one half of Bonnie and Delaney." Heavens. One of the top duos in the country! No wonder he laughed. Shows how much I'm up on what's happening, I thought. Good for him!

They had started serving dinner when Harlan joined me at the table. Each of us talked to people around us but not to each other. I was ready for this masquerade to be over.

One by one Frances Preston (by now a top executive with Broadcast Music Incorporated) was reading off the names of the winners. As each one was announced, the proud writer and publisher would walk up, receive their award, and stand while their picture was taken. My heart was pounding! I wished I had worn something besides this dress that I now felt like a hooker in. I didn't think I'd ever be able to walk up there. Too late. "And now . . . for the gold medal award of the year. 'It's All Over but the Crying'—Jan Howard, writer, Harlan Howard, publisher." It wasn't my imagination that I heard some laughter among the applause. With my head high, I walked in front of Harlan to receive my award, stood there while the flashbulbs blinded me, then walked back to the table. Later, people came over to congratulate me, and now and then someone would lean over close and whisper, "Is it really true that you and Harlan are separated?" I'd nod and go on to the next.

As soon as decently possible, I asked Harlan, "Would you please take me to my car? I've had all this phoniness I can stand."

On the way home from the office, I tried to cry but lost the battle. I felt like a princess whose carriage had turned into a pumpkin.

Turning into our driveway, knowing the kids would be waiting, I turned off the key and sat there. I wished I could tell them the whole truth but I couldn't. I wished I could put things back together again but I wasn't a magician. My heart was so heavy, and my shoulders felt like I was carrying the weight of the world, but I put a smile on my face, opened the car door, and walked up the walk to the house.

The only thing that kept me from losing my mind was work and my boys. With the TV show and some dates, I was kept busy. Otherwise, my activities consisted of cleaning house, cleaning closets, working in the yard—exciting things like that. I was grateful for them.

Bill and I had worked a date in East Tennessee. They were going on that night to the Lake of the Ozarks and I had planned to stay over and fly home the next day. Suddenly, the thought of spending the night in another lonely motel room was unbearable. "Bill," I asked, "are you all going anywhere near Nashville?"

"Sure," he said, "we're going right through Elizabethown, Kentucky."

"Is that near Louisville?" That would be only a thirty-minute flight.

"Yeah . . . not far." He said I was welcome to ride with them.

Arriving there sometime in the wee hours, I slept till mid-afternoon, then called a cab to go to the airport. A flight was leaving at four.

When I told the driver to go to the airport, he turned around and said, "Where ya goin'?"

"I told you . . . the Louisville airport."

"No, lady . . . I mean your final destination."

"Oh . . . Nashville."

"Hell, lady, you're halfway there now!"

"Well, I can't walk!" I was irritated.

"I'll drive you to Nashville for thirty-seven fifty."

"How much to the airport?" I asked.

"Seventeen-fifty." Let's see . . . seventeen fifty and fifty dollars plane fare . . .

Stretching out in the seat, I said, "Head south!" Maybe it wasn't a limousine but it would do until one came along!

"Miss Howard. You told me to wake you when we got ten miles out of Nashville." The cab had stopped and the driver was talking to me.

"Oh, yeah, go someplace where I can use a phone." I had to call David so he wouldn't go to the airport to meet me.

"David?"

"Are you at the airport already," he asked.

"No, I'm taking a cab. You won't have to go to the airport."

"You're taking a cab from the airport?"

"No, David. From Elizabethtown."

He choked. "You mean from Elizabethtown, Kentucky?"

"It's a long story. I just wanted to save you a trip to the airport."

"Only my mother would do that." I guess sometimes they did think their mother was a little crazy.

"See you in a little while," I said, and hung up. I could see him standing there shaking his head.

Several times I'd called Mr. Norman's office, but each time I got the same answer from his secretary: "I'm sorry . . . Mr. Norman's in conference." Well, this time that wasn't good enough!

"Well, get him out of conference. I have to talk to him!" Every time I'd left word, I might as well have left it with a wooden Indian. He never returned the calls. This time a few seconds later he came on the line.

"Yes, Mrs. Howard. How are you?"

"I didn't call to talk about my health, Mr. Norman. I called to see when we're going to have some kind of hearing."

"Well, these things take time. Have you talked to Mr. Howard?"

"Hell, no, I haven't talked to Mr. Howard! And I don't intend to!"

"Sometimes, given enough time, these things work themselves out," he said. "We like to give a couple every chance to get back together."

"Mr. Norman, this is not going to work itself out. I suggest you get to work immediately!"

"All right . . . if you're sure."

"I'm sure!"

"Well, with the holidays coming up, I doubt if we can get anything done before the first of the year, but get all your monthly expenses, groceries, clothing, school expenses, medical, dental . . . everything you can think of together and bring them to my office. We'll get started then, all right?"

It wasn't all right. But I did as he asked.

Christmas wasn't in me but, for the boys' sake, I wanted to have everything as near normal as possible. I baked cookies, shopped until I was numb, decorated the house to the hilt. We even bought a beautiful flocked tree for the living room. Without even asking, Jimmy climbed up and put the angel on top.

Christmas Eve, Harlan called and said he would be out that evening to bring the boy's presents. I thought, *Oh, well, it's Christmas.*

"Would you like to stay for dinner?" I asked.

"Sure, I guess so." After I hung up, I hated myself for asking but started dinner anyway. I'd already planned something special so the only thing different would be to add his place at the table.

Dinner was ready to be put on the table when Harlan walked in and started joking around with the boys as though he still lived there. Not wanting to dampen the atmosphere, I said, "Okay, everybody, sit down. I'll put dinner on the table."

Harlan, who hadn't taken off his coat, said, "Oh, I gotta be somewhere else. Just wanted to drop these off." He handed the boys their gifts. Their faces fell. *Damn him! Damn him!* That was it! He might hurt me time and time again but, if I could help it, he'd never hurt my sons again!

"And a Merry Christmas to you, too, Harlan," I said.

Mr. Norman's secretary called and said the preliminary hearing was set for nine o'clock on Monday . . . finally! Twice before I'd been told to be there and when I showed up at the courthouse, Earl McNabb, another attorney in the Norman law firm, had been there and said it had been postponed. It better not happen again.

Once more, I was there an hour early cooling my heels in the courthouse hallway. Right about nine o'clock, I saw Earl McNabb walking toward me. Damn!

Before he could speak, I said, "Where's Mr. Norman!"

"He's in courtro—" I didn't wait for him to finish.

"I know . . . on the fourth floor. Well, damn it, I want him here! I didn't hire you, I hired him!"

"But this is just to get it on record. It won't take five minutes. You didn't even have to be here."

"But I am here! And I'll tell you what. You can give Mr. Norman a message for me. Tell him forget it . . . I've changed my mind. If he's too damned busy or doesn't care enough about my case to handle it himself, I'll get another attorney! He's not the only one in Nashville!" I turned on my heel and walked out of the courthouse.

That afternoon about four o'clock, I answered the phone and a familiar voice said, "Mrs. Howard?" It was Jack Norman, Jr.

"Yes. Mr. Norman."

"I understand you have a message for me." I could tell he was smiling.

"Ten to one you've already gotten it or you wouldn't have called. And I hope he gave you the complete message."

"Yes, he did. And I do care about your case. Why don't you come down to the office about noon tomorrow and we'll talk."

"Are you inviting me to lunch?" Now, I was smiling.

"I think that would be a good idea. That way we won't have any interruptions."

"I'll look forward to it. See you then."

The next day, when I walked into his office, he was all smiles and looked awfully smug about something. I liked his smile, it made him look a lot less formidable.

Over lunch, he told me that Harlan had hired an attorney, Charlie Warfield, and that he was mean. "Not near as mean as I am though," he said. Then he told me he had hired a private detective to follow Harlan.

"I didn't tell you to do that," I said.

"I know but it never hurts to have an ace in the hole."

After lunch, we went back to his office and went over some details that would come up at the hearing, which he promised would be soon.

"Will you be there?" I asked. He laughed.

"I promise. . . . From here on, I'll be there." And then added. "Whenever you need me."

Except for a few people, the courtroom was empty. Mr. Norman and I walked in and took our places at a table on one side of the room. Harlan and his attorney were directly opposite. Neither of them looked our way.

I was asked to take the witness stand. After being sworn in, the judge looked at some papers in front of him, then asked, "Is this the amount you figure it takes to support your household for a month?" The amount I had given Mr. Norman was the exact amount of the bills I had paid the month previous, plus an average for medical, dental, etc. "Yes, sir," I answered. Seeming satisfied, he dismissed me.

Harlan took the stand. His attorney, Charlie Warfield, stood and began a long dissertation as to why Harlan couldn't afford this amount of support. "Why?" the judge asked—all the while looking over some more papers—Harlan's I supposed.

"Well, sir," Mr. Warfield said, "Mr. Howard is in the public eye and has certain needs, such as clothes." I wondered how many pairs of jeans Harlan needed, since that's all he wore. His attorney went on to say that Mr. Howard had to dress well and paid two hundred dollars each for his suits. The judge looked at Harlan, who had dressed for the occasion.

"Mr. Warfield, are you saying that Mr. Howard can't afford to support his family because he has to pay two hundred dollars for his suits?" Without another question, the judge granted exactly the amount I had turned in.

All spring and summer, I worked every date possible. Bill Anderson and I had put the road show together and now I was working strictly with him and his band. To a lot of people, I supposed I was classified as the "girl singer" with Bill Anderson, but to me it was a relief not to have to face bad bands night after night. And riding the bus with them relieved some of the loneliness. Since Bill wasn't getting paid all that much, I adjusted my pay accordingly. And, if for some reason he didn't get paid, neither did I.

One of those times was a big ballroom show somewhere in Texas. After doing two shows to a packed house, Bill and I were out on the bus. The band was busy tearing down the equipment and loading up. All this took about an hour, after which they came on board to change clothes. Then the piano player went to collect our money. First, he tried the door out of which they'd brought the equipment. It was locked. Next, he went around to the front. A few minutes later, he came back and said, "You're not gonna believe this but the whole place is locked up tight."

Sure enough, when we all went to investigate, it was true.

The parking lot was empty, the house was dark, and the doors locked. In nothing flat we were in town at the nearest sheriff's office. No one had ever heard of the promoters. We headed back to Nashville, poorer in money but richer in experience. From now on we would get half the money in advance.

After a lot of thinking, I told Mr. Norman to go ahead and start divorce proceedings. And the sooner the better. There was no use in putting it off any longer. I had to get on with my life. A meeting was set up between Harlan, myself, and the two attorneys.

Except for the absence of a judge, it was almost like being in a courtroom. His attorney threw every obscene question in the book at me. Harlan sat there like a bump on a log, and so did Jack Norman, Jr. During a break, I said to him, "I thought you were supposed to handle this."

"You seem to be doing all right," he said. "If you get in trouble, I'll bail you out." He seemed pleased with the way things were going and had told me before going in that he had Harlan right where he wanted him.

When we went back in, Harlan dropped the bombshell that destroyed my mind! He said that Wilderness Music and his songs were his brainchildren and I had done nothing to contribute toward his success. In other words, I deserved nothing. I thought about all the times he'd asked me to put melodies to his lyrics. All the times he'd written ideas I'd given him. All the demos I'd made. All the times I'd put up with having drunks in our home just so we could get a song recorded. All the work I'd put into getting Wilderness started. If all that counted for nothing, he was right. I didn't deserve anything. Not wanting Harlan or his attorney to see me cry, I left the room. Mr. Norman followed me.

Turning to him, I said, "Let him have it."

"What are you talking about!" He knew where I was coming from.

"I don't want anything. Just the divorce," I said.

Mr. Norman was furious! "You don't know what the hell you're saying! Do you know you can have half of everything he's written since the day you were married! Plus half of Wilderness Music!"

"I don't care," I said, "I just want out. He can have it all." Turning my back, I walked over and stared out the window at scenery that looked as blank as my life. I heard the door shut as he went back into the room.

Coming back out, he escorted me from the building and we walked back to his office. "Jan," he said, "I think you'll regret your decision. But if that's the way you want it, that's the way it'll be. I'll tell you one thing though, the bastard will pay dearly for my services."

August 1967. The divorce was set for nine o'clock that morning. I'd never dreaded anything more in my life. When I gave Harlan everything, I figured the final thing would just be a formality. But he had countersued. I wondered what was left that he would want. Not me. Not the kids. Maybe now he wanted the car which I had paid for, or the furniture that I'd bought a piece at a time from each tour, or maybe he wanted the lousy three thousand dollars which came from "our money" that we'd put down on the house. I didn't know and was at the point of not caring.

Jimmy walked into the room as I was dressing. "I'm going with you," he said.

"No, I don't want you there." All this time, I'd tried to keep the ugly details from them. Until now, all the kids knew was that Harlan and I had agreed to get a divorce.

"I don't care," he said. "I'm not letting you go there by yourself." He was right. I needed someone.

The hallway outside the courtroom was filled with people. As Jimmy and I walked by, I could hear whispers, "That's Jan Howard . . . you know . . . the one on television." They started filing into the courtroom.

Mr. Norman had Jimmy and me wait in a small room and came to get us when it was time. Holding onto Jimmy's hand, I felt like I was walking down the last mile.

Once more, Harlan and I were seated on opposite sides of the room beside our attorneys. He never once raised his eyes from the table.

Harlan took the stand and my attorney did exactly as I had asked him to do . . . asked only the necessary questions.

Expecting the same treatment, I took the stand. After I was sworn in and took the stand, Harlan's attorney approached. I couldn't believe the questions he started firing at me.

"Mrs. Howard, isn't it true that you work with a lot of men?"

"Yes, but . . ."

"No buts! Just answer yes or no!"

I looked at the judge. "Sir, may I explain?"

"Yes," he said. "Let Mrs. Howard explain."

"It's true that I work with a lot of men, almost everyone in country music. And all of them are friends of Mr. Howard's." Charlie Warfield glared at me.

"Isn't it true that you see these men outside of your work?" I knew where his questions were leading.

"Yes, sometimes we run into each other on airplanes."

"Don't you stay at the same hotels?"

"Sometimes. Same hotels but different rooms."

"Don't you see these men at the hotels?" I knew exactly what he was trying to do. Suddenly, I wasn't nervous anymore. His questions were totally ridiculous! And Harlan knew they were! I couldn't believe even he could be so low as to allow this line of questioning.

"Yes, sir. Sometimes we run into each other in the coffee shop."

Before Warfield could ask another dirty question, the judge said, "I've heard enough. Divorce granted to Mrs. Howard." With the sound of the gavel hitting wood, it was over.

Jimmy, standing in the aisle, took my hand as I walked by. Outside the courtroom, I broke down. Mr. Norman came over and said, "I'm sorry this has hurt you so much."

At that moment, Harlan walked out of the courtroom, stopped, and looked at me. Jimmy walked over and stood in front of him. "Dad," he said, "I used to think you were ten feet tall. Right now, you'll do good to measure one inch."

Walking back to me, he said, "Come on, Mom, he's not worth it." As we walked past Harlan and out of the courthouse, I thought, *Jimmy is the one who is ten feet tall.*

I came out of the divorce with the house, car, and a thousand dollars a month until David was eighteen . . . which was less than three years away.

Corky and David were waiting as we drove up. "It's over," I said, and went into my bedroom. Sitting on the side of my bed, I tried to think. I felt so damned lost. All I wanted to do was pull the drapes and not come out. The kids didn't deserve this. How many times had their lives been torn apart? How many times could their security be washed away like a sand castle on the beach? Corky had graduated and would be entering college this fall, but in a lot of ways, he was still a little boy. He tried to act so grown up, like he could handle anything but, inside, I knew he was hurting. Sometimes I'd see him sitting alone out in the yard and I'd want to go out, put my arms around him, and say everything would be all right. But I didn't know if it would help. Of all the boys, he was the closest to Harlan and the divorce hurt him deeply. And David, right at the age when a boy needs a father most, just wandered around as though he were lost. Jimmy seemed to be handling it best, but I didn't know what was going on in his head. The only thing we could do was hold on to each other and, God willing, go on living.

What with the race riots, the anti-Vietnam marches, and everything else that was going on, the whole damned world seemed to be in a mess and our lives reflected it.

The kids took turns mowing the lawn. Today was Jimmy's day. No one really made a fuss over it because we had the riding lawn mower. I'd even tried it once but the yard was on such a slope and the darned thing got to going so fast I couldn't get it stopped. Corky, standing on the steps laughing his head off, was no help. I was screaming, "Somebody stop this thing!" when Jimmy walked around the corner and yelled, "Just jump off!" Without hesitating, that's what I did . . . and fell flat on my face. The lawn mower stopped as though it was waiting for me. Mustering what dignity I could, I said, "Okay, boys, it's all yours."

Jimmy had taken his shirt off and was mowing in his cut-off jeans and tennis shoes. For a while, I watched. Then went in to wash dishes.

Hearing him scream I ran to the door. He was running toward the house screaming, "Mom! Mom! Help me! I'm dying!" Dear God! He was clawing so hard at his back and chest he was actually bringing blood!

I grabbed him and ran some lukewarm water in the bathtub and dumped a box of soda in. "Get in there!" I said. Trying to keep calm, I kept pouring the water over his back. Nothing helped . . . he kept screaming, "Mom! Please help me!"

I ran for the car, and with him screaming every step of the way, drove to the nearest clinic—the hospital was too far away.

Before I turned off the engine, someone came out and gave him a shot which knocked him out immediately. With me following, a man carried him into a room and laid him on a bed. I stood there crying and brushing the curls back off his forehead. "What's happened to him?" I asked the doctor.

"He has a severe case of sun poisoning," he said.

"But would sun poisoning do this?"

"Well, I've never seen it before but yes, it could." I was still confused.

"But what would make him in such pain?" The doctor stood there looking at Jimmy and taking his pulse.

"Do you know how it feels when you have a nerve in your tooth exposed?" he asked. "Well, that's exactly what every nerve in his body is . . . exposed." Dear Lord!

For twenty-four hours, every time Jimmy would start to regain consciousness, he'd start screaming, "Mom! I'm dying!" and they'd give him another shot. I never left his side. Just kept praying that the next time he came to, he wouldn't scream. Finally, that time came . . . Thank you, God.

For two days, in bed at home, Jimmy took pills every four hours, but outside of being more than a little weak and a little pale, there were no more effects. I thought, *What in the world is going to happen to you next, my son.*

It wasn't long before I found out—a severe case of monocucleosis which kept him confined to bed for fourteen days and in the house for over a month.

A recording session was set up to begin work on my second album for Decca. Songs had been the last thing on my mind and I'd left most of the listening to Owen. With my mind so messed up, I doubted if I'd know a good song if I heard one. "Jan," Owen asked. "Would you object to doing one of Harlan's songs?"

"Owen, I'd record a song written by a garbageman if it was a hit."

"Good, now we can get on with it," he said.

The night before I was to record, David asked if he could drive my car over to his friend, Larry Baker's. "Please, Mom. I promise not to go anywhere but there." He looked so pitful. Poor David, he was the only one without a car—Corky had gotten a black Corvair for graduation—and had to beg every time he wanted to go somewhere. But he knew how I felt about my Cadillac. It was the first one I had ever ordered to my specifications—royal blue with white vinyl top and all-white leather interior. Even though it was two years old, I planned to keep it for a long time. With reservations, I handed him the keys and said, "Okay. But promise you won't go anywhere near where Corky and the others are shooting off fireworks. And be home by ten."

"I promise," he said, and was gone before I could change my mind.

Ten o'clock came and went and still no David. This just wasn't like him. He wasn't perfect but he usually did exactly what I asked him to do. I was beginning to get worried when I heard a car. *Finally,* I thought, and went to the sun-deck door. The two figures I saw hardly resembled my two sons who had left home earlier. Covered with some kind of black soot (all except what I could see of their ashen faces) and their clothes torn half off their bodies. "What in the world has happened!" I said. My God! They looked like they'd been in World War III. Corky was trying to nudge David on around me. "Wait a minute," I said to David. "I thought I told you to be home by ten." He hadn't said a word.

"Mom, let David go upstairs and I'll explain," Corky said.

"No," I said. Then I looked outside. "Where's my car?" Corky's was the only one out there. While my attention was diverted, David had inched his way around me and upstairs.

"Well," Corky said, "it's at the Madison Garage." He was shifting from one foot to the other.

"What's it doing there?"

"It got burned a little," he said real quick. Now *he* was trying to get around me.

"Corky, how did you get all that black stuff on you?"

"Mom, I'll explain in the morning, okay?" he pleaded. Without waiting for my answer, he scooted up the stairs. *Something mighty strange is going on,* I thought. Then, like the light bulb being turned on, I had it figured out. They must have been experimenting with cigarettes, burned the seat, and wanted to get it fixed before I saw it. But . . . why all that black soot? Oh, well. I'd find out in the morning.

The next morning, I called Bud Stokes, my insurance agent. "Bud? Something's happened to the car. Would you like to come out and go with me to look at it?"

"Anything serious?" he asked.

"No. I think the boys were experimenting with smoking and burned the seat."

"Okay, I'll be out around ten."

When Bud came, I walked out to the den and found all three boys like See no evil . . . Hear no evil . . . Do no evil—all lined up on the sofa. No one said a word. "Bud and I are going to look at the car, then I have to go to the studio." No one even looked at me. "Well, doesn't anyone want to talk this morning?" They looked at each other, waiting for someone to be spokesman. No one volunteered. "Okay, I'll see you later," I said. I couldn't figure out what I'd done to get the silent treatment.

Bud pulled up to the garage. "Hi, I'm Jan Howard," I said. "Is my car here?"

"You're mighty calm," the attendant said.

"Is there something I should know? How much damage is there?"

"It's around back . . . I think you'd better see for yourself." Bud drove around to the alley and, telling me to wait there, got out and walked around where the wrecked cars were. Suddenly, he stopped and called out, "Jan, what's your license number?"

"Why?"

"Just tell me the number. Then hold on to something."

I told him the number but, looking around, I still didn't see my car. Why, in the midst of all this junk, it would stand out like a sore thumb. I got out and walked to where Bud was standing. He took my arm. "Jan . . . turn around slowly. Is that your license number?" I looked to where he was pointing and almost fainted. Good Lord! It was nothing but a burned-out chassis and a license plate . . . mine! "Bud! I've got some important papers in the glove compartment!"

"Jan, there is no glove compartment."

When we walked into the house, the boys were still sitting exactly as we'd left them. The three monkeys. Only this time, their antics were not too funny. Sitting down in a chair, I asked, "David, have you seen the car?" His face was white as a sheet.

"Yes, ma'am."

"Corky . . . have you seen the car?" I couldn't believe this calm voice I was hearing was mine.

"Yes, ma'am."

"Jimmy, have you seen the car?"

"Yes, ma'am."

"All right. I want to hear what happened . . . Somebody talk." Corky volunteered. David and his friend, Larry, had done what I'd told them not to—gone to the park where Corky and his friends were shooting off fireworks—and taken along a big box of firecrackers in the backseat. On the way, they'd lit up their cigarettes. But, before getting to the park, they'd rolled down the window to throw the cigarettes out. Only, they didn't go outside . . . they went into the box of fireworks. Suddenly, it was the Fourth of July at a county fair . . . only this time the Roman candles were shooting out the windows of the car! Corky and his friends, seeing what was happening, ran to the car and got there just in time to see David and Larry dive out the windows and the car explode! I realized now that they could have both been killed. Suddenly, the car didn't mean a thing. It could be replaced.

"All right, David, I hope you've learned your lesson. Jimmy, take them both down and all of you take another good look and see what happens when you do things you're not supposed to do. Then, I want all of you to stay out of my sight until I tell you!"

The session had just started when in walked Harlan. "Hi, L.G.," he said. Then, just like nothing had happened, he walked around, joked with the musicians, and went into the control room with Owen. Trying to ignore him and not wanting to cause a scene, I went on rehearsing. Then, he came out and began to give his opinion on how the song should be done. "Harlan, did it ever occur to you that I'm not interested in your opinion?"

"I don't know what you're so uptight about," he said.

"Well, I'll tell you what I'm so uptight about." And told him the events of the morning. He laughed.

"Hell, it's just a piece of machinery," he said.

"But, Harlan, David could have been killed!"

"Well, he wasn't, was he?" he said, and turned to say something to a musician. All my resolutions went to the wind. Grabbing his arm, I said, "You insensitive bastard. You could care less what happens to any of us." I knew I was screaming but didn't care. No one in the studio had ever seen me like this. Owen came out of the control room and over to me. "Owen!" I said. "Get this son of a bitch out of here and don't ever let him in one of my sessions again!" Harlan shrugged his shoulders and, taking his stupid grin with him, left. I'd lost all control and was crying. Owen said, "Never mind. We'll cancel the session and try again tomorrow, okay?" He was right. I sure couldn't sing. Able to or not, the little stunt had cost me over five thousand dollars' studio and musician costs.

A few days later on a flight to Cincinnati, a woman sitting next to me started the usual airplane conversation.

"Do you live in Nashville?"

"Yes," I answered, not wanting to drag it out. But she continued.

"Well, I live in Indianapolis but I'm thinking about moving down there since my daughter has to have medical treatments at Vanderbilt."

"I'm sure you'll like it," I said thinking *Now she'll probably give me her whole family history.*

"Oh, I might get used to it," she said. "But you've sure got some weird people down there."

"Really?"

"Yeah, I met one last night. Me and a friend was sitting in a bar and this weird-looking guy was at the other end. He just kept leaning over staring at me." I could tell she wanted me to ask her to continue. When I didn't, she did anyway. "Suddenly, he came over and propositioned me . . . right in front of my friend. And not in too nice a language either!" Then she said something that got my attention. "He was a songwriter."

"Really? What was his name?"

"Harlan Howard." The Seven-up that had been halfway down my throat came back up through my nose. "Why? Do you know him?" she asked.

When I got my breath from laughing, I said, "Well, slightly, he's my ex-husband."

"Oh Lord! I'm sorry!" she said.

"Don't be. I'm not."

The boys had been moping around the house and I decided what we needed was some diversion. "How about going to a dude ranch?" I asked.

"Where'd you get that idea?" one of them asked.

"Well, it sounded like fun. I've found one near Gatlinburg. Wanta go?"

Corky was really enthusiastic but Jimmy and David had reservations. When we got there, so did I. *Surely this must be the wrong place,* I thought when I saw the plain old farm with a few run-down "bunkhouses" scattered around. The ad had sounded so great. "Horseback Riding and Fresh Air!" it said. Well, the fresh air part was right . . . especially through the cracks in the wall of our quarters. Thank God there was a bathroom. I was beginning to think we'd have to go to the woods! Jimmy and David almost wouldn't get out of the car. And even Corky looked at me like I was crazy! But, putting all my false enthusiasm into my voice, I said, "Okay, who's for roughing it?" Reluctantly, they followed me inside. Seeing the Army cots covered with olive drab blankets and nothing else, my brave smile slithered off my face. But, being the brave, adventurous souls we were, we decided to stick it out.

Before daylight, some awful sound jarred us out of bed. It was the breakfast bell! For a minute, we all looked at each other . . . then laughter caught us off guard. We literally rolled on the beds! "You know, Mom, they got golf courses in Gatlinburg," Jimmy said.

"Yeah," David said. "And miniature golf courses—and restaurants—and swimming pools."

"And horses!" Corky chimed in.

As though it had been rehearsed, they all said, "Let's rough it at the Holiday Inn!" Within a few minutes we were loaded and on our way.

Driving through the mountains, we saw a small brown bear run across the road in front of us. "Stop the car!" Corky yelled. I slammed on the brakes and he was out of the car and over to the side where the bear had disappeared. Suddenly, he turned and ran back. "Let's go!" he said as he jumped in the car. And I could see why. The little bear was running back, and right behind it was Mama or Papa bear. "Don't take me long to look at a bear," Corky said.

From the day Bill and I recorded the first time, we'd been looking for just the right song to follow it with. In Roanoke, Virginia, we found it. We stopped at a radio station where King

Edward IV (a disk jockey and longtime friend of country music) worked. He played us a song out on a small label by writer Steve Karliski called "For Loving You." It was a recitation, which Bill was good at with a short singing chorus. After listening to it several times, we decided to play it for Owen. With his approval and after waiting nine months for the right space between our individual releases, we went in to record.

The next day, I learned that about two hours after the session, Bill had been admitted to the hospital for exhaustion. When I called, he laughed and said, "It was recording with you that put me here." I wasn't sure if he was serious or not.

When the record was released, it went to number one on the national charts, and we were more in demand than ever. The television show was, at least in our opinion, the best on the air. And it was being shown everywhere. Before we went back into a town, we'd completely change the road show. The hard work paid off. Outside of my sons, work was all I was interested in.

One day I had been shopping and, coming in through the basement, I could hardly get through for the boys, Corky's gang at one end, and all Jimmy's at the other. David, not belonging to either bunch, was in the middle, just watching. Looking at them, I thought *They're as different as night and day.* And they were. Jimmy's group was the white shirt-sport coat type. And Corky's was the blue jean, yellow filling station cap group. Hearing sounds that resembled an argument, I went on upstairs. My policy had always been "If you don't see blood, don't interfere."

Putting away my things, I walked out to the den and switched on the TV. Suddenly, the kitchen door to the basement banged open and Corky stomped out to the den. He didn't even look at me, but when I looked at him, I gasped! His T-shirt was torn, his face was red, and he was crying. That last part scared me because when Corky cries, he's not only mad, he's dangerous! He slumped down in a chair. Then, I looked up and here came Jimmy . . . in the same shape! Good Lord! What had happened! Totally ignoring me, Jimmy walked over to where Corky was sitting, knelt down, and said, "Corky, I just want to be proud of you. You're my brother and I love you."

Corky said, "I love you, too," They put their arms around each other and I couldn't take it. Silently, I slipped from the room, went to my bedroom, and cried. I doubt if either of them ever knew I was there.

Jimmy had started his second year at M.T.S.U., and Corky had started at Austin Peay in Clarksville. David and I were home alone—with Solona. Jimmy and Corky were back and forth a lot but it wasn't the same. David was heavy into the theater—it was all he talked or thought about. The house was lonely. If only Mom were still here. She sure wouldn't be in anyone's way now. But it was too late. Since my brother Dick had taken little Keith and gone back to California, she'd never been happy here and had gone back to West Plains to live in an apartment in the Senior Citizens Towers. There, she could have her sewing and doll collection all over the place and it was all right. Besides, she knew everyone in West Plains and Tiny was there.

Once in a while a date would come in for Bill or for me, separately, and we had an agreement that if it didn't interfere with the TV show or dates booked together, we could work them—especially if the money was right. And I couldn't afford to turn down anything, bad bands included.

Tiny went with me a couple of times . . . what an experience! One show was in Atlanta, where I was booked to work some godawful club. Things got off to a bad start immediately.

As soon as we got there and got checked into the Holiday Inn, I had to go to a radio station. "Wanta go with me?" I asked Tiny. "I'll only be about an hour."

"No, I'll just wait here."

"Well, why don't you put on a bathing suit and go out by the pool."

"I didn't bring one," she said.

"Mine's in the suitcase . . . wear it."

"Well, I'll see."

I knew when I got back she'd be sitting right there in that room. Wrong!

When I walked up the steps, there she was standing outside the door in a pair of shorts. "Tiny, what are you doing out here?"

"I went out for a Coke and locked myself out."

"Why didn't you go down and ask for another key?" I asked.

"I wasn't going down there dressed like this! Besides, I didn't know if they'd give me one." The more I laughed, the madder she got.

"How long had you been out there?" I asked when we got into the room.

"An hour," she said sheepishly.

We'd come down a day early so I could take her out to a really nice place for dinner. Looking over the menu, she gasped! "Lord. I could buy a week's groceries for what this cost!"

"Don't worry about it," I said. "Would you like a shrimp cocktail?"

After giving it some serious thought, she said, "Well, that might be nice."

When the waiter put it in front of her, she said, "What's that?"

"A shrimp cocktail," he said. Tiny looked like she might throw up any minute.

"But I thought a cocktail was something to drink! These things look like grub worms!" The waiter stuck his nose in the air and walked off. I remembered a time in Home Economics when I was in the ninth grade that I thought the same thing. My, how I had changed.

The next night I worked in one of the worst places ever. The band was creatively lousy and the dance floor was alive with drunks! Money was the only thing that got me up on that stage.

The third set, I was singing one standard after another. A drunk who had been there all night was standing, weaving back and forth, in front of the stage. He started hollering something at me. At first, thinking it was probably an insult, I ignored him. Then, deciding to be real brave, I leaned over the rail that surrounded the stage and said, "What's that, sir?"

"I said, can you sing 'Your Cheatin' Heart' in the key of C?" I'd taken many requests but had never been given the key to sing them in.

"No, sir, but I'll bet you can."

"I sure can!" he said, and leaped over the rail.

Handing him the microphone, I signaled the band to start it off. Listening to as much as I could stand, I wondered what on earth made him think he could sing in the key of C, or any other key for that matter. If ever anyone sang in the crack, he did, and he was totally oblivious to the fact. Between him and the out-of-tune electric fiddle, I was darned near deaf when the evening was over. But, when I counted my money, I thought, *It's better than robbing a bank.*

The next day we started for Tampa, Florida, where I was to work four days in another club. Tiny was real edgy about going there because of the race unrest going on. And I wasn't too fond of the idea myself. Before leaving home, I had purchased a small, .25 automatic pistol, which lay between us on the seat. Solona had insisted I carry it. "Mrs. Howard,you got no business going down there with all that's goin' on."

"Well, Solona," I said, "if you're so worried about me, come and go with us."

"No, ma'am! I got sense enough to stay outa where I'm not wanted!"

"But, Solona," I said. "If you were there we wouldn't be in trouble with the blacks or whites!"

We checked into a nice motel on the causeway near the club. And since it was early afternoon, I put on my bathing suit and started out to the pool. Tiny said, "I hope you're not going to wear that out where anyone can see you!"

"Why not?" I asked.

"That bikini wouldn't cover a postage stamp!" she said.

"Well, since I'm not a postage stamp, I'm going out to the pool."

"You can go if you want to, but I'm not going with you!"

"Whatever you say," I said, and closed the door after me.

At the club, I seated her with wives of the band members while I worked. Several times, I'd look over and see a man asking her to dance. Looking embarrassed, she'd shake her head no and he'd walk away.

At intermission, I kidded her. "Were those men asking you to dance?"

"Men!" she said. "Why, one of them wasn't as old as my son Mickey. I told 'em I had heart trouble."

"What!"

"Yeah, all of em except one believed it. He said he'd be back for the next slow dance."

Sure enough, before long I saw her out on the dance floor with the slow dancer.

Going back to the motel about three in the morning, I got lost and ended up right smack in the middle of a black neighborhood! And about a dozen men were standing in the middle of the street I had to go down. As I got closer, they didn't part like I thought they would to let me through but came directly toward my car. One of them carried a ball bat and hit the side of the car! Tiny screamed but I just kept on driving.

All the way to the motel, Tiny kept saying, "I'm going home. I'm going home."

The next morning, I awoke to find her completely dressed and packed. "Where you going?" I asked.

"I told you last night. I'm going home! There's a bus in an hour."

"You're crazy, Tiny! It'll take you twenty-four hours to get home by bus. If you insist on going, let me buy you a plane ticket to Memphis and you can catch a bus from there."

"One way or another, you're going to get me killed!" she said.

As she walked up the steps to the plane, she turned and yelled so I could hear, "If this thing crashes, it'll be your fault!"

All through the divorce, Mr. Norman had remained Mr. Norman, even though we had become good friends. He was easy to talk to and I knew I liked him more than I should. And several times, when we were having lunch or a drink near his office, he'd talked about his children—Pia, fifteen, and the twins Melody and Valeria, thirteen. I knew he was married . . . I'd seen his wife's picture on his desk, but all he told me about her was that she was an ex-circus performer of some stature. Mostly, we talked about other things—like skydiving, which he was into, and flying—he had his own twin-engined plane. One day we talked about my fear of flying.

"You know how to get over that?" he asked.

"No," I said. "I wish I did."

"Take flying lessons."

"You're crazy. I just told you I'm afraid to fly!" He laughed that soft laugh of his that I liked so much.

"Yes, but if you learn what keeps the plane up, you won't be so scared."

"I'll think about it," I said.

It was such a pretty day. The leaves were just beginning to fall and I was out in the yard enjoying God's great creations. It was sweater weather, my favorite time of year. Solona came to the door and interrupted my thoughts. "Mrs. Howard . . . telephone!" As I got to the door, she smiled and said, "It's Mr. Norman." She knew how I'd come to look forward to his calls.

"Hello?"

"Miss Howard?"

"Yes, Mr. Norman." I smiled.

"I've decided that before you go sign up for expensive flying lessons, you should go flying."

"You mean, just go out to the airport and say I want to go up with somebody?"

"No, I mean with me. Can you be ready in an hour?"

"Sure," I said.

"Okay . . . I'll pick you up. How do I get to your house?"

After giving him directions, I hung up and went running to my bedroom. "Solona, help me find something to wear flying!" In the next hour, I'd changed clothes three times.

On the ride to the airport, I learned that Jack owned all or part of Cornelia Fort Airport and kept his plane, a twin-engined Cessna 310, there. I felt a little better thinking the one we were going up in had two engines. But, when we got there, he walked me to a little red and white Cessna 150, a single-engine plane. Just looking at it made me nervous.

"You're not serious!" I said, "We're not actually going *up* in this thing?"

"Sure . . . climb in." He was already seated. Seeing my nervousness, he said, "Trust me."

Against my better judgment, I climbed in beside him and buckled up tight.

Watching as he went through the preliminaries, I thought, *Well, he seems to know what he's doing.*

We taxied out to where they do the "run up" and I listened as he got take-off clearance. Now he was like I knew him—all business. We began to roll down the runway and I fastened my seat belt so tight that if we flew over twenty minutes, I'd be a good candidate for gangrene.

The take-off wasn't bad—in fact, I enjoyed it. It was exciting! He was explaining everything that was about to happen. But I was caught up in the view and didn't pay a lot of attention. "Do you know where we are?" he asked.

"I haven't the faintest idea!" I looked down at what looked like a row of toy houses. He pointed down.

"Right there—that's your house." Looking down, I saw three tiny figures waving. It must be the kids! This was great. Then he took off in another direction.

"Now, I'm going to show you some things you'll be required to do." He banked the plane right and left then started climbing.

"What are you doing?" I yelled.

"I'm going to put the plane into a stall," he said.

"Like hell you are," I screamed. He was still climbing.

"You'll be required to do this to get your license." He was ignoring me.

"Listen," I yelled. "I see no reason for messing with a perfectly good running engine. And if I have to do more than you've already done, forget it!"

"Before the engine stalls, you'll feel the plane shudder and a horn will come on," he explained calmly, and drew the plane back almost vertical. I started screaming at the top of my lungs. "No. Please don't! Don't stall the engine . . . please!" About this time, I felt the plane shudder. Oh, God! I was holding on for dear life! A loud horn sounded and the plane seemed to stop in midair. Suddenly, he nosed the plane over and left my stomach two thousand feet above me. "You son of a bitch!" I screamed. He was laughing. Not a giggle, but a full-blown laugh.

After he straightened the plane into a normal straight and level, he said, "I wondered what it would take for you to call me something besides Mr. Norman. I never dreamed when you did it would be son of a bitch."

On the way home, Jack was quiet. Once or twice, he'd reach over like he was going to touch my hand. Then, as though he thought better of it, didn't. Several times, though, he'd look at me and shake his head. I wished I knew what he was thinking.

When he pulled into the drive, I said, hesitantly, "Would you like to come in?" My bravado of a little earlier had disappeared.

He hesitated, then got out and followed me up the walk. I fixed us some iced tea. He sat at the kitchen table and told the boys all about my flying experience. It was great seeing them laughing and talking together. He'd met Jimmy at the courthouse but it was the first time Jack had met David and Corky. I could tell they liked him. *Now, why in the world should I be glad about that,* I thought. *After all, he's just my attorney.* Nevertheless, I was glad. Glancing at his watch, he stood up to leave, said good-bye to the boys, and I walked out to the car with him.

Before getting in the car, he took my hand and said, "Miss Howard, you're something else." For a moment, we just stood there looking at each other. Then he got in the car and, once more, slowly shook his head, as if to clear it of something. I hoped it wasn't me.

"I'll be gone to Vietnam with the Guard for a couple of weeks but I'll call you when I get back." I knew he was a major in the Tennessee Air National Guard but didn't know they made trips like that.

"That's a long way off," I said thoughtfully. Actually, I didn't know how far it was. All I knew was what they said on the news—that it was somewhere in the Far East and there was trouble there. But, suddenly, I hated to think of two weeks without hearing from him. I watched as he backed out of the driveway, then ran into the house. "Solona! I think I'm in love!"

"Oh, Lordy no, Mrs. Howard! He's married!" She was right to remind me. For a short while, I'd forgotten. And I had no right to forget. Neither of us needed the kind of hurt divorce could bring. But, right now, the memory of his hand holding mine overshadowed everything.

That night, I dreamed of a tall, good-looking man in an Air Force uniform standing beside a military plane. It was Jack. And just before he boarded the plane, he slowly shook his head.

Several things happened, right in a row, that made me consider putting on my waitress uniform again.

I had to leave for Michigan at ten one night and the boys and I had just sat down to dinner when the phone rang. It never fails—get in the shower or sit down to eat and it will ring every time. Otherwise, days on end can go by and you think you must be the only one left on earth with a telephone.

"Hello?" I said, figuring it was for one of the boys, since they received most of the calls these days.

"Mrs. Howard?" Surprise! It was for me.

"Yes, this is Mrs. Howard." I didn't recognize the woman's voice.

"I just want you to know that I know where the bus is leaving from and what time you're leaving and I'm going to blow your brains out before you get there."

"Who is this?" A weird laugh was my answer. "Who is this?" She hung up.

I sat there looking at the dead phone in my hand and started trembling all over.

The kids were all waiting for me to explain my outburst.

"Mom, who was that?" David asked.

"Some woman said she was going to blow my brains out before I got to the bus," I said.

"Well, you're not going!" they all said.

I dialed the number for the police. After telling the officer of the call, he said, "There's not a lot we can do about it unless a crime is actually committed."

"What the hell do you call this?"

"Well, ma'am, what I mean is, unless she actually shot you, we have nothing to go on."

"I see. Well, it's nice to know that if she does kill me, you'll take some action," I said sarcastically. "Well, I'll tell you what, I'm going to carry a gun!"

"Do you have a permit?" he asked.

"No, I don't. But, if I have to use it, feel free to do whatever you have to." I slammed down the receiver.

The kids were having a fit! "Mom, you're not going!" All thoughts of dinner had been forgotten as far as I was concerned. My stomach was in so many knots a drop of water couldn't have gotten through.

Realizing that I had to pull myself together, I said, "Hey, it's going to be all right. People who call and warn you are usually too cowardly to commit a crime." Someone, somewhere, had said that. I was sure.

All the time I was packing, I was a nervous wreck. My brave speech had convinced everyone but me. I tried to think logically. Okay, the creep who had called would expect me to drive my own car . . . right? Sure! I called Jimmy Gately, a member of Bill's band, and asked if he would pick me up on his way to where the bus was parked across town. With some excuse about my car not running well, I told him I'd wait downstairs for him about nine.

As soon as I saw his car, I ran out, scooted as far down in the seat as I could get, and said, "Drive!" He looked at me like I was crazy but didn't ask any questions. All the way across town, I stayed that way.

When he stopped beside the bus, I peeked out and, seeing no one I didn't know, jumped out, dashed onto the bus and all the way to the back. In answer to the questions of "What's the matter with her?" Jimmy Gately said, "Don't ask *me*. She was like that when I picked her up!"

When we'd gotten about ten miles out of town and I figured it was safe, I emerged from the back. Seeing their inquisitive looks, I explained what had happened.

Jimmy said, "Hey, Howard, at least you could have told me. I might have gotten shot!"

"Yeah, I know," I said, slightly ashamed.

The bus was an old Flex. A horrible, green thing Bill and the boys had nicknamed "The Green Goose." I didn't have a room. You just slept in whatever bunk happened to be empty at the time.

It must have been nerves that caused my stomach to be upset. Before, it had been knots . . . now, I felt like everything I'd eaten for a week was about to come up. One bunk after another, I tried to find one where I wasn't sick. Bill finally suggested the one over his bed, which hung by chains from the ceiling. Very carefully, I climbed up. But, just as I got settled, the bus hit a bump and down we came . . . bunk, chains, and all . . . right on top of Bill.

"Damn, Howard! You're trying to kill me!" Bill yelled as he pushed me off onto the floor. "Go find someplace else to sleep!"

Like Linus, I walked down the aisle of the bus, dragging my blanket behind me, until I found an empty bunk, which happened to be our drummer, Snuffy Miller's.

Sometime in the night, I woke and realized we had stopped. Pulling back the curtains, I saw we were in a truck stop and I could see some of the guys in there eating. By now I wasn't sick—I was hungry.

As I walked in, they all looked up and smiled. "Feeling better?"

"Yeah," I said as I slid in the booth next to one of them. "But, you know, after sleeping in all your bunks, I've decided Snuffy's is the best." I heard silverware hit the table.

Turning around, I saw two women, who were sitting in back

of us, glaring at me. "It's all right," one of the guys said. "She's just a real good sport and we believe in share and share alike."

The women said, almost as if on cue, "Well!" and huffed out of the restaurant.

Bill's television show had been moved to Windsor, Ontario, for quite a while now. Where before I could drive to Charlotte, now I had to fly to Detroit every two weeks or so and rent a car to drive across the river to Windsor. The porters even knew me by first name.

We'd only been home a few days when I had to go up there. For some reason, I didn't want to go. I hadn't been sleeping well. Jimmy and Corky were dating a lot and even when they were home they were out constantly. I worried about having to leave David so much. Solona was there and David had his friends, but sixteen was very young to have to fend for yourself. Yet, I had to work. If there was a solution I couldn't find it. I promised him, as soon as I had some time off, just the two of us would go somewhere.

After finding the note when I'd gotten home the last time, I wasn't too fond of leaving Corky and Jimmy. "Corky," it said. "We've got to quit having parties in the den when Mom's gone, or, at least, clean up the mess before she gets home. *(Signed)* Jimmy."

The day before I left, I went down to see Hubert. "Have you made your plane reservations yet?" he asked.

"No, I was waiting until the last minute."

"Well, this is the last minute," he said, and got on the phone and made me one on American Airlines at ten-sixteen the next morning. Hanging up, he said "What's the matter, Redhead? You look worried."

"I don't know, Hubert. I just don't think I should go."

"Oh, come on now, you just don't want to fly." He knew I was still chicken.

Resigning myself, I started to leave the office when his secretary said, "Jan, there's a Mr. Carruthers with American on the phone for you."

Thinking it was something about the reservation Hubert had just made, I said, "Yes, Mr. Carruthers, this is Jan Howard."

"I'm sorry to bother you, but are you flying to New York tomorrow on American?"

"No, I'm not. Why?"

"Well," he sounded relieved, "I've gotten some wrong information then . . . sorry I bothered you."

"That's all right. I'm not going to New York but I *am* going to Detroit."

"On American?" His voice took on a different tone. Anxious.

"Yes."

"At ten-sixteen?"

"Yes."

"Well, in that case there's something I have to tell you. A man called this morning and said that Jan Howard would be on a flight to New York at ten-sixteen tomorrow morning and there would be a bomb on board."

The phone fell out of my hand. "Hubert!" I screamed. He came running out of his office and I just pointed to the phone . . . I couldn't even speak. I guess he could see the terror on my face.

All the time he was questioning Mr. Carruthers, I kept saying, "I'm not going, I'm not going," and shaking my head. Something was real scary. That man had called this morning and Hubert had made my reservation only a few minutes ago!

While he was still on the phone, I left.

At home, I walked the floor. Why these sudden threats? The one from the woman who was going to blow my brains out, one when I was at the radio station, from a woman who said I had stolen her song, one from a woman who said she was going to throw acid in my face when I left the TV station, and now this. *Is this what fame is all about?* I thought. Well, if it is, the hell with it. The other threats, as bad as they were, I hadn't taken very seriously, but a bomb on a plane? Whoever it was knew exactly how to hit a nerve!

The kids came home and there was no way I could conceal my fright. "That's it!" they said. "You can't go." They went into my bedroom and started taking clothes out of my suitcase. As scared as I was, as they were taking them out, I was putting them back in. I didn't know what to do.

About ten o'clock, Bill Anderson called. "Now, Jan, you know you can't take things like this seriously."

"Ha!"

"You know I'm booked on that same flight. What I want to know is how come you got top billing?" He was laughing.

"I don't think it's funny!"

"Well, you can do whatever you want. You can drive or go on the bus with the guys or not go. Or, you can go with Hubert and me on the train."

I knew he was just trying to make me feel better but, no matter what anyone said, I knew this threat was real. Why were my suitcases still packed?

All night long, what little sleep I got, I dreamed of planes crashing, bodies covered with white sheets waiting for someone to identify them. One of them was me. Finally, I gave up and got up. All the time I was swearing I wasn't going to go, I was dressing.

Once again, telling the boys that we couldn't put our faith in some crank, I kissed them good-bye and drove to the airport, all praying I was doing the right thing.

As I walked into the airport, I saw Bill, Hubert, and Archie Campbell (he was booked to do the TV show) standing at the ticket counter. When a man walking toward me said, "Mrs. Howard?" I almost jumped out of my skin. "I'm Mr. Carruthers." He smiled and held out his hand. I just nodded. "We feel that you'll be flying on the safest plane in the air today. Every piece of luggage and every passenger has been searched." He seemed quite pleased with himself.

"You feel it's really safe then?"

"By all means!" he said.

"Okay, then I'll tell you what. If you think it's so darned safe, you go with us."

"I can't do that. I have a luncheon at the Hermitage at eleven o'clock!"

"That settles it then," I said. "If you don't go, I'm not going." I walked toward Hubert and Bill. Mr. Carruthers, right behind me, said, "All right. I'll go."

"Fine," I said, and walked to the gate.

Bill, catching up to me, said, "Your face is as white as a sheet!" I didn't doubt it.

When I saw the plane, I thought, *Lord! Why did it have to be an Electra!* Three of them had crashed recently. As I walked up the steps, I said a silent prayer. "Lord, if I'm not supposed to get

on this plane, please tell me." Not getting any heavenly sign, I
walked back and to my seat. A highly irritated Mr. Carruthers sat
in front of me, Archie beside me, and Bill and Hubert across the
aisle.

We were supposed to fly to Cleveland and change planes but,
about twenty minutes out of Nashville, the plane began to vi-
brate. I knew something was wrong! Then the pilot came on the
intercom. "Ladies and gentlemen, we're going to make an un-
scheduled landing in Louisville for a change of equipment.
Nothing to be alarmed about, though." My foot! Suddenly, instead of being more frightened, I was calm. I now knew we were
going to make it.

As we got off the plane, I asked Mr. Carruthers, "What was
the destination of that plane?"

"Buffalo, New York," he said.

My next trip out was to do The Tommy Hunter Show in Toronto,
Canada. I'd known Tommy since 1960 and usually enjoyed doing
the show, but this time it was hard work. I missed the boys,
worried about David, and wanted to be home.

Since I had to be in town five days, I decided to stay in the
Four Seasons Hotel downtown. It had a nice dining room, shops,
and a drugstore to while away what time I wasn't at the studio.

Every evening I'd had dinner in my room, but the last night I
decided to splurge and go to the dining room. With all the couth I
could muster, I called the maître d' and said, "This is Mrs.
Howard. I'd like a reservation for eight o'clock and I don't want to
be seated by the door or near the kitchen." I was quite proud of
myself.

"Yes, ma'am, I'll take good care of you!"

After a nice dinner, during which I was treated like Miss
Astor herself, I browsed through the drugstore for things like
toothpaste, magazines, etc., then walked to the elevator. A man
whom I'd noticed in the drugstore followed me but I didn't pay
much attention. *Just going to his room,* I thought. As I got on the
elevator, he got on. Neither of us spoke. When I got off, he got off.
Oh well, I thought, *his room is on this floor.* My room was the last
one on the right. All the way down the hall, he followed me. *Well,*
I thought, *his room must be across the hall.*

When I stopped at my door, he turned to the room across the

hall . . . just like I thought he would. But . . . when I opened my door, quick as lightning he pushed me inside, shut the door, and leaned against it. Totally flabbergasted, I said indignantly, "What can I do for you, sir?" Now, that was a stupid question! He stood there looking me up and down. Somehow, I wasn't frightened— just angry!

"You are a model, yes?" His accent was German or something like that.

"I am a model . . . no."

Still sizing me up, he said, "I watched you in the dining room and in the drugstore. You wear clothes very well."

I've got to be cool, I thought. *I can't make him angry.* Somehow, he didn't look dangerous, just curious. "Thank you," I said. Then, "Well, as long as you're here, you might as well be comfortable. Won't you sit down?" I motioned to a chair across the room . . . away from the door. He hesitated, then walked over and sat down. I did the same . . . on the bed nearest the door. The phone was beside the bed but I knew better than to reach for it. Suddenly, he walked back across the room and jerked open the closet door. "I like this one . . . I like this one, I don't like this one." He went through every outfit there. Holding out two dresses, he said, "Here, put these on."

"I will not!" I said. Then, thinking of a plan of action, I said, "All right . . . tell you what—you come back and sit down and I'll model one of them." He walked back and sat down. Looking him over (expensive suit, alligator shoes), the picture of a rapist or murderer didn't fit. "Tell me, what is your occupation?" I asked, curious.

"I'm a dress designer," he said. Then, getting angry, he said, "Try on the dress . . . now!" Now was my chance.

Casually picking up the dress, I walked toward the bathroom door . . . which just happened to be next to the outside door. Suddenly, instead of going into the bathroom, I jerked open the other door and screamed, "Now! Get out of my room, you son of a bitch!" Before I had finished the first word, he was out and running down the hall. Quickly, I ran back inside, locked and bolted the door, and called Security. After telling them what had happened, I hung up. When I thought about what could have happened, I broke out in hysterics.

The next morning when I went to pay my bill, I asked if

Security had caught the man who broke into my room. "What man?" the clerk asked.

"Excuse me, where is Security?" I asked

"Over there," she said, and pointed to the desk a few feet away.

Walking over, I asked to see the list of complaints from the night before—there was nothing from my floor. They hadn't even bothered to check out my call.

Walking back over to the desk, I asked for my bill. With it in hand, I said, "See these charges for the five days I've stayed here?"

"Yes," she said.

"Well . . . sue me." I tore up the bill and walked out.

Another time, in the Hyatt Regency in Flint, Michigan, at one o'clock in the morning, someone knocked on my door.

"Who is it?" I asked

"Room service," a man's voice answered.

"I didn't order room service," I said, and walked over to look through the peephole in the door. Three man were standing outside. Quickly I walked back and called the operator. "There's three men trying to get into my room," I said softly. "Don't open the door," she said unnecessarily.

"Lady! This is Security! If you don't open this door, I'll break it down!" the man outside said. The operator said, "Stay on the line. I'll send up Security."

I walked back to the door and looked out again. They were still there. "Are you going to open this door or do I have to break it down!" he said again.

Loud enough for him to hear, I said, "No, I'm not going to open the door and if you do break it down, you'll find a .357 Magnum aimed at your head!"

One of the men said, "Holy shit! Let's get the hell out of here!" They turned and ran down the hall.

A few seconds later, the real security man came. When I saw his identification through the door, I told him he'd probably passed the men in the hall. After he left, I settled down to another sleepless night.

The next morning, it was the same old story. They hadn't

actually committed a crime, therefore, all the action that was taken was to escort the men out of the hotel. Damn! I'd about had it!

We were in Windsor doing the TV show and, unlike other times when I was full of energy and raring to go, I was awfully tired and couldn't seem to function. My heart, which had a habit of getting out of rhythm now and then, was really acting up. But, not wanting to say anything, I went ahead and rehearsed even though I couldn't seem to concentrate or remember lyrics.

The camera was rolling and I was singing "I Don't Mind," one of the few songs I attempted to strum on the guitar. One minute I was singing . . . the next I was lying on the floor and Ferlin Husky—booked on the show along with his wife Mavis—was pouring water on my face. "Don't mess up her makeup!" Mavis said.

"To hell with her makeup!" Ferlin said . . . and that's all I remember until I woke up in a hospital with Jimmy standing by my bed. When I asked how long I had been there and what had happened, he said it had been three days and at first they had thought I was having a heart attack. Later, thank God, they had decided I was suffering from exhaustion. They had sent for Jimmy to take me home. Bill and the boys had already gone.

It had been a couple of weeks since the hospital and they must have been right about the exhaustion, because I was feeling a lot better. Being home had been the cure. I wished it could stay that way, but I couldn't think of anything I could do in town to make a living. I was a lousy secretary and hated to think about going back to being a waitress. What else could I do? I'd thought about trying to get in with some of the background singers but knew no one would take me seriously . . . and besides they all read charts and to me charts looked like a bunch of chicken scratches.

Deep in thought, I looked out the kitchen window and saw Jimmy drive in. He looked up, saw me, and waved. Then he called, "I'm going out to get the mail!" I went on peeling potatoes for their favorite meal . . . pot roast. Solona had fixed her specialty, brownies, and was setting the table. It had been a while since all of us had been home at the same time and this was going to be a special dinner.

Jimmy came back in and, holding up a letter, said, "Guess what? I got a letter from the President!"

"You got a what?"

"Yeah," he said. "It says 'Greetings.'" My God! He'd been drafted. I grabbed the letter out of his hands and read it. He was to report for a physical in a few days! They weren't supposed to draft boys who were in college, especially students with a B average! There must be a mistake.

The night before his physical, I didn't sleep much and was up long before he was sitting at the kitchen table drinking a cup of tea. He came down dressed in his stay-pressed pants, open-necked shirt, and V-necked sweater, just as though he was going to school. Oh, how I wished!

Attempting a smile, I said, "Do you have those letters?" Right after he'd gotten the notice I called Dr. Goldner for copies of his medical records, which stated that he had a heart murmur, a damaged liver from the severe mono he'd had, and defective stomach muscles from the spinal meningitis. Surely, with all that, he wouldn't pass. Of course, all three of the boys had heart murmurs and Dr. Goldner had said it was just an extra sound in the heart and not dangerous, but I'd known a boy in West Plains who had been rejected by the Army because of it. I was hoping that would be the case this time.

Shortly before noon, he was back . . . all smiles. "Well?" I asked. He told me that he and a boy with flat feet had been sent home.

"Does that mean that you don't have to go?" I asked hopefully.

"I guess so. They said to come back in the morning at eight-thirty as a formality."

"Did they read the letters?"

"No, they tore them up. They said too many guys were turning up with back trouble." He laughed. After a kiss on my forehead, he ran upstairs to his room. I breathed a sigh of relief.

That night, I couldn't figure it out. If Jimmy wasn't going, why couldn't I sleep? Why did I have a feeling of dread?

Once more, I was up before dawn. As Jimmy came downstairs, I asked, "Got time for breakfast?"

"No," he said, "I'll be gone only an hour. I'll eat when I get back." He kissed me and walked, slower than usual, down to his car. I stood there and watched as he stood beside his car for a minute, then walked out to where Bucko was lying in the yard, kneeled down, and hugged his beautiful, furry neck, and walked back to his car. Before getting in, he looked up, waved to me, and drove out the driveway.

Waiting for him to come back, I smoked one cigarette after another and paced the floor. When the phone rang, I grabbed it before it finished the first one.

"Mom?" The sound of his voice told me before he could. "I'm on my way to Fort Knox, Kentucky." Dear God. They hadn't even let him come home to say good-bye.

As the days went by, I'd catch myself thinking that Jimmy would come home from school and the Army was all a bad dream. Then, I'd look out and see his car sitting in the driveway, and know it wasn't. He was in the Army and there was nothing I could do about it. Corky and David missed him, too. But they seemed to draw closer together. They still had their arguments but everything was different, in an indefinable way.

Every few days, we'd get a letter from Jimmy describing the horrors of basic training. Even though he made a joke out of it, he knew I could read between the lines. To assure us of one good laugh, he sent some dime-store pictures of him making faces and showing off his new skin-head crew cut haircut.

It was three weeks until Christmas. We were trying our best to act normal. For a few years now, we'd been supplying Christmas for a needy family—the boys felt that was what Christmas was all about and they were right. I remembered the days I wished someone would help us out. Thank God, now I could do it for someone else.

I always had the boys make out a wish list. This way I'd have something to choose from. But Jimmy wasn't here to make out his list. And he could only use so many shaving kits and boxes of stationery. What else could he use in the Army? Then I decided he wasn't going to be in the Army forever. I'd buy presents for him just like I did for Corky and David. We would save them until he came home. I didn't know if he would get a leave to be here for Christmas.

I thought about having a party, but most of the people I'd counted on as friends dropped out of sight along with Harlan. At the last minute, I invited Hubert and Bobby and Jeanie Bare over for dinner. With Corky and David's help, we decorated the house, inside and out, and bought big tree.

A few days before Christmas, we got a big present. Jimmy was coming home for ten days!

Corky and David picked him up at the bus station while I waited at home. It was important for them to have time together. When they walked in the house, after giving me a big hug and kiss, the first thing Jimmy did was put the angel on top of the tree. Now it was complete.

For ten wonderful days, they were three kids again—playing in the snow, building a snowman, wrestling with Bucko. I never wanted it to end. I tried not to think about it.

Christmas Eve, I fixed a special dinner—candles—the whole nine yards. The evening was spent just enjoying each other. When it got yawning time, I went to my room and left the three boys by themselves. When everything got quiet, I went to make my usual rounds of taking one last peek at each one of them asleep. I discovered Jimmy asleep on the sofa in the living room. Next to the tree. With the soft glow of the lights on his face, he looked about fifteen years old, and so peaceful. I prayed to God to watch over him.

The next morning when I woke and saw it was nine o'clock, I knew they were really grown up. More so than the night before, when, as a joke, they'd set out a glass of milk and some cookies for Santa Claus—which I'd removed after everyone was asleep.

Corky and David couldn't wait to get to the presents but Jimmy lay on the sofa and let his be brought to him. "Mom," he said. "This is the most comfortable sofa in the world and the only one long enough for me to lay on. You can sell everything else in the house but not this, please?"

"I promise," I said.

All too soon, Christmas season was over. Corky and David were back in school, Jimmy was back at camp, and I was going on a thirty-day tour.

Several times after Jack had come back from Vietnam he'd called, but that's as far as it went. I think both of us knew that if we saw each other we would be playing with fire. By silent, mutual agreement neither of us suggested it. He did say, though, now that Jimmy was in the Army, if I ever needed him, call. We left it at that. I did miss talking to him, though. It's a good thing I'm going on this tour, I thought, or I just might break our mutual agreement. I did need him.

As far as I'm concerned, thirty days is too long to be on tour. Starting out in Texas, we continued on to New Mexico, California, up the coast to Washington State, Oregon, and then on to British Columbia, and across Canada. My body was on the bus and at the shows but my mind was home.

Every couple of days, I'd call, sometimes talking to Solona, but usually to David or Corky. If it was David, always before hanging up, I'd have to ask, "Are you sure there's nothing else I need to know?" One time, while Jimmy was still home, it was "Oh, yeah, Jimmy broke his collarbone playing football in the backyard." But then he he reassured me, even though it was in a sling, it was all right. Another time it was, "Oh, the house got burglarized and they took your mink jacket." Just the little tidbits I needed to make me know how much I needed to be home.

The next time, I talked to Corky. Even though we only had a few more days left on this tour, I needed to be reassured that everything was all right. But it wasn't. He told me that David had been at some party and, for some reason, it had been raided and David had spent the night in jail. "Jail?" I said. "What for?"

"Well, there was talk of dope or something."

"But David wouldn't have anything to do with that!"

"I know, Mom, but he was there. Anyway, it might have done him good to see what happens if you hang out with the wrong people. But he's okay now. Don't worry." His voice told me he was trying to convince himself as well as me. We'd talked before about David having to be alone so much. Solona was there but he needed more than she could give—more supervision—more love. And I didn't know exactly how to provide those from a distance.

The bombshell came at the end of the conversation. "Oh, yeah, I joined the Army."

"You what?"

"I joined the Army," he repeated.

"But, Corky, with Jimmy in, they can't draft you, too."

"They didn't, Mom. I volunteered. If Jimmy's going, I'm going."

"Dear God, Corky, I can't handle you and Jimmy both being gone. Please tell me you didn't actually do this."

"It's too late, Mom. I leave in the morning. Dad's going to take me to the bus."

"In the morning? Corky, if you had to do this, why didn't you wait until I got home?"

"Well," he said, "I thought about it. But thought it would be easier on you this way.

"Easier? How could you think it would be easier for me not to even see you before you left?" I was so hurt I started crying.

"I'm sorry, Mom. I know I should have waited, but it's done now. I won't be far away. Fort Campbell, Kentucky."

It might as well have been to the moon. Oh, God, he was only eighteen—just a kid! It was January twenty-ninth, exactly two months to the day from when Jimmy was drafted.

The rest of the tour, I might as well have been absent. Cues, songs, everything went right over my head. *God, what else was going to happen?*

Don Bowman, the comedian from the television show, and Kenny Price, another entertainer, were on the show and did everything possible to take my mind off problems at home by making me laugh. Things like pushing a broom across the stage in back of Bill when he was singing a sad song. The audience laughed with me but Bill didn't. Another night, Don, who was about five feet six and didn't weigh a whole lot, got in a grocery cart (I don't know how it got backstage) and Kenny, whose nickname is "The Round Mound of Sound," pushed him across the stage, again, in the middle of one of Bill's sad songs. Then there was the night I sneezed in the middle of one of Bill's recitations. Poor Bill. If we hadn't all been on separate contracts, we'd have all been fired.

Oshowa, Ontario, was the last night of the tour. Bill and I had been singing "For Loving You" every night and sometimes twice a night for thirty-three days and it had become very difficult for either of us to keep a straight face. Every time I'd look into his eyes, I'd start laughing. Finally, to keep from breaking up, he'd look at my forehead. "Don't do that," I'd say. Can you imagine talking to someone with him looking at your forehead? Yet, he continued to do it.

One night, after doing my part of the show, I was in the

dressing room waiting to go back on for the duets and the finale. Thumbing through a *Mad* magazine someone had left behind, I saw the picture of a horrible, bloody eye! Just a big, round eye! I'd found my solution. Getting out my fingernail scissors and eyelash glue, I cut it out, pasted it on my forehead and pulled my bangs down over it. Now I was ready to sing the duets!

Walking onstage, I kept my face turned to the audience. The band started the music for "For Loving You" and, after the opening chorus, I turned to Bill. He began his recitation. "For loving you . . . my life is." I parted my bangs. He started again. "For loving you . . . my life is." He'd seen the eye but he couldn't believe it. Then, he did. "My God! It's an eye!" he said, and literally fell to the floor, white suit and all. The audience didn't have the faintest idea what was happening but, seeing me laughing, they joined in. Then I turned to the band. It was all over. They went into hysterics and I had completely lost it. Bill, half furious and half laughing, got up from the floor and turned to the audience, which was out of control. "Wait a minute!" he said. "Wait a minute! Stop! Stop laughing! You've got to hear what this idiot has done to me!" In detail, he explained, and that was all it took . . . the roof came off! There was nothing I could do but leave the stage—quickly.

Going to my dressing room, I changed clothes and went out to sit high in the stands until he finished his show.

About an hour later, with the auditorium empty now, he found me still sitting there. "Well," he said. "You said you were going to do something and you did."

"Yeah, I did."

"I guess you knew I'd be a good sport, though, or you wouldn't have done it, right?"

"Bill," this time, I could look him in the eye straight-faced, "it wouldn't have mattered if you had fired me on the spot. I'd have done it anyway."

"Yeah, I guess you would have." He got up and walked to the bus. Taking my chances that my things wouldn't be sitting out on the street, I followed. For hours, "the eye" was the topic of conversation and laughter. Even Bill couldn't stay in a bad mood and finally admitted it was the funniest thing he'd ever seen.

Don Bowman was famous for staying awake days at a time, roaming the halls trying to find someone to keep him company.

At the beginning of the tour, it wasn't bad to be awakened at three o'clock in the morning with, "Jan, this is Don and I need someone to talk to." But as the tour stretched out, everyone tried to be as invisible as possible.

After leaving Oshowa, everyone was just waiting for the "fuel and eat" stop to crawl in our bunks and sleep to Nashville. Everyone but Don. When I got back onto the bus, he said, "Jan, whatever you do, don't let me go to sleep."

"But, Don, you've got to sleep." I could see, in spite of himself, he was already nodding.

"No! I can't sleep! Promise me you won't let me sleep!" He and I were the only people up . . . Everyone else had sacked in. Very softly, like you would talk a baby to sleep, I started talking. Like someone had hit him over the head, he started snoring and was out like a light. Getting one of the boys up, we dragged him to the nearest bunk and rolled him in.

Just as we were pulling into Nashville, he came out of the back like a streak of lightning! "Damn," he said. "Why did you let me sleep!"

"Don, now you'll be rested when you get home," I said.

"Yeah, that's just the trouble!" he said. "If I go home tired my wife Ruth will know I've been working hard. If I'm rested she'll swear I've been in somebody's bed."

I was now used to no one being there when I got home, but this time it was strange. Corky's room, which always had that "lived in" look, was now neat as a pin, too neat. I couldn't stand it. Walking through the rest of the house, it almost looked like no one lived there. Thank God for David's room, which was a mess. That evening, we had a long talk and he explained that he had no idea what had been going on at that party until the raid. He said he never wanted to spend another night in jail!

All night, I thought about it. I knew something had to be done. He was sixteen years old, too old for a baby-sitter and too young to be left with only Solona. The next morning I called Harlan. With every part of me, I didn't want to but, it was all I had left.

A woman answered. "This is Jan," I said. "Could I please speak to Harlan?"

A minute later, he came on the phone. "What is it?" he said, not overly friendly.

For a second, I started to hang up, but then I continued. "Harlan, with Jimmy and Corky both gone, I have to think of what's best for David, and he can't continue to stay here with just Solona."

"What's that got to do with me?" he said. He sure wasn't making it easy for me.

"Would it be possible for him to stay with you when I'm on the road?" By his silence, I already knew what his answer would be.

"No, Jan, it wouldn't be possible. I'm getting married again."

"Sorry I bothered you," I said, and hung up. I vowed never to call him again.

The next morning after David left for school, Solona said, "Mrs. Howard, I'm worried about David."

"What about?"

"Well, he's running around with boys I never saw before and comes home at all hours. And when I tell him he can't go, he says I can't tell him what to do. I'm afraid he's going to get himself in some kind of trouble." She was right.

Searching my mind, I remembered another entertainer, Jack Green, saying his boy went to Castle Heights Military Academy and what a fine school it was. I made the call.

That evening, when I told David, his face fell. "Is it some kind of reformatory?" he asked.

"Oh no, honey! It's just a school where you'll have some supervision. You can't stay here by yourself anymore. Too many bad things could happen."

"I'm old enough to stay by myself," he said.

"No, David, you're not. You're not sixteen. And I couldn't bear it if something happened to you." He was looking so down, I almost backed off. "It will only be until school's out, and we'll think of something else then. Will you try it?"

Seeing this was tearing my heart out, he came over, put his arms around me, and said, "Sure, I'll try it. Who knows, I might even like it." I knew he was only trying to make it easier on me and it only made it worse. Damn. If there was only another way. Our lives are like a picture puzzle. Yet, instead of the pieces fitting together, they are scattered out of place. He couldn't start until the next quarter. So we had time.

The dreams started coming. Every time I'd close my eyes, I'd see an explosion, fires burning, something that looked like an Army tank overturned, and Jimmy's body lying on the ground . . . someone was taking his rings and watch off. I'd wake up screaming, "*Jimmy!*" It got so I was afraid to go to sleep. Many nights David would hear me screaming and spend the rest of the night lying beside me on the bed patting me like I was a little child.

I tried to tell myself my mind was working overtime. Jimmy was still at Fort Knox. What would happen to him there? And why was it always Jimmy? Corky was in the Army, too. Sometimes, since I was afraid to sleep at night, I'd nap in the afternoons. It didn't matter . . . daylight or dark . . . it still happened. Often, when I'd be crying, the phone would ring and it would be Jimmy. Instead of hello, he'd say, "What's the matter?" Our minds had always been in tune, but now more than ever.

Since the dreams had started, David was sticking close to home and was in the den watching television. It was ten o'clock and I went into the bathroom to clean my face. Suddenly, feeling dizzy, I sat down on the side of the tub. It wouldn't go away. "David!" I called. The next thing I knew I was in Madison Hospital, and Jimmy was sitting by my bed, holding my hand and crying. I reached out to touch his head. "Mom," he said, "you can't do this to me. I can't stand to see you hurt or see you cry. Now, Corky and I have a job to do and you have a job to do. You're always telling us to act like adults, now it's your turn."

No matter how much I had wanted to see him, I hadn't wanted it to be this way. I couldn't stand to see him hurting like this. It was all my fault. He told me that the doctor had called and said I was seriously ill and had kept calling for him. He had gotten a ten-day emergency leave, four of which had already been used up. As far as he knew, it was caused by overwork. Thank God David hadn't told him about the dreams. And he would certainly never find out from me.

He said a serious thing: "Mom, guys in Vietnam get killed worrying about their families at home. I don't know if Corky or I will have to go there or not but, if we do, we know we won't have to worry about you—right?"

Smiling, I reached out and touched his face. "You're so right, my son." Then and there, I made up my mind, no matter what, they'd never hear anything but good news from home. No matter how I thought of them, he and Corky were men now and had enough things to worry about without me adding to them.

I told Jimmy to spend the time with his friends and David. But, every afternoon, Jimmy, and whoever was with him, came to the hospital for a game of penny-ante poker. One day, just as we got all the money and cards spread all over the bed, the chaplain walked in. Seeing us trying to cover up the evidence, he smiled and said, "Carry on, folks," and left.

Right after I got out of the hospital, David had to leave for Castle Heights. It was one of the worst days of my life.

David and I made a deal. If I was home on weekends, he would come home. If not, he'd stay at school. And on Wednesdays, the afternoon he had off, either he'd come home or I'd come up there. It was only twenty miles away.

Since he'd be wearing a uniform, he didn't take many clothes. With the few things he was allowed to have, we drove to Lebanon, Tennessee, where the school was located. Driving up the long tree-lined drive, David said, "I guess this is how a guy feels when he goes away to college." Lord, I hoped I was doing the right thing.

The commandant looked like a kind but strict man. "Don't worry, Mrs. Howard," he said. "There are boys here from seventh grade through high school."

David and I walked to his room, which was in one of the big red brick buildings on campus. Opening the door, we both stared. Talk about spare. There was an army cot, a chest of drawers, a sink with a small mirror over it, and that was it. The window was bare. I started to cry. David walked around the room and said, "You know, with a little fixing up, this could be almost livable." He turned to me, smiling, but I knew it was strictly for my sake. As I drove out the drive, I thought, *Please God, let this nightmare be over soon.*

David came home fairly often, and as far as I could tell, he seemed to be getting along fine. One day, when I couldn't be there on Wednesday, he called and said, "I'd already seen the movie. So I went down to the square to watch the old men spit and whistle." He said that was the primary excitement Lebanon had to offer.

With the boys gone, Bucko was lost. Every afternoon, he'd wait for the school bus. And when the boys didn't get off, he'd come in the house, tug at my clothes, and take me to each of their rooms. Then, he'd stand there looking as if to say, "Where are they?" It broke my heart. He'd follow me back downstairs and lie on the kitchen floor making terrible sounds, and I'd see what seemed like tears coming from his eyes. He wouldn't eat and kept running off. I knew he was looking for the boys. The vet said he was grieving himself to death and the only solution was to have him around children. And that meant give him away. I wrote to all three of the boys and got the same answer. "No! That would be like giving away one of us!" I decided to try it awhile longer. I needed him, too. He was all I had left.

Outside of a few phone calls and lunch now and then, I hadn't seen much of Jack Norman. After the day we went flying, we both knew it was best that way. He'd once said, "You don't need any more hurt." He was right. A couple of times he jokingly asked, "When are you going to fix dinner for me?" But that's all it was—a joke.

The phone's ringing jarred me back from my private thoughts. "Miss Howard? When am I going to get that dinner you promised?" I could hear his smile.

"Well, Mr. Norman (by now the Miss Howard and Mr. Norman had become nicknames). It's nice to hear from you."

"I asked a question," he said. He was used to getting answers.

"How about this evening," I said, never dreaming he was serious.

"I can be there by six, but I have to leave at nine-thirty. Is that okay?"

My heart was beating ninety miles an hour. "Of course," I said, trying not to let my excitement show through. "I'll see you at six."

Glancing at the clock I saw I'd have just enough time to put a roast in the oven. Heavens! I didn't even know if he liked roast! Oh, well, it would have to do. The most important thing was what to wear.

Rummaging through the closet, I chose a long "at home" thing I'd bought recently.

Promptly at six, I heard his car. Taking another look in the mirror, I dashed out to check on the roast and to make sure the table looked as inviting as it had the dozen other times I'd looked. The best china, silver, and tablecloth. Lights turned down low and candles ready to be lit.

Instead of coming in the front door, he came to the one off the dining room . . . the one leading up from the patio. As I watched him walk across the sun deck, I thought, *What ever made me afraid of this man?*

Offering him a drink, I showed him where everything was. He knew the extent of my knowledge of how to fix a drink was to open a bottle of beer. We walked to the den.

After walking around looking at the awards and mementos on the wall, he sat down on the sofa and motioned for me to sit beside him. But, self-consciously, I'd already seated myself behind the desk. *How stupid,* I thought, *here all this time, I've wanted him here and now I'm acting as nervous as a schoolgirl.*

Knowing I'd just finished another album, he said, "Why don't you play your new album for me?" After I got it started, he walked over, took my hand, and led me back to the sofa. All the time the album played, we sat there not saying a word. We didn't need to. The most natural thing in the world was for him to put his arm around me.

As the song "You'd Better Sit Down, Kids" came up, he listened closely. It was a story of two people who had separated, and the mother was telling her children to sit down, she wanted to explain that even though their father wouldn't live there anymore, he still loved them. As the music stopped, he said, "You put a lot of yourself into your songs." Turning me to face him, he said, "Miss Howard, I think I love you." I thought my heart was going to stop.

"I think I love you, too," I said very softly.

"What did you say?"

"I said, I think I love you, too." There was no thinking about it. I did. I didn't want to love him and I knew he didn't want to love me. But we were fighting a losing battle. Dinner was completely forgotten.

At nine-thirty precisely, an alarm went off on his watch and he got up to go. As we stood at the door, arms around each other, he said, "I may not call you for a few days. I have to think. But I do know that I love you." That was all I needed to hear.

Two whole weeks went by. As much as it hurt, I knew it was

best. There was no solution. Just when I was beginning to be resigned, he called.

"I've avoided calling you on purpose," he said. "I've tried to get you out of my mind but I can't. Do you still mean what you said?"

"Yes, Jack."

"Then I've got to see you." Yesterday wouldn't have been soon enough.

After basic training, Jimmy came home for ten days before going to Fort Polk, Louisiana, for Advanced Infantry Training. While he was home he decided to sell his Corvair to some friends of ours, Joe and Rose Lee Maphis, and get another one he'd had his eye on, a Chevy dual carburetor Super Sports. I knew it was silly but he had his heart set on it and I couldn't say no. But then I wasn't very good at saying no. Between polishing his new car and his golf clubs, it took up most of his time. But it made him happy, and that was all that mattered.

The day before he left, he came running in the kitchen. "Mom, come and go somewhere with me," he said.

"Where?" I asked.

"Never mind," he said. "You'll see when we get there."

All the way across town it was like he had some fantastic surprise for me. "You'll just love it," he kept saying. We stopped in front of a pet store.

"What's this?" I asked.

"Come on," he said, practically dragging me from the car. In the front door we went directly to the back, where he pointed to a chimpanzee in a cage. "There!" he said.

"There *what*?" I said. Jimmy was all smiles.

"That's just what you need to keep you company until we get back!" he said.

"Jimmy, believe me, I don't need an overgrown monkey to keep me company! Besides, I already have three monkeys . . . you, Corky, and David!"

"But, Mom, he's so cute and it'll just be for a little while," he said as I pulled him from the store.

The bad dreams, which had ceased for a while, began again. Now they were more real than ever. But I couldn't let on—even to

David. This was something I had to handle myself and a promise I had to keep. I told Jack about them but he said I was just worrying unnecessarily. When I told Dr. Goldner, he suggested a psychiatrist. They all thought I was crazy but I knew the dreams were nothing as simple as that. Each time, they began and ended the same way. An explosion, fires, an overturned tank, and Jimmy lying in the ground with someone taking his rings and watch off. I couldn't see a wound. The only person I could talk to was a friend in Atlanta, Mary Ann Summers.

The years I'd been in country music I'd met a lot of nice people but Mary Ann was special. From the moment we'd met when she came along to a show somewhere in Georgia with a man named Zell Miller, who was running for Congress, we became friends. I really don't know why. She was so heavy into politics, we certainly had nothing in common. But her smile was beautiful and her positive attitude was something I wished I had. She'd only been to Nashville and my house just once, but we'd talked often. And when I'd think I couldn't handle the dreams, I'd call Mary Ann, who was quick to talk about funny things that had happened. Like the time, when I wasn't along, that Jimmy had gone on a tour with Bill and the band. He and the band had gone on ahead and gone deep-sea fishing and when they picked Bill up at the airport, there was a big fish tied to the front of the bus. And about the time he and five of his buddies had gone to Florida and stopped on the way back just to say hello and had ended up staying five days. She was that kind of person—adopting everyone, including me.

Since I had joined Bill's show, my Opry spots depended on him. It seemed now I was just the girl singer with the Bill Anderson Show. Even though I'd had number-one hits of my own and was one half of the successful duets, I felt like a spare part, and began to lose my confidence again. Even the disk jockeys that came to the show took me for granted, and it hurt. And sometimes, to my regret, my hurt showed in public.

The day before we were to work the Mid South Coliseum in Memphis, a reporter wrote a whole column about the Bill Anderson Show appearing there, not once mentioning me. Another newspaper did, but the one that did not was the only one I worried about. Onstage, Bill went out of his way to thank the paper that hadn't mentioned me. And I, having my own micro-phone, said, "And I'd like to thank him also, for nothing." Bill could have cut my throat. Later, I felt so bad, I wished he had.

Bill wasn't the easiest person to get along with. But then, neither was I. Especially at this point. My nerves were raw and exposed and I was so edgy every little thing upset me.

One day, while rehearsing the television show, I laughed during one of Bill's songs. He was furious! "Don't laugh when I'm singing!" he said. Hell, we weren't filming. I couldn't see what he was so upset about.

"Okay, I won't laugh," I said. "I won't even smile."

All afternoon it was tension time. Since everyone took their cues from us, everyone was snapping at each other. I was fixing to do my song when the floor director came over and handed me a note. "If you think I acted like an ass—you're right. If I should say I'm sorry—I do. Now, will you please smile?" I looked over to where Bill was standing at the side. Walking over, I hugged him and said, "You were right on both counts, but I love you anyway, Star."

To make matters worse, that was the day I also had a run-in with his then wife, Betty. Bill had warned me that she had been told by her hairdresser that he and I were having a hot love affair and she was coming out. "Fine," I said. "Let's get this out in the open."

Sure enough, when I walked out of the makeup room, she was waiting for me. Before she could say a word, I said, "Betty, I understand you've been told Bill and I are having an affair." I could tell she definitely didn't expect me to take the offensive.

"Well, that's the rumor," she said.

"Betty, that's exactly what it is—a rumor," I said. "Now let's get one thing straight and then I'll never discuss this again. Bill and I work together—that's all. When the show's over, I doubt if either one of us enters the other one's mind. If we seem to be really caught up in these love songs, it's strictly for the cameras and the audience. As a man, he doesn't appeal to me, and as a woman I don't appeal to him. And that's great. We're friends—nothing more. Okay?" I walked away without waiting for an answer.

Except for a few shows, we were home for a while and I was glad for that. David got to come home more often and Corky came home for his leave before going to Fort Sill, Oklahoma, where he'd be taking his A.I.T. The house felt like a home again. Once more, there were boys everywhere. I never knew how many there would be for breakfast. They'd come up from the rec room, out of the den, and down from upstairs . . . everywhere there was a bed, and sometimes where there wasn't. I couldn't keep track of all of them but a few I could always count on being there—Jamesy Baker, "Butterball" Lane, Steve Moore, and Dennis Onyx. Between them, they could eat more pancakes than a football team.

Talk about perfect timing—I was booked on a show in Shreveport, Louisiana, just a hundred and fifty miles from where Jimmy was stationed. After calling to see if he could get off that weekend, we decided Corky would fly down with me.

I have never been so proud as when I introduced Jimmy and Corky to the audience just before I sang, "Where No One Stands Alone." When they stood, both in uniform, I didn't think I'd ever be able to get the first note out. But I had to. This was for them and them alone—my sons.

So we could all be together, I had booked a suite at the hotel. After dinner, talking until we were out of breath, I left them alone. But, with the door open between the bedrooms, I could hear as they wrestled and played like two little kids. During a rambunctious pillow fight, someone called to object to the noise. "I'm sorry," I said, "you must have the wrong room." Slowly, they wore down and I peeped in to see them both sound asleep. Tiptoeing in, I pulled the covers over them, leaned down and kissed their foreheads and stood looking down at my two boys. Even though in the morning they'd have to put on the uniforms that hung in the closet, tonight they were little boys again. Walking out, I closed the door, then opened it again. I knew that several times during the night, I'd come back to cherish the scene before me.

As we were getting ready to leave the next day, I heard them making plans. Jimmy would be finishing his A.I.T. about the time Corky would be finishing his at Fort Sill and maybe—just maybe—they'd be home at the same time. In my heart I knew that's all they were, just plans. It was difficult to watch Jimmy get on the bus back to camp, but they were laughing and kidding around. We had already decided that if something happened so they couldn't both be home at the same time, when Jimmy came home, he, David, and I would fly out to Fort Sill.

Corky's leave was up all too soon and he had to return to the real world.

One night, Jimmy called from Alexandria, Louisiana, collect as usual.

"Hey, Mom! Guess what? A bunch of us are at this place here and they have *your* record on the jukebox!" He sounded amazed. One by one, I talked to each of his buddies and assured them that I was indeed the real Jan Howard. Before hanging up, Jimmy laughed and said, "Maybe now I'll get some respect."

His training was finished, but still Jimmy was kept at Fort Polk. Every few days he'd call and say, "Surely they'll let me come home soon." I could tell he was homesick. "All they do is send me out on maneuvers," he reported. "I'm the enemy and if I get this white stuff on me, I've been killed. Well, I've been killed so many times I'm sick of it."

Late May I was doing the afternoon Ralph Emory television show. Ralph invited me home to have dinner with him and his wife, Joy. "Let me call home first," I said. Before I even got out the question "Has Jimmy called?" David said, "Mom, you're not gonna like this. Jimmy called. He's being sent to Vietnam. They're not gonna let him come home."

"Like hell they are!" I said. Ralph heard me and took the phone. After listening, he hung up and said, "Come on home with me and I'll see what I can do."

All the way to his house I was crying so hard I could barely see the road. "Surely they can't do this! Surely he'll get to come home!"

After several calls, Ralph located Congressman Richard Fulton having dinner in a restaurant in Washington, D.C. He explained what had happened, and after hanging up, said to me, "He said to go home and someone would contact you."

Daylight came before sleep did. The next morning David, Solona, and I waited by the phone. It rang at nine o'clock. "Mrs. Howard, this is the Secretary of the Army's office. Please stay by your phone. Your son will call within the hour." You couldn't have pried me away. Sure enough, thirty minutes later, Jimmy called.

"Mom! What did you do? The Secretary of the Army himself called down here! My sergeant came and got me and said, 'Howard! Go call your mother, then be prepared to work your ass off!' "

"But do you get to come home?" I held my breath.

"Yeah! For twenty-one days! I told 'em not to mess with my mom!" Thank God!

It was like the Army didn't exist. Jimmy played golf, taught kindergarten-aged children in Sunday School, ran around with his buddies. It was like old times. Whatever I felt, I didn't want to show it. I noticed, though, that he spent extra time with David and was home early at night. I told him he didn't have to be but he said, "I like to be home."

Ever since the divorce I had been meaning to have my will updated. It just happened to come at this time. I suggested that Jimmy meet me for lunch afterward.

After eating, I said, "Jimmy, I have to discuss something with you."

"I know, Mom."

"Well, you know I've been redoing my will and since you're the oldest, I've named you as guardian for Corky and David."

"That's fine." He was looking so serious, I wished I hadn't brought it up.

"Anyway, I just wanted you to know. I don't want to talk about it anymore." I started getting out the money to pay the check. Reaching across the table, he put his hand over mine.

"Wait a minute, Mom. Since this has come up, there's something I have to discuss with you." Suddenly, I knew what it was.

"No! I won't talk about it!"

"But, Mom . . . we have to discuss what could happen."

"I refuse to discuss it and that's all there is to it!" I got up and left the table. If it was me we were talking about, that was one thing. But him? No.

As we had planned, David, Jimmy, and I flew to Fort Sill. For four wonderful days we played tourist, with Corky as our guide. Climbing hills, taking pictures, swimming—anything as long as we were together. One day, while they were in the pool, I was dozing on a chaise with my eyes closed when I heard a familiar voice. "Jan? Is that *you?*" I looked up to see Jimmy Dean. "What are you doing here?" he asked.

"I'm here with my sons," I said, pointing to where they were having a water fight in the pool.

"Those are your sons?"

"Yes. Corky, the middle one, is stationed here at Fort Sill and Jimmy, the oldest, is on leave before going to Vietnam."

"Damn!" he said. "I'm doing a show at the base tonight—if you all can come, I'll have reserved seats for you."

"Thanks, Jimmy," I said, "but I think we'll just spend the time here together."

"I don't blame you," he said. Walking away, I saw him look again to where the boys were playing and shake his head.

That afternoon, Jimmy and Corky said they were going somewhere for a beer and would be gone for a couple of hours. They were gone four, and when they returned they were a lot more serious than when they'd left. I didn't ask why.

It was our last night at Fort Sill and, at eleven o'clock, they decided to go swimming. "You can't," I said. "The pool's closed."

"Well, I guess you'll just have to stand watch!" they said, and ran for the pool, Diving in, they swam under water in a race to the end. Corky and David swam straight, but Jimmy headed for the side. Before I could stop him, his head hit the concrete. When he came up, blood was running down his face. But, after checking, I saw the blood made the cut look a lot worse than it really was. Corky climbed out, came running around the pool, and said, laughing, "Hey, big brother, it takes more than that to get a Purple Heart!" Jimmy grabbed his feet and, ready or not, Corky went back in.

Back in the room, Corky and David never let up on Jimmy about not being able to swim straight and it ended in a huge pillow fight. I was busy playing "shutter bug" with my camera.

Time was running out and we all knew it. No one wanted to go to bed. But, one by one, they drifted off, and the only noise came from the television. I was the last one to fall sleep. There'd be plenty of time for that. Right now, all I wanted to do was fill my eyes with memories.

The next morning in the parking lot, a man passed by and I said, "Sir, would you mind taking a picture for me?"

"Sure," he said, and took the camera. We all stood together but no one smiled. Then I took one of all three of the boys together. Again, no one was smiling.

Knowing we'd see him in a few weeks, David and I said our good-byes to Corky and walked on to the plane. I watched out the window as Jimmy and Corky shook hands. Then, Jimmy walked toward the plane and Corky toward the rental car. Suddenly, at the same instant, they both turned, ran back, and hugged each other. The tears I'd been holding back overflowed. Jimmy ran to the plane and sat in the seat across from me. Tears rolling down his face, he said, "That's the last time I'll ever see Corky, Mom."

"Jimmy! Please don't say that!"

"It's true, Mom. I'll never see him again." He turned his face to the window and never spoke another word all the way to Nashville.

As soon as we got home, I was getting ready to take David back to Castle Heights. He only had a few more days of school and I'd tried to get him dismissed early but he had one more test the next day. As long as I could, I left him and Jimmy out on the sun deck talking. Then, when I couldn't put it off, I said, "Okay, fellas, it's time to go," and watched the same scene as I did at Fort Sill. After they hugged each other, David walked slowly to the car. Jimmy stood there, tears running down his face, and said, "That's the last time I'll see David."

"Jimmy. Don't *say* that."

Looking at me, he said, "Mom, we both know it's true," and went upstairs to his room.

All the way to Lebanon, except for David's sobs, we were silent. I kept patting his hand but couldn't say a word. My heart was so heavy.

Jimmy went out for a while but was back before ten o'clock. I was in bed trying to read but hadn't turned a page for hours. He came in, kissed me, and went on to his room.

About one o'clock, he came back down. "Mom," he said softly as he tapped on my door, which was only partly closed, "can I talk to you?"

"Always," I said. He came in, knelt by my bed, and laid his head on my breast. He was crying as I had never seen him cry.

"Mom, I'm scared," he said. Oh, God, I couldn't stand to see him hurt like this.

"Honey, it takes a brave man to admit he's scared. That doesn't mean he's a coward."

He looked up and held my hand. "You know, I've been thinking. All I want to do is stay home with my friends and my family, but I guess if everyone did that, we'd be in trouble, right?"

"Right," I said, sounding a lot braver than I felt.

"Until a short time ago I never heard of Vietnam and now I'm going there. And I don't believe in taking another man's life but I know God will guide me in whatever I do. So, if I have to give one year of my life to protect my friends, my family, and the way we believe, I'll gladly do so. You'll be all right, won't you, Mom?"

I ran my hands through his curly hair. "Yes, darlin', I'll be all right."

"I love you, Mom."

"I know. And I love you, too." For a few moments we held each other, not saying a word; then he went back upstairs.

I thought about what Harlan had said the week before when I'd called and told him Jimmy was being sent to Vietnam. "Don't worry about it," he'd said, "only one in every four hundred gets killed."

The sound of the riding lawn mower woke me. Looking out my bedroom window, I saw Jimmy, in his cut-offs and tennis shoes (he called them "tenny pumps"), mowing the lawn.

Taking a glass of lemonade down to him, I said, "Honey, you don't have to do this today."

"I know, Mom, but I want to. Who knows, I may never get to mow this lawn again." I hoped he was talking about the fact that I planned to lease the house and move to an apartment until they came home. Until Hubert had sent me a clipping of some new town houses being built across town with an inscription that said "This is your new home," I hadn't even thought about it. When I called, he said he and the boys had decided that the house and all the upkeep would be more than I could handle by myself. And with them gone, I needed a smaller place. I knew it made sense but, on top of everything else, I couldn't think right now about giving up my home.

Hubert called. "What are you two still doing at home! The party's already started!" Lord. I'd forgotten! Hubert, knowing we'd spend the day thinking about when Jimmy had to leave, had planned a party at his lake house. He was right, this wasn't a day for thinking.

After Jimmy had polished his golf clubs and carefully placed them in the back of the walk-in closet, then polished his car and made me promise that whoever drove it would take good care of it, we put everything he had to take in my car and started out the drive. Suddenly Jimmy said, "Wait, Mom," got out, and stood there and looked . . . for a long time. Then he got back in the car. "Okay, I'm ready," he said.

The house was full of Jimmy's friends . . . everyone Hubert could think of to invite plus the whole office staff. And Owen and Katherine Bradley, Dick and Pat Blake (a promoter I'd worked for many times who had a lake house near Hubert), and some people I didn't even know. It was like a Fourth of July party! All day long there was fishing, swimming, water skiing, and some lively liquid flowing. And Hubert, in his fishnet T-shirt, was at the grill cooking hamburgers. Audie Ashworth, one of Hubert's staff, was taking pictures of everything and everybody. The later it got, the more often I looked at my watch. Hubert saw me and finally took it off my arm and put it into his pocket. "When it's time, I'll tell you," he said.

Jimmy's flight was on American at 3:05. Until one o'clock, I made it fine. Then, when he went in to take off his bathing suit and T-shirt and put on his uniform, I couldn't stand it and went out to the deck. Hubert came out, put his arms around me, and said, "Not now. You can't let him see you cry." I knew he was right and went back into the house.

At two o'clock a caravan started to the airport. When one of his buddies started to get in the car with us, Jimmy said, "I'd like for just Mom and me to ride together." All the way to the airport, we just held hands, not saying anything. There was no need to.

At the gate, everyone but me was trying to keep the mood going. I couldn't fake it any longer. But, each time I'd feel the tears welling up, Hubert would look at me and shake his head and I'd swallow them back down. When the flight was announced, Jimmy went around shaking hands and hugging everybody. Then, he came to me and there was no way either of us could muster a smile. I walked with him as far as they'd let me go. Then he hugged me and said, "I love you, Mom," and walked out to the steps of the plane. Suddenly, he turned and ran back to where I stood. "Mom, promise me you'll always sing 'Where No One' for me."

"I promise, my son." He ran back to the plane and disappeared inside. I couldn't hold back any longer. I ran to the parking lot. Hubert followed. Putting his arms around me, he said, "Now you can cry." But his words were too late. The tears I'd saved for so long were running down my face.

The plane was late in taking off and I thought, *They're using time we could have had together.* As it took off, I clung to Hubert

and cried, "Oh, God, Hubert. My son is gone!" With someone
following in his car, he drove me home and stayed until he knew
I'd be all right.

The only evidence of Jack that day was when he'd flown over
the house in his plane and dipped his wings.

Three nights later, at midnight, the phone rang and the
operator said, "I have a collect call from Wake Island. Will you
accept the call?"

"Yes!"

Jimmy said, "Mom, I know it's a long ways and it costs a lot of
money but I just had to hear your voice one more time."

"Honey, I wouldn't care if it cost a million dollars. I'm so glad
you called." There was just time for one more "I love you" before
the phone went dead.

David was out of school. Corky called to report he was going to
Fort Benning, Georgia, for paratrooper training and wouldn't be
home for another few weeks.

My dreams came almost every night. I'd wake up in a cold
sweat, shaking all over. *Please, God, make them stop!* I wouldn't
watch the news on television. Every day there were more and
more casualties from Vietnam. I knew then I had to do something, or lose my mind.

"David, how would you like to go to Disneyland?" My question took him by surprise.

"Do you mean it?" he asked, "Really?"

"*Really!* I promised we'd so something together. Well, this is it
if you want to go."

"You bet I do! When do we leave?"

"As soon as we get packed," I said. He ran up the stairs and I
went to the phone to make reservations.

The flight out was great until we got to L.A. Then, due to the
smog conditions, we couldn't land at L.A. International and had
to go back to San Diego. This was David's first flight and he was
more than a little nervous. As we kept circling over the ocean,
two sailors in back of us kept laughing and talking about ditching
procedures. David turned around and said, "Would you please
talk about procedures for landing, not ditching." We landed at
L.A. two hours late. David was the first one off the plane.

We had only four days but not a minute was wasted. We rode

every ride, ate every kind of food, bought souvenirs until we were loaded down. We visited Universal Studios, where, since I was a Decca artist, we got the V.I.P. tour. David sat for a caricature of himself, yet when he suggested I have one done, I told him I was a living caricature. When it was time to leave, we were happy but tired. Except for changing planes in Dallas, we slept all the way home.

Later, I had to go back to work—and thank God, there was work. It was the only thing that helped me keep my sanity. The first date was with Bill Anderson in Knoxville. When I checked into the motel, the clerk said, "There's a surprise waiting in your room." I didn't know if it was a person or a thing. It was several things . . . a dozen long-stemmed red roses. The card read, "To the best mom in the world. I love you, David."

The next date was a fair in Virginia. The stands were packed with nearly five thousand people. The bus was parked right near the stage, and when it was time, I dashed out and onstage. After doing several songs, the microphone, which was electronic and rose up from the floor, just sank all the way down. One minute I was singing to the crowd . . . the next . . . to thin air. I stood there looking stupid. Then, like a stiff snake, it came back up. When it stopped, I said, "Well, that's the first time I ever had one go down on me." At first, from the audience, there were just giggles here and there. Then it began to spread until it became an uproar. I couldn't figure out what I had said that was so funny. I turned around to the band. The drummer (Snuffy Miller) was laughing so hard he had to leave the stage . . . The others were doubled over. In my mind, I went over what I had said. They'd taken it all the wrong way. I was so embarrassed I left the stage, and ran for the bus. Bill said, "What did you say?"

"Don't ask!" I said.

When it came time for the duets, it started all over again. There was nothing to do but shrug my shoulders and join in. This time, it was Bill who couldn't keep a straight face.

Jack Norman had become more and more important to me. Several times he'd been out to the house but mostly we met for lunch, or I'd meet him at an apartment he and some other men had rented (I imagine for this purpose), or wherever he named. I cared so much for him, I'd have gone to the moon. Sometimes, he'd have me meet him somewhere for dinner, always with a friend of his in attendance. That way everyone was supposed to think I was with his friend. The pretense was all in vain . . . everyone knew, and neither of us tried to hide it. Somehow, even though he was married, it wasn't a "slipping around" affair. I knew he loved me. He knew I was having a rough time and needed him. Every day, whether I saw him or not, he'd call. And he said if I ever needed him at night to call his house. But, since I tried not to even think about him at home, I'd never do that. There were times when I'd actually forget he was married . . . or perhaps my guilt pushed it aside. But I was reminded when the small alarm on his watch went off and he'd say it was time for him to leave. I had no illusions about a future for us, and knew I was going to be hurt, but I couldn't have stopped if I'd tried. I didn't. After all these years, I knew what being "in love" felt like. Wonderful and terrible, all at the same time.

I'd read that they wouldn't send brothers to Vietnam at the same time, so it never entered my mind that Corky would go, too. Then he called and said he'd gotten his orders. "But, Corky, Jimmy's there! They can't send you, too!"

"They're not *sending* me, Mom, I volunteered."

"But what on earth for?"

"Because Jimmy *is* there. And since he's there, I'm going, too." I knew, Corky being Corky, that all the arguing and crying in the world wouldn't change his mind. But I tried.

"Corky, please don't go. I'll call a congressman or somebody and get your orders changed."

"Don't do that, Mom. I have to go," he said.

"You are going to get to come home, aren't you?" I was afraid they'd do what they almost had done with Jimmy.

"Yeah. I'll be home in a few days for thirty days. We'll talk then." I hung up. My heart was now twice as heavy as it had been. Jimmy being in Vietnam was bad enough. But Corky would be there, too. I couldn't bear it. My sons, my sons. I knew other mothers all over the country were going through this and my heart ached for all of us.

With the boys' permission, I'd finally given Bucko to Del Reeves and his family. Suddenly, I had to see him and be with someone I knew loved and missed the boys as much as I did.

I drove in Del and Ellen's driveway. Bucko recognized the car.

Before I could get out, he was all over it. When I got the door open he whined and jumped around trying every way he could think of to get in. He licked me from head to toe. I couldn't stand it and called for Del to come and get him. With him straining to get away, Del led him around to the backyard. I knew it was the last time I would ever come to see him. It wasn't fair to either of us.

With the understanding that I would keep the house until after Corky came home on leave, I had leased it to Joe and Rose Lee Maphis, but only until the boys came back home. They had three children and, like Bucko, this house needed children.

Corky came home the last day of July and I noticed a difference in him immediately. Before, he was always laughing and playing pranks. Now he was very serious. At night, when I was alone, I thought back to the times he used to love to scare the living daylights out of me. When he'd caught a big snake, pickled it and put it in a gallon fruit jar and set it right where he knew I'd find it, at the end of the clothesline beneath the rose bush. He knew I always stopped there and smelled the roses. That day, I noticed him standing on the sun deck watching me. I should have known something was up but I went on with what I usually did, stoop to smell the roses. Then I saw the snake. "Corky! Come and get this snake!" He knew I was scared to death of them. Coming down the stairs, he said, "Roses don't smell so good now, do they?" and laughed. Grabbing a wet towel, I swatted at him and missed. I remembered all the times when I'd turn back the covers on my bed to find some rubber monster there. And the time I thought they were all gone and went upstairs to clean out the walk-in closet. Suddenly, all the lights went out. It was dark as pitch! All I could think of was that a fuse had blown and felt my way down the stairs. Just as I got to the bottom, there was a blood-curdling scream. I darned near fainted! It was Corky! As he switched on the light, he was laughing so hard he couldn't stand up. As crazy as it sounds, I wished those days were back.

I thought about trying to get his orders changed whether he wanted me to or not, but how could I say: "This one goes . . . this one stays." Besides I knew Corky would hate me for doing it. It had to be his decision and, like it or not, I had to accept it.

Corky spoke about his paratrooper training and said the only thing that got him through it was hate for his sergeant. From

what he said, it was mighty rough and I gathered the sergeant
had used a psychological approach: "If you hate me enough, your
anger will push you through it." Corky realized it now. For all his
training, he was still barely nineteen years old.

At least two or three times a week, I wrote Jimmy. Usually I
tried to tell him things about his friends or what was going on at
home—anything happy. This letter was different and I couldn't
change it. It seemed I had no control over what came from my
pen.

*My son, my son, I pray that you'll come home to me . . . my
son, my son. It seems only yesterday the most important thing
on your mind was whether you'd make the baseball team or get
the new school jacket like all the other kids had. And I remember
how your eyes lighted up when you got your new rod and reel for
that big fishing trip . . . just you and your dad. And I remember
wiping the tears away when you hurt yourself on your sled. In
those days the house was filled with laughter and joy . . . filled
with your friends, and they were all such good boys. And then
came the day that you walked down the aisle to receive that all-
important diploma. I couldn't believe that tall young man was
my son . . . my wonderful son. And then I remember the little girl
that was always around . . . kinda tagging after you. She's not so
little anymore, but she's still around . . . who knows . . . maybe
someday? Then you received the call that I guess we knew would
come someday, but it came so quick and now you're so far away
. . . in a land that, until a short time ago, I didn't even know was
there. I know the time will pass and you'll be home again but,
until that time, my darlin', take care . . . take special care. My
son, my son, I pray that you'll come home to me . . . my son . . .
my son.*

"Mom, you should put this to music," Corky said when I
showed him the letter.

"No, it's just a letter to Jimmy," I said.

"But it could be any mother talking to her son. And Jimmy
would be so proud."

I folded the letter and put it away. "I'll think about it," I said.
"Right now it's too personal."

Corky's thirty days were up far too quickly—and once more
Hubert had planned a party. This time with all of Corky's friends
and David, too. Once more there was fishing, swimming, skiing,
hamburgers, and drinks. When Hubert fixed Corky his specialty,

a "bitch" (Scotch and Fresca), I said, "Hubert! He's only nine-teen." Then, I realized if he was old enough to go to Vietnam, I guess he was old enough to drink. Once more Audie was snapping pictures. It was like a rerun of a movie that was too sad the first time. Even his plane left at 3:05 A.M. The same day, the same hour, two months apart, the twentieth of August, 1968.

When it came time for him to change into his uniform, I went out on the deck. Hubert came out and said, "We've been through this before, remember?"

"Yes, Hubert, how well I remember. And I won't let him see me cry."

Corky, David, and I rode to the airport together, each thinking our private thoughts. I knew if I talked, I'd cry, and I couldn't cry—not yet.

The walk to the gate was like the last mile. Every step, I wanted to grab Corky's hand and run in the opposite direction. But I kept on walking. They announced his flight and Corky shook hands and joked with everybody, then turned to David. "Take care of yourself and Mom, little brother. Remember, you're the man of the house now." Corky hugged him and turned to me. "Don't worry, Mom. I'll be fine. And I'll try to see Jimmy. I love you." He kissed me and was gone.

With David and Hubert right behind me, I ran to the car. David drove and with someone else driving Hubert's car, he held me and let me cry. My sons were my life, and two thirds of my life was gone.

At eight o'clock, the movers came. Even though I'd had very little sleep, it was the best thing. With all the confusion, I couldn't think.

There was one thing the boys and Hubert didn't take into consideration when they decided I should move from a ten-room house to a six-room apartment—the furniture. Everything in the rec room had to be left—pool table, jukebox, sofa, chairs, rugs, barrel table, chairs, bar and stools. Everything in the workshop—lawnmowers, etc., two bedroom suites, one dinette set, and sev-eral other things—stayed. The thing I had to remember was, "It's only temporary." And "I'm just renting the house, not selling it." With the Maphises' promise to take good care of everything and one last look at what had once been a happy home but now looked like a lonely house, we drove toward a new way of life.

Even with everything we'd left behind, the apartment still

looked so small compared with our house, and the furniture looked very big. With boxes everywhere, there wasn't room to move. David and I worked until midnight and still hadn't made a dent. Finally, I sat down in the middle of the floor and cried. David put his arms around me and said, "Don't worry, Mom, we'll get it straight."

Looking around at the mess, I said, "Do you really think so?" He shook his head. "No."

We did, though. Working steadily, in a few days it almost resembled a home, ours, mine and David's. Because that's where I'd decided he was to be from now on . . . home.

Besides David, the most important man in my life was the mailman. He knew Jimmy and Corky were in Vietnam and if he had a letter from them, instead of putting it in the box, he'd ring the doorbell. With a big smile he'd hand it to me and say, "I know you're waiting for this."

"You bet I am," I'd say, and have it opened before closing the door. At least twice a week I'd hear from Jimmy, and despite Corky's warning that he hated to write letters, he'd write at least once a week. Their letters kept me going.

One day, opening a letter from Jimmy, a picture fell out . . . a picture of an A.P.C. (Armored Personnel Carrier) with Jimmy sitting on top. Dear God, it looked like the tank I'd seen in my dreams. But I tried to put it out of my mind. On the back was written: "Mom, this is what I drive, ride in, sleep in, and fall off of." He'd written that he was driving an A.P.C. but, until now, I had no idea what one looked like. He wrote: "How am I supposed to drive this thing when I've never even seen one before." Also, he thought it was funny that he had been assigned to "F" Troop. To him, that was the comedy series on television in which the whole cast was zany. "I should fit in real good," he said. He wrote funny things about raiding a "hootch" and finding a water buffalo inside. "Needless to say, we ended that raid real quick." Then he wrote things like "I don't know why there's so much hurt and poverty in the world. Maybe that's why Corky and I are here, to ease some of that hurt." He'd heard that Corky was somewhere near and, in each letter, said he was trying to see him but hadn't yet. Also, that he was trying to get Corky sent home. "One of us in this hellhole is enough."

Corky wrote that he was a forward observer. When I asked Jack what that was he said, "It's the toughest job in the Army. Helicopters drop them behind enemy lines and they call in artillery fire." Now I understood why he had paratrooper training. In one letter Corky told about calling in fire to protect our jets and got in a slight bit low. One of the pilots yelled, "Some son of a bitch is trying to get us blown out of the air!" Corky lowered the fire and blew a mountain off the face of the earth. I had read about it in the paper but, until Corky told me, I didn't know that he was one of the soldiers responsible. In each of his letters he'd say, "I haven't seen Jimmy yet but I'll keep trying." Corky thought that they were about eleven miles apart. Eleven miles! The distance from Madison to Nashville and they couldn't meet each other! One of Corky's letters said, "I almost got to where Jimmy was today but they stopped me. Next time, they won't. With me here now, maybe they'll send him home." Now, I knew why he had volunteered.

I couldn't understand why the Army wouldn't let them be together but Jack explained it was so both boys wouldn't be in the same place in case "something" happened. I didn't need to hear this.

I've never prayed so hard in my life. Every night I'd ask God to please take care of my sons. And we all counted the days. On each of their letters the number of days to go would be at the top and each day I'd put that number on my calendar. I wouldn't really start living again until that number was zero for both of them. I'd read each letter over and over until it was frayed at the edges and then put it on my bedside stand, next to their pictures. And when another one came, I'd put that one in the drawer with the rest and replace it with the new one.

The day we started doing the television show in Nashville was a real blessing. Now, instead of having to go to Windsor, Ontario, every two weeks, I could be home. One day, while we were filming, one of the crew came running. "Jan!" he said. "You've got a ham radio call from Corky!"

Dropping everything, I ran to the phone and talked to a ham operator somewhere in Pennsylvania. After giving me instructions how to say "Over" when I finished saying something, he told me to hold for Corky. After an eternity and amidst loud crackling noises, I heard, "Mom! It's me . . . Corky! How are you? . . . Over."

"Oh, Corky, it's so good to hear your voice . . . are you all right? . . . Over." I could barely hear him but I've never welcomed anything more in my life. He only had three minutes, so after each of us assuring the other that we were all right and him saying "Hi" to David and telling me that he was still trying to see Jimmy, we only had time for one more "I love you" before hanging up. The rest of the day I was walking on air!

When Corky came home from basic training, he'd had a big color portrait done in his uniform . . . a sixteen by twenty. Then David had one done in his Castle Heights uniform. So, while Jimmy was home on leave in June, he'd put on the top of his uniform (shirt, tie, jacket, and hat) and went to have his made. The rest of his uniform that day was cut-offs and tennis shoes. "They'll only see the top," he said. That made sense. But it was now September, and I hadn't seen the pictures. Every day I'd call and they'd tell me they were working on it. Finally, I lost patience. "What in the world is taking so long?"

"Mrs. Howard," the photographers studio said, "I don't know how to tell you this but we've lost the negative to Jimmy's picture." I hit the ceiling.

"Well, I'll tell you what! If you don't want a bomb put under your building, you'd better find it!"

"We'll keep looking," he said. From the tone of his voice, I didn't have a lot of hope.

After showing "My Son" to Bill, he said, "Jan, you've got to record this!"

"I don't know if I can, Bill. I can't even read it without crying."

"Let's do a demo on it, then we'll see," he said. We set a time for later on that week at the studio.

Since all I had was the lyrics, the melody came with the help of the musicians who had just started playing some background music. Singing it didn't come that easy. I couldn't get the words past the tears in my throat. After getting it down roughly one time, I quit.

Bill convinced me to show it to Owen Bradley, who said, "Jan, you've got to record this . . . It's your masterpiece." But when we went into the studio, once more I couldn't sing it.

Owen said, "Jan, remember this is just another song."

"No, Owen," I said. "It's Jimmy's life." He saw that it was tearing me apart.

"Tell you what, if you can get throught it once, we'll take it, okay?"

"I'll try," I said. Then prayed silently *God, please help me.*

The music started. Trying to keep my voice under control as much as possible, we got through it one time. "That's it, Owen," I said. "I can't do it again."

When I left the studio, I had a seven-inch tape to send to Jimmy . . . I wanted him to be the first to hear it. Since Corky had already heard the lyrics, I couldn't wait to write and tell him I had actually recorded it and sent it to Jimmy.

Hubert had become a sort of "godfather" to my three sons. I think Jimmy and Corky wrote him as often or more often than they did me. Every few days he'd call and say, "Hey, I got a letter from Corky," or "I got a letter from Jimmy."

"What did they say?" I'd ask.

He'd just laugh and say, "That's between us men." But he must have kept the mailman hopping, too, because almost every letter I'd get from them they'd say they got a letter, funny card, or package from Hubert. Thank God for Hubert.

I tried to keep the packages going. One time it was cookies I'd baked. And to make sure they knew I'd baked them, I put a layer on top of the last batch which I'd burned. They always said that when I was in the kitchen it was a disaster area.

When I received word that they'd gotten them, Jimmy's response was "the guys loved your cookies but I ate the burned ones. I knew *you* baked those." Corky wrote, "I knew, without looking below the top layer, that you baked the cookies."

The deadline for sending Christmas boxes to Vietnam was the fifteenth of October and the limit was fifteen pounds per box. David and I went to the market and bought everything that could possibly be mixed with water—hot chocolate, soup mix—and everything dried. Also, small cans of V8 juice. With that and all kinds of cookies (which I baked but didn't burn this time) and candy, we ended up with four boxes each . . . sixty pounds. The man at the post office said, "Those are might lucky boys to have you for a mother."

"No, sir, it's just the other way around," I said.

Jimmy wrote that he had received the tape but couldn't find

anyone with a tape recorder to play it on. He'd keep looking, though, and would write me as soon as he heard it. I'd written that I had a surprise for him but didn't tell him what it was. He also had a surprise for me—he'd learned to play the guitar.

At a cocktail party I ran into Joe Allison, who was now hosting a radio show for Armed Forces Network which was heard in Vietnam. "Guess who I got a letter from? Jimmy! He wrote that he was the official requester for 'F' Troop and asked me to please play more Jan Howard records." Joe laughed . . . He'd known Jimmy since he was nine years old.

"Did you answer it?" I asked.

"No. I never answer any of those letters. They might not be there to get it."

"Joe! Don't say that!"

"I'm sorry, Jan. I promise I'll answer Jimmy's letter." I knew he'd give a lot to take back what he'd said. I walked away thinking about that.

A horrible feeling of dread followed me everywhere. I couldn't shake it. It seemed to fill my every thought. It was as though my mind and body were encased in some kind of darkness. Except for when I was working, I wouldn't let David out of my sight. He seemed to sense what I was feeling, and stayed close to home.

The road dates had slacked off and, except for TV shows, I was home and I was glad of that. I wanted and needed to be home. I did everything I could think of to keep busy. I had new drapes made for the whole apartment, had the furniture re-upholstered, and polished and shined everything that didn't move. Sometimes, I'd have dinner with Jack or Hubert but mostly I just wanted to be home.

I'd been working on a new album and had only one last session to do. We were recording at Bradley's Barn, a studio Owen had built in Mt. Juliet, about thirty minutes from Nashville. The session ended at 1:00 A.M. but, with listening to the playbacks, it was 2:30 before I started home. I was used to driving by myself at odd hours so I didn't pay any attention to the car behind me until I noticed that every time I made a turn, so did that car. Whether I drove slow or fast, it did the same. I began to get uneasy. All I could make out was that it was a black Cadillac but, in Nashville, there are hundreds of black Cadillacs.

Arriving at my apartment, I jumped out and ran for the door.

Footsteps were right behind me! I was so nervous I couldn't get the key in the lock. All I could think of was that it was one of those "nuts" who had threatened me over the telephone. Suddenly, this voice said, "L.G., it's kinda late for you to be out by yourself, isn't it?" Shit! It was Harlan!

"What the hell do you mean scaring the daylights out of me! It's none of your damned business what time I get home!"

"I just wanted to talk to you," he said.

"Well, we have nothing to talk about!" I finally had the key in the lock.

"But I don't have anyone that I can talk to," he said.

If I hadn't been so mad, I'd have laughed.

Getting the door open, I turned for a parting word to Harlan. "That's what you get for marrying an idiot!" I said, and slammed the door.

As small as the apartment had seemed when David and I first moved in, it now was quite comfortable and attractive. Downstairs was a large living-dining room combination, a small kitchen-breakfast area, and den. Along the whole length of the apartment was an enclosed patio which I'd had planted with all kinds of shrubbery. Two sliding glass doors gave it an indoor-outdoor effect. Upstairs were three bedrooms. At the left, at the top of the stairs, was David's bedroom and bathroom. In the middle was a bedroom I had turned into an office-studio. And, at the other end, was my bedroom and bath. The only thing I didn't like about the whole apartment was the enclosed stairway. A leftover from my claustrophobia days, I guess.

As I walked into the house, I worked off my anger at Harlan by going through straightening pillows on the sofas, putting dishes in the dishwasher, and putting things in "getting up" shape. My days always started off better if I didn't have to face a mess.

Walking up the stairs, I turned to go down to David's room. His door was shut but, gently, I turned the knob and opened it. I didn't care if he was seventeen, I still had to see that he was home safe and sound in his bed. He was sound asleep. I stood there looking at him. With that "baby" look which I hoped he'd never lose, he looked so innocent. His curly hair was tousled and I smiled thinking about how much time he spent trying to get it straight. Plastering it down with lots of gloop and drying it under the hair dryer. Then, within an hour curls would start springing up everywhere. My hair was fine and thin, unless I had it permed, and I wished many times I had thick, curly hair like my sons.

Closing David's door, I walked down the hall to my bedroom. But, as tired as I was, I hated to go to bed. The dreams had been coming every night. A couple of nights before, I'd attended a party at the home of June and John Cash and, before leaving, had told them, "Something is going to happen—and soon." I didn't know what that "something" was but I knew it was coming.

The knots in my shoulders and back felt as big as eggs. The doctor said it was tension . . . But that was his answer for everything. Tension or nerves. Well, I suppose I did have both.

The next day, I was trying to get ready to leave for Atlanta to work a club called The Playroom for a week, but my heart wasn't in it. Hubert called to see if there was anything he could do for me while I was gone. "No," I said, "but you can do something before I leave."

"What?" he asked.

"Cancel the Playroom. I just don't feel up to going."

"Well, Redhead, I guess we could, but I think it will do you good to get out of the house and get your mind off things."

"Hubert, if you mean the boys, that won't help." I said. But I agreed to go. Maybe he was right, at least I'd be busy.

The week at the Playroom was pure hell! Sunday afternoon while I was rehearsing the band, the cleaning people began to vacuum. If the dust they stirred up didn't go in my throat, it would at least have filled a rodeo arena. I felt the effects immediately. By night my throat felt like sandpaper and I was so hoarse I couldn't talk. For three nights I sounded like a bull frog on a dry day.

Mary Ann Summers and a lot of her friends were at the club almost every night. She tried to get me to stay at her house but I begged off. I couldn't sleep. I'd work till 2:00 A.M. and cry and walk the floor until daylight. I called Jack. "Please, is there some way you can check on the boys?"

"Now, Jan, everything is all right or you would hear," he'd say.

"Damn it, I *do* know! That's why I'm calling! Something is wrong!"

"All right, calm down. I'll see what I can do," he said. But I knew he wouldn't. He thought it was my imagination. I knew it wasn't.

One night, while I was onstage, a waitress brought me a note. "Dear Mom. Have a good show. I love you, David." He had called the club. Bless his heart, he knew what I was feeling. That night, when I got back to the hotel, there were a dozen red roses on the dresser. I knew without reading the card they were from David.

The record of "My Son" had been released two weeks before and I kept getting requests for it. Each time, I'd thank them and use the excuse that I hadn't learned it yet. Every word was burned into my mind but it was too hard for me to sing it.

Onstage, I tried to be the happy Jan Howard the audience deserved to see. Telling jokes, kidding with the band, singing every uptempo song I could think of. I couldn't bear the sad ones.

The Playroom was a honky-tonk. The customers were died-in-the-wool rednecks. One night there were about a dozen rodeo riders in the audience, each with a big white cowboy hat on. They were having a ball. One, in particular, came up and introduced himself as Goat Mullis, a bull rider, and invited me to a party after I got off work.

"But I don't get off until 3:00 A.M.," I said with absolutely no intention at all of going.

"That's fine," he said. "The party don't get a good start till then." I thanked him but said I thought I'd pass.

The manager came up to the bandstand and said, "Jan, would you tell those cowboys to please remove their hats?"

Looking at "Goat"—a good head taller than anyone else in the room—I said, "Sir, if you want those cowboys to remove their hats, which is against their principles, I suggest you tell them." He looked at Goat and got my drift. Goat went right on dancing with his hat on and the manager went back where he belonged—behind the bar.

By the end of the week I was a nervous wreck. If it hadn't been for Mary Ann, I wouldn't have made it. Her husband, Stump (Charles), even took me to some radio stations to promote the new record, but I'd walk out in the middle of the interview. Nothing I did made any sense. I was so jumpy. If a bobby pin was dropped, I heard it. Finally the date was over. I had one more date to work, in Des Moines, Iowa, the next night.

Since I had my car in Atlanta, I drove back to Nashville, and

Jack had a pilot fly me to Des Moines in his plane. Ordinarily, I would have spent the night, but I told him we had to fly back to Nashville right after the show. He didn't know what the big rush was, and neither did I. I just knew I had to get home.

At 3:00 A.M. Monday, I finally got home and fell into bed exhausted, but woke up in a hour, shaking all over. My gown was soaked with cold sweat. The dream had been the most vivid ever. It was so real I could almost reach out and touch Jimmy lying so still on the ground. Getting down on my knees, I laid my head on the bed and prayed until daylight. "Dear God, please take care of my sons!"

Bright and early, Jack called. "Hi, Redhead! How'd the shows go?"

"Okay, I guess," I said. But I didn't want to talk about shows. "Jack, did you ever check on the boys?"

"No, honey. But remember what I told you. Everything's all right or you would know." It was no use talking to him. He thought I was just a nervous mother.

"How about meeting me at Mario's for dinner?" he asked.

"No thanks, Jack. I've got to stay here," I said.

"I'll call you later. Are you sure you're all right?"

"No, Jack. I'm not all right," I said, and hung up.

David stuck to me like glue. Except for school, he never left the house. He knew something was wrong but, like me, didn't know quite what it was.

Monday afternoon the florist delivered more red roses, this time from Jack. I'd told him roses always made me feel better but this time they didn't seem to help. All I did was walk the floor and cry. I called Mary Ann. "Get back on a plane and come down here," she said.

"I can't leave," I said, hanging up and promising to call her later.

Tuesday, the feeling deepened. Every time the phone rang, I'd jump out of my skin. There were all kinds of errands I needed to do but couldn't force myself to leave the house. Hubert called and asked if there was anything he could do. "No, Hubert. There's nothing anyone can do."

Wednesday night, Jack and a friend of his from the Guard, Al Powell, came over. As always, I invited them back to the den. I sat down in a chair and waited until Jack had fixed himself a drink and sat down on the sofa beside Al, then said, "Jack, how do they notify you? They don't send telegrams anymore, do they?" Seeing I was very serious, Jack's mood changed to fit mine.

"No, Jan . . . Two uniformed officers would come to your door." He looked very uncomfortable, as though he wished he could say something to ease my mind but he didn't know what. He looked at his watch and I knew he was leaving—I didn't even question it anymore.

As I walked them to the door and opened it, he turned and said, "Are you going to be all right?" There were tears in his eyes.

"Yes, I'll be fine," I said. It was almost as though someone else was talking.

David had gone out somewhere and, to keep busy, I got out the bills that were waiting to be paid and started writing checks. Coming across the premiums for a small insurance policy I had on all three of the kids and myself, I wrote checks for David's, then Corky's, then mine. But I couldn't write the check for Jimmy's. Each time I'd try, it was as though my pen wouldn't move across the paper. Finally, I laid his premium aside.

The next morning, Thursday, the 30th of October, 1968—the day before Halloween—I was awake before sunup. I lay in bed feeling the weight of the world on me. For some reason, the dream hadn't occurred the night before. The sound of a door closing told me that David had left for school.

Ordinarily, my routine was to get up, turn on the *Today* show, wash my face, take a shower, brush my teeth, and put on clothes and makeup. But, this morning, when I started to switch on the TV, I stopped. No. No TV this morning.

Getting out of the shower, I put on a pair of light blue jeans, a blue and white shirt, and reached for my tennis shoes. Then, after a minute, put them back in the closet.

Looking in the mirror, I thought, *There's no use putting on makeup today,* and sat down on the side of the bed. Just sat there. Not thinking. Just looking at my bare feet on the floor.

The phone rang. It was Jeanie Bare and I could tell she was crying. "Jan," she said, "are you okay?"

"Yes, I'm all right." My voice sounded far off.

"I . . . I'll call you back. One of the kids is crying," she said, and hung up. That's funny . . . I didn't hear anyone crying. Not anyone except Jeanie.

The phone rang again but I ignored it. It would ring awhile . . . Stop . . . Then start ringing again. The bedside clock said nine o'clock. *Why is everyone calling me so early?* I thought. Finally, I picked it up.

"Hello?"

"Jan, this is Penny." Penny Lane, my hairdresser. Why was she calling? This wasn't the day for her to do my hair. "Will you come down and open the door?"

"No."

"Jan, please, come down and open the door for us," she said.

"Who's us?" I asked.

"Jan, please! We've been ringing the doorbell and knocking on the door for half an hour." I hadn't heard any doorbell or anyone knocking. I was in a trance. Placing the receiver back on the hook, I slowly walked down the stairs and to the front door.

With my hand on the knob, I could hear voices outside. I opened the door and my eyes fell on two uniformed officers. David, his face white as a sheet, rushed past them and grabbed me. Then Jack . . . Then Hubert. I was backing up. "No. No." I ran for the den! Someone was screaming. It was me! I kept screaming . . . Jack grabbed me and I tried to get away. "I don't want to hear. Please. No!" David was crying harder than I'd ever seen him cry. Jack, tears running down his face, said, "Jan. Honey . . . you've got to listen!"

David, holding on to me for dear life said, "Mom! Jimmy's *dead!*"

"No, David! No!" I screamed. He and Jack were holding me to keep me from falling. One of the officers spoke.

"Mrs. Howard, we regret to inform you your son is dead."

"Oh, dear God! It's Jimmy! Jimmy!"

Jack said, "For God's sake, tell her which one!"

"My God," one of the officers said. "We didn't know there were two! It's James."

"Jimmy! Jimmy! Jimmy!" I could hear myself screaming. David, all one hundred and thirty-five pounds of him, lifted and carried me upstairs.

The world was black. I prayed for death. The room was filled with people . . . Tiny, Beulah, Mom, Jeanie, Mary Ann, June and John Cash. One by one they filed in. Owen, Hubert, my brothers, Junior, Pete, Dick, and Bob . . . So many more. Each time I'd open my eyes someone would put a pill in my mouth. Merciful sleep. Voices kept coming through. Someone said it would be ten days before they could get the boys home. Then I heard Dr. Goldner say, "She can't live ten days."

I heard water from the fountain outside my window and kids yelling "Trick or treat?!" Every time I'd open my eyes, I'd start screaming, "Jimmy! Jimmy! I want Jimmy! Don't tell me he's dead. No! No!" I wanted to die. "God, where are you! I prayed to you to take care of my sons . . . where are you!"

Penny Lane said, "Now, Jan, you'll get over this." What a stupid-assed statement. How in the hell would *she* know! She kept talking about God's will.

"Don't talk to me about God!" I screamed. "I don't want to hear about God!"

Jeanie was talking on the phone. "Jack, we can't get her quiet. She keeps screaming for Jimmy."

Then I felt him holding my hand. "Jan, honey, you've got to sleep."

"I don't *want* to sleep," I screamed, fighting away the pill he was trying to give me, "I want to *die*."

Then he said, "David and I are going to help you downstairs. There's something you'll want to see." With him on one side and David on the other, I walked down the stairs. They led me past the people standing silently to one side and into the living room. There, above the piano, was the portrait Jimmy had had made last June. "Oh, God! Jimmy! Jimmy!"

Holding an eight-by-ten of the same picture to my breast, I was helped back upstairs.

Time was measured by pills. Every four hours. Sometimes I'd wake to see David kneeling by my bed crying. Someone said, "Shhh . . . you'll disturb your mother," and I wanted to say, "Leave him alone! Let him cry!" but I'll never know if the words came out or not.

Jack had pulled strings, and the plane that was bringing Jimmy and Corky home was due at eight o'clock on Sunday morning. The airport manager, Frank Knapp, Sr., had closed the airport to all traffic except the one American Airlines plane. All the cars drove out to the runway and waited until the plane touched down and rolled to a stop. Then, the black hearse drove to the rear of the plane. An honor guard, with Jack at the head, stood at attention as the door opened and Corky stood at the top of the stairs. He saluted the guard and walked down the steps and around to the back of the plane. The honor guard marched around and they all stood at attention as the ramp opened and the casket that carried my Jimmy was lowered. They couldn't hold me back any longer. "Corky!" I screamed and ran toward him. Someone said, "Let her go." Corky ran toward me. "Mom!" His arms went around me and we cried together. My son, my precious son! With him on one side and David on the other, we watched as the hearse drove away.

All the way back to the apartment, I couldn't hold on to David and Corky tight enough. Both of their faces showed the grief and strain. Corky's face was ashen. No longer was he a nineteen-year old boy . . . he was a man who was suffering terribly. Except for the one word he had spoken, he didn't talk. None of us talked.

That evening we drove to Phillips Robinson Funeral Home on Gallitin Road. My feet didn't want to walk up the steps, but I forced myself. I had to see Jimmy. Jack kept saying, "You can't break down, Jan. He deserves dignity." Except for him, Corky, and David, the other faces were a blur. I saw the casket and his picture (the one I'd seen for the first time three nights ago) sitting on the floor beside it. One rose was lying on top of the casket.

With Corky and David on each side of me, I walked to the casket and looked down at my son . . . my wonderful son. He looked as though he were asleep. Looking closer, I saw one small V-shaped wound in his temple. That was why I didn't see a wound in my dreams . . . it was so small. But big enough to kill him. His hair was lying in curls on his forehead. Reaching down to smooth it, my hand touched glass. I screamed, "He can't breathe with this over him! Get it off!" Someone was pulling me away. Jack said, "Remember—dignity."

"To hell with dignity!" I screamed. "I want my son." They led me back to the car.

Ever since they'd notified me, I'd told everyone who'd listen, "When Jimmy's letter comes, I want it."

"Jan," they'd say sadly, "there won't be any more letters."

"Yes there will! And when it comes, I want it!" There will be another letter!

Jimmy's funeral was on Tuesday, and I wished it were mine.

Tiny chose the dress I wore . . . navy blue with white lace at the collar and on the cuffs. Jimmy had never liked me in black. I sat there like a mannequin as someone fixed my hair, put some makeup on my face, and dressed me.

Corky and David had chosen the pallbearers—all Jimmy's friends. One of them was stationed at Fort Benning, Georgia, and Mary Ann and her husband, Stump, had flown him up in a private plane.

The service was at the church Jimmy had loved so much, City Road Methodist. It was filled to overflowing with friends who had loved him. As I walked down the aisle, I saw Solona waiting in the section reserved for the family. As I sat down I touched her hand. I knew she was hurting, too. Up until I'd moved to the apartment, she'd been with us eight years and loved my boys. I looked across the aisle to where Harlan was sitting.

Corky and David were on each side of me, and we watched as the honor guard walked down the aisle to stand at attention near the casket. Flowers. There were so many flowers. Someone was singing.

The minister, Reverend Wray Tomlin—Jimmy had baby-sat for his children many times—was talking about Jimmy. I didn't want to listen. My mind went blank.

The graveside services were at National Cemetery in Madison. We were seated in a small tent with the casket in front of us. My body was numb but my mind was screaming. David, in a gray suit, was on one side of me. Corky, in full dress uniform and white gloves, was on the other. He stood as the flag which covered the casket was folded three-cornered, accepted it, and turned to me. His face was white and his hands were shaking. His voice trembled as he said, "In grateful appreciation, I present to you this flag." He laid it in my hands. The honor guard stood at attention as the bugler played taps and the guard fired the rifle salute. My Jimmy was gone.

When we got home and I was in my bedroom, Jimmy's letter was given to me. It had arrived on Saturday. When I asked why it hadn't been given to me, someone explained that Penny, the hairdresser, had intercepted it and took it upon herself to keep it from me. If I had had the strength I think I would have choked her but now I just wanted his letter.

Gently, I opened it and, as I read, I knew he was giving me

instructions for the future. "Don't get behind in your washing and ironing," he said—he knew that was my downfall—"and promise you'll take time to take a vacation now and then. You're not as strong as you let on." Tears kept getting in the way of the words. "I know Christmas will be there before you know it," he wrote, "and, though I won't be there in person, know that I'll always be with you in spirit." It was signed, "Your loving Son, Jimmy Van." The only time I had called him that was when I was mad at him or teasing.

Jack called every morning, and Hubert came by to go through the mail. There were so many letters. Letters from the government, letters from fans and friends, letters from Jimmy's buddies in Vietnam. And letters from strangers. Hubert and Corky decided which ones I should see.

I couldn't eat. I couldn't sleep. All I could do was cry. Grief was swallowing me. I knew Corky and David were hurting, too, and it hurt them more to see me grieving myself to death but I couldn't stop. I was crying when I woke up, and crying when I went to sleep. For two weeks, I'd watch the clock to see if it was time to take another pill. I read Jimmy's letter until every word was memorized and slept with his picture in my arms.

One morning, the minute I woke up I reached for the pills. But, instead of pouring one in my hand, I poured the whole bottle. When I started to put them in my mouth, it was if someone had jerked my hand and they fell to the floor. I realized what I had almost done.

Going through the medicine chest, I took down every bottle, emptied them in the bowl, and flushed it. My mind was clear for the first time. I loved Jimmy but I also loved Corky and David. They needed their mother. In my grief, I had forgotten about theirs. All I was thinking about was myself. And even with me cursing God and begging Him to let me die, He'd somehow seen fit for me to live through this—I knew now, He'd help me to live with it. It wasn't going to be easy but I had to try.

I looked in the mirror and saw a stranger looking back at me. Someone whose hair hadn't been combed in days, whose eyes were terribly swollen with dark circles under them, and whose face was almost gray. I looked horrible.

Getting in the shower, I let the hot water run over my body

until I felt almost human, put on a fresh gown and robe, and ran a brush through my hair.

As I walked into the den and saw the relief on Corky and David's faces, my efforts were worthwhile.

David had to go back to school but Corky never left the house. Now that I had a clear mind, I realized, with a shock, how much weight Corky had lost. He'd never been a heavyweight but he now weighed less than David. When I asked him why, he said, "The bark off a tree isn't very nourishing, Mom." He said he didn't want to talk about it. I never asked him again.

One day, he received a manila envelope with several letters in it. After looking at them, he went upstairs and shut the door.

At night, he'd pace the floor and turn on every light in the house. And as much as I tried to get him to sleep in a bed, he wouldn't. Just slept on the sofa, either in the living room or the den, with all his clothes on. Sometimes, after he was asleep, I'd go down and turn the lights off. In the morning, they'd all be back on. I understood why when, in answer to my question about it, he said, "The Vietcong would wait till it was dark to attack."

Several times, he'd cautioned me never touch him if he were asleep. Just stand across the room and call his name until I was sure he was awake. One night I forgot. He was asleep on the living-room sofa and I walked over to wake him and try again to get him to sleep in a bed. As I touched him, he shot up like a bolt with both arms raised toward me! His eyes were wild. "Corky!" I screamed. Suddenly, he stopped and slumped to the floor crying. "God, Mom! I could have killed you!" I sat beside him until he quiet down. Then he said, "You know those letters I got the other day?"

"Yes."

"They were ones I had written to Jimmy that he never got. And there was one telling me that the team I worked with in Vietnam . . . all seven of them . . . had been killed by mortar fire." Dear God!

Each night, I'd make down the hide-a-bed in the upstairs den, hoping he'd come upstairs to sleep. One night, I woke to see a light on in there. Softly, I walked down the hall and looked in. Fully clothed, he was lying on his stomach across the bed . . . sound asleep. As I watched, he reached out and started patting the bed in a circular motion. Suddenly, he sat straight up. "My weapon's gone!" he screamed. Then, realizing where he was, he said, "Oh God! In Nam, if your weapon's gone you're dead. They sneak in at night, steal your weapon and kill you with it." He put his head in his hands and cried. "I feel so guilty," he said. "I'm here sleeping between clean sheets and all my buddies and my brother are either dead or sleeping in mud." I felt so totally helpless. Corky had said there was a chance he would be sent back but I vowed, if he were, I'd put a bomb in the White House.

It had been thirty days and Corky hadn't been out of the house. I called one of his friends and asked if he would try to get him to go somewhere with him that night. It was time for him to start living again, and time for me to try to be alone.

David had gone somewhere, too, and the house was quiet. At first I walked from room to room. Then, got into bed but left the light on. Since I'd chosen not to take the pills, sleep didn't come easy. I reached for Jimmy's letter and, even though every word was burned into my mind, I read it again. Just to see his handwriting. Suddenly, he was beside me on the bed . . . dressed in his stay-pressed pants, open-necked shirt, and V-neck sweater . . . the clothes he wore to school. But his face was so sad. "Mom," he said, "I've tried to get through to you but I can't. Read the chapter before the book of Ecclesiastes."

"Jimmy!" I cried, and reached to touch him . . . but he was gone. At that moment Corky walked in.

"Mom? What's the matter?" he asked, and walked over to the bed.

"Corky, Jimmy was here," I said.

"Now, Mom . . ." I stopped him.

"Corky, I'm not crazy and I know what you're going to say. But he was here!" I told him exactly what Jimmy had said.

"Well, did you read it?" he asked.

"No, it just happened." Corky got the Bible and turned to the chapter before the book of Ecclesiastes, which was the last chapter of Proverbs.

Sitting down on the side of the bed, he said, "Let's read it together."

It tells the words of Lemuel, King of Massa, which his mother taught him. Advice to him about life. It says, "Give strong drink (as medicine) to him who is ready to pass away and wine to those in bitter distress of heart." And it tells about the rareness of a capable, intelligent, and virtuous woman. "She is far more precious than jewels." It tells of everything she does for her household and it says, "Her children rise up and call her blessed." It goes on . . . "Many daughters have done virtuously, nobly, and well but you excel them all." I knew Jimmy had spoken to me. He knew the Bible—I didn't. I didn't even know there was a book of Ecclesiastes in the Bible.

From the look on Corky's face, I knew he accepted it, too. Handing me the Bible, he kissed me and went to bed. For the first time, I slept with some sort of peace.

Hubert called and said, "I'll be there in an hour to pick you up. We're going for a ride." He hung up before I could answer.

I rode—Hubert drove and talked. Out through Brentwood, a suburb south of town, and back toward town. Then he turned and I saw where he was heading. "No, Hubert, I don't want to go there" He was driving to the golf course where Jimmy used to play. He ignored me and kept on driving. "Look how beautiful the trees are! Jimmy would have loved to be playing golf today." He wanted me to see the world through Jimmy's eyes—and I tried. Then, he drove to the National Cemetery in Madison and turned in. I had never been to the actual gravesite, but when I saw the big beautiful tree in the corner, I remembered the day when Jimmy was home on leave, and we'd stopped at the red light there. Jimmy had looked at that tree and said, "That's got to be the most peaceful spot on earth." Now, his grave is right near that tree. As we walked over to the marker that said *Corporal James Van Howard,* it was more than I could bear. Hubert held me as I fell apart, then took me back home. But we both knew I'd taken a giant step.

A few nights later, after everyone was asleep, I drove out there, climbed over the wall, and sat by his grave. No one could see me now, I could cry all I wanted to. From now on, my grief would be private.

The twenty-first of November Bill and I were supposed to work a date in St. Louis. I wanted to cancel but Hubert said it would do me good to work. David had to be in school but, with Corky and Jack going with me, I agreed.

Several other people, Kitty Wells, Johnny Wright, Carl Smith, and I don't remember who else, were on the show. I accepted their condolences but tried not to dwell on them. I knew I'd never get through the show if I did. As always, I closed my part with "Where No One Stands Alone." The next thing I knew, I was lying on the floor of my small dressing room with my head in Carl Smith's lap. All the other times I'd seen Carl, he'd been teasing and joking—usually in a vulgar way—but now he was sitting there bathing my head with a wet washcloth and looking very somber. For a minute, he didn't say anything, he just let me cry. Then he said, "Jan, I've got to ask you something."

Between sobs, I said, "All right."

"You know I'm your friend, right?"

"Yes." I couldn't see what he was getting at.

"I'm your buddy, right?"

"Yes."

"Okay, here goes. How in the hell do you ever expect to get screwed if you keep singing 'Nearer My God To Thee.'"

"Carl Smith!" I yelled, and jumped up from the floor. He was laughing!

"See, got you up off the floor. If I'd given you sympathy, you'd have been out cold again." He was probably right.

Every day there were new steps to take. Corky's leave was up and he was now stationed at Fort Campbell, Kentucky, the same place he'd taken basic. Just sixty miles from home. Even though he had top secret clearance, his orders hadn't caught up with him, and he was assigned to guarding the stockade. He'd usually come home one night during the week and on weekends—bringing with him all his dirty clothes to be washed or cleaned.

Going through his pockets, I found a wrinkled sheet of paper. Not knowing whether to throw it away or not, I read what was written there. And, as I did, tears of pride rolled down my face. It was entitled "I Am."

"I am a soldier, I'm a slave of power, power so great that it can destroy God's world with one mighty blast. I'm a machine, a computer, an engine programmed to reap destruction wherever I go. I'm a bad risk for my credit is only backed up by the United States Government. My reputation is that of a braggart, sex

*fiend, cheat, and rustic hero. I'm a killer, paid and trained to hit
first before being hit, and I do.*

"*I'm a soldier, so who cares how dirty the job is, if it has to be
done, it's done, right? But I'm also a human being. I'm myself,
good or bad.*

"*I smell the flowers in the spring, hear the birds sing in the
early morning. I feel the warmth of a fire in the winter, I feel the
rain as it moistens my brow.*

"*I'm part of a family with God as my Father and me the
obedient child. I have wants and needs and the strength and
faith to fulfill them. I have passion, the kind that brings forth a
love so great that no war, tragedy, or other being could destroy
... I'm a human being and I feel things around me and I'm
grateful.*

"*I am an American and I'm proud. I have the right to worship
God as my master. To love a wife, children, mother, and father
without the fear of political reprisal. My country gives me the
right to build, destroy, and to rebuild to better proportions.*

"*I am an American. I have a right to listen to the 'Star
Spangled Banner,' to feel a chill through my entire body when I
look at the flag, our flag. I have the right to defend, to honor, to
pay tribute to the great ones who have come and gone before.
Why? Because I am an American.*

"*I can also cry, cry for my lost brother who died defending us
... I am an American and I'm proud, so very proud!*"

Corky walked in as I finished reading and told me the story
behind his writing it. One of the prisoners he was guarding
walked up to him and asked, "Tell me, what's so great about being
an American and living in this country?" "I Am" was Corky's
answer.

"I'd like to record this if it's all right?" I asked. Until that
moment I hadn't even thought about ever going into the studio
again.

"I don't know," he said. "Those are my private thoughts."

"I know. But they're words a lot of people should hear," I said.
He finally agreed.

With much planning, and with "I Am" included, I went in to
record a patriotic-inspirational album dedicated to Jimmy. All of
the musicians had known him. Several times during the session,
I'd see one of them leave the studio with tears in his eyes.

It was the most difficult album I'd ever recorded yet one that would always be the closest to my heart.

Jack—as Major Jack Norman, Jr., Tennessee Air National Guard—Bill Anderson and Bobby Bare wrote the liner notes.

As yet, I hadn't been back to the television show. One day Bill called and said they were doing a special show in tribute to Jimmy and asked if I'd like to come and sit in the control room. David went with me.

As they did the TV show, I sat there holding David's hand. My record of "My Son" was playing, and Jimmy's pictures, from the time he was little to the most recent one in uniform, flashed across the screen. I knew Bill had taken a lot of time preparing it. In fact David had gathered the pictures for him. Yet at times, it was almost more than I could handle.

Then George started singing, and I remembered. My God! He'd sang "Where No One Stands Alone" at Jimmy's funeral! The whole thing came back so vividly, as if it was happening all over again. No wonder he had looked at me so strangely. I jumped up and ran to him. "Oh, George, I'm so sorry! I didn't remember!"

"I knew you didn't. And I was afraid when you did, it would upset you."

I hugged him. "God bless you, George. And thank you." I knew I must have asked him to sing. Now I also remembered the Jordinaires singing the "Lord's Prayer," the long, long line of cars—so many things. *Oh, God, give me strength!*

December 1, 1968. The fair buyer's convention was being held in Chicago this year. Hubert, being agent *and* buyer, always attended. He never missed anything that had to do with business or fun. From what I'd heard, this was a combination of both. The night before he was scheduled to leave, he called. "Why don't you come with me?"

"I can't, Hubert," I said. "I just don't want to see anyone."

"I think it's time you got out of the house," he said. "Besides, Jack will be there." He knew that would bring a smile to my face. Jack was Hubert's best friend and he knew there was much more than a client-attorney relationship between us.

"Yeah," I said, "and so will his wife." Hubert laughed.

"But you'll be with me," he said. "My new girlfriend. And we don't want to beat Nashville out of a new rumor, do we?"

I could just hear the tongues wagging if I showed up in Chicago. "Well, I don't know," I said, "I'll think about it."

"Tell you what," he said. "I'm leaving in the morning. If you decide to come, I'll have a room for you at the hotel. Just come on up, I'll be expecting you." A few minutes later, he called again. "Just in case, I've made you a plane reservation for day after tomorrow."

As I got off the plane and felt the cold Chicago wind, I wished I was back home curled up in a warm robe. But it was too late. I wondered if Hubert had told Jack. Anticipating his look when he saw me, I had to laugh. Jack wasn't too much on surprises.

After getting checked in and settled in my room, I called and left word for Hubert to call me. In the meantime, I took a shower and lay across the bed with my eyes closed. Just as I was about to drift off, the phone rang.

"Redhead! You made it!" Hubert said. "Meet me in the lobby in ten minutes."

As we walked into the bar, the first two people we saw were Delores Smiley and Bob Neal—agents from Nashville. Doing a double take, they said, "Jan! What are *you* doing here?"

Hubert said, "Oh, you all know my girlfriend, Jan Howard." I could see they didn't know whether to take him seriously or not. Other heads in the room started turning and I could hear the whispers. Hubert was right. Nashville needed a new rumor and it was now evident we were it. The news would be back in Nashville before we were.

Everywhere we went, I expected to see Jack at any moment. Worse yet, his wife. "Hubert, what does she look like?"

Looking innocent, he said, "Who?"

"You know who, Duina Norman!"

"Oh, that who." He laughed. "Well, if you see a leopard coat walking around with a leopard in it, that's Duina."

We went from the hotel to Trader Vic's for dinner and Hubert insisted I have a Mai Tai.

"Hubert, I don't know," I said hesitantly. "I'm afraid it'll make me sick."

"No it won't," he said, "it'll just make you relax." He was right. After the second one I was so relaxed I couldn't see.

After dinner, Hubert said we were going to the Playboy Club. Since I was more than a little tipsy, Hubert's capable arm assisted me out of the cab and up the steps to the club where, once again, we ran into Bob Neal, this time with his son, Sonny. The look they exchanged meant, "What in hell's going on?" Hubert just smiled, said, "Good evening, gentlemen," and guided me on in. He was having a ball, and so was I. To every Bunny that walked by, Hubert would say, "I think we'll take that one home to Corky," or "Do you think Corky would like that one?" The one he was pointing to was black and beautiful.

"No, Hubert," I said, "I think Corky can pick out his own."

The next night was the formal banquet, and I began to worry. Jack had come to my room that morning. When I said I didn't want to cause him any trouble, he laughed and said, "No trouble, I know you'll handle it." He was getting a kick out of this. Yet, I couldn't stay mad at him, not after he held me and said how glad he was that I was here. Even so, Jack had arranged for us to be seated at the same table with him, his wife, and her family.

That night, I got a real good look at the "Leopard." She was sitting directly across from me. I knew I richly deserved it, but I've never been more uncomfortable in my life.

All evening, except when I was dancing with everyone who asked me, my attention was focused solely on Hubert. Except for one time when Jack insisted the waiter bring me the proper glass for my champagne. Everyone else at the table, including his wife, was drinking out of plastic glasses. If I had been in her place, I'd have poured the champagne on him, or, better yet, christened his head with the bottle.

Somehow, we got through the evening but I was glad when it was over. Deceit didn't feel good. I resolved to leave the next morning.

Christmas was coming and I dreaded it. I remembered what Jimmy had said about "being with us in spirit." I wondered if he'd received any of his packages. Corky said he hadn't gotten any of his and we hoped that somebody had them, who wouldn't otherwise have gotten any.

The letters kept coming. One from Jimmy's chaplain said, "Your son Jimmy set an example that few men can follow but all men should try." He went on to tell me of Jimmy's spiritual outlook. That every morning, before going into "the field," he had come to him and they'd read the Twenty-Third Psalm.

There was a letter from a man in Jimmy's troop who said it was his tape recorder that Jimmy used to hear "My Son," and that he had been so proud he had cried.

And I knew he was there when I went, with Corky, in full dress uniform, as my escort, to acknowledge the Grammy nomination for best female performance on the recording of "My Son."

As I Christmas-shopped, I'd look around at all the happy faces in the stores and wonder if some of them, like me, were just going through the motions. But I'd smile and say, "Merry Christmas to you, too."

David and I bought presents for everyone we could think of, then went shopping for a tree—the biggest one we could find that would fit in the apartment. It wouldn't be like the one at the house, but a lot of things would never be the same.

I wanted to see the house and Jeanie Bare drove me out. But the minute we turned in the drive and I saw Jimmy's blue Corvair (the one we'd sold to the Maphises) parked beneath the basketball goal, I said, "Get me out of here!" I now knew I could never go back.

After talking it over with the boys, and not even going to pick up the things I'd left there, I sold the house to the Maphises.

David and I worked until midnight putting up the tree but waited for Corky to help trim it. With every last ornament on and the lights lit, we stood back to admire our work. Then, as if on signal, we all turned to the lonely angel still laying on a chair. No one made a move. Then Corky, in a voice choked with tears, said, "Damn it, Jimmy, this was *your* job!" and grabbed it, climbed up on a chair, and stuck it on top. A little crooked maybe, but it was there.

Christmas morning, we exchanged our gifts. David's to me had a note attached. "Something you don't want, don't need, and will probably hate." It was a crocheted vest, a bit too small, but I put it on anyway. Corky's present was two Early American lamps for my French provincial living room. But their main gift to all of us—and to Jimmy—was a regulation-size American flag and stand which was placed next to Jimmy's picture.

Jack had been in Florida since the sixteenth and would not be back until after the fourth of January, but his secretary delivered my gift—a twenty-dollar gold piece on a solid gold chain and a charm bracelet filled with gold coins. It was pretty, but I would rather have had a candy bar delivered in person.

Except for work, and dinner with Jack now and then, I very seldom left the house. David was such a comfort. He was my baby, but suddenly, he was a man. Just seventeen but a man. He was sensitive to my every mood. I had to be careful because when I hurt, he did, too. We'd sit for hours talking and drinking hot chocolate. Or he'd fix his special soup. Some horrible concoction of tomato sauce, chopped raw onions, and Tabasco, but I'd drink it anyway. One night, he decided he was going to fix dinner and spent all afternoon preparing it, not wanting or asking assistance. While he finished, I put on my best "at home" outfit, did my hair and makeup, and waited for him to call me to come down. When he did, I saw the table set with the best silver and china, candles lit, and David in slacks and a velvet jacket, holding my chair for me. It was a special evening.

Then, when everything was ready, he brought in the chicken he'd been baking, set on a silver platter and surrounded with red crab apples. It was very pretty—and we should have left it that way. Because when David cut into it, blood spurted everywhere. It was raw! After the initial shock, we broke down and laughed until we were weak. Then David said, "Hold everything! I'll be right back!" and he ran out the door. A few minutes later he returned with fast-food hamburgers and french fries which we ate by candlelight. Sirloin steak couldn't have tasted better.

After my first initial flight with Jack, I decided to take flying lessons. And, after getting over most of my fear, I'd learned to love it and couldn't wait for the next lesson. Before I was notified of Jimmy's death, I had been ready to solo. But since then I hadn't been interested in anything—not even the health club which I'd attended regularly. I decided to go back. Gathering my workout things, I left a note for Corky, who was home on leave, and David and I went to the club.

I walked a mile, then started on the exercises. It felt good, I did more than usual. About a block from home, I felt a tightness in my chest. Then I began having trouble breathing. By the time I pulled into the parking lot the pain involved my whole chest. *Oh God,* I thought, *I'm having a heart attack!* I prayed someone would be home. I made it to the door and leaned against the doorbell. David opened it and I fell into his arms. "Get Dr. Goldner on the phone," I said. He dialed the number.

"Dr. Goldner! This is Jan Howard . . . I think I'm dying! I can't breathe and my heart is beating very, very fast!"

"Lie down," he said. "I'll be right there."

David helped me to the sofa. "Find Corky, David!"

I heard the ambulance and saw Dr. Goldner and Corky run in the door at the same time. "Corky," I said, "promise me you'll take care of David."

He said, "Mom, you're going to be all right." I saw the fear in his face. We were in the ambulance, Dr. Goldner gave me a shot. The pain was getting worse. I knew I was going to die.

Through a fog, I opened my eyes and could make out faces. Corky, David, Dr. Goldner. "Did I have a heart attack?" I asked.

"No, Jan," Dr. Goldner said. "You didn't have a heart attack." He was taking my pulse.

"But what happened?"

"I don't know but you must believe me. You did *not* have a heart attack." I wanted desperately to believe him.

For ten days, I lay in bed afraid to move, afraid it would happen again. Then, with help from everybody, I accepted my good fortune and tried to regain strength enough to go home. The day I left, Dr. Goldner said, "Just stay away from health clubs for a while." He needn't have worried. It would be a good while before I tried the club again. His explanation was I was still weak from all the medicine I took and my heart had had some kind of spasm.

It took a long time for me not to panic at every little pain. I was very afraid of death—not dying, just death.

When Corky's leave was up and he was on his way to Fort Campbell, I asked him if he would mind not wearing his uniform when he came home. "I don't ever want to see another uniform," I said. All of them represented one thing . . . the morning I was notified of Jimmy's death. So, respecting my request, every time he came home, he'd wear his blue jeans.

I'd been shopping and when I pulled into the parking lot, I saw Jimmy's car. Even though Corky was driving it now, it was still "Jimmy's car." *It is Wednesday,* I thought, *what's he doing home?*

Opening the door, I called out, "Corky? Are you home?" and walked on back to the den. I stopped short. Corky was there in full dress uniform! "What are you doing here in that uniform?" I said. "I asked you not to wear it home." Getting up from the sofa, he walked over, put his hands on my shoulders, and sat me down in the nearest chair. "Mom," he said, "I want to talk to you." He sat down. "In answer to your question, do you remember the two officers that came to your door that day?" I nodded. How did he think I'd ever forget. "Well," he went on, "that's what I've been doing today." I stared at him. "There's a woman in Murfreesboro who just lost her eighteen-year-old son. He'd been in Vietnam only two weeks. She has five younger children and, right now, they don't know if she'll survive or, if she does, whether she'll end up in a mental hospital." I was trying to grasp what he was telling me. He went on. "I think it's time you stopped wallowing in your self-pity and realize there are others out there who are just as bad off, or worse off, than you are. I suggest you either get on the phone or go to Murfreesboro and see if you can help this woman." Tears were rolling down my face. I sat looking at him. His words had hit home. I started to say something when he interrupted me. "And another thing, you'd better get used to seeing this uniform. I'll be wearing it for another two years. Besides, this uniform and what it represents is what Jimmy died for."

I was ashamed. He was right. I'd only been thinking of myself, drowning in self-pity. I knew he and David were hurting but not as much as I was. Not only didn't Corky and David want me to pity myself, but Jimmy wouldn't have, either. And it took Corky to make me realize this. I had lost my oldest son, but we had had twenty-one beautiful years together. Some people have their children all their lives but are never close to them. I still had two wonderful sons. I had so much to be thankful for.

"Corky," I said. "You are right. You're a lot taller than the tape measure says. I'm proud of the uniform you wear. I can't promise things will change overnight, but I'll try, okay?"

"Okay, Mom," he said, and walked over and hugged me.

As I was changing clothes, I thought of the time after Harlan had left when Jimmy had shaken me and said, "My mom has more guts than any woman I know . . . It's time for her to *show* it." Corky had shaken me, in a different way.

Nothing changes overnight. There were still times when I'd

walk the floor and cry for hours. And, many nights, I'd call friends, mostly Hubert, and tell him: "I can't make it! I can't handle it!" They'd either stay on the phone until I calmed down or come over and sit with me, sometimes all night. But, except for a few people, I tried not to show that side of Jan Howard to anyone. Whatever, it had to be kept between me, Jimmy, and God.

In March of 1969, Bill, myself, Conway Twitty, Loretta Lynn, and George Hamilton IV, and all the band members, went on tour in Europe. I'd never been there and looked forward to it, especially since Hubert would be along. It promised to be a fun trip. But, after fifteen hours of flying, I decided fun could wait. All I wanted was a bed.

Landing in Frankfurt, West Germany, we went straight to the hotel, where Hubert took over. After talking with the clerk, he came back with a puzzled look on his face. "The reservations have been messed up," he said. "They don't have all the rooms." Everybody said, "Oh no!" He went on. "But they do have rooms for five people in a private home about thirty miles from here . . . who wants to go?" I was the first to raise my hand.

The house looked like one I'd seen in magazines. A big, old, two-story frame house with flowers all around . . . sitting right at the foot of a small mountain, and the family out front waiting to greet us. I tried to appreciate everything, but I was so tired I couldn't think. *I'll appreciate everything after I've had some sleep,* I thought.

The lady showed me to a room about the size of a walk-in closet . . . but the cleanest walk-in closet I'd ever seen. In one corner was a washbasin and a chair. Against the wall was an old-fashioned chifforobe and, in what space there was left, a three-quarter-size bed piled high with feather comforters. I couldn't wait to get in it.

Since neither of us understood the other's language, I made motions indicating I wanted to take a bath. She smiled, "Ahh, ja. Bat," then got a look of dismay on her face. I followed her down the hall to the "bat." Opening the door, she pointed to the bathtub. Now, I now understood her look of dismay. It was filled with clothes soaking in water. "I vasha clothes," she said, and shrugged her shoulders. I patted her shoulder and walked back to the room. She came in all smiles, reached down in the bottom of the chifforobe and brought out a thin, well-washed washcloth. "American," she said, so pleased with herself. Thanking her, I made a few swipes at my face, stood on the stool placed near the bed, and jumped in, sinking in the soft feathers. I know I was asleep before I stopped sinking.

The next morning at breakfast, I was trying to figure how to tell them what I wanted. Looking over at some fresh fruit one of them was eating, I pointed to that and nodded my head. Everybody started snickering. When the lady brought it out, I knew why—it was swimming in wine! But I ate it anyway. It was strange sitting there not being able to understand a word anyone was saying. But I loved it.

The show that night was at a military base. During my part, several of the men shouted out, "Sing 'My Son'!" At first I planned to refuse. But looking out over the audience of young men about Jimmy and Corky's age, I thought, *They deserve it,* and did the best I could.

Afterward, several of them came up and said hearing it was like hearing their mothers talking to them. Now I understood why I had written it. It wasn't just Jimmy and me, it was for all mothers and all their sons.

After the show, we drove eighty miles up in the mountains to a village that seemed to have been there for centuries. And there, right in the middle of it, this pink stucco hotel with a pink wall all around it . . . But when I learned that Hitler had it built and it had been one of his favorite places, I understood . . . As far as I was concerned, he had bad taste.

On the bedside table in my room were all kinds of buttons. Trying to figure out what they were for, I pushed one and then another . . . nothing happened. Then, someone knocked at my door. I opened it to find the bellman standing there smiling and pointing to my shoes. I couldn't understand what he was trying to say. Then, he pointed up. A red light was shining above my door. "Oh, no!" I said. "You've got the wrong room!" To me, a red light above a door meant only one thing, prostitution! My father had told stories about the old red-light district in San Francisco, when he was a young man. Now I had one of my very own!

About that time Hubert came walking down the hall. "Hubert," I said. "Tell this man that I don't want his services." Looking up to where I pointed to the red light, he laughed.

"No, Jan. He thinks you want your shoes shined."

"My shoes?"

"Yeah . . . If you want your shoes shined, you turn on that light and put your shoes outside your door. Then, in the morning, they bring them back." No wonder he was pointing to my shoes. I felt West Plains sticking out all over me.

The tour went well! And I saw some of the most beautiful country I'd ever seen, particularly Bergen, Norway. As we flew in, it seemed like a picture postcard. Mountains surrounded this gorgeous fairyland village on a beautiful clear blue lake on which rode two white yachts, one larger than the other. The stewardess explained that they belonged to the king and queen of Norway. The queen's was the smaller one. I'd heard of people having separate bedrooms but this was ridiculous.

I never got used to daylight almost twenty-four hours a day. At three o'clock in the morning, there were children out in the streets. *When do they sleep?* I wondered.

At the show, when I sang "Where No One Stands Alone," the audience started stomping their feet. It grew until it was like thunder! I didn't know what I'd done! Turning to Steve Chapman, the guitar player, I said, "What's happening, Steve?"

"I don't know," he said, "but I'm following you!"

Then someone yelled out, "Sing more!" I got it . . . They wanted an encore!

"Well, why didn't you tell me," I said, and started singing the chorus again.

In Oslo, the hotel was right in the middle of the town square and we were told this was where Hitler had the town officials executed. That made chills go down my spine. With my vivid imagination, I could almost see the blood.

As I looked into the history of the old buildings, some hundreds of years old, I realized how very young our country was— still a baby—and how very lucky I was to have this experience.

Loretta had been her usual good-natured self on the whole tour except for Stockholm, Sweden, where she was mad as hell at Doo (Doolittle, her husband Mooney's nickname). "Where's Doo?" I asked.

"Where else!" she said. "Out in the bus, asleep. All he wants to do is spend all day in those old dirty bookstores and make love all night!"

"Loretta!" Well, Loretta was not one to mince words!

In Amsterdam, besides the tulips and windmills, Hubert had

something else to show me. Hailing a cab, we rode down a
narrow street. "Look!" he said, and pointed to a window in this
small house where a woman was sitting with a sheer negligee on
and nothing else. And all of the houses were the same . . .
Women on display. It dawned on me that we were on the famous
Canal Street, Amsterdam's red-light district. I was fascinated!
The pedestrian traffic needed a traffic cop. Then, at one house,
the woman smiled and motioned Hubert to come in. I *thought*
she was motioning to Hubert. But, looking again, I saw she was
motioning to me. Hubert was laughing his head off. "Hubert," I
said. "I think you should take me back to the hotel, then you can
'window shop' all you want." Now, if they'd had a good-looking
man in the window, I could have forced myself to look a little
longer.

From London, I called home, and a voice I had never heard
before answered. "Hi," I said, "this is Jan Howard . . . is David
there?"

"Oh . . . hi, Miss Howard! No, David isn't here. He's out in
Madison."

"Oh. Well, is Corky there?"

"No," he said, "he's out in Madison, too." I could hear other
voices in the background. The person I was talking to said, "Hey,
guys, hold it down . . . it's Miss Howard!"

"Listen," I said, "I'm calling from London. Would you mind
telling me whom I'm talking to?"

"Oh, sure. This is Al Strenyak, a friend of Corky's from Fort
Campbell. He brought a few of us home for the weekend. But,
don't worry, we'll clean up all the mess and clear out all the
bottles and stuff." *Bottles?* "We sure do appreciate this, Miss
Howard. You sure got a nice apartment."

"Glad you like it, Al." I wasn't too surprised. Corky had done
this before, and I knew his reason. All the boys he brought home
were either just back from, or going to, Vietnam. "Well, I gotta
hang up. Tell the boys I called, will you?"

"Sure thing, Miss Howard. Sure good to talk to you."

Before I hung up, I said, "By the way, Al, have a good time." I
meant it.

All during the tour, at different hotels, I had letters waiting for
me from Jack. Each one written on a yellow legal pad when he

was in court. (His clients probably thought he was hard at work on their case.) Each one saying how much he missed and loved me. In the last letter, he'd said there was something very important he had to ask me when I got home. Now, we were almost there, and I was more than ready to hear his question.

When we touched down, I thought *Gosh, it's great to be home!* The last few days, I'd been extra homesick. I'd been on long tours before, but somehow being in Europe made coming home very special. I knew Corky was at camp and David was at school, but Jack had written that he'd meet me.

Sure enough, there at the gate in the midst of all the wives and kids stood Jack—all smiles. And, right in front of everybody, he grabbed and kissed me as though I'd been gone for a year. Everybody gathered round with questions, like, "When's the wedding?" There was no denial from either of us.

In the car, Jack said, "Miss Howard, how does the name Jan Norman sound to you?"

"It sounds wonderful," I said, and threw my arms around his neck.

"Well," he said, "I've decided I like the sound of it, too." But there was one hitch. He was still married and still living at home. When I voiced those thoughts, he said, "I'm working on it." Up to now, no mention of any future together had ever been mentioned by either of us.

He made a turn in the opposite direction from my house. "Where are we going?" I asked.

"Birmingham," he said.

"Birmingham! Jack, I've just gotten off a plane after flying for seventeen hours. I don't want to get back on one!" He kept on driving . . . to Cornelia Fort, where his plane was. "Honey, please, if you have to go to Birmingham, just take me home and I'll talk to you when you get back."

"No way," he said. "I'm not letting you out of my sight. Besides, there's a lot we have to talk about. Important things."

In the hotel, we discussed things like where we'd live. He said he knew I wouldn't want to live in the house where he lived now, and he was right. It was beautiful, but it would never be mine. Finally, we decided it would be the apartment above his office where his folks lived now. They were moving to a farm and it would be perfect. I'd been to the apartment and, as it was, it was beautiful. But, he said, "After we're married, I'll give you a re-decorating allowance and you can do anything you want to with it." I was happier than I'd ever been in my life.

With the new direction of our relationship had taken, and being back full time with the show, my mind and my outlook were slowly coming back into focus. Whenever I'd feel a "down" period coming, I'd go shopping. Always having to have different things to wear on the TV show, shopping for new clothes was a necessity. I never had pretty clothes as a kid, but now I loved dressing in the beautiful long gowns I usually wore onstage. Either that or silk or satin pant suits. It was like playing "dress up." At home, though, even though they might have advanced from Salvation Army to designer, I still liked my blue jeans and sweat shirts.

My hair was another thing I was constantly changing. The color ranged from dark brown to strawberry blond—depending on what came out of the bottle and my mood at the time. And the length depended a whole lot on how much attention I paid to the hairdresser with the scissors in his hand. One time, in Toronto, I decided to visit the famous salon of Vidal Sassoon and came out with hair about an inch long all over. I was sick.

That night, when I walked out onstage the first time, one of the band members said, "Jan! You look just like a turtle that just stuck his head out of the shell!" All through the show I was so self-conscious I could barely sing. And for days, I'd pull and try to stretch my hair until I decided if I didn't stop, I'd be bald.

Before, when Jo Coulter, the makeup lady at the studio, did my makeup for the television show, I'd just let her do it and not pay much attention. But now, I watched every move she made to get pointers, Since my eyes were deep set—inherited from my father—I noticed she put light eye shadow on the lids and dark on the brow bones . . . and a lighter eyebrow pencil than I was used to using. And loads of dark brown mascara. Then, instead of the brown-toned blush I was using, she used a mauve. It made all the difference in the world. And she showed me how to place it in the hollow of my high cheekbones so they'd stand out. Next came lipstick. Since it turned dark on me, she took away the red and replaced it with a coral or rose color. But, to cap it off, she made me wear false eyelashes! And for a long time, I really *tried* to wear those things. At the studio, with her putting them on, I learned how. But at home, when I ended up sticking them in my eyes instead of on my eyelids, I gave them up and eventually discarded them altogether. It sure took a lot longer getting ready to go somewhere but, little by little, I began to feel like a halfway attractive woman!

Sometimes, no matter how good I was feeling, out of nowhere would come a feeling that made chills go all over me.

One day, right in the middle of getting my makeup done, I turned to Jo and said, "Four years."

"Four years what?" she said.

"I don't know, Jo. I just know it'll be four years for something." *Why did I say that?* I thought, and tried to put it out of my mind.

When I was home, I was fine. But out on the road there were still rough moments. Thank God I was with friends. I needed to work but still I dreaded the lonely motel rooms.

Most of the time, after the shows and all the autographing was done, I'd go to my room (or on the bus) and cry all night. If Bill or the band noticed my red or swollen eyes, no one mentioned them. Sometimes, if we were traveling from one date to another on the bus and I could get anyone to join me, we'd play poker until all hours. Bill wasn't much on cards, and the players would end up being me, Jimmy Gately, and one or two others. Funny thing about "Gate"—he never seemed to win, not even when everyone else lost. "Just came out about even," he'd say. I loved Gate. Most of the time he was in a world all his own but you could always count on him for a laugh.

When I'd worked with Bill and started traveling on the bus with them, I'd told them all that I didn't want them feeling uncomfortable with a woman around. "Just think of me as one of the boys," I said. I knew the amount of respect I got depended a lot on me. One day, I got an example of just how much they thought of me as one of the boys.

Getting dressed for the show, I was standing behind my curtain with just a blouse and a pair of panty hose on, when the curtain was jerked back and Gately said, "Hey, Jan, how does this tie look?"

"Gately!" I said, and jerked the curtain back closed. "I'm standing here with just a blouse and panty hose on, and you ask how your stupid tie looks!"

"You were?" he said. "I didn't notice." Damn! "Well, you didn't answer my question."

"What question!"

"About my tie?" I had to laugh.

"Yeah, Gate, your tie's fine. Only, your head is warped!"

Later that night, when I was relating the story to the rest of the guys, I said, "Some night I'm going to wear a flimsy negligee and see if anyone notices."

"Don't do it!" they said.

One night I was put to the test. Bill was flying to the next date and I was on the bus with the boys. Very seldom did any of them drink—and *never* on the bus—but the old saying "When the cat's away the mice will play" was in effect.

I was in bed reading but in the front of the bus the booze was flowing freely. There was a lot of laughing and now and then, I'd hear someone say, "You'd better not, she'll kill you!" Suddenly, the door slammed open, my curtain was jerked back, and the steel guitar player, more than a little drunk, said, "Tonight's the night, baby!" and fell on top of me! As he fell, his hand caught my wig (which I sometimes wore onstage), which was lying on a shelf over my bed. As drunk as he was, and with one push from me, he was off me and on the floor. "No, darlin'," I said, "tonight's not the night!" He looked down, saw the wig, which was still clutched in his hand, and said, "My God, I've pulled her hair off!"

As he scrambled up and out the door, I jerked my curtain back closed and almost smothered myself with the pillow to keep them from hearing me laughing. Poor guy, for the next two days he couldn't look at me without his face turning red. Then, to put an end to his embarrassment, I said, "Hey, forget it! In a way it's a compliment. After all, you are young enough to be my son."

"Well," he said. "At least now you know we really don't think you're one of the boys."

Country music fans are wonderful. They love the person . . . not just her current record. And during the very difficult period right after Jimmy's death, they were all so considerate. If they said anything, it was usually "I'm sorry about your son" or a request for "My Son," which I'd tried a few times but got to where I couldn't sing it without crying all night afterward. And when I couldn't, they understood. I loved them all. All, that is, except one woman. After a show, while I was signing autographs, this woman said, "Didn't you just lose a son in Vietnam?"

Expecting the usual "I'm sorry," I said, "Yes, I did," and went on signing.

"Well," she said, "you certainly don't act like it!" I dropped my pen. I was angry.

"Lady, if you have a problem with what I'd doing, then I'm sorry. But I'm doing exactly what my son would want me to do. Would you prefer that I crawl in a hole and die? Would that make you happy? Or is it that you want visibly to see my grief? Well, I'm sorry, it's private," I said and ran to the bus.

Bill, following close behind me, said, "That stupid bitch! Don't let her get to you."

His advice was too late. I was crying. I said, "She already did. But she won't have the satisfaction of knowing it."

I'd always wanted to know what it felt like to drive that big bus. Several times, always where Bill could hear me, I'd said I would someday. "Not while I'm the owner, you won't," Bill would say.

One day, while rolling down the open highway in Texas, Bill was in his room in the back of the bus, the band was all playing cards, and I was sitting on the jump seat up next to the driver. "How difficult is it really?" I asked.

"Not difficult," he said. "Wanna try it?"

"Really?" Looking around, I saw the boys all engrossed in the card game and Bill was still in his room. "Yeah," I said.

Still holding onto the wheel but sliding out from under to make room for me to slide in, he said, "It's all yours." I sat down in the jump seat.

Seeing the looks on several truckers' faces when they passed, I really felt in command. "Hey, this is great!". . . Then I looked in the mirror and saw Bill coming out of his room. *Uh, oh,* I thought. Yawning and scratching his head, he walked toward the front and started to say something to the driver in the jump seat. Then he saw the relief driver playing cards. His face went white. When he realized I was driving the bus, he said, "Good God! Get her out from under that wheel! She'll kill us all!" He and half the band ran for the back of the bus. Quickly, I exchanged seats with the driver and wondered which one of us would get fired first. I couldn't see what all the fuss was about . . . I thought I was doing great.

One day, right after Bill bought the new Silver Eagle, we

pulled into a drive-in to get hamburgers to go. Someone over-heard one waitress say to another one, "Gosh, Ernest Tubb and Loretta Lynn came in a gold Cadillac. All they got's an old bus!" That "old bus" cost a hundred thousand dollars.

We weren't always on the fancy bus, though. One time, down in Georgia, it broke down and we rented a yellow school bus to go the rest of the way. As the old saying goes—the show must go on.

Fans were always curious about the bus. With the old one, their question was "How did you all make it here?" With the new one, they always wanted to know what was inside. The band always had an answer. At a fair in Michigan, one of them told a fan that the reason Bill couldn't come to the door was that he was downstairs taking a dip in the pool.

With the TV show being shown in Canada, we were in and out of there so much that most of the border guards knew us. But, one night at three o'clock in the morning, even after the driver had presented all the necessary papers, the guard still insisted on seeing Bill, who was sound asleep in his room. Nothing would do. He had to see Bill. The driver had no choice but to wake him.

In his pajamas, and with his hair standing on end, a very perturbed Bill walked to the front of the bus. "You wanted to see me?" he asked the guard.

The guard stood there looking at Bill. Then, shaking his head, he said, "Nope, it's not my television." And walked off the bus.

Another night, they made us unload all our suitcases from the bus and went through every piece. As the guard opened my wig box, he jumped back and said, "Cheez! It's a bloody head."

Thank God for those moments. They were often all that kept us going.

After the trip to Birmingham, Jack never mentioned getting married again. If I hadn't heard it with my own ears, I'd have sworn I made up the whole conversation. Still, I lived for his phone calls. Sometimes, just a hurried, whispered, "I love you." But it was enough. I knew the situation was hopeless but I loved him so much I couldn't break away. I tried to—several times. And being a typical female, twice I'd gone out with someone else. Once, at Jack's suggestion, with his friend, Al Powell.

When Al called and said Jack had given him my phone number, I knew Jack just wanted to see if I'd go. It made me so mad, I did! But, after dinner, when Al took me home and kissed me good night, he said, "When I kiss someone good night and they don't even know they've been kissed, I know they're in love with someone else." He was right.

Another time, at a cocktail party where I just happened to run into Jack and his wife, I was introduced to one of his friends from New York—another attorney by the name of Jerry, who only knew that Jack was my attorney. After the party, when Jerry suggested we to go to dinner at Mario's, an Italian restaurant in Nashville, I accepted.

As we walked in the door, Mario, with his wonderful Italian accent, said, "Jane! (he never could pronounce Jan) Good to see you!" I introduced him to Jerry. "Hey," Mario said, "Jack's got a big table. I know he'll want you to join him!" I looked across the room where Jack, his wife, and several friends were sitting. *Oh sure,* I thought, *I'll just bet he would.* Too late, Jerry had spotted them too and was walking toward the table. Oh, Lord! There was nothing to do but join them.

At the table, everybody but Jack and I seemed to have a big appetite. Jerry started talking about a murder case. Duina turned to Jerry and said, "Tell me, if I kill Jack, will you defend me?" I choked! I decided it was time for us to leave.

Since we were in my car and I was tired of playing this game I suggested I take Jerry back to his hotel. "A gentleman doesn't let a lady go home by herself," he said. "No, I'll see you home, then take a cab back."

Arriving at my house, I said, "Would you like a drink?" and started back to the den. He stood there watching me get out the glasses . . . one for my iced tea and one for his drink.

"You really invited me for a drink, didn't you?" he said.

"Yes, what did you think?" I knew what he thought and felt stupid.

"I thought I was going to see the inside of Jan Howard's bedroom," he said.

"I know you did, but you know what?"

"Yeah. I'm not. Damn! That's the first time I've been turned down in two years!" he said.

"Well, in that case," I said, "you must be exhausted! We'd better call your cab so you'll get a good night's rest before you go back to New York."

At the door, he handed me his card and said, "If you ever need an attorney, and can't find a good one in Nashville, call me. It won't cost you a cent." Then, after looking at me a long moment, he added, "I think I get it. It's Norman, right?" It was more of a statement than a question and I left it at that.

Corky was dating a girl in Madison by the name of Pam Chance, a sweet girl whom I liked very much. They'd gone to church together since they had been twelve, but, after he'd come back from Vietnam, they seemed to be together constantly. She was quiet and very southern—an accent you could cut with a knife— but a lot of fun. And that's what Corky needed now. Fun. He still dated other girls, one in particular whom he'd known for a long time and whom I also liked, Nicky Joyner, but lately it had been Pam more than anyone. As time passed, he seemed to get more adjusted and be happier. It did my heart good. And I was doubly thankful that he was able to come home often. Not only did I need him but David needed him. He seemed very lost at times and I didn't know what to do. He liked and accepted Jack but they were never buddies. Jack represented the "legal" world, and David was a little in awe of him.

David loved to sing and did so much better than average. I called Harlan and asked if he'd let David do some of his demos. He said he'd think about it but we never heard from him. Several times, David had gone down to Harlan's office to see him and came home crying. When I asked what had happened, he said, "His secretary went in to tell him I was there, then came back out and said Mr. Howard wasn't in. Then I saw Dad going out the back door."

One day, David and I went to the Pancake Pantry for lunch. In the whole place, there was one empty table . . . right next to Harlan and his new wife Donna Gail. Not wanting to make a scene by leaving, we went ahead and sat down. Harlan looked up, saw us, got up, and walked out, leaving his wife sitting there. Even she was embarrassed. Getting up to leave, she turned and said, "I'm sorry."

David looked at me with tears in his eyes and said, "Why does he hate me so?"

"I'm sure he doesn't, David," I said, trying to convince myself as well. "Maybe he just doesn't have the nerve to face you."

Don Williams, one of my favorite artists and writers, came

over one day to play some songs. David sat there and listened.
Don asked "Do you like to sing, David?"

"Yeah," David said. "I asked Dad to do some demos but he
hasn't let me yet."

Don said, "Well, you can do some for me." I appreciated that.

Several weeks after Jimmy's death, his personal belongings were
sent from Vietnam. And try as I would, every now and then I
couldn't keep myself from going through them. Each time, it
would bring the sorrow back. I just had to touch things that he
had touched. That's what I was doing this day, several months
later. Sitting there on the floor, crying and touching everything.
Some photograph albums with pictures of his buddies around
and on the A.P.C., several pictures of Corky and of David and of
the three together, some of Bucko, and eleven pictures of me,
some which I had sent him and some I didn't even know he
had—in a bathing suit in Panama City, one of me onstage, with
Kenny Price and Bob Luman, and one of me beside the little
plane I took lessons in. There was one pair of stay-pressed pants,
one Banlon shirt, some rubber thongs with the name Howard
written with marker pen on them, his New Testament which the
Church had given him before he left; letters, his rings and watch
(with the crystal broken)—the very things I'd seen someone
removing in my dreams, and a few other things. Not much for
twenty-one years of living. I sat there caressing every single
thing, crying and thinking, *Oh, God! Will it never be better?* The
doorbell rang, jarring me back to the present.

Drying my eyes, I went to the door and opened it to see two
uniformed officers. I almost fainted! "Corky!" I screamed, and
started to run. One of the men grabbed me. "Oh, Mrs. Howard,
we're sorry. Corky's all right. We just came to present you with
some medals. We should have called first."

I sank down on the sofa. Medals! I didn't want their damned
medals! I wanted my son! I tried to pull myself together.

As they handed them to me, they said, "These are the two
highest medals the Vietnamese government presents." I looked
at them and thought, *They're not worth the price he paid.*

Just about the time I'd take one step forward, something
would happen to set me back two. A man from the insurance
company came to present me with a check from the small policy I

hadn't been able to pay the premium on. "Please," I said, "just lay it on the table." I couldn't touch it. After he left, I stood there looking at it and decided where it would go—to the new youth addition of the church. That way, even though he wasn't here, Jimmy would always be a part of the church he loved so much.

The money from the government insurance had been put into a special account and, when the time came, I'd know the right thing to do with it. I just knew even if I were starving, I could never touch a cent of it.

Touching the small gold and diamond star that Jack had given me shortly after that horrible day, I was reminded once more that I was and would always be a "Gold Star Mother." I remembered, in World War II, every time we'd move to another house, the flag with the five gold stars, which represented my three brothers and two brothers-in-law who were in Europe and the South Pacific, was hung in the window. Thank God, my mother never had a reason to wear one forever.

J ack had a small houseboat down on the river. It was the ugliest thing I'd ever seen. But the times we spent there were so precious it became beautiful. Either way, I loved it. One afternoon, he called and said he'd decided to take it upriver to Hubert's lake house. "After all," he said, "that's where we spend most of our time."

"But, Jack, it is freezing cold!" I couldn't believe he had chosen this season to take the houseboat upriver.

"It'll be warm enough," he said. "Put on a big sweater." Even though the only heat on the boat was a small kerosene heater that you practically had to sit on top of to keep from freezing it wasn't the weather that concerned me, it was his ability to pilot the boat! I'd heard stories about the many times he'd run it aground and up on the bank, and the only thing that kept it from sinking was the fact that it had a steel hull. Yet if he were game, so was I.

Jack, Hal Hardin, a young attorney friend of Jack's, and I left the river dock at four-thirty in the afternoon with the expected arrival time at Hubert's at nine o'clock. *Ha!* At nine o'clock we weren't even halfway! Hal and Jack were drinking—to keep warm, they said—and I stood as close as possible to Jack. In fact if there were more than two people on the boat, you had to be close.

Locking through the dam was an experience in itself. There were no lights on the boat except the dim ones inside, and none at all on the outside. And it was dark as pitch! While Jack and Hal were outside trying to tie the boat to the side, I was inside turning the wheel. Every time I'd hear Jack say "son of a bitch!" I knew I was turning the wheel the wrong way. Finally, the big concrete walls swung open and we were in the lake. But still a long way from Hubert's house. Jack headed the boat in what he thought was the correct direction.

Seeing some strange-looking things . . . some black and some red . . . sticking up out of the water, I asked, "What are those things?"

"How the hell should I know!" Jack said. Suddenly, it was like the *Titanic* hitting the iceberg. The engine quit and we came to an immediate halt! God, it was dark! I just sat there waiting to hear the water seeping in.

Jack fixed himself another drink, went in the back, and came out with his swimming trunks on. "Jack," I said, "you can't go in the water . . . you'll freeze to death!" Ignoring me, he went out, slid over the side and under the boat. Hal and I, with the one flashlight we had on board, stood on the deck shining it to see what he was doing. Every few seconds, Jack would come up for air, then back down again. Next time he came up, he said, "Hand me the damn c . . . c . . . cotter key!" His voice was shaking so I could hardly understand him.

After a few more dives, he climbed back on board, his whole body shaking and so cold he couldn't talk. I just knew he'd get pneumonia! But, when he came back out after changing clothes, it was as though he'd never been down there. When I asked what had happened, he said, "The son of a bitch was sittin' on a mud bank!"

After a few feeble tries, the engine started and we chugged our way on up the lake, Jack steering and Hal and me taking turns standing on deck with the flashlight. When a bank came up in front of us, he'd just turn the other way or go around it.

Twice the engine quit and twice Jack went through the same routine, over the side in swimming trunks and under the boat. Finally, twelve hours after we'd left the river, we saw a light

swinging back and forth on the bank. Thank God. It was Hubert!
"Where the hell have you been!" he said.

"Hell," Jack said, "it was farther than I thought! We kept
getting tangled up in trash."

"Why didn't you follow the buoys?" Hubert asked.

"Buoys?" we all said together. Hubert explained that was how
to tell if you were in the main channel. The red ones on your right
going *up* river and the black ones on your right going *down* river.
He was amazed we had even made it. And so were we. If the hull
hadn't been made of steel, we'd have probably now be at the
bottom of the lake.

Jack had been telling about his expertise as a skier and promised
to take me sometime. But my first trip came unexpectedly. It was
snowing like crazy. Jack called. "Can you be ready to leave in an
hour?" he asked. Knowing him, I'd learned to keep a makeup kit
packed at all times.

"Sure," I said. "Where are we going?"

"To Sugar Mountain," he said. He'd told me about going over
there skiing. Sugar Mountain was near Boone, North Carolina, a
six-hour drive from Nashville. I'd never been there.

"Have you considered the fact that I can't ski?" I asked.

"Yeah," he said. "But you can learn." I had my doubts but
began packing.

Jack and his ever-present friend, Al Powell, picked me up, and
at nine o'clock we checked into the Sugar Mountain Lodge. It
was a good thing it was dark so that I couldn't see the mountain
that would challenge me the next morning.

At seven-thirty, Jack was up and dressed in his ski clothes.
Looking out the window, I watched as he and Al carried their skis
down the path to the slope and lodge where I was to meet them
for breakfast. Lord, the mountain looked dangerous. And there
were people actually upright coming down it on skis!

Dressing as warm as I could in what I had with me, I carefully
made my way down the path. After the quick bowl of oatmeal,
Jack took me into the pro shop and told the clerk: "Outfit her with
whatever she needs."

"Don't you think we should wait until I see if I can stand up?"
I asked, knowing full well if he bought all this stuff, there'd be no
way I could chicken out.

Walking out in my new clothes—red and blue ski suit, goggles, and red down mittens—I looked like a pro. Little did they know. Next came the skis, boots (which weighed a ton!), and poles. The only thing I had on that wasn't new was my fur hat, which was pulled tight around my head to keep my ears from freezing off.

After enrolling me for lessons with an instructor, Jack and Al skied off, leaving me standing there with four six-year-olds and a woman who appeared to be about eighty. There was no way I could weasel out of this . . . Jack had spent over five hundred dollars! I was the best-dressed idiot on the slopes!

With great apprehension, I stood there trying to understand what the instructor was saying. Suddenly, my feet flew out from under me and I was flat on my ass in the snow. With help from two of the six-year-olds, I untangled myself and got back up. I could see right now, this was going to be an interesting day.

Little by little, I began to get the hang of it. First, you learn to stand up. Then, you learn to fall, backward, not forward. After an hour or so of this, came what I'd been dreading. "Okay," the instructor said, "now we go to the lift." God help me! Several times I'd seen Jack ski by, look over, and give me the old "thumbs up" sign. *One more time, my friend,* I thought, *and I'll tell you what you can do with that thumb!*

On the lift and looking down at the bottom far below me, I said to the instructor, "I thought we were going on the kiddie slope."

"You'll love it once you get up there," he said, and laughed. *Well, I'd take odds against that!*

The top of the mountain was coming up fast. "Okay, get ready to push off," the instructor said. Push off! I was hanging on for dear life! "How about if I just stay on and ride back down?" I asked hopefully.

"Push off!" he yelled. *Okay, here goes nothing!*

Miraculously, my skis hit the snow and I stayed upright—at least for a few seconds at a time. On the way down, at least forty people offered to help me. Each time, I'd smile through my pain and say, "No thanks, I can make it," untangle myself, and try it again. *Jack,* I thought, *if I ever see you again, I may kill you.*

At the bottom, I decided to quit while my arms and legs were still intact. Then Jack slid to a stop beside me and said, "Come on, I'll ride up the lift with you." Yet, at that moment, I wouldn't have quit for a million dollars! Not with him looking at me with that "shit eating" grin on his face. Giving him a weak smile, I half walked, half slid to the lift.

As soon as we reached the top, he was off and gone and I was on my own. This time it was a little better. I was almost to the bottom when I heard "Look out!" and a girl, about sixteen, slammed into my back and knocked me into a double back flip. I lay there, sprawled facedown in the snow, and wondered what I should try to move first. My back felt like it had been broken. The girl skied off without even an "I'm sorry."

As I lay there, Jack and Al skied up, stopped, and said, "Need any help?" They were both laughing.

"No thank you. I'm fine," I lied. *Fine, hell! I felt like every bone in my body was broken!* But I was more determined than ever.

By four-thirty, I was more physically tired than I had ever been in my life but, also, I was surprised to find that I had really enjoyed myself. Standing at the bottom, I waited for Jack. And when I saw his expression of pride in me, it was worth every bit of the pain and agony. Putting his arm around me to help me up to our room, he said, "One thing about you, Miss Howard, is that you're not a quitter."

After dinner, a hot shower, and a rubdown with the skier's companion, Ben-Gay, I fell into a tired but happy sleep.

David had finished the last year at Hillsboro High School but I was still concerned about him being on his own so much of the time. So, after a lot of checking around, he decided, since he now had his very own little Volkswagen and could come home whenever he wanted to, that he'd go to Columbia Military Academy, about thirty miles away. The school was highly recommended. He seemed to like it and be adjusting well. But I still worried. I'd cook food for him and leave it in the freezer but, when I came home, it would still be there. "Too much trouble," he said.

He was eighteen and, by the time Jimmy and Corky were that old, or a little older, they were in the Army. But David was different. He was my baby. He wasn't old enough to be on his own, not emotionally, anyway. In so many ways, he was just a little boy. My favorite times were when he'd curl on my bed beside me and watch television. Or tell me about all the plays he'd tried out for and everything that had happened while I was away.

One night, as I sat in the audience and watched my handsome talented son playing Rutledge in 1776, a woman in front of me said to her companion, "Who is that handsome young man playing Rutledge?" I tapped her on the shoulder and said, "David Howard, my son." I was so proud of him. He had so much talent and his dream was to go to California, or to New York, to study acting. But I just couldn't let him go so far away. Not yet.

There was a lot on television about the drinking age being lowered to eighteen. It was all David talked about. So, on his eighteenth birthday, I took him out to dinner. When the waitress came around and asked if I'd like a cocktail, I said, "Yes, I'll have a glass of Chablis. What about you, David?" I could almost see his chest swell.

"I'll have a martini," he said, as though it was an everyday thing.

When she brought the drinks, we clicked glasses and I said, "Happy birthday, my son, you're old enough to drink."

Taking a big swallow, he gulped a couple of times and said, "Am I old enough to cuss?"

"If you think you have to," I said.

"*Damn*," he said. That did it. The rest of his drink remained untouched. He'd decided drinking wasn't such a big thing after all. But that night we made an agreement—if he were going to drink, he would do it in front of me, not behind my back.

My relationship with Jack was at a standstill. As much as I cared for him, seeing him at only at his convenience was getting stale. It hurt never seeing him on weekends, and knowing the few hours we were together were stolen hours. I'd tried to end it, but the longest I'd been able to keep my resolve was four days. David would laugh and say, "If this is what it's like to be in love, I don't think I want to try it."

When I wouldn't talk to Jack, he'd talk to David and ask him to give me a message. "He loves you, Mom," he'd say. "And he wants to marry you when he gets a divorce." At those times, I hated him for using David. I knew we'd never be married. He'd said he and his wife weren't living together and hadn't been for some time but I knew he was just saying it to keep me happy. He led two lives. I wondered sometimes how he kept his lies straight. One Sunday, after he'd called, I sat on my bed and wrote a song called "Love is a Sometimes Thing" just for him.

A few days later, while we were on the bus, I was singing it and Bill said, "What's that you're singing?"

"Oh, just a song I wrote for Jack," I said.

"I like it," he said. "Can I record it?" I was flabbergasted! Bill was one of the top songwriters and he wanted to record one of my songs! *Stick around, Norman,* I thought, *and I'll make a million dollars off you.*

About the time I'd swear I'd never see Jack Norman again, he'd call and say be ready to go somewhere, and I'd start packing. His red and white Cessna 310 and I were getting well acquainted. Even though I'd never gotten my license, Jack had taught me well. I'd end up flying and he'd go to sleep. I knew I must be pretty good. He was too good a pilot to trust me otherwise. The only time he got slightly nervous was when I flew into a cloud and got vertigo. "Jack," I said. "I think you'd better wake up. I've got vertigo." He came wide awake quick! After getting out of the cloud, I was okay but he kept the controls.

I don't know how he managed it, but we had four whole days together. The first night we flew to Fort Lauderdale. Sitting in the bar for hours, we couldn't seem to get enough of just talking to each other. For every drink Jack ordered for himself, he ordered me a champagne cocktail. For some reason, they weren't making me drunk—just giggly. The waitress kept her eyes on me. Finally, she walked over and said to Jack, "Sir, is this your wife?"

Jack looked at me, smiled, and said, "Not yet."

She said, "Well, do you realize that she's had nine champagne cocktails?" and laid the bill on the table. I got the drift and so did Jack. If I weren't his wife, she wanted him to know how much the night was costing him.

"She's worth it," Jack said.

The next day we flew to Nassau. The following day we flew at six hundred feet all the way up the coast to New Orleans.

The Roosevelt Hotel was beautiful! It had Old Money written all over it. Jack had told me to bring a long dress, and that night we dressed in all our finery and went down to dinner. I'd never felt so elegant. Sitting there at our table, holding hands, Jack whispered something to me. I couldn't hear him and said, "What?" Then, in a voice loud enough for everyone in the room to hear, he said, "Fifty dollars!" For a minute I didn't know what he was talking about, then it hit me! The old joke about a prostitute asking fifty dollars for her favors. I could have killed him. After only a few drinks, how could Jack do something like that?

The next day, after brunch, we lay by the pool drinking Planter's Punches. After one, I quit but not Jack. By dinner time, he was on his way. We'd already decided to have dinner at the Court of Two Sisters but Jack refused to make reservations. "I can get a table anywhere!" he said.

But when we arrived, we were told, "There will be an hour wait." Well, Jack wasn't going to wait an hour for anything and proceeded to make one hell of a fuss. The waiter, not too kindly, asked us to leave but Jack had to have the last word. "To hell with it," he said. "I didn't want to eat in the Court of The Damned Two Sisters anyway!" and promptly stumbled over a chair which was in back of him. I couldn't hold my laughter back. Glaring at me, he got up and stalked out.

Brennan's was the same way. We finally gave up and went back to the hotel. By this time, Jack was in the mood to drink, and the more he drank, the more belligerent he became. After a while, when I became more irritated by the minute, we went back to the room and promptly fell asleep.

The next morning, while he was still asleep, I got up, dressed as quietly as I could. Then went to the table and wrote a note. "My Darling, when you are 'you,' there's no more considerate, kind, loving, compassionate, and wonderful man. But when you're drinking, there isn't a more egotistical, conceited, selfish, inconsiderate, mean son of a bitch on earth. Written by the one who loves you very much, body and soul, in the first instance . . . and hates you intensely and could cut your damned throat in the last instance! Jan Howard."

Leaving the note propped up on the table, I went down to breakfast. Not too long after, with a sheepish grin on his face, Jack came down to join me. "You do love me, don't you?" he said.

"Didn't you read the last part?" I asked. He ignored me and ordered breakfast.

As each day went by, I learned a lot from Jack. How to eat (and enjoy) escargot and caviar, how to fly a plane, how to ski, and how to have fun. But, most of all, how to love and be loved.

Just before his graduation, David came down with the flu and couldn't attend. I was upset, but he didn't seem to care. All he

could talk about was going to California. "After all," he said,
"Jimmy and Corky went to Florida when they graduated!"

"Yes, David," I said, "but that was only for a week. You're
talking about all summer!"

"Please, Mom," he said, "it's my one big chance." I never
could say no to him but he worried me. We had friends in L.A. he
could stay with but he'd be so far away. I just wasn't sure. I knew
he was nineteen years old but I had to think on it, and talk it over
with Corky.

Finally, we decided he should have his chance. With his car
loaded to the hilt and another boy riding with him, I watched as
he drove off to chase his dream.

With David gone, the house was so empty, I couldn't stand it.
He called twice a week and wrote often but I missed him terribly.
Even though he'd promised faithfully to obey all the *Can do's and
Cannot do's* I still worried. There were so very many temptations,
I just hoped he was strong enough to resist them.

For a few weeks, everything was fine. Then, David's calls
began to worry me. I could hear the homesickness in his voice.
Several times I'd suggested that he come home but he wouldn't
hear of it. While he was objecting, I got the feeling that he really
wanted to come home. *Then why is he staying?* I thought.
Finally, I took the bull by the horns and called him.

"David, are things going well out there?"

"Sure, Mom . . . why?" Even his "Sure, Mom" wasn't con-
vincing.

"Well, I get the feeling you're kinda homesick . . . are you?"

"Well . . . yeah."

"Okay, that's it," I said. "I'm wiring you three hundred dollars
today. As soon as it arrives, I want you to get in that little bug and
head east."

"But, Mom," he said. "You've spent all that money on my
lessons . . . I can't quit now!" So that was it!

"David, all the money in the world isn't worth your unhappiness. Besides, I miss you." I really did. I wanted him home. His
voice took on a different tone.

"Well . . . if you're sure . . ."

"I'm positive," I said. After cautioning him to stop at nice
motels every night and not to pick up anyone, we hung up. My
boy was coming home where he belonged.

Three days later, sooner than I had expected, he drove in, very tired but happy to be home. "L.A. isn't all it's cracked up to be," he said. I could have told him that.

Laughing, he told me stories about the teacher trying to get rid of his southern accent by making him talk with an apple in his mouth. "Hey, I can do that," I said, and grabbed an apple and crammed it in his mouth.

"If you don't mind," he said, "I'll just eat this one." Gosh, it was good to have him home.

After much discussion, we decided he would enroll at M.T.S.U., where Jimmy had attended, in Murfreesboro. He would take business administration and, of course, music, art, and drama. Knowing David, I knew the business course was strictly an order.

It had been almost two years since Jimmy's death—two years going on yesterday. My grief was neverending and the pain was still very real, yet I knew it would always be there. Time helps, but time never heals. I decided it was high time to have a few people over. Not many, just a few friends. But the more I got into it, the longer the guest list became. A lot of Jack's friends—from attorneys to senators—Dr. Fred Goldner and his wife, Owen Bradley, Hubert . . . The list went on and on. I called Tex and Dorothy Ritter, two people I loved dearly. Tex answered. "Jan, my darlin' . . . how are you?"

"I'm fine, Tex," I said. "The reason I'm calling is I'm having a few people over and I'd like for you and Dorothy to come if you can." I told him the night.

"Well," he said, "I'm doing the Jim Ed Brown show that night and won't get through until ten o'clock. But we might stop by for a few minutes."

"Well, I'd love to see you, but if you can't make it, I'll understand." Hanging up, I stood there thinking about Tex, how dear he was and what a big part of my life he had been. From the first time I'd sang on a microphone to now. I remembered the first time I'd seen him after Harlan and I had separated. It was at the Opry. He walked up and put his arm around my shoulders. I expected some words of sympathy. Instead, he said, "I hear you and Ole Harlan split the sheets." Only Tex would have said that. It was just what I needed—seeing the humor in the situation.

Not long before, Tex and I had worked a date just outside Baltimore together. Afterward, there was a one-thirty flight back to Nashville and we drove like crazy to make it. As we walked into the airport, Tex said, "Hell, there's that little piss ant—just what I need." I looked in the direction he was looking and saw Jerry Lee Lewis. Not noticing us, he was giving the ticket agent a hard time and we walked to the other end of the counter, got our tickets, and went on to the gate. We were lucky, so far Jerry Lee hadn't seen us. They still weren't there when we boarded. *Good,* I thought, *maybe they're going in another direction.* We got on and sat down in the second row of first class. Tex leaned his head back and closed his eyes. At that moment, Jerry Lee and all his entourage walked on. He was giving the poor stewardess hell because some of his group had to fly tourist. Tex never opened his eyes and I kept my head turned to the window, but I could see Jerry Lee in the reflection. Suddenly, he turned his attention to us.

"Hey, Tex, old buddy, are you asleep?" he asked. Tex didn't answer.

Jerry Lee reached over and nudged Tex's shoulder and said, "Tex, it's me, Jerry Lee. Are you asleep?"

Without ever opening his eyes, Tex said, "I'm trying to, piss ant."

When we landed in Nashville, it was raining cats and dogs and my car was at home. Usually I parked it at a nearby Shell station, but this time David had brought me to the airport. *Oh, well,* I thought, *I'll take a cab.*

Walking down the corridor, I saw Dorothy walking toward us. "Tex, darling!" she called. She never ceased to amaze me. Here it was three o'clock in the morning, raining like crazy, and she looked like she just stepped out of *Vogue.* A beige silk suit, a soft pink blouse and scarf, and her ever-present hat. I was suddenly conscious of the fact that I probably looked like a snake. Learning that I was planning to take a cab, they insisted on taking me home.

As we got into the car, Dorothy was rattling on a mile a minute about the paper boy. "Tex, darling," she said, "you've just got to do something about that paper boy. He *never* puts the paper in the mailbox when it's raining!"

Tex snorted a couple of times, then said, "Dorothy (he pronounced all three syllables . . . Dor-o-thy), I don't give a damn where the paper boy puts the paper. And I don't give a damn if the paper gets wet." Then, looking over at her and smiling, he said, "By the way, my dear, did I tell you you look lovely tonight?" To me, that was the most beautiful thing. He had chewed her out and all in the same breath told her how lovely she looked. Dorothy never even heard the chewing out part, she just went right on talking.

Arriving at my house, Tex started to get out of the car. "Oh, no, Tex," I said, "don't get out . . . it's raining."

Going right ahead, as if I hadn't spoken, he walked around, opened my door, and said, "I never let a lady walk to her door alone." God broke the mold when he made Tex Ritter.

The night of the party, I was going around trying to be the "hostess with the mostest." But there was one guest who didn't talk much—he didn't talk at all. Since Bobby was out of town, Jeanie Bare had brought a life-size poster of him as her escort. Every now and then, when she'd walk by, she'd say, "We sure are having a good time, aren't we, Bobby?"

Tex and Dorothy arrived about ten. "Now, we can't stay long," he said. But at three A.M., with all the guests sitting on the floor at his feet, Tex was telling stories as only he could do. No one made a move to leave until they did—about four A.M.

Before they walked out the door, Tex leaned over to me, and said, "I'm going on a tour of Vietnam . . . for Jimmy and Corky."

While we were still doing the TV show in Charlotte, one of the guests was Charlie Pride—his first television appearance. Before he'd ever recorded, I was at RCA Victor one night doing some demos when Jack Clement (writer and producer personified) came in and said, "I want you to listen to something and tell me if you think this guy is any good." We went upstairs to his office and he played a tape. As I listened, I said, "He's really good. Who is he?" There was a uniqueness in his voice I hadn't heard before. Jack handed me a picture. I stared at it, thinking Jack was playing some kind of joke. The picture was of a black man, but the man singing didn't sound black at all—just different. I couldn't believe it. He was fantastic! Jack said he was going to record him and I said, "When you do, I want to be there."

Not long after, Charlie came to Nashville for his first recording session. And except for one word—car—there was not the slightest trace of black dialect. After Jack (Clement) coached him a few times and Charlie went around saying "car . . . car . . . car" there wasn't even that. Very few people impress me, but I was impressed that night.

For several years, Jack Norman and Hubert had produced the show at the Mid South Fair in Memphis. One night, the three of us were having dinner at Mario's restaurant and they were discussing who to book for the talent. "Why not Charlie Pride?" I asked.

"Who's Charlie Pride?" Jack asked, not being up on show biz.

"Only the next superstar," I said. Charlie's records had just begun to get a lot of attention and I knew his career was fixing to snowball.

They took my advice and bought him for twenty-five hundred dollars . . . a third of what he was getting by fair time. That night, the coliseum was packed and Jack and Hubert walked away with eighty thousand dollars.

As the three of us were driving home, they kept talking about their good fortune in booking Charlie Pride. Handing me two thousand dollars, Jack said, "Here, Redhead, this is your finder's fee." *Hmmm,* I thought, *I must be in the wrong end of this business.*

Concerning the Mid South Fair, a few weeks before, something interesting had happened. When I'd read about our spaceship landing on the moon and bringing back samples of its surface, I never dreamed I'd actually touch it. But I hadn't counted on Jack.

One day he called and said, "How would you like to go to Bemidji, Minnesota?"

"Where?" I asked. I'd never heard of the place.

"Bemidji, Minnesota," he repeated. "We're going to go get a moon rock and take it back for exhibition at the Mid South Fair."

"You've got to be kidding," I said.

"No, I'm not," he said. "How soon can you be ready?" That was a silly question. I wouldn't miss it for anything!

Stopping in Memphis to pick up Joe Pipkin, who was a friend of Jack's and an official with the fair, and a reporter, we headed straight north for Bemidji. And when I say north, I mean way north. On the flight to Memphis I had looked at the map and saw that Bemidji was only a short distance from Canada, at the top of Minnesota.

The weather was bad and the farther we went, the worse it got. Bumpy was not the word! Joe and the reporter kept saying, "How much longer?"

After what seemed like the longest flight on record, we landed in this pretty town of about ten thousand people. Even though it was September, it was very cold.

Once in the motel, Jack immediately opened his briefcase, which was filled with miniature bottles of booze, and he promptly downed several.

Asking the clerk to recommend a place for dinner, he suggested Jack's restaurant. By the time we got there, the booze had taken effect. He changed from a dignified businessman to a surly, belligerent and plain hateful boor.

As we walked into the restaurant, a group of about twelve men, all weighing at least two hundred and fifty pounds, were seated at a table near the one the waiter showed us to.

Excusing himself, saying he was going to the men's room, Jack lagged behind while the rest of us were seated. In a few minutes, we watched as he walked toward our table. Then, when he got to where the "giants" were sitting, he just stopped and stood there. Joe said, "Lord, I hope he doesn't say anything. Those bruisers will kill him!" Quickly, I got up, smiled at the men, and, taking Jack's arm, aimed him toward our table.

All during dinner he kept mumbling something under his breath. Having no idea what he was so angry about, the rest of us ignored him. But Joe and I both knew, with several glasses of wine and a brandy after dinner, something was happening.

As Joe paid the check, I tried to guide Jack past the big men's table. I almost made it. Suddenly, he jerked his hand from mine, walked back a few steps to their table, and said, loud and clear, "I don't like the Minnesota Vikings!" Every head in the place turned in his direction.

Joe said, "Jan, go get him, or he'll get us killed!"

I walked back, grabbed Jack's arm, and practically dragged him from the restaurant and to the car.

When Joe came out, he said, "Do you know who those guys were?"

"No, who?" I asked.

"None other than the Minnesota Vikings!"

The next day, flying to Memphis, I was holding the moon rock in my hand. It just looked like a piece of burned cinder to me. *All of that for this?*

Corky was still dating Pam. But he was still seeing Nicky now as well, and another girl from Clarksville, whom I'd never met, named Rita. He said Rita only came now and then to fix dinner for him at his off-base apartment.

One afternoon, I came home to find him sitting in the den in his uniform . . . grinning sheepishly.

"Hey, it's good to see you," I said. "What's the occasion?"

"Well," he said. "I came home from work and Rita was there fixing dinner for me. Then Nicky called and said she was on her way over. Then the doorbell rang and when I answered it, there stood Pam. Figuring it would be safer here, I said 'Come on in,' and then I left." As usual, he'd used good judgment. But I figured it was choice-making time, and I knew the choice would be Pam. Neither of them had said anything. But it was just a matter of time.

Jack had Guard on Wednesday nights and usually he'd stop by afterwards, sometimes like tonight, for dinner. I kept glancing at the clock. He should be here by eight o'clock, and it almost that now. I fixed the salad, put the steak in to broil, and saw that the table was set just right before starting upstairs to change from my blue jeans, sweat shirt, and sneakers. He'd seen me like this many times but tonight was special. The doorbell rang. Glancing at the clock, I thought, *Gosh he's early.* Oh, well, so much for dressing up.

Opening the door, I said "Hi, hon—" The word "honey" never got out of my mouth. It wasn't Jack . . . it was his wife! My first inclination was to quickly shut the door. My second was to invite her in. I chose the second.

"Hello, Mrs. Norman, won't you come in?"

She walked past me into the living room, over to the boys' pictures hanging over the piano, looked at them, then turned back to me. "You're younger than I thought," she said. I was conscious of the way I was dressed and felt like a kid caught with her hand in the cookie jar. A burning odor came from the kitchen. I ran in, reached for the broiler, and took out what had been a juicy sirloin steak. Now, it resembled the bark off a tree. She'd followed me and looked at my burned disaster. "My, what a shame," she said. "Now Jack won't have his dinner." I couldn't help it, I laughed. If the situation had been different, I would have liked this woman. I take that back, I *did* like her. She walked over and sat down on the sofa. Nervously, I glanced at the clock. Jack would be there any moment!

"Can I fix you a drink?" I asked.

"Well," she said, taking off her coat, "I don't usually drink but this occasion calls for one. Yes."

"Would you mind fixing it," I asked. "I'm not too good at it." We sounded like any two women getting acquainted. It was crazy! I wondered when the bomb would drop. I didn't have long to wait.

Taking a sip from her drink, she said, "You do know you're not the first, don't you?" I'd heard of a couple—a nurse and someone else. But that was before. She went on. "You do know he's had an affair with his secretary for years, don't you?"

"His secretary?" That did surprise me.

"Oh, yes," she said. "She's been in love with him for years. I called his room in Memphis one time and he was stupid enough to let her answer the phone."

"Maybe it was business," I said. She laughed.

"Yes, of course, business." I wished I could find some way to end this conversation. No matter who it was, I didn't like discussing Jack behind his back. At that moment, the doorbell rang. Oh, Lord, it was Jack! Well, so much for conversation!

I opened the door and, before I could say a word, Jack said, "Hi, darlin'," and started back to the den. I stood there. "Jack, we have company." I said.

He turned and said, "Who?" At that moment Duina Norman walked out of the kitchen. Jack turned white! "Son of a bitch!" he said. "I'd rather be in hell without a fire extinguisher!" and started for the door. But I stood in front of him.

"No, Jack. If you go out that door, don't expect to come back in," I said. "We both knew this would happen someday . . . It's time to face the music." I didn't know where all my bravery was coming from. I just knew it had to be settled. I led the way back to the den. They both sat down on the sofa.

Even though it was my house, I felt like an intruder. "I think this should be between you two," I said. "I'm going upstairs."

Over an hour passed. Intentionally, I ran water, turned on the television set—anything so I couldn't hear what was being said. I didn't want to. Waiting as long as I could, I turned the TV off and listened . . . there was no sound coming from downstairs. I walked to the head of the stairs. Nothing. Walking down the stairs to the den, I saw Jack sitting there with his head in his hands. I knew what I had to do. Walking over, I put my hand on his shoulder and said, "Jack. Go home. I know you want to. And we've known all along we couldn't build our happiness on someone else's grave." I was an expert at that. I knew I'd lost him. I turned and walked back upstairs and listened until I heard the door shut behind him. Then, I lay across the bed and cried.

Four days later, he called. "No, Jack," I said. "No more. I don't want to talk to you."

"Listen to me," he said. "It's over. I've moved out."

"Where are you now?" I asked.

"Right now, I'm at the Sam Davis Hotel." The Sam Davis! Compared to Jack's house, that was the slums!

"Jack, you can't stay there."

"Well," he said, "I am here and it's okay for now. Will you come here to see me?" He sounded doubtful.

"You know I will. I'll be there in an hour."

As I walked in, the clerk looked at me and said, "Aren't you Jan Howard?"

"That's me," I said, and walked to the elevator. From now on, no more hiding!

January 1971. Two weeks before Corky's enlistment was up, an officer from Fort Campbell called me. "Mrs. Howard, would you consider talking Carter into reenlisting?"

"No, sir, I can't do that," I said. "He has a mind of his own and I'm sure he's given a lot of thought to whatever he plans to do." I remembered the last, and only, time I'd talked to Colonel Siebert.

Corky was in a top-secret job and had given me the "hot line" number to use only in case of emergency. He had come home on Wednesday night and, too tired to drive back to camp, had set the alarm for five o'clock and brought the clock to my room. "Be sure to wake me, okay?" The clock was one of those metal things whose alarm sounds like a four-alarm fire. I started to remind him that it would work just as well by his bed, but didn't.

"Okay, I'll wake you," I said, and went on to bed. Right at five o'clock, it darned near jarred me out of bed. Walking downstairs, I shook Corky, who was asleep on the sofa. "Okay, I'm awake," he said.

"Are you sure?"

"Yeah, I'm awake." He was sitting up so I figured it was safe to go upstairs and back to bed.

The next time I awoke, it was past seven. Needing coffee desperately, I went downstairs and saw a form on the sofa. Good heavens! It was Corky, sound asleep with his clothes on! "Corky," I said, shaking him, "it's after seven o'clock!" He was up and halfway out the door before I got the sentence finished. All I heard was "Shit! I'm AWOL!"

I fixed some coffee, sat there a minute, then picked up the phone and dialed the hot-line number. A voice said, "Colonel Siebert speaking." I started to hang up, then gathered my courage and said, "Colonel Siebert, this is Jan Howard, Corky Howard's mother."

"Corky?" he said. "Did you say Corky?" He was laughing and I knew I'd messed up.

"I'm sorry, sir," I said. "I mean Sergeant Carter Howard's mother."

"Oh no, I prefer Corky," he said. "Now, what can I do for you, Mrs. Howard?"

"Well, sir, I know he's late, but it's my fault and I was hoping you wouldn't be too hard on him." I knew I was talking fast but I had to get the words out before I lost my nerve. Again he laughed and I knew why. I was acting and sounding like a mother making excuses for her child who was late for school. And Corky was a sergeant in the Army! I'd goofed!

Colonel Siebert said, "Mrs. Howard, Carter, or rather, 'Corky' is a good soldier and we're not going to be too hard on him for being late, but let's just keep this between you and me, okay? We'll probably razz him a little bit." I knew Corky was in for it and so was I. Apologizing for using the hot line, I hung up and hated myself for calling. A short while later, Corky called.

"Mom! Why did you call up here! Now the whole base is calling me Corky!" He was doubly angry and I didn't blame him. To me, he might be a little boy, but to the world he had proven himself a man. Colonel Siebert's voice brought me back to the present.

"Well, Mrs. Howard, if you change your mind, Carter is, in Army language, a damned good soldier and we'd like to keep him."

"Sir, I appreciate your words," I said. "But I would never try to talk Corky into or out of anything. It's his life and I know he'll do whatever he thinks is best. And, whatever it is, I'll accept his decision." I thanked him and hung up. Two weeks later, Corky was home.

For a while, he just ate, slept, and goofed off with his friends. Then, I could see him begin to get edgy. He was too military-minded to waste his life doing nothing, and he went to work as a laborer for a construction company.

After three weeks of coming home every night covered with cement and dirt, he said, "This manual labor stuff is not for me. Do you think Jack could get me a job with the city?" My, how he had changed. I called Jack.

A few days went by, then Jack called back and said, "Tell Corky he has an interview with George Rooker in the General Sessions Court Clerk's office. Also, you can tell him I went out on a limb for him and if he lets me down, his ass is mine." I think he knew he had nothing to worry about.

Every weekend, Corky, all of his friends, and sometimes David went out to Hubert's lake house. It was a constant party. Hubert loved it, but I worried that they were taking up too much of his time. "Maybe you should cool it awhile," I said to Corky. "You know Hubert is single and might just like to have some time with someone else." They agreed. For three weeks he didn't go out to the lake. One day Hubert called.

"Where are the boys?" he asked, and I thought his voice sounded hurt.

"They're here. Why?"

"It's been three weeks since they've been out. I thought something was wrong."

"No, Hubert," I said. "It's my fault. I just thought they were taking up too much of your time."

"Miss Howard! I'll tell them when I don't want them here!" I could just see him straightening up and with that In Command look on his face, he said, "Now, you tell them to get their asses out here!"

"Yes, sir!" I said. The boys were already out the door.

Solona called one night and said, "Hi, how ya doin'?" It was her usual greeting.

"I'm fine, Solona. Are you okay?"

"Yes, I'm fine," she said, and hesitated.

"What is it? Solona. What's wrong?" I asked.

"Well, I hate to carry tales and don't tell Corky I called, but I don't think he and his friends should be going in black places. They might get hurt."

"What?" I said, but had some idea what was coming next.

"Last night," she said, "I was out at that black tavern on Walton Lane—you know the one?"

"Yes, Solona."

"Well, Corky and Jamesy Baker walked in and I told them they'd better leave. It's just not a good idea." I agreed with her and promised her I'd talk to him. But I'd have to tell him she'd called—otherwise how would I have known. She said she guessed it was okay.

When Corky came home, I said, "Corky . . . Solona called."

He laughed. "She told you, didn't she?"

"Yes, and she was really concerned." Then, he told me the real story. He and James had always been curious about that place and the previous night had decided to check it out. He said they walked in the door and were standing there trying to get their eyes adjusted when they heard this voice. "Corky Howard! Jamesy Baker!" They recognized Solona's voice. Before they could do anything, she had them by the arms, marched them outside, and said, "You get your white asses out of here before you get your throats cut!" She was still taking care of her boys. As Corky told the story, he was laughing so hard he could hardly talk. I could just see Solona. To her, they were still little boys.

Had my sons turned into slobs? Every time I came home the house looked like a dozen people lived there. Clothes were scattered everywhere. It looked like they'd undressed one piece at a time—all the way from the living room to the bedroom. Shirts here, sweaters there, pants and shoes somewhere else. I was busy picking them up when Corky called. "Corky," I said, "how in the world did you make it in the Army? This place is a mess!"

"Mom, remember when I was in Vietnam and you wrote and

said you'd give anything to see just a sweater laying across a chair?"

"Yes. But I said one sweater, not your whole wardrobe!" After that he and David were both on House Patrol.

Not long afterwards he and Richard Lane, a longtime friend, decided to get an apartment together. I was now sorry I'd gotten on to him about being a slob. "Why, because I got on to you?" I asked.

"No." He laughed and said, "It's just that I've spent three years in the Army and it just isn't right for me to come home and live with Mama." I understood. He was twenty-one years old and certainly deserved the right to have a place of his own. But I knew that once he moved out, the last apron string would be cut. I didn't like that kind of surgery.

Since I had joined the Bill Anderson Show, the only times I worked the Opry were with Bill. I was always given a solo spot and usually we did one of our duets but more and more I just felt like "one of the band." The greatest moment came in March of 1971. While attending a party at Bill's house, I was talking to Bud Wendall, the manager of the Opry. He was fixing to leave and turned to me and said, "See you tomorrow night." He was talking about the Friday Night Opry and I assumed he thought Bill was scheduled to work.

"No, Bud," I said. "Bill won't be there tomorrow night."

"Aren't you working?" he asked.

"No. I only work when Bill does," I said. "I'm not a member."

"You're not?" he asked.

I laughed. "No. I've never been. I guess I've just been around so long I'm a fixture."

"Well," he said, "we'll see you Saturday night. .You will be there then, won't you?"

"I plan to be unless I get fired before then," I said.

Saturday night, after I'd finished my song, Bud walked out onstage and officially made me the newest member of the Grand Ole Opry—one of the honored, select few. As far as my career went, nothing would ever equal this. I just wished my dad, who had spent so many years listening to the Grand Ole Opry and was the first one to ask me to sing, could have been here. But then, maybe he was. To this day, each time I stand center stage and remember all the "greats" who have stood there, I feel deeply humble and honored.

School was out and David was home for the summer. All he talked about was the theater and getting a part in this play or that play. That was fine, but until his dreams came true, I suggested he get an ordinary job. He was shocked! "Me? Get a job?"

"Yes, David. A job!" I said. "You know, one that gives you what is called a paycheck—money."

"But what kind of a job?" he asked, amazed that I should suggest such a thing.

"I don't know. Pumping gas, sacking groceries, anything that's honest." I could see by his expression that his ego was very deflated. David would soon be twenty years old. The thought of an ordinary job had obviously never crossed his mind. I hugged him and said, "You may not believe this but it may be for your own good."

"You're right," he said. "I don't believe it."

The next night, looking as if he'd just been sentenced to twenty years at hard labor, he came home and said, "Well, I got one."

"Where?" I asked.

"A gas station on Nolensville Road . . . Pumping gas." Reality had hit home and David didn't like it at all.

A week went by. Each night he'd drag home, flop on the sofa, and fall asleep. I felt sorry for him, but only for his fatigue. Each morning, he looked like he was headed for eight hours on the rock pile.

One afternoon, I pulled into the gas station where he worked. He walked out to the car and said, "Fill 'er up?", not even saying hello.

"Yes, please," I said, trying not to laugh. I didn't dare. Never once looking at me, he went through the whole routine . . . wiping the windshield, checking under the hood. When I paid him, he just said, "Thank you, come back," and walked away. My heart went out to him. He looked as though he had been transplanted from another planet. And, in a way, he had.

All afternoon I thought about the way he looked. Finally, I made up my mind. When he came home and after he'd flopped on the sofa, I said, "David, you really hate that job, don't you?"

"It's a job," he said, but his heart wasn't in it.

"You can quit, if you want to," I said. For a minute, it didn't sink in. Then he looked at me, not really believing he'd heard right.

"You mean it? I can quit?"

"Yes, you can quit. I never knew you would be so unhappy."

The tiredness gone, he jumped up and threw his arms around me. Then, when he calmed down, he said, "Mom, it's not that I don't want to work, it's just that there's something different in me. I've got to be an entertainer." From the time he was thirteen and entered the Little Theater group, it was all he'd talked about. Most kids, when asked what they want to be when they grow up, have two or three answers. Not David. His was always the same— "an entertainer."

"You will be, my son. You will be." I didn't have a doubt in the world.

Since Jack and Hubert had had such success with the Mid South Fair, they were putting together the talent for the Memphis Cotton Carnival, which was held in May. They decided on Charlie Pride, Ray Price, Merle Haggard, and me.

"Jack, I can't do it," I said. "I don't have a band!" Things like that meant nothing to him. He had no idea the agony I went through each time I worked with a local band. To him, only making the money was important.

"Okay," he said. "Hire one! Hell, all you have to do is thirty minutes!"

It was no use explaining that when the band is going into every chord but the right one that thirty minutes can seem like eternity. I started searching for six musicians who would play for a hundred dollars apiece. That would leave me four hundred, enough to make a down payment on a nervous breakdown.

The night of the show, a terrible storm hit Memphis and a tornado watch was issued for the entire county. The eleven-thousand-seat coliseum was packed and I was to open the show.

The stage was about twelve feet high with no railings around it. The only way up was a narrow staircase leading up from the back.

I'd finished the first few songs and was counting the minutes until I could get off stage when suddenly every light in the building went out. It was pitch black. The audience screamed, and I could hear panic about to begin. Damn, I was scared! And afraid to move! One wrong step and it was twelve feet straight down to a concrete floor.

Then, a light hit me in the face. Somebody had hooked up a small auxillary "trooper" spotlight . . . just one. I tried my microphone. Thank God, it worked!

"Ladies and gentlemen," I said in a normal tone of voice. The sounds of panic in the audience drowned out my words. I repeated, "Ladies and gentlemen!" They quieted down some. "Please," I said. "There's been a power failure due to the storm but everything's all right. Now, this stage is twelve feet high and I can't see to get off so you're gonna have to put up with me for a few minutes, okay?" The panic turned to laughter. The guitar player walked over to me and said, "Jan, we have no power for the instruments." Evidently the only power was on the mike I was using.

"Okay," I said. "Bring your flattop over here and stand real close." Then, to the audience, "All right, ladies and gentlemen, I need your help. There's no power for the instruments so it's you and me all the way. Will you help?"

They yelled, "Yeah!"

Starting out with "He's Got The Whole World in His Hands" and "You Are My Sunshine," for the next forty-five minutes we had one heck of a sing-a-long. And, when I ran out of songs, I told every Minnie Pearl and June Carter joke I could think of. The audience was wonderful! They even sounded like they were having a good time!

Just as I had run out of everything I knew to do, the lights came on and the audience roared with applause. I wasn't too sure how much was for me and how much was for the lights but it didn't matter. I thanked them for hanging in there with me and left the stage.

As I walked down the steps, Jack and Ray Price were standing at the bottom. Ray hugged me and said, "Hon, I wouldn't have done that for a million dollars!"

"Yeah, you would," I said. "If you had no other choice."

It had been a hectic summer. A lot of dates were booked. Many times Jack would fly me there and back home. When people would smile and ask if he was my husband, he'd say. "No, her pilot." As though I could afford a pilot! At times, I'd think he really wanted them to believe that and it made me feel that I'd never quite measure up to what he wanted me to be. I was doing well, but got the feeling he expected so much more of me.

After that one time, he'd never mentioned again our getting married. A few times I had, but then he'd get that look on his face that said, "I don't want to talk about it." I knew he loved me but he seemed to be satisfied with things the way they were. I also knew that as long as I went along with him, that's the way it would be. After all, he had all the advantages and none of the disadvantages. Twice more, for several days at a time, I'd refused to see him and each time, he'd call and say, "I can't make it without you, Redhead," and I'd go back on my word. I loved him so much that I had no willpower, but each time, it became harder. I knew, in my heart, if there was no future for us, I had to get out. I couldn't live like this for the rest of my life.

I was tired. I wanted to stay home but couldn't . . . there were so many obligations. I began to be sick a lot and Jack had no patience with illness. "It's all in your head," he'd say. I knew it wasn't. Something kept nagging at me. For a while, I thought it was the imminent death of my brother, Bill, who had been ill for a long time. But, when he passed away in June, the feeling stayed, I knew it was something else. I just couldn't put my finger on it. *I'm just tired,* I thought.

Jack decided it would do us both good to get away for a few days and he was right. We flew to New Orleans and stayed at a little French hotel, the Bienville House, right in the middle of the French Quarter. This time Jack wasn't in a partying mood and in the daytime we played tourist and at night just had dinner and went to our room. He was as loving and considerate as he'd been in a long time. I loved him for it.

On Sunday, Jack had to go back. But, since there was a clinic there—the Oshner Clinic—that was supposed to be one of the best in the country, I decided to stay and have a thorough checkup. He wasn't much in favor of it but, before he left, he moved me to a motel near the clinic. "It will only take a day or so," I told him, "and then I'll know once and for all."

The next morning, after talking to a clerk, I was told to come in at one that afternoon. After talking to me and jotting down little notes, the doctor said I should come in the next morning for some routine tests.

At seven-thirty A.M. I checked in with the clerk and was told to go to a certain room for a proctoscope . . . I had no earthly idea what she was talking about. But once I was in that room, draped in a very embarrassing position on the examining table, I found out! And, right in the middle of the most painful examination I've ever had, a technician came in the door, looked at me and said, "Miss Howard, I watch you on television all the time. Could I please have your autograph?" and stuck a piece of paper in my face. I was so embarrassed I could have died right there.

"Sure," I said, "if you'll take this damned examination for me I'll be glad to give you my autograph!"

After they finished, I went to the ladies' room to recuperate. As I was coming out of the stall, zipping up my slacks, a flashbulb went off in my face. "*Please!*" I said to the woman standing there with a camera in her hand.

"Oh, I'm sorry," she said, "I didn't mean to startle you, but the technician told me you were here and I knew this was the only chance I'd have to get a picture." She was right. *If I ever get out of this place,* I thought, *I'm never coming back!*

I had one more test to go through, an exercise test. After having me run up and down steps until my heart was pounding so hard and fast I could hardly breathe the doctor took my pulse and listened with his stethoscope. He listened for a long time. "Can you check into the hospital?" he asked.

"What for?" I asked. "Is something wrong?"

"Well, before this exercise test, I would have said no, but now I'd like to do a heart X ray, and it will be more convenient if you're here in the hospital."

At first I started to say no, then thought, *Okay, Jan, you're here, you might as well get it all done.* I went back to collect my things at the motel.

The following morning, the nurse came with two pills. "What are these?" I asked.

"Just some preparation for the test," she said. Thinking it was something like a gall bladder test, which I'd had before, I swallowed them. But, within a few minutes, I started getting dizzy. *Damn,* I thought, *what the hell did she give me?* She came back and shoved a paper in front of me. "What's this?" I asked, barely able to see the paper.

"Just permission for the test," she said and pointed to an X where I was supposed to sign. Not thinking, I scrawled my signature, leaned back, and closed my eyes.

I felt someone lifting me from the bed onto something else, and I knew I was being wheeled down the hall, but I had no resistance. We stopped moving and I opened my eyes enough to distinguish a white room, very hot lights, and two white-coated figures. I felt a stick of a needle and someone said, "This won't hurt." It didn't, but my right leg was cold and tingly.

"My legs are cold," I said. "I can't feel my leg."

The last words I heard were, "We've got to operate immediately or lose the leg."

Back in my room, I woke to see the doctor sitting by my bed. "Don't you have any family?" he asked angrily.

"Yes."

"Well, where in the hell are they? Don't you know you could have died!"

"What do you mean?" I asked, suddenly frightened.

Leaning back in his chair, he explained that the paper I had signed gave them permission to do an arteriogram . . . a procedure where a dye is injected into an artery in the groin and, while it goes through your body and around your heart, they take X rays of it to show if there's a blockage.

"But," I said, "I thought it was just an ordinary X ray . . . that's what you said."

"Well, it is an X ray," he said, "But this one is very dangerous. Some people are allergic to the dye or get blood clots and lose their limbs or worse. That's what happened to you." Now, I was angry. Sitting straight up in bed, I said, "Why in the hell didn't you tell me this beforehand!"

"I thought someone had," he said.

"What day is this?" I asked.

"Wednesday."

"Wednesday?" Lord, I had lost two days! But, after he left and I lay there thinking about it, I decided I was lucky that was all I'd lost.

Upon leaving, I didn't know much more than I did before . . . except that I didn't have hemorrhoids.

David was happier than I'd seen him in a long time. Opryland, a music-theme park, was opening and he'd gotten a part in the *I Hear America Singing* cast. He was in hog heaven. The show wouldn't be opening for a few months, but it was all he talked about. And except for music, art, and drama, Middle Tennessee State University might as well not have existed. He was failing every other subject. After a long talk with his counselor, she and I both agreed college was a waste of his time and my money. A trade school, whether it be in acting or what, was the answer. But I decided to wait until the year was over to talk to him about it.

In the meantime, if there was an audition being held anywhere, David was a part of it. This time, it was a play called *The Fantasticks* which was being held in Murfreesboro, and David had the young male lead. To hear him talk, opening could have been on Broadway—it was that important to him. Unless you understood the lingo, grease paint, stage right, stage left, you couldn't carry on a conversation with him. He even went out and had some special pictures made for his "promo" kit. I tried to talk to him about the real world, but he refused to listen. It didn't exist for him. The theater was his real world.

Opening night, the theater was packed. Not wanting to upset David, I didn't try to see him beforehand. But it wouldn't have mattered. During the play, nothing else existed for him. He *became* the character, no one could take him out of it. He was so talented. I watched him and prayed that he'd get his chance. I was so proud of him, but he and I both knew there were a lot of talented people out there who had had to give up their dreams in order to make a living. If that happened to David, I just hoped he'd be strong enough to handle it.

When the play was over, I watched as he signed autograph after autograph. When he was finished, he ran over, threw his arms around me, and said, "Well? Was I a star or was I a *star!*" He was beaming!

"Yes, my son," I said, "you were and are a star."

A couple of days later, I received a note from Charlie Monk, a friend who worked for ASCAP (American Society of Composers, Authors and Publishers), saying, "Jan is not the only talented member of the Howard family. David was Fantastic in *The Fantasticks*." The note went into David's growing scrapbook.

Giving school one last try, I told David about the talk with his counselor. "You know," I said, "when you are a success, you need to know how to handle money" or "You may have to supplement your income until you get started." Nothing sank in. He was going to be a star and that was all there was to it. End of conversation! I often thought if I'd had his drive and ambition, I'd be a superstar. That's what it took.

Since school was out of the question, I decided, from then on, to get behind him one hundred percent.

After checking with everyone we could think of in the theater in Nashville, we found what was supposed to be a reputable theater workshop in Atlanta. The course was six weeks, starting immediately, and would end just in time for him to start rehearsals with Opryland. I called my friend Mary Ann, who lived in Atlanta, and with her promise to check on him periodically, I let him go. But, even with her there, I was still troubled. Maybe it was just a mother's natural reservation at seeing her youngest leave the nest, but something I couldn't identify was bothering me.

David was supposed to call when he arrived in Atlanta . . . it was only a five-hour drive and he'd left home at noon. At midnight, he called.

"David! Where have you been! I've been worried sick!" I said.

"Oh, I went over to some friends," he said. "I just forgot."

"What friends?" I asked, "I didn't know you knew anyone but Mary Ann in Atlanta?"

"Oh, just some guys," he said. "They're nice—they really are. And I don't have to be there until eight o'clock tomorrow morning."

"That's besides the point, David," I said. "You made me a promise and you broke it." It didn't matter that he was almost twenty years old, David still often thought like a fifteen-year-old.

After two weeks, David's calls didn't sound as enthusiastic as they had at first. When I asked what was wrong, he said, "Oh, just some requirements I hadn't counted on."

"What kind of requirements?" I asked.

"Oh, just some school stuff. You know."

"No," I said, "I don't know." Then, hearing a silence at the other end, I said, "David, you don't have to stay there, you know."

"I know, Mom," he said.

Hanging up, I called Mary Ann and asked if she would check on him. A while later, she called back and said, "David's here with us. I went over to that school and, after taking one look at David, I brought him home."

"What's wrong with him?" I asked.

"Well, that place isn't what it's cracked up to be. David was white as a sheet and looked like he hadn't slept in a week." She said, "I think he needs to be around Stump and the kids for a while. Is it okay if he stays here for a week?"

Maybe she was right. I knew he'd be in good hands. With me working so much and Corky living his own life, I knew David must get lonesome at times. I also knew he still missed Jimmy terribly. Many times, when he thought I wasn't looking, I'd see him talking to Jimmy's picture. But since I did that myself I didn't see anything odd about it. Now, when I was so worried about David, was one of those times. "Please, Jimmy, help me watch out for David." I still couldn't talk to God. Not really. Several times I'd tried but wasn't sure my prayers were being heard. But I did have a good middleman up there. Some people who claimed to be Christians had told me that God caused the war that took Jimmy's life, I didn't believe that. How could the God that I prayed to be that kind of God? I didn't know what I believed. But I did know that Jimmy was up there. I still felt his presence strongly, especially when I was troubled.

A week later, David came home, ashamed that he'd let me down. "Hey, don't worry about it," I said, "it's as much my fault as it is yours—okay?" I tried to make my voice lighter than my heart felt. From the look on his face, I knew I'd succeeded. But it's hard to put on a front you don't feel. Sometimes I felt my face would crack with its ever-present smile. It was a mask, one big, smiling mask for the world to see.

The tour we had just finished ended in Chicago. The band had gone on to Alaska, where we were to open in a couple of days, so there wasn't time enough to go home. Bill had some friends there he wanted to see and I planned on two days of rest and breakfast in bed.

Before going to sleep, I called David. Since the *I Hear America Singing* rehearsals had started, he was his old self . . . in high spirits. I asked the usual questions. "Are you sure there's nothing else I need to know?"

"Well, the apartment got robbed and they took your fur coat."

"What?"

"Yeah," he said. "But they took some of Jimmy's things, too." I could hear the hurt in David's voice.

"I could care less about the fur coat," I said. "But why did they have to take Jimmy's things?"

"I don't know, Mom," David said. He went on to tell me that, evidently, the burglars had used a ladder, climbed up to the second-story window, gone in through David's room, taken what they wanted and gone out the front door. The odd thing they took—and one I'd miss the least—was my wedding ring from Harlan. After telling him not to worry about the material things and to be sure and keep the doors and windows locked, I hung up.

My mind was clouded with worry as I turned out the light. I wished I was going home instead of Alaska. Damn it.

I can't breathe was my first thought. My chest felt like a ton of bricks was on it and my heart was beating like hummingbird's wings. I could feel it in my throat and it was choking me! I felt myself passing out. I couldn't raise up to turn on the light but reached for the phone.

"Operator, Operator." I could hear her voice but couldn't answer.

I knew I was in a hospital. The familiar bright light was blinding me and I heard a doctor say something about intensive care. The pain was spreading across my chest and I felt the stick of a needle.

Time meant nothing. In and out of my vision, I saw faces but they were all strangers. Every time I'd wake up, the nurse gave me another shot. I felt like I was dying and didn't have the strength to fight. There were other beds in the room and I thought, *They're all dying, too.*

I must be crazy, I thought, *I see Dr. Goldner.* No, I wasn't crazy. It was Dr. Goldner. "Are you in Chicago?" I asked weakly.

He leaned over my bed. "No, I'm in Nashville," he said, "and so are you. How do feel?"

"I don't know."

"Well, you're here now and we're going to get you well."

"How did I get here?" I asked. Things were still so fuzzy.

"Never mind," he said, "we'll talk later. Right now, sleep." He was right.

Over the next few days he tried to explain what had happened. A lot of it, even he didn't understand. Once again, he tried to convince me that I hadn't had a heart attack. If I had, he said, it would show up on some tests . . . and nothing did. "What then?" I asked.

"I honestly don't know," he said, "possibly another spasm of some kind." I looked at the monitor beeping every heartbeat. I was still very weak, and it was an effort just to talk. "How did I get here? And what day is this?" When he told me, I gasped! My God! It had been ten days! He tried to fill in the gaps.

Bill Anderson, whom I didn't even remember seeing, had called Jack. Jack, in turn, had called Dr. Goldner, who had called the doctor in Chicago. But, for some unknown reason, the doctor in Chicago refused to talk to him and said he would only release me to go to Nashville if I was under the care of another doctor. His excuse was that Dr. Goldner had me on the wrong medication. But I wasn't taking any medication. I didn't understand any of this. Finally, with the assistance of Dr. Jim Thomison, Hubert's doctor, Jack and Al Powell flew to Chicago, brought me to Nashville, and turned me over to Dr. Goldner. I didn't remember one thing. Not even the flight! It was like a nightmare!

Four days went by and I was still in intensive care. Dr. Goldner came for his morning rounds and was taking my pulse. I watched his face. If he were smiling, I knew I was over the hump. He was. "How do you feel?" he asked.

"I'd give a thousand dollars for a cigarette," I said, knowing that would get a rise out of him. For years he'd tried to get me to quit.

"Well," he said, "the only way you can have one is to be in that room across the hall."

"Then, how about getting me unhooked from all this crap and across the hall," I said. Within ten minutes, I had my favorite vice in my hand and, for once he didn't object. I was the only patient, he said, who had been carried in—and walked out of intensive care.

That summer, when finding out that Owen Bradley was selling his fifty-foot houseboat for a bigger and newer one, Jack sold the "Paddlin' Madeline" and bought it. It was beautiful! And what made it even more so was that Jack said this one was half mine, on paper! "From now on," he said, "everything will be ours." Knowing it had to be his decision, I'd given up asking him about the divorce. After all, I told myself, a piece of paper doesn't make a marriage—look at mine and Harlan's. And look at Jack's. As long as we loved each other, that was all that mattered. Several times, when Jack and I would be a little miffed at each other, Hubert would say, "Why don't you two get married, you already act like it." That would bring the quarrel to an end.

For the past several months, Corky only saw Pam. I knew it was only a matter of time before they told me what I already knew. The time finally came. I was busy doing something in the kitchen when they walked in holding hands, happiness written all over their faces. But I waited for them to tell me. I thought they'd never say it. "Mom," Corky said, "how would you like to have Pam for a daughter-in-law?"

"I thought you'd never ask!" I said, and hugged them both. They looked disappointed at my reaction.

"Is that all you have to say?" Corky said. I didn't understand.

"What do you mean?" I asked.

"Well," he said, "Pam's mother cried."

"Why in the world would I cry? It's what I've been *hoping* for! When's the great day?" They said, right now, they thought it would be the first week in June . . . just three months away. After they left, I sat there thinking about their disappointment that I hadn't cried. Now I wished I had.

Bill and I were working a tour that ended in St. Louis and, like many times, Jack was flying up to take me home. This time, he was bringing along Hubert and Lucy Coldsnow, the girl Hubert had been dating for some time. As I walked into the hotel I saw Hubert and Lucy in the lobby.

"Where's Jack?" I asked. Lucy had a confused look on her face.

Hubert answered. "I don't know," he said . . . almost sounding angry. "We're going home!"

"Home!" I said. "You just got here! Didn't you fly up with Jack?"

"No," he said, "I'm not flying on that little plane!" This wasn't like Hubert at all. He'd flown with Jack many times. But, more than that, Hubert was usually all smiles. This was a Hubert I didn't know.

"Hubert," I said, "you're not serious about going home, are you? The show's in a couple of hours."

"We're going home now," he said. "Besides, Lucy didn't bring the right clothes." That was ridiculous! Lucy always looked nice. Besides, Hubert knew that people came to the shows dressed in everything, from black tie to blue jeans. Lucy and I looked at each other in total confusion. Hubert grabbed her arm and marched her out the door. I was still standing there when Jack came in. "What's wrong with Hubert?" I asked. I told him what had happened. He said when he had called Hubert to tell him what time take-off time was, Hubert had said they were flying commercial. That was only three hours ago. Good heavens! They had just gotten there!

When we got home, I called Hubert and, after talking to him, I wondered if I had imagined the whole conversation in St. Louis. He was the old Hubert. Laughing and making plans to have dinner with Jack and me that night at Mario's. I decided to forget the whole thing. Maybe he and Lucy had had a fight. That would explain it.

That night, after dinner, we were talking about parents' responsibilities at the wedding. It came down to the rehearsal dinner. Instead of Hubert joining in, though, he just sat there looking sullen. I decided on the dinner being held at Mario's, upstairs in a private dining room. Turning to Hubert, I said, "What do you think?"

He said, "I don't know why you're asking me. I'm not even invited."

"Hubert," I said, "you don't have to be invited . . . you're family." He refused to discuss it further.

The next week was my birthday . . . March thirteenth. Hubert never forgot. He called and asked, "What are you and David doing for dinner?" He sounded like Hubert again.

"Nothing, why?" I said, knowing he had something planned.

"Well," he said. "You are now! I'm taking you to dinner at the House of Choy! That way, we'll get a fortune cookie. I'll pick you up at five o'clock." That was another thing that was unusual. Hubert was not an early-dinner person.

When the doorbell rang, I opened it to find Hubert standing there, his hands behind his back and grinning like a little kid. Handing me a box, he said, "Open it . . . open it" and began to help me unwrap the package. I stared at the gift inside! It was a dime-store piece of costume jewelry, something a child might have picked out for his mother. It wasn't that it was inexpensive that got me . . . it just wasn't Hubert's taste. He stood there looking at me expectantly. Putting the necklace around my neck, I hugged him and said, "It's the most beautiful necklace I've ever had." His pleased look was all the birthday present I needed.

All through dinner, he rattled on about this and that, not making any sense. The only thing I could figure out was, since Hubert was a diabetic, his blood sugar must be messed up. "Hubert," I asked, "have you seen Dr. Thomison lately?"

"No," he said. "He's on vacation."

"Will you promise to see him as soon as he gets back?" I asked.

"Yes . . . I promise," he said, and was silent the rest of the time. He didn't even open his fortune cookie or smile when I opened mine and it said I would take a trip.

Two days later I had to leave for California, but the night before, Jack, Sumpter Anderson, a doctor and a mutual friend of Jack's and Hubert's, and I went to dinner. Jack and Sumpter were big into running several miles a day and working out at the Y. "That's what you need, Hubert," Jack said, "more exercise." Hubert didn't answer.

"Leave him alone," I said. "I don't think Hubert feels well."

"You're right, Redhead," Hubert said. "I don't feel good. I have a headache." It was the first time he had admitted anything was wrong.

Three days later, Jack called me in San Diego. "I have bad news, Redhead," he said. "Hubert's in the hospital."

"What's wrong?" I asked.

"He has a brain tumor."

"Oh, God! What room is he in? I'm going to call him," I said.

"Well, be prepared," he said, "he may not know you. But here's two numbers—they're both in the suite." I told him I'd be home as soon as I could get out, then called one of the numbers. Hubert answered.

"Hubert," I said, "this is Jan."

"What are you doing calling this number!" he said, and hung up. I called the other number and he answered again.

"Hubert, this is Jan."

"Hi, Redhead . . . where are you?" He didn't remember I'd called the other number. My heart was breaking. My friend . . . My beautiful friend. I flew home that night.

On the way to the hospital, Jack cautioned me that Hubert wouldn't know me but nothing could keep me away. Hubert had so many friends and many of them were in his room. I walked over, leaned down, and kissed his forehead. He smiled and said, "There's my redhead in the Mexican pants suit." I was relieved! He couldn't be as bad off as Jack had said he was if he remembered the nickname he had for the conglomeration of colors in this pants suit. Then, he looked right at Jack and said, "Where's our friend?"

"Which one?" Jack said.

"Jack Norman." Oh, God, he didn't know his best friend! Surgery was scheduled for the next morning.

About two in the afternoon, Jack called with the news. It was malignant but they said they'd gotten it all. "He'll just be in the hospital a couple of weeks," he said, and I knew he believed it, but I didn't. He asked me to meet him at Mario's. "That's where he'd want us to be," he said. "Drinking a toast to his health."

Walking into Mario's, I saw Jack sitting with Dick Blake, another friend. All through dinner, they talked about how great it was that the tumor had been removed. Suddenly, for no reason, I said, "No. They didn't get it all. He'll be dead in six months." They looked at me as though I were crazy. I just wanted to go home.

Only family was allowed to see him but his sister said, "If you're not family, no one is," and showed me into his room. As I kissed his bandaged forehead, he looked at me through vacant eyes and I knew he didn't know me. I stood there, tears rolling down my face, and held his hand. "Please, Hubert, don't leave me. I need you. And I love you." If he heard me, he gave no sign. I stayed as long as they'd let me. Five minutes. The next day, Corky, saying he was Hubert's nephew, got in to see him but with the same result—no recognition.

The houseboat had become Jack's and my second home. His folks had moved to their farm and his actual residence was the apartment over his office, but every minute he could, he spent on the boat. For a long time, we couldn't think of an appropriate name. Then the perfect one came along. The Poaj—which stood for "Pissed Off At Jack" or "Pissed Off At Jan." One or the other was happening a lot lately. But, when anyone asked about the name, we just said it was an old Indian name.

I loved the boat. Especially the times when we'd take rides up the lake. Or, when we were the only boat on the dock. There was nothing more peaceful. I'd spent many days cleaning it, having drapes made, buying a new sofa and chair for the main cabin, buying pots and pans, electric broilers, even a nine-hundred-dollar Oriental rug. Because it was ours, nothing was too good for it. Jack offered to pay for a lot of it, but I thought since he'd bought the outside, the least I could do was contribute to the inside. He let me have my way. Eventually, our boat got to be a gathering place. For his kids, who had accepted me by now, and my kids, and for everybody on the dock. The kids I loved, but the "commune" less so. Oh, I liked most of the people, but not all the time. But Jack was happiest when there were lots of people around, no matter who they were.

Tammy Wynette and George Jones, who were married at the time, had a boat near ours. One night after Tammy and I had spent all day cooking and washing dishes, she said, "How come everybody else has the good times and all we do is cook and wash dishes?"

"I don't know," I said, "maybe that's what we get for being the nondrinkers."

"Come and go to Memphis with me," Micki Brooks said. She and I had been friends for years and she'd caught me in one of my Feeling Sorry for Myself moods.

"What for?" I asked.

"I've got to go over there—just for the day—and there's someone there I want you to meet."

"Who?" I asked.

"Never mind," she said "I'll tell you about her on the way."

It turned out that there was a friend of Micki's who never did anything without consulting a black psychic, and Micki thought it would be fun to go see the psychic. I wasn't sure. I believed that people had this gift to a degree, but I didn't believe in messing with it. But, what the heck, it might be fun as long as I took it with a grain of salt. We made an appointment for that afternoon.

The psychic's "office" was in the rear of a beauty shop that catered to blacks, and when Micki went in, I waited in the car, which was parked in the alley in back of the shop. After weird looks from the people passing by, I was glad to see Micki finally coming out. Now, it was my turn.

I walked into what looked like the back room of any beauty shop. The black lady sitting at the table seemed about eighty years old. As I sat down, she didn't say a word, just started shuffling a deck of cards. Without my saying a word, she started talking. I was involved with a man whose last name resembled a woman's first name, she said. Norma. She went on to describe him to a T. Tall, dark but graying hair, a winning smile. She said she saw legal books, airplanes, uniforms, and clowns—Jack produced the Shrine Circus every year. She also said she saw no legal papers between us. "You can have him if you have patience," she said. "But when you can, you won't want him."

Then, she said, "Your middle son's first name is like a last name—Carter." That blew my mind! "He knows where he's going, that boy," she said. "He sets goals and reaches them. You'll never have to worry about him. But David is a different story." She called him by name and I had never spoken a word. "He is troubled and has problems. He is so mixed up. He needs extra love, and tell him to be careful with his car. I see an accident . . . Nothing serious but an accident." Then she looked hard at me and tears came into her eyes. "And I'm so sorry about Mr. Jimmy," she said, and stopped talking. I laid some money on the table and walked out of the room shaken. How could she have known? She had never seen me before in her life and I knew she certainly wasn't a likely country music fan. As we drove home, I tried to rationalize the things she had said but couldn't come up with an answer.

Arriving home, I saw David's car parked in its usual place . . . only . . . the whole front end was caved in. I ran into the house. "David! What happened to your car!"

"I ran into a brick wall," he said. I got cold chills. What the woman had said came back to me, but I never told David about seeing the psychic. Right now, I wanted to forget it.

Sometimes, being well known is not good, especially if someone disreputable wants to use that name.

Jack and I were having dinner downtown when a man who
Jack said was a judge from another town came in, loaded to the
gills. I'd never seen anyone so drunk who could still walk. He
weaved on past us to another table and sat down. "I hope he gets
home in one piece," I said.

"Oh, he will," Jack said. "He does this every once in a while."
We finished dinner and Jack walked me to my car. Sometimes,
Jack had a late appointment and I'd driven down to meet him. It
was eleven o'clock when I got home.

The next morning, he called and said, "Where did you go
when you left me last night?"

"What do you mean, where did I go? I came home!" He
laughed.

"That's not the way I heard it," he said. "Joe Pipkin has
another story." Joe was a friend of Jack's who lived in Memphis.
Also, he was my insurance agent. He went on. "You remember
that judge we saw last night, the one who was so drunk?"

"Yes."

"Well, as Joe tells it, the judge called him this morning, all
upset because he thought he'd spent the night with 'my girl.'"

"What?"

"Yeah, wait'll you hear the rest," he said, and proceeded to tell
me. It seemed that after the judge finished dinner, he had
wandered down to the Black Poodle, a place that played country
music just a few doors down, and the manager had brought over
a girl and introduced her as Jan Howard. The judge said all he
remembered was the name and that was because he had heard it
from Jack. That, and the fact that she was complaining about her
manager sending her to Phoenix the next day for one day. Also,
she said she was on Decca Records! But, to top it off, she offered
to spend the night with him for five hundred dollars. And when
he had counteroffered with forty dollars, she had accepted. Anyway, the judge woke up this morning with the girl, his money and
most of his memory gone. He couldn't even remember if he'd
gotten his forty dollars' worth. The thing he did remember was
the name Jan Howard, and being sure that she was "Jack's girl."
He had called Joe, who told him he had been royally taken! That,
in fact, he did not spend the night with Jan Howard but someone
impersonating her. But, whether they were convinced or not, this
was terrible! Jack laughed it off but said, "From now on, I'm
going to keep better track of your activities."

For a while, it was funny. But not after David came home one day looking like his face had met up with somebody's fist. It had. When I asked what had happened, he said he was defending my honor. Evidently, the girl was at it again and someone who knew about it had told David. "Not my mother," he'd said, and waded into a guy twice his size. Angry now, I told David the story, then called the police. A couple of days later, they called and said I wouldn't have to worry about it happening again. She had approached the wrong person, a plainclothesman who happened to know the real Jan Howard.

Two weeks later, Jack called and said he had some business to take care of in the judge's hometown and asked if I wanted to ride along. "Ha," I said. "You just want to see if he recognizes me!" And I wasn't too sure that he didn't.

I waited in an outer office while Jack went in to tend to his business. When he came out, he was accompanied by the judge, who looked at me with no sign of recognition. "Oh, by the way, Judge," Jack said, "I'd like you to meet Jan Howard." The judge did a beautiful double take! I stood up to shake hands.

"Judge," I said, "it's so nice to meet you. I've heard so much about you." He looked very uncomfortable. "But you really should know one thing."

"What's that?" he asked.

Leaning over real close, I said, "You wouldn't get my body for the five hundred dollars, let alone forty." He spun around to Jack. "You son of a bitch," he said. "You told her!" I had a feeling that was exactly what the judge didn't need to make his day, but it made ours.

Corky and Pam's wedding had been set for June tenth at City Road Methodist Church. I'd been there only a few times since Jimmy's funeral, it hurt too much to go. But this was a happy occasion and I was determined there would be no sadness. With their approval, we'd set the rehearsal dinner at Mario's, asking him to plan the dinner, which would be topped off with baked Alaska and champagne. Wanting everything to be just right, I called Harlan and invited him and Gail.

"How much is this gonna cost?" he said.

"Harlan, if you mean how much is this going to cost you the answer is nothing. I wouldn't dream of asking you for a cent. But if you would be so good as to grace us with your presence, it would please the kids." He promised to be there. The next day, his wife Gail called back.

"Harlan's changed his mind," she said. "He's not going to attend the rehearsal dinner or the wedding. He's against the Establishment." It was so dumb I had to laugh.

"Gail," I said, "you tell that bastard to look in the mirror—he is the Establishment!"

"But he doesn't own a suit," she said. "And I don't have a long dress." I wondered what had happened to all those two-hundred-dollar suits he'd used as an excuse for not paying me any money.

"Gail," I said, "I don't care if you wear sackcloth! And you tell Harlan he can rent a suit! Just be there!" She said she'd try.

Jack and Norro Wilson (a songwriter, producer, and one of the "boat bums") flew to West Plains to get Mom and Tiny for the wedding. About an hour before they were due to land in Nashville, a terrible storm hit. I had every confidence in Jack as a pilot, but I worried about Mom—I knew she'd be terrified. And Tiny would be no help. I knew she'd probably had to take serious nerve medicine to even consider getting on the plane. As I drove to the airport, it was raining so hard I couldn't see, and the wind was whipping my car around like a toy. The radio said there was a tornado watch out for this county. I just hoped they had landed somewhere until it passed, But, as I drove into the parking lot, I looked up to see Jack's plane. Storm or no storm, he was bringing it in for a landing. Suddenly, like someone had waved a magic wand, the rain slowed to a drizzle. I ran out to the plane as Norro was helping Mom down the steps. "Mom! Are you all right?" I asked. She was saying over and over, "Oh. Oh."

"Yes," she said. "Or I would be if this young man would let go of my arm. He's hurtin' my carbuncle." Now, for those of you that don't know, a carbuncle is something like a boil and it hurts like hell! I'd had one when I was a kid and I remember. Other than that, though, she looked fine. Tiny was a different story. She looked scared. "I've never been so glad to touch ground in my life!" she said.

Mom said, "Oh, Tiny, you're just carrying on for nothing. We made it, didn't we?" But Tiny was not to be quieted and, between her and Norro, I was filled in on the details. First off, they said, there was no one at the small airport in West Plains to fill the plane with gas. According to them, Jack took off with the tank registering empty. But since I had flown with Jack all over the country and knew he was not that stupid, I just let that pass by. Then they had run into the storm and Jack climbed to get over it. Mom had looked down at the clouds and said, "My, look at all that snow down there." And when they had explained that it was clouds, not snow, she had said, "Well, it sure looks like snow to me." The fact that the turbulence didn't bother her, I took credit for. A few years before, my niece Barbara—Beulah's daughter, twenty-seven years old—had died suddenly of a heart attack in Kansas City and I was flying with Mom to the funeral. The weather was awful, and to prepare Mom for the turbulence I said, "Now, Mom, it's going to be a little bumpy but no more than if you were in a car on a bumpy road." As much as I had flown, I was still a white-knuckle flyer and when we hit really bad turbulence over St. Louis, I said, "Now, don't be nervous, Mom . . . it's going to be all right."

She was crocheting and, never dropping a stitch, said, "I don't know what you're so concerned about, I've been on worse roads than this many times."

Norro was trying to get a word in edgewise to fill in the story. He said at first Jack had tried to land at Metro Airport and with the rain pouring down so bad and the turbulence turning the plane every way but loose, he had told Norro to watch for the rabbit. But Norro, being a novice flyer, thought he hadn't heard right. "What did you way?" he asked.

"Watch for the rabbit, Damn it!" Jack yelled (the rabbit is what they call the string of lights that direct you to the runway).

"Hell," Norro said, "I can't even see the runway, let alone a rabbit."

Anyway, they had passed up landing at Metro and came on across the river to Cornelia Fort where I'm sure Jack had planned to land anyway. The story was so confused, Jack and I just stood there shaking our heads. But they had landed safely and that was all that mattered.

The next day, Tiny and I took Mom shopping for dresses to wear to the wedding and to the rehearsal dinner. But first, we decided to take her to 100 Oaks Mall shopping center just so she could look in the stores. Mom could spend all day in a dime store and never buy anything.

As we were walking through the mall, Tiny and I noticed she

was walking funny . . . her legs real close together and taking little bitty steps. "Mom," I asked, "do you have to go to the bathroom?" She started laughing.

"Well, yes, I believe I do," she said. I was afraid if we didn't get her to one soon it would be too late and went into the nearest store.

"Excuse me," I said to the clerk, "do you have a rest room my mother could use?" She looked at Mom, who was standing there with her legs still in that funny position, laughing, and nodded to a door in front of us.

When Mom came out, she was walking normal. "Do you feel better?" I asked.

"I sure do," she said. "It was awful trying to walk with both my legs in one side of my pants." It was a good thing Tiny and I didn't have to go to the bathroom or it would have been all over.

We finally chose her dresses . . . a soft silk print for the rehearsal dinner and a beautiful pink silk suit for the wedding.

The next day, as I was fixing her hair, I couldn't help but notice how feeble she was getting . . . but she still had her sense of humor.

She'd always been tender-headed, and I guess I got a little carried away putting the rollers in. "It feels like you're boring a hole in my head," she said. Then, since her hair was so fine and thin, I tried to back-comb it a little bit. "I don't understand it," she said. "First you roll it, then you brush it, then you put all those rats in it . . . you might as well have left it alone." But, that night, it was worth it all. With her white hair brushed in soft waves around her face and her eyes twinkling as I'd never seen them, she looked like everyone's grandmother should look.

The rehearsal dinner went perfectly. Harlan didn't choose to show up, but nobody noticed. Everybody else was there—Pam's parents, her grandparents, me, Jack, Tiny, Mom, David, and all of the wedding party, fifty in all. Knowing neither Pam's parents, grandparents nor Mom drank, I had also arranged for ginger ale to be served for the toasts. But, before the night was over, the nondrinkers were leading the toasts. The only comment Mom made about the champagne was "These bubbles sure tickle my nose."

A couple of times during the evening, Jack reached over and pressed my hand and I knew we were both missing Hubert.

The wedding was one of the proudest moments of my life.

The church was filled solid with family and friends, including Solona. As Corky walked down the aisle, he looked so handsome, his dark curly hair looking even darker against his unusually pale face, I felt the tears welling up in my throat. I'd never seen him so nervous. I looked at David, so handsome in his white tuxedo—as all the grooms and ushers were dressed. As he watched Corky, his eyes were filled with pure brotherly love and pride.

The wedding march began and all eyes turned to watch Pam walk down the aisle on the arm of her father. She was breathtakingly beautiful! And as she and Corky looked at each other and I saw all the love they felt for each other, it was all I could do to keep from crying. If ever there was a time for happy tears, this was it. Saying a silent prayer for them, I listened as they exchanged their vows and became man and wife. I knew, as I watched them walk back up the aisle, their marriage would last.

Opryland was open and I never got tired of seeing *I Hear America Singing*. The whole cast was great but, needless to say, I was especially proud of David. All the time he'd spent these last few weeks learning the songs and routines had paid off. He was fantastic. At last, he was doing what he loved better than anything. He was a star!

Before Mom and Tiny went back to West Plains, I took them to see the show. Upon entering the park, I got a wheelchair for Mom and started pushing it down the ramp. I don't know how it happened, but it got away from me and Mom went flying down the walk with me running after her. But, before I could catch her, the chair hit a wall and dumped Mom on the sidewalk, kerplunk! She was leaning over and her shoulders were shaking. I just knew she was hurt bad. "Mom! Are you all right?" I asked. Then, I saw the shaking was from laughter. About that time, David came running up. "Grandma, are you all right," he asked.

"Yes, I'm fine," she said. "Just don't let this crazy girl get hold of this wheelchair again," she said, pointing at me.

David carefully helped Mom back in the chair, then took off running with it, hollering to anyone in the way, "Clear the way! Lady in a hot wheelchair!" They were having the time of their lives, and Tiny and I were right behind them.

As David placed Mom's chair in a special place where she could see well, he said, "Watch, Grandma, you're gonna see me be a star."

During the show, I looked over and saw her crying. I knew it was from pride.

Later that afternoon, Bill and I were doing a show in another part of the park. As I was signing autographs, a woman came up and said, "Would you sign this, please?" I looked at her program and saw, at the top of the page, where David had signed "David Howard, Jan Howard's son." Right underneath, I signed "Jan Howard, David Howard's mother."

Hubert was getting progressively worse. Each time I saw him, I could notice the difference. Some so-called friends of his said, "Jan, don't go out there, he won't know you." How callous. If it were me, he'd be there whether I knew him or not. With a twenty-four-hour attendant, he was living at his precious lake house, the same one where we'd had so many great times with Hubert, the life of the party. This was where he should be and where he'd want to be. There were so many memories there: Jimmy and Corky's parties before they'd gone to Vietnam, Christmas parties, the days, when the boys were in Vietnam, when he and I would walk along the country road and he'd try to convince me they would be all right. The times Jack and I and Hubert and Lucy had spent there and on the lake together. Yes, there were a lot of memories. And behind that vacant look in his eyes, somehow, I hoped he could remember them. But, no matter what anyone said, there were times when I'd walk into the room and his eyes would light up—just for an instant—and I knew he knew me. That was good enough for me.

One day, Jack docked the boat at Hubert's dock. While he went into town on business, I took Hubert down to the boat and he stayed with me three hours while I cleaned the boat . . . just sat there on the sofa or following me around while I worked. Then I took him by the hand and we walked along the shore, where he'd pick up rocks and lay them in my hand as though he was giving me presents. And he was, because I knew, before long, even this would be gone. I had to talk to him, even if he didn't hear me.

David had been acting strange lately and I couldn't persuade him to tell me what was bothering him. I'd thought once Opryland opened, he would be fine. And he was—for a while. But now, he seemed depressed. He was losing weight he couldn't afford to lose. He'd never been a heavyweight.

In answer to my questions, he'd just say he was tired from doing four shows a day. Perhaps that accounted for the weight loss but not the depression I saw in his eyes and in his actions. I made an appointment for him with Dr. Goldner. After David returned, I asked him what Dr. Goldner had said. "Oh, nothing much," he said. "Just take some vitamins." I had a feeling he wasn't telling me the whole truth. That night, Dr. Goldner called me.

"Jan," he said, "did David tell you what I suggested?"

"Well, he said you suggested he take some vitamins."

"Yes, but that's not quite all," he said. "I think he needs to see a psychiatrist."

"What on earth for!" I said indignantly. "I know he's depressed but he isn't crazy!"

"Jan," Dr. Goldner said, "David is in a state of deep depression, and I think he needs professional help." We talked some more and I hung up with the name of a psychiatrist he suggested.

David usually got home around ten but, that night, it was three o'clock in the morning before I heard his key in the lock. Before he came home, I was worried, but the minute I saw him my mood turned to heartsick. He was so white and drawn looking. Something was terribly wrong. All the words I had planned to say stuck in my throat as I watched him climb the stairs that a few months before he would have taken two at a time. Tonight, it was as though he could barely put one foot in front of the other.

The rest of the night, when I wasn't walking the floor, I was tossing and turning in bed. Finally, about nine, I went downstairs to fix coffee, trying to be quiet since I figured David would surely sleep until at least noon. But then I heard him in the shower. *Well,* I thought, *maybe he is like me and couldn't sleep.* I started fixing breakfast. A few minutes later, he came bouncing down the steps as though last night had never existed. "Hmm, that smells good," he said, walked over, and switched on the TV and came and sat down at the table. He didn't even look like the same boy. Maybe my imagination was working overtime again.

Waiting until he had wolfed down two eggs, bacon, and three pieces of toast, I said, "David, Dr. Goldner told me what he suggested to you." His expression changed. I wished I hadn't mentioned it.

"Mom," he said sadly, "do you think I need it?"

I walked around the table, put my arms around him, and said, "Honey, all of us have problems. Some we can't handle without help. I know. I've been there." I waited. I could see he was giving it some thought.

"Okay," he said, smiling again. "Make me an appointment." Without saying anything else, he was out the door and gone.

For three weeks, twice a week, he had an appointment and, from his actions, on the "up" side, I thought they must be going well. But, each time I'd ask, he'd just say "okay," and drop the subject. Not wanting to push it, I dropped it, too. But I was still worried. Even Tiny knew something was wrong. She'd called a few nights before and said, "David called me and didn't sound like himself. . . . Is anything wrong?" Not being willing to admit there was something wrong even to myself, I used the same excuse David had: "He's just tired."

Bill and I had a few days booked up in Ohio, Michigan, and Indiana. But some things had been happening that made me really decide not to go. The phone would ring and when I'd answer, the person would hang up. Either that or a voice I wouldn't recognize would ask for David, and if he wasn't home they didn't leave a name or number. David always had an explanation, but I didn't accept any of them. And when I'd try to pursue the questions, he'd get belligerent. "Damn it, Mom, I'm twenty-one years old!" I tried to tell myself he was twenty-one and I was treating him like a kid. But I was worried!

The night before I left, he came to my room and said, "I'm sorry I yelled at you, Mom. I'm just tired." Who could stay mad at him? As he sat on the floor next to the chaise longue where I was watching television, and laid his head on my lap, I ran my fingers through his thick curly hair and thought, *I don't care what he says . . . he's still my baby.* But, looking at him, I knew different. He was a troubled young man and my heart ached for him.

The tour ended in Indianapolis. After the show, we drove about an hour before stopping to fuel the bus and our bodies. Almost always, everybody except Bill would get off to eat. Tonight, though, it was just me and the driver. Everybody else was yawning and heading for their bunks.

While Tom, the driver, and I were eating, I saw John Potter, a man who lived in Indianapolis and whom we'd seen just two hours ago at the show, walk in the door. *What in the world is he doing here?* I thought. Everybody knew John—and John knew everybody, or at least he said he did. He was a deputy sheriff of sorts and at all the shows around Indianapolis. I waved at him and thought it was strange that he sat down in another booth instead of joining us. But then, even Tom was acting strange, insisting I have another cup of tea or another piece of pie, anything to keep me from going back to the bus. Finally, full to the brim, I said, "I've had it . . . I'm going back to the bus." Tom followed me and I noticed, as we passed John Potter, he shrugged his shoulders, but I didn't pay too much attention.

As I climbed on to the bus and saw the front part empty, I thought, *Boy, they really did go to bed early tonight.* Then, I heard voices coming from Bill's room, not only the band members and Bill's but female voices! I turned to Tom, who was standing there looking stupid. "Is that what John Potter is doing here, importing girls?" I was furious! One thing we'd agreed upon was that there would be no unauthorized women on the bus. Away from home, this was our home and it was supposed to be treated that way. Somebody must have changed the rules.

I sat there waiting until, one by one, all with sheepish looks on their faces, they filed in. No one said a word and no one would look at me. Then, just ahead of Bill came two of the cheapest-looking females I'd ever seen. Micro-mini skirts, white vinyl boots, hair that looked like bleached straw, and makeup so thick you'd have to scrape it off. Getting up from my chair, I said, "Open the door, Tom," grabbed the first one by the arm and dragged her to the front and, with one foot, kicked her out the door. She landed facedown on the gravel. The other woman tried to get past me but wasn't quite quick enough. My foot caught her ass and she joined her friend on the gravel. As I closed the door, I heard one of them yell, "You bitch!"

"Drive on, Tom," I said, and turned to face the boys. But all I saw were curtains closing as they slid into their bunks. Bill was already in his room with the door closed. I was so mad I couldn't see straight.

As I saw the lights of Louisville coming into sight, I said to Tom, "Take me to a motel near the airport. I'm not staying on this bus a minute longer!" I began getting my things together, and heard Tom on the phone to Bill.

"Yeah! She really means it!" he said.

As soon as I got into my room at the motel, I called the airport. "What time do you have a flight to Nashville?"

"Six o'clock tomorrow night," he said.

"You mean six o'clock this morning, don't you?" I asked. It was now three A.M.

"No, ma'am, I mean six o'clock tomorrow night."

"But . . . that's fifteen hours from now!" I said. He explained that there was only one flight a day to Nashville and that was six P.M. Damn, the bus would be home in three hours and, because of my darned temper, I was stuck in Louisville! I could have disinfected the whole bus in that length of time. *From here on,* I thought, *I'd better carry an airline guide.*

I started to call David but, realizing what time it was, I decided to wait until morning. But, when I tried at ten, there was no answer. *Oh, well,* I thought, *he probably has an early show.* Sometimes he'd start at ten, sometimes at two. I never knew which schedule he was on. Just before getting on the plane, I called again . . . still no answer.

When I pulled into the apartment parking lot, I was relieved to see his car in its usual place. Opening the door, I called, "David?" He didn't answer. I walked on back to the den and stopped cold! David was lying on the sofa staring blankly at the ceiling. I walked over and shook him. "David? What's the matter with you?" His eyes came around to me, stopped, then went back to staring at the ceiling. "David!" I shook him again. He looked at me again and what I saw in his eyes scared me to death. Nothing. No recognition. Nothing! He was white as a sheet! I grabbed his shoulder and forced him to look at me. "David! For God's sake, what's the matter with you?"

Then, in a slurred speech I'd never heard before, he said, "Wha do you want?" Oh, my God. He was drugged.

Like something was pulling me, I walked into the kitchen, knelt down, and reached as far back into a cabinet as I could reach and brought out a coffeepot I hadn't used in years. Opening it, I found what I knew was marijuana. I'd never seen it before but I knew that's what it was.

Walking back over to the sofa, I held the stuff where David could see it. "Where did this come from?" I asked, angry. His eyes grew wide with surprise.

"I don't know," he said.

"David! Don't lie to me. Who brought this here?" Realizing I was almost screaming, I lowered my voice. "David, please tell me." He just turned his face to the wall. It was useless. Even if I were getting through to him, I knew I'd get nothing out of him until he was himself again. Gently, I helped him up the stairs and into his bed. His arms and legs were like rubber. His eyes immediately closed and I sat on the side of the bed patting his shoulder as I did when he was a baby. With his eyes closed in sleep, he looked so innocent . . . how could this have happened? I walked out and softly closed the door behind me.

Walking into my room, I started to call Corky . . . then changed my mind. He would be furious. And I knew David needed help, not anger. I thought about calling Jack, but, knowing he would look at it from a legal standpoint, I didn't. Instead, I called the psychiatrist David had been seeing. When he came on the line, I said, "This is Jan Howard . . . I'd like to talk to you about my son."

"Who did you say this is?" he asked.

"Jan Howard." For a second he didn't answer. Then . . .

"Oh yes . . . Mrs. Howard. You're calling about David?"

"Yes."

"Well, I'm sorry," he said. "I only saw your son once. He never came back for his next appointment."

"Thank you," I said, and hung up the phone. It didn't take a genius to figure out where the hundred dollars a week I'd given David for the doctor had gone. For the first time in a long time, I prayed. "God, please show me what to do. Please help David."

David slept around the clock. Several times I'd gone in to check on him but, seeing he was sleeping normally, I didn't disturb him. There'd be time enough for questions. The questions that wouldn't let me sleep. Surprised that no one from Opryland had called, the only thing I could figure out was that David had called in sick.

The next morning, I was fixing breakfast—just like it was a normal day—when David walked down the stairs looking sick, sorry, and ashamed. He sat down at the table. Not saying a word, I set his breakfast in front of him. He took one look and started to get up. "No, David," I said. "You've got to eat." He started picking at his food. Then, as I watched, the tears welled up in his eyes and ran down his face. I couldn't stand it any longer. Walking around the table, I held him as he cried. Not since Jimmy's death had I seen him cry like this. "Oh, Mom, I'm so sorry," he said in between sobs. I cried with him.

Later, after we'd both calmed down, we talked. He still wouldn't tell me where he got the stuff, but he promised never to touch it again. "Just please don't tell Corky," he begged. I promised. Then, with what small smile he could muster, he said, "God's promise?" That was something I'd began when they were little. If you broke a promise, it was bad. But if you said "God's promise" and broke it, that meant it was forever unforgivable.

"God's promise," I said.

August 23, 1972. It was supposed to be a secret, but the word leaked out that there was to be a Jan Howard Day in West Plains. I had no idea what it involved, but Bill and I were doing a show in Springfield, Missouri, the next day. He and the band would be there so we could do a show. It would just mean an extra day on the road.

Jack flew me down in his plane and, when we landed, I saw half my family standing there. Beulah, her husband, Don Duce, her son Sonney and his family; my brother Bob, Tiny, her son Mickey and his family. Freddie had been sick a long time, but they said he would come that night. I saw the mayor and several town officials, Dennis Kostik, the producer of Bill's TV show, Hubert's brother Isom, Dick Blake, Jo Coulter, the makeup lady from the studio, and her fiancé, Chic Dourghty from Decca Records. It blew my mind! Turning to Jack, I said, "You knew about this, didn't you?" He smiled the smile I knew so well, the one that meant he'd put something over on me.

The first stop was at the Harlan Museum, where one whole wall was dedicated to me. Pictures, albums, a stage dress I had sent some time ago, and memorabilia I had forgotten about.

Then, on to the square, which had been roped off for the crowd. The mayor asked me to make a speech. *Me? Lula Grace Johnson, make a speech,* I thought. I looked across the square to the little café where I had worked when I was twelve to bring home food instead of money. Then, at the drugstore where I'd

worked to earn money for school clothes. And down the street to
the grocery store that had refused me credit when my children
were hungry, and the stores where I'd looked longingly at things
in the windows knowing I could never buy them. Down the
street I saw one of the many houses in which we'd lived. I
thought, *Well, Jan, you've run the gamut. Now make the speech.* I
can't tell you what I said but, summing it up, it was "Thank you.
I'm grateful for all the things that have brought me to this point."
And I was.

Next came cutting the ribbon for the Jan Howard Ex-
pressway, the new four-lane highway that circled West Plains.
Tiny said she had lived there all her life and didn't even have an
alley named after her. "You can have one lane if you're good," I
said.

That night it was "This Is Your Life" time. One at a time, my
family and people I knew, and some I didn't, came onstage with
remembrances. Then, by way of tape recorders, were voices of
people like Owen Bradley and Tex Ritter congratulating me. All
in all, it was a beautiful night and one I will always remember for
two reasons. The honor that was bestowed upon me, and the fact
that the two most important and precious people in the world to
me weren't there, Corky and David. I was told they had had to
work, but the excuse rang hollow to me. I had a horrible feeling
that whoever had put this together had just not thought about
that part, and I wished to God I had known. But it was too late
now.

It got to where, more and more, I hated to go on the road. The
main reason was David. To my knowledge, he had lived up to his
word. But I still worried. His behavior had changed dramatically.
Before he had always been "Mr. Neat," now his room was a mess
most of the time. I'd clean it up but he never seemed to notice it.
There was a time when he'd change his clothes several times a
day, never wearing the same thing for days at a time. Now, when
he took his clothes off, they lay wherever they fell. I didn't
understand. And If I pressed him, he'd just get angry and say,
"Maybe I need my own apartment." It was the last thing I
wanted.

I decided to use some reverse psychology and took him shopping. He'd always loved clothes, and if he expressed interest in

anything, I bought it. Jackets, pants, shirts, everything. Each day, I'd hope to see him in one of the new outfits, but they just hung in the closet with the tags still on them. I called the psychiatrist again, this time for me. I had to talk to somebody and didn't want to break my word to David by telling Corky. I'd tried to talk to Jack but he just said what David needed was strict discipline. Maybe so, but who in the hell did he have to turn to? Corky, yes. But I knew what David feared—losing Corky's love and respect. And I couldn't take the chance. Wrong or not, I felt this was something David and I had to work out together. If only Hubert were here.

Leaving the psychiatrist's office, I felt as helpless as I had before I went. All he said was to get David to come in. I knew there was no use asking. The doctor agreed it was best not to push him but he had no other suggestions.

The checks from Harlan had ended two and a half years ago, so I worked constantly. Several times, I'd canceled and I knew Bill was getting fed up with it. We had disagreed more often than we agreed. With the problems at home and Jack constantly reminding me I would never be more than "Bill Anderson's girl singer" as long as I stayed with the show, I couldn't think straight.

One night, in Fort Worth, Texas, the band was inside the building where we were working. Just Bill and I were on the bus. I had on my stage clothes and was sitting in the front of the bus doing my nails when suddenly Bill slammed out of the bathroom where he'd been brushing his teeth, with this look of panic on his face. He kept reaching over his shoulder and trying to pound himself on the back. I just sat there and looked at him. *What in the world is he doing,* I thought. He kept doing it. My God, he was choking! I jumped up and, with all my strength, hit him on the back, knocking him into the wall. I'd been wanting to do that for a long time but not for this reason. He sucked in air and I've never seen him so scared. "Thank God you were on the bus," he said. "I could have choked to death!" The next time we had an argument, I said, "I knew I should have gotten off the bus in Fort Worth." I didn't mean it, of course, and told him so. But it got so hardly a tour went by that we didn't have words of some sort. It was largely my fault, but I was pulled in so many different directions. Thinking about David—and wishing I had the ambition that Jack wanted me to have. I knew he got disgusted because I wouldn't assert myself, but my heart wasn't in it. Sometimes Jack would apologize and say, "It's all right—you don't have to work anyway. You're going to be my wife." But I'd just let that statement pass without an answer. I still loved him, but I didn't believe him. And I had long ago given up trying on the name "Jan Norman."

It was September, 1972. Jack and I had been planning for a long time that the next time I worked in New York, he'd come up and we'd spend a few days in the city and stay at the Plaza. During my trips to New York City, all I'd seen was the airport and the hotels where we stayed or worked. They strictly weren't the Plaza.

One time, a few years before, Bill and I worked a full week at the Taft, more or less a second-class midtown hotel in New York City. Maybe, at one time, it had been better, but that had obviously been some time ago. With Mary Ann, her sister-in-law, and some other friends coming up from Atlanta, it promised to be a fun week.

Since my duets with Bill were hotter than a firecracker, the opening night the audience was filled with record and radio people and we were given the "grand treatment." The second night, of all things, I slipped in the bathtub and broke my foot. It hurt like hell and became swollen so fast I couldn't get my shoe on. Mary Ann came to the rescue—she went to a store and bought some sequined material which we wrapped my foot in. *Not real classy, Jan,* I thought, *but better than nothing.*

After the first show, the pain became so bad, I couldn't bear it. Mary Ann and Steve Karlisky, who wrote "For Loving You," took me to an emergency room which turned out to be a hospital where they took gunshot victims, people who had been knifed, and worse. Lying there in a small cubicle with my eyes closed waiting for the shot they had given me to take effect, I felt the presence of someone else in the room. Opening my eyes, I saw a big black man staring at the diamonds on my hands. Quickly, I put my hands under the covers and screamed, "Mary Ann! Where are you!" She came running in, shooed the man out, then stood there laughing. "I don't see what's so funny," I said.

Still laughing, she said, "I didn't know your name was Lula Grace!" She'd gotten out my insurance card for the hospital and

there it was, Lula Grace Howard. It was no secret, I had just
never told her.

Jack kept his word, and at the end of the tour I met him at the
Plaza Hotel. As we walked into the room, I looked around and
said, "You better watch out, I could get used to this."

After a quiet dinner, we decided to turn in early for a good
night's sleep before the full day of sight-seeing and shopping we
had planned for the next day.

As tired as I was, it took me a long time to fall asleep. And
when I did, I dreamed of Hubert. The "old" Hubert. We were
out on the boat and he was laughing up a storm. I had on the
Mexican pants suit he was always teasing me about. I heard the
phone ringing, but Jack reached it before I could. As he listened,
I watched his face sadden. Hanging up, he turned to me.
"Hubert's gone, darlin'." We held each other and cried. Our dear
friend would suffer no more. Just forty-eight years old, he had
just reached the financial point where he could do anything he
wanted. Now he was gone.

The next morning, before leaving for Nashville, Jack bought
me a solid gold charm of the Plaza to go with all the others he'd
given me. Each one stood for something. Even though he didn't
intend it to be that way, this one stood for the place we were when
Hubert died.

Before Hubert's last trip to Europe, Jack had tried to get him
to make out a will, but he'd just laughed it off. Therefore, the only
one they found was a handwritten joke that said, "First thing, call
Red O'Donnell [a columnist who wrote a daily column in a
Nashville newspaper]. Next, if there aren't enough flowers, buy
more and charge them to me. If there's anything else, call Jan.
She'll know what to do." How like Hubert. He even named his
pallbearers, and I was one of them. But at the funeral me, Jo
Walker, who was executive secretary of the Country Music Asso-
ciation, and Frances Preston, Vice President of Broadcast Music
Inc., were honorary pallbearers.

As I walked down the aisle for the last farewell, I tried to
remember, "Dignity. He deserves dignity." Leaning over the casket, I touched his hand and whispered, "I'll miss you, my friend."
Then I walked away. For me, he had died six months before.
Later that night, Jack reminded me of that night at Mario's just
after Hubert had been operated on, when I'd said, "He'll be dead
in six months."

For quite a while now, David had been like his old self. Dancing around the house and practicing with the tape recorder. It was like old times. He was even talking about, when Opryland closed, putting his own group together and working in lounges. I knew a lot of people who did that, and it hadn't seemed to hurt them. Whatever would put the light back into his eyes, I was enthusiastic about. I had to go on the road for a few days, but I felt better about leaving him than I had in a very long time.

The night before I left, David fixed his special "soup" concoction for both of us. Then we sat around and drank hot chocolate and talked for hours. It was good to have my David back. "As soon as I come home," I said to him, "we're going to take a few days and go to Gatlinburg . . . Okay?"

"Hey, all right," he said. My mind was at ease when I left the next day.

Several times, I'd tried to call home from the road, but there was never an answer. I had an uneasy feeling I couldn't shake, I called Corky.

"Mom," he said, "I didn't want to tell you while you were on the road, but David's been in the hospital."

"What! What happened?"

"He's all right now but—" I knew there was something he didn't want to tell me.

"But what?" I coaxed.

"Well, he took an overdose of sleeping pills."

"Oh, God, Corky!" I said.

"He's okay now," he said. "He's here with us and we'll keep him until you get home. Don't worry." I hung up and called Bill. I had to go home. I had to be with David. Oh, God! What could I do to help him?

When I arrived home, David wasn't exactly his old self, but he seemed alert and said it was just an accident. He hadn't been sleeping well and didn't realize how many pills he took. "Where did you get the pills anyway?" I asked.

"From Dr. Goldner," he said. I knew that wasn't the truth. Dr. Goldner would never give him sleeping pills. I didn't push it, but later called Dr. Goldner, who confirmed what I had suspected. He had not given David sleeping pills. I knew now I had to break my promise.

That night, Corky and I had a long talk, but neither of us came up with any answers. Corky was concerned about the type of people David was associating with and so was I, but we didn't know what to do about it. He said that one night when I was gone, he had gone over to the apartment, walked back to the den, and saw someone he had never seen before. David wasn't even home. When Corky had asked this man who he was and what he was doing in my apartment, he had called Corky a son of a bitch, which was the wrong thing to do. According to Corky, he had knocked him from the den to the living room, then from the living room to the front door. And from the front door to the iron gate in front, where the guy's face went through two of the bars, scraping the skin from both sides of his face. Then Corky had picked him up, thrown him in his car, and driven to Vanderbilt Hospital, where he had kicked him out. Before leaving the hospital, though, Corky had gotten the name of the boy's father, who happened to be a judge, called him and told him where his son was, what had happened, and where he could reach Corky. The judge had never called him.

I told Corky about the phone calls, which had been coming frequently. Only now, instead of them hanging up when I'd tell them David wasn't home, they'd call me every dirty name in the book. Without David's knowledge, I called the police and a tap was put on the phone. But, each time, the caller would hang up before a trace could be put on the call. I had no idea where to turn next.

Thank God, it was the time of year when, except for doing the television shows, I was home. Eventually, things began to appear more normal. David began to get some color back into his face and I started to relax.

Christmas was coming and, thinking the spirit would rub off on David, I threw myself into it. It worked. With Opryland closed, he got a job decorating windows at Cain Sloan department store. For the first time in a long time, he seemed to be content and happy. I hoped it would last; from past experience, I did not take it for granted.

When he wasn't working, we shopped, and shopped, and shopped. The presents began to pile up in the living room waiting for the giant tree we planned to buy. Ten days before Christmas, we looked for the tree. We looked at the wreaths, one for the door and one for Jimmy's grave. Seeing two white-flocked ones, I started to tell the clerk I'd take them when David said, "You know Mom, if it were me, I'd rather have just a plain green wreath with a big red bow on it." I bought two of them. The next day, he and I drove to National Cemetery and placed one wreath on Jimmy's grave. Both of us knelt and said our private silent prayers. Mine was usually, "God, please take care of my son." This time, instead of "my son," it was "my *sons*."

That night, for the first time, David and I put up the tree alone. With everything done except the angel, which was still lying on a chair, David walked over, picked it up, and said, "I guess it's up to me now." Standing on a chair, he placed it at the very top, then walked over to Jimmy's picture and said, "I did it, Jimmy." I had to leave the room. I didn't want David to see me cry.

Every year I always resolve that "I will not be a last-minute shopper." But, characteristically, two days before Christmas, I was out battling the crowds.

It was three-thirty in the afternoon. I had just come home from shopping and, knowing David would be home soon, was right in the midst of wrapping presents when the phone rang. Picking it up, I held it to my ear with my shoulder and went on wrapping. "Hello?"

Jack said, "Hi, baby. Are you coming to the party at Cornelia Fort?"

"I'm sorry, I can't," I said, "I've still got wrapping to do and David is coming home soon."

"If I come and get you, can you come for an hour?" he asked.

"Where are you?"

"At Cornelia Fort," he said.

"Jack, it would take an hour to get here with all the traffic."

"Never mind that," he said. "I'll be there in thirty minutes. Be outside." Not waiting for an answer, he hung up.

Quickly, I stuffed the remaining unwrapped presents in my closet, scribbled a note to David, grabbed a coat, and went outside to wait.

I stood there watching for his car when I saw a helicopter approaching the empty parking lot across the street. *Gosh,* I thought, *It's actually going to land there.* Then it did! And, lo and behold, it was Jack! Half the neighborhood was outside watching. Feeling a little like Cinderella, I ran across the street and climbed in. As we flew over the lights of Nashville, I yelled over the roar of the engines, "Do you suppose this is how Santa Claus feels?"

Later, when Jack brought me back and landed, David was

waiting for us. "When I got home," he said, "the woman next door came over and told me she didn't know for sure, but she thought she'd seen you take off in a helicopter." I laughed just imagining the woman's face. David said, "I told her it *had* to be my mom—I couldn't think of anyone else around here who would be picked up in a helicopter."

Christmas Eve, Corky and Pam came over for dinner, and for the first time, we opened our presents Christmas Eve. It seemed sacrilegious, but most important, we were together and the shadow of what David had been going through seemed to be fading.

The next morning, with no gifts to open, David and I were sitting around with a "What do we do now?" look on our faces when Jack called with, "How would you and David like to get out of town for a few days?"

"We'd love it!" I said.

"Okay," he said. "Be at the airport in an hour." One thing I'd learned by being around Jack: Be prepared for anything. One time, with no notice at all, he'd called and said, "How would you like to go skiing?" Thinking he meant the five-hour drive to Sugar Mountain, North Carolina, I said, "Jack, I don't think there's any snow there."

"Sure there is," he said. "I just heard on the radio that the snow is perfect in Vail, Colorado." That short conversation led to five of the most wonderful days of my life.

Back to the present, I said, "Where are we going?"

"It's a surprise," he said.

"Okay, just tell me one thing—cold weather or warm."

"Warm," he said, and hung up.

When I told David the news, we both came to life and ran upstairs to pack. For how many days, we didn't know . . . and where, we didn't know, but it didn't matter really.

When Jack said one hour, he meant exactly that. Pulling into the parking lot at Cornelia Fort, I saw him checking the plane and within a few minutes we were airborne. When he checked the weather for Orlando, Florida, I knew we were going to Disney World!

The first part of January, Bill and I were booked back in England as part of a big festival which is held there every year. But, for some reason, a feeling of *Don't go* came over me. Trying to reason it out, I thought, *It's only for a week, surely David will be okay.* David assured me he would be fine and I knew, if I didn't go, he'd know I didn't trust him. I couldn't let that happen, but, still, I couldn't shake the feeling.

In New York, before boarding the plane, I called home and was relieved when David answered and told me everything was great. I knew, from his voice, that it was. Why, then, did I have this feeling I couldn't get rid of? Waiting until everyone else had boarded, I forced myself to walk on the plane. As sometimes happens, it was oversold and someone else had my seat. Any other time, being put in first class might have made me feel better, but not this time. We'd been out of New York three and a half hours when I felt my heart go into the same kind of spells I'd had before. Usually, I could get it stopped, but not this time. There was a woman doctor on the plane who gave me a pill and instructed the stewardess to put the oxygen mask on me. But even then I had trouble breathing. Oh, God, would we never get there? I kept fading in and out of consciousness. The next thing I knew I was in a hospital somewhere in London, so weak I couldn't move. When I asked how long I'd been there, they said four days. Four days! Then they handed me a note from the promoter's office in London which said even though I hadn't been able to work, they had paid Bill my money and that Bill and the band had gone back to the States. I had never felt so alone in my life. Again I listened as they said they didn't know what had happened.

Releasing me with explicit instructions to go to the hotel and to bed, I left the hospital. In my room, I checked my purse and found that I had about five hundred dollars and my return ticket. I had to get home. I didn't know if Bill had told anyone where I was. Calling the airport, I asked what time the next flight was and if I could use the ticket I had. But, when I told them my name, they said, "I'm sorry, ma'am, we have instructions not to let you board a flight." I hung up feeling like a woman without a country. Then, I called back and after finding out I had just enough money for a ticket and a little left over, I gave an assumed name for the reservation on a flight that evening. I just hoped they wouldn't have reason to ask for identification.

Trying to look like I felt a lot better than I did, I boarded the plane and took the sleeping pill the doctor had given me. Telling the stewardess I was tired, I asked her to please not wake me and hoped I could sleep all the way to New York.

Dog tired, I drove home from the airport—David's car wasn't there. I called Corky. "Mom," he said, "David's in the hospital." Oh, God.

"Where, Corky?" I asked, afraid to know what was wrong.

"Memorial. He has hepatitis." He went on to tell me that David had spent the night with him and Pam and at four o'clock in the morning had started vomiting blood. Corky rushed him to the emergency room, where an East Indian doctor had admitted him. It had been a couple of days. My tiredness forgotten, I grabbed my purse and drove like mad to the hospital. Finding out what room he was in, I walked in and David was asleep. But the longer I sat there, the more I knew it wasn't a natural sleep . . . I couldn't wake him. He was completely drugged.

Walking out to the desk, I asked the nurse, "Why is my son drugged?"

"The doctor ordered pain medication," she said.

"Is this ordinary for hepatitis?" I asked.

"Evidently," she said, "or he wouldn't have ordered it." I didn't like her answer and called the doctor's office. When he came on the line, I asked, "What's wrong with my son, David Howard?"

In broken English, he said, "Your son has hepa-ti-tis."

"I know that," I said. "Why is he drugged?"

Again he said, "Your son has hepatitis." That's all I could get out of him.

I said, "I'm coming over there. I want to talk to you." The last remark was to a dead line.

Finding out from the nurse that his office was right across the street, I walked over there and barged into his office. "I'm Jan Howard," I told the nurse. "I want to see the Doctor. As she left the desk, I leaned over to see where she went and saw her talking to an East Indian—the doctor, I presumed. She motioned to where I was standing and I saw him shake his head. Quickly, I stepped back to where they couldn't see me. The nurse came back and said, "I'm sorry, Doctor isn't in."

"What the hell do you mean," I said angrily. "I just *saw* him!"

Acting like she hadn't heard me, she said, "You can call tomorrow between the hours of ten and four." Before she could stop me, I was around her desk and down the hall to where they had been talking . . . just in time to see him go out the back door and get in his car. "That son of a bitch!" I said, and ran back to the hospital and to the nurse I had talked to before.

"Did the Doctor come back here?"

"No," she said. I slammed my hand down on the papers she was sorting.

"Well, when will he be here!" There was no mistaking the anger in my voice.

"I . . . really don't know," she said. Realizing I was taking my anger at him out on her, I walked back to David's room. For a while, I sat there watching him sleep, then kissed his forehead and went home.

For three days, I practically camped at the hospital trying to see this creep that called himself a doctor. He was slippery as an eel. What I couldn't understand was *why* he was avoiding me. If he was any kind of doctor at all, he should *want* to talk to me.

I tried to get another doctor to take over David's case but, because of some sort of ethics, no one would do it. Seeing the shape David was in, I didn't think it was the time for "ethics."

On the third day, David was coherent but still high as a kite. When I asked if he was in pain, he said, "What pain?" I knew I had to get him out of there.

As soon as I got home, I called Dr. Goldner's office, which I should have done at the outset. Trudy, his receptionist, said he was out of town for two weeks. Damn! What do I do now? There was one other person I could call—the psychiatrist. If David didn't need him, I did. After telling him the story, he said he never heard of hepatitis behaving that way, or requiring strong pain medication. "If possible," he said, "get him out from under that doctor's care." I could definitely do that!

The next morning, bright and early, I went to a book store and bought a medical reference book. Looking up hepatitis, I read: "Treat with bed rest and liquids"—nothing about pain. I drove to the hospital and, for the first time, David was fully awake. Pale and weak but awake.

Trying to act cheerful, I said, "I'm glad you're finally awake! What'd you do, get tired of my cooking?" His smile looked like it needed a doctor. I began gathering up his things.

"What are you doing?" he asked.

"It's not what *I'm* doing," I said. "It's what *we're* doing . . . we're going home." Helping him out of bed, I somehow got him into his clothes and told him to wait there for me.

When I told the nurse I was checking him out, she said, "You can't do that," and reached for the phone.

With my hand, I stopped hers in midair, "Don't do that," I said. "I'm checking my son out with or without a check-out slip. Do you want to give me one or not?" Jerking her hand away, she reached again for the phone. Going back to David's room, I got him and we walked past her and into the car. She was talking a mile a minute on the phone. All the way home, I kept looking in the rearview mirror. I felt like I had broken someone out of jail. David just sat there holding a group caricature picture the Opryland cast had given him. He didn't seem to care where he was or where he was going.

As the drugs began to wear off, I practically had to hold him in bed. He'd scream, thrash around, yell at me. Then he would cry and apologize. I knew he couldn't help what he was doing. Wild horses couldn't have dragged me away from the house. I just kept pouring the liquids down him and the strongest B vitamins I could buy. With those and good nourishing food, he began gaining strength day by day.

Several times someone had called and asked for David. The same voice I'd heard before. I'd would say he wasn't home and hang up. But one night I wasn't quick enough. David answered the phone and I literally saw his face turn white. "Leave me alone," he said. "Please leave me alone." I jerked the phone from his hand and slammed down the receiver.

"David . . . you've must tell me who these people are!"

"I can't, Mom," he said. "They'll hurt you. They said they would."

"David," I said, "they can't hurt me. All you have to do is tell me who they are and they'll be put in jail."

"But they said they'll hurt Corky, too, Mom. And Jimmy's memory." The bastards. They knew just where to hit David.

Kneeling down in front of him, I said, "David, please. Corky isn't afraid of them, and neither am I. And Jimmy would be the first to suggest that you tell me." He wouldn't budge.

"I can't, Mom. Please don't ask me." I gave up.

"All right, David." My heart was breaking for my son. He was suffering terribly and not from the hepatitis. I thought of the gun upstairs in my bedside table. If the bastard who was doing this to him would have the nerve to show his face, I'd kill him.

One afternoon, thinking David was asleep, I was watching television in the den. Hearing a sound, I looked up and thought, *My God! It's Jimmy!* Then I realized it was David standing there in his Castle Heights uniform. I knew my face had betrayed my thought. Trying to sound calm, I said, "David, what are you doing in that uniform?" He hadn't worn it in several years.

"You thought I was Jimmy, didn't you," he said. His voice sounded so strange.

"Of course not," I said. "You just startled me." He stood there.

"But I *do* look a lot like Jimmy, don't I, Mom?" he said. God help me to say the right thing.

"Of course you look like Jimmy—you're brothers. But you're also you—a very important, wonderful you. Yes, I loved Jimmy, but no more than I love you and Corky. You know that, David."

I waited for his answer, which didn't come. Instead, he walked into the living room and stood looking at Jimmy's picture. Then, he turned and went back upstairs. After I heard his door close, I covered my face with a pillow. I didn't know where to turn.

The next morning when I went up to wake him for breakfast, I saw Jimmy's twenty-two rifle standing beside his bed. Until now, it had been on the top shelf of David's closet. While he was still asleep, I took the rifle downstairs and called Corky. After telling him where I'd found it, he said he'd come over that evening and get it. Until then I hid it in the laundry room.

When David came downstairs, he never said a word about the gun. Neither did I.

Even though it was the first week in February, it seemed almost like spring. I opened the patio doors and was enjoying the fresh air. David came downstairs all dressed up in one of the new outfits I'd bought him several months before. He looked brand new. *It's going to be okay,* I thought.

Switching on the TV he said, "What's for breakfast?" It was the first time I hadn't had to force-feed him.

Joining in his mood, I said, "Anything you want, sir," and I tousled his hair.

"Hey," he said, "I just spent an hour getting it straight." It was good to be able to joke with him again.

I started his favorite—pancakes.

After wolfing down two helpings, he said, "I'm going out for about an hour . . . okay?" My heart almost stopped.

"David, you're supposed to rest, remember?" My face must have conveyed my thoughts because he walked over, put his arm around my shoulder, and said, "Mom . . . I'm fine. Really, I am. And I promise to be back in an hour. Then, I've got someplace I want us to go, okay?"

Even though I wanted to, I couldn't keep him prisoner. "Okay, but first, God's promise?"

He smiled. "God's promise."

In the next hour I must have looked at the clock a hundred times and until I heard his key in the lock, I didn't take a good breath. It had been exactly an hour. Thank you, Lord.

"Are you ready?" he called.

"Yes, I'm ready," I called down from upstairs. "But I really don't think you need to be out."

Without waiting for me to come down, he came up to my room and handed me a piece of paper with a phone number written on it. "This will be fun," he said. "Just call this number."

I saw it was long distance. Columbia. "David, whose number is this?"

"It's a goofy old woman in Columbia who tells fortunes and I want her to tell mine." I remembered the woman in Memphis.

"David," I said, "you know you can't believe what these people tell you. It's a waste of money."

"Oh, come on," he said, "it'll be fun. And maybe she'll read yours."

"Oh, well," I said, "it's a pretty day for a ride anyway. Okay." I dialed the number.

"Hello," said this squeaky little voice.

"Yes, I wonder if you could do a reading for me this afternoon?" I said, not giving her my name.

"Well, I guess I can about three o'clock if you'll bring me some of that malted milk stuff. I can't get it here in Columbia." It entered my mind, how did she know I wasn't calling from Columbia. I motioned to David and held my hand over the receiver. "This woman's crazy," I said. Then, back to the woman. "Yes, I'm still here." Then, I gave a questioning look to David. "Tell her we'll bring it," he said.

"All right," I said to the woman. "We'll bring the malted milk and be there at three." She gave me directions to her house.

All the way there, we laughed and joked like we hadn't done in two weeks. I was glad David had suggested it. Not the psychic maybe, but just getting out of the house was doing us both good.

Following her directions, we stopped in front of a run-down house badly in need of paint about two miles out of Columbia. Leaving David in the car, I took the malted milk mixture and, expecting a dog to come running out of the bushes any minute, I walked around to the back of the house. There, I saw a woman who appeared to be in her fifties. She was about five feet tall with thin wisps of yellow hair straggling down her face, and she sat on the back porch patting a cat. *Why do they always have cats?* I thought.

Looking up, she said, "Did you bring my malted milk?"

"Yes," I said, holding out the jar to her.

Taking it from my hand, she got up from her chair and said, "Come on in."

Following her, I walked into her "parlor," a dingy room filled to overflowing with overstuffed chairs and floor lamps. There must have been a dozen of them. We sat down at a card table and she began shuffling the cards. I was familiar with the routine.

She told me about the man I was involved with and hoped to marry. "But you won't," she said. "He's a cheat and already married." This gave me a start. Then she rattled on a bunch of other stuff about sprinkling salt around my door to keep out the evil spirits. And some other things I couldn't associate with. *As I said,* I thought, *it's a waste of money.* When she finished, I asked, "Will you read for someone else?"

The drapes in the front of the house were pulled and she had never looked out to where the car was. She looked at me so long I was beginning to think my head was on backward. Then she said, "Usually I don't read for men—they're so skeptical—but I'll read for your son."

When I walked back to the car, I said, "Okay, David, it's your turn." Even though the woman had shaken me with a few of her statements, I tried to keep my voice calm.

"What did she tell you?" David asked anxiously.

"Oh, just a bunch of crap," I said. "But, you'll see."

He got out and walked to the house. Lighting a cigarette, I leaned back and prepared for a good thirty-minute wait. But fifteen minutes later he was back. His expression was puzzled.

Expecting him to be bursting with whatever she had told him, I was surprised by his silence. "Well?" I asked. "What did she say?"

"Well, she told me I was an entertainer and all about my past. But when I told her I knew all that and asked about my future, she said she didn't see any future." I could see he was really taking it seriously.

"David," I said, "remember I told you not to take anything these people say seriously? This was supposed to be fun, remember?"

"Yeah," he said, still troubled. "But that was a stupid thing for her to say, wasn't it? Everybody has a future."

I reached over and touched his hand. "And you, most of all," I said. Now I wished we had never come here.

A couple of nights later, I said, "How would you like to go out to dinner?" I didn't think it would do any harm. He'd been getting enough rest. In fact, all he did was sleep.

"Yeah," he said. "That would be great. Where do we go?"

"You choose," I said.

"Okay . . . Nero's." The same place we'd gone on his eighteenth birthday.

At the restaurant, he barely picked at his food and was unusually quiet. I thought he was just tired.

When we got back home, David walked on ahead of me to open the door. Gathering up some things in the backseat I wanted to take in, I took my time, and as I walked through the gate I was surprised to see him still standing outside the door. As I got closer, I saw why. A black wreath was hanging on the door and on it, in big letters, was David's name. His face was white with fear. Grabbing the wreath, I took it and threw it in the outside trash can.

When I got back, David was sitting on the sofa in the den, crying. I ran over and put my arms around him. "David, who could be this cruel? Who did this to you?" He wouldn't answer.

After he went to bed, I called Jack. "Just keep the windows and doors locked," he said, "and I'll see what I can find out tomorrow."

As I walked upstairs, I saw that David had his door closed, but I doubted if he was asleep any more than I would be that night.

For hours, I walked the floor and thought. I thought about the people who were doing this to David. I hoped they would burn in hell! And again, I thought about the gun. Walking over to my bedside table, I took out the little twenty-five automatic. Just the feel of it burned my hand. *No,* I thought, *this is not the way.* And, even if it were, the people I was hating were nameless and faceless. Quickly, I removed the cartridges and put the gun in a dresser drawer. I didn't want the two of them together.

I turned out the light and, even though my eyes were closed, I saw David as he used to be . . . such a short time ago. He'd even put together his group and was supposed to open on the fifteenth in the lounge at St. Clair's restaurant. He'd spent hours and days learning songs, putting them on the tape recorder, and playing them back for me. "Is that the *new* Glen Campbell or *not?*" he'd say, and I had to admit he was pretty darned good. Damn it, these bastards are not going to destroy my son's life. The fifteenth was still ten days away and if he was strong enough to do it, I planned to be in the front row cheering. He deserved this chance and no drug pusher was going to ruin it for him. Yes, I'd finally admitted it to myself. For a long time, even after finding the marijuana, I refused to admit that David was on drugs, I'd seen all the warning signs on television and in newspapers—certainly, I'd been around enough people who used or smoked marijuana to recognize it. Yet, since David was my son, it couldn't happen to him, I had reasoned. And then, even having firm evidence before my eyes, I'd thought, *Give it time and it'll go away.* I think it's called burying your head in the sand. Well, I was wide awake now and the facts were hard and cruel. Some evil thing had a strong hold on David and we had to have help. We both did.

Within a couple of days, David had seemed to have put the black wreath out of his mind. And I wished I could. I called Dr. Nat Winston, a friend and psychiatrist. He was out of town and I left word for him to call as soon as he returned. I didn't tell David, but I intended for both of us to see him. Together, or separately— either way, David was going to need help.

After the wreath incident, no strange calls came, only calls from David's friends from Opryland. When they'd come over to see him, he was like his old self, laughing and saying things like, "Now that we've rehearsed for a season, do you think they'll hire us back?"

The working relationship between Bill and me had just about come to an end. We still had a few dates booked together but I wasn't mentally or physically able to keep up the pace doing the show full time. With Jack needling me that I was nothing more than Bill Anderson's "girl singer," he brought my self-esteem to an all-time low. He repeated constantly that all I had to do was show a little ambition and I could be a star. *Funny,* I mused, *I thought I already was one.* No, I take that back. That was my problem—I never thought of myself as a star. As far as I was concerned, the only stars were the ones I saw shining in the sky on a clear night. The rest were just people who made their living a different way. I'd tried hard to be normal, perhaps I was. But I had to admit Jack was right. The job with Bill was comfortable. I didn't have to worry about the band or transportation. I'd just show up and do my well-rehearsed show. I'd gotten so used to taking a back seat, I might have stayed indefinitely, or until Bill got tired of me. But we'd had so much success together, it was tough to pull away. Bill said I was a fool and perhaps he was right. Dick Blake, who had taken over Hubert's talent agency, said if I would break loose, he'd put me on all the Ray Price dates. Of course, there was a drawback—since Ray worked most of the time with an "orchestra" instead of a "band," I had to have charts written on enough songs to do a forty-five-minute show. I did—to the tune of three thousand dollars. And so far only one date had been booked, in Lexington, Kentucky. If my mind had been capable of thinking of anything but David, I might have worried. But now there were more important things to worry about.

Jack had been understanding about us not spending much time together. And, ever since I'd called him about the wreath, he had either called or come over every night. He knew I was worried sick but without names, there wasn't much anyone could do. It was the same old story. Until a crime is committed, there is no criminal.

One day, I got a idea. When a woman is feeling down, take her shopping. Well, for some time, David had been talking about a new car, his old one had about had it. I'd checked into having it completely restored, but the cost would be more than it was worth. Several times he'd mentioned a baby-blue Super Beetle he'd had his eye on and told me how good he'd look driving it. I thought now was the time.

I could hear the hair dryer going. Sick or well, the routine was the same. Every morning he washed his hair, plastered it down with gloop to get it straight, and sat under the dryer. To me, it was a waste of time because in an hour it was back in a mess of curls. I shouted, "David!" but he couldn't hear me. Walking up to his bathroom, I shouted, "How long will you be?"

"Why?" he asked.

"I want you to go shopping with me," I said. I could see the idea didn't thrill him.

"For what?"

"Never mind, "I said. "There's just something I want your opinion on. Will you go?"

"Yeah, I guess so."

Lately, I never went anywhere without making sure all the windows and doors were double-locked. David watched as I went through the drill, then walked ahead of me to my car.

"No," I said, "I want you to follow me in your car." For the first time, I saw a flicker of excitement in his eyes. I think he knew where we were going.

When we pulled into the Volkswagen dealer, David stopped just long enough to plant a kiss on my cheek before going into the showroom. I followed, checkbook in hand. Before leaving home, I'd called and talked to the salesman David had mentioned talking to and found that the difference between David's old car and the new one was eighteen hundred dollars. A lot of money but, seeing the happiness on David's face, it was worth every cent. As the temporary tags were put on, he was almost jumping up and down. "Hey, calm down," I said. "Or you'll bounce all the way home." It was better medicine than a doctor could have prescribed.

In the next few days, he almost polished the paint off. "Slow down," I said, "this car's going to last you for a long time." He'd just grin and go on polishing.

Jack's birthday was February eleventh but we decided to wait until the fourteenth, Valentine's Day, to have some friends over to his apartment. I'd been missing from the scene so long, there were rumors that we'd broken up. We knew better, of course. I said that if things were good at home, I'd come for a little while. Even though, for the past two weeks, David had been better, I still didn't want to leave him alone. I also knew he was beginning to resent the fact that I was around all the time.

David sat on the chaise and watched me as I put on makeup. "Are you sure you'll be okay?" I asked. Seeing his eyes cloud over, I wished I hadn't asked.

"Sure, Mom, don't worry so much!" Then he said, "Just go and have a good time. I'll catch up on some TV."

Trying to hide my worry, I said, "Okay." And finished dressing. As I walked to the door, I said, "Remember, keep the door locked." Giving me an irritated look, he nodded his head.

Jack's apartment was filled with people, and I tried to get into the party mood but it was hopeless. He saw I was nervous and said, "Why don't you call home?"

"No, I've got to go home. You understand?"

"If you think you should," he said. "But call me when you get there, okay?" My coat was already on, and I grabbed my purse and ran down the steps to my car.

All the way home, I was shaking. It was as though I was having a hard chill. But I wasn't cold. I recognized the feeling—it was fear!

I pulled into my parking place, jerked to a stop, and ran to the door. After two tries, I got my key in the door and opened it. Walking back to the den, I began shaking harder than ever. Then, I stopped and stared in disbelief. David and a man I had never seen before were sitting on the sofa . . . stoned out of their minds! The dirty rotten bastard had finally gotten to him! They were in a world of their own and didn't even see me as I ran upstairs. Walking over to my bedside table, I took out my gun. Then, I got the clip from the dresser drawer and clicked it into place. I knew what I had to do.

As I got to the bottom of the steps, I saw the man weaving toward the front door. David saw the gun in my hand and screamed, "No, Mom! Don't." He jumped in front of me.

"David," I said, "get out of my way! I'm going to kill that son of a bitch."

"No, Mom, you can't!" he said, and knocked the gun from my hand. It went flying across the room. Before I could reach it, David was past me and out the door. As I stared after him, the look he had given me hit me full in the heart. It wasn't fear, it was hate. The drugs had not only taken my son's body, they had taken his mind. I called Jack. The only thing I remember saying is, "I'm going to kill someone."

I don't know how or when, but he found me wandering around Green Hills without a coat on and the gun hanging from my hand.

All night long he stayed and held me. At eight o'clock the next morning, he said he had some appointments and had to go to the office. "Will you be all right?" he asked. It seemed he was asking that a lot lately.

Like a robot, I answered, "Yes." I was numb. I had no feeling. After Jack left, I started cleaning house like a machine. Washing windows, clothes, anything I could think of to keep busy. I didn't want to think. The phone rang. It was Corky.

"Mom," he said, "David spent the night with us." Thank God! I wished he had called me but all that mattered was that he was alive. "I'm down at the courthouse, but I'm putting him in a cab to come home. Mom," he said, his voice so sad. "He's out of it." I could hear the worry in his voice. I didn't know if Jack had called him or not.

"All right, Corky," I said, "I'll be here." I hung up and waited. A few minutes later, the phone rang again. It was Owen Bradley's secretary.

"Jan," she said, "David is here and something's wrong with him. He thinks he's home."

Not bothering to explain, I said, "Just put him back into the cab and give the driver this address. I'll talk to you later."

A few minutes later, the doorbell rang. I knew it was David because I'd found his keys by his bed this morning. As I opened the door, he almost fell into my arms. Dear God.

Helping him back to the kitchen table, I tried to get some black coffee down him. He pushed it away and laid his head on the table. "David," I said as I lifted his head back up. "What did you take?"

"Nothing!" he said angrily. I'd never seen him like this. I tried again to get him to drink some coffee. After a while, his eyes settled on my face. He looked so pitiful. My heart was breaking.

"David," I said softly, "if I go with you, will you go to the hospital?"

For a minute he was silent. Then he said, "Mom, do you really think I need to?"

Putting my arms around him, I held him like he was a little baby. "Yes, David, I really think so."

"And you'll go with me?" he asked, looking up at my face.

"All the way, my son. All the way."

"All right, I'll go," he said. "But first, I've gotta take a nap." His voice was so slurred, it was as though he were talking in slow motion.

I watched as he got up and slowly walked up the stairs. As soon as I heard his door shut, I called Nat Winston. His nurse said, "I'm sorry, he's still out of town. Would you like to leave a message?"

"Yes, please," I said. "This is Jan Howard. Would you please tell him it's urgent that he get in touch with me immediately?" I hung up and started clearing the table. Every few minutes, I'd glance at the phone and think, "Ring, damn it, ring!"

At ten, Corky called. "Mom, did David get home all right?"

"Yes," I said. "But, oh Corky, what's happened to him!"

"Let me talk to him," he said.

"He's asleep. Do you want me to wake him?"

"No," he said. "I'll call back in an hour."

At eleven, he called again. "He's still asleep, Corky," I said.

At twelve, he called again. "He's still asleep," I said. "But I'm fixing some lunch and if he's not awake in a little while, I'll get him up."

He called back at one. "Mom," he said. "Is David still asleep?" His voice sounded odd.

"Yes," I said. "But I was just going up to wake him, he's slept long enough. Can you call back in a few minutes?" He said he could.

I walked up the stairs and down the hall to David's closed door. I knocked and, getting no answer, I tried the door. It was locked. We never locked our bedroom doors. Without even thinking, I ran to my room, got a credit card out of my purse, ran back, and slipped it between the door and the lock. "Please God," I prayed. "Let me be in time!"

I pushed the door open and stared at what faced me. The bed was covered with blood and David lay facedown in the middle of it. I thought, *David, how can you sleep with all that blood on the bed?* Then, realization hit me. *Oh, God.* I ran to the bed and touched his hand . . . it was warm. Quickly, I put my mouth to his and tried to breathe life into him. *God, please make him breathe. Please!* Oh, God, I have to call someone! I ran to the phone and

called Dr. Goldner's office. "Trudy!" I screamed to his receptionist. "Please tell Dr. Goldner to come quickly. I think David is
dead!" I hung up and called Jack. "Jack . . . Oh, God, Jack, I
think David is dead!"

"Get out of there!" he said. "Go next door!" I dropped the
phone and ran back to David's room. He hadn't moved. I had
expected him to move. Dropping to my knees, I wrapped my
arms around him and rocked back and forth. Oh, dear God! I ran
downstairs to Jimmy's picture. "Oh, Jimmy," I prayed. "Please
help David. You always took care of him. Please help him now!" I
ran out the door. The woman next door heard me screaming and
ran out and grabbed me. "David's *dead!* David's *dead!*" I
screamed over and over. I heard a siren. *Thank God! Oh, thank
God!* Dr. Goldner, followed by two ambulance attendants, rushed
past me. As I started to follow them, Jack grabbed me. Then
Corky. I fell to the floor. *"David! David,"* I screamed. Corky
carried me to the sofa in the den. "Oh, Corky," I cried. "David's
gone. Please let me go to him!" He sat there holding me, his tears
falling on my face. Then, I saw Dr. Goldner walking toward me.
Behind him, the two attendants were carrying a sheet-covered
form on a stretcher. *"No! No!"* I screamed. "Not David! Not my
David! Oh, Dr. Goldner, please tell me he isn't dead!" He nodded
his head.

"Where the gunshot wound was, Jan," he said, "if he had
survived, he would have been a vegetable." Dear God, he had
shot himself with my gun! I heard myself screaming and felt a
needle go into my arm.

The faces were blurred, but I could make out Pam, sitting
beside me holding my hand and crying. Jack and Corky were
standing nearby. I heard someone say David died at approx-
imately ten minutes to one. Oh, God! If I had gone up ten
minutes sooner he would be alive. "Oh God, where *are* you!" I
said. And heard myself repeating over and over, "And now there
was one." Oblivion.

It was night. Something hitting the window reached my
unconciousness. I heard Jeanie Bare say, "We'd better call Jack."
Then another voice, Tammy Wynette, said, "We'd better go
downstairs so we don't wake her." I couldn't open my eyes.

Once again, the house was filled with family and friends.
Someone kept putting pills in my mouth and saying, "Jan, swal-

low this." As though I didn't have a mind, I obeyed. I wanted to die. My baby was gone and I didn't want to live.

I'd see Corky and knew he was hurting. *Thank God he has Pam,* I thought. Bless her heart, she stayed right by his side. He was sitting by my bed asking about the arrangements. I didn't want to hear, but he insisted. Then I said, "City Road. His service will be at City Road."

Someone in the room said, "No, Jan. Corky and Pam have to go to church there. You should have it somewhere else." Her words brought me straight up off the bed. "His service *will* be held at City Road!" Corky glared at her, ushered her out the door, and said, "I'm sorry, Mom. Of course his service will be at City Road."

The next few days were a blur. I remember going to the funeral home, holding on to Corky and Jack. But seeing my David lying there was more than I could bear. "Oh, David," I cried. "We could have handled it. I know we could have." But it was too late. I wanted to cradle him in my arms. The faces all ran together. Corky kept saying, "He isn't suffering anymore, Mom."

Looking down at David's peaceful face, I said, "I know, Corky—I know." He would never suffer again.

The morning of the funeral, it was as though I was playing a part I'd been rehearsing for four years. Four years. I remembered telling Jo Coulter, "Four years, Jo." She said, "Four years, what?" "I don't know," I'd said. "Just four years." Now I knew what I had been talking about. It was another warning. For four years I had been gathering strength for this. Now, my strength was gone.

Even with my grief, an intense hate was growing inside me for Harlan. He hadn't had the decency to come to the funeral home, and now he wasn't even at the service. I remembered that David had begged to see him—just for a minute—and Harlan had turned his back on him. I couldn't get out of my mind the picture of David crying and saying, "Why does he hate me, Mom?" Perhaps it was best he didn't come.

All of my family was present—all except Mom, who had been in a nursing home for almost a year. Tiny said she had worried about telling her about David. But when she did, and suggested that Mom not try to make the trip, she just said sadly, "Whatever you think." Thank God for her lapses of memory. The news wouldn't stay with her long.

I sat in the church, never taking my eyes off my precious son's face, knowing, when the casked was closed, the memory of him would have to last the rest of my life. I heard the minister talking, but couldn't comprehend what he was saying. Ray Walker, of the Jordinaires, was singing "Where No One Stands Alone." Dear God, hold my hand. How many times David had asked me to sing that for him. It was one of the songs he had put on tape. That and "Remember the Good" were his two favorites of all the songs I ever recorded. That's what I would try to do now— remember the good.

David's body was laid to rest in Spring Hill Cemetery . . . near Hubert and right across the street from where Jimmy was buried.

When we arrived back at the apartment, the first thing I saw was David's little blue Beetle . . . the car he had loved so much. I went all to pieces. All I could think was how happy he had been the day we got it. I could just see him polishing it and remembered what I had said. "David, remember that car's got to last a long time."

As we walked in the door, the sight of the stairway leading up to David's room hit me in the face. I didn't want to walk up those stairs, someone had to help me. Trying not to look, my eyes were drawn automatically to the closed door. Just as though he were inside, asleep.

Several times, I heard the phone ring. But the only person they let me talk to was Nat Winston, the psychiatrist. "Nat," I said. "If only you had been here, you might have helped him."

"Jan," he said, "when you called, it was already too late."

For days, I lay in bed. Time for me was measured in pills. One every four hours. Asleep, I didn't have to think. Somewhere, in the back of my mind, I thought, *I've been through all this before.* I knew some of my family was still there, but no one really existed.

Everyone was downstairs, and when the phone rang I automatically picked it up. "Grace?" The voice sounded vaguely familiar. But who would call me Grace? "This is Mearle."

"Mearle?" I said. For some reason, I didn't hang up. "What do you want?"

"First," he said, "I want you to know I've got all your albums. And where did you get all that hair?" Albums? Hair? What the hell was he talking about?

"Mearle, what do you want?" I said.

"You didn't answer my question," he said. "Is it a wig or what?" The bastard must be crazy!

"No, Mearle, it isn't a wig," I said weakly. "I've got to hang up."

"No, wait," he said. "It's too bad what happened to Jimmy." Jimmy? That was four years ago!

"Yes, Mearle," I said. "It was too bad."

Then, as I started to hang up, he said something that reached through the pills. "But if you'd raised David to be a man, he wouldn't have shot himself. Only a coward does that." I sat straight up.

"You no-good bastard. What the hell do you know about being a man! You never were a man! *Just a crawling WORM!* David was more of a man in his little finger than you could ever hope to be. You don't deserve to even mention his name!" I threw the phone across the room and hoped it had burst his eardrums.

Tiny came running up the stairs. "What happened?" she said. In between uncontrollable sobs, I told her. She reached for the pill bottle. *Oh, yes,* I thought, *by all means another pill. They solve everything.*

The house was quiet. So quiet, I couldn't bear it. Everyone had gone home except Tiny, and she was staying to help me pack a few clothes. For a while I would stay at Corky and Pam's. After that, I didn't know. It didn't really make that much difference.

One day was like another, a deep fog. I knew Corky and Pam were worried about me, but I couldn't help it. Reality was too much to face.

Jack would call, but since all he talked about was going back to work, I didn't even want to talk to him. I knew he had my best interests at heart, but I never wanted to sing again. All the beautiful melodies seemed to have died with David.

The Johnny Cash Show was leaving for Australia on the tenth of March and June and John said everything had been arranged for me to go with them. "It'll do you good," they said. Suddenly, everybody but me knew what would be "good for me." Sometimes, I wanted to say, "Leave me alone!" but I didn't. That would have taken emotion, and I didn't have any left.

"I can't," I said. "I can't sing anymore."

"That's okay," they said. "If you can fine, and if you can't it's still okay." Like a robot, I let myself be led through the motions of living.

The beauty of Hawaii somehow escaped me. It might as well have been the Mojave Desert. The only thing I saw was the inside of a hospital room for four days. I didn't need the doctor's diagnosis of "She's dying of grief" to tell me the reason. The day I was released was my forty-third birthday, but I felt a lot older.

I had already decided to go home, but June said, "Home to what? To whom?" She was right. There was no reason to go home. There never would be again.

Over the Pacific Ocean, I saw a beautiful sunset. Yet, instead of appreciating it as everyone else did, I thought, *Like all God's creations, it will soon be gone.*

Before leaving Hawaii, June suggested I buy some needlepoint to pass the time. I'd always hated things like that but worked at it incessantly. One day, John was walking back through the plane and, seeing me with my glasses on and working diligently with my needle and thread, he stopped and said, "You know, Grace, you'd look more natural with a deck of cards in your hands than that needlepoint." Until now, he was probably right but the Jan he was talking about was dead. The one he was talking to was like a wind-up doll . . .

With everyone else leading the way I followed like a mindless child. From airports to hotels, from hotels to airports—they all looked the same. Sometimes I'd go to the shows, but, more often than not, I stayed in my room. I was watching everything from far off. My days were filled with memories, my nights with nightmares.

In Sydney, Australia, my room was on the eleventh floor that overlooked the street below. Everyone else had gone to dinner. With the balcony door open, I was standing there watching it rain and thought, "I wonder if David is eating right. He's lost so much weight lately." But David was dead. My sweet David was dead. I couldn't understand why the room was so silent. Without even thinking, I walked out onto the balcony and put my hands on the rail. *It would be so easy,* I thought. *Never to have to think again.* Then, someone knocked at the door. They knocked again. Halfway to the door, I turned and looked back to the balcony. *It'll wait,* I thought.

Carl Perkins, an entertainer on the show, stood there. "Jan," he said. "Do you have a tape recorder?"

"Yes," I said, and went to get it. He looked across at the open door to the balcony, walked across the room, and shut it.

"You know you could get wet with this open?" he said. I didn't answer, just handed him the tape recorder and waited for him to leave.

Instead, he said, "I've got this new song I just wrote. I'd like for you to hear it. I'll just go get my guitar and put it down on tape here." Before I could answer, he was out the door.

A few minutes later, he was back, carrying his guitar, and sat down on one of the twin beds. He started singing, but, from the look on my face, he guessed I wasn't into music appreciation, stopped and started talking. "Jan, I know you're having a hard time, but that"—he nodded his head in the direction of the balcony—"isn't the answer." He talked . . . for two hours he talked, about conquering his drinking problems, about his frustrations as an artist, words that meant nothing to me. Most of the time he was talking, my mind shut out his words. Finally, seeing he wasn't getting through, he asked, "Do you have some sleeping pills?"

"Yes," I said. The doctor in Hawaii had given me some.

"Well, I want you to take one right now," he said, handing me my purse, which was lying on the floor near him. Then, he walked into the bathroom and came back with a glass of water. As I swallowed the pill, he began to talk about God.

"I don't want to hear it, Carl," I said. "The God I believe in wouldn't have taken my sons. No!" Carl went right on talking.

"Yeah, I think you do whether you know it or not," he said. I could feel the pill taking effect. He got up to go.

"Are you gonna be okay?" he asked.

"Yes, Carl," I said. "I'm fine." I didn't know whether I was or not. I closed the door after him.

Before going to sleep, part of what Carl had said seeped into my mind. The part about God saving me for something, and that it was wrong to go against His will. I couldn't think anymore.

The rest of the tour, I found the best way to cope was to pretend nothing had happened. All of this was a bad dream. One day I'd wake up and it would be over.

Day by day, I began to gain strength, both mentally and physically. In places like the Outback, in the midst of five hundred aborigine natives, home and all that had happened there seemed unreal. One day, standing looking out the window of my room at the beautiful seaport of Hobart, Tasmania, I thought, *Jan, what in the world are you doing here?*

Back in Los Angeles, instead of staying a few days as June and John planned to do, I decided to go home. I needed to be home.

Before I left for the airport, John said, "Jan, you've been out of touch with reality for a while. But, when you get home, be prepared to hit the lowest low you've ever known." His words really didn't really sink in.

At the airport, seeing Corky and Pam's smiling faces, I automatically looked for David's. *No, Jan,* I thought. *Don't do this to them* and began rattling on about the trip. I could see relief on their faces. That evening, when Jack came over, we talked about everything but the past.

Corky insisted I not go to the apartment alone and, for a few days, I obeyed his request. Then, one day while they were both at work, I felt compelled to go.

Walking to the door, I unlocked it and walked into the living room. But I couldn't go any further. Seeing the staircase had turned my legs to stone. Feeling for the sofa, I lowered myself to it. My heart pounding so hard I couldn't breathe, I tried talking to myself. "Okay now . . . you can do it. One step at a time . . . you can do it." Getting up my courage, I walked back to the kitchen, avoiding looking at the staircase. My ears were ringing with the silence . . . the nothingness in the apartment.

Slowly, I turned and faced the stairway. Then, like a force of some kind was pulling me, I walked up the stairs . . . down the hall to David's room, and opened the door. Dear God! It was just like I had seen it that horrible morning. His clothes laid across a chair . . . his rings, watch, and broken glasses were on the nightstand by the bed, along with his New Testament. The only things that were missing were the bedclothes and the mattress. My legs gave way and I sank to the floor. Oh, David! David, my baby! Where are you? I love you! I got up and ran downstairs. I felt like I was dying! The nearest person I could think of was Dennis Kostik, the TV producer, whose office was a block away. Trying to control the shaking of my hands, I dialed his number. When he came on the line, I said, "Dennis, this is Jan. Can you please come over? I'm at home and I can't stand it."

"Are you by yourself?" he asked.

"Yes."

"Good God!" he said. "I'll be right there."

Crying so hard I couldn't see, I went to Jimmy's picture and prayed . . . not to God but, to Jimmy. "Please, Jimmy. Please take care of your little brother."

My mind was with Jimmy and David, I hadn't heard Dennis come in. He put his arms around me and said, "Jan, you shouldn't be here by yourself."

"I know, Dennis," I said. "But I just had to come." He led me back to the sofa. We sat there until I was calm, then he walked me back to my car. Before I got in, I walked to David's car, took what things of his were in the glove compartment and seats, and put them in my car, then drove to Corky's. That night, I asked Corky to sell the car. I never wanted to see it again and I didn't want to know who bought it. He said he'd take care of it.

Next, I called Tiny and asked if she could come for a few days. I had to go through David's things, and knew I couldn't go back there alone. She said she'd be there the next morning.

After picking her up, I drove straight to the apartment. All the way there, she kept saying, "Maybe we should go to Corky and Pam's first." I knew she didn't want to go to the apartment.

"No, Tiny," I said. "I don't want anybody going through David's things but me. But I need you here."

Corky had already moved David's car. Like my heart, his space was empty. We walked in and, with Tiny leading the way, we walked to the stairs and, not looking toward David's room, on back to my bedroom.

After being on the bus for twelve hours, she was exhausted and lay down on the bed. I sat on the chaise and talked until I saw her eyes close in sleep. Then got up and walked down the hall. Unlike yesterday, I was calm. For a minute, I stood outside the door and, just in case God was listening, I prayed, "Please give me strength." Then opened the door and went in.

Very carefully and touching every piece of clothing with love, I took his clothes out of the closet and laid them across the bed. Some of them still had the plastic bags and tags on them. Never worn. Going through the drawers, I felt guilty. We'd always respected each other's privacy and this was invading his. Over and over, I kept saying, "I'm sorry, David." In my heart, I knew I was asking forgiveness for more than just going through his personal things. For tearing his life apart by moving from Madison, for sending him to military school, for being gone when he needed me, for being blind to what was happening to him and not admitting it when I saw it, for so many things that could now never be undone.

For hours I worked, gently separating the things I would keep—his scrapbooks and mementos, his personal things, his rings, watch, glasses, and New Testament. These, I carefully wrapped and put in a box to be kept. The rest I gently folded and put in stacks to be given to someone Corky would choose.

When everything was done, I took one last look around, walked out, and closed the door on the past. But it would never be locked.

Gently, I touched Tiny's shoulder. She jerked awake. "Are you ready to start?" she asked.

"It's all done, Tiny," I said. "Let's go."

Without ever going back to the apartment again I found another one in three days, called the movers, and said, "Just pack everything and move it."

Right across the hall from my new home lived one of Nashvile's leading producers, Larry Butler. And downstairs, my first producer, Joe Johnson. Sometimes, we'd see each other going in or coming out, but I wasn't interested in the music business. But Jack never let it drop. What I was afraid of had happened. After I got home from Australia, he'd never mentioned the divorce again, just said that I needed to go back to work on the road and also do something with the songs I had written and filed away in a notebook. One night after Larry had been over for a drink, Jack said, "I've been talking to Larry and he's interested in producing an album on you."

"But Owen is my producer," I said.

"Yes, but let's face it," he said. "You haven't been exactly setting the world on fire." His words hurt. I didn't need to be reminded that the last few records had been flops.

After Jack left, I thought about what he'd said. If I were going to work, and I had no choice about that, I had to record. And, if I was going to record, it might be smart to have a different producer. Owen and I had been together so long, like everyone else I thought he was taking me for granted. My heart wasn't in it, but I went to see Owen. It was the first time I'd seen him since David's death.

After a few uncomfortable moments of "How are you?" and

oblique talk, I mentioned the idea of a new producer. He disagreed. In a way, it made me feel good to know that he wanted to keep me but, in another way, it didn't. I failed to understand his reasoning, but couldn't convince him otherwise. Once, he asked what producer I had in mind. When I said Larry Butler, his face clouded over and he said, "No. It's me or no one." I gave up. As I started to leave, I asked a question I'd been wanting to ask for a long time. "Owen, why, in eight years, has Decca never promoted Jan Howard? Even with number-one records, the only ad I've gotten is the quarter-page ad in *Billboard*. The rest I've done myself."

"Now that you've asked," he said, "I'll tell you. One of the top-selling artists with the label said that if you were promoted, they would leave." He named the artist. I'd known that person for years, and what Owen had said hurt me deeply. As I got to the door, I turned and said, "This won't change, will it?"

"I doubt it," he said.

With a heavy heart, I walked downstairs to the lobby. As I started out the door, one of the promotion men came to the door of his office and said, "By the way, Jan, I'm sorry about that little thing that happened." I didn't know what he was talking about.

"What little thing?" I asked.

"David's death," he said. I was stunned! Little thing?

Not letting on how much his words had hurt me, I said, "Yes, that little thing. Thank you." Knowing I would never walk back in again, I walked out the door.

Jeanie Bare came over one day and, during a conversation, she said, "Jan, do you remember hearing something that sounded like rocks hitting the window the night David died?"

"Yeah," I said, "I think I do."

"Well, I've got to tell you what happened." She said she and Tammy Wynette were sitting with me when whatever it was hit the window. They knew about the threats and their imagination went wild. I told her I remembered hearing them say they'd better go downstairs so as not to wake me.

"Yeah," she said. "We went down and called Jack and he told us to call the police and keep everything locked until he got there. Well, we went around and checked everything and it was all locked but we were scared to death. And when this knock came at the door, neither one of us wanted to answer it." I could tell that if anything was funny at that time, Tammy and Jeanie had found it. "Well," Jeanie said, "I told her it had to be the police! But Tammy said 'What if it isn't?' Anyway, she went to the door and looked out through that little peephole and saw a blue uniform. Tammy asked, in a little-bitty voice, 'Who is it?' A big gruff voice said 'Police!' and Tammy said, 'Do you promise?' "

Picturing the scene in my mind, I laughed and said, "Did she actually think, if they weren't the police, they would have said so?"

"Gosh," Jeanie said. "We never thought of that."

I had turned the second bedroom into a den, and knowing thank-you notes were long overdue, I was sitting on the floor going through the cards and the flowers at David's funeral. Most of them were the same: "Sincere sympathy," or words to that effect. But one stood out from the rest. "What more to make them see," it said. I was trying to figure it out when the phone rang. The minute he spoke, I recognized the voice. A cold chill ran over me.

"It didn't do any good to move," he said. "As you see, we know your phone number and also where you live. We're coming to see you." Suddenly, I wasn't afraid but very angry!

"Fine!" I said. "You come right ahead. I'd like to see your face, but bastards like you would never have the nerve to show up. But, just in case you do, let me warn you, the minute I open the door, I'll blow your head off!" Click! The receiver went dead. I doubted very much if I'd ever hear from the creep again.

Another person I would have liked in my clutches was the East Indian doctor. Right after I'd returned from Australia, I was going through the mail and came across a bill from a pharmacy for two prescriptions for Seconal two days in a row, the fourteenth and fifteenth of February. The day before, and the morning he died. Altogether there were forty pills. It blew my mind. Why would any doctor give a normal, healthy, twenty-one-year-old boy, two prescriptions for sleeping pills? I knew why . . . The same reason he'd kept him drugged in the hospital. He had to be David's drug source. I also knew how David had paid him. Going through my checkbook, I'd found several pages of checks torn from the back. And when I received the statement, the checks, with my signature forged in David's handwriting, were there. They were all made out to cash. As much as I knew he had loved me, drugs had forced him to do something he would never have done otherwise.

I went through the motions of living, but sometimes it got unbearable and I couldn't handle it. One day, it was smothering me and I thought, *I need help. I've got to be with somebody!* I got in my car and drove to Corky and Pam's house. The tears were blinding me. I thought about pointing my car in front of an oncoming one, but I knew that would only hurt someone else. I thought about hitting a concrete wall! I don't know why I didn't. I felt so alone.

Without knowing how I got there, I pulled into their driveway, but they weren't at home. I leaned my head on the steering wheel and gave way to my grief. Hearing a car drive in behind me and expecting to see Corky, I looked up. But it wasn't Corky, it was a friend of his. He walked up to my car.

"Jan, I really don't think it's fair of you to shadow Corky and Pam's marriage with your unhappiness," he said. "And you shouldn't burden other people with your problems." Not believing anyone could be so cruel, I just stared at him. Then, wiping my face with the back of my hands, I started the car and turned to him.

"Yes, maybe you're right," I said. "But let me tell you something. You're very blessed to have three healthy children. God willing, they'll be with you the rest of your life. But, God forbid, something should happen to them and some stupid bastard says to you exactly what you just said to me! Now, if you'll move that darn car, I'll leave."

He went back to his car, and as soon as the way was clear, I backed out scattering gravel in all directions and drove home. Then and there, I made up my mind. No matter how difficult it might be, I'd never show my feelings to anyone again. I wouldn't leave myself open to the hurt it brings.

From then on, except for rare occasions, the only one who saw or heard my grief, and feelings of guilt, was the psychiatrist I saw once a week for several months.

Jack had taken me to David's grave one time but seeing the fresh dirt and no marker was too much for me to take. I'd chosen the marker—a simple bronze with his name, dogwood leaves and music notes on it—and Jack, at his insistence, had paid for it. But it had taken six weeks to be put in place. When they called and said it was ready, I called and asked Corky if he would go with me to see it.

I've never been able to go to one grave without going to the other so, after going to Jimmy's grave, we drove across the street to David's. As I sat on the ground with tears in my eyes, Corky walked a few steps away and, standing with his back to me, looked up at the sky. For a few minutes, he let me give in to my grief, then came back and gently lifted me from the ground. "Mom," he said, "I came with you today because you asked me to, but I'm not coming back here anymore."

"What?" I didn't understand. I knew he was hurting as much as I was.

"I don't mean to hurt you," he said. "But, see, I know they're not here. They're with God and I know I'm going to see them again one day." I stood there listening as he went on. "Just because I don't come here, sit on the ground, and cry doesn't mean I don't love my brothers . . . You know I do. But I'm going to live my life just as they'd want me to, and look forward to the day when we're together again. I'd want you to do the same. I think they would, too."

He was right. Yet, I knew it would be a long time before I was the "man" he was. If Corky hurt, and I knew he did, he hurt silently and inside. No one would ever see it.

Holding my hand, and not looking back, he led me back to the car.

Ready or not, I had to go back to work. My financial resource was me and only me. I'd heard rumors that Jack was supporting me and, at times, I wished it were true. It wasn't.

The last date I worked with Bill was the first since David's death two and a half months before. He had already hired my replacement, Mary Lou Turner, and I could tell she was uncomfortable. I told her that this had been decided before she came along and to please relax. I asked the promoter if it was okay if I didn't do the duets and he said it was. Not that I disliked Bill. It was just that Mary Lou did the finale and it just would add to her strain. That night was the first time I ever left the show without signing autographs.

The dates began to straggle in, but none where I could use

the three thousand dollars' worth of charts I'd had written. Most were as a single with bands that would have made good electricians. One of them consisted of three guitars, and no other instruments. And the stage that night was the back of a flatbed truck in a supermarket parking lot. After a few dates like that, I felt like I should apologize to the audience at the end of the show instead of thanking them. Many nights, I'd be so depressed and ashamed, I'd go back to the motel, cry and go to sleep. But, as bad as the bands were, the thing I dreaded the most was the loneliness—the empty motel rooms I had to return to.

One date was at a club somewhere in Louisiana. After driving all the way down by myself, I checked into the motel, then drove to the club so I'd know how to get there. I saw what looked like a boarded-up barn. I thought, *Surely this can't be it?* But it was. In all the years I'd worked, I'd never seen worse. Ray Price had a name for them—"Skull Orchards," places where they put chicken wire around the stage so the performers wouldn't get hit with flying beer bottles. No amount of money would have made me go into that place. I went back to the motel and called the agent who had booked it. "You know that club you booked in Louisiana?"

"Yeah," he said. "What about it?"

"Well, this is one time, my friend, if you want it worked you'll have to do it yourself." Before he could say a word, I hung up. Then, after a hot bath, I had a nice dinner and went to bed. I didn't care if I got sued or not.

All summer, Jack and I spent every possible moment on the boat. But things had changed. No longer was it a place of peace and rest and being together. I take that back. It was togetherness all right but together with everyone on the boatdock. The drinking never ended and the party never stopped. We saw the same faces week after week from Friday evening to Monday morning. And most nights during the week, we'd see the same people for dinner. Sometimes, it was fun, but, eventually, it got boring. I felt guilty. Guilty when I'd see certain looks on friends' faces. Guilty when I didn't go to church. Guilty when I'd see Corky and Pam. They knew I loved Jack and accepted and liked him, but I knew their disapproval of the way we lived. They began to come around less and less.

There were a few funny moments that took my mind off my troubles and broke the monotony. Like the time George Jones came out to the dock drunk and started throwing hundred-dollar bills in the lake. "George, stop!" I yelled, and tried to take them away from him. He just laughed and kept on throwing. Determined to retrieve some of them, I dove in the water. Then, remembering I couldn't swim, I hollered for someone to pull me out. Later, when a diamond ring followed the money, I considered taking a chance on drowning.

Another time, when one of the boat owners had had more than a few drinks and had gone into his boat and passed out, several of us towed his boat to an island in another part of the lake and left it there. The next afternoon, we saw his boat headed to where all of our boats were tied together in a cove. He pulled alongside of our boat but, unlike everybody else, he wasn't laughing. "Okay," he said. "Who did it?" Nobody snitched. Finally, he told the story of his rude awakening. Waking up in the middle of the night to go to the bathroom, he flipped the light switch. When nothing happened, he thought the power was off. Feeling his way to the bathroom and back again, he went back to sleep. When he woke up again, it was dawn. He walked out on deck. During the night, a heavy fog had set in and was still so thick he couldn't see. He decided to walk out on the dock, but stopped just in time. "Shit!" he'd said. "That's not the dock, it's water." We were all in hysterics. He said it had taken him over an hour to figure out where he was and what had happened, and now he was angry! "It's not funny, you bastards! I could have drowned!" That stopped the laughter. He was right, he could have and it was a stupid thing to do. Yet I couldn't blame that prank on everybody's drinking—it had been my idea.

Without talking to anyone, I started reading the Bible, searching for answers to banish the unrest in my heart. I knew they had to be somewhere. I had so many questions. And when I couldn't find answers to them, I'd get frustrated. "God," I prayed. "Please help me! Please give me strength!" I realized I wasn't praying to Jimmy and David, I was praying to God. Somehow, I knew that He hadn't taken my sons. The world had taken them and He was crying with me. I wish I could say that something akin to a bolt of lightning struck me, but I can't. I just know that little by little, I began to feel a kind of peace. Yet I knew I still had a long way to go, and a lot to learn.

In July, Jack flew me down to see Mom. She seemed physically all right, but when she asked, "How are the boys," I knew her mind and memory were slipping fast. In a way, it was a blessing. I just said, "They're fine, Mom." No need to remind her. One minute she'd be lost in another world. Then she'd be her old feisty self. Until now, she'd always called Jack "that guy" . . . now she called him by name. "Jack," she said. "Are you still a lawyer?"

"Yes, Mrs. Johnson," he said.

"Well," she said, "I may need one." Jack laughed. The mere thought of Mom needing a lawyer was enough to make anyone who knew her laugh.

"Why would you need a lawyer?" he asked.

"Well," she said. "There's an old woman who lives here who keeps sitting in my chair at the table. And the next time she does, I'm gonna dump her out of that chair and onto the floor."

"That's right, Mrs. Johnson," Jack said. "It's your chair and if she sits in it again, dump her. I'll defend you." I loved him for going along with her.

When Mom lived in the highrise, she'd had a canary and she missed it. Tiny said that's all she talked about. Her canary. Before we left, I went to every store in town until I found what I was looking for—an artificial canary in a little cage. At the bottom was a key which, when you wound it, would make the canary swing and chirp for some time. Taking it back to the nursing home, I wound it real tight and hung it over Mom's bed. A week later Tiny called and said, "I thought you'd like to hear what happened with the canary." She went on to tell me that after we'd left, at midnight that night, Mom had come out to the nurses' desk and complained that she couldn't sleep. When the nurse asked why, Mom told her it was "that darn canary chirping and swinging." She said she had covered it up, like she always did with her other one, and it wouldn't stop. "It's just not a normal canary," she said. The nurse had gone in, disconnected the chirping and swinging box, and when it stopped, Mom said, "Now, that's more like it," and went to sleep.

Another time when I sent her a dozen red roses, she said to the nurse, "Why that silly girl must think I've passed on."

I had three dates booked—one in Illinois and two in Waterloo, Iowa. I didn't want to go. I hadn't been feeling well and it was a long drive. But I went, anyhow.

In Illinois, the small auditorium was packed and there wasn't enough air to go around. At least for me. Onstage, I had trouble breathing. Then, right in the middle of a song, I felt my heart go into the all-too-familiar rapid beating. But, no matter how familiar it was, it was still frightening. I turned my back to the audience and did all the things I had been told to do, press on my eyelids, press an artery on my neck, hold my breath. But it didn't work. My heart beat faster and faster and I felt faintness coming over my body. There was nothing to do but leave the stage while I could still walk off. I made it to the back and someone got me to a sofa and helped me to lie down. I heard a siren and knew I was in an ambulance. The next thing I knew, it was morning and I was in the hospital hooked to monitors. My heart was beating normally, but I was weak. And scared. With the shots they gave me, I slept most of the day and that night. But, the next morning, when the doctor came in and said, "Mrs. Howard, we're going to do an arteriogram," I came fully awake."

"Hell no, you're not!" I said. "I had one done in New Orleans and it darned near killed me."

Then he said, "We have reason to believe that there's a blockage that's not letting the blood get through to your heart and that's what caused this attack." Now, I didn't know what to do. I was afraid to move.

I asked the nurse to call Jack. Whatever happened, the dates in Waterloo would have to be canceled. She came back carrying the phone.

"This is strictly against the rules," she said. "But he insists on talking with you." She handed me the phone.

"Hello?"

"Jan! What in the hell are you doing in the hospital!" he said, not the least concerned. Instead he was angry.

"Jack," I said, "I . . . I had another heart spasm." I sounded like I was *apologizing!*

"Shit," he said, his disgust clearly showing through, "there's nothing wrong with you and you know it. Now, get the hell out of that bed and go to Waterloo!" Without speaking to him again, I hung up and began unhooking the monitor. I thought, *I'll go to Waterloo and take my chances! What did it matter anyway!* As soon as the first wire was disconnected, the nurse came running in.

Seeing me out of bed, she said, "You can't do this!"

"I am doing it," I said, and went on dressing. She ran out again and came back with the doctor.

"Mrs. Howard," he said. "If you leave here against my orders, I won't be responsible."

I stopped dressing long enough to say, "No one ever has been, Doctor. No one ever has been."

Halfway to Waterloo, I realized why Jack had behaved that way. He wasn't heartless, he just knew if I got mad I'd start fighting back. And he was right. It had happened many times before, each time unexplained by doctors. But each time it was no less frightening than the time before. And I had no control over it.

I got to Waterloo, checked into the Holiday Inn, and began to rehearse with the local band. As soon as I returned, I got undressed and fell into bed. All of a sudden, I knew I had to call Tiny. In all these years, I had never called her from on the road. I always waited until I got home. Now, I knew I had to. I sat up and called her number. Her husband Freddie answered and told me she was at the hospital with Mom.

"You mean the nursing home, don't you?" I said. Tiny worked there.

"No," he said, "the hospital."

The feeling I had come to dread so much had made me call Tiny. I called the West Plains Hospital and asked to speak to Minnie Downen, Tiny's married name.

She came on the line. "Grace, where are you? I've been trying to find you for two days!"

"I'm in Waterloo, Iowa. What's wrong with Mom?"

"She has a kidney infection and pneumonia. I think you'd better come. They don't think she'll make it."

"I've got my car here," I said. "It will take me twelve hours, but I'll be there as soon as I can." I hung up and called Dick Blake, who had booked the date, and told him what had happened. He said not to worry about anything. He'd take care of it. I was on my way.

Driving twelve hours gave me a lot of time to think, and regret. Regret the rebellion I had felt as a child, regret all the times I could have gone to see Mom, and didn't; regret that I hadn't brought her to live with me. There were lots of excuses, but none of them worked. I felt guilty. I kept praying she could hold on until I could tell her I loved her. And that I was so sorry that I hadn't been a better daughter. *Please, God. Give me a chance to make it up to her.*

I thought back to what the psychiatrist had said. "Jan, you can say 'if' all you want to. And you can live in guilt. But the fact is, it doesn't do any good. What's done is done and you can't change the past. Some things are just out of your hands."

I pulled into the hospital parking lot, jumped out, and went down the corridor to the nurses' station. Tiny was coming out of the room they pointed out as Mom's. She was crying. I stood there.

"Tiny . . . is she . . . ?"

"No," she said. "But she went into a coma ten minutes ago."

"Oh, God! Now, she'll never know I was here!"

"Yes," Tiny said. "She knows." She told me that just before I'd gotten there, she'd gone into Mom's room. Mom had opened her eyes and said, "Grace, is that you?" Tiny had answered, "Yes, Mom, it's Grace." Mom had closed her eyes again.

For five days, we never left the hospital except to change clothes and take a bath in a room I'd gotten at the Holiday Inn. Everybody took turns. Me, Tiny, Beulah, Bob, Junior, who had come in from Kansas City. Dick was in California, and Pete was ill in Springfield.

The fifth day, my eyes felt like two burned holes in a blanket. I told Tiny I was going to the motel to take a bath and lie down for just a few minutes. Mom had been in a coma the whole time. I didn't figure in an hour there'd be that much change.

Back at the motel, I cleaned my face, took a hot bath, and started to crawl into bed. Then, suddenly, I was wide awake! I knew I had to get back to the hospital.

I threw on some clothes, and drove like mad to the hospital. As I ran down the corridor, I saw Bob coming out of Mom's room crying. He came toward me. I tried to run past him, but he grabbed my arm. "She's gone, Grace," he said.

I began sobbing uncontrollably.

"Take this," a doctor said. I think I must have hyperventilated. Automatically, I swallowed the reliable Valium. The answer to everything, or so they believed.

Arrangements had to be made. We chose the casket and the

dress she would be buried in, the same pink silk she'd worn to Corky and Pam's wedding. But there was one thing I had to do myself.

Several times in the past, Mom had said, "When I die, I want you to sing at my funeral."

"Mom!" I'd said. "I can't do that!"

"Why not?" she'd said. "You sing for all those other people." Like most people who think that the time would never come, I'd promised.

Calling around town, I finally found someone to play the organ. Then a man from the radio station came and, in a small room in the back of the funeral home, I sang and taped "Just A Closer Walk With Thee," "Just As I Am," and "Where No One Stands Alone."

The service wasn't very long or very large. Just family and a few friends. On the program it listed Jan Howard as the vocalist. I wished I had told them to say Lula Grace. That's what she had named me, and who I really was—Lula Grace.

She was buried near a beautiful tree in the new cemetery. She was seventy-nine years old. It was September 30, 1973.

Bob drove home with me, but he stayed only a few days. Once more, I became depressed, not leaving the house for days at a time. All I did was read and reread David and Jimmy's letters and notes. I'd pull out from under my bed the storage boxes which held the only things, except memories, I had left of them. To their things, I added Mom's glasses and a few poems she'd written. Her doll collection—except for a few each of her children had kept—we'd given to the museum in West Plains. She'd always loved people to come and see them. Now they could. The one I kept was the "Jan Howard" doll, which she'd dressed in the costume I wore onstage the first time. A white blouse and blue skirt . . . both trimmed in gold, some little gold sandals on the feet and tiny gold earrings.

After Jimmy's death and then David's, the Born Again Christians started coming to visit. They were back again. I knew they meant well, but I didn't want to hear what they had to say. Some of them chose the wrong words. Things like, "Jan if you'd been a better person, these things wouldn't have happened." Or, as one so-called evangelist said, "Jan, if you ever need to talk to God, I can intercede for you." I told him that if I ever needed a "middleman," I had two boys up there a lot more qualified than he was. Another asked me not to deceive myself into thinking that David was in heaven. Suicide, she said, was the devil's work and an unforgivable sin. It was all I could do not to throw her out of my house. "I'm sorry," I told her, "but I believe that God is a loving God. And David was sick. I believe that the world took my sons, not God." I never invited any of them back. Whatever I felt deeply was between me and God.

The relationship between Jack and me was a like a yo-yo. Up one minute, down the next. The good times were great, but the bad times were terrible. There would be days when we didn't talk. Then I'd find a note under the windshield of my car with an apology and signed "Bad Ass." He'd named himself that, not I.

It got to the point that I hated to go out to the boat. But Jack wasn't happy anywhere else. And if I suggested we spend more time alone, he'd say I was antisocial and didn't know how to have a good time. He was right about the last part, anyway.

He knew the guilt I was feeling, but if I ever mentioned divorce, he'd get angry and say, "Is that all you can think about? Getting married?" It had been six years. After a while, he'd apologize and say he was working on it. I knew he was just saying it to pacify me. He was the best divorce attorney in Nashville. And if anyone could get a divorce, he could. He didn't want one, and I knew it. But the alternative was hard to face.

One day, out of the blue, he said, "I promise we'll be married by Christmas and go to Vermont skiing on our honeymoon. Would you like that?" I didn't try to hide my happiness. Yet I was afraid to expect anything. There had been too many broken promises.

When I told him so, he said, "Honey, those who don't expect or ask very seldom get."

Only one more date had been booked in Lexington, Kentucky. Dreading to face another local band, I took Steve Chapman, a guitar player who used to work with Bill Anderson, and who knew my songs, with me. I'd told Jack I wouldn't be back until the next day, but after the show I asked Steve if he felt like driving back. As tired as I was, I felt the need to be at home. And I wanted to be with Jack. I'd decided that if it took ten years, I'd wait. I loved him and that was all there was to it. Suddenly, it didn't matter what anyone thought and I had to tell him so.

Dropping Steve off at his car, I started to go to the boat, then changed my mind. It was almost dawn and I knew he'd be sound asleep and from past experience I knew it was useless to talk to him then. I wanted him wide awake when I told him. I went home.

About four the next afternoon, and after carefully rehearsing my speech, I drove out to the boat. Jack was standing on the dock talking to some of the regulars. When I walked up, they drifted away. Jack's greeting was less than I had expected. Just, "Hi, Redhead," as though I'd never been away. I walked into the boat and to the back. Seeing the bed unmade, I started to make it. As I shook the spread, some bobby pins fell out. I hadn't used bobby pins in years. I walked to the bathroom and saw big wire hair rollers lying by the sink. I didn't use those, either. My heart refused to accept the evidence right in front of me. Sticking them in a drawer, I walked to the kitchen, where evidence of two people having had dinner still remained. Two plates, two wineglasses, two knives and forks. I washed and put them away. Instead of coming on the boat, Jack had walked down the dock to where the cronies had drifted and I could see them down there laughing and talking. After a while, mustering up some false hilarity, I went down and joined them. Later, when we were alone, I started to question Jack but decided against it.

Several times in the next few months, without my even asking, Jack would tell me that there was never and never would be anyone else. One time, I smiled and said, "Thou dost protest too much, my dear." I'd heard that somewhere. It applied now.

In early October, Jack and I attended a cocktail party. Tammy Wynette was there. Jack was in another part of the room and I was talking to a casual acquaintance. Tammy came over and said, "Can I talk to you for a minute?"

"Sure," I said, and we walked to a corner where it was fairly quiet. "What is it?" I asked.

She hesitated, as though she'd changed her mind, then said, "Jan, you may hate me for this, but you need to know." I thought, *Why do people always think you* need *to know*. With no encouragement from me, she went on. "Every time you're out of town, Jack has someone else on the boat, and you don't deserve it." I knew she expected me to get angry or cry or do something dramatic, but my response was to get up and walk over to where Jack was standing. I knew she did what she thought was best, but what she didn't know was that I didn't need her to tell me what I already knew.

Christmas came and my gift to Jack was an Ultrasuede trench coat. He gave me a bracelet made up of sixty-four pearls with a blue sapphire between each one. I'd have gladly traded it for a plain gold band. Reading my mind, he said, "By your birthday . . . I promise."

We did go to Vermont. But it was different from the time before, in more ways than one. Previously, the weather had been like a picture postcard, snow falling softly on the slopes, cold but beautiful. And at night, we'd laugh and talk about the excitement of the day and plan for the next one.

This time, it was cold and icy, both in our room and on the slope.

The first day, going up on the lift and seeing the ice shining on the slope below, I knew I was liable to break more than my leg—possibly my neck. Even experts knew better than to ski on ice, and I was far from an expert.

Halfway down, and after taking several bad falls, I made it to the side, took off my skis, put them under my arm, and walked down. When Jack saw me doing this, he was furious! "You just don't do that!" he said.

"Jack," I said, "I may be stupid in many ways, but this is one time I don't intend to be a fool. I'm not going back up."

I waited in the clubhouse until he tried it a few more times, then he came in and grudgingly admitted I was right. We drove to another slope a few miles away. He told me to wait in the car until he checked it out. I agreed, because I could see the ice shining from the car. I watched as he walked to the bottom of the slope and looked up. Suddenly, his feet flew out from under him, and I knew without hearing them that he'd said several colorful cuss words. I jumped out of the car and ran to help him. Angrily, he pushed me away. "I can make it!" he said.

I stood up and said, "Okay, macho man," and walked to the car. Jack limped after me.

Driving to one of the inns Vermont is famous for, we checked in and he lay on the bed as I removed his shoe. His ankle was swelling fast, and I knew he must be in pain. "Jack," I said, "don't you think you should have it X-rayed?"

"No!" he exploded. "I'm not going to a damned hospital! Just get me some aspirin!"

By nighttime, his ankle was in pretty bad shape, but he was in a better mood and insisted on going to the dining room for dinner. We did it up right. Pheasant under glass, a great wine—everything.

The mood and togetherness we had that night wore thin on the drive back to Nashville. But it had been a long drive and we were both tired. A few miles from home, I switched on the radio and heard the news of Tex Ritter's death. He had suffered a fatal heart attack. I was saddened by the loss of a dear friend.

I dreaded going to the funeral because Harlan would be there. For the past months, I'd prayed to God to put forgiveness in my heart, but it hadn't come. I still hated him. So much so that at times it consumed me. I knew that I was only hurting myself, but it didn't matter. I didn't know what I'd say when I saw him.

After the service, when I walked from the church, I found out. Harlan was standing right in front of me talking to some friends. From the look on his face, I could tell he didn't know what to expect. I didn't, either, but I walked right up to him. Silently, I stood there and looked at him. He looked twenty years older, his shoulders were stooped, and his hair was completely gray. Suddenly, the hate was replaced by something else—pity. He was a stranger who didn't even resemble the man I had been married to for ten years.

The other people had moved away and I could see my silence had made Harlan uncomfortable. He hadn't said a word. With a smile, I said, "Hello, Harlan," then turned and walked to my car. For a few minutes I sat there unable to do anything but say, "Thank you, Lord." I felt as though a heavy burden had been lifted from my shoulders.

In the next few weeks, I did a lot of thinking. I shouldn't have done this. Someone once told me a long time ago, "Don't think, Jan. You're not too good at it." I think they were wrong. I was an expert at thinking, but I never seemed to come up with answers, only more questions. And there was one question now weighing heavy on my heart: Jack. I drove out to the boat, where he was expecting me.

As usual he was drinking a glass of wine, and I could tell it wasn't his first. Some other people were on the boat and I asked them to leave. "I'd like to talk to Jack," I said. "Alone."

"Did you hear that, Jack," one of them said. "She asked us to abandon ship." Jack didn't answer and they walked off laughing. I sat down in a chair across from him. If I were too close to him, I knew my courage would fail me.

"Jack," I said. "Are things ever going to be any different for us?" He could hear a difference in my tone of voice.

Setting his wineglass down, he said, "I honestly don't know, Redhead."

I sat there savoring his answer. Then, I said, "I've been thinking a lot about us and I can't live like this anymore. As much as I love you." Tears came into his eyes, but I went on. "I've tried and so long as there was hope, I could handle it. But now that I know there's no hope, I can't. I don't know what I'll do or how I'll live without you, but when I leave here today, I'm never coming back." Jack sat there taking in my words, which had completely sobered him. I stood up to go.

"I'm proud of you, Redhead," he said. "I never thought you'd do it. I know now I was wrong." I walked over, kissed him lightly, walked out the door, and pulled it shut behind me.

Several times on the way home I almost relented. But I knew if I did, I'd never have the courage again. It was over. I'd lost the only man I'd ever really loved.

The Opry was moving from the Ryman Auditorium to the grand new Opry House at the Opryland complex. Since David's death, I'd never been out there, and knew there was no way I could go. Every last ounce of my strength was gone and I just couldn't fight anymore. I called Bud Wendall, who at the time was manager of the Opry.

"Bud, I have to talk to you," I said. He thought I meant over the phone.

"Sure," he said. "What is it?"

"I . . . uh . . ." The words didn't want to come from my mouth. "I have to leave the Opry."

"Why?" he asked.

"There's just no way I can come to Opryland," I said. He knew what I was talking about.

"Before you make a decision," he said, "why don't you come out one day and let me walk you through it. Then decide." We set up a time for the following afternoon.

The Opry House was truly beautiful! Forty-four hundred seats and not a bad one in the house. As I walked out and stood center stage on the circle that had been cut from center stage of the old Ryman, I was sorry that I wouldn't be performing here. I loved the Opry and the Opry family, but there was no music or song left in my heart.

We walked out to the park. The sun was shining but the silence was strange. I'd never been in the park when it was empty. I was like Sleeping Beauty waiting for the someone to awaken her.

As we walked, we talked about nothing in general. But the closer we got to the theater where David had worked, the slower my steps became. The last time I had been here was a happy occasion. This time I found it hard to breathe. Not wanting Bud to see me cry, I choked back the tears. Then, when we got in front of the entrance to the theater, I stopped. "Bud, I can't! I just can't!" I said, and turned and walked back in the direction from which we'd come. At his office, I thanked him for taking his time and told him I'd think about what I'd told him.

He said, "Jan, you won't ever have to go into the park if you don't want to. Think long and hard about your decision." I promised I would. I was glad he didn't ask for God's promise.

The next two weeks, I spent in self-pity, grief, and indecision. Several times, Jack had called and asked me to have dinner with him, but I'd refused. I knew, if I did, it was all over. I still loved him and, what made it worse, I knew in his own way he loved me, too. But I also knew, no matter how hard I tried, I'd always come up short of what he wanted me to be.

Just to hear another voice, I had the television on. I sat down to watch someone else's love scenes when the phone rang.

"Hi, Redhead," Jack said. "This is your Bad Ass." It was all I could do not to say, "I'm sorry . . . I didn't mean it," but I didn't.

But while my heart was saying that, my mouth said, "Yes . . . I know." I couldn't believe this calm voice was mine.

There was a pause. Then he said, "You really mean it, don't you?"

"Yes, Jack. I do." Another pause. I thought I'd heard a tear in his voice. *Oh God,* I thought. *Another minute and I'll give in.* But before I could speak, he did.

"I want you to know something, darling. You're the only

woman I've ever really loved. And, in your little finger, you're
more woman than all the rest put together." I thought, *Oh, Jan,
you fool!*

"Thank you, Jack," I said. Was this actually me talking?

"And you know if you ever need me, I'll be there."

"I know," I said. "The same goes here."

"What are you going to do?" he asked.

"I don't know," I said. "I really don't at this point."

For a moment, neither of us said anything. Then he said, "I
love you, Redhead."

"I love you, too, Bad Ass," I said. He laughed . . . There didn't
seem to be any more to say. Very gently, I hung up the phone.
With every part of me, I wanted to call him back. My heart was
breaking, but I'd glued it back together with false promises so
many times that, next time, it would shatter.

I didn't talk to Corky. I knew he wouldn't understand any of this.
And whatever I did had to be my decision. I'd already decided
that continuing to live in Nashville was out of the question.
Except for Corky and Pam, all I had left here were memories.
Besides, if I wasn't going to be in the music business any longer,
what could I do? Maybe somewhere else, I could start over. Oh,
God! I've started over so many times and I didn't yet have it down
pat.

The last performance at the Ryman was on Friday, the fourteenth of March, and I wanted to be a part of it. Only Bud and I
knew that it would be my last performance. No, I was the only
one who really knew.

Usually, only about half the cast appears at any one performance of the Opry. But, that night, everyone you could name was
there. Artists canceled dates on the road just so they could be a
part of it. Each person I talked to said it was all they could do to
keep from crying when it came their time to sing. That included
me.

That night was almost sacred. When the last song was sung
and the curtain came down, never again would the Ryman be
filled with music and applause. There was a rumor that it might
be torn down, but I hoped it was too much a part of history for
that to happen. With a feeling of great sadness, I drove home. No,

I take it back. *Home* stands for happiness and people around who love you. I was going to an apartment. An apartment, to me, meant a place where, if you were lucky, you existed.

Before going to bed, I pulled the drapes so not a ray of light would wake me. I wanted and intended to sleep the day away. There was nothing to get up for. But, instead, I woke at dawn. Not being able to go back to sleep, I got up, fixed a cup of tea, and sat down at the kitchen table. There didn't seem to be a reason to do anything. My thoughts took over.

I thought back over the years and tried to figure out why things had happened the way they had. And the more I thought, the more my negative thoughts turned into positive thoughts.

I thought back to the days on Graycroft when we'd all been so happy. My mind brought back pictures of the boys romping with Bucko and playing ball in the backyard. Of Jimmy practicing basketball by the hour so he'd be good enough to make the team. Of David showing me his first fish and my making *him* clean it. Of Corky putting rubber snakes and spiders in my bed and laughing his head off when I'd find them and scream. I thought of Harlan and the good relationship we'd had for seven years. And I thought of Jack and how he was always there when I needed him and the love we'd shared. My God. I could have missed out on all those things! Some people never have one of them! I could still be a waitress or a secretary in Los Angeles. Or, worse yet, starving somewhere. I thanked God I still had my health. There was still a lot for me to do and, God willing, still a lot of life for me to live.

Once more, Jimmy's words came back to me. "My mother has more guts than any woman I know . . . for God's sake get up and show some!"

The anger that I had aimed at everything and everyone else turned around and aimed itself at me. I'd been living with self-pity and yet I had so much to be thankful for. The twenty-one beautiful years I'd had with Jimmy and David. And Corky . . . my rock of Gibraltar. Thank you, God, for Corky. Oh, God, forgive me. All the time I was asking where you were, you were here with me.

I couldn't wait to call Bud and tell him I'd changed my mind. I'd be there tonight! God had given me my talent and an opportunity and place to use it. If I could help it, I wasn't going to blow it.

I chose the most beautiful dress I owned. A black silk, with all colors of embroidery down the front, around the hem, and on the sleeves. The last time I'd worn it was with Jack at the Roosevelt Hotel in New Orleans. He'd been proud of me then and, even though he wouldn't be there tonight, I knew he'd be proud of me anyway. I could just see him giving me the old Thumbs Up sign.

Ready long before I usually was, I drove out early. Even with my new strength, it was still a big step and I wanted to be there in time to "get my feet wet."

As sad as last night had been, tonight was just that happy. The excitement was electrifying! There was a constant hum of people oohing and aahing over the beauty of the new building. There was always camaraderie among the Opry family, but tonight it was even more so. It was like a big reunion.

The music started and the curtain rose. The audience, which was filled with dignitaries of all sorts, roared with applause.

Right in the middle of the show, everything stopped as the President of the United States, Richard Nixon, was introduced. He had come especially for the opening. Next was me. I stood there filled with my own thoughts. Just before I stepped onstage, silently I said, "This is for you, Jimmy. This is for you, David. This is for you, Corky. This is for you, Lord. And this is for me." Yes, for me! I felt the song welling up in my heart long before it reached my throat! I wanted to sing!

Driving home, yes, home, I felt an exhilaration I hadn't felt in a long, long time. I didn't know what the future held. I didn't want to know. I did know, though, that whatever life dealt me, God would be there to help me handle it. I'd asked Him many times what He was saving me for. Well, I still didn't know, but I trusted Him. I didn't know if there was to ever be another man in my life but, that, too, I'd leave up to Him.

The last time I'd talked to Corky, he'd said, "Mom, you don't sound like yourself." Thank God, he'd recognized the difference. It was too late to call him tonight because I knew if he heard the new "life" in my voice, he'd be awake the rest of the night trying to figure out what had happened.

But, tomorrow, this glorious brand-new tomorrow, I'd call him and say, "Hey, Corky, guess what—your mom's back!" And I could just hear his answer now. "Amen to that!"

EPILOGUE

Several years ago, a friend of long-standing said, "Jan, you should write a book."

"What on earth for?" I asked. But the seed was planted and every now and then I'd work on the outline. When I finished, at a hundred and thirty-three pages it was almost a book in itself. But not the book I wanted written. It just wasn't right. For three years, I put it aside. Then, one day, it came to me . . . I knew how it was to be written. Not a "show biz" book but a book about life. My life.

I hope, through the pages, you've come to know me and my sons. I hope you've felt the love between us and the strength I prayed for and received from God. Without that, I couldn't have lived the life I wrote about or written this book.

I know there are some parts and some words that possibly might offend someone . . . and I'm sorry. But that's the way it was and that's what I said. If I had lied about those, then the whole book would have been a lie and there would have been no reason to write it.

There have been a lot of highlights in my life. In my career, being made a member of the Grand Ole Opry is by far the greatest. I still appear there regularly and love every minute I'm on that stage and the Opry "family" I'm a part of. When I think of all the Greats who have stood on that same "center stage," I feel very humble and grateful. In spite of the times I fought against it, due to my insecurities and family problems, I'm grateful to God that He saw fit for me to be a part of the world of country music.

In my life, it goes without saying that the highlights have been my sons. I am so grateful for the twenty-one beautiful years I shared with Jimmy and David. And for Corky . . . my rock of Gibraltar.

Corky is now a successful businessman in Madison, Tennessee. President of his own company, the Carter Company (from his first name), he deals in commercial real estate, syndications, and investments and he and Pam are the parents of two beautiful daughters, Mitsi Ann, age 11, and Anita Marie, age 9. Being a typical grandmother, they're the apples of my eye. When they asked if they were going to be in the book and I had to say no, they said, "Well, Jana (which is what they call me), you'll have to write another one!" Funny they should say that because that's exactly what I plan to do. In fact, I'm already working on my first novel.

This past year, since I've devoted every minute to writing this book, I had to cancel all road dates, but I'm already filling in my calendar for next year. Not nearly as much as I used to but, remember, Jan Howard is older, and wiser. I still love my fans, though, and thank them for hanging in there with me.

My latest album was for MCA Dot, and I'm currently looking for material for a follow-up. I love to sing and hope that, for a long time to come, God will give me the opportunity to do so. And, when He tells me to quit, I hope I have the sense to follow His advice.

Not being one to "rest on my laurels," I also have my real estate license and, now and then when the opportunity comes up, I will work at it. I love people and beautiful homes . . . this gives me a way to see both of them. And what's great is putting the right two together.

There's still so much I want to do I'll need at least two lifetimes. I'd love to travel—just be a tourist—I'd like to learn another language . . . it always amazes me when I hear people speaking a language other than English. I've always been a "ham" and I'd like to act. I even studied acting for a year and loved it. But, if I do, I hope the part is in a comedy.

I'm still single, but if a "prince" instead of another "frog" comes by, I'm willing to give love another try. Who knows?

Well, I'm wasting time just sitting here, I could be doing instead of thinking. And the opportunity might come today. Is that my doorbell ringing? So if you should call and I'm not home, don't worry . . . Just say, "Jan's out living life to the fullest, every single day!"